THE ROUTLEDGE COMPANION
TO DRAMATURGY

Dramaturgy, in its many forms, is a fundamental and indispensable element of contemporary theatre. In its earliest definition, the word itself means a comprehensive theory of "play making." Although it initially grew out of theatre, contemporary dramaturgy has made enormous advances in recent years, and it now permeates all kinds of narrative forms and structures: from opera to performance art; from dance and multimedia to filmmaking and robotics.

In our global, mediated context of multinational group collaborations that dissolve traditional divisions of roles as well as unbend previously intransigent rules of time and space, the dramaturg is also the ultimate globalist: intercultural mediator, information and research manager, media content analyst, interdisciplinary negotiator, social media strategist.

This collection focuses on contemporary dramaturgical practice, bringing together contributions not only from academics, but also from prominent working dramaturgs. The inclusion of both means a strong level of engagement with current issues in dramaturgy, from the impact of social media to the ongoing centrality of interdisciplinary and intermedial processes.

The contributions survey the field through eight main lenses:

- world dramaturgy and global perspective
- dramaturgy as function, verb and skill
- dramaturgical leadership and season planning
- production dramaturgy in translation
- adaptation and new play development
- interdisciplinary dramaturgy
- play analysis in postdramatic and new media dramaturgy
- social media and audience outreach.

Magda Romanska is Visiting Associate Professor of Slavic Languages and Literatures at Harvard University, Associate Professor of Theatre and Dramaturgy at Emerson College, and Dramaturg for Boston Lyric Opera. Her books include *The Post-Traumatic Theatre of Grotowski and Kantor* (2012), *Boguslaw Schaeffer: An Anthology* (2012), and *Comedy: An Anthology of Theory and Criticism* (2015).

"With its 85 contributions by leading theoreticians, practitioners and scholars, *The Routledge Companion to Dramaturgy* will become a basic handbook and a critical source of inspiration for practicing artists as well as researchers in the performing arts.

This companion will serve as a basic map for this ongoing and future project, by (1) presenting a complex and multi-faceted picture of the dramaturgical strategies that have been and most likely will continue to be applied to the more traditional forms of drama and theatre; by (2) posing fundamental questions that will continue to open up new horizons for post-dramatic, avant-garde performance practices and experimentation; by (3) exploring the role of dramaturgy within popular, more commercially oriented forms of entertainment; and by (4) confronting the challenges and potentials of the more recent artistic expressions based on innovative 'new media' technologies.

The international scope of the contributions within these fields is impressive, presenting the readers with a wide variety of socio-ideological contexts from which a very complex, sometimes even disturbing, but still, always very stimulating picture of the state of the arts emerges."

Freddie Rokem, *Tel Aviv University, dramaturg and author of* Philosophers and Thespians: Thinking Performance

"This collection demonstrates the considerable breadth and depth of dramaturgy today. Giving voice to a generation, it is bound to become the major reference point in the field for years to come."

Martin Puchner, *Chair in Drama and in English and Comparative Literature, Harvard University*

"With this exquisitely curated volume, Magda Romanska has gathered perspectives as sophisticated as they are varied from an impressive cohort of international scholars and practitioners, veterans and young lions, keepers of the flame and visionaries. The result doesn't seek a definitive answer to "What is dramaturgy?;" it simply renders the question entirely beside the point. *The Routledge Companion to Dramaturgy* cracks the entire discipline open for examination and, what's much more, for new avenues of exploration."

Catherine Sheehy, *Chair of Dramaturgy and Dramatic Criticism Department, Yale School of Drama*

"In a field of study which has long eluded easy definition, this marvellous compendium of essays makes the case that we should stop trying to pigeonhole dramaturgy and rather ask how we as artists and scholars can use our knowledge to make a more vital theatre for a rapidly globalizing culture. This book can and should inspire established and emerging professionals to see dramaturgy as a platform on which to seize agency as generative artists and original thinkers."

Christian Parker, *Head of Dramaturgy Concentration, Columbia University*

THE ROUTLEDGE COMPANION TO DRAMATURGY

Edited by
Magda Romanska

LONDON AND NEW YORK

First published 2015
by Routledge
2 Park Square, Milton Park, Abingdon, Oxon OX14 4RN

and by Routledge
711 Third Avenue, New York, NY 10017

Routledge is an imprint of the Taylor & Francis Group, an informa business

British Library Cataloguing in Publication Data
A catalogue record for this book is available from the British Library

Library of Congress Cataloguing in Publication Data
The Routledge companion to dramaturgy / [edited] by Magda Romanska.
pages cm
Includes bibliographical references and index.
1. Theater--Production and direction. 2. Dramaturges. I. Romanska, Magda, editor of compilation. II. Title.
PN2053.R78 2014
792.02'3--dc23
2014002637

ISBN: 978-0-415-65849-2 (hbk)
ISBN: 978-0-203-07594-4 (ebk)

Typeset in Goudy
by Taylor & Francis Books

Printed and bound in Great Britain by
TJ International Ltd, Padstow, Cornwall

CONTENTS

CONTENTS

CONTENTS

CONTENTS

CONTENTS

CONTENTS

ILLUSTRATIONS

Figures

Tables

CONTRIBUTORS

Jessica Kaplow Applebaum has been working as a dramaturg in New York City for the past thirteen years. She is literary manager and dramaturg for One Year Lease Theater Company and collaborates with companies such as Enthuse Theater and Yinzerspielen. In 2004 she earned her Master's Degree in Performance Studies at NYU and served as editorial assistant for *TDR: The Drama Review*. In 2012 she finished her M.F.A. in Dramaturgy at Columbia University. The culmination of that work was a trip to Prague where she presented part of her thesis: "Standing the Dramaturg on Her Head:A Call for New Perspectives on Training" at the Prague Quadrennial's symposium Devised Dramaturgy: A Shared Space.

Jane Barnette was the resident dramaturg of the Department of Theatre and Performance Studies at Kennesaw State University from 2007–2014, before joining the Department of Theatre at the University of Kansas. She is a theatre historian who does archival research on train culture and American pageantry. She has published reviews and articles in *Theatre Journal*, *Theatre Symposium*, *Theatre InSight*, and *TPQ*. Barnette serves as LMDA's regional vice president for the Southeast, and was the conference co-chair (with Celise Kalke of the Alliance Theatre) for the 2012 LMDA conference in Atlanta.

Bruce Barton is a creator/scholar who teaches playmaking, dramaturgy, and intermedial performance at the University of Toronto and whose research focuses on physical dramaturgies in devised and intermedial performance. He has published in a wide range of scholarly and practical periodicals, as well as several national and international essay collections. His book publications include *At the Intersection between Art and Research* (2010) and *Collective Creation, Collaboration and Devising* (2008). Bruce is also an award-winning playwright, and he works extensively as a director and dramaturg with many of Canada's most accomplished physical theatre and intermedial performance companies.

Robert Blacker has worked as a dramaturg for 35 years at New York's Public Theater, La Jolla Playhouse (California), and the Stratford Shakespeare Festival of Canada. Over fifty projects from Blacker's eight years as artistic director of the Sundance Theatre Labs went on to production including: *I Am My Own Wife* (Tony, Pulitzer), *The Laramie Project*, *The Light in the Piazza*, and *Spring Awakening* (Tonys for the latter two). He was interim chair of playwriting at Yale School of

Drama and has taught playwriting and Shakespeare studies in graduate programs at Columbia, Iowa, and Yale. Blacker was the first dramaturg at the Public Theater and Des McAnuff's associate artistic director at La Jolla Playhouse, where he worked on The Who's *Tommy* and Steppenwolf's *The Grapes of Wrath* (Tonys for both); and has dramaturged 18 productions of Shakespeare at these theatres and the Stratford Festival, where he was dramaturg for the past five years. He is a graduate of Cornell University.

Marin Blažević, Ph.D., is associate professor and head of the Dramaturgy Department at the Academy of Drama Arts, University of Zagreb. He publishes widely on performance studies and postdramatic dramaturgy. Recent publications include the MIS-performance issue of *Performance Research*, co-edited with Lada Čale Feldman (2010), and a monograph *Izboren poraz* (A defeat won) (2012) on the theory of new theatre and its peculiar history in Croatia. He will be a curator and dramaturgy director of the Performance Studies International dispersed conference project Fluid States in 2015.

Mark Bly was the chair of the Playwriting Program at the Yale School of Drama from 1992 to 2004 while being the associate artistic director at the Yale Rep. Over the past thirty years he has served as a dramaturg, director of new play development, and associate artistic director at such theatres as the Arena Stage, Alley Theatre, Guthrie Theater, Seattle Rep, and Yale Rep, dramaturging and producing over 150 plays. He has dramaturged on Broadway Emily Mann's *Execution of Justice* (1985) and more recently Moisés Kaufman's *33 Variations*. Bly has served as the dramaturg for the world premieres of plays by Rajiv Joseph, Suzan-Lori Parks, Tim Blake Nelson, Sarah Ruhl, and Moisés Kaufman. Bly has written for numerous publications: *Yale Theater* as contributing editor and advisory editor, *Theatre Forum*, *American Theatre*, *Theater Topics*, and *LMDA Review*. In 2010 Bly received the Literary Managers and Dramaturgs of the Americas G. E. Lessing Career Achievement Award, only the fifth time the award was bestowed in the organization's history.

Anne Bogart is the artistic director of SITI Company and a professor at Columbia University, where she oversees the graduate directing concentration. With SITI: *A Rite*, *Café Variations*, *Trojan Women*, *American Document*, *Antigone*, *Under Construction*, *Freshwater*, *Who Do You Think You Are?*, *Radio Macbeth*, *Hotel Cassiopeia*, *Death and the Ploughman*, *La Dispute*, *Score*, *bobrauschenbergamerica*, *Room*, *War of the Worlds*, *Cabin Pressure*, *War of the Worlds: The Radio Play*, *Alice's Adventures*, *Culture of Desire*, *Bob*, *Going*, *Going*, *Gone*, *Small Lives/Big Dreams*, *The Medium*, Noël Coward's *Hay Fever* and *Private Lives*, August Strindberg's *Miss Julie*, and Charles Mee's *Orestes*. Anne Bogart is the author of five books: *A Director Prepares*, *The Viewpoints Book*, *And Then, You Act*, *Conversations with Anne*, and *What's the Story?*

Catherine Bouko holds a Ph.D. in Performance from the Université Libre de Bruxelles (Belgium), where she is now associate professor in the Department of Performing Arts. Her works primarily concern immersive and digital performances. She has published dozens of articles and book chapters on theatre and performance, in French and in English. She published *Théâtre et réception. Le spectateur postdramatique* in 2010 (Peter Lang) and edited *Corps et immersion* in 2012 (L'Harmattan).

Kate Bredeson is Assistant Professor of Theatre at Reed College. A theatre historian, director, and dramaturg, she has published on French theatre in journals including *Theater, Modern and Contemporary France, Theatre Symposium,* and the books *May 68: Rethinking France's Last Revolution* and *International Women Stage Directors.* As a dramaturg, she has collaborated with theatres including Portland Playhouse, Yale Repertory Theatre and the Guthrie. Former Resident Dramaturg of Chicago's Court Theatre, Kate has an MFA and a DFA from the Yale School of Drama.

Debra Caplan is Assistant Professor of Theater at Baruch College, City University of New York. She is working on a book about transnational networks among itinerant Yiddish theatre artists between the two World Wars, and her work has appeared in *Comparative Drama* and *New England Theatre Journal.* Debra holds a doctorate from Harvard University, where she was also the founding executive director of the Mellon School for Theater and Performance Research. She is also a director, translator, and dramaturg specializing in bringing turn-of-the-century Yiddish dramas to the contemporary stage, and a dramaturg and consultant for Target Margin Theater.

Andrew Ian Carlson holds a Ph.D. in Theatre History from the University of Illinois and an M.F.A. in Acting from Purdue University. He teaches dramaturgy and theatre studies at the University of Texas, Austin, where he is the managing director of the Oscar G. Brockett Center for Theatre History and Criticism. Andrew has published his work in *Theatre History Studies* and recently contributed to the revised editions of Oscar Brockett's *The Essential Theatre* and *Plays for the Theatre.* Andrew is also an active practitioner: he regularly works as a dramaturg at Austin Shakespeare and the Zachary Scott Theatre and is an artistic associate with the Great River Shakespeare Festival, where he has performed over a dozen Shakespearean roles.

Faedra Chatard Carpenter is a freelance dramaturg and an Associate Professor of Theater and Performance Studies at the University of Maryland, College Park. She has served as a dramaturg for Arena Stage, Crossroads Theatre Company, Center Stage, the John F. Kennedy Center for the Performing Arts, African Continuum Theatre Company, Theater J, Black Women Playwright's Group, and TheatreWorks. Her scholarly interests focus on race, sexuality, and gender in performance; and she has published in *The Cambridge Companion to African American Theatre, Review: The Journal of Dramaturgy, Theatre Topics, Women & Performance, Text and Performance Quarterly,* and *Callaloo.*

Anne Cattaneo is the dramaturg of Lincoln Center Theater and the creator of the LCT Directors' Lab. A past president of LMDA, she received its first Lessing Award for lifetime achievement. She has worked widely as a dramaturg on classical plays with directors such as Bartlett Sher, Robert Wilson, Adrian Hall, Jack O'Brien, Robert Falls, Mark Lamos, and JoAnne Akalaitis. For the Phoenix Theater she commissioned Wendy Wasserstein's *Isn't It Romantic,* Mustapha Matura's *Meetings,* and Christopher Durang's *Beyond Therapy.* For the Acting Company, she created *Orchards* (Knopf and Broadway Play Publishing) and *Love's Fire* (William Morrow). Her translations include Brecht's *Galileo* (Goodman Theater, starring Brian Dennehy) and Botho Strauss' *Big and Little* (Phoenix

Theatre, starring Barbara Barrie) (Farrar, Straus and Giroux). In 2011, she was awarded the Margo Jones Medal.

Ken Cerniglia is dramaturg and literary manager for Disney Theatrical Group, where during the past decade he has developed over forty shows for professional, amateur, and school productions, including 2012 Tony Award–winners *Newsies* and *Peter and the Starcatcher*. He has written articles for numerous publications and recently edited *Peter and the Starcatcher: The Annotated Script of the Broadway Play* (2012) and *Newsies: Stories of the Unlikely Broadway Hit* (2013). The co-founder of Two Turns Theatre Company and the American Theatre Archive Project, he holds degrees in theatre from UC San Diego, Catholic University of America, and University of Washington.

Michael Chemers is Associate Professor of Dramatic Literature at the University of California, Santa Cruz. He was the founding director of the Bachelor of Fine Arts in Production Dramaturgy program at Carnegie Mellon University. He is the author of *Ghost Light: An Introductory Handbook for Dramaturgy* (SIU Press, 2009), and has been involved in the development of social robotics and digital gaming since 2009.

Walter Byongsok Chon is a doctor of fine arts candidate at Yale School of Drama. He recently received his M.F.A. in Dramaturgy and Dramatic Criticism from YSD and served as artistic coordinator at the Yale Repertory Theatre. As a dramaturg, he worked on productions and staged readings at the Yale Rep, YSD, the Eugene O'Neill Theater Center, and the Great Plains Theatre Conference. His other accomplishments include translation (English and Korean), conference presentation (ATHE, PTRS), and publication of his articles in *Praxis* and *Theater*.

Marié-Heleen Coetzee is Professor and Head of the Drama Department of the University of Pretoria, South Africa. She has been involved in drama/theatre/performance education and training in the higher education sector since 1994. She has written on theatre/performance practice in South Africa, as well as on drama/theatre as embodied pedagogies. Her publications include the practice-as-research project *Shiftings*, the production *Mapungubwe Stories* for the UP centenary celebrations, and articles on Zulu stick fighting as modes of performance. She has acted as instructor for, and served on the artistic advisory committee of, the International Organisation of the Sword and the Pen for a number of years. She currently serves on the directorial board of the Aardklop/Clover National Arts Festival in South Africa.

Marianne Combs reports on the arts for MPR News. Combs joined Minnesota Public Radio in 1993. Since then, she has hosted *State of the Arts*, a weekly program dedicated to Minnesota's arts community, and worked as a reporter, producer, and anchor at stations in Duluth, Rochester, and St. Paul. In 1997 Combs left Minnesota Public Radio to work with the Peace Corps in Cote d'Ivoire, West Africa, where she served for three years.

Graça P. Corrêa, affiliated with CFCUL, University of Lisbon in Portugal, holds a Ph.D. in Theatre and Film Studies from the Graduate Center of the City University of

New York, an M.A. in Theatre Education from Emerson College, Boston, a Licentiate in Architecture from UTL-Lisboa, and a B.A. in Dramaturgy from ESTC-Lisboa. She is a playwright, director (theatre and television), set designer, dramaturg, translator, and professor of Theatre Theory, Dramaturgy, and Acting. A Fulbright Scholar and recipient of fellowships from Gulbenkian Foundation and FCT, she authored the book, *Sensory Landscapes in Harold Pinter: A Study on Ecocriticism and Symbolist Aesthetics* (2011).

Agata Dąbek is a doctoral candidate at the Jagiellonian University, Cracow. Her main areas of research include twentieth and twenty-first-century European drama, especially German and Polish practices of writing for the stage. She authored the monograph *Polski Faust. Wątki faustyczne w polskiej dramaturgii XX wieku* (Polish Dr. Faustus and Faustian motives in Polish drama of the twentieth century, Cracow, 2007) and co-edited the collective monograph *Publiczność (z) wymyślana. Relacje widz-scena we współczesnej praktyce dramatopisarskiej i inscenizacyjnej* (Invented audience: the relationship between the audience and stage in contemporary theatre, Cracow, 2009). With Wojciech Brojer, she co-authored the book *Bertolt Brecht. "Die Dreigroschenoper." Marian Bogusz* (Warsaw, 2012).

Ketaki Datta is Associate Professor of English, Bidhannagar College, Kolkata. She is a novelist, critic, and a translator. Her debut novel, *A Bird Alone*, has won rave reviews in India and abroad. Her paper "Human Values and Modern Bengali Drama," which was read out at an IFTR conference at Lisbon, was published in the Festival Issue of *The Statesman* in India. Other notable publications include *Indo-Anglian Literature: Past to Present* (Booksway, 2008); *New Literatures in English: Fresh Perspectives* (Book World, 2011); *Selected Short Stories of Rabindranath Tagore in Translation* (Avenel, 2013); *The Black and Nonblack Shades of Tennessee Williams* (Book World, 2012); and *The Last Salute* (Sahitya Akademi, 2013).

Tanya Dean is a D.F.A. candidate in Dramaturgy and Dramatic Criticism at Yale School of Drama, where she also received her M.F.A. Her current research focuses on fairy tales and folklore in European theatre. Her production dramaturgy in Ireland includes *Caligula* by Albert Camus (Rough Magic SEEDS), and *The Yellow Wallpaper* by Charlotte Perkins Gilman (Then This Theatre Company). Production dramaturgy at Yale School of Drama includes *The Droll {or, a Stage-Play about the END of Theatre}* by Meg Miroshnik, *Othello* by William Shakespeare, and *Eurydice* by Jean Anouilh. For Long Wharf Theater, she dramaturged *The Glass Menagerie* by Tennessee Williams.

Matt DiCintio is pursuing a Ph.D. in Drama at Tufts University. He received an M.A. in Romance Languages from the University of North Carolina and an M.F.A. in Theatre Pedagogy from Virginia Commonwealth University. His publications include *The Columbia Encyclopedia of Modern Drama*, *Tennessee Williams Annual Review*, *Theatre Symposium*, and *American Theatre Magazine*, where he was an affiliated writer. DiCintio was a founding producing director of Emigrant Theater in Minneapolis and has served as dramaturg at the Guthrie Theater, PlayMakers Repertory Company, the Playwrights' Center, Richmond Triangle Players, and Park Square Theatre, among others.

Julie Felise Dubiner is associate director of American Revolutions at the Oregon Shakespeare Festival. She has served as dramaturg at Actors Theatre of Louisville and the Prince Music Theater, and guest dramaturg at the O'Neill Playwrights Conference, Defiant, and more. She holds degrees from Tufts and Columbia, and has taught at University of Evansville, KCACTF, and elsewhere. Julie is co-creator of *Rock & Roll: The Reunion Tour* and co-author of *The Process of Dramaturgy*. Her essays are published in HowlRound, *LMDA Sourcebook*, and several blogs and newsletters. She is lead mentor of early career dramaturgs and a board member of LMDA.

Peter Eckersall is Professor of Asian Theatre in the Graduate Centre, City University New York. Recent publications include *Theatre and Performance in the Asia-Pacific: Regional Modernities in the Global Era* (with Denise Varney, Barbara Hatley, and Chris Hudson, Palgrave, 2013) and *Performativity and Event in 1960s Japan: City, Body, Memory* (Palgrave, 2013). He is a visiting fellow in the Center for Interweaving Performance Cultures in Berlin. He was the co-founder of Dramaturgies (Australia) and was the resident dramaturg for the performance group Not Yet It's Difficult (1995–2012).

Andrew Eggert is a freelance stage director and dramaturg based in New York City. In the 2012–13 season, he directed the US premiere of *Clemency* by James MacMillan for Boston Lyric Opera and *Bluebeard's Castle* for Opera Omaha. He has enjoyed a longstanding relationship with Chicago Opera Theater, where he directed *Mosè in Egitto* and *La Tragédie de Carmen*. His new production of *Mourning Becomes Electra* was selected as a winner of Opera America's 2009 Director-Designer Showcase. Eggert is a graduate of Yale University and is currently pursuing a Ph.D. in historical musicology at Columbia University. He has been appointed director of Opera Studies at the Chicago College of Performing Arts at Roosevelt University, from 2013–14.

Margarita Espada has traveled the world in her careers as a Puerto Rican artist, educator, and cultural organizer, training in physical approach to theatre practice. She is the founder and executive-artistic director of Teatro Yerbabruja, an organization formerly based in Puerto Rico and Long Island that uses the arts as a tool for social change. Her work has also been featured in media outlets such as *Newsday*, *The New York Times*, and the *Associated Press*. Margarita is a faculty member for the Department of Theater Art at Stony Brook University.

Elinor Fuchs has been Professor of Dramaturgy and Dramatic Criticism at Yale University since 1997. She is the author or editor of five books, including *The Death of Character: Reflections on Theater after Modernism* (1996); *Plays of the Holocaust: An International Anthology*; and, with Una Chaudhuri, *Land/Scape/Theater* (2002). Her work has won numerous awards, among them the George Jean Nathan Award for Dramatic Criticism, the Excellence in Editing Award of the Association for Theatre in Higher Education, and the Los Angeles *Drama-Logue* Best Play award for her documentary play, *Year One of the Empire: A Play of American War, Politics and Protest*. Elinor Fuchs has taught at Harvard, Columbia, New York, and Emory universities, and at the *Institut für Theaterwissenschaft* of the Free University in Berlin, and has offered dramaturgical workshops in Europe and the UK. A recipient of two Rockefeller Foundation awards and a Bunting fellowship, she was awarded the 2009 Betty Jean Jones Teaching Award by the American Theatre and Drama Society.

Jacob Gallagher-Ross is Assistant Professor of Theatre at the University at Buffalo, SUNY. A contributing editor of *Theater*, his writing has appeared in *TDR*, *PAJ*, *TheatreForum*, *Theater*, and *Canadian Theatre Review*. He was for many years a frequent contributor to the *Village Voice*, and worked for several seasons as a dramaturg under Robert Blacker at the Stratford Shakespeare Festival. He is a graduate of the Yale School of Drama.

Jackson Gay is a freelance director based in NYC. Her recent projects include David Adjmi's *3C* and Lucy Thurber's *Where We're Born* at Rattlestick. She directed Rolin Jones' *The Jammer* and *The Intelligent Design of Jenny Chow* for the Atlantic Theater Company. Her production of *Jenny Chow* received the Best Production Connecticut Critic's Award at Yale Rep. Her production of *A Little Journey* at The Mint received the 2012 Drama Desk nomination for Outstanding Revival of a Play. She is currently developing *These Paper Bullets* with Rolin Jones, Billie Joe Armstrong, and choreographer Monica Bill Barnes. Jackson teaches directing at Columbia University and received her M.F.A. from the Yale School of Drama.

Martine Kei Green-Rogers is a Raymond C. Morales Postdoctoral Fellow in the Theatre Department at the University of Utah. Her Ph.D. is from the Department of Theatre and Drama at the University of Wisconsin-Madison. Some of her dramaturgical credits include: Classical Theatre Company's productions of *Uncle Vanya*, *Antigone*, *Candida*, *Ghosts*, and *Tartuffe* (Houston, TX), *The Mountaintop*, *Home*, and *Porgy and Bess* at the Court Theatre (Chicago, IL), *Comedy of Errors*, *To Kill A Mockingbird*, *The African Company Presents Richard III*, *A Midsummer Night's Dream*, and *Fences* at the Oregon Shakespeare Festival (Ashland, OR).

Helena Grehan is Associate Professor in English and Creative Arts at Murdoch University. She is the author of *Mapping Cultural Identity in Contemporary Australian Performance* (Peter Lang, 2001) and *Performance, Ethics and Spectatorship in a Global Age* (Palgrave Macmillan, 2009). She writes essays on performance and technology, art and politics, and spectatorship and ethics. She is currently working with Peter Eckersall and Edward Scheer on a large research project about new media dramaturgy. Her focus in this project is on the politics of spectatorship in new media performance. She is co-editor of *Performance Paradigm*.

Anne Hamilton is a New York City–based freelance dramaturg and the founder of Hamilton Dramaturgy, an international consultancy. She holds an M.F.A. from Columbia University School of the Arts, and has worked with Andrei Serban, Michael Mayer, Lynn Nottage, Niegel Smith, and Classic Stage Company, among others. She created Hamilton Dramaturgy's TheatreNow! Her specialties include new play development, production dramaturgy, new musicals, career development advising, advocacy, and oral histories. She is a dual citizen of the United States and Italy and was a Bogliasco Foundation Fellow.

Tori Haring-Smith is the current president of Washington & Jefferson College. Previously she served as Vice President for Educational Affairs at Willamette University. She has taught as a member of the theatre faculty at Brown University and the American University in Cairo, served as artistic director of the Wallace

Theatre in Cairo, and worked as a dramaturg at Trinity Repertory Company and at the Jean Cocteau Repertory.

Jessica Hinds-Bond is a doctoral candidate in the Interdisciplinary Ph.D. of Theatre and Drama program (IPTD) at Northwestern University. Her research focuses on contemporary Russian drama and its engagement with the pre-Soviet Russian literary canon.

Eiichiro Hirata is a theatre researcher in Tokyo. After studying German Literature and Theatre Studies in the doctoral course at Keio University, Tokyo, and at Humboldt University, Berlin, Hirata was associate professor (from 2004 to 2012) and professor (since April 2012) at the Department of German Literature of Keio University. Published books and essays include *Theater in Japan* (German, co-ed., Theater der Zeit Berlin, 2009), *The Dramaturg, toward Promoting the Theatre Arts* (Japanese, Sangensha-Publisher, 2010), "The Absence of Voices in the Theatre Space: Ku Nauka's Production of *Medea*" (English, in Markus Hallensleben (ed.), *Performative Body Spaces: Corporeal Topographies in Literature, Theatre, Dance and the Visual Arts*, Rodopi, 2010).

Gitta Honegger has translated the plays of Elias Canetti, Thomas Bernhard, Peter Handke, and is the authorized translator of 2004 Nobel Laureate for Literature Elfriede Jelinek's performance texts *Death/Valley/Mountain* (Totenauberg), *Jackie*, *Snow White*, *Sleeping Beauty*, *The Merchant's Contracts*, *Rechnitz*, and her opus magnum, the novel *The Children of the Dead*. She was resident dramaturg and a stage director at the Yale Repertory Theatre and Professor of Dramaturgy and Dramatic Criticism at the Yale School of Drama. Currently, she is Professor of Theatre at Arizona State University and contributing editor of *Yale Theater* magazine.

D. J. Hopkins is an Associate Professor and the Director of the School of Theatre, Television, and Film at San Diego State University. He is author of *City / Stage / Globe: Performance and Space in Shakespeare's London* (Routledge, 2008), and co-editor of a collection of essays entitled *Performance and the Global City* (Palgrave, 2012), and *Performance and the City* (Palgrave, 2009). All three of these scholarly volumes explore the relationship between performance and the production of (urban) space. As dramaturg Hopkins has worked with numerous writers, directors, choreographers, and theatre artists including Les Waters, Tina Landau, Joe Chaikin, Robert Woodruff, Chay Yew, Greg Gunter, José Rivera, Naomi Iizuka, Chuck Mee, Joé Alter, Liam Clancy, and Eric Geiger. Hopkins is the 2012 recipient of the Elliott Hayes Award for Outstanding Achievement in Dramaturgy, in recognition of ten years as editor of *Review*, the online journal of dramaturgy. He is now serving as co-editor of *Theatre Topics*.

Klaus P. Jantke studied mathematics at Humboldt University in Berlin. He has a Ph.D. in computer science (1979) and a habilitation in computer science (1984), both at Humboldt. His research areas include algorithmic learning theory, abstract data types and formal semantics, planning in dynamic environments and process control, meme media technology, technology-enhanced learning, digital games, artificial intelligence, and interactive storytelling.

Barbara Johnson was an American literary critic and translator. She was a Professor of English and Comparative Literature and the Fredric Wertham Professor of Law and Psychiatry in Society at Harvard University. Her scholarship incorporated a variety of structuralist and post-structuralist perspectives, including deconstruction, Lacanian psychoanalysis, and feminist theory, into a critical, interdisciplinary study of literature. Johnson helped make the theories of French philosopher Jacques Derrida accessible to English-speaking audiences in the US at a time when they had just begun to gain recognition in France. Accordingly, she is often associated with the Yale School of academic literary criticism.

Jodi Kanter is Associate Professor of Theatre at the George Washington University, where she teaches dramaturgy and directs the interdisciplinary major in dramatic literature. She serves on the editorial board of *Text and Performance Quarterly* and holds a Ph.D. in Performance Studies from Northwestern University. Her book, *Performing Loss: Rebuilding Community through Theater and Writing* (Southern Illinois University Press, 2007) explores how devising new work for the theatre can help communities navigate collective experiences of loss.

Gad Kaynar is the Chair of the Theatre Arts Department at Tel Aviv University (2009–13), and initiator of Dramaturgical Studies. He was a guest professor at Hebrew University in Jerusalem, LMU University in Munich, and Venice International University. He was also the dramaturg of three major Israeli repertory theatres (1982–2005). Currently, he is co-editor of the quarterly *Teatron*. He was knighted by King Harald V of Norway for his Ibsen translations and research (2008). His publications include: *Another View: Israeli Drama Revisited* (edited with Prof. Zahava Caspi, the Ben Gurion University Publications, 2013); *The Cameri Theatre of Tel-Aviv* (2008); *Bertolt Brecht: Performance and Philosophy* (edited with Prof. Linda Ben-Zvi. Assaph, Tel Aviv University, 2005). He also edited with Prof. Freddie Rokem, the "Special Focus: Dramaturgy" section of *Theatre Research International* 31:3 (October 2006).

Amy Kenny received her Ph.D. in Early Modern Literature and Culture from University of Sussex on Shakespeare's representation of the family. She has dramaturged for 15 productions at Shakespeare's Globe and conducted over 80 interviews with actors and directors on architecture, audiences, and performance. She has also dramaturged at the American Shakespeare Center in Virginia, USA, and has lectured at King's College London, University of Sussex, Shakespeare's Globe, University of Concordia, and University of California, Riverside.

Kristin Leahey is the resident dramaturg at Northlight Theatre and formerly the literary manager at Woolly Mammoth Theatre Company in Washington, DC. Her dramaturgical credits include productions with the Goodman Theatre, the Kennedy Center, the Indiana Repertory Theatre, Cleveland Play House, Victory Gardens Theater, Notre Dame Shakespeare Festival, Collaboraction, Teatro Luna, Teatro Vista, Eclipse Theatre Company, Redmoon Theater, Next Theatre Company and A Red Orchid Theatre (where she formerly served as the literary manager), and the Galway Arts Festival, among others. Her publications include articles in *Theatre Topics*, *Theatre History*, and *Theatre Studies*. Leahey received her doctorate in Dramaturgy and Performance Studies at the University of Texas at Austin, her M.A. in Theatre at Northwestern University, and her B.A. at Tufts University.

Hans-Thies Lehmann is one of the most distinguished international theatre scholars; he made a significant contribution to the study of contemporary theatre and performance practice with his groundbreaking book, *Postdramatic Theatre* (1999; English 2006), which has been translated into more than ten languages. Lehmann is also one of the leading international Brecht scholars, and president of the International Brecht Society, as well as a prominent expert on Brecht's disciple Heiner Müller. Education credits include: Chair in Theatre Studies at Johann-Wolfgang-Goethe University, Frankfurt/Main (Germany), Visiting Professor at the Universities Paris III (Sorbonne), Paris VIII (St. Denis), Paris X (Nanterre), Kaunas/Lithuania, Krakow/Poland, and the University of Virginia/US.

Gideon Lester is Director of Theater Programs at Bard College, where he curates theatre and dance at the Richard B. Fisher Center for the Performing Arts and chairs the undergraduate Theater and Performance Program. He is co-curator of Crossing the Line, a cross-disciplinary international arts festival in New York City. He frequently adapts and translates texts for theatre. Lester previously worked at the American Repertory Theatre as acting artistic director, associate artistic director, and dramaturg, and chaired the A.R.T. Institute's M.F.A. dramaturgy program. He taught at Harvard University, and directed the Arts Collaboration Lab at Columbia University School of the Arts.

Jason Loewith is the Artistic Director of the Olney Theatre Center. As a playwright, Jason won Lucille Lortel and Outer Critics Circle Awards for Best New Musical for *Adding Machine: A Musical*, which he co-wrote with composer Joshua Schmidt. Recent work as a director includes the NNPN Rolling World Premiere of Steven Dietz's *Rancho Mirage* (Olney Theatre Center), the world premiere of Janece Shaffer's *Broke* (Alliance Theatre, Atlanta), and a dozen plays for Chicago's Next Theatre Company, where he served as artistic director from 2002–08. Before joining Olney Theatre Center, Jason proudly served four years as executive director of the National New Play Network. His book *The Director's Voice, Volume 2* was published by TCG in 2012.

Jodie McNeilly is a researcher, writer, and choreographer from Australia. She holds a Ph.D. in Performance Studies (University of Sydney), and she is a Research Scholar at the Centre for the Philosophy and Phenomenology of Religion (Australian Catholic University). Her research has been published in a number of academic and non-academic contexts. She is the founder of a dance dramaturgy group that inquires into experimental dramaturgies.

Toby Malone is a postdoctoral fellow in the Department of Drama and Speech Communication at the University of Waterloo, Canada. He holds a Ph.D. from the University of Toronto's Centre for Drama, Theatre, and Performance Studies, where he pioneered performance edition–based parallel-text analysis. His work has appeared in *Literature/Film Quarterly*, *Shakespeare Survey*, *Canadian Theatre Review*, and several forthcoming collections. Toby is founding co-artistic director of

Toronto's Unit Dramaturgy Collective, and has worked with companies including Canadian Stage, Young People's Theatre, Soulpepper, the Stratford Festival, the Shaw Festival, the Australian Shakespeare Company, Kill Shakespeare Enterprises, Arizona Theatre Company, and the Bell Rock Company, Scotland.

Marjan Moosavi is a doctoral student at the University of Toronto's Centre for Drama, Theatre and Performance Studies. She won Iran's International Fadjr Theatre Festival Special Acting Award and Iranian Women's Theatre Award for her research on gender dynamics in plays by Iranian women playwrights. Marjan is originally from Iran, but her life, work, and studies have taken her across Iran, the US, and Canada. As a dramaturg, researcher, practitioner, and translator, she has lectured at various conferences on contemporary Iranian theatre. Her current studies focus on transgressive dramaturgy and resistant aesthetics, and their interventionist roles in the growing dynamics of resistance in the context of Iran's (inter)national theatre tradition.

Michael Leonard Kersey Morris is a doctoral candidate at Tufts University. He received an A.B. in Russian from Harvard and an M.B.A. from Brigham Young University. His research focuses on the organizational sociology of theatre, particularly of commercial theatre. Michael is also a performer in theatre and opera and member of the American Guild of Musical Artists.

Allan Munro is a Research and Innovation Professor in the Department of Drama and Film at the Tshwane University of Technology, South Africa. He has an M.A. and a Ph.D. in Theatre from Ohio State University. He has presented and published nationally (in South Africa) and internationally. He attempts to blend art-making and research, and has developed a course demystifying research in the arts, which he has taught at several universities. He has written on the problems in *Practice-Led Research in Playwriting*. His current research focuses on ethics in research, arts research ethics (an example of which can be found in the conferences of the Design Educators Forum of South Africa), and the ethics in art-making.

Sandra Noeth has been Head of Dramaturgy and Research at Tanzquartier Wien, center for contemporary dance, performing arts and theory, since 2009. She is internationally active as dramaturg and curator and was Research Associate at the University of Hamburg in Performance Studies from 2006–9. Main areas of research, teaching posts, and artistic-theoretical projects focus on the ethics and politics of the body and dramaturgy in contemporary dance and performance, with a specific engagement in non-Western body practices and concepts. Recent publications in English include "Working (with) Dance. Notes on Contemporary Dance in Morocco and Tunisia" (*Performance Research* 18.1, 2013), "On Addressing: The Bodies of Religion" (SCORES, ed. by Tanzquartier Wien, 2013), *Emerging Bodies. The Performance of Worldmaking in Dance and Choreography* (co-edited with G. Klein, 2011) and MONSTRUM. *A Book on Reportable Portraits* (co-authored with K. Deufert/Th. Plischke, 2009).

Jules Odendahl-James is the resident dramaturg at Duke University. Recent work appears in *REVIEW: A Journal of Dramaturgy*; *Journal of the Fantastic in the Arts*; *Theater Survey*; and *Crime, Media, Culture*. Her current book project, *Over My*

Dead Body: Documentary Performance and the Forensic Imagination, explores connections among individual trauma, public memory, and social activism by tracing the complimentary narrative constructs of contemporary documentary performance and forensic media. As a director and dramaturg in North Carolina she has worked with Playmakers Repertory Company, SLIPPAGE, Manbites Dog Theater, Little Green Pig Theatrical Concern, and UNC-Chapel Hill's Department of Dramatic Art.

Thomas A. Oldham is an independent scholar and dramaturg with an M.F.A. from Columbia University and a Ph.D. from Indiana University. His experience includes theatres from Lincoln, Nebraska's Rough Magic to The Atlantic Theater in New York. He has taught at Indiana State University and Indiana University, where he served as dramaturg for new work from M.F.A. playwrights. Tom is working on his first book, *Towards a Poetics of Violence: The Early Modern and Postmodern English Stage*.

Shelley Orr teaches theatre history and dramaturgy in the graduate and undergraduate programs in the School of Theatre, Television, and Film at San Diego State University. Her publications have appeared in *Theatre Journal*, *TheatreForum*, and *Theatre Topics*. She co-edited a collection entitled *Performance and the City* (Palgrave, 2009). She holds an M.F.A. in Dramaturgy from University of California, San Diego, and a Ph.D. in Theatre Studies from the UCI/UCSD joint doctoral program. She is a past president of Literary Managers and Dramaturgs of the Americas (LMDA).

Jens Peters holds a B.A. in English Literature from the University of Cambridge, an M.A. in Text and Performance Studies from King's College London and the Royal Academy of Dramatic Art. He has recently completed his Ph.D. on a comparison of British and German contemporary theatre at the University of Exeter. He has worked as assistant dramaturg at the Soho Theatre, London, and at the Deutsches Theater, Berlin, and has directed a range of plays in the UK. Jens is currently working as Assistant Dramaturg and Personal Assistant of the Head of Drama at the Badische Staatstheater Karlsruhe.

Dassia N. Posner is Assistant Professor of Theatre at Northwestern University. Her research interests include Russian modernist theatre, the history of directing, dramaturgy, and puppetry. Her books in progress include *The Director's Prism: E. T. A. Hoffmann; Russian Theatricalist Directors, and the Rise of Theatre Thinking*; and *The Routledge Companion to Puppetry and Material Performance* (co-edited with John Bell and Claudia Orenstein). Her articles have appeared in *Theatre Survey, Theatre Topics, Slavic and East European Performance*, and *Puppetry International*. Recent dramaturgy projects include *Russian Transport* and *Three Sisters* at Steppenwolf Theatre Company. She was formerly resident dramaturg at Connecticut Repertory Theatre and holds a Ph.D. from Tufts University.

Gerry Potter is a writer, dramaturg, director, filmmaker, screenplay consultant, and teacher. He founded Workshop West Playwrights' Theatre in 1978 and was artistic director and dramaturg there for 17 years. He later served as artistic director of Fringe Theatre for Young People, and is currently artistic producer of both Peregrine Productions and Rising Sun Theatre. He has written 12 produced plays and 6 produced films. He holds an M.F.A. from the University of Alberta, where he taught for 12 years. He now teaches screenwriting at Macewan University and drama at the University of Lethbridge, Edmonton campus.

Patrick Primavesi teaches Theatre Studies at the University of Leipzig and is Director of the Dance Archive Leipzig. He wrote his Ph.D. on Walter Benjamin's theories of translation and theatre. He also worked as a dramaturg and co-directed a master's program in dramaturgy at the University of Frankfurt am Main. He has published widely on contemporary theatre, on voice, gesture and rhythm, and on interrelations between theatre, film, and new media. His current research projects connect the issues of representation and the public sphere with the development of theatre, dance, and performance art.

Robyn Quick is a Professor and Chair of the Department of Theatre Arts at Towson University, where she teaches courses in theatre history and dramaturgy. She holds a Ph.D. in theatre from the University of Michigan. Her articles have appeared in *American Theatre*, *The New England Journal of Theatre*, and *Slavic and East European Performance*, among others. She served as a production dramaturg for the Baltimore Shakespeare Festival and the New Russian Drama Project at Towson University, and received the 2010 Elliott Hayes Award for Excellence in Dramaturgy from the Literary Managers and Dramaturgs of the Americas.

Brian Quirt is Artistic Director of Nightswimming, a Toronto dramaturgical company that has commissioned 30 works of dance and drama by artists including Judith Thompson, Jason Sherman, Carmen Aguirre, Anosh Irani, Don Druick, Anita Majumdar, and Ned Dickens (www.nightswimmingtheatre.com). Brian is also director of the Banff Centre Playwrights Colony. He was interim artistic director of the Great Canadian Theatre Company; company dramaturg at Factory Theatre; dramaturg at the Theatre Centre; and dramaturgical associate at the Canadian Stage Company. He is the past president of the Literary Managers and Dramaturgs of the Americas, and two-time recipient of LMDA's Elliott Hayes Award for Outstanding Achievement in Dramaturgy.

Duška Radosavljević is a Lecturer at the University of Kent. She has worked as the Dramaturg at the Northern Stage Ensemble, an education practitioner at the Royal Shakespeare Company, and a theatre critic for *The Stage* newspaper. Her work in theatre translation resulted in the world premiere of *Huddersfield* by Uglješa Šajtinac – the first Serbian play ever to be produced in Britain. Duška is the author of *Theatre-Making: Interplay Between Text and Performance in the 21st Century* (Palgrave Macmillan) and editor of *The Contemporary Ensemble: Interviews with Theatre-Makers* (Routledge). She has also published numerous academic articles on dramaturgy and contemporary British theatre, and is working on a Methuen Bloomsbury volume on theatre criticism.

Katie Rasor is the co-founder and Director of New Work for the Hilton Head Island New Play Festival. She holds an M.F.A. in Dramaturgy from the American Repertory Theatre/Moscow Art Theatre School Institute for Advanced Theatre Training at Harvard University. As a dramaturg, she has worked with the American Repertory Theatre, Williamstown Theatre Festival, Actor's Shakespeare Project,

South Carolina Repertory Company, and Theatre of NOTE. She has served as a teaching fellow or guest lecturer at Harvard University, Boston University, and Georgia Southern University, and as a Visiting Assistant Professor at Bridgewater State University and the University of Evansville.

Magda Romanska is a writer, theatre theorist, and dramaturg. She is Visiting Associate Professor of Slavic Languages and Literatures at Harvard University, Associate Professor of Theatre and Dramaturgy at Emerson College, and dramaturg for Boston Lyric Opera. Her books include *The Post-Traumatic Theatre of Grotowski and Kantor* (2012), *Boguslaw Schaeffer: An Anthology* (2012), and *Comedy: An Anthology of Theory and Criticism* (forthcoming in 2014). A former exchange scholar at the Yale School of Drama and fellow at the Mellon School of Theatre and Performance Research at Harvard University, Romanska graduated with honors from Stanford University and holds a Ph.D. in Theatre and Film from Cornell University.

Judith Rudakoff has worked as dramaturg throughout Canada and in Cuba, Denmark, South Africa, England, and the US. Recent books include *TRANS(per)FORMING Nina Arsenault: An Unreasonable Body of Work, Between the Lines: The Process of Dramaturgy* (with Lynn M. Thomson), and *Dramaturging Personal Narratives: Who am I and Where is Here?* Her articles on theatre and performance have appeared in *The Drama Review, TheatreForum,* and *Canadian Theatre Review.* Rudakoff is a member of the Playwrights Guild of Canada and Literary Managers and Dramaturgs of the Americas. She received the Elliott Hayes Award for Outstanding Achievement in Dramaturgy for her work on *Revealed by Fire.* Rudakoff is Professor of Theatre at York University in Toronto.

Pavel Rudnev is a theatre critic, producer, and special project director at the Moscow Art Theatre and Moscow Art Theatre School. He graduated from the Russian Academy of Theatre Arts in 1998 as a theatre researcher and critic. From 2005 to 2011, he was the artistic director of the Moscow Meyerhold Center, the first open venue in Russia. From 1995, he has published more than one thousand articles on contemporary theatre and drama. He specializes in new Russian and world writing. Since 2003, he has taught courses in theatre criticism and contemporary drama at the Russian Academy of Theatre Arts.

Edward Scheer is a Professor in the School of the Arts and Media at the University of New South Wales. He is the author of *Scenario*, a study of new performative media work from the iCinema Project (UNSW Press and ZKM, 2011), and his latest book is entitled *Multimedia Performance* (Palgrave, 2012) with Rosie Klich. Scheer's study of Mike Parr's performance art, *The Infinity Machine* (Schwartz City Press, 2010) is the first comprehensive account of this aspect of the artist's practice. He was president of PSi, Performance Studies International from 2007 to 2011.

Tom Sellar is a writer, editor, and curator. He is editor of Yale's international journal *Theater* and Professor of Dramaturgy and Dramatic Criticism at Yale School of Drama. Under his editorship since 2003, *Theater* has published articles on a wide range of contemporary topics and global artists. (A complete list can be found on www.theatermagazine.org). Sellar's arts writing and criticism has appeared in national publications including the *New York Times*, the *International Herald Tribune*, *TheatreForum*, and *American Theatre*. Since 2001 he has been a frequent contributor to the *Village Voice*, covering theater and performance art nationally.

Sarah Sigal has recently completed a Ph.D. from Goldsmiths College. She is a writer, dramaturg, and director working in physical theatre, radio, devised work, live art, site-specific performance, and new writing. She is the writer-in-residence for Fluff Productions and has made work for the Shunt Vaults, the Union Theatre, the Cheltenham Everyman, the Arcola, the Edinburgh Festival, the Bike Shed, the Rondo, the Etcetera, the Old Red Lion, and Horse Trade. She is currently writing a book about the role of the writer in collaboration for Palgrave Macmillan.

Fadi Fayad Skeiker is Assistant Professor of Theatre Arts at the University of Jordan. He served as an assistant dean of the College of Arts and Design at the University of Jordan, and as a Visiting Assistant Professor at the University of Minho in Portugal. In addition to his academic work, Skeiker has facilitated applied theatre, shadow theatre, and improvisation projects in Jordan, Egypt, Canada, Portugal, and the US. He has led workshops and directed plays which focus on human rights, equality for women, youth, and personal development issues.

Janine Sobeck is the Dramaturgy Specialist at Brigham Young University, the executive producer of the Dramaturgy and Marketing Department at Utah Repertory Theater, and a freelance dramaturg. She is also the VP of Communications for the Literary Managers and Dramaturgs of the Americas. Previously, Janine worked as the artistic associate at Arena Stage in Washington DC, where she was the head dramaturg, literary manager, and producer of new work. In 2009 she was awarded the Dramaturgy Debut Award from the Association for Theatre in Higher Education.

Edward Sobel has served on the artistic staffs of Steppenwolf Theatre Company, Arden Theatre, Delaware Theatre Company, and was artistic director of the Playwrights Center of Chicago. At Steppenwolf, he founded and was the director of the First Look Repertory of New Work, for which he received the Elliott Hayes Award for Outstanding Achievement in Dramaturgy. He is currently on the faculty at Temple University.

Teresa Stankiewicz is an interdisciplinary artist whose career spans the intersections of dance, theatre, writing, and music. She worked as a dramaturg for the Black and Latino Playwrights Festival at Texas State in 2009, 2012, and 2013; the William Woods University 2011 production of *Amadeus*; and as resident dramaturg for Theatre NXS in Columbia, Missouri. She received her Ph.D. from the University of Missouri in May 2013.

Bernd Stegemann works as a dramaturg at the Schaubühne am Lehniner Platz Berlin and as a Professor for Theatre History and Dramaturgy at the Academy of Dramatic Arts "Ernst Busch" Berlin. He gained his doctorate for a work on systems theory under Manfred Brauneck and worked for numerous theatres and festivals.

He founded the *Lektionen* series at Theater der Zeit press. Published so far are book 1, *Dramaturgie*, 2, *Regie*, 3 and 4, *Acting* (Berlin 2009 and 2010). He has also written many publications about dramaturgy and the art of theatre, most recently *Die Kritik des Theaters* (Berlin, 2013).

Johannes Stier is a Ph.D. student and Junior Lecturer at the Department of Media Culture and Theatre at the University of Cologne. He studied Theatre, Film and Television Studies, Philosophy and German Philology at the University of Cologne, where he graduated in 2011.

Vicki Stroich is executive director at Alberta Theatre Projects (ATP) in Calgary, Alberta, Canada. She was interim artistic director of ATP for the 2012–13 season and has been a member of the artistic team for 12 years in the roles of artistic associate festival and dramaturg. Her focus during her time on the artistic team was dramaturgy and programming for the Enbridge playRites Festival of New Canadian Plays. Even as executive director she still dramaturgs new plays for ATP. She freelances as a dramaturg, facilitator, and director. Her work has included dramaturgy of dramatic texts, devised theatre, and performance creation. Vicki is president of the Literary Managers and Dramaturgs of the Americas and was conference chair of the international 2010 LMDA conference in Banff. She is the proud recipient of a Betty Mitchell Award for Outstanding Achievement for her contributions to new work.

Gwydion Suilebhan is a DC-based playwright and theatre blogger. The author of *The Butcher*, *Reals*, *Hot & Cold*, *Abstract Nude*, *The Constellation*, *Let X*, *The Faithkiller*, *Cracked*, and *The Great Dismal*, Gwydion serves as DC's representative for the Dramatists Guild. His work has been commissioned, produced, developed, and read by Centerstage, Ensemble Studio Theatre, the National New Play Network, Forum Theatre, Theater J, Active Cultures, Theater Alliance, Source Theater Festival, and HotCity Theatre, among others. A founding member of The Welders, a DC-based playwrights' collective, Gwydion consults, lectures, and writes widely on the intersection between theatre, the arts, and technology. His clients include the Dramatists Guild, the Playwrights Center, and the National New Play Network, among others.

William Huizhu Sun is Professor, playwright, and director at Shanghai Theatre Academy, and consortium editor for *TDR*. He received his Ph.D. from NYU in 1990, and he taught at Tufts and other universities in North America before returning to Shanghai in 1999. Major research interests include: social performance studies, intercultural theatre, and theatre narratology. His publications include: *Theatre in Construction and Deconstruction*; *Conflicts on Stage and Clash of Civilizations*; *What to Imitate? What to Express: On Chinese and Western Aesthetics*; *Social Performance Studies*; *Reinventing Western Classics as Chinese Operas*. He is the author of 150 Chinese and English papers; 14 plays/Chinese operas, including *China Dream*, *Shalom Shanghai*, *Oedipus*, *Miss Julie*, *Hedda*, seen in 15 countries. He created the Chinese opera series *Confucius Disciples*.

Lawrence Switzky is Assistant Professor of English and Drama at the University of Toronto. He works on modern dramatic literature, modernity across the arts, media theory, the legacies of modernisms and avant-gardes, and the history of theatre directing. He is currently completing a manuscript on the rise of theatre directing as an aesthetic, ethical, and administrative problem and on the reciprocal influence of playwriting and directing throughout the early twentieth century. His essays have appeared in several collections and in *Modern Drama*, *Shakespeare Bulletin*, *TDR*, *The Annual of Bernard Shaw Studies*, and *The London Sunday Times*.

LaRonika Thomas is completing her PhD in Theatre and Performance Studies at the University of Maryland, researching the performance of urban planning, and cultural space and cultural policy in twenty-first-century Chicago. A professional dramaturg, LaRonika has worked in literary management, arts education, producing, and dramaturgy in Chicago and in the Baltimore/DC area. She is the vice president for regional activity for the Literary Managers and Dramaturgs of the Americas (LMDA), and has presented papers and chaired panels at several LMDA conferences and at ATHE.

Ilinca Todoruţ is a D.F.A. candidate at Yale School of Drama, where her research centers on interdisciplinary art and political performance. She served as production dramaturg in the program and at the Yale Repertory Theatre, with credits including *The Seagull*, *The Winter's Tale*, and a number of new plays. She also worked as literary assistant for the Yale Rep, as translator of theatre texts into Romanian, and is currently devising community-based projects. Her essays have been published in *Theater*, *Romanian Journal of Performing Arts*, *Scena.ro*, and *Journal of Poverty*, among others.

Katalin Trencsényi is a London-based dramaturg. She received her Ph.D. at the Eötvös Loránd University, Budapest. As a freelance dramaturg, Katalin has worked with the National Theatre, the Royal Court Theatre, Deafinitely Theatre, Corali Dance Company, and Company of Angels, amongst others. She was literal translator of three contemporary Hungarian plays, published by Oberon Books (*The Fourth Gate* by Péter Kárpáti, *Portugal* by Zoltán Egressy, *Car Thieves* by Ákos Németh). From 2010 to 2012 Katalin served as president of the Dramaturgs' Network. For her research on contemporary dramaturgical practices, she was recipient of the Literary Managers and Dramaturgs of the Americas' Dramaturg Driven Grant.

Brian D. Valencia is a D.F.A. candidate in dramaturgy and dramatic criticism at the Yale School of Drama. As a composer, musical director, dramaturg, and performer, he has collaborated on numerous theatrical productions in New York, Washington, DC, and New Haven, Connecticut. As a scholar, he has written on musical theatre for the New York Public Library and for *Theater* magazine. Brian also holds an M.F.A. from New York University's Tisch School of the Arts in Musical Theatre Writing and a B.S. from Yale College in Chemical Engineering.

Marianne Van Kerkhoven was one of the leading dramaturgs and critics/essayists in Flanders and beyond. Her aesthetic and political views have inspired generations of directors and choreographers. In the early 1970s she launched the first political theatre company in Flanders, and from the early 1980s she worked at the Kaaitheater with countless artists such as Anne Teresa De Keersmaeker, Jan Lauwers, Jan Ritsema, Josse De Pauw, and Guy Cassiers. Right before her death in 2013, she was working with a new generation of artists, including Emio Greco, Hooman Sharifi, Kris Verdonck, Kate McIntosh, and Merlin Spie.

Adam Versényi is Professor of Dramaturgy at the University of North Carolina and senior dramaturg for PlayMakers Repertory Company. A theatre scholar, dramaturg, critic, translator, and director, he is the author of *Theatre in Latin America: Religion, Politics, and Culture from Cortés to the 1980s* (Cambridge University Press, 1993, 2009) and *The Theatre of Sabina Berman: The Agony of Ecstasy and Other Plays* (Southern Illinois University Press, 2002), among others. He has written widely on Latin American theatre, US Latino/a theatre, dramaturgy, theatre production, and theatrical translation. He is the founder and editor of *The Mercurian: A Theatrical Translation Review*. His essay in this volume is a revision of a keynote address he delivered at the Drama Translation in the Age of Globalisation Symposium at the University of Salford in Manchester, England in March 2013.

András Visky is an Associate Professor of Dramaturgy and Performance Studies at the University of Babeş-Bolyai in Cluj, Romania, and the associate artistic director of the Hungarian Theatre of Cluj. As dramaturg he has worked with directors Gábor Tompa, Karin Coonrod, Robert Woodruff, Robert Raponja, Mihai Măniuţiu, Dominique Serrand, and David Zinder. He has been a Visiting Professor at the Moholy-Nagy University of Art and Design, Yale School of Drama, Northern Illinois University, Josai International University, the University of California, San Diego, and Calvin College. His plays have been produced in New York, Avignon, Bucharest, Budapest, Cluj, Chicago, London, Edinburgh, and Paris.

Julie Ann Ward is a UC-MEXUS postdoctoral fellow at the University of California, Riverside. In 2013 she earned a Ph.D. in Hispanic Languages and Literatures from the University of California, Berkeley, with her thesis "Self, Esteemed: Contemporary Auto/biographical Theatre in Latin America," and holds an M.A. in Spanish from the University of Kansas. Her work has appeared in *Latin American Theatre Review*, *Revista de Literatura Mexicana Contemporánea*, *Paso de Gato*, and *Lucero*. Her research interests include contemporary Latin American theatre, documentary theatre, and self-representation onstage and in print.

Vessela S. Warner is Associate Professor of Theatre at the University of Alabama, Birmingham, and dramaturg of Overground Physical Theatre Company, New York. She has contributed to *Theatre and Performance in Eastern Europe: The Changing Scene* (Scarecrow Press, 2008), *Performing Worlds into Being: Native American Women's Theatre* (Miami University Press, 2009), and *International Women Stage Directors* (University of Illinois Press, 2013), and published articles on South Slavic drama and post-communist theatre in *Slavic and East European Performance*, *TheatreForum*, *New England Theatre Journal*, *Balkanistica*, *Serbian Studies*, and others. Warner holds a Ph.D. in theatre history and dramatic theory from the University of Washington.

Miriam Weisfeld is the associate artistic director of Woolly Mammoth Theatre, where she dramaturged several world premieres, including Anne Washburn's *Mr. Burns*, Aaron Posner's *Stupid Fucking Bird*, and Robert O'Hara's *Bootycandy*. Additional credits include work for New York Theatre Workshop (projects with

JoAnne Akalaitis and Ivo van Hove); A.R.T. (with Robert Woodruff and Anne Bogart); Two River Theatre (with Teller); Steppenwolf Theatre; Actors Theatre of Louisville; and Lookingglass Theatre. She has lectured at Harvard, MIT, George Washington University, Northwestern, the Kennedy Center, and the Moscow Art Theatre School. She holds an M.F.A. in Dramaturgy from the A.R.T./MXAT Institute at Harvard.

Tomasz Wiśniewski teaches in the Institute of English and American Studies at the University of Gdańsk, Poland. He is the author of *Kształt literacki dramatu Samuela Becketta* (*The literary shape of Samuel Beckett's dramatic works*, Kraków, 2006) and several articles on modern literature and theatre. Wiśniewski has edited five books, which were published by the University of Gdańsk Press and Maski Publishers. He is on the editorial board of the scholarly quarterly *Tekstualia* (Warsaw) and the literary bimonthly *Topos* (Sopot). He is also artistic director of the project BETWEEN.POMIĘDZY, which organizes literary/theatre festivals, academic seminars, and theatre workshops.

Miriam Yahil-Wax is a dramaturg, writer, and translator. Among her plays are *The Shit Path*, about Israeli-Palestinian conflict, and *The First Stone*, the tragedy of an abused Arab woman. *Without Premeditation*, poems, was published in 1977. She translated Charles Dickens, Carson McCullers, Doris Lessing, Peter Carey, John le Carré, E. L. Doctorow, Molière, Brian Friel, and others. Formerly a Lecturer in Drama (Stanford, UCSC), artistic director of the National Theater for the Young, and artistic director of Haifa Theatre Festival, Miriam Yahil-Wax also lectures at Tel Aviv University Porter School of Cultures.

Randi Zuckerberg is the founder and CEO of Zuckerberg Media and editor in chief of *Dot Complicated*, a newsletter and website helping us navigate and "untangle" our wired, wonderful lives. As an early executive at Facebook, Randi created and ran the social media pioneer's marketing programs. Randi was nominated for an Emmy Award in 2011 for her innovative coverage of the 2010 mid-term elections. Since starting Zuckerberg Media, Randi has produced shows and digital content for BeachMint, The Clinton Global Initiative, Cirque du Soleil, the United Nations, Condé Nast, and Bravo, and has a wide range of projects in the works.

Milan Zvada studied English and Philosophy at Matej Bel University (2001–6) in Slovakia. In 2010, he graduated from the Erasmus Mundus M.A. program in International Performance Research at the University of Tampere and University of Amsterdam. His interests range from reading lyrics and poetry to cultural policy, theory of theatre, and translating. He publishes reviews and articles in theatre journals and online. He works as a teacher, theatre critic, and cultural manager. He is in charge of program dramaturgy and international artistic projects at Záhrada (Garden), a cultural centre based in Banská Bystrica, Slovakia.

Introduction

Magda Romanska

Dramaturgy: an overview of the concept from *Poetics* to *Smash*

In its broader and earliest definition, dramaturgy means a comprehensive theory of "play making." The original Greek compound word, *dramatourgos*, meant simply a play maker, play composer, that is, a playwright. According to Aristotle, the root word "drama" came from the Attic verb that simply meant "action" (δραν = "to do" or "to make"). The second morpheme, "tourgos," was derived from the Greek word "ergo" (έργο = "work" or "composition"), which meant "working together." Aristotle often used it in its vernacular meaning, as the connector "therefore." (This meaning eventually entered Latin, where it was most famously used by Descartes in his maxim *cogito ergo sum* – "I think therefore I am.") Thus, originally, *dramatourgos* simply meant someone who was able to arrange various dramatic actions in a meaningful and comprehensive order. To this day, in many modern languages, including French, Spanish, and Polish, the word *dramaturg* also can mean playwright, adding to the confusion as the two roles continue to be conflated. As dramaturgy attempts to define itself separately from playwriting, the etymology of the word can help us illuminate its many historical and modern uses. Everyone can be a playwright (or, at least, everyone can write a bad play), but not everyone can be a dramaturg (that is, not everyone will actually know how to fix it). Dramaturgy requires the analytical skill of discerning and deconstructing all elements of dramatic structure.

We can say that although Aeschylus was the first Western playwright, Aristotle, whose *Poetics* was the first Western book attempting to define the formal rules of well-structured drama, was the very first Western dramaturg. Trying to find the optimal recipe for a successful piece of dramatic work, Aristotle deconstructed all its components, including plot, character, theme, language, rhythm, and spectacle. In *The Poetics*, he considers *plot* (μῦθος = mythos) as the most important element of drama, defining it as "the arrangement of the incidents." A plot must have all the necessary elements: unified and logical beginning, middle, and end. The arrangement of the incidents must be such that the cause-and-effect chain reaction (*desis*) leads to climax and eventually to believable and internally coherent unraveling (*lusis*). A successful plot has all the elements in the proper order; it includes reversal (*peripeteia*), recognition (*anagnorisis*), and the scene of suffering (*pathos*), and it leads to a cathartic purging of emotions. A plot is not a story or a narrative but rather a dramaturgical scaffolding that arranges the order of storytelling incidents in an order that culminates in cathartic release. In this earliest Aristotelian model, the dramaturg concerns him- or herself foremost with plot, the arrangement of incidents – in other words, with dramatic structure.

This definition of dramaturgy as a comprehensive theory of dramatic structure is the cornerstone of modern dramaturgical practice. This is also how the concept of dramaturgy is viewed in popular culture. In the February 2013 episode of the hit TV series *Smash*, titled "The Dramaturg," a dramaturg is referred to as "the book doctor." His job is to fix the structural errors afflicting the script of the new musical. This particular example of the pop culture use of the word "dramaturg" reflects a broader understanding of the concept of dramaturgy to mean any purposeful arrangement of events, as in the dramaturgy of one's life, war, or political campaign.

Evolution of the dramaturg: from Germany to America

The concept of dramaturgy as a separate theatrical function originated with Gotthold Ephraim Lessing (1729–81), whose collection of essays, *Hamburgische Dramaturgie* (1769), introduced both the actual term and the figure of the "in-house critic," whose role was to assist a theatre in the process of play development. Employed as a resident critic at the Hamburg National Theatre, Lessing, who was also a playwright, advised the theatre's management on its selection of plays and offered his own criticism of each production. Lessing understood dramaturgy as "the technique (or poetics) of dramatic art, which seeks to establish principles of play construction."[1] He saw his function within the theatre foremost as that of a kind of "public educator" whose role was to "enlighten the mass and not confirm them in their prejudices or in their ignoble mode of thought."[2] Challenging public tastes and promoting the highest aesthetic standards was part of Lessing's dramaturgical mission. Although Lessing's influence on his contemporaries was negligible, his occupation set the precedent. In 1775, von Gemmingen wrote *Mannheimer Dramaturgie*. In 1789, von Knigge published *Dramaturgische Blätter*, and in 1791, Albrecht completed *Neue Hamburgische Dramaturgie*. The second most renowned dramaturg following Lessing, however, was the German poet and critic, Ludwig Tieck (1773–1853), who together with August Wilhelm Schlegel (1767–1845) translated Shakespeare's collected works into German. The project, which began in 1797 and was completed in 1833,[3] widened the scope of the dramaturg's functions to further include translation and adaptation. With Lessing and Tieck, dramaturgy established itself as an essential practice in the German theatrical landscape.

Following World War II, Bertolt Brecht (1898–1956) introduced the new notion of production dramaturgy. In Brecht's theatre, "The dramaturg became the director's most important theoretical collaborator. Dramaturgy in Brecht's sense comprises the entire conceptual preparation from its inception to its realization."[4] With Brecht, the task of the dramaturg broadened further to include researching and clarifying the "political and historical as well as the aesthetic and formal aspects of a play."[5] The dramaturg was to participate in rehearsals and to convey his research and knowledge to other members of the production team, particularly the director, before and during the production process. He was also to function as a liaison between the team and the audience, writing program notes and theoretical articles on the production. Following Brecht, another German playwright, Heiner Müller (1929–95), established the tradition of dramaturgical training as an essential component of playwriting. By the time Müller became the dramaturg at the Berliner Ensemble in 1972, Germany already had established as an institution the literary manager, the idea of which had slowly begun spreading beyond German borders. Britain's first well-known literary manager was Kenneth Tynan (1927–80), who was brought to the National Theatre in the early sixties by the then artistic director, Laurence Olivier. Tynan established his position in British theatre and the position of the National Theatre in particular through his function as the country's chief dramaturg, one responsible for the national dialogue in addition to (or perhaps a byproduct of) his dramaturgical role.

Around the same time, in the early sixties, the US landscape of regional theatres slowly began developing, with the Guthrie Theater (founded in 1963) and the American Conservatory Theatre (founded in 1965), among others, leading the way. In 1966, the Yale School of Drama's theatre criticism program was launched, and eleven years later, in 1977, the first MFA in dramaturgy was conferred. The event is generally acknowledged as the turning point for American dramaturgy in that it established dramaturgy as an official field of study, a theatrical function, and a profession in the US. In 1978, Yale *Theater* magazine published a dramaturgy issue, edited by Joel Schechter, which crystalized and defined the program and the field. In 1986, the magazine issued another dramaturgy issue, edited by Mark Bly, which further defined the role of dramaturg in American Theatre. Following the Yale School of Drama, many other dramaturgy programs, both graduate and undergraduate, appeared, and the major US theatres began creating their own literary offices that would eventually employ the graduates of these programs. For the next thirty years, American dramaturgy developed alongside European models, guided primarily by the German example of production dramaturgy and literary office management, with each regional theatre developing its own models suitable for its particular sociocultural and economic circumstances. As Mark Bly notes, during that time "[i]n addition to growth within the field, several dramaturgs have chosen to become artistic directors of major theatre organizations, a logical result of the dramaturg's wide-ranging, yet in-depth, knowledge of dramatic literature and the theatrical process. A few enterprising dramaturgs have also ventured into opera, dance, film and television, extending the profession into other disciplines."[6] Funded primarily through private donations, American regional theatres served traditionally different functions than that of state-funded European theatres. In most cases, American dramaturgs working at regional theatres weren't as concerned with preserving the national theatrical legacy as they were with creating work that reflected the current social and cultural moment. Since then, a number of seminal books and handbooks on dramaturgy have been published, among them the most important: Mark Bly's *The Production Notebooks: Theatre in Process, Volume One* (1995) and *The Production Notebooks: Theatre in Process, Volume 2* (2001); *Dramaturgy in American Theater: A Source Book* (1996), edited by Susan S. Jonas, Geoffrey S. Proehl, and Michael Lupu; Bert Cardullo's *What Is Dramaturgy?* (2000); *The Process of Dramaturgy: A Handbook*

(2010), by Scott R. Irelan and Anne Fletcher; and Michael Mark Chemers' *Ghost Light: An Introductory Handbook for Dramaturgy* (2010).

Dramaturgy of life: sociological and vernacular context

The vernacular understanding of the concept of dramaturgy as a purposeful arrangement of events evolved simultaneously from the fields of both theatre and sociology. In 1959, the term was used for the first time as a sociological category by Erving Goffman in his book *The Presentation of Self in Everyday Life*. Goffman's dramaturgical theory of human behavior viewed everyday life as a series of theatrical events, performed along the lines of pre-established social scripts. (It is this sociological notion of the dramaturgy of everyday life that gave rise to performance studies, which defines performance as existing between "theatre and anthropology."[7]) With everyone performing a "character," Goffman argued, human identity is not stable, but constantly reframed and redefined by the dramaturgy of one's role performed in response to external interactions. We become who we are and develop our own self-image based on dramaturgical analysis of our social relations and the roles we are constantly asked to perform. In other words, we are the dramaturgs of our lives and of ourselves because we create meaning out of the lived events (choosing some and discarding others to create a coherent and meaningful life story). Following Goffman, other sociologists used the term to further define social relationships in terms of the dramaturgical model: for example, Gregory Adams in *All the World's a Stage* (1963); Dennis Brissett and Charles Edgley, eds, in *Life as Theater: A Dramaturgical Source Book* (1990) and Charles Edgley, ed. in *The Drama of Social Life: A Dramaturgical Handbook* (2013). The blending of theatrical and sociological jargons has further broadened the concept of dramaturgy. Most recently, dramaturgy has entered the newest interdisciplinary field of technoself studies, which focus on analyzing the construction of human identity vis-à-vis technology, particularly virtual environments, such as video games and online identities. In both theatrical and sociological contexts, virtual dramaturgy is the latest frontier of dramaturgical pursuits.

Postdramatic dramaturgy

In the last decade, the digital, new-media revolution and the changes in the theatre-making process that it inspired have influenced not only the global theatrical landscape but also the function and role of dramaturgy in and outside of the theatre. Some of these recent changes have been long in the making and grew out of earlier cultural and aesthetic trends. Starting in the 1960s the postdramatic performances "repeatedly disconnected individual theatrical tools from their larger contexts."[8] The idea of postdramatic theatre was first introduced by Andrzej Wirth (1927–), a Polish theatre theorist and the founder of the famous Institute for Applied Theatre Studies in Gießen, Germany, to describe the type of postmodern, abstract theatrical forms that were no longer dialogic, linear, or realistic. Wirth's concept of postdramatic theatre was influenced by a Hungarian theorist, Peter Szondi (1929–71), whose book *Theory of Modern Drama* (1965, first published in English in 1987) defined Drama as a particular dramaturgical structure that emerged in the seventeenth century and that was both Dialogic ("consist[ing] only of the reproduction of interpersonal relations") and Absolute ("conscious of nothing outside itself"). In Drama, Szondi writes, "accident is domesticated; it is rooted in the heart of drama itself."[9] In other words, in Drama, dramaturgical contingency is absorbed into the internal logic of the dramatic structure. Not so with postdramatic "theatre without drama," which escapes the Aristotelian logic of plot and character in favor of a non-dialogic, non-linear, and non-narrative form that is, like modern art, often guided by accidental and abstract modes of representation.

Following Wirth and Szondi, Hans-Thies Lehmann (1944–) in his pivotal book *Postdramatic Theatre* (1999) continued to define the type of postmodern, postdramatic theatre which emerged after World War II and "which is no longer even based on 'drama'."[10] Twentieth-century theatre, Lehmann agues, has undergone "the transformation that has *mutually estranged theatre and drama and has distanced them even further from each other.*"[11] Consequently, "the idea of theatre as a representation of a *fictive* cosmos in general has been ruptured and even relinquished altogether, a cosmos whose closure was guaranteed through drama and its corresponding theatre aesthetic."[12] With the advent of the twenty-first century, the new-media revolution has accelerated the transformation towards non-linear, non-narrative, immersive theatrical experience that is increasingly reflective of a changing and fragmented global cultural landscape and its audiences. As Robert Lepage put it: "We are confronted with audiences whose narrative vocabulary has evolved ... They can read stories backwards now, and jump cut, and can flash forward."[13] The changes of the last decade have altered both the very nature of the theatre-making process, which is increasingly moving towards a devised, collaborative, and globalized mode, and the relationship between theatre and the audience, which expects increasingly sophisticated and challenging narratives. These changes in theatre-making and its reception in turn have affected the field of dramaturgy on multiple levels: the production process, research, literary office management, and audience outreach. With new times comes new theatre, and with new theatre comes new dramaturgy.

Dramaturgy of now and of the future

The Routledge Companion to Dramaturgy is intended to serve as a primary sourcebook for dramaturgy students, practitioners, and academics. The goal of this collection is to frame dramaturgy in the contemporary context, taking into consideration the new-media revolution and the increasingly interdisciplinary and intermedial nature of performance-based artworks. This book is intended to serve as a primary survey of the increasingly expanding field, offering the broadest possible theoretical and practical application of dramaturgical practice: one that encompasses collaborative works, musical theatre, dance, opera, multimedia, film, and video game design – art forms previously neglected in the discussion of dramaturgical practice. Since the dramaturgical method of research and analysis can have broad application across multiple art forms and disciplines, the potential career options for dramaturgs have been expanding to venues outside of theatre. Because contemporary dramaturgs engage in a variety of tasks related to the production process, audience outreach, and institutional management, the goal of this anthology is to provide a framework for different aspects of the ever-expanding field.

Dramaturgy in the global context

Part I, "World dramaturgy in the twenty-first century," offers a global survey of the field as it currently stands across six continents. In some countries, like Germany, the UK, the USA, and to a lesser degree Canada and India, where dramaturgy has an established tradition, the recent changes have been rooted in past practices and reflect the evolution of the field as it attempts to adjust and respond to the modern paradigm shift. In other countries, such as France, Poland, and Russia, where dramaturgy has always existed as a skill but where it has only recently began establishing itself as a function and a field separate from playwriting, dramaturgical practice develops in congruence with the information age and globalization, while simultaneously responding to the postmodern "crisis" of the dramatic text as reflected in and by the crisis of national identity that it has traditionally embodied (from Racine to Chekhov). Dramaturgy in these countries often finds itself deconstructing and reconstructing a sense of national identity, while preoccupied with "adaptation, the rewriting of classic texts, and literary assemblage" (see Rudnev, p. 62, this volume).

In some countries, like Brazil, Chile, Australia, and South Africa, which continue to struggle with their own postcolonial legacies, dramaturgy has been developing as an interdisciplinary tool of cultural transformation aiming to bridge the post-traumatic gaps in the sociopolitical fabric of the respective nations. As Peter Eckersall puts it, "symptomatic of the history of domination and colonialism's violent ruptures" (p. 103, this volume), postcolonial dramaturgy attempts to negotiate the many conflicting narratives of history that are fraught with trauma, subjection, and dispossession. Similarly, in counties like Japan and Syria, dramaturgy's main function is to navigate the hybrid performances that blend multiple theatrical forms, particularly traditional ethnic traditions and Western-influenced modern theatrical modalities. In yet other countries, like China and Iran, where theatre is fully subsidized by the state and where it remains foremost as its ideological arm, dramaturgy has been forced to face its own internal politicized division between the "unofficial" dramaturgs who often censor and control theatrical language and the "official" ones who attempt to circumvent them. The spectre of this type of politicized dramaturgy still haunts Central and Eastern Europe, manifesting itself in its own postcolonial legacy.

Part II, "Dramaturgy in the age of globalization," builds on the previous overview of world dramaturgy. With the rise of the new information age, theatre-making has not been immune to the fast-paced global exchange of goods and ideas. Thanks to the internet and the digital revolution, average theatregoers are now more aware than ever of their interconnected and interdependent relationships with people and places other than their own. Like cultural artifacts and mimes, theatre artists move between countries, continents, and neighborhoods with greater ease, creating works that must necessarily negotiate between specific local and global identities. In this new context, dramaturgy emerges as an essential interlink that translates and connects the vast and varied cultural paradigms. As Tom Sellar puts it in his essay, "The dramaturg as globalist":

> In the era of digital media, theatre practitioners around the world find themselves interconnected as never before; productions, plays, and proposals circulate with fluidity, assisted by a globalized economy and its infrastructure; collaborations and partnerships form readily and regularly across national borders as a de-centered art world orientates itself to new opportunities and imperatives. International collaboration is today a structural necessity rather than an isolated ideological or artistic gesture. The dramaturg, scholar, and critic must offer a practice informed by global currents, maintaining links to multiple theatre cultures as well as supplying expertise and context both at home and externally.
>
> (p. 117, this volume)

Although globalization can threaten local theatre ecosystems (as Jens Peters argues with regard to the National Theatre's live streaming of their shows), it can also offer unprecedented opportunities for theatre to become part of global cultural and political dialogue. In the USA in particular, the rise of the internet, and the replacement of virtual spaces for physical interactions, goes hand in hand with the decline of communal and civic life (as Robert Putnam famously argued in his 2001 classic, *Bowling Alone: The Collapse and Revival of American Community*). Jacqueline Olds and Richard S. Schwartz (2009) warn us further that despite greater virtual interconnectivity, the "increased aloneness" and "the movement in our country toward greater social isolation" are detrimental to our health and well-being.[14] The paradigm of American loneliness is slowly becoming a global phenomenon as other developed and developing nations replicate our lifestyles. Rather than fearing the challenges of globalization, theatre should and must embrace them as an opportunity to find for itself a unique space of communal interaction that can bridge the gaps between virtual and physical spaces, both global and local identities. Because of its roots and historical tradition (going back as far as Tieck and his project of translating Shakespeare into German), the role of the dramaturg has always been quasi-globalist. Now, more than ever, the dramaturgical function, its theoretical and practical methodologies and applications, faces an enormous opportunity to seize the challenge and to assert its central position on the global stage.

The changing role and place of the dramaturg

Since its Aristotelian origins, dramaturgy has undergone many transformations, and Part III, "Dramaturgy in motion: demolitions, definitions, and demarcations," looks at the current redefinition of the term as it develops in the contemporary multimedia landscape. Modern dramaturgy sees itself as a field, profession, skill, and verb; as a tool of inquiry, a liberal art, and theatrical practice. The increasingly interdisciplinary nature of theatre-making demands new tools, which, in turn, affect dramaturgical practice. As Hans-Thies Lehmann and Patrick Primavesi put it:

> Transdisciplinary theatre projects attract new audiences by deviating from the familiar interpretation of dramatic texts on stage. Thus contemporary dramaturgy is facing a challenge: to develop creative ideas in cooperation with authors and directors; to ensure the quality of theatrical work based on a fruitful communication process within the production team; to invent helpful concepts for season schedules and for cultural institutions in general; to enhance unconventional modes of exchange and discourse.
>
> (p. 169, this volume)

How do dramaturgs see themselves and their work in these new contexts of trans-disciplinary, collaborative, and devised theatre? Some, as Jessica Kaplow Applebaum argues, define themselves through hyphenated titles which designate their many multidisciplinary positions. Others use their dramaturgical training to expand their reach into other fields and industries. Dramaturgy increasingly is becoming detached from the specific theatrical function and becoming a skill necessary for the entire creating team involved in the theatre-making process to employ in the process of development and audience outreach. The dramaturgical skills of analysis, critical and structural thinking, and interconnectivity also become tools that can cross artistic boundaries and gain applicability in a world outside of theatre. There is danger in that the dramaturg, as Lawrence Switzky tells us, risks becoming a specialist without a specialty. If everyone can do dramaturgy, and the dramaturg can do everything, who is she, then, and what is her métier? How dramaturgy and dramaturgs define themselves and their profession in the next decade will be essential not just for the future of their field but for theatre itself and for its potential to participate in the new information age.

The dramaturg's artistic leadership and vision is the subject of Part IV, which focuses on the privileges and responsibilities of the literary office. In their participation in season planning and new play development, dramaturgs have always had leadership and quasi-producing roles, but their full impact only recently has gained national and international attention. As Gideon Lester rightly notes, in Europe, the artistic leadership positions are held more often than not by dramaturgs and literary managers. Lester also notes that transplanting this model to US soil would require redefining the what and how of American dramaturgy:

> Rather than keeping them in supporting roles, perhaps the theatre world might begin by readying them to compete for leadership positions, that is, to become artistic directors, curators, programmers, creative producers, beyond the limitations of the institutional dramaturg's traditional function. This would entail an expansion of the definition of dramaturgy to include the articulation of a broadened institutional vision, so that the shaping and running of a theater or cultural center itself becomes a dramaturgical practice. … Some of the most entrepreneurial performing arts organizations in the United States have leaders who operate on a dramaturg-curator-producer-programmer

continuum, even if they don't consider their primary work to be dramaturgical.

(p. 226, this volume)

In many European countries with a well-established dramatic tradition, theatre often shapes the national dialogue, and the dramaturgs shape what's shown at the theatres. If you want to influence social and political debate in your country, one sure way is to become a playwright or a dramaturg (Václav Havel, for example, was a writer, dramaturg, and playwright who became Czechoslovakia's first democratically elected president). In the US, where the majority of theatres are either not-for-profit or commercial ventures, the selection of the season has artistic as well as financial implications. The two goals, artistic and financial, often are viewed as incompatible. European governments have had a time-honored convention of heavily subsidizing their cultural institutions, particularly their performing arts. In exchange, the performing arts have tacitly fulfilled a specific social function: they are tasked with funneling and promoting the voice of the nation as an expression of the cultural and national identity of its people. Without such social, cultural, and artistic pressures, but with plenty of financial concerns, the season-planning aspect of artistic and dramaturgical leadership in the US is wrought with challenges. As a result, theatre's implicit mission often becomes to be an extension of the voice and vision not of the people it is supposed to serve, but of its artistic director.

Historically, the American regional theatres have been run by white males, who have promoted the work of other white males, catering to predominantly white audiences. The changes in the US population have led to the decline of these traditional audiences, provoking re-examination of these longstanding leadership models. Looking at two case studies with two different season-planning strategies, one at the Guthrie Theater and the other at the Oregon Shakespeare Festival, illustrates some of the most salient aspects of literary office management and dramaturgical leadership. The Guthrie is one of the best, but certainly not the only, example of outdated season-planning practices, as illustrated by the short-lived outburst over its all-male, all-white 2012–13 season. Although sharply at odds with its much-lauded explicit mission of cultural diversity, the Guthrie nonetheless continues to demand the support of its increasingly diverse communities and taxpayers. In response to the outrage at the uniformity of its season, Joe Dowling, the Guthrie's then artistic director, called the demands for greater diversity at his theatre a "self-serving argument," thus promulgating the assumption that everyone's "self-serving" impulses, except his own, are ethically questionable (p. 256, this volume). Dowling feels fully entitled to treat the theatre in his care as an extension and expression of his own white, male identity. What's more, he assumes that it is morally just – the way of the world – that others unquestionably serve his singular vision, supporting it with public and private money.

Oregon Shakespeare Theatre's dramaturgically driven season planning and literary leadership present a new alternative to the Guthrie's leadership. As Julie Felise Dubiner, associate director of American Revolutions at the OSF, puts it, "The long view is that whether we are responding from an ethical impulse or a desire for survival, we need to keep striving towards creating institutions that are welcoming to artists and audiences" (p. 252, this volume). The Oregon Shakespeare Festival has been a leader in inclusive initiatives since 1991, when it first formed the Diversity Council. Since then, the OSF has been committed to diversity and inclusion in all aspects of theatre work, including "play selection, hiring, casting, marketing and public relations efforts, education and outreach programs, recruitment of volunteers, and the composition of the Boards of Directors" (p. 253, this volume). Driven by Lue Douthit, the director of Literary Development and Dramaturgy, the OSF's dramaturgical leadership has been crucial in making both the theatre staff and the audiences aware of the numerous issues at stake in the process of representation.

The changing makeup of American audiences will eventually force all theatres to restructure their season-planning practices, as will the emergence of new technologies that are altering our theatre-going habits. With Netflix, YouTube, and other internet services providing any type of entertainment on demand, in the privacy of one's own home, the ritual of going to the theatre is becoming increasingly endangered. In the December 2013 issue of *The Wall Street Journal*, drama critic Terry Teachout observes: "The idea that you might voluntarily go out at night to see a half-dozen human beings act out a story in person … is now alien to most Americans, especially younger ones."[15] If it is to survive these two major paradigm shifts (the changes in population and the emergence of new streaming technologies), American theatre needs dramaturgical leadership to both broaden and maintain its audience base. As Ken Cerniglia notes in his essay, to reach a broad audience, theatres must start considering the dramaturgy of appeal. New collaborative technologies, peer-to-peer exchange platforms, and user-driven feedback create new opportunities for virtual literary office management that can change our season-planning practices. In Europe, such an approach has been implemented in a number of countries for over a decade. This includes the searchable database of plays in translation developed by the Information Centre for Drama in Europe (ICDE) (www.playservice.net) with founding partners from Finland, England, Germany, France, and the Netherlands; the Polish database of all plays produced in Poland since 1900, including scanned reviews, posters, and programs (www.e-teatr.pl), and the UK database of English-language plays (www.doollee.com). In the US, the National New Play Network (www.nnpn. org) is leading the way in transforming the practice of literary office management and dramaturgical leadership. Other virtual networks such as New Play Map (www. newplaymap.org), New International Theatre Experience (www.nitecorp.com and www.nitenews.org), and The Playwrights' Center (www.pwcenter.org) provide additional tools for virtual office management, play exchange, and peer-to-peer collaborations. It is up to the dramaturgical field at large to see how to use the new technology to remain relevant and to advance the practice of theatre in the most inclusive way.

Dramaturgy in context

Part V, "Dramaturg as context manager," provides an overview of one of the most salient dramaturgical practices: contextualization of the theatrical experience. At the 2014 Consumer Electronics Show, Marissa Meyer, CEO of Yahoo, proclaimed that "the future of search is contextual."[16] If for IT businesses the future is contextual, for dramaturgs the past has been contextual since the beginning of the profession. Researching historical background, maintaining the coherence of a project, and explaining its context to an audience has been one of the main tasks of the many production dramaturgs since the 1800s. For dramaturgs, managing the context is often akin to the process of translation. In dramaturgy, however, the concept of "translation," like the concept of dramaturgy itself, has many meanings. It can mean literal (or literary) translation from one language to another. It can mean translating (adapting) a project from one medium to another (from film to theatre, from novel to theatre, from theatre to novel and film). During the process of new play development, it can also mean translating the world of the play between the playwright and the director. And finally, it can also mean translating the same world from the rehearsal room to the wider audience, through various audience outreach methods, program notes, lobby displays, social media, and other digiturgical tools.

Beatrice Basso, an American translator of Italian drama, once wrote that in the process of translating drama from one language to another, one must

> live through two main phases: the linguistic translation and the transmutation of the physical /cultural essence of the piece into another culture. Sensitivity both to the linguistic issues of the original text and to the culture from which the play stems, is ... necessary to any translation aimed at production. ... The more the sociological and cultural aspects of a text are taken into consideration, the more you can trust the original writing and understand its tone.[17]

In addition to mastering the plays' sociological, cultural, and linguistic context, one must capture their intricate musical structure: the rhythm and tonality of language. Just as she must seamlessly move between two languages and two cultures when focused on linguistic translation, the production dramaturg as the context manager must move between the different "languages of the stage," to quote Patrice Pavis, or sometimes even between different art forms.[18] Whether during linguistic translation, the new play development process, or adaptation, understanding and moving between two different contexts is an essential aspect of the dramaturgical experience. Katalin Trencsényi, Gitta Honegger, Jane Barnette, and Mark Bly analyze different strategies for contextualizing the world of the play as applied to various dramaturgical practices, from translation to adaptation to new play development.

The same ability that allows the dramaturgs to move between contexts permits them to move between different disciplines and artistic mediums. Part VI, "Dramaturgy among other arts: interdisciplinarity, transdisciplinarity, and transvergence," provides an overview of dramaturgical practice as it's applied to other artistic disciplines, including musical theatre, opera, dance, film, multimedia projects, interactive theatre, experimental works, new media, and video game design. Since dramaturgy concerns itself with the issues of dramatic structure, the dramaturgical tools and strategies used in theatre are transferable to other mediums that also rely on dramatic structure. In opera, Andrew Eggert notes, for example, "composers and producers have called on the knowledge and experience of a dramaturg – a knowledgeable theatre practitioner – to help give direction to the creative process" (p. 354, this volume). Likewise, dramaturgical research strategies are applicable to many other forms beyond live stage. To quote Gerry Potter, who writes about film dramaturgy, "As it is in theatrical dramaturgy, research is a primary activity for screenwriters, directors, actors, designers, cinematographers, editors, composers, and craft departments in motion pictures" (p. 359, this volume). Increasingly, dramaturgs can be found working in new areas. In the latest developments, dramaturgy expands into the fields of new media, virtual worlds, and video game design, where structuring the user's emotional experience is fundamental to the very process. As Klaus P. Jantke notes,

> Dramaturgy is the design of emotional experience. For digital games that are intended to tell a story, game design includes the anticipation of the players' experiences which will lead to excitement, fascination, thrill, perhaps to immersion and flow. What players will experience takes place over time. Events that happen are linearly ordered and those that may potentially happen form a partially ordered space, the game's story space. Dramaturgical game design is the anticipation of varying experiences and their thoughtful arrangement in a partially ordered space of events that players may possibly experience when playing the game.
>
> (p. 370, this volume)

Dramaturgy has concerned itself with structuring the emotional experience of the audience since its very beginnings. Starting from Aristotle's *Poetics*, through Eugène Scribe's concept of the "well-made play," Gustav Freytag's dramatic "triangle" (*Technique of the Drama*, 1863), and Layos Egri's famous book, *The Art of Dramatic Writing* (1942), to the multitude of modern how-to guides, among which Jeffrey Hatcher's *The Art and Craft of Playwriting* (2000) is one of the best-known, these dramaturg-playmakers attempt to provide the most reliable recipe for the well-designed dramatic structure. On the other end from the new play development process are production dramaturgs whose job is to break down already existent dramatic structures in order to translate the dramatic text into theatrical language. These dramaturgs have been developing different methods of play analysis for years, using Aristotle, Scribe, Egri, and others to unlock the playwright's purpose behind the arrangement of dramatic events. The best-known modern play-analysis guides, such as David Ball's *Backwards and Forwards: A Technical Manual for Reading Plays* (1983) and David Rush's *A Student Guide to Play Analysis* (2005), however, concern themselves with classic, Aristotelian dramas, which rely on internally coherent dramatic structure (often based on the unity of time, space, and place), domino-like causality, and linear arrangement of events and characters which are consistent, realistic, and believable. Thus, many of these play development and play-analysis strategies are inadequate when faced with postdramatic dramaturgy of non-realist dramas, devised performances, and avant-garde multimedia works. Part VII, "Dramaturg as systems analyst: dramaturgy of postdramatic structures," focuses on this long-neglected area of dramaturgical practice. The part opens with Gad Kaynar's essay on "Postdramatic dramaturgy," which delineates the challenges and issues involved in working with non-linear, anti-Aristotelian narratives. Further, the part includes some of the iconic essays on play analysis, like Elinor Fuchs' legendary "EF's visit to a small planet," Tori Haring-Smith's "Dramaturging non-realism," and D. J. Hopkins's "Research, counter-text, performance," as well as new articles by leading international dramaturgs working in new media, dance, and digital performance. Some of the methods of play development and analysis included in this part can apply to realist dramas, but all of them can also apply to postdramatic works that might not even have a dramatic text. This part also includes one older essay, Barbara Johnson's "Teaching deconstructively," first published in 1985. The essay has been staple reading in comparative literature and English departments, but it is barely known in theatre studies and performing arts courses. Yet the reading strategies provided by Johnson are very suitable for theatrical texts, particularly those whose dramatic structure is not easily discernable. As theatre moves towards a collaborative, devised model, developing works that reflect our current, global, mediated, and fragmented reality, new analytical tools will need to be developed.

Dramaturgical outreach

The final part, "Dramaturg as public relations manager: immersions, talkbacks, lobby displays, and social networks," provides an overview of traditional dramaturgical outreach tools, like talkbacks and program notes, as well as the latest trends, including immersive dramaturgy, pre-show talks, lobby displays, production blogs, podcasts, preview videos, social media outreach, theatre apps, geo-turgy, photo-turgy, blogo-turgy, and tweeturgy. Miriam Weisfeld's article on theatre lobby displays is the first essay ever published on the topic. As audiences demand more interactive, immersive experiences, lobby displays will become part of the dramaturgical process. Likewise, the revolution in online dramaturgy and social media creates unprecedented opportunities for dramaturgs to build online components into their traditional dramaturgical audience outreach. Some theatres, like the Oregon Shakespeare Festival or the National Theatre in London, have developed elaborate online educational sites to supplement their on-site outreach. The National Theatre, in fact, is one of the very first theatres to have an entire digital department devoted solely to developing and promoting the theatre's online content. In October 2013, the National Theatre pioneered an app, specifically designed to commemorate their 50th anniversary. The app consists of an "extensive collection of content from a selection of fifty seminal productions, [f]eaturing exclusive content from the National Theatre's archive," including "an interactive timeline of production posters; hundreds of production and rehearsal photographs, costume illustrations, set designs, technical images, annotated scripts and other content from a selection of National Theatre productions; exclusive video interviews; [and] an overall introduction and an introduction to each production."[19] As more and more dramaturgs across the globe engage in online digiturgy, the future of dramaturgical outreach lies in mobile and context-driven search and networking technology. Dramaturgs should embrace these tools, as they can help the field to grow and further develop while expanding audience experience and making theatre more accessible and interconnected.

If there ever was a time for a profession to flourish, our new digital information age creates a perfect storm for the dramaturgical mode of analysis to dominate how we process, shape, and structure the information overload. Although it initially grew out of theatre, contemporary dramaturgy has made enormous advancements in recent years, and it is now permeating all kinds of narrative forms and structures: from opera to musical theatre; from dance and multimedia to filmmaking, video game design, and robotics. The definition of dramaturgy is expanding and the concept is being redefined as we speak, as verb, skill, and function, to include many modes of making meaning. In our global, mediated context of multi-national group collaborations that dissolve traditional divisions of roles as well as unbend previously intransigent rules of time and space, the dramaturg is also the ultimate globalist: inter-cultural mediator, information and research manager, media content analyst, interdisciplinary negotiator, social media strategist. If the twentieth century can be called the century of the auteur director, the twenty-first century will be the century of the dramaturg.

Notes

1 Patrice Pavis, *Dictionary of the Theatre: Terms, Concepts, and Analysis* (Toronto: University of Toronto Press, 1998), 24.
2 Quoted in Joel Schechter, "In the Beginning There Was Lessing ... Then Brecht, Muller and Other Dramaturgs," in *Dramaturgy in American Theater: A Source Book*, eds. Susan Jonas, Geoffrey S. Proehl, and Michael Lupu (Fort Worth, TX: Harcourt Brace College, 1997), 18, 16–24.
3 See W. Habicht, "Shakespeare in Nineteenth-Century Germany: The Making of a Myth," in *Nineteenth-Century Germany, A Symposium*, eds. Modris Eksteins and Hildegard Hammerschmidt (Tübingen: Marr, 1983), 141–57; and W. Habicht, "The Romanticism of the Schlegel-Tieck Shakespeare and the History of Nineteenth-Century German Shakespeare Translation," in *European Shakespeares: Translating Shakespeare in the Romantic Age*, ed. Lieven D'hulst and trans. Dirk Delabastita (Amsterdam: John Benjamins, 1992), 45–54.
4 Quoted in Schechter, 21.
5 Schechter, 22.
6 Mark Bly, *The Production Notebooks: Theatre in Process, Volume 2* (New York: Theatre Communications Group, 2001), xv.
7 Richard Schechner, *Between Theater and Anthropology* (Philadelphia: University of Pennsylvania Press, 1985).
8 Erika Fischer-Lichte, *The Transformative Power of Performance: A New Aesthetics* (Abingdon: Routledge, 2008), 140.
9 Peter Szondi, *Theory of the Modern Drama*, ed. and trans. Michael Hays (Minneapolis: University of Minnesota Press, 1987), 10.
10 Hans-Thies Lehmann, *Postdramatic Theatre* (Abingdon: Routledge, 1999), 30. (Emphasis author's).
11 Lehmann, 30.
12 Lehmann, 31.
13 Quoted in Craig Fleming, "CUI BONO? A Critique of the Conscripted Audience and, Perforce, a Manifesto," *HowlRound*, February 3, 2013, available online at www.howlround.com/cui-bono-a-critique-of-the-conscripted-audience-and-perforce-a-manifesto.
14 Jacqueline Olds and Richard S. Schwartz, *The Lonely American: Drifting Apart in the Twenty-First Century* (Boston: Beacon Press, 2009), 135.
15 Terry Teachout, "How Theatres Can Combat the Stay-at-Home Mindset," *The Wall Street Journal*, December 25, 2013, available online at http://online.wsj.com/news/articles/SB1000 14240527023048669045792668822201324884 (accessed December 25, 2013).

16 Adrian Covert, "Marissa Meyer Reveals Yahoo's Big Plans for 2014," *CNNMoney Tech*, January 7, 2014, available online at http://money.cnn.com/2014/01/07/technology/marissa-mayer-ces-yahoo/index.html?hpt=hp_t2 (accessed January 8, 2014).

17 Beatrice Basso, "Italian Dramaturg in a Translation Process," *Theatre Topics* 13.1 (March 2003): 161, see also 162–3.

18 Patrice Pavis, *Languages of the Stage: Essays in the Semiology of the Theatre* (New York: PAJ, 2001).

19 "50 Years of the National Theatre" [App], October 12, 2013, available online at https://itunes.apple.com/gb/app/50-years-national-theatre/id720763482?mt=8 (accessed October 14, 2013).

Part I

WORLD DRAMATURGY IN THE TWENTY-FIRST CENTURY

1

Robert Blacker looks at the past and future of American dramaturgy

Jacob Gallagher-Ross and Robert Blacker

Dramaturgy in America was a European ideal grafted onto native aspirations. Arising in the 1970s, it became widely disseminated as a job description and a set of emerging ideas in the 1980s, as a new generation of artistic directors took over regional theatres. This piece attempts to indicate macrohistory by relating anecdotal microhistory, revealing snapshots of the evolution of American dramaturgy. In a series of interviews conducted over the winter and spring of 2013, Robert Blacker and I discussed the role of the dramaturg in a trio of theatrical institutions that represent three kinds of theatre organizations – regional, developmental, and classical. We talked about where the profession has been, and where it's going, as the founding generation prepares to retire and new cultural and financial constraints produce new definitions of the role. The following is excerpted from Blacker's remarks.

Jacob Gallagher-Ross

On the La Jolla Playhouse

In only our second season La Jolla was nominated for a Tony for Best Regional Theatre. La Jolla emerged so quickly in prominence on the national scene because of the caliber of the artists that its artistic director, Des McAnuff, and I were able to bring there. Artists are always the foundation of good work. I had worked as dramaturg with Des on two of his productions for Joe Papp in New York, and he invited me to join him at La Jolla as institutional dramaturg and later associate artistic director (different title, same function). We planned seasons together, and I admired his willingness to take the best idea in the room and bring in directors as good as he because he was secure in his talents. Insecurity is the death of collaboration.

We worked from personal connections, and Peter Sellars, Robert Woodruff, Bill Irwin, Stephen Sondheim, and James Lapine were a critical part of our early seasons. We also took advantage of an historical moment. A talented group of young directors who were soon to become artistic directors at theatres across the country were still available: Mark Lamos, Emily Mann, and Peter Sellars, among them, as well as Garland Wright, who withdrew from La Jolla when he got the Guthrie. Suddenly, in the 1980s, a new generation of artistic directors inherited the American theatre from its not-for-profit founders. It was a seismic shift that moved the energy away from a handful of urban centers, where these young directors developed their ideas, to theatres across the country.

Most of these directors had worked in small theatres, and Des saw the importance of giving them the opportunity to mount productions on our Broadway-sized mainstage, often letting them choose plays and projects such as rarely produced Brecht and Sophocles that normally would not be done on this large a scale. I learned when I worked for Joe Papp that it's as important to provide opportunities for an artist to develop their skills as focusing on the project at hand. That's how you create an exciting theatre scene.

A larger stage often meant for these directors the opportunity to tackle large cast classics that they could not afford to do in smaller theatres. We put together seasons in a fashion that was very important for Des McAnuff. He hated when an artistic director asked: "Do you want to do *Pygmalion*?" "Why would *Pygmalion* be the classical play out of all the classical plays I want to do," he told me. "Ask me what I want to do." So we worked off of lists of plays from our directors, making sure that our seasons still offered variety. Our productions were successful because they were driven by passion that these directors brought to projects that came from their gut.

There was another reason as well. The most important artistic function of the artistic leadership of a theatre, after choosing artists and projects, is to guide productions, *as they need it*. Des and I were very good about helping to shape material and productions. Seeing run-throughs in the rehearsal room. Attending dress rehearsals. Continuing to give notes during previews. Des has the eye of a director and is amazing with detail. For example, he is constantly scanning the stage so he can remove anything that throws the focus. My strength was complementary – in the area of text, particularly with clarity and meaning, and using structure to achieve both. That's what a dramaturg can do. But there is no need for rigid guidelines for any of this. Des is also the best dramaturg I know because as a playwright himself he understands a writer's process. As collaborators you bring your own strengths to the table and that will change with each collaboration. The ability to guide productions makes the difference between a good theatre and a great theatre and surprisingly is often lacking.

Of course, work on a new project starts before rehearsals begin with conversations and readings, and sometimes a workshop – the focus of my work for Sundance.

On the Sundance Theatre Labs

I was invited to Sundance to restructure its annual Playwrights' Lab, which was then a two-week plus summer event at the Sundance resort in the Utah mountains. I was artistic director for eight years, and each year I made a number of changes in collaboration with Philip Himberg, the director of the Sundance Theatre Programs.

First, I proposed changing the name. Because the theatre that I found interesting was generated in multiple ways – by playwrights, by directors, sometimes through the collaboration of a group, sometimes by solo artists – I wanted to honor every way that theatre work is generated. And I wanted to bring in projects that ran the full range of American theatre, from the avant-garde to traditional musicals. So I suggested changing the name to the Sundance Theatre Lab. Playwrights were understandably concerned that their access to the lab was more limited and protested. More on that later.

Another change I implemented for our first season was based on my experience attending the annual O'Neill Playwrights Conference. The admirable success of their workshops turned the conference into a marketplace for artistic directors and others to shop for product. I was concerned that the pressure to be at your best when an important producer attended a presentation of your play would curtail the freedom of artists to explore and experiment. And so the Sundance Theatre Lab became a private affair. The artists loved it. The only audiences for presentations at the end was the community of artists and staff who were working there. With one exception. If you were already committed to producing a project at the lab, you needed to see it in its latest state to help move it forward thereafter. Those visitors, however, were only allowed to see their project.

Feedback sessions in front of an audience, the surest way to shut down a writer, also became private and limited to a handful of participants. We tried not to hold them immediately after a presentation when artists were still digesting what they had seen. I began then by asking what the creators learned from watching their work and then continued by requesting questions that they wanted us to answer. We moved on to our own questions and comments thereafter.

If I felt a young project was not ready for a presentation and the writer agreed, we did not do one. If a writer was timid about presenting something I thought would benefit from the presence of an audience, I would ask artists to consider doing so. The secret to the success of any workshop where the projects are at different stages of development is to give them the individual treatment that they need and deserve.

Changes continued through seven out of my eight years there and were based on our observations and feedback from the artists. One of the most important was implemented for our second year. Rehearsing every day, writers had little time to rewrite, sometimes putting in all-nighters to turn in rewrites based on what they had seen the day before. This seemed unproductive to me, and so for our second season we lengthened the lab to three full weeks and cut down rehearsals to every other day, so that the writers would have a full day in between to write – and to think. One of the most important things that any artist needs is think-time. At Sundance they could take a long walk on the incredible mountain that towers over the resort. In that solitude, an important idea may come to you. Well, the artists agreed, and the Sundance Institute was extraordinarily generous in giving us more money to expand the length of our residency there.

I brought in dramaturgs on two levels: those who worked on a pair of projects and would be present at those rehearsals; in addition, I brought in two mentors, who helped me visit rehearsals, occasionally giving feedback, but also to help Philip and me track how projects were doing. This also gave them the opportunity to get to know artists and projects before they became part of the feedback sessions at the end. For mentors, I often chose artistic directors I knew who were good at giving notes. For the first season I invited Des McAnuff and Emily Mann. Later I included playwrights who were also teachers, such as Marsha Norman.

The people who attended the final critique sessions were the writer, director, and dramaturg who were working on the project, the two mentors, the dramaturgs who were working on other projects, in addition to me and Philip. I made it clear that it was perfectly fine to make limited observations. I think it's a trap to think that you always must have something to say. Not everyone understands or is sympathetic to every project. Sometimes the best thing you can offer is keep your mouth shut. I would lead the sessions and we'd try to keep them, as much as possible, as a dialogue. This kind of session is always very sensitive, and when a writer showed signs of fatigue, I would bring it to an end if I had not already done so. The stage the project was at was also an important consideration. If you try to get a writer to cerebrate about a project that is in the earliest stages, they may articulate something which should not yet be verbalized. Once you verbalize something, you're beginning to freeze what the piece is.

After three seasons, we expanded the Sundance theatre programs. We created a writing retreat for playwrights, in part to help address the criticism that the Theatre Lab had cut down on opportunities for writers. (On average, six of our eight projects at the lab still had a playwright at the center). Philip found an arts colony on a cattle ranch in Wyoming – in February – run by the amazing Ucross Foundation. Only we theatre folk were crazy enough to go to Wyoming in the winter. We usually brought seven playwrights and a composer there each year.

I learned the value of the austere beauty of the Wyoming plateau and the lab in the majestic Utah mountains for our urban-bound art. We usually make theatre in cities, but these rural retreats offered the opportunity to reflect on the immensity of the world and to ponder something outside of yourself. And that informed the breadth and depth of the work. The format at Ucross was simple. You were there to write. You didn't need to show anyone what you were working on, but ad hoc private conversations took place. Solitude until dinner. (Lunches were even brought to our work rooms). Conversation and community over the dinner table. There were always two events at the lab and the retreat, the project you were working on and community among the artists who were there. Conversations about the art; practical exchanges about the commerce. Friendships formed, lasting and fleeting. Watching the artists gathered at these events, it began to feel as if there really was an American theatre in this vast country where we seldom meet. It was ironic that this occurred at a ski resort and a cattle ranch thanks to the visionaries who brought our visionaries there.

On the Stratford Shakespeare Festival of Canada

Going to Stratford was intimidating because its amazing acting company included actors who had been there for twenty to thirty years, and whose knowledge about Shakespeare made my eighteen productions seem a flirtation. It was a great opportunity to learn more about my favorite writer. In my early career, Joe Papp showed me the importance of changing your focus regularly, so you don't go stale. Having worked in New York, regional and developmental theatre, the classics were next.

Stratford's first two artistic directors, Tyrone Guthrie and Michael Langham, were pioneers, strong directors with new ideas. But as the festival had evolved over decades, it had become better known as an actor's theatre. Des restored the balance between director and actor and sought to put the playwright back at the center of the work. With Shakespeare, we encouraged everyone to dig into the texts and find what is really there. Very often what we see in productions of Shakespeare are sentimental notions that come from false traditions which have evolved over the centuries. Tradition in theatre, Des would say, is often the last five productions you've seen of a play. And what we most often see are productions that are overcut and so have diminished the magnificence of the wide canvas that Shakespeare is presenting. I was shocked to see that in the seven productions of *Henry V* produced at Stratford in its first fifty years, all but two had cut the most onerous action Henry takes in the play. At the battle of Agincourt, when he is badly outnumbered by the French, he orders the execution of his prisoners so he can use the soldiers guarding them on the battlefield. How can a king who is the presumed model of a *good* leader do this? Well, Shakespeare is more complex than usually presented. In *Henry V* he actually makes an implicit comparison between Henry and Machiavelli by paraphrasing one of *The Prince*'s most famous lines. My job as institutional dramaturg was to fight for the complexity in Shakespeare's writing and promote the excavation of the text. Scenes that seem irrelevant are often clues to what issues were circling in his head. I knew from my work with living playwrights that they are always reflecting their times, and so we looked to the history of Shakespeare's time for other clues. The Guy Fawkes Gunpowder Plot to blow up the king and Parliament is key to understanding *Macbeth*.

Des also brought more living playwrights to Stratford. He believes it's important to do classical work and new work side by side because they inform each other. You don't have to reinvent the wheel, he would tell you. If you're having a problem as a writer, perhaps you can find a solution in a classic play. And by doing new work alongside the classics, you are reminded that classics are not museum pieces. He expanded the number of playwriting commissions, and I created a playwriting retreat based on the one I had instituted at Sundance. Canadian playwrights got to know us, and we got to know them. There were spirited discussions over dinner, and I learned so much about the mechanisms of contemporary Canadian theatre and how Stratford could perhaps help solve some of the problems they encountered. An institutional dramaturg must always have his/her eye on the big picture, as well as the project at hand. That is how you move our art form forward.

On the state of American dramaturgy

I began working as a dramaturg at the Public Theater in the 1970s and seen many changes in the decades that I've been working in the theatre. When I began there were only a handful of dramaturgs. As university programs have expanded, I wonder how we are going to employ all the graduates that come out of them. I've seen the impact that dramaturgy has had on the profession. I see the talent, but I also see a lack of opportunity in these difficult economic times. Opportunity and money are always related. And so I feel my job in my later years is to hang in there long enough to help ignite the next great age of theatre. Theatre is always a marathon race and we're constantly passing the baton. That's why I am hanging in here: to pass the baton.

2

Contemporary new play dramaturgy in Canada

Brian Quirt

Canadian dramaturgy takes many forms depending on the nature of the work, the region, and indeed the language of the artists. I will speak only of dramaturgy in English-Canada, where over the past 25 years the profession has evolved into a significant and central component of the country's new-play creation movement. A growing number of emerging artists identify themselves as dramaturgs, seek and find work in the field, and are mentored by a generation that carved out, defined, and brought tremendous artistry to the landscape of dramaturgy.

This was not always the case. When I entered the dramaturgical profession in the late 1980s, fresh out of the M.A. Drama program at the University of Toronto, I'm not certain how much I knew about dramaturgy. The then head of the M.A. program, Ronald Bryden, had left Canada in his youth to become a newspaper critic in the UK and ended up as the literary manager of the Royal Shakespeare Company for five years in the 1970s. His tales of discovering Tom Stoppard must have inspired my desire to become a dramaturg; I knew that I wanted to work as one, but was aware at the time of precious few role models in Toronto or anywhere in Canada. So I wrote to local artistic directors asking to be considered for a dramaturgical position. I was invited to a number of interviews, but there were, in fact, no positions to be considered for. I was, fortunately, offered a short-term intern position as the (newly created) assistant to the literary manager of what has since become the Canadian Stage Company, a job that offered me a window into the artistic engine house of that company, though one that involved little actual dramaturgy, at least initially. I quickly became aware of a heated, ongoing debate in the Toronto, and Canadian, theatre community about the value, role, and status of the dramaturg.

In 2009, I attended the regional finals of the Sears Ontario Drama Festival, a gathering of high-school theatre productions, to watch a student version of one of my adaptations. I was surprised and delighted to note that several of the student productions included dramaturgs as part of the creative team. This suggested to me that a sea change had occurred in the understanding and appreciation of the role of the dramaturg in Canadian theatre. If even high-school students are claiming the title for themselves, and are finding creative ways to contribute to the work of their colleagues, then much of the work my generation undertook to promote, inspire, and work as dramaturgs has indeed had a huge impact.

In English-Canadian theatre of the past 40 years, creating and producing new work has been at the core of the majority of our theatre companies (with of course some significant exceptions), as artists, audiences, and arts councils have prioritized a national need to generate a canon of Canadian plays and performance pieces. This has been paralleled in other creative fields such as novels, visual arts, movies, and so on, with varying success, as this small country (at least in terms of population) has striven to assert its creative energies in the face of the overwhelming and often stifling colonial influences of the United Kingdom and the United States. In our field, one result is that dramaturgy in Canada has largely been focused on new work; production dramaturgy certainly occurs in the new-work field, and in some arenas of classical theatre production, but the majority of English-Canadian dramaturgs specialize in collaborating with living playwrights.

The artistic directors that were skeptical about making a living as a dramaturg in 1980s Toronto were largely right. My personal solution to this was, like many freelance theatre artists, to find a community of theatre-makers whose work inspired me, largely through festivals focused on new plays, and who responded to the ideas, analysis, and inspiration I, as an emerging dramaturg, could offer them. Even that network may not have been sufficient to support me, so I created part-time dramaturgical positions at Toronto's Theatre Centre and then at Factory Theatre. These offered me the stability of (modest) regular fees and expanded my network of collaborators to include, at the Theatre Centre, dancers, choreographers, and an increasingly diverse group of theatre artists, and at Factory, the ability to work with both senior and emerging playwrights from across Canada.

Ultimately, however, my desire to explore dramaturgical issues and ideas led me to establish my own company (founded with producer Naomi Campbell): Nightswimming. Though initially created to develop and produce a show that I was dramaturging, it soon evolved into a non-producing, commissioning company that explicitly placed dramaturgy at the heart of its mission: to advance the field of dramaturgy and play development in Canada through the exploration of theatrical stories and how they are told. Since 1995, Nightswimming has provided a fertile environment in which I have been able, with many colleagues, to explore the boundaries of theatrical storytelling in theatre, dance, and music. We have commissioned adaptations of novels and poetry, contemporary dance, an a cappella musical, a seven-play cycle of classically inspired plays, physical theatre, new works by leading South Asian and Latina writers, and plays by some of the country's leading playwrights. It has been conceived as a forum for exploration through the making of new performance. We currently place all of our work in three interconnected categories.

The category of *Research* includes all of our exploratory initiatives, from our Pure Research program to our investigations of form and genre, and soon reaching into an international collaboration with like-minded theatre research organizations in Europe. *Creation* is at the heart of all that we do, including commissioning artists, developing their work, conducting readings and workshops, hosting residencies, and partnering with companies to ultimately produce the works we create in collaboration with each artist. *Performance* acknowledges that public presentations of our works-in-progress are crucial to our creation process: our goal has always been to ensure that the plays we commission and develop reach the stage through partnerships with producers, presenters, festivals, and theatre schools. Through performance we refine our work and tell stories to audiences locally and nationally.

The work I do as a dramaturg – though I also serve as a director on many of the projects we develop – is itself focused on three broadly defined areas: ideas, communication, and process. The first refers to the *ideas* that underlie any work of performance, both intellectual and emotional, and my search for the core set of ideas at the heart of the work's inspiration. Understanding and being able to work with those ideas prepares me for the second element, *communication*. Dramaturgy, to me, is always focused on how a piece is communicated to an audience by whatever means is selected by the artist, and my role is to scrutinize those devices for their effectiveness in communicating the desired ideas to the ultimate spectators. The goal is not to clarify, but to deepen and enrich the expression of the core ideas. The third, and equally critical, role is that of *process*. Designing, or helping to design, the process by which a new work is created is a vital part of the dramaturgical contribution at Nightswimming. Determining which activities happen and when and with what agenda is a central part of our collaboration with our commissioned artists. Throughout all three components (which, of course, often overlap one another; little in our dramaturgical world is perfectly sequential) I am searching for the core ideas and how they evolve, looking for new ways to inspire the creators to dig deeply into the material they have selected, and exploring the theatrical effectiveness of the work by examining both the challenges and the rewards of the piece for its eventual audience. That Nightswimming has thrived over the past 18 years is a testament to how much the culture of dramaturgy has evolved throughout our theatre community and the degree to which writers and theatre companies have accepted the role and its functions.

Dramaturgy in English-Canada is confident of its place in our theatrical milieu – clearly a substantial change from the situation 20 years ago. Today there are literary managers and staff dramaturgs at a dozen major theatre companies from Vancouver's Arts Club Theatre to Toronto's Tarragon Theatre, including the Stratford and Shaw festivals. The role is embraced by students and emerging artists seeking to contribute their voices to the theatrical process, eager to generate creative environments in which storytellers (including playwrights) are provided the tools to make their work and bring it to audiences. Not every play or playwright works with or needs a dramaturg, but the fluid nature of the dramaturgical profession in Canada effectively accommodates the ways in which artists want to create. In general, the days of prescriptive approaches have faded away, replaced by wide acceptance amongst dramaturgs that it is the artist that must define the nature of the process in collaboration with dramaturgs and other colleagues. The role is also increasingly common in new-play festivals (as we've seen even at the high-school level). And while many theatres maintain a focus on text-based plays that can seem old-fashioned in this internet-driven age, the flexibility of the dramaturgical community enables many of its members to move between disciplines and media with great ease; it has long been said that dramaturgs can contribute to any form of storytelling, and this is increasingly the reality in English-Canada.

From my perspective, three factors have had significant impact on the field of dramaturgy and play development in Canada over the past decade. The first is the growth and evolution of new-play festivals such as the Fringe, Summerworks, Rhubarb, Groundswell, Rock.Paper.Sistahz, Panamerican Routes, De Colores, and NextFest, to name some of the major events in Toronto each year; many other cities host similar festivals. These festivals provide not only practical and supportive environments for playwrights to produce or present new work, but they also offer work for freelance dramaturgs and opportunities for actors and other theatre artists to collaborate directly with writers. As well, these festivals give writers (and their creative teams) direct access to audiences, which is always the best and most productive element of any play development process. They also suggest a more expansive approach to collaboration in which the writer is empowered to be a central member of the creative team with responsibility for mounting the production. And they are an increasingly useful training ground for dramaturgs.

The second factor is LMDA Canada (Literary Managers and Dramaturgs of the Americas: lmda.org). The Canadian arm of this service organization has, since its founding in 1997, presented five international conferences on dramaturgy, eleven editions of the Toronto Mini-Conference on Dramaturgy, developed a substantial national network of dramaturgs and artists committed to the creation of new work, and brought Canadian dramaturgs into increased contact with our colleagues in the United States and beyond. LMDA Canada has had an active membership of more than 100 for over a decade, demonstrating the growth of practitioners across the country. The impact of this type of network is always difficult to quantify with any precision, but I believe that LMDA Canada has offered a forum for artists to express and explore a multitude of approaches to creating new plays. A more articulate conversation about this work and about dramaturgy itself has resulted.

The third factor is the growth and maturity of our network of play development centres. This national network was formalized under the name Playwright Development Centres of Canada (PDCC). The eleven organizations share a commitment to supporting the work of playwrights through a profusion of services and programs. Some have national mandates, like Vancouver's Playwrights Theatre Centre, the Banff Centre Playwrights Colony, and Montreal's Playwrights Workshop Montreal, and they provide essential meeting places for writers and theatre artists from across the country. Several are designed to serve artists in particular regions or cities. Exchanges between companies, festivals run by several centers, and regular meetings of the network have strengthened the bonds between dramaturgs, and between dramaturgs and playwrights. Nightswimming is a member, though it is least like any of the other centers in that it doesn't have a service or regional mandate. But even here, the flexibility of the dramaturgical scene to include outliers is a hallmark of our community.

Having arrived at this comfortable plateau, I see four priorities ahead of us. The first, and most important, is a continued focus on diversity – cultural and creative. We are in danger of falling far behind the cultural mixture of our cities, our audiences, and other media. There are more stories by a diverse body of artists drawing on more forms and traditions that we must cultivate by offering them access to the resources of theatre companies and festivals. As mainstream theatrical storytelling increasingly embraces other media and conventions, our dramaturgs must change our institutions from within by advocating for the leading edge whenever possible.

To that end, play development programs must continue to develop more theatrical approaches to creating new works by emphasizing on-the-feet workshops, presentations, and productions incorporating design, technology, movement, sound, etc. Choreographers, designers, performance artists, visual and new-media artists must be welcomed into our theatres to remind us of the vitality of other disciplines and how much they can offer to the theatre. We must return play creation and development to our theatres and get it out of rehearsal halls. Working in a theatre space is different: it inspires more imaginative choices and reconnects us to our audience, even when they are not yet in the room. And, when necessary, we must embrace (as many artists have) theatre that is not interested in theatres at all, while also welcoming the bravura of such artists into our theatres whenever possible.

Finally, play development will only ever be as good as the plays and the directors who interpret them. Dramaturgs and new-play development organizations must support director training and internships. This is a vital need. If the imaginative visions of our best playwrights are to truly flourish, we must have inspired, trained, and able directors to bring their works to life. And to return to the insights of that artistic director who challenged my career choice so many years ago, we must foster a more effective collaboration between our theatre-makers, our directors, and our dramaturgs. This communication gap still, at times, exists; it curtails creative impulses and can hold us back from the boundaries that many are challenging.

Dramaturgs are flourishing in Canada today and often taking leadership roles in our theatres and support organizations. But there is much work to do to welcome and inspire the artists that should be making the theatre of the twenty-first century. In my roles at Nightswimming and the Banff Centre I'm proud to be able to help define the need, articulate the way forward, and design the pathway toward a more richly integrated theatrical and dramaturgical landscape.

3

Collaborative dramaturgy in Latin American theatre

Margarita Espada

We must invent our own theatre; to create our own utopias … to create another language; the language of those who are different … to use the imagination to find that space of freedom; since there is not just one absolute truth but a union of different truths.[1]

With this speech, Argentinean theatre director Osvaldo Dragún traveled the world creating spaces to share practices and conversation about the alternative theatre that emerged in Latin America as a result of the political turmoil that characterized 1960. Dragun was a founder of the Latin American and Caribbean Theatre School, which provided an intensive theatre encounter with masters of Latin American theatre, with the goal of creating a professional forum to exchange experiences and training with professional actors. The school traveled through different countries exchanging experiences with other followers of the Latin American masters. My experience as a member of that school offered me the opportunity to learn the principles of Latin American theatre, including the culture of theatre as a group, the concept of *creación colectiva*, collaborative dramaturgy, and the approach to actor training and physical theatre.

A full discussion of Latin American theatre would not be complete without an explanation of popular theatre that encompasses this style of visual dramaturgy. Unlike dominant European bourgeois theatre forms, Latin American popular theatre encourages audiences to become active members of society and to engage in the transformative process of their own community. Latin American popular theatre was born from the people and gives back to the people; it is a theatre that debates ideas and mobilizes the audience, a new theatre that incorporates the individual responsibility and collective effort of the participants with the goal of taking active participation in the process of transforming society. This theatrical insurgence in Latin America is very well represented in groups such as La Candelaria, the Experimental Theatre of Cadiz in Colombia, the Galpon in Uruguay, Teatro Libre of Argentina, Escambray in Cuba, the Arena Theatre of Sao Paulo in Brazil, and the Yuyachkani Group in Peru.[2]

The focus on group collaboration and the rejection of the concept of a traditional theatre company, which, according to these groups, economically exploited artists for the financial benefit of the producers, became a signature format of Latin American theatre.[3] These groups had political agendas and used theatre as a tool to fulfill them. Artists approached their daily lives as a fundamental expression of the political movement by living together in communes. A group experience tried to live beyond the performance, exchanging ideas and anxieties, developing a dramaturgical work, and engaging "in an intensive investigation process of space, historical memory and the personal and social identity of the actor."[4] The approach to the creation of the performance was done collaboratively.

This approach of *creación colectiva* (collaborative writing) emerged as a response to the desire to develop a structure of equal collaboration between the members of the group. They proposed a participatory playwriting approach where the power created by the theatrical structures was destroyed, giving every member of the group an active and equal participation. This new dramaturg/playwright rescued native cultures and stories that were repressed and classified as myths, legends, and oral tradition, introducing them to the stage. This new dramaturgical approach incorporated elements like music, dance, and poetry into the creative process with the need of building a new structure that reflected their reality.

One of the most important elements that dominated Latin American theatre was the development of a new language on stage using the actor's physicality as the lynchpin of the creative process that produced the performance. This tendency was in part a consequence of not having the economic resources available to build extravagant sets and of reconnecting with and rescuing indigenous dances and traditions.

Actor training, group culture, collective creation

One of the groups that exemplified Latin American theatre practice is the Yuyachkani Theatre Group of Peru. In the Quechuan Indian language, "Yuyachkani" means "I am recalling." This group has worked together for about 30 years, building models of work for an alternative theatre. The Yuyachkani Theatre Group looks for new ways of rediscovering their roots and reconstructing their identity working with indigenous traditions as source material for their performances. In the beginning, the Yuyachkani Theatre Group took a political position as theatre that educated and entertained. One of their goals included communicating with a new audience: with people who had never stepped into a theatre. Furthermore, they planned to work toward a popular theatre that spoke to vital issues and provoked reflection. In the process of building their dramaturgy, they realized that the reality that they wanted to speak about was not written; they had to develop a way in which the worker, the indigenous, the poor would speak in the play. Their desire to search for these new audiences and stories took them to faraway towns and villages. As Miguel Rubio, director of Yuyachkani, explained: "In these travels we came to know another Peru, one that had been unknown to us."[5]

The artistic approach of the Yuyachkani Group was to put the actor in the center of the creative process, based on the notion that the actor is the most important element in the theatre. It is the actor who is responsible, as part of the collective process, for developing the poetic that will be used to create the spectacle. He will write on stage the images that later will be organized to create the show. This is an approach that had been conceived by, and has been a tendency of, a number of theatre groups in Latin America.

In the search for a new theatre, new actors must be formed out of the theatrical tradition, an actor training that includes proposals from the "master" constructors or reformers that constitute the theatrical culture such as Stanislavski, Meyerhold, Artaud, Brecht, Grotowski, and Barba, among others. But this knowledge, as Raquel Carrion said, cannot be a "dogmatic reproduction" of these investigations and positions, "The utilization of this theatrical knowledge must occur within a dialectical relationship between assimilation and differentiation."[6] Assimilation must be understood as the active appropriation of these techniques, but subject to a new investigation within a new historical and cultural context. The combination of training system, acculturation of the body with indigenous traditions, and the political agendas of Latin American theatre created a unique work system for this group.

In order to achieve a new theatrical body, the actor must first deconstruct himself socially. This training must take place in a workshop that permits him to experiment without the pressure of a performance. This laboratory must be a moment of freedom that permits the discovery of new forces, energies, and physical possibilities without making any judgment. This training is based on a series of exercises in which the body is challenged. The exercises should have their own rules and technical operations that will help the actor to increase his or her levels of "pre-expressivity."[7] The next step in this process is the creation of sequences or phases of movements. These are an articulation of actions that constitute the body in movement, a tracing or displacement of the body in space. The sequences do not necessarily bear any "meaning" but must be precisely executed; they help the actor to increase his or her corporal memory. The next level in actor training is improvisation, which enables the actor to collect a series of movement phrases that will help him or her keep in physical shape, building energy, and that will carry on to the writing of the presentation in a subsequent phase.

The construction of the spectacle: the applied training

Once a common physical language is discovered within the group, Latin American mythology, traditional songs, dances, and oral stories are then introduced. The dilemma is how to convert this material into a scenic language during a subsequent phase. The actors then are taken through the improvisational process of what Yuyachkani calls "accumulation sensible" (sensorial accumulation), where the material is processed using the body and intuition, moving away from intellectual or psychological analysis.[8]

It is here that the first sketches of creative work flourish. Each actor will tell his or her own history according to the stimulus received as a motivation for the improvisation. In this process the actor accumulates ideas, associations, images, and sensations of other types (sound, rhythmic, olfactory) specific to the story that they are exploring.

From that phase they move to the third level, called "dramaturgy of the representation." By "dramaturgy of the representation" we should understand the set or fabric of actions that shape the "text" of the scene. In this new improvisational stage, possible characters, sketches, spaces, relationships, and actions emerge. Here the work of the director/dramaturg is essential. In the Latin American group theatrical model, the director fulfills a dramaturgical role, not as an outside critic or scholar, but as someone who has shared the same physical training as the actors. As simultaneous director/dramaturg, this person must help the actor find his or her obstacles, locate new difficulties in his or her training, and help him or her to discover problems – the director/dramaturg is a mediator between the members of the group. S/he will never impose decisions, but will suggest ways of organizing the actors' materials.

This dramaturgical approach is well demonstrated in the Yuyachkani's 1990 production of *No me toquen ese valse* (Do not play that waltz). During this time Peru suffered political and economic instability after an indecisive presidential election. Violence was in the streets, and the Peruvian government imposed a national curfew to restore order. The Yuyachkani Group was forced to lock themselves inside their theatre space, canceling all outside tours and workshops in the community. This physical confinement led to the group's existential search. They developed a play that included elements of their own personal crises, loss of families, and loneliness. For the first time, the Yuyachkani explored their own experience, oppression, and destabilization as the dramaturgy of their performance. During the piece, they doubled as actor-characters as they reflected on their personal experiences during the curfew.[9] The story revolves around two dead musicians who return as ghosts unaware that they are performing in an empty bar destroyed by war. An actress/singer in a wheelchair was anchored at one end of the stage and the other actor/musician sat at the opposite side behind his drum set. Each of them had their own territory and never moved from their places.

The first raw material shown by the actors to the director/dramaturg was a sequence of movements in which they ran around the stage to exhaust themselves and to project an identity crisis. The director/dramaturg, dissatisfied with the image, asked the actors to do the same sequence, but this time in a more confined space. In another exercise, the actress presented an improvisation inspired by t'ai chi. In this instance, the director asked her to hide the movement phrase inside the body. From this working relationship emerged a type of "sitting dance" (in a wheelchair), which gave the basic pattern of retained energy that characterizes the work. Another directorial/dramaturgical intervention was to ask the actors to imagine a heavy ceiling falling on top of their heads and at the same time the walls closing in from the sides. These obstacles developed images of compressed movements, creating an illusion of the actors' bodies constricting in a dome. These interventions of the director/dramaturg produced a powerful fragmented presence that became the main body content of the production: the dilemma between paralysis and vitality.

The intense training and use of the human body in the Latin American theatrical experience is a response to the minimal resources available, with identity searches and political movements driving the development of a new aesthetic that prioritizes physical dramaturgy over the traditional written text. Theatre groups were born as a social and creative alternative in response to the political and economic struggles suffered in Latin America. Latin American theatre is rich in images and varied in stories that embrace a diverse population unique to each country. A chaotic reality full of political repression and economic struggles stimulated collective creation as an alternative theatre. Still today, Latin American theatre continues working in non-traditional spaces and with audience participation. These are theatres that permit communities to understand their own struggles and imagine what a future society might be like. Latin American theatre continues to flourish, to reinvent itself, using the imagination to find that space of freedom and the development of alternative poetic dramaturgies written from the actor bodies.

Notes

1 Osvaldo Dragún, master class lecture, XVI Training Section, International School of Latin American and Caribbean Theater Forum (Perú, 1996).
2 Elena De Costa, *Collaborative Latin American Popular Theater* (New York: Peter Land, 1992), 29.
3 Beatriz J. Ruiz, *El Nuevo Teatro Latinoamericano: Una Lectura Historica* (Minneapolis, MN: Prisma Institute, 1987), 10.
4 Raquel Carrion, *Recuperar la Memoria del Fuego* (Lima: Grupo Yuyachkani), 24.
5 Miguel Rubio, my notes from the Yuyachkani's 25th anniversary celebration (Lima, June 1996).
6 Carrion, *Recuperar la Memoria del Fuego*, 24.
7 Eugenio Barba and Nicola Saverese, *El Arte Secreto del Actor* (Mexico City: Escenologia, 1990), 19.
8 Rubio, notes.
9 Magali Mugercia, *Lo Antropologico en el discurso Latinoamericano* (Havana: Conjunto Magazine, 1990), 15.

4

Documentary dramaturgy in Brazil

Julie Ann Ward

In Latin America, documentary dramaturgy has been an important aspect of the dramatic arts, especially beginning with Brazilian theatre practitioner Augusto Boal's *Teatro Jornal* (Newspaper theatre) in 1971. The purpose of *Teatro Jornal* was, in Boal's words, "to demystify the supposed 'objectivity' of journalism: *Teatro Jornal* demonstrates that a news piece published in a newspaper is a work of fiction. ... In this case, the newspaper is fiction, newspaper-theatre is reality."[1] Boal's other stated objectives with *Teatro Jornal* were to popularize theatre as well as to show that theatre can be practiced by non-actors. A later manifestation of Boal's philosophy, *Teatro do Oprimido* (Theatre of the oppressed), put actors and audiences into everyday situations, allowed audience members to participate and influence the outcomes of the staged scenes, and had as its intention the effect of real change through the practice of revolutionary art. As we will see, this socially driven vision of reality in the theatre will continue to affect documentary drama and theatre of the real up to the present day.

In the twenty-first century in Latin America, so-called theatre of the real has seen an explosion in popularity among companies and dramaturgs, and Brazil is no exception. In the past decade, there has been a growing tendency toward exploring the real in theatre. Artists in this genre push the boundaries of what constitutes theatrical space, a character, or theatricality. Diverging from the traditional definition of documentary theatre, Carol Martin posits the broad term "theatre of the real" to attempt to categorize this trend. She defines theatre of the real as "a wide range of theatre practices and styles that recycle reality, whether that reality is personal, social, political, or historical."[2] She gives the following list of manifestations of theatre of the real to give an idea of how varied a field it is:

> [D]ocumentary theatre, verbatim theatre, reality-based theatre, theatre-of-fact, theatre of witness, tribunal theatre, nonfiction theatre, restored village performances, war and battle reenactments, and autobiographical theatre. ... The array of terms indicates a range of methods of theatrical creation that are not always discrete, but may overlap and cross-fertilize. ... In this kind of theatre, there is an obsession with forming and reframing what has really happened.[3]

Many plays and dramatic projects emerging in Brazil form part of the tendency Martin describes. While Brazilian manifestations of theatre of the real are far from being considered mainstream or commercially successful, as is the case in, for example, Argentina, it is a growing tendency that promises to continue to provide an outlet for the nation's dramaturgs to stage specific, unique versions of Brazilian reality.

In Portuguese, the term *dramaturgo* refers to the author of dramatic compositions. In documentary theatre, however, the dramaturg's role is distinct from that of a playwright. Using historical documents, personal objects, and journalistic footage, the documentary dramaturg must go beyond authorship, as well as cede authority to other sources. The term *compiler*, used in criticism on *testimonio* literature, is apt here. Rather than inventing something from nothing, as perhaps the most extreme example of authorship might be considered as doing, the documentary dramaturg's creation is limited by the archive. The work of compiling evidence to create a play rooted in the real is the work of the dramaturg in this sense. However, while the dramaturg is limited by the documentary, there is also the possibility of going beyond traditional authorship. The nature of interview and testimony allows for a collaborative process in which authorship is shared with the actors or the people portrayed in the play. The dramaturg often retains authority, albeit tacit, over the lives of others and real events by compiling them into a play.

An especially relevant vein of theatre of the real in Brazil involves site-specific theatre, in which the dramaturg is inspired by and uses the constraints of an unconventional space, like a church, prison, hospital, or street, to create the play. Such interventions allow dramatists to make political and social statements and test the boundaries of theatre. For example, in the 1990s, São Paulo theatre company Teatro da Vertigem (Vertigo theatre) brought elements of the real into their dramatic projects to give new life to ancient forms and themes. Their "Biblical Trilogy" premiered in 1991 in the Santa Ifigênia church in São Paulo with *O Paraíso Perdido* (Paradise Lost) and continued with the 1995 production of *O Livro de Jó* (The Book of Job), which was staged in the Hospital Humberto Primo. Spectators walked through the building from scene to scene. The trilogy closed in 2000 with *Apocalipse 1,11* (Revelation 1:11), which was staged in a defunct prison, the Presídio do Hipódromo.[4] While the subject matter is of mythic origins, the use of unconventional spaces forces audiences to confront the reality of modern issues such as AIDS and a culture of criminality.

In 1997, also in São Paulo, the group Teatro de Narradores (Narrators' theatre) was formed. Their goal has been to insert their own social experiences and lives in the city into their productions. For example, their 2006 production, *Cabaré Paulista – Do Manifesto Contra o Trabalho* (São Paulo cabaret – from the manifesto against work), is a musical featuring testimonies from the actors on their experiences of working in the world of theatre. More recently, with *Cidade Fim Cidade Coro Cidade Reverso* (End city chorus city flip-side city) the company explores the limits of documentary theatrical production, mixing real-life testimonies by workers with those of actors as well as with fictional testimonies. The end of the play has the company leading the audience out to "occupy" a bar near the theatre, further extending the relationship between reality and performance.[5] Such use of testimony, in which the role of the dramaturg is not only to write the play, but rather to compile, research, and arrange the words of others, will resurface throughout the twenty-first century in Brazil.

In 2004, Brazilian director and playwright Christiane Jatahy opened her trilogy *Uma cadeira para a solidão, duas para o diálogo e três para a sociedade* (One chair for solitude, two for dialogue, and three for society) with the play *Conjugado* (The studio apartment), a monologue that uses performance, documentary film, and installation to recreate the life of a woman. Part two, *A Falta que nos Move ou Todas as Histórias São Ficção* (The lack that moves us, or all stories are fiction), debuted in 2005 and has actors onstage preparing supper and awaiting a mystery guest, all the while conversing with the audience.[6] Finally, in 2010 the trilogy closed with *Corte Seco* (Cut), a piece that further blurs the lines between fiction and reality by placing cameras in the surrounding areas of the theatre and projecting their feeds onstage. The director and technical team are plainly visible, and their interventions are unavoidable, which draws attention to the theatrical process.[7] By drawing attention to her own role in manipulating the testimonies of the actors onstage, Jatahy questions the role of the dramaturg as author, a move which is also evidenced by her crediting the actors as co-creators of the play.

The Paulista group Companhia Teatro Documentário (Documentary theatre company) was founded in 2006 and constructs its theatrical proposals upon interviews and testimonials with different people and groups in the city. Their first production, *Desde quando eu ainda era Travesti ou Lamentos do Palácio das Princesas* (Ever since I was still a transvestite, or lamentations from the palace of the princesses), in 2007, staged the story of a Brazilian transvestite who had, after having lived in Europe, begun dressing like a man upon returning to Brazil. Their 2008 play *Consumindo 68* (Consuming '68) looks at the way that icons of the 1960s are manufactured and consumed by young people today.[8] More recent projects, like the 2012 *Vértice* (Vertex), a collection of documentary scenes that portrays the residents of a certain street, the Rua Maria José, are more geographically specific, focusing on one particular space and its theatrical possibilities.[9]

Also in 2006, the Núcleo Argonautas de Teatro (Argonauts of theatre nucleus) decided to answer the question "Is it possible to create a poetics by editing documents from reality?" In the resulting project, *Terra Sem Lei* (Lawless land), participants selected documents from which to create their experimental scenes. Their presentation always includes an element of being "in process," emphasizing the experimental nature of the proposal.

Emanuel Aragão's 2009 *Nãotemnemnome* (Itdoesn'tevenhaveaname), a two-part play, involves *"encontros"* (encounters) between the playwright and individual spectators, and between the actors and the collective audience. The encounters are based on questions that arise during the personal interviews with spectators.[10] Another work that puts the "real" onstage is Coletivo Improviso's (Improv collective) *OTRO (or) weknowitsallornothing* (2010). To prepare this work, artists followed instructions as if on a scavenger hunt through Rio, in which they were to take the first bus that passed, get off at the third stop, talk to the fifth person they saw in the street, and so on. One artist would ask the person a question, and the other would observe. The interviews with strangers provided the fodder for putting on scenes.[11]

Other dramatic representations of the real and personal on the Brazilian stage include Márcio Freitas's 2010 *Sem Falsidades* (Without makeup), in which the director interviewed young actresses about being young actresses, then, in his words, re-mixed their responses into a play that questions the uniqueness and specificity that self-representation in the theatre seems to assume. The play strips its actors of specificity and indispensability while conserving the postdramatic concept of situation. The audience is made aware of the process the play represents as it calls attention to the interview process and the dramaturg's role in manipulating their answers for the stage.

Nelson Baskerville, a Brazilian director and actor, has tried his hand at documentary theatre as well. In 2011 Baskerville directed the scenic documentary *Luis Antonio-Gabriela*, which deals with a transgender individual, Luis António, who would be known as Gabriela in Spain.[12] That year another company, Factual Experimentações Cênicas (Factual scenic experimentations) took up the figure of Anne Frank to produce *O Medo* (The fear), a documentary play based on Frank's life as well as other feminine historical figures.[13] Baskerville joined forces this year with the Cia Provisório-Definitivo (Provisional-definitive company) to produce *As Estrelas Cadentes do meu Céu sao Feitas de Bombas do Inimigo* (The falling stars in my sky are made of the enemy's bombs), based on Zlata Filipovic and Melanie Challenger's book *Stolen Voices: Young People's War Diaries, From World War I to Iraq* and *The Diary of Anne Frank* with Brazilian elements.[14]

All of these plays and films add up to a cultural moment that is highly concerned with reality. Marcelo Soler, of the Cia Teatro Documentário, published his treatise *Teatro Documentário: A pedagogia da náo ficção* (Documentary theatre: the pedagogy of nonfiction) in 2011. Hearkening back to Boal's socially driven Theatre of the Oppressed, Soler sees in documentary theatre an essential educational nature, citing Swiss director Stefan Kaegi and Argentine Lola Arias's 2007 intervention in the Brazilian theatre scene with their documentary play *Chácara Paraíso* (Paradise ranch) as a contemporary example of documentary theatre. However, as we've seen here, there has long been an interest in staging reality in Brazil, with a significant increase in the late twentieth century and first decade of the new millennium that continues today.

These new plays don't occur in a vacuum, but rather are representative of a rich cultural scene that focuses intently on the real and its place within the theatre. Whether allowing the space to shape the performance or using the randomness of reality to let interactions on a city street determine a play's contents, the dramaturg in Brazil is becoming a porous, malleable figure. Rather than attempting to create a world onstage, now the theatrical practitioner allows the world to intervene in the staged. The place of the dramaturg is now examined onstage, and the creative process revealed from within theatre itself. This liberation has its roots in Boal's theories, which called for theatre to go out on to the streets to change reality; now reality is being invited into the theatre.

Notes

1 "[D]esmistificar a pretensa 'objetividade' do jornalismo: demonstra que uma notícia publicada em um jornal é uma obra de ficção. ... Neste caso, jornal é ficção, teatro-jornal é realidade." Augusto Boal, "Teatro Jornal: Primeira Edição," *Latin American Theatre Review* 4.2 (1971): 57.
2 Carol Martin, *Theatre of the Real* (New York: Palgrave Macmillan, 2013), 5.

3 Ibid.
4 "Teatro da Vertigem," Artes Escénicas, available online at http://artesescenicas.uclm.es/index.php?sec=artis&id=106, accessed March 30, 2013.
5 Teatro de Narradores, last modified 2012, available online at www.teatrodenarradores.com.br/index.php?option=com_content&view=section&id=12&Itemid=32.
6 "Jatahy, Christiane (1968)," Itaú Cultural, last modified November 22, 2010, available online at www.itaucultural.org.br/aplicexternas/enciclopedia_teatro/index.cfm?fuseaction=personalidades_biografia&cd_verbete=5902.
7 Lucas Neves, "Diretora 'edita' peça ao vivo no espetáculo *Corte Seco*," *Folha de S. Paulo* (February 4, 2010), available online at http://www1.folha.uol.com.br/folha/ilustrada/ult90u689183.shtml, accessed August 30, 2013.
8 "Descrição," Companhia Teatro Documentário, available online at http://3.bp.blogspot.com/_PmCwB_92C_M/TC-Iso3PjjI/AAAAAAAAAII/WiZj9sosj74/s1600/descrição+cia.jpg, accessed March 30, 2013.
9 "Cartaz Vértice," Companhia Teatro Documentário, 2012, available online at http://4.bp.blogspot.com/-jb4aTRA3TEM/UJpBPoPn1EI/AAAAAAAAAgw/H3EjRfwaRBE/s1600/cartaz+vertice.jpg, accessed March 30, 2013.
10 "Nãotemnemnome – Programação Cultural," Cultura.rj, October 29, 2011, available online at http://www.cultura.rj.gov.br/evento/naotemnemnome, accessed March 30, 2013.
11 Andrezza Czech, "*Otro*, com Enrique Diaz, aborda as diferenças no palco," *Época São Paulo* (June 2, 2011), available online at http://epocasaopaulo.globo.com/cultura/otro-com-enrique-diaz-aborda-as-diferencas-no-palco, accessed August 30, 2013.
12 "Documentário Luis Antonio-Gabriela estreia na Funarte São Paulo," Funarte – Portal das Artes (October 3, 2011), available online at www.funarte.gov.br/teatro/documentario-"luis-antonio-gabriela"-estreia-na-funarte-sao-paulo, accessed August 30, 2013.
13 André Lisboa, "Inspirada na história de Anne Frank, a peça O *Medo* representará o Maranhão no Festival de Teatro de Curitiba," *diário do andre* (March 24, 2011), available online at http://diariodoandre.com/2011/03/24/espetaculo-o-medo-representara-maranhao-no-festival-de-teatro-de-curitiba, accessed August 30, 2013.
14 "*As Estrelas Cadentes do meu Céu* … Nelson Baskerville dirige espetáculo sobre guerra," *Globo Teatro*, available online at www.globoteatro.com.br/reportagem-1466-nelson-baskerville.htm, accessed March 4, 2013.

5

The place of a dramaturg in twenty-first-century England[1]

Duška Radosavljević

Between 2002 and 2005, I was one of few people in the UK with the job title of dramaturg, having been recruited to the post jointly by the Northern Stage theatre and Newcastle University. Even when confronted with the friendliest of dispositions, being a "dramaturg" in England[2] inevitably goes hand in hand with having to explain what your job title means. Having continental roots (especially German, Scandinavian, or Eastern European) appears to bestow more of a natural entitlement to the D-word; however, this by no means guarantees freedom of access to the English rehearsal room.

Under Alan Lyddiard's leadership (1992–2005), Northern Stage was a largely atypical and exotic British theatre.[3] One of my first projects in my new job was a devised piece consisting of Romani music and folk tales, which would form Northern Stage's own contribution to an international festival the theatre would host in June 2003, called the Newcastle/Gateshead Gypsy Festival. Tasked with writing brochure copy in which I would attempt to explain to our potential audience why this particular topic was relevant and timely, I cited the increased mobility of the contemporary lifestyle as a form of cosmopolitan nomadism, which should bring us closer to understanding the "gypsy-condition":

> [W]e live in a time and place of mobile communications, information highways and space holidays. In the global village of multilingual families, we are all up-rooted. If the place of birth is anything to go by, most of us are displaced too. We are not Gypsies, but our condition is increasingly gypsy-like. And even if we cannot change the world, we can try to let the world change us. Hopefully for the better.[4]

In *Staging the UK*, Jen Harvie identifies literariness as the most distinct feature of British theatre. She notes that this literary genealogy inevitably runs back to Shakespeare as the most prominent exponent of British theatre, but also points out that the Lord Chamberlain's office, active until 1968, inevitably required theatre to be script-based in order to facilitate censorship prior to performance.[5] She uses Aleks Sierz's, Dan Rebellato's, and Simon Shepherd's writings on British theatre histories to further substantiate this view and tease out several more particular characteristics – namely, anti-intellectualism and anti-theatricality:

> By celebrating individual creativity, seeking isolation, indulging anti-theatricalism, and maintaining a hostility to theory, dominant British theatre culture resists collaborative practices, healthy miscegenation, and a recognition of creativity as labour, material practice and intellectual practice.[6]

Mary Luckhurst, too, recognizes that both British and American theatre features an underlying degree of anti-intellectualism, which she discerns for example in Terry McCabe's attack on dramaturgs as "creatively bankrupt and destructive forces," confined to not-for-profit theatres.[7]

Lyddiard's decision, therefore, to appoint a dramaturg in conjunction with the university, in order to work with her on non-literary theatre, was unprecedented and unrepresentative of British theatre trends in every way.

Place

My practice as a dramaturg has by and large consisted of bridge building, on the one hand, and, on the other, a negotiation of frontiers between theory and practice, between writers and directors, between the show and the audience, between theatre and academia. When I left Northern Stage in order to join the Learning Department at the RSC, my brief was a bridge-building exercise between the RSC and the UK higher-education sector. On the understanding that my main area of activity would be to bring a kinesthetic approach and the RSC's rehearsal room methodology to the teaching of Shakespeare at university level, I considered this particular work a form of dramaturgy too – but one that was oriented towards the audience rather than towards the production. As opposed to the work of the literary departments and the idea of "production dramaturgy" occurring in rehearsal rooms, I would call this kind of dramaturgy "reception dramaturgy." Reception dramaturgy, as such, is concerned with facilitating an engagement of the audience with the inner workings of a piece of theatre (and includes the work of education departments, marketing departments and theatre critics).

What particularly struck me about the way in which some of the RSC rehearsal rooms were arranged – especially in the first stages consisting of lengthy sessions sitting around the table and grappling with the text – was that the sheer number of people (the twenty-odd-member cast would initially be joined by an army of designers, voice coaches, movement directors, stage managers, and technical crew) required everyone present to arrange themselves into two concentric circles. The actors, the director and his assistant(s) would be sitting in the inner circle, with everyone else on the margins around them.

Thinking about the place of a dramaturg in English theatre, one therefore encounters "bridges"[8] and "frontiers,"[9] not unlike those discussed by Michel de Certeau,[10] the tackling of which eventually may even necessitate a kind of "delinquency":

> If the delinquent exists only by displacing itself, if its specific mark is not to live on the margins but in the interstices of the codes that it undoes and displaces, if it is characterized by the privilege of the tour over the state, then the story is delinquent.[11]

Interestingly, in the UK, those seen at the top of the theatres' managerial pyramids are often Oxbridge graduates – and therefore not graduates in drama or theatre or performance studies. Although it is easy to see how this might have led to the literariness of British theatre, one wonders how the trend of anti-intellectualism came about? Meanwhile, the literariness of British theatre would also, according to Dwight Conquergood for example, seem to imply a privileging of the textual over the embodied knowledge. This is the "apartheid of knowledges" Conquergood tried to address by calling for an elevation of the experiential and participatory epistemologies to the level traditionally held by the textual and critical-intellectual ones. Taking inspiration from de Certeau, Conquergood acknowledges the changing nature of "place" at the time of increased mobility: nowadays the "'location' is imagined as an itinerary instead of a fixed point", "we now think of 'place' as a heavily trafficked intersection, a port of call and exchange, rather than a circumscribed territory".[12] This view of "place" provides some optimism in relation to my enquiry as to how a dramaturg might inhabit an English rehearsal room. De Certeau's "story cuts across the map" with a certain "delinquency", moving from "the margins" to the "interstices of the codes that it undoes". Meanwhile, England itself is increasingly a "heavily trafficked intersection". In other words, it is the "gypsy-like" condition and increased cosmopolitanism[13] of contemporary life that will hopefully enable new ways of working, new kinds of theatre-making and new hierarchies of knowledge to move from the margins towards the mainstream.

Dramaturg

Turner and Behrndt's *Dramaturgy and Performance* departs from an acknowledged position of the term's own instability. Dramaturgy, they suggest, can be understood as composition, architecture, analysis, playwriting, research, producing, interpreting, critique, engagement with the context; "indeed the more precise and concise one tries to be, the more one invites the response: 'Yes, but ... '"[14] Conceptually, however, Turner and Behrndt signal that the "millennial dramaturgies," as they call them, are marked by a whole new set of approaches to and variations on the theme of "narrative". I am particularly intrigued by the account of Maaike Bleeker's "'consideration of the interaction between stage and audience' in terms of movement."[15] Instead of emerging from the decoding of signs, meaning is no longer considered as static or fixed but in terms of how the performance "moves" the audience. "The implication is that we might look for the politics of work in terms of what it does, rather than what it says."[16] This of course is not a particularly new phenomenon but it is a useful way of transcending some old text and performance struggles. The audience is by and large heterogeneous and will potentially follow a multitude of trajectories in response to any given mechanism – even if seated in a most conventional theatre space all the way through the performance. What the dramaturg can begin to monitor here are the vectors of movement, the force, the intention, the impact, and the effect of the "movement" on the frontiers and boundaries of experience. Or more specifically, for example, as in the case of the Belgian company Ontroerend Goed's production *Internal*, the dramaturg (Joeri Smet) might well be taking part as a performer, alongside four others, in the show featuring probing and questioning of the audience and culminating in a one-to-one dance with a chosen audience member.

It seems that amid such a proliferation of potential functions for a dramaturg, the question is certainly not "what does the dramaturg do?" but "what is the dramaturg's domain?"

In his consideration of spatial stories, de Certeau offers two modes of description: "the map" – the official organization of a series of "facts" about a particular space – and "the tour" – an account of a journey through the space. In this respect, the domain of a dramaturg is neither solely the map (which I would say belongs to the director) nor the story (which may start with the writer but ultimately belongs to the actor) but the journey itself (which is an experience and therefore immaterial, speculative, personal as well as potentially shared). Regarding the distinction between the dramaturg and the director further, I would add that at least in the UK context, both of these figures are equipped with the tools of making work and of dramatic composition, although perhaps the director is more the figure tasked with finishing the product and putting it in front of the audience, whereas the dramaturg is the figure whose process of reflection and co-creation of meaning can continue well after this point.

Anne Bogart raises the question of the dramaturg's ownership within a context where everyone else has a clear domain and suggests that this must apply to "archival materials and structural ideas," while Anne Cattaneo seems to reinforce the same view by proposing that dramaturgs are "good at thinking structurally" and "sensitive as to how something is shaped and how this shape or structure affects interpretation."[17] I agree and identify with this. During my time at Northern Stage, due to various international collaborations, I ended up traveling more than usual – to Hungary, Denmark, Russia, Spain, the United States. In addition to my various duties as part of my job description, I also regularly wrote travelogues for the internal newsletter. Often these journeys were related through the narratives that would be of interest to my readers, reflecting on patterns and leitmotifs shaped to resonate with the particular works we were developing. But most interestingly, when I eventually moved on from Newcastle, my suitcases were full of "archival materials and structural ideas" – as well as a few maps and stories.

In reflecting on how the "gypsy-condition" might affect us, it is perhaps worth noting the following commonly held assumptions: unlike most other cultural minorities, Romanies tend to transcend or at least resist the question of cultural integration, as it is traditionally an inherent part of their culture to stay on the move. Although often seen as a delinquent element within the host culture, nevertheless Romanies have historically also generated their own appeal by embodying the values of freedom from societal constraints, deep passions, and a spirit of adventure.

In conclusion to his chapter on spatial stories, de Certeau proposes that

> ... in matters concerning space, [the] delinquency begins with the inscription of the body in the order's text. The opacity of the body in movement, gesticulating, walking, taking its pleasure, is what indefinitely organizes a *here* in relation to an *abroad*, a "familiarity" in relation to a "foreignness."[18]

In short he reiterates his departure point that "space is a practiced place."[19] This paper could be seen to result from an implicit understanding that there is no pre-existing defined space for a dramaturg in an English rehearsal room. However, it is particularly worth acknowledging here that old hierarchies between text and performance appear to be on the move and subject to change,[20] thus requiring a new means of engagement between the meaning being created and the audience response. It seems therefore that the best "tactic" for a dramaturg in dealing with the "strategies" of the English theatre and performance context (whatever that may mean in the climate of globalization) is simply to continue practicing his or her craft, wherever he or she happens to be, and under whatever name seems suitable.

Notes

1 The full version of this article originally appeared as: Radosavljević, Duška "The Need to Keep Moving: Remarks on the Place of a Dramaturg in 21st Century England," *Performance Research: On Dramaturgy* 14 (3) (Taylor and Francis, 2009), 45–51.
2 I speak of 'England' because England has been the main site of my practice. I am quite aware that the word 'dramaturg' tends to have a bit more currency in Scottish and Northern Irish theatre, for example, while I am not fully acquainted with the status of a dramaturg in Wales. Having originally written this article in 2008/09, I am also compelled to acknowledge that in 2013 the situation in England is changing in favor of the term "dramaturg" and "dramaturgy."
3 I have written more extensively about this project in "Shared Utopias? Alan Lyddiard, Lev Dodin and the Northern Stage Ensemble" in Jonathan Pitches (ed.) *Russians in Britain: British Theatre and the Russian Tradition of Actor Training* (London and New York: Routledge, 2011).
4 Radosavljević, Duška, "Programme Note," *Spring Brochure* (Northern Stage, 2003).
5 Harvie, Jen, *Staging the UK* (Manchester and New York: Manchester University Press, 2005), 116.
6 Ibid., 119.
7 Luckhurst, Mary, *Dramaturgy: A Revolution in Theatre* (Cambridge: Cambridge University Press, 2006), 211.
8 "The bridge is ambiguous everywhere: it alternately welds together and opposes insularities. It distinguishes them and threatens them. It liberates from enclosure and destroys autonomy. Justifiably, the bridge is the index of the diabolic in the paintings where Bosch invents his modifications of spaces." de Certeau, Michel, *The Practice of Everyday Life* (Berkeley: University of California Press, 1984), 128.
9 "The theoretical and practical problem of the frontier: to whom does it belong? The river, wall or tree makes a frontier. It does not have a character of a nowhere that cartographical representation ultimately presupposes. It has a mediating role" (Ibid., 127).
10 Ibid., 126–9.
11 Ibid., 130.
12 Conquergood, Dwight "Performance Studies: Interventions and radical research," *TDR* 46 (2) (Summer) (2002): 145–56.
13 Dan Rebellato's distinction between the terms "globalization" and "cosmopolitanism" is particularly pertinent here, and the latter term is taken in the sense defined by Rebellato as a positive manifestation of the trend. Rebellato, Dan *Theatre and Globalization* (Basingstoke: Palgrave Macmillan, 2009).
14 Turner, Cathy and Behrndt, Synne, *Dramaturgy and Performance* (Basingstoke: Palgrave MacMillan, 2008), 17.
15 Ibid., 92.
16 Ibid., 93.
17 Ibid., 164.
18 de Certeau, 130.
19 Ibid., 119.
20 In re-examining the changing relationship between text and performance and the strategies for their creation, Patrice Pavis also concludes that this new trend "encourages us to go forward, to move our feet and not get stuck in the same position forever." Pavis, Patrice "On Faithfulness: The difficulties experienced by the text/performance couple," *Theatre Research International*, International Federation for Theatre Research, 33(2) (2008): 117–26.

6

On German dramaturgy

Bernd Stegemann

Translated by Johannes Stier

In German, the word "dramaturgy" implies two meanings. Following the literal translation of the term from ancient Greek, it means the philosophical dimension of the "architecture of the action." Dramaturgy is also the name of a function in the German theatre system. In the latter case it stands for the department of a theatre in which the dramaturg works as well as for the intellectual authority which "dramaturgy" has over the invention and communication of theatre. Because of that, the work of a dramaturg is equally multifaceted: s/he belongs to the management of the theatre and is the creative director and curator of new teams and projects. A dramaturg also edits the literary source material of the play and is the first observer of a new production next to the director. As such s/he can add his or her opinions and interpretations to the artistic process during the rehearsals.

The important place of dramaturgy in the German-speaking theatre originates from its historical birth during the eighteenth century. Lessing's *Hamburg Dramaturgy* (*Hamburgische Dramaturgie*) was instrumental for the self-reflection of theatre producers and a guide for the audience to acquaint it with the new art of bourgeois theatre. The emerging bourgeoisie in the politically tattered country saw itself as unfit to overthrow the traditional political relations in an act similar to the French Revolution. The unique path that Germany took was often described as an escape into the arts. The art of Romanticism and the German city theatre (*Stadttheater*) are the two most distinctive examples of this sublimation. During the nineteenth century every city tried to build a theatre in its centre as a sign of its self-confident citizens. The performances there were of varying quality and covered every genre: opera, operetta, ballet, play, musical comedy, melodrama, etc. The thriving market for plays offered a range of different texts, so the repertoire of the city theatre could satisfy the lust for entertainment and the wish for representation even-handedly. The birth of city theatre lies in the idealism of Lessing's *Dramaturgy*, which was carried on by the dramaturgies of the theatre. People worked on and are still working on the idea of theatre as a political art of self-reflection. This idealism combines the philosophical and institutional dimensions of dramaturgy.

At the beginning of this development stands the dramaturgy of the bourgeois tragedy (*Bürgerliches Trauerspiel*), which sought for a different and new relation between the audience and the theatre, other than that of the folk theatre and the French tragedy, which provided either amusement or lofty elevation. A new dramaturgy of the action as much as a new dramaturgy of the performance was needed. The new characters had to show their inner lives, which led to a new dramaturgy of the psychological action. The characters knew about, and fought against, the constraints that social conventions imposed on them. The phantasm of the natural form was in the centre of this representation. Likewise, a new kind of acting had to be invented. To demonstrate the new situation believably, the actors had to learn to play in a new way. They had to be able to show the external constraints and the internal struggles at the same time, and they had to learn to play on two different levels at once. The characters of psychological theatre feel and reflect their emotions; they are looking for something and are insecure whether this desire is right. They have to conceal something and nevertheless want to be acknowledged as individuals. The identificatory potential of the new theatre consists in the fact that the audience possesses the same technique of self-expression in their everyday lives. In civic society trust arises not through conventions of role-playing and the coding of the costume as it did at court, but by showing one's inner, true, and therefore invisible personality. But how will someone be able to show these hidden qualities if their authenticity lies in the fact that they cannot be deliberately shown? Self-expression just has to happen, has to appear unintentionally and against the will of the subject. The border of desire and suffering, of feeling and thinking becomes the main difference in this bourgeois dramaturgy. This is why there is so much crying and sighing in the bourgeois tragedy. These borders of the sayable give an insight into the "true" self. In this way, the aspiring bourgeois class, which wanted to experience itself as true in its own feelings, found the adequate art for its self-discovery and self-affirmation in the theatre.

The subject of modern history is characterized by this self-reflection, which became the theme and the means of the presentation in the new dramaturgy of realism. During the nineteenth century, realism and naturalism brought this new method to perfection, which in turn had an impact on the art of acting. Until the reinvention of theatre as a bourgeois art, new inventions came from theatre authors and actors and originated from ritual and traditional sources. Now a new actor enters the stage. The new style of play desired by psychological realism necessitates rehearsals during which the new effects of playing behind the "fourth wall" can be reviewed. The direct contact between actor and spectator is broken; the act of representation has to be invisible. Through this new kind of play, the audience disappears for the actor as much as for the spectator him or herself. S/he is not part of the audience anymore but the only one feeling in the dark stalls. The development of this new impression requires a surrogate for this lone spectator: the director enters the theatre. The director sits in the auditorium as a representative of every future member of the audience, and next to him or her sits the dramaturg as the first critic of the event. From here, the handling of concentration, attention, and sympathy is organized. The dramaturgy of the action is staged with the dramaturgy of a performance. The theatre text does not become theatre within a convention or a tradition of a play, but every performance becomes an original production which bestows upon the text its own form of presentation.

The goal of realistic theatre was the representation of bourgeois contradictions which originated in the necessary ambiguous communication between the market and alienated labour. Because capitalism turns everything into a commodity that receives its price on the market, life gets shaped by a double alienation of work on the one hand and the negotiation of prices on the other. As the new bourgeois class experiences itself as the winner of this alienation, the art of realism loses its critical potential and becomes a form of entertainment. The once dialectical representation of the world becomes "commercial realism," which adopts the strong effect of identificatory moments without the desire of showing the contradictions behind it. The enlightening power of realistic theatre loses itself in the lulling stream of feelings which eventually ends in the cinema.

In the twentieth century, epic theatre turns against this tendency by taking the self-reference of the modern subject seriously. It re-establishes the contradiction as the foundation of a dialectical theatre. According to Brecht, the simplest definition of the epic manner of acting is the actor showing one thing while at the same time showing him or herself. By doing so, s/he establishes a relationship between showing and what is shown as well as between the one showing and the spectator. By this, the dispositive of the fourth wall gets abolished, the once direct contact, which characterized folk theatre, is established again and is expanded by the dimension of a reflecting actor. For dramaturgy, the epic theatre has far-ranging consequences. The architecture of the epic scene is different from the dramatic situation insofar as it is no longer written to create suspense or a sense of identification but for the act of showing. Likewise, the dramaturgy of a performance is no longer built towards a closed story arc (geschlossener Wirkungsbogen) but for the demonstration of certain aspects of the contradiction. The contradiction of the drama, which started the need for the characters to act, becomes the contradiction in society which the exemplary presentation shall make understandable by the exemplary presentation of specific facts. Therefore, the dramaturg's collaboration during the rehearsals is no longer limited to aesthetic questions but broadens into the horizon of the social relevance of the theatrical event: how are the social contradictions reflected in human souls and bodies?

The consequences of the political demand placed on theatre are hardly to be overemphasized for the German-speaking theatre system. They are connected to the enlightened idea of theatre as the art of an emancipated middle class as much as to the ideological feuds of the twentieth century. As a result of this, the dramaturg moves again to the center of the intermediation between theatre and reality. The rehearsals become enriched by his or her research, which subsequently becomes available for the audience in the form of the theatre program. The dramaturg's vision, which is marked by the attitude of "include me out," becomes the touchstone of social relevance. The art of epic theatre thereby frees itself from the desperate attempt of late bourgeois art to be meaningful because of the artist's uniqueness, while rediscovering collective work as the natural state of theatre.

The ramifications of psychological and epic theatre are similar for German theatre, but since the 1980s they have become increasingly overlaid by postmodern theory. This development operates under the name of the "postdramatic" but assembles numerous and sometimes contradictory characteristics of a postmodern theatre. Two manifestations of postdramatic theatre can be roughly distinguished. On the one hand, it stands in the tradition of visual arts, especially that of the early-twentieth-century avant-garde. This can be seen in the use of collages, which cause sensory and semantic effects from the clash of unexpected materials. In this way, the dramaturgy of the performance no longer is structured by the dramatic action but by energetic, rhythmic, and other aesthetic phenomena. In this case, the dramaturg is not so much a mediator between the fictional world of the drama, the reality of the performances, and the social presence as the co-author of a fable of the production that needs reinvention. Through the abandonment of the dramatic structure, the collective presence, as evoked by theatre, changes. One can say that dramatic theatre produces a community of feeling and identifying spectators whose presence is sentimental because it is directed backwards. On the other hand, epic theatre in contrast produces a community of astonished spectators, who come to know the familiar as strange in order to experience the changeability of the world as possible. Their present is coined by a faith in the future. The postdramatic theatre produces pictorial puzzles in which the audience can no longer decide whether what they are seeing is a sensual irritation or a semantic effect, whether it is play or reality, whether it is meant or it really happens. This oscillation in perception generates a special form of presence. The self-reference of the modern subject, which is always experienced as a relation between at least two conflicting levels, becomes an aesthetical paradox of a self-referent perception. Thus, the presence of perception becomes aware of itself and expands into a broader presence. One perceives and realizes one's own perception at the same time. In this way, the broad presence lays itself over the past and the possible future. The oscillations of postdramatic theatre become a feast of self-referentiality in which the contradictions are no longer psychologically or socially justified but rather become aesthetic games.

The other tendency of postdramatic theatre derives not so much from visual arts but from Brecht, to the extent that it could also be called post-epic theatre. Here, the play on two different levels, as Brecht asked for, gets adopted, but without having recourse to the social position of the actor. It is no longer the political individual that tries to become aware of his or her class and, emancipated, stands in front of the audience, now the performer makes his or her own presence become the foundation of the stage presence. As a result, the techniques of realistic acting become mostly expendable because of the mimetic ability of creating a different situation on stage so that the actual theatre situation is no longer necessary. The actor becomes a performer, which means that s/he enters the stage not as an acting subject but as one who is experiencing the world and reality. The performer is the always responsive employee that emotional capitalism demands.

The dramaturgy of such a post-epic performance evolves from the scenic material which emerges during the rehearsals. There is no dramatic template from which the effect and structure of the dramatic arc could be developed, but the scenic inventions must be composed by their different dimensions. The dramaturgic assistance here becomes the central authority of artistic invention, requiring not only the techniques of drama but also the effects of mash-ups, music, and dance, to arrange the specific material into something more than a scenic essay about a certain topic. The specific character of scenic inventions and the deliberate approach to them are part of post-epic theatre. Because of this, the self-referentiality of the scene becomes central again, which previously – in its performative form – had its roots in performance art and in poststructuralism. During the performance, the scenic reality acquired an intrinsic value, because of self-referential plays and their continuity. Through this, the material emerges from behind the semiotic dimension. In poststructuralism, the sign becomes analyzed in view of its intrinsic value. Its power to signify something covers that which is hereby signified. Through the practice of such a deconstruction, all certainties crumble into discursive games. In a postmodern theatre that is critical towards representation, both techniques are often practiced. The categories of drama, mimesis, and catharsis as a banishment of spectators, who unite to form an audience in order to experience theatre as a collective, become replaced by the postmodern categories of self-reference, performance, and paradox.

The diversity of the different dramaturgic techniques is striking. In German theatre, all four traditions (dramatic, epic, postdramatic and post-epic) exist simultaneously, and the lines between official city theatres and independent theatres become increasingly blurred. As a result, not only actors have to expand their skills. Above all, dramaturgy always has to invent and comprehend new architectures of actions and effects. This variety of theatrical expressions has wide-ranging consequences for the education of young dramaturgs. There are two different training routes in the German-speaking theatre. One runs through art colleges where dramaturgy is taught alongside acting, scenery, costume design, and directing. The other route is through theatre studies, which has diverse offers in applied theatre studies. In this case, what is taught is not a specific skill but a theoretical understanding of theatre and theatrical events. As the foundation of applied theatre studies fell into the high phase of postmodern cultural theories, their aesthetic paradigms have been highly marked by them. The openness of the scientific education still dissociates itself from the classical, technical art forms of theatre and its mimetic claim. Applied theatre studies fosters a remarkable alliance of virtuosic perception, discursive processing, and production of new forms of theatre. The accusation that theatre is produced purely for theatre studies is certainly true for some of these self-referential formats. The production of more and more essay collections, which elevate a just-seen performance to the level of indispensable knowledge of the field, surely fuels this cycle further. It cannot be overlooked that the innovative energy of the technical theatre education is in danger of weakening and that the forms inspired by these discourses frequently appear more modern and animated. Since public attention to theatre is rather diminishing, we have to ask whether this animosity is really useful, especially since this strong differentiation only furthers the exhaustion of mimetic energy and the encapsulation of postmodern aesthetics towards a complacent game. The prime task of the dramaturgs and dramaturgies is to build a connection between the dramatic art and the more discursive theatre. What is needed for this purpose is an intense engagement with the technical-mimetic side of theatre as much as with the discursive procedure. Such an engagement, however, has to break through the dividing barriers instead of getting entangled in more fights for distinction. And whose job would be more appropriate for this than that of the mediator, the dramaturg?

7

The making of *La Dramaturgie* in France

Kate Bredeson

The cover image of the January 1986 special issue of *Théâtre/Public*, "Dramaturgie," offers a glimpse of what dramaturgy looked like to French theatre scholars and practitioners at the time: a photo of a hand lightly touching a single typewritten piece of paper on a desk, with other overturned pages nearby. It is dark. A small lamp illuminates the stack of paper; it is a script. In her preface to this issue, which proposed to assess the state of dramaturgy in France, Michèle Raoul-Davis made the distinction between the "literary side of the dramaturg, the person responsible for the programming and publications for productions"[1] and "the dramaturg that Jean-Marie Piemme calls the 'stage dramaturg.'"[2] Raoul-Davis asserted a mandate to dwell primarily on the latter, as "The utility [of the former] at least in the big theatres, seems evident."[3] This distinction between stage dramaturg and literary dramaturg permeated the issue, conversations about dramaturgy at the time, and continues to do so today in definition, theory, and practice. This is amplified by the fact that in French, as in other romance languages, the word for dramaturg, *dramaturge*, has long meant "playwright." In her "dramaturgically staged"[4] interview in *Contemporary Theatre Review*, in which she edits and arranges excerpts from interviews with several dramaturgs and one playwright, British scholar Clare Finburgh argues that the terms "dramaturgy" and "dramaturg" remain "diverse and unresolved"[5] in France in 2010. My purpose here is an examination of the evolution of French dramaturgy, to ask when and how French theatre developed its own unique practice of dramaturgy. Tracking the status of the French dramaturg is not only compelling for the story of dramaturgy in France, but also illuminates key moments in French theatre history.

Jacques Scherer's 1950 book, *La Dramaturgie classique en France* (Classical Dramaturgy in France),[6] is a detailed study of dramatic technique through close readings of plays, and marks the beginning of a discourse around contemporary French dramaturgy. While others had written extensively about the playwrights he considers – including d'Aubignac, Molière, and Corneille – Scherer's innovation was to isolate and analyze the elements of dramatic structure, and to call this approach dramaturgy. In the 2004 *Dictionnaire du théâtre*,[7] Patrice Pavis provides three definitions of *dramaturgie*; here, Scherer, a literary scholar, employs the word *dramaturgie* in its first sense: "the art of the composition of plays."[8] Scherer's methodology reflects the ongoing dominance of Aristotelian and Corneillian dramatic theories and the lingering reign of neoclassicism.

In French theatre, the early 1950s saw the advent of the movement later called theatre of the absurd or *le nouveau théâtre* and, in 1954, the Berliner Ensemble's first visit to France. During this time of reconsideration of dramatic structure and language, "dramaturgy" became a way to talk about the plays themselves in rehearsal and on stage. A few individuals emerged who called themselves dramaturgs, including Brecht translator Maurice Regnaut, whom Jean Jourdheuil notes as "the first dramaturg in France who actually went by that name."[9] With Brecht's arrival, dramaturgy emerged as an active part of theatre production, and for the first time dramaturgy became a practice, named as such, in French theatre.

This new role of the French dramaturg was that of an intellectual who specialized in critical thinking and often worked as a translator and writer. The *Dictionnaire du théâtre* defines this idea of *dramaturgie*: "Dramaturgy, activity of the dramaturg (second sense), consists of putting in place textual and scenic materials, to unpack complicated significations of the text and to choose a particular interpretation, to orient the spectacle in the chosen sense."[10] Still, Finburgh writes, "dramaturgy in France existed as a function before it existed as a profession."[11] While Brecht popularized dramaturgy, and some went on to use the title of dramaturg, his visit to France sparked the *idea* of dramaturgy as a mode of thinking, rather than an artistic practice.

Early French dramaturgs provoked some skepticism, particularly since they were primarily philosophers and academics instead of trained theatre practitioners. Michèle Raoul-Davis noted in 1986, "One of the main reasons why production dramaturgs are sometimes seen poorly, badly resented by certain actors ... is, I think, because ... they appear as the intellectual *among* the artists, and in a position of power in the creative team. It seems to me that many theatre people in France have a very angry complex about the University."[12] A link between dramaturgy and a political bent in theatre – what Bernard Chartreux calls when "dramaturgy also immediately put a political flag in its pocket"[13]– is a refrain in reports from French dramaturgs of this period. Bruno Tackels recalls that the dramaturg was seen as "a Janus-faced figure who brought intellect that was no doubt valuable, but that could quickly become authoritarian. So the reputation for steering a production in a specific political direction led to dramaturgs having a reputation for controlling."[14] Joseph Danan notes that:

> From the start, the relationship between French theatre and the dramaturg was never simple and was, to my mind, marked by what I'd call failure. The problem was that the French imported what they thought to be the Brechtian conception of dramaturgy. The first dramaturgs ... turned Brecht's theories into a doctrine, into what in France we call "Brechtism" – a term that's now an insult. ... Dramaturgs seemed to be employed with the remit of conceiving and imposing a specific political line.[15]

He recounts that during this time, director "Antoine Vitez called dramaturgs *les flics du sens* – 'the meaning police.'"[16]

The events of May 1968 signaled an upheaval on all levels of French society – from politics to theory to cultural production. Dramaturgy evolved as theatre-makers experimented with innovative collaborations, international inspirations, and new ideas about the role of theatre in society. Raoul-Davis notes in an interview with Jean-Marie Piemme, "It is always said that the twentieth century is the century of directors. It's certainly not by accident that work with dramaturgs developed in France following '68."[17] Major directors like Antoine Vitez, Roger Planchon, and Patrice Chéreau worked with dramaturgs in some capacity, even if the word "dramaturg" wasn't consistently or officially employed. Jean Jourdheuil, who worked as a dramaturg between 1968 and 1974, proposes, "From 1968 onwards in France, the dramaturg was to constitute an element of disruption … Dramaturgy for me involved not simply the elucidation of the text, but an attempt at thinking, with respect to the play we were creating, about the politically transformatory potential of theatre. We heralded the advent of a 'new theatre' similar to those initiated by Lessing or Brecht."[18]

By the 1980s, the split between the dramaturgs of the page and stage was more clear, as was an ongoing division between the German tradition and a new, particular French practice. By the 1986 *Théâtre/Public* dramaturgy issue, the revolutionary mandate of French theatre had waned, the *théâtre populaire* movement had taken off, and the visionary director-centered theatre of Planchon, Chéreau, Vitez, and Ariane Mnouchkine reigned. Dramaturgs now worked in a variety of capacities in major dramatic centers, operas, universities, and even the Comédie Française.[19] Bernard Dort, who worked at the Théâtre National de Strasbourg, started his first dramaturgy course at the National Dramatic Conservatory in 1981. He notes that dramaturgy is not really a function, but a way of thinking about text and scenic practice; he writes of "a *dramaturgical state of spirit*, meaning, a certain attention to modalities of passage from the text to the stage."[20] For Dort, what is more important is "To ask questions, in the practice itself, of what is being represented? What does it mean to play a text? That's what I would like to call my dramaturgical vocation."[21] Michel Bataillon's 1985 lecture in Lyon, reprinted in the same journal, remarks, "Dramaturgy is born of reading, or of the work of studying, or of inspiration. Dramaturgy takes shape on the stage, is material, is sensual."[22] After a pigeon-holing of dramaturgy as intellectual practice aligned with Brecht, in the 1980s a redefinition capturing a more fluid, expansive notion of the profession emerges.

What follows Dort's opening essay in *Théâtre/Public* is a three-part series of conversations about the state of the profession. In a continuation of France's orientation towards Germany on this subject, a full quarter of the issue is devoted to interviews with German dramaturgs and directors, including Peter Stein and Heiner Müller, about German dramaturgy history and practice. In his interview, "L'avocat de l'auteur" [The author's advocate], Wolfgang Wiens introduces the idea of a "dramaturgie de production" (production dramaturgy). The following two sections instigate a discussion about dramaturgy in France. In "Le 'dramaturge'," Michel Bataillon, Bernard Chartreux, Jean-Pierre Vincent, Daniel Besnehard, and Jean-Marie Piemme discuss their visions of French dramaturgy. Piemme proposes the idea of the *dramaturge de plateau*, or stage dramaturg, the phrase that will come to define contemporary production dramaturgy.[23] Piemme defines this simply: "For me dramaturgy is an activity of transformation. It consists of transforming ambient conceptual knowledge into a tool that serves actors, directors, and scenographers. It's an extremely specific activity, and shouldn't be confused with university research activity."[24] Finally, Antoine Vitez, Emile Copfermann, Christian Drapon, and Gérard Lépinois ask, "What good is a dramaturg?" As articulated in *Théâtre/Public*, a major leap forward for French dramaturgy emerges in terms of its definitions, clarification of major trends and figures, and public prominence. That all of the dramaturgs interviewed are men reflects the ongoing male dominance of French theatre at this time; the only woman cited is dramaturg Michèle Raoul-Davis, who edited the issue and wrote the introduction. In 2006 and 2009, *Théâtre/Public* published special issues on *la dramaturgie*; the journal is a leader among French publications in ongoing discussion about the practice and profession.

If the 1986 *Théâtre/Public* conveys the state of the profession at that key moment, Anne-Françoise Benhamou's July 2012 *Dramaturgies de plateau* (Stage dramaturgies) provides an insight into the profession today. Benhamou is perhaps France's best-known contemporary dramaturg to work within a collaborative, practical model, based on a longstanding artistic partnership with a director. From 1993 to 2012, she worked with director Stéphane Braunschweig, current artistic director of Paris's Théâtre National de la Colline. After writing her dissertation with Dort, Benhamou began her career as a professor in 1990 at the Institut d'Etudes Théâtrales at the Sorbonne and moved to the École Normale Supérieure in 2012. Like many French dramaturgs, she works as both scholar and practitioner, and founded and edited the theatre journal *Outre Scène*. In 2001 she helped found France's first dramaturgy training program, at the École Supérieure d'Art Dramatique du Théâtre National de Strasbourg, where dramaturgy is offered in tandem with directing training. She directed this program from 2001 to 2008.

Dramaturgies de plateau traces her work with Braunschweig since 1992, giving particularly in-depth discussions of plays on which the two of them worked, from classics including *The Cherry Orchard* and *Tartuffe* to operas and projects at the Théâtre National de Strasbourg theatre school. These discussions include notes, letters to Braunschweig and others, and thoughts recorded during rehearsals for different productions; in this way Benhamou provides a French collection somewhat akin to American Mark Bly's *The Production Notebooks* – a rare glimpse into the thought processes behind particular productions. Her substantial introduction offers her contemplations on the profession, beginning with the provocation that "We must be able to stop saying *the* theatre. And instead, *the dramaturgy.*"[25] She advocates for a practice that is both artistic and critical, and defines dramaturgy: "It's this process of contamination of thought by action, and its reciprocation, that I call *stage dramaturgy.*"[26]

One of Benhamou's mandates is, through her book title and her professional title, to question the terms *dramaturge* and *dramaturgie*. This is clear in her comments at a 2008 roundtable at the École Normale Supérieure de Lyon:

> If I am not called dramaturg in the programs, even if I am doing dramaturgy, it's because we are all doing dramaturgy. It would be, from our point of view, kind of absurd to say that someone is a dramaturgy specialist. If there is dramaturgy in Stéphane Braunschweig's productions, and there is, it's because it's a common terrain for all of us: the costume designer makes dramaturgy in his proposals, the lighting designer too, and of course the actors. There's no reason to ascribe it to one person, and I'll add that it

would be impossible to do dramaturgy as I do if the director didn't have the head of a dramaturg. … It's for that reason that I chose, from the beginning of my collaboration with Stéphane, the title of artistic collaborator.[27]

Also a part of the roundtable was Joseph Danan, writer, dramaturg, and professor at the Institut d'Études Théâtrales at the Sorbonne, where he teaches a course called "Dramaturgical Questions." Alongside Benhamou, he is one of the best-known contemporary French dramaturgs. In several essays in the mid 2000s, he proposed some of the ideas that would shape his 2010 book *Qu-est ce que la dramaturgie?* (What is dramaturgy?). In his 2005 interview with Christian Biet, Danan, continuing the split proposed in *Théâtre/Public* twenty years earlier, takes care to divide dramaturgy into two different meanings: "We know that the word *dramaturgy* has *grosso modo* two senses. In its first, it designates what we call less and less 'the art of dramatic composition.' In its second sense, dramaturgy means this other practice, that considers the conditions of putting onstage a theatre text, in this it is very close to directing."[28] Calling the dramaturg "the ghost that haunts the theatre,"[29] Danan discusses the emergence of stage dramaturgy and the idea of the dramaturg as stand-in for the audience:

> Then, we saw appear, at the end of the 1970s, stage dramaturgy. What the dramaturg was reading, thus, was not just the text, but the production. He became the first reader of the signs proposed by the stage, … this type of dramaturgy avoids fixing one preconditioned reading of the stage work, and elaborates the reading based on scenic practice. So, the position of the dramaturg is one of someone who doesn't direct the work, but is the first "audience member," the first spectator facing the stage.[30]

Danan stresses that, as opposed to the earlier model of the dramaturg imposing a particular viewpoint, this conception of the dramaturg is one premised on invisibility: "The dramaturg is invisible by excellence, even more than the director … The dramaturg is invisible and the dramaturg is herself the invisible dimension of the production."[31] In his 2006 essay of the same title, Danan asked if we have reached the "end of dramaturgy?"[32] He remarks that with the advent of postdramatic theatre, the textual basis of French dramaturgy has been upended: "There is today a clear crisis in dramaturgy in its first sense – a crisis that Hans-Thies Lehmann radicalises as part of 'postdramatic theatre.'"[33]

As they attempt to unpack and situate the state of French dramaturgy today, both Benhamou and Danan locate themselves in a lineage of theatre history. Benhamou notes, "Brecht and critical theory then continued to be dominant forces in the theatres of successive generations of French directors such as Vitez and Patrice Chéreau, who had trained with Planchon, and also with Giorgio Strehler, who had introduced Brecht to Italy in the same way that Planchon had introduced him to France. Then, Braunschweig, for whom I'm dramaturg, worked with Vitez, and he continues the tradition of incorporating critical theory into mise en scène today."[34] Danan writes, "André Antoine distinguished, in directing, a material and an immaterial dimension, and Dort said that directing and dramaturgy were 'two sides of the same activity.'"[35] Bruno Tackels finds the practice fluid and even omnipresent, though warns of lingering mistrust of the specific vocabulary of practice and practitioner: "Therefore, I am not saying dramaturgy doesn't exist in France; on the contrary, many people perform the function of dramaturg, but the term itself has become taboo for reasons I've explained."[36] For dramaturgy in France today, Bernard Dort was prescient in his 1986 comment: "The word 'dramaturgy' has multiple accepted uses. These reflect the evolution of theatre practice. But they are less different than they seem."[37] While there are multiple definitions for it, dramaturgy in France remains an ongoing profession and tradition that reflects flashbulb moments in French theatre history.

Notes

1 With the exception of quotes from Finburgh's essay, all French-English translations are my own.
2 Michèle Raoul-Davis, "Profession 'dramaturge,'" *Théâtre/Public* 67 (January/February 1986): 4.
3 Raoul-Davis, 4.
4 Clare Finburgh, "External and Internal Dramaturgies: The French Context," *Contemporary Theatre Review* 20.2 (2010): 203. An excerpt from this interview is reprinted in Finburgh's collection *Contemporary French Theatre and Performance*, co-edited with Carl Lavery (New York: Palgrave MacMillan, 2011).
5 Finburgh, 203.
6 Jacques Scherer, *La Dramaturgie classique en France* (Paris: Nizet, 1950).
7 Patrice Pavis, *Dictionnaire du théâtre* (Paris: Armand Colin, 2004).
8 Pavis, 106.
9 Finburgh, 205.
10 Pavis, 106.
11 Finburgh, 205.
12 Raoul-Davis, 5.
13 Bernard Chartreux and Jean-Pierre Vincent, "Celui qui est dehors tout en étant dedans," *Théâtre/Public* 67 (January/February 1986): 47.
14 Finburgh, 207.
15 Finburgh, 207.
16 Finburgh, 207.
17 Jean-Marie Piemme, "Une activité de regard," *Théâtre/Public* 67 (January/February 1986): 56.
18 Finburgh, 206.
19 Jean-Pierre Vincent worked as dramaturg at the Comédie Française.
20 Bernard Dort, "L'était d'esprit dramaturgique," *Théâtre/Public* 67 (January/February 1986): 8.
21 Dort, 12.
22 Michel Bataillon, "Une connivence fluide et aléatoire," *Théâtre/Public* 67 (January/February 1986): 41.
23 Piemme, 52.
24 Piemme, 54.
25 Anne-Françoise Benhamou, *La Dramaturgies de plateau* (Besançon: Éditions Les Solitaires Intempestifs, 2012), 15.
26 Benhamou, 11.
27 Roundtable, "Dramaturges et Dramaturgie," École Normale Supérieure de Lyon, organized by Marion Boudier and Sylvain Diaz (29 January 2008), transcript available online at http://agon.ens-lyon.fr/index.php?id=1049.

28 Christian Biet, "Entretien avec Joseph Danan: Le dramaturge, ce spectre qui hante le théâtre," *Critique: Le théâtre sans illusion* (Paris: Les Editions de Minuit, 2005), 619.

29 Biet, 619.

30 Biet, 625.

31 Biet, 626.

32 Joseph Danan, "Fin de la Dramaturgie?" *Frictions: théâtres_écritures* (Montrouge: Frictions, 2006), 46–51.

33 Biet, 620.

34 Finburgh, 205.

35 Danan, 626.

36 Finburgh, 207.

37 Dort, 8.

8
Dramaturgy and the role of the dramaturg in Poland

Agata Dąbek

Translated by Michael Leonard Kersey Morris

"The dramaturg is in a similar situation to Caliban. Closely watched and difficult to understand."[1] At first glance a facetious reference to William Shakespeare's creation, Peter Gruszczyński's statement made in 2009, which rings with a slight hint of self-irony, still accurately reflects the condition of this profession in our country. Indeed, Poland still lacks a precise definition of the occupation; there is no agreement on the actual scope of competencies of the dramaturg in the theatre. The practice of dramaturgy, although present with us for more than fifteen years, is still often seen as new and, above all, due to cultural mediation, as foreign to our soil, a transplant from the theatrical practice of the German-speaking world.

Nevertheless, one can observe, presently, an increasing number of theoretical attempts to adapt the functions of the dramaturg to Polish theatrical soil. These attempts consist mainly of giving the profession features relevant to our historical-cultural context as well as placing dramaturgy into the framework of a specific Polish theatrical-dramatic tradition. What emerges is a clear image of the Polish dramaturg, albeit framed by its historical-ideological basis. The emergence of dramaturgy as a profession in Poland entailed a change in how we think about theatre as an institution.

The first significant initiative aimed at launching a national debate on the role of the dramaturg was the opening of the Dramaturgy Forum at the Theatre Institute in Warsaw in 2009. Its organizers have tried to outline prospects for the development of the profession and to specify the dramaturg's field of activity in Poland and abroad.[2] The educational activities carried out under the auspices of the forum were to normalize the dramaturg's presence in the minds of the Polish audience and directors, in particular, by demonstrating the continuity of the tradition of that profession with the basis of our theatre practice.[3] This was supported by the issue of *Notatnik Teatralny* (Theatre Notebook) entitled "Profession: Dramaturg," comprised of the edited insights gleaned from the initiative. In addition to articles by foreign authors, the issue featured the first comprehensive texts on the dramaturgy profession in our theatre, including works by Rafał Węgrzyniak and Jolanta Kowalska.

However, the analysis in the issue raised some doubts as to the success of attempts to lay down roots in Poland for this profession by demonstrating its historical, local pedigree.

Węgrzyniak, in an article entitled "But the Dramaturg, Who Is He? Dramaturgs and Their Ancestors in the History of Polish Theatre,"[4] dedicated a significant amount of space to Leon Schiller, the eminent Polish theatre director and educator who introduced the term "dramaturg" to Polish from the German cultural tradition in the interwar period.[5] Schiller, before becoming a director at the Polish Theatre in Warsaw, himself served as the dramaturg and music director, working on scripts and adaptations, preparing stagings, and also co-creating a number of productions. Schiller pointed out that the most appropriate place for a dramaturg is on the stage, next to the director and the actor, with whom he must cooperate closely. Already during the Second World War, Schiller had prepared a program in the dramaturgy faculty of the State Institute of Dramatic Art in Warsaw, which specified the functions of a dramaturg in the postwar Polish theatre. These included the assessment of plays and suggestion of any corrections; dramaturgical development of non-stage plays; modernizing old plays; preparing commentary and materials necessary for the actors, director, and set designer; analysis of the content of the work; outlining the ideological concept of the production as part of the work on compiling the acting script; presence at rehearsals; monitoring the overall shape of the staging; overseeing the archive and theatre library; and taking care of the layout of the poster and program; as well as editing the theatre magazine.[6] After the war, accepting the leadership of the State Theatre Academy in Warsaw, Schiller organized a dramaturgy faculty, which existed until mid 1953.

In fact, if you look at how broadly Schiller construed the dramaturg's sphere of activity, you can see the extent to which it overlaps even with this sphere as it currently exists in Germany – a country considered, quite rightly, the birthplace of this profession.[7] The frequent invocation of Schiller – and Węgrzyniak is no exception[8] – is meant to show the Polish and not the mediated, German pedigree of the profession in our country. After describing the merits of Schiller in introducing the functions of the dramaturg to the Polish theatre, Węgrzyniak says that, in the end, after Schiller was not able to fully realize all his proscriptions, he, paradoxically, dispensed with dramaturgs. Thanks to his talent and erudition, he independently edited Old Polish texts and folk scenarios, adapted novels, modernized old plays, and found in each its own approach.

According to Węgrzyniak, the majority of directors in twentieth-century Polish theatre operated similarly to Schiller, including Tadeusz Kantor, Mieczyslaw Kotlarczyk, Tadeusz Dejmek, Jerzy Grotowski, Andrzej Wajda, Jerzy Grzegorzewski, Jerzy Jarocki, and Krystian Lupa.[9] The major difficulty in adapting the function of the dramaturg to the Polish theatre is not found in the fact that the profession was transplanted from abroad but in the distinct profile of the Polish theatre, largely as a result of the system for training directors that has been in place for many years. Inadvertently, rather than legitimizing the existence of the dramaturg in Polish theatre, Węgrzyniak only confirms the impact of the Polish model of the theatre director – a total artist, who usually dispensed with (and also today dispenses with) his help. Węgrzyniak does mention the young generation of directors of the Variety Theatre, who at the end of the twentieth century collaborated with dramaturgs, though the impetus for this collaboration came from the influence of the Volksbühne on Rosa Luxemburg Square in Berlin. The presence of the dramaturg in the theatre landscape in recent years clearly promotes not so much the shape of our theatrical tradition but the relationship between Polish and German artists.

When discussing directors' work, Węgrzyniak primarily focuses on the process of developing their theatrical scripts and creating adaptations of the classic plays. Since he describes these directors as doing the work of dramaturgs, he automatically assigns the dramaturg (absent in the theatrical narrative) essentially just these functions. He does not fully follow Schiller's model. Emphasizing the process of writing and rewriting texts limits the dramaturg's field of action to literary treatments carried out from behind his or her desk, as if bypassing the whole sphere of his or her presence on the stage and active participation in shaping the drama of a theatrical event: monitoring its progress, rhythm, and emerging meanings. The tendency to reduce the activities of the dramaturg to strictly literary procedures is also evident in Justyna Kowalska's article "A Brief History of the Betrayal of the Author."[10] Kowalska describes the adaptation strategies of placing old texts in a current context and examines the variation of the boundaries of consensus between the rights of the theatrical adaptor and the integrity of the vision of the text's author, charted in Poland over the last two centuries, noting that these boundaries were significantly shifted by Jerzy Grotowski and his literary manager collaborator, Ludwik Flaszen. While describing the practices of Grotowski and his productions, Kowalska speaks most of all about reversing theatrical signs in order to disrupt the internal logic of the text (Grotowski changed very little in the text). Analyzing the directors of the younger generation – Maja Kleczewska, Michał Zadara, Wiktor Rubin, and Jan Klata – Kowalska points out their practices of playing with the literary text: over-writing their own issues on the original dialogue, compiling motifs, and building intertextual collages. She adds, "There is no lack, evidently, of more radical practices. We have now dramaturgs who – following in the footsteps of Bertolt Brecht and Heiner Müller – write their own play on the themes of classical works."[11]

Kowalska paints a picture of the Polish dramaturg as the person responsible mainly for literary matters (as opposed to Brecht and Müller). To illustrate some of these "radical adaptation practices," she analyzes the works of Paweł Demirski. Although his plays are always directed by Monika Strzępka, with whom he closely collaborates, Demirski considers himself more a playwright than a dramaturg. In fact, as in France, in Poland too for many years the two terms "playwright" and "dramaturg" have been used interchangeably.[12] The consequences of this confusion in terminology are significant: rather than strengthening, they have effectively weakened the position of the dramaturg in the Polish theatre. On the one hand, reducing his or her role to purely literary activities makes the dramaturg a literary craftsman subordinate to the director, exclusively supplying textual material that conforms to the director's sensation of the world and interests. On the other hand, this supports the still strong model in Poland of theatre remaining in the power of director.

This "working" definition of the function of a Polish dramaturg as author of the text subordinate to the will of the theatre producer persists to this day, as evidenced by even the last debates on the working conditions of Polish playwrights. In the battle between "old" and "new" writing for the stage, the issue of the alleged sub-ordination of the shape and content of theatrical scripts to the director's vision has become a strong argument in favor of the devaluing of the literary achievements of dramaturgs.[13] Just as often the reason for this devaluation is the "undramatic" nature of their scripts: fragmented, discontinuous, full of mediations, etc. Such theatrical scripts are also appreciated, especially by advocates of new strategies for communicating with the viewer beyond the traditional communication scheme of the dramatic theatre.[14] Both supporters of drama and of theatrical scripts often do not notice the valuable features in the works of the other side or see them in their own works, where in fact they are not. In discussions on the dramaturgical practice in the Polish theatre, the major concern is invariably not so much theatrical dramaturgy, of which the text is just a component, as much as the dramaturgy of the text. Inter-estingly, this is occurring at a time when the Polish theatre is defined in the pages of the trade press under the heading of "postdramatic theatre."[15]

Dramaturgs themselves have quite a different vision of the dramaturgy profes-sion.[16] For example, some dramaturgs, such as Piotr Gruszczyński, Dorota Sajewska, Sebastian Majewski, Weronika Szczawińska, Bartek Frąckowiak, Jola Janiczak, Iga Gańcarczyk, Aśka Grochulska, Marcin Cecko, or Michael Buszewicz, emphasize the revolutionary and, at the same time, unpredictable aspect of their operations, describing their role as a "positive virus." Gradually, they beneficially infect our theatre, bursting its rigid hierarchical structures, both formal-artistic and organizational. This happens mostly not so much as a result of their literary activities, but primarily as a result of close collaboration with directors: directors such as Paweł Miśkiewicz, Krzysztof Warlikowski, Krzysztof Garbaczewski, Wiktor Rubin, and Jan Klata see their dramaturgs as equal partners in the process of shaping the dramaturgy of theatrical productions.[17] In addition to writing texts, the collaboration of our dra-maturgs with directors often involves introducing new interpretive tropes and formal solutions, which emerge as a result of creative disunity and clashes, by observing actors' improvisations and, above all, by taking into account the perspective of the potential viewer. In the Polish theatre, the dramaturg is increasingly seen as a necessary intermediary in communicating between the stage (the director) and the audience. The dramaturg is considered as the first viewer and, at the same time, the most important, who by considering the expectations and perceptual processes of the audience serves as a guarantor of the understanding and establishment of the dialogue. This allows the active participation of the audience in the performance.

The theatrical paper *Didaskalia* has served to extend the image of the dramaturg as a public-relations manager by supplementing the published reviews of productions with interviews with dramaturgs.[18] Its editors have initiated a sort of national discussion about strategies for writing about productions, which might eventually resemble in their fervour that which concerned the "invisible" contributions of Bertolt Brecht's collaborators in the shaping of his dramatic-theatrical vision of epic theatre.[19] Although Polish theatre is dominated by a rather classical scheme of communication between the stage and the audience, significant changes actually have occurred in the last two years. Not without its impact on this change is the increasingly noticeable presence of the dramaturg in the Polish theatre. By urging a dialogue, the dramaturg subsequently is repositioning this communication scheme in the entire space of the theatre. Some theorists do argue that it is not the presence of the dramaturg that has changed the face of today's Polish theatre, but simply that the changes taking place in it, as if spontaneously, allow the dramaturg to emerge from out of the shadows. This too reveals a strong desire to subjugate the dramaturgy profession to the Polish theatre establishment with its tradition and history, which, however, Polish dramaturgs oppose with increasing effectiveness.

Notes

1 Piotr Gruszczyński, "Człowiek czy ryba?" *Dialog* 9 (2009): 124.
2 The Opening Forum conference with the participation of foreign guests – Cathy Turner, Synne K. Behrndt, David Williams, Thomas Kraus, Rok Vevar, Beate Seidel, and Dunji Funke – was the starting point of an annual cycle of drama workshops conducted by Polish and foreign dramaturgs and researchers.
3 See Marta Keil, "Dlaczego teraz?" *Notatnik Teatralny* 58–9 (2010): 74–6.
4 See Rafał Węgrzyniak, "'Ale dramaturg, kim on jest?' Dramaturdzy i ich protoplaści w historii polskiego teatru," *Notatnik Teatralny* 58–9 (2010): 12–23.
5 Schiller, before becoming a director at the Polish Theatre in Warsaw, himself served as the dramaturg and music director, working on scripts and adaptations, preparing stagings, and also co-creating a number of productions.
6 See Leon Schiller, "Wydział Dramaturgiczny PIST. Program studio," ed. and introduced by Jerzy Timoszewicz, *Pamiętnik Teatralny* 3 (1987): 341–68.
7 See Thomas Irmer, "Mózg i jego pomocnik. Dramaturg na tle przemian w niemieckim teatrze," *Notatnik Teatralny* 58–9 (2010): 98–103.
8 See Marzena Sadocha, "Dramaturdzy, czyli jajko Kolumba," *Notatnik Teatralny* 58–9 (2010): 9–11.
9 There were occasional exceptions to this rule. For example, Jarocki collaborated on the production *Dream about the Sinless* with Józef Opalski, and Lupa engaged Iga Gańczarczyk and Magdalena Stojowska to work on the production *Factory 2*.
10 See Justyna Kowalska, "Krótka historia zdrady autora," *Notatnik Teatralny* 58–9 (2010): 36–43.
11 Kowalska, 43.
12 See Dorota Jarząbek, "Niewidzialna profesja," *Dialog* 9 (2009): 135–41.
13 See Zbigniew Majchrowski, "Dekada dramatopisarek," *Teatr* 4 (2011): 5.
14 This is confirmed by theoretical texts by Marzena Sadocha, Jagoda Hernik-Spalińska, Anna Wojciechowska, Paweł Sztarbowski, and Rafał Węgrzyniak contained in the latest edition of *Theatre Notebook*. See *Notatnik Teatralny: Nowe Teksty* 68–9 (2012): 32–98.
15 For more on the confusion arising from the specific reception of Hans-Thies Lehmann's *Postdramatic Theatre* in Poland: see Agata Dąbek, "Teatr postdramatyczny i teksty dla teatru w Polsce," *Dialog* 10 (2012): 131–9.
16 See Joanna Targoń, "Wirus, strażnik, negocjator, partner ... Rozmowa z Szymonem Wróblewskim, Magdą Stojowską, Bartoszem Frąckowiakiem, Igą Gańczarczyk, Dorotą Sajewską, Mironem Hakenbeckiem," *Didaskalia* 77 (2007): 9–17.
17 See "Intelektualiści czy artyści. Z reżyserami rozmawiają Iga Dzieciuchowicz, Anna Herbut, Joanna Targoń," *Didaskalia* 78 (2007): 12–17.
18 See *Didaskalia* 109/110 (2012): 127–45.
19 See Joanna Wichowska, "*Iwona Księżniczka Burgunda* Krzysztofa Garbaczewskiego," *Dwutygodnik* 81 (2012). See also Marcin Cecko, "List do recenzentki," *Dwutygodnik* 81 (2012).

9

The new play dramaturgy in Russia

Pavel Rudnev

Translated by Jessica Hinds-Bond

The movement for the renewal of the repertoire and new playwriting in Russia is hardly more than fifteen years old. In that time a powerful network has been created, an infrastructure that covers Russia and the former Soviet republics. This network has become involved with the selection and cross-country distribution of plays; experimental work; the education of playwrights, directors, and actors in the new aesthetic; and the presence of the contemporary play in social networks. Today, dramaturgical life is both highly saturated and fiercely active. Seminars, laboratories, readings, student performances, festivals, discussions, and competitions extend across all of Russia, significantly influencing the theatrical climate of the country. There is a living reaction, a rebirth of the community, direct contact with spectators. And there is a conception of theatre as a dialogue in the literal sense of the word, as an agon, in which the most alarming problems of contemporaneity are debated. The spectators' discussion teaches us that the new art reflects the unpleasantness of contemporary reality, which hides behind the unpleasantness of its art. In this new reality of the Russian theatre, one of change and transition, the dramaturgical function is vital.

"Dramaturgs" in the German sense of the word do not exist in Russia. The Russian word *dramaturg* indicates the person who writes plays, not necessarily an affiliate of the theatre. Literary functions in the theatres are usually undertaken by the so-called "*zavlit*" (literary manager) or the associate artistic director. Russia, unfortunately, lacks a form of artistic residency for the dramatists inside the theatrical organism, but I am not dismissing the possibility that this Western experiment may be applicable to us in the near future. The need has now become urgent in that, as a rule, the question of the evolution of the dramatist (*dramaturg*) in Russia is to a great extent a question of the close collaboration between author and theatre. The techniques of the postdramatic theatre are already appearing in Russia, and the dramatist's work is more and more frequently demanded in adaptation, the rewriting of classic texts, and literary assemblage.

The ethical atmosphere of today's Russia is extremely complex. We have lived twenty years outside of the Soviet order, but just as before we have not fully organized our conception of reality, not named that country in which we now live, not finished constructing it. An important motif of contemporary Russian life was recently recorded in *Transfer* (dir. Vladimir Pankov), a notable performance piece based on the work of contemporary playwrights. It is set in a pedestrian underpass, which links one side of the street with the other, as individuals stand still for a long while: a holdup in the day that is life, the impossibility of turning backwards and the fear of coming out. The performance ends with a moment of triumph, as all the characters (around 40 people) go up to the forestage and sing a grand anthem, in which the anthems of tsarist Russia, the USSR, and the new Russia are all blended together. For those who do not know, I'll explain: the melody of the new anthem partially coincides with the Stalinist, although some poet has rewritten the words. Here then is the spiritual state of the country: Russia can only rely upon something that exists in reality, a history that was truncated, "nullified" in the epoch of Lenin. To depend on the contemporary era is impossible because everything is unstable. Russia lives only insofar as its basic foundations, those laid in the Soviet system, continue to stand as they did back then. But the problem is that these foundations are decaying, if they are not already completely decrepit. There is nothing, or almost nothing, that is new. Putin's Russia – especially in his second and third terms – raises the question of the rebirth of the Stalinist system, the rebirth of Sovietism. This historical preamble will be very important to keep in mind when we talk about the aesthetics of the new play.

The problem of contemporary play development is many layered. The last surge of new drama in Russia before the fall of the USSR was in the era of Perestroika. All at once, censorship collapsed, we discovered texts previously banned from the stage, theatrical life was decoupled from the state, and some of our most brilliant playwrights found themselves "liberated": Lyudmila Petrushevskaya, Vladimir Sorokin, Aleksei Shipenko, Venedikt Yerofeyev. On the one hand, this was a playwriting of pain and despair. The plight of Soviet man was suddenly revealed: the automatism of his existence, the dislocation of his consciousness, the mundane routine of daily life, the savagery. Yet, on the other hand, these were the first experiments of postmodern deconstruction: the Soviet style turned into pop art and the related Sots Art (Socialist Art); and the Soviet mythology was imposed on the colossal cultural legacy of pre-revolutionary Russia, begetting freaks of nature, waxworks, and the insanity of an era in which the empire broke up and came to ruin. Following the fall of communism, dramatists began organizing various forms of social activity; they were called upon to defend the honor of their genre and simply to shout: "We are here." The problem of the 1990s was also one of communication, which is crucial in our vast country. All the Soviet connections were in flames, books stopped being published, but the internet did not yet exist. Therefore, there was a pervasive need to inform all the theatres of Russia about the new plays, the new points of view.

And then came silence. In the history of the theatre, the 1990s began as years of stagnation: the crisis of financing and administration, the drainage of spectators (above all, the intellectuals, for whom theatre had been a beacon of liberal ideas, but the democratic spectators as well), the growth of the bourgeoisie, the gutterization of the repertoire. And due to several factors, the link between the theatre and dramatic literature snapped. First, the mechanism for circulating plays through the theatres vanished. The internet did not yet exist (although since the 2000s it has been the main propulsive force of the contemporary play in the Russian world), and the theatre journals ceased publication. For the vast, fragmented country without stable lines of communication, this fact led to the widespread claim: "we have no contemporary play." Second, Soviet playwrights ceased writing overnight. If they did still write, it was with a lost sense of time: reality had been so abruptly exchanged, and it was still changing every day. Some other sort of brains and methods were needed to nail down this world. But it was the spirit of the time that was the most important factor in the parting of the theatre and the new play. The contemporary character vanished from theatrical productions, as stagings of classical prose became the phenomenon of the 1990s. It was precisely then that the celebrated theatre school of Petr Fomenko was cultivated and strengthened, a school famous for its particular method of theatrically realizing the prose through the irony of the narrator. Reality was terrible, criminal, hopeless, and unrecognizable – and so it completely vanished from the stage; the theatre did not wish to work on its own reflection in the mirror, and so it departed into nostalgia, dreams, and reveries.

The paradox of the Russian path towards a change in the repertoire and an interest in contemporaneity lies in the fact that it was the playwrights themselves who began the movement for renewal: having rallied together, the first post-Soviet generation began to campaign for the staging of new plays and the advancement of new drama into theatrical practice. This playwright-driven change is characteristic of Russian theatrical tradition. Russia is a literature-centric country, and the history of the theatre at all times has assumed that the playwright goes ahead of the process of change, writing his dream play rather than a text for the existing theatre. The playwright leads the theatre to change. And the theatre is reformed only through the word, through a sense of meaning, through logos. There has been extremely little non-verbal theatre in Russia up to now. The system of actor training is now, just as before, very dependent on the words and the established arrangement of performance roles. From the end of the 1990s to the start of the 2000s, many things were established for these dramaturgic populations: a whole network of mini-festivals, public readings of new plays, the electronic distribution of texts, discussions, and training seminars.

But there is a more complex aesthetic problem. Today, as never before, we see how Russian culture suffered under Soviet censorship, the system of prohibitions, and the cultural isolation of the era of communism. Today we see how the patriarchal theatre still struggles against contemporary culture, having armed itself with a system of taboos that was long ago overcome in the cinema and the art world. Theatre in Russia often resembles a museum or an archive of "eternal" values, which need to be protected from the dominating influence of contemporaneity. Because of the cultural isolation and censorship, Russian theatre could not pass through a crucial phase in the development of the European stage – the theatre of the absurd of the 1960s and 1970s. That style destroyed faith in scenic logic, in the logos, in life on the stage, in the meaning of the word, and in the linear construction of the plot.

Russian theatre did not pass through this essential stage of theatrical deconstruction. And therefore, Russian psychological theatre of the Chekhovian and Moscow Art Theatre type still prevails, inhibiting the experimental theatre. If we were to interrogate the society of today as to its cultural priorities, we would see that the majority would still name the Soviet phenomenon of art as a cultural ideal, full of virtue, harmony, imperial grandeur, and complacency. One significant topic arises in conversation with western colleagues who have seen much Russian theatre: Russian theatre is painfully antisocial. It does not speak to the contemporary spectator and it generally does not need the spectator, because the fourth wall stands in his place. Our theatre does not notice contemporaneity, its problems or psychoses. Our theatre is either nostalgic or else it appears to be an anachronism. One of the strongest taboos of the stage is that it is considered bad form for art to be topical – it must speak about the eternal and the high-spiritual. The cultural legacy of Russia is so extensive that the majority of the efforts of cultural establishments must be spent on maintenance and restoration. These establishments are essentially a part of the structure of the state's cultural policy (we are frighteningly dependent on the policy, since government sources account for three-quarters of the operating expenses of Russian cultural products). Very little place is devoted to contemporary art. The contemporary play is somehow optional. It may be in the repertoire, but it certainly does not have to be.

Strictly speaking, the contemporary playwriting movement is born in that moment, when some sort of simple renewal of the repertoire is no longer enough, when it becomes imperative to put a contemporary person on the contemporary stage. When we need to understand our time, to name it and begin to contribute to it. The new play recognizes man's need for self-identification, which is essential in order for him to function properly. The contemporary play in Russia is a manifestation of enormous social unrest and even of social irritation. It lies in the field of inevitable societal conflicts. The most important result of the fifteen years of this resistance movement is that, together with the new play, a whole new generation has arrived on the scene: new directors, new ideas, new theatres, and most importantly the new spectator. Today it is widely accepted that a young director may enter the greater theatre world only through the staging of a new play. In fact, the practice of "double debuts" – when the young director makes his own debut with a new text in hand – has become firmly established. In other words, the playwrights began the reform of the theatre through the renewal of the texts, often incorporating cinematic elements. The contemporary text brought with it a series of problems, which were sooner or later resolved. At first, the spectator could not be found, so they cultivated him. Then the large theatres did not permit new texts, so they created small theatres. And when the system for distributing texts crashed down, they turned to the internet. And so forth.

The new play has raised a wave of public discussion about the theatre. Moreover, as a socially active art form, the new play resembles sociopolitical journalism, protest-oriented and broaching disputed issues – the new drama has returned a public significance to the theatre. This is above all due to the fact that it elicits dialogue from and arouses reactions in the spectator. Is it possible today to hope that the new phase of the theatrical experiment will depend on the text, on literature? All the same, how are young playwrights writing? And about what? The naturalistic verbatim style of documentary theatre prevails: a changeable reality demands the fixing of the reality that is slipping away, the fixing of the mechanics of life. The phenomenon of the contemporary play in Russia is for the most part a provincial occurrence. Among Muscovites and St. Petersburgians there are few playwrights. The playwrights mature outside the theatre, outside the institutions. The verbatim form offers both an apparatus and an excellent welcome for those who are writing their fifth or sixth text. It allows them to rise up and to break away from the experience of understanding oneself to the experience of understanding the other.

A pessimistic view is common to the new plays, as is extremely sharp dramatic effect, even tragedy – or rather, as in Nietzsche, tragic optimism. Comedies in Russia are simple, laughing. Not yet ready to part with the past, they instead take up the popular notion of the rebirth of the Soviet system. New drama is concerned with the subject of the little man, in this sense continuing the greater tradition of Russian literature. Its trajectory is extremely interesting: at first, the theatres of the capital city began to stage contemporary plays, and only today, towards the end of the first decade of the 2000s, has contemporary drama rolled over into the provinces. Now the provincial spectator and the regional theatres are the main "testing mechanism" for new plays. This is not a sign of the marginalization of the new play, but rather evidence of its profound evolution: the new play, which was written by provincials, returns home to finally appear to those to whom it was addressed. Ivan Vyrypaev's play *Oxygen* confronts neopositivist values, while parodying and reinterpreting the Ten Commandments. The play's protagonist maintains that we all live in the face of a future ecological or cosmic catastrophe, the final generation before the destruction of civilization. Essentially, the play states that it is important today to preserve our oxygen, the vanishing resource that is of singular importance for the safeguarding of life. A central motif in both Vyrypaev's *Oxygen* and the Presnyakov brothers' *Playing the Victim* is the renunciation of false national values and priorities. There is a theme: the man and the megalopolis, the man and mass communication, the effect of a totally open world on a person's consciousness. There is the theme of antiglobalization, of the resistance to capitalism.

The new play conquers the taboos of society and the taboos of the theatre. In society there are three topics about which almost no one speaks: the demythologization of the Soviet soldier in World War II, the interfaith and international relations in Russia, and finally the topic of the church. Russia is becoming an increasingly clerical country, with the Orthodox church having entered into the government and its cultural policy. This connection has led to many prohibitions of theatrical productions, bans initiated by the church and supported by the authorities. Of course, there are no overtly antireligious plays in Russia. But there is another, even more pressing topic: the crisis of traditional faiths. Take for example the play *The Polar Truth* by Yury Klavdiev, who writes about new legends of urbanity. This play depicts members of the AIDS generation who live life as if they have begun humanity anew, a makeshift community of squatters disconnected from the outer world. The play treats AIDS as an illness, which peels off layers of immunity – the history of mankind, its protective crust. As if nullifying history, it burns out everything false so as to bring the genuine out into the light. Traditional Russia is dying, the nation – especially the provinces – is becoming extinct, and traditional values are departing. To save them, one can either exit to the depths, there to vanish, or else become a museum, a tourist center. In the 2010s, when Russians have again begun to speak about the repressive mechanisms and the premature rollback of liberal reforms, the playwright has appeared: speaking about the salvation to be found in illusion and the therapeutic effect of escapism and social phobia.

10

Dramaturgy in post-revolution Iran

Problems and prospects

Marjan Moosavi

To write about dramaturgy in post-revolution Iran demands a comprehensive grasp of Iranian theatre tradition from past to present, as well as a broad and diverse understanding of political and religious dynamics in contemporary Iranian society. Providing such an overview of the contemporary challenges and accomplishments of the dramaturgical tradition in Iran can help us shed more light on the existing paradoxes and prospects for its practitioners, researchers, and even authorities. Iranian contemporary theatre has been developing and flourishing in a country where revolution, war, economic sanctions, and cultural transformations have all marked its recent history.[1]

This article looks at the roots and effects of the Islamicization and politicization of dramaturgy as both a practice and profession in Iran during the last 30 years, starting from the 1979 revolution. Through elaborating the ways in which dramaturgy has been shaped by political/religious motivations and interventions in Iran, I will discuss how the dramaturgical tradition has been influenced by the transformation of political objectives, a transformation that in the context of Iran has led to the formation of a new political and artistic intelligentsia in the realm of theatre. Within the Iranian context the social and political dynamics in the years following the revolution – the Iran-Iraq war, Reformation era, and finally the current decade – have produced new dramaturgical strategies, functions, and approaches that have been influential in the formation and development of a repertory of Islamic agitprop theatre as well as avant-garde and experimental theatre. In what follows, in addition to a brief historical overview, I will explore the unique features of Iranian dramaturgy based on Bert Cardullo's discussion of major dimensions of dramaturgy. According to Cardullo, "production research" and "organization of the many facets of repertory theatre activity," irrespective of geographical, political, and artistic specificities, are two principal aspects of dramaturgy.[2]

With the advent of Islamist political groups after the 1979 revolution, the necessity to change the fundamentals of the social and cultural dispositions of Iranians gained prominence. The Islamists' determination to Islamicize the educational system, cultural structures, and political directions led to the establishment of several bureaus, organizations, and committees, namely the Supreme Council of the Cultural Revolution, the Center for Dramatic Arts (CDA),[3] and the Islamic Development Organization in the immediate years after the revolution. The underlying purpose of such institutions is to promote the ideological visions and values of the so-called Islamic revolution and to integrate its religious political system into various aspects of Iranian culture, through funding and supporting numerous artistic events and practices.

During the Iran-Iraq war era (1980–88), most of the state-sponsored productions were categorized as Holy Defense Theatre (referring to the Iran-Iraq war). Regardless of their genre, almost all of these productions glorified the theme of Iranian warriors' resistance and sacrifice.[4] The government's considerable investment in this type of theatre is easily understood by looking at the numerous festivals that were organized throughout these eight years in various venues, including war-stricken provinces. The end of the Iran-Iraq war (1988), however, was followed by the growth in theatrical-funding opportunities as a result of government's recognition of the aesthetic/cultural values of theatrical productions. The Ministry of Islamic Culture and Guidance started investing in the training and producing of theatre as an apparatus to promote and showcase the Islamic and revolutionary ideology for (inter)national audiences while enhancing Iranian nationalistic values for its national spectators. It organized and sponsored various institutes, groups, festivals, and conferences under the auspices of the CDA. Both before and after the revolution, the underlying notion in this formative stage of dramaturgy in Iran has been the development of a national theatre by either writing plays about and for Iranian people or re-writing and appropriating foreign texts to satisfy the aesthetic, religious, and political tendencies of Iranian authorities and audiences. Since the 1980s, the objective to preserve the Islamic-Iranian self-image entailed directing ample attention toward works by Iranian playwrights. This project of advancing a national theatre resembles similar nationalization projects in countries like China or various Eastern European countries under the Soviet regime, in the sense that certain theatrical traditions and functions, and in particular dramaturgical practices, have been regarded by Iranian theatre's officials and con-servative practitioners with suspicion as being instances of strategic practices which import Western, anti-Islamic, or Imperialistic intentions into Iranian theatre.

On the other hand, like other countries' dramaturgical traditions, translation, adaptation, and re-writing have been sanctioned practices of Iranian dramaturgy.[5] The 2000s boom in academic institutions and global communication generated pro-fessionally translated plays and technical texts which played a significant role in raising awareness of and interest in dramaturgy.[6] It should be noted, however, that Iranian dramaturgical politics and practices are still far away from the celebrated German, British, or American dramaturgical traditions. With respect to dramaturgy's institutional/official status, or its professional identity in Iranian theatre, it suffices to say that there is no officially appointed literary manager or resident dramaturg, nor is there a prize of any kind for its practitioners. Unlike the words "director" and "playwright," the word "dramaturgy" has no equivalent in Persian.

While affirming that the scope of dramaturgical collaboration varies from one theatrical group to the next, Nasim Ahmadpour, one of the self-proclaimed dramaturgs, describes her professional career as precarious due to its unrecognized status in the process of unionization and funding. Admitting that state limitations impose problems for the production process, she highlights the authoritative presence of theatre directors alongside theoretical weaknesses and lack of dramaturgical experimentation as the main reasons that cause artists and officials to disregard the necessity of dramaturgical practices and the profession. Consequently, many theatre groups lose the opportunity of a permanent and trusting collaboration with dramaturgs.[7]

In the current decade, a number of playwright-director-dramaturg teams have been formed, mostly among the young generation of experimental and avant-garde theatrical groups. Owing to the scarcity of desirable Iranian dramatic pieces, these collaborative dramaturgies have been directed to adaptation, assimilation, and appropriation of an array of highly political works of Western drama. Aware of these texts' potential to improve the critical awareness and intelligence of Iranian audiences, these practitioners have discovered and exercised textual and directorial strategies to challenge state authoritative interventions in framing their theatrical tradition. This, of course, has been possible through a wide range of textual and performative treatments of the plays, from subtle interpretational shifts to deliberate transformation to strategic recontextualization.[8] One of these young director/ dramaturgs is Rouhollah Jafari, who by creating a repertory of Matei Vişniec's plays – namely *The Spectator Sentenced to Death* and *Horses behind the Window* – has created a stage from which to discuss critically issues that are generally prohibited, such as judicial justice, war, and totalitarianism. Jafari's *Spectator* was observed meticulously and on more than eight occasions by the Supervision Committee before getting license for public performance in 2011. Despite the committee's insistence on omitting one of the roles, Jafari ultimately kept the role, but accepted to omit politically offensive parts of dialogues.[9]

Such revisions and recontextualization of foreign dramatic works for the Iranian context and audiences have paved the way for new waves of theatre practice in Iran to not only enter into "a dialectical relationship" with other theatre practitioners,[10] but also, as Arrigo Subiotto notes about Brecht's adaptations, have a dialectical treatment of history through "bring[ing] out the latent social comment in the play" and "suggesting that the audience should go on to reappraise the contemporary moment."[11] Obviously, in the current restraining political atmosphere in Iran, where even scant questioning of Islamicized political hegemony is barely tolerated by the government, adaptation as a model of dramaturgy allows Iranian adaptors and dramaturgs to rethink and thus to investigate their relations toward sociopolitical life, the artistic world, and enthusiastic audiences. Furthermore, within Iran's sanction-stricken economic system, adaptation is an inevitably safe solution that can also guarantee the financial success of a show. One of these successful adaptations was Reza Servati's 2012 revisioning of *Macbeth* in which a man played the role of Lady Macbeth.[12] Cross-gender casting was a source of dramaturgical intervention through which the dramaturg and director could cross and thus question the distinctly defined gender boundaries on an Islamicized stage. In another example of transgressive dramaturgy, *Drought and Lie* (an outstanding Iranian production by M. Yaghoubee, 2009), actors went through their movements in slow motion style and silence to signify the sentences that had to be changed due to censorship. Repeated success of such disguised counter-hegemonic dramaturgy delineates the resilience of its practitioners in invigorating their aesthetic visions with their ideological progression.

Nonetheless, it is equally important to mention that such dramaturgical models have objectionable aspects as well. The increasing number of adaptive productions which are sometimes devoid of a dialectical relationship with their similar Iranian and foreign productions, runs the risk of positioning Iranian dramaturgy on a unidirectional path. Some critics, such as M. Hossein Mirbaba, also consider these adaptive strategies "excessive" and at points "not fully informed and disciplined." Mirbaba also asserts that lack of conceptual consistency and also excessive attention to formal innovation and visual creation rob performances of their conceptual vigor and interrogative potentials, and thus result in a theatre repertory of a "politically harmless strand of physical and visual theatre that has been ironically more favored by the state officials." According to Mirbaba, the epistemological and ontological differences between non-Iranian dramatists and Iranian director/dramaturgs generate complications and gaps in interpretation and performance, a problem that urgently calls for recognizing a substantial role for the dramaturg, independent from that of director or designer.[13] Accordingly, other than sporadic endeavors to realize individual dramaturgical ambitions, in today's Iranian theatre one of the principal dimensions of dramaturgy, "specific production research" to borrow the term from Bert Cardullo, has been pushed to the sideline.[14]

Cardullo's second important dimension of dramaturgy, organization of repertory theatre, has been controlled in Iran recently by a diverse array of conditioning elements, from the state's financial policies, afflicted by international sanctions, to spectators' religious sensitivities. A brief discussion of state evaluative and supportive policies will help us take note of the key features of Islamicized and politically inflected theatre repertory and its related dramaturgy in contemporary Iranian theatre.

In the 1980s the Supreme Council of the Cultural Revolution played a decisive role in legislating and maintaining art-related regulatory principles which were later updated in 2000. According to the two major principles of these regulations, Iranian theatre productions must not refute the principles and ideals of the Islamic faith, and also must not contribute to the cultural, political, or economic influence of foreign enemies.[15] The combination of these principles and the mainly unwritten regulations based on religious and moral codes form a body of rules that are not only general in scope and nature, but are most importantly based on attitudinal imprecision and subjective arbitration. These rules control issues including costumes, dialogues, placement of males and females on the stage, body language, stage designs, musical rhythm, and dance movements. In fact, all aspects of the theatre-making process are so much influenced and contained by the censorial intervention of the state that we cannot discuss their influence on dramaturgy independent of other facets of Iranian theatre. Therefore, in the dramaturgical domain, not only are the composition or selection of the text and its thematic features infiltrated at the very initial stages, but directorial practice and representational strategies should also pass through a religious and political filtering process to be licensed for public performance.

As one of the main subdivisions of the CDA, the Committee of Theatre Supervision and Evaluation is the most authoritative bureau in contemporary Iranian theatre that directly examines and evaluates the appropriateness and Islamic decency of all theatrical productions. The evaluation process begins by examining the dramatic pieces (whether Iranian or foreign); once texts are cleansed of their implicit or explicit interpretive threats, theatrical groups can obtain a license for their rehearsal. A second evaluation is usually scheduled after the rehearsal period. Since the Supervision Committee is very well aware of the transgressive potential of live performance, all groups must stage their production before the Supervision Committee. Most often, the Supervision Committee's comments and suggestions are production-oriented. Differently put, having observed the run-through performance, the committee prepares a list of objections and "corrective" suggestions for cutting and changing offending parts of the performance. A situation that can consequentially mean, albeit strangely, that in today's Iranian theatre the members of the Supervision Committee form an Islamist group of resident dramaturgs who have been actively preparing and assembling dramaturgical protocols and casebooks specific to each production.

In addition to their attitudinal features stemming from the political and religious dispositions of the committee members, these corrections vary depending on the occasion and venue of the performances. For instance, during the selection and evaluation process of performances for the Fadjr International Theatre Festival (FITF), where there is much ground for showcasing the government and international/intercultural exchanges, the committee shows more flexibility and tolerance in terms of the regulations concerning music, costumes, and movements.[16] On the national level, however, since its inception in 1983, FITF has actually operated as a kind of repertory theatre. Practically, very few theatrical productions can obtain a license for public performance unless they perform once at the festival, a fact that clearly delineates the consistent and systematic reinforcement of these regulations.[17] Nonetheless, in the Reformation era, known as Esla-haat (1997–2005), and its following years, the committee and other officials began to realize that in their politics of dramaturgical analysis, they should incorporate some degree of religious flexibility and artistic sensitivity.

Minimizing the role of controllers and their ideological impositions, religious officials tend to maintain that such imposed changes stem from Iranian audiences' expectations to see their moral and religious values recognized and respected on the stage. In contrast, many non-conservative artists, critics, and even officials contend that the interventions of the Supervision Committee are unquestionably repressive and thus a form of censorship. Whatever the origin of this evaluation and correction can be, it invariably conditions and controls not only the possibilities for selecting and interpreting a play, but also the methods of emphasizing and dramatizing its theatrical elements.

Although there is always a political and religious dimension to Iranian dramaturgical practice, enough credit must be accorded to state funding and administrative policies as well. Except for very rare instances of private funding in the last couple of years, financial policies and administrative procedures in relation to venue and the duration of performances have been determined and enforced by the Support Committee, a newly established committee under the supervision of the CDA. On this account, similar to other countries in which market and state funding condition a theatre production, the impositions of the Support Committee, which is in fact a masked oppressive apparatus, affect in parallel with other forces the employment opportunities of dramaturgs.

Last but not least, the entire conceptual and representational preparation of a production is influenced by the self-censorship committed by playwrights, translators, dramaturgs, and directors, as a compromise to be done if they want to maintain their artistic vision and agency. Interviewing several Iranian dramaturgs, I realized that quite similar to other members of the Iranian theatre family, by finding their position as double outsiders, they can hardly see any prospect of acting according to their own personal aesthetic convictions.

My intervention in the ongoing scholarship on the concept of dramaturgy intended to situate contemporary dramaturgical directions in Iran in relation to the state's interventionist role in theatre-making, by identifying one of the most decisive ways in which religious politics has spurred on dramaturgy in Iran. Briefly speaking, in recent decades and within the Iranian context, the Islamicization and Iranianization of dramaturgy, the explosion of dramaturgical knowledge and experience, and the tensions arising from their confrontation have played pivotal roles in shaping dramaturgical models and have brought about a rethinking of different aesthetics and representational strategies. While the dramaturgical incoherence and ignorance are due to financial and regulatory constraints, the general tendency to focus on directorship and translation rather than dramaturgy has to do with the paucity of technical knowledge in this realm. Nevertheless, it should be emphasized that politically and religiously informed dramaturgies have offered new ways of negotiating and legitimizing their roles as critics and censors or creators and practitioners of theatre to the members of the Supervision Committee as well as dramaturgs and directors. The prospect of such discourse and practice is positioning the Iranian performance tradition in a condition that is nationally growing and internationally becoming recognized.

Notes

1 The information and viewpoints presented here are from official records, the blogosphere, and personal observations during my recent stay in Iran, and interviews and (never-ending) conversations I have conducted with various theatre practitioners and critics. All the translations are by myself.
2 Bert Cardullo, *What Is Dramaturgy?* (New York: Peter Lang, 1995), 5.
3 Although the organization is well known in English scholarship as the CDA, its name has been officially translated as the General Directorate of Performance Art in Iran. See the CDA's website at www.farhang.gov.ir/en/depuThies/artaffairs.
4 Hossein Farrokhi, "Contemporary Iranian Theatre and the State of Theatre of Holy Defense," accessed July 14, 2013, available online at www.theatermoghavemat.ir/ebook/article/1387/07/post_17.php.
5 These adaptations include works by a variety of playwrights in genres ranging from Greek and Shakespearean to contemporary European and American drama.
6 Iran has not joined international conventions on the protection of literary, artistic, and scientific works yet.
7 Personal interview, July 23, 2013.
8 One of my research challenges in this area has been how to introduce and explore these transgressive practices without sacrificing the resilient endeavors of theatre practitioners.
9 For his views on this and other productions of Vişniec's plays, see www.kaleme.com/1392/05/01/klm-152680/, accessed July 22, 2013.

10 For this point, I am indebted to discussion of Brecht's practices of adaptation by Cathy Turner and Synne Behrndt in their seminal book *Performance and Dramaturgy* (New York: Palgrave Macmillan, 2008).

11 Arrigo Subiotto, *Bertolt Brecht's Adaptations for the Berliner Ensemble* (London: Modern Humanities Research Association, 1975), 5.

12 In spite of its homosexual implications, which were overlooked by the Supervision Committee, the production ran successfully for 40 nights in one of the state-subsidized venues in Tehran.

13 Personal interview, June 23, 2013.

14 Cardullo, 5.

15 *The Overview of Theatre in Iran: An Analytical Report of Theatre in Iran 2005–2009* (Namayesh: Tehran, 2009), 100, translated by the author.

16 Organized and funded by the government each February, the Fadjr International Theatre Festival was initiated and developed as part of the ten-day Fadjr celebrations in 1983 to commemorate the (Islamic) Revolution. In the last decade, as the most celebrated international theatre festival in Iran and the region, FITF has hosted on average 140 Iranian productions and 10 to 15 international productions.

17 For an in-depth study of the politics and practice of organizing this festival, see my MA thesis "The Politics of Festival Performing and Conforming: A Critical Analysis of Iran's Fadjr International Theatre Festival" (York University, 2013).

11

Performing dramaturgy in Syria

Observations and interview with Mayson Ali

Fadi Fayad Skeiker

Let us imagine a scenario together.[1] You are finishing high school in Syria and you want to get into the vibrant theatre scene in Damascus or become a part of the celebrated TV industry in Syria. What would you do?

You pay a visit to the prestigious Higher Institute of Theatrical Arts in Damascus, an independent higher education conservatory in Syria[2] and present your application. You are asked which department you want to enroll in,[3] and you automatically think to register in the Acting Department. They ask you, what about joining the Theatre Studies Department and becoming a dramaturg? Your conversation might go like this:

"Drama what?"

"*Dramaturg.*"

"What does *that* mean?"

"It means you can adapt Western plays to a Syrian context, you can be a cultural
    administrator, you can be a critic, you can be a director, you can be a dramaturg
    for a theatre company or for a performance."

"Drama what?"

You decide to give it a shot. You ask about the requirements to enter the department, expecting it to be easier than the Acting Department, which usually requires preparing a monologue and auditioning. You are surprised when you're asked to read plays by Shakespeare, Brecht, Tennessee Williams, and Arthur Miller, as well as works by Aeschylus and Arab plays, and then be prepared for a written entry exam, as well as an interview before admission. You look at the reading requirements and think to yourself, "I thought I would study these while I am at the institute, not before." The answer slowly dawns on you: you will do that and much more. You will spend four years of your life at the institute, putting in 12-hour days that are divided carefully between class time, theatre projects, and library time so that you will be a public intellectual creating theatre.

In the call-out[4] for Arab theatre artists, the Damascus Theatre Festival in 2008 invited interested Arab artists and scholars to engage in a dialogue on dramaturgy, a cry that reflected how Syrian theatre artists look at this concept. The call-out was more than simply a manifesto on the state of dramaturgy in Syria. The main points of this 2008 call-out are highlighted in this paper and will conclude with a brief interview about the state of dramaturgy in Syria with Dr. Mayson Ali, a dramaturg and head of Theatre Studies Department at the Higher Institute of Theatrical Arts in Damascus.

Three major changes in the landscape of theatre in both Syria and the Arab world are identified in the call-out, including, 1) the introduction of interdisciplinary theatrical forms; 2) the beginning of new theatre companies which drift away from traditionally controlled governmental theatre companies; and 3) the global aspects of theatre in our modern world. The call-out identifies the work of the dramaturg in these changing times as a cultural mediator who is able to transform theatre practice from one place to the other, culturally speaking. According to the call-out, the work of the dramaturg becomes a necessity for dramaturgical work on the following levels:

- collaboration with directors and scenographic artists to examine new channels of creativity;
- ensuring the creative production is both intellectually and artistically appropriate for the audience;
- actively participating, programming, and selecting plays to be performed;
- leading theatre labs where dramaturgs can experiment with new forms of theatre that encourage interdisciplinary collaboration;
- connecting the local work to the surrounding theatre community, the Arab community, and to the world.

In addition to these more comprehensive assignments, the most influential Syrian dramaturgs such as Mary Elias, Nabeel Hafar, Hanan Qasab Hasan, and Mayson Ali call for enlarging the traditional dramaturgical role to encompass broader definitions within the theatre profession. Dramaturgy throughout the Middle East appears to be going through a parallel process of broadening the role of dramaturg. Nihad Saleeha,[5] for example, an influential theatre scholar from Egypt, offers these roles of a dramaturg:

- suggesting texts for directors or theatre companies; texts that reflect the community where the play is produced;
- re-writing, adapting, and modernizing classic texts;
- helping the director formulate a clear directorial vision;
- in an improvisational workshop, taking notes in order to document the work of the company;
- mentoring new playwrights;
- adapting novels for theatrical performance.

All of these roles of the dramaturg are very different from the ones that were conventionally considered dramaturgical duties, such as helping playwrights to develop plays, serving as in-house critic for a play production, serving as a cultural/intellectual consultant for the director, and the most traditional role which is adapting works for the theatre.

One of the important roles that a dramaturg holds is the script adaptor.[6] In Arab theatre as well as in Syria, adaptation is a very complex act because it involves working on different levels of language. For example, *Hamlet* has been translated into Arabic several times, and each time the Arabic that is used in translating the play is archaic, not smooth enough for the stage. Almost every director who decides to direct *Hamlet* will solicit the assistance of a dramaturg to rewrite the play using language that is closer to a simplified, standard Arabic or even slang Arabic. Another consideration when "translating" the text from classical Arabic into standard Arabic (or simplified standard Arabic or slang) is making decisions about what to do with the text. Should it be Arabized, which means changing the names of the characters and even twisting the plot or the story to make it appear as if it were written by an Arabic playwright? Would Hamlet be called Ahamad? Is Ahamad the son of a tribal sheikh? Usually such twists on the original play require alteration by a dramaturg to make the play more appropriate and accessible for Arab audiences.

However, dramaturgy as we know and practice it now is not restricted to adaptation only; dramaturgs now have many more roles. The new roles that the call-out proposes contextualize the work of the dramaturg and require the dramaturg to imagine and map out not only the present state, but, ultimately, the future state of theatre in a specific community; as theatre scholar Saleeha puts it, "The dramaturg becomes a bridge between theory and practice, between practical experience and academic knowledge, between literature and theatre, between what is envisioned and what is possible, and finally between past and present."[7]

To achieve this vision, the call-out advocates for a revision of dramaturgical study. In Syria, for example, the Theatre Studies Department at the Higher Institute of Theatrical Arts takes on the role of preparing dramaturgs; and the call-out made by Syrian dramaturgs was understood as an invitation to revise its curriculum planning.

This invitation to open up the role of the dramaturg was not without controversy. When the dramaturg position was introduced in the mid 1980s, many directors avoided using dramaturgical services because they viewed dramaturgs as a threat to their work. One of the challenges the dramaturgical profession faced in the Middle East in general and in Syria in particular is the fact that it developed very fast. The Theatre Studies degree that prepared future dramaturgs was introduced in 1984, originally focusing on preparing theatre critics to write reviews for plays in local newspapers. In the beginning, the department was called Theatre Criticism and Literature, and the degree was offered at the Higher Institute of Theatrical Arts, an independent academic institution that operates independently with no affiliation with a university. It is supervised by the Ministry of Culture in Syria.

The first generation of graduates of the Theatre Criticism and Literature Department established themselves as public intellectuals with distinctive opinions about theatre productions seen and reviewed. Directors were encouraged to invite them to witness rehearsals to give opinions before opening night. Directors began to hire critics as permanent in-house critics during the full rehearsal time. The expansion of the services that a dramaturg might offer affected the way the department operated, so its name was changed from Theatre Criticism and Literature to Theatre Studies Department and is still known by that name. It logically followed that the course offering would also change and broaden. New practical courses were introduced – directing and playwriting, cultural administration, theatre programming, and more – while the departmental focus shifted from preparing critics to preparing dramaturgs and theatre-makers. Later, the graduates of the department started to gain more credibility and acceptance in the theatre scene and moved into leading positions in the national theatre as well as in private theatre companies. For example, one graduate, Imad Jalol, became a manager for the directorate of theatre and music in Syria, the directorate that supervises all theatre and music activities in Syria and steers the national theatre activities in Syria.

Note that graduates of both the Theatre Criticism and Literature Department and the currently named Theatre Studies Department were called dramaturgs, and that most of the graduates of that program insisted on being called dramaturgs whether they were working as critics, theatre artistic leaders, playwrights, or in other capacities. In a way, it was felt the title was broad enough to give the freedom to be able to be theatre practitioners or theorists, or even administrators as needed. This evolution in Syria took an interesting path that was organic and relatively fast since the early 1980s. Even though it was informed by the Western development of the term, it was neither forced nor proscribed by the Western model. It took a natural growth, as evidenced by the graduates of the department and their work.

To learn more about dramaturgy in Syria, the way of studying it, and the way it is practiced on the ground, there is no better expert than Professor Mayson Ali, who is the chair of the Theatre Studies Department and has been teaching there for many years. Her students shaped the course of dramaturgy in Syria and continue to shape its future. I conducted the following interview via email.

Fadi Skeiker (FS):	Can you tell me about your work and study?
Mayson Ali (MA):	I am the head of the Theatre Studies Department at the Higher Institute of Theatrical Arts in Damascus, Syria. As professor of contemporary Western theatre at the Higher Institute of Theatrical Arts, I have participated in workshops with directors such as Peter Brook, Eugenio Barba, and many others. I served on the committee to develop the curriculum of the Theatre Studies Departments in 1997 and in 2008. I have been on the selection committee for accepting new students for many years. I have supervised many graduation projects in the department and have published in Syrian and Arab theatre journals. I have worked as performance dramaturg on many plays, some text based and others dance based. When working on a text-based play, I would bring the play closer to the Syrian audience; and while working on a dance-based play, I would develop a scenario script based on each of the dancers alone at the beginning, then as a group. I also practice dramaturgy while teaching when I ask my students to trans-form mythical stories or fables into texts and when I lead dramaturgy workshops both in Syria and in the Arab world.
FS:	How is dramaturgy studied in Syria?
MA:	The Theatre Studies Department at the Higher Institute of Theatrical Arts was established in 1984. Those who teach are academics and practitioners from different theatrical disciplines

such as acting, directing, criticism, etc. However, the curriculum of the program focuses on three main courses: theatre-text analysis, theatre lab, and playwriting. Other courses include theatre literature, reading performance, development of theatre performance, etc. All of these courses help students gain a prolific knowledge of theatre and teach them to work as dramaturgs after they have finished their studies. Over the years, many new courses have been introduced, and there are now two year-long courses called "Dramaturgy" offered for students in their third and fourth years. New courses emphasize the broader concept of dramaturgy, such as a course on cultural administration.

FS: How important is the presence of a dramaturg in Syrian theatre practice?

MA: Utilizing a dramaturg in each performance in Syria has become commonplace and accepted. Sometimes there will be two dramaturgs in one performance. Usually, there are two kinds of dramaturgs working in Syria. The first is a producing dramaturg, where the dramaturg strikes a partnership with a director and helps select a play, conducts research on the play, and documents the performance after it is done. The second type of dramaturg is a stage dramaturg, who translates and adapts the play. Sometimes the dramaturg will be asked to write a play based on a novel.

FS: How important is having a dramaturg in a theatre performance? In a theatre company in Syria?

MA: It is reaching the point where it is necessary for any theatre to have a dramaturg working in it. The number of graduates of the Theatre Studies Department at the Higher Institute of Theatrical Arts has contributed to the growth of this profession. These graduates enter the theatre scene in Syria and the region after they are fully competent in terms of knowledge and experience that qualifies them to work as dramaturgs. Dramaturg-influenced performances have increased during the past ten years as dramaturgical practice in Syria has moved toward a more comprehensive theatre practice, a practice that is not solely defined by writing or directing a play, but which is concerned with connecting the performance to the audience. The concept of dramaturgy now means any activity that is related to performance.

FS: Did dramaturgy in Syria reach a stage where it formulated its own traditions?

MA: Even though Arab critical discourse does not have an Arabic translation for dramaturgy or the dramaturg, we have been working on teaching dramaturgy and preparing dramaturgs. The issues that dramaturgy addresses, such as text adaptation, dealing with a foreign text, translation, theatre language (standard Arabic or slang), actor preparation, etc. are all very evident in our theatre practice. Each of these issues is addressed separately during each performance. Having a dramaturg will connect all the missing dots on these issues and others.

FS: How will dramaturgy change in the midst of all the social and political changes currently happening?

MA: When a dramaturg is working on a text or a performance, the dramaturg has to connect the vision of the work to a broader social/political/aesthetic vision. Dramaturgy has to present a vision of coexistence and contribution to find a new future that has nothing to do with the illusions of the past and monsters of the present.

Notes

1 Information in this article is derived from personal experience, official records, interviews (formal and informal), and web pages. Most of the information is based on personal experience. All Arabic-English translations are my own.
2 The author of this article studied his BA in the Theatre Studies Department at the Higher Institute of Theatrical Arts in Damascus.
3 The Higher Institute of Theatrical Arts started in 1977 with only the Acting Department; now it has many departments including Acting, Theatre Studies, Theatre Technologies, Dance, and Theatre Decoration.
4 "Theatre Dramaturgy," *Theatre Life* 67–8 (2009): 9–10.
5 Nihad Saleeha, "Dramaturg and Translation for Theatre," *Theatre Life* 67–8 (2009): 45–56.
6 Menha Albatrawi, "Translator of the Text: Translator of the Perfromance," *Theatre Life* 67–8 (2009): 31–4.
7 Saleeha, 45–56.

12
Official and unofficial dramaturgs
Dramaturgy in China

William Huizhu Sun

Various meanings of the term

Dramaturgy is a hard-to-define word to begin with, even in Germany and other parts of Europe. It is even more bewildering in China. That is why there is still no commonly accepted Chinese translation of the word in mainland China, nor such a position as a formally and clearly defined dramaturg in any theatre company. For those Chinese with some knowledge of Western languages and cultures, the word can mean three related yet quite different things: 1) theatre studies; 2) approaches to, structures and techniques of playwriting; and 3) the work of a dramaturg, a profession not yet clearly established in China. Two fairly well known and studied Western books in China's theatre circles, Gotthold Ephraim Lessing's *Hamburg Dramaturgy* and William Archer's *Playmaking*, in their Chinese translations, have not helped in clarifying the word, let alone promoting the related profession. The former book, which is in fact an anthology of papers on theatre theory and criticism, as its Chinese title *Hanbao Juping* (Hamburg drama review) indicates, is no longer a relevant use of the word "dramaturgy" as discussed in this book. The latter book, whose Chinese title *Juzuo Fa* literally means *Methods of Playwriting*, really refers to one of the two meanings of the word today. Yet Archer did not use the word "dramaturgy" in his title. The most important third meaning, the focus of this book, however, has not been seen in any Chinese-language books so far.

In the People's Republic of China (PRC), beginning in October 1949, the government has set up many state theatre companies in which the choice of plays is of the utmost importance, especially in terms of dramatic themes. Therefore dramaturgy was badly needed from the very beginning of those theatre companies. By the same token, it was badly needed by the new regime eager to overhaul the entire theatre system. Without knowing the term "dramaturgy," or the exact meaning of the word, they usually set up an office or a department called the Artistic Office or Office of Artistic Creation, into which they assigned playwrights, directors, and critic/editors. In a large state theatre company, such as the Beijing People's Art Theatre, Shanghai

People's Art Theatre, or China Youth Art Theatre, each with about a hundred or more people in total, this office/department is always the smallest group, compared to the other two major office/departments – the actors' group and the group of designers and shop workers.

Official/unofficial dramaturgs

The most important dramaturgical institutions in China are certain national or provincial offices that have been virtually given dramaturgical responsibilities. For example, shortly after the PRC was established on October 1, 1949, the Ministry of Culture opened a Bureau of Chinese Opera Improvement (BCOI), headed by Tian Han, China's foremost playwright of both Western-style modern drama and Chinese opera, who was also the president of the brand-new semi-official Chinese Theatre Association. In a sense, Tian Han was not dissimilar to Goethe in Weimar in terms of position and stature, albeit on a much larger scale, as the New China's de facto chief dramaturg. Tian was working hard mostly to carry out the order of the national leader, Mao Zedong, who decreed the immediate reform of the "stale and feudal" Chinese opera. The BCOI quickly issued a list of banned Chinese operas and another list of Chinese operas that needed to be severely revised before any performances. Tian personally rewrote a few Chinese operas, including the much-performed *Story of the White Snake*, based on folk operettas, and *The Story of the West Chamber*, based on a thirteenth-century Yuan dynasty drama, to demonstrate how the old pieces of Chinese opera could be reformed, mainly by eliminating the elements of so-called superstitions and highlighting the Maoist view of the progress of history, to serve the people of the New China.

Tian Han was politically persecuted and physically abused during the Cultural Revolution and died in prison in 1968. He was exonerated in 1979, after the end of the Cultural Revolution. Since then there has not been such a "chief dramaturg" on the national scene. This function has been loosely taken over by various Chinese Communist Party (CCP) and government officials. Their work includes conceiving and announcing dramatic themes periodically according to the needs of the CCP and governments on different levels, oftentimes to coincide with specific anniversaries such as, in recent years, the 60th anniversary of the PRC in 2009, the 90th anniversary of the CCP, and the 100th anniversary of the Xinhai Revolution, resulting in the ROC (Republic of China), both in 2011. They also need to review proposals and drafts of related plays and decide to which they should award grants of how much money, before supervising the rehearsal process until the productions. These unofficial dramaturgs, individuals or collectives, are crucial forces in Chinese theatrical circles, yet they are usually not credited in the programs, almost anonymous to outsiders.

For example, months before the 90th anniversary of the CCP in 2011, a play titled *Kaitian Pidi* (Opening of the world) by Meng Bing, a Beijing-based prolific playwright with an army general's rank, head of the Drama Company of the General Political Department, People's Liberation Army, was turned down by the Shanghai Dramatic Arts Center (SDAC). The explicit reason was that the SDAC had already commissioned a play to commemorate the 90th anniversary of the CCP, focusing on Chen Yuan, the late highest ranking CCP leader next only to Deng Xiaoping and a native of Shanghai. The other, more implicit reason was, however, that Meng Bing's play portrayed all 12 delegates attending the first CCP Congress in July 1921 in Shanghai, and more than half of them later turned out to either quit the Party or even became notorious traitors, leaving only a handful of the earliest Chinese Communists, including Mao Zedong, loyal members of the CCP throughout their lives. The SDAC was afraid of being seen as painting a stained picture of the CCP when people should be celebrating her glorious history. Nonetheless, the Information Department of the CCP, Shanghai Committee, learned about this and believed that Shanghai, the birthplace of the CCP, must put on a play about the CCP's birth in Shanghai. By that time Meng had already given his play to Zhejiang province, which also had a connection to the birth of the CCP in 1921, because during its first congress in Shanghai, police detectives became suspicious and checked on its site, which caused the delegates' to decide to rush to a lake in Zhejiang to conclude the congress. The Zhejiang CCP Information Department officials happily accepted Meng's play and asked him to revise it to focus on the Zhejiang part of the First CCP Congress. When the Shanghai CCP Information Department wanted to get the play back, they learned that a Zhejiang drama company was already working on Meng's revision. They quickly decided to get permission from Meng for his original Shanghai-focused version and gave it to the Shanghai Theatre Academy (STA), Shanghai's other major producing institution with many high-caliber theatre artists. The Shanghai CCP Information Department asked Meng and the STA director to put more emphasis on today's glossy Shanghai, making his piece a memory play from young people's perspective, hence reducing the political risk associated with those CCP delegates who later strayed away or even betrayed the CCP cause.[1] Meng ended up having two simultaneous productions with different dramaturgical emphases. Who was behind all these unusual maneuvers? People guessed it was the head of the Information Department of the Shanghai CCP Committee, often represented by his staff members, who frequently read drafts of plays and gave politically oriented dramaturgical advice. Yet none of those "official" dramaturgs' names appeared in the program, which in fact made them "unofficial dramaturgs." This is quite typical of many of the "official" Chinese dramaturgs, who are political and administrative officials but virtually unofficial dramaturgs hovering above the professional theatre circles.

These unofficial dramaturgs can also be catalysts for long-lasting works, if their ideas are not just for a specific anniversary or other government commission. For example, *Confucius Disciples* is a series of short plays about China's greatest educator, Confucius (551–479 BC) and his three fictional teenage disciples, conceived by myself, written mostly by my students, and directed and performed by my colleagues and students, all of the STA. I have never had the title of dramaturg, but in fact have functioned as a general dramaturg in giving prospective playwrights theme/plot ideas and supervising their writings and rewritings and the directors' rehearsals. Modeled after the classic novel *Journey to the West* about Buddhist monk Xuanzang (602–64) and his three disciples, including the Monkey King, this project is set during Confucius's historic travels to various warring states, promoting his philosophy and statecraft. While the plays are essentially allegories dealing with issues relevant to today's audiences, all characters are based on role types of traditional Chinese opera, rendered in stylized movement patterns, somewhat similar to those of *commedia dell'arte*. This ongoing series has been created with two rationales: for Chinese students, it is a medium of educational theatre; for the international community, it is an introduction to traditional Chinese culture, including basic Confucian ideas and classical Chinese opera. So far the STA team has toured the series to Korea, India, the USA, Italy, and Bulgaria. American and Bulgarian students have joined the STA team in performing the series, including a joint presentation at the UNESCO International Theatre Institute World Congress in Xiamen in 2011. Similar things have been done at other theatre academies. Xie Boliang, professor and chairman of the Dramatic Literature Department at the National Academy of Chinese Theatre Arts (NACTA), conceived and supervised a series of four short plays based on characters from the classic novel *Dream of the Red Chamber* for his playwriting students to write for Yue opera acting students at the Zhejiang Professional Arts Academy. This general dramaturg's project is titled *Shows of Red Chamber Characters*.[2]

Dramaturgs in professional theatres

Like those unofficial dramaturgs who are in fact officials in various other capacities, in the professional theatre companies there are also unofficial dramaturgs whose official titles could be archivists, critics, playwrights, directors, and/or administrators. Take the SDAC as an example. Arguably China's best-managed state theatre company, somewhat modeled after the British-styled Hong Kong Repertory Theatre, the SDAC was established in 1995 as the result of merging the Shanghai People's Theatre (founded in 1950) and the Shanghai Youth Drama Company (founded in 1957). Its artistic office is headed by Yu Rongjun (Nick), the SDAC's deputy general manager and its best-known playwright, who has written and produced more than 30 plays internationally since 2000. Without the exact title, he is virtually the SDAC's chief dramaturg, because the duties of his artistic office include:

1 Maintaining relationships with playwrights, directors, and experts of all types.
2 Coordinating major creative artists' theatre-going regularly and sending them to attend academic symposia.
3 Organizing juries to screen plays the SDAC receives, replying to their authors, and submitting sort-listed plays to the artistic committee.
4 Regularly organizing the office of the artistic committee's meetings to discuss the selection of plays for productions, to recommend various contests, and to make season plans.
5 Training young playwrights and directors and commissioning new works.
6 Editing *Drama*, the SDAC's journal.
7 Recording, editing and publishing the SDAC's historical documents.
8 Planning and promoting the SDAC's productions, especially key plays; discussing with playwrights how to improve their plays; contacting and deciding on directors and other personnel; appointing producers to work on approved plays.

9   Planning production seasons by utilizing all possible plays and coordinating the SDAC's personnel and resources.
10 Supervising rehearsals and productions when needed, organizing critical symposia to improve the running shows.[3]

It is not difficult to see that much of the office's work is dramaturgical, even though none of the staff members has the official title of dramaturg. Yu Rongjun has been writing three plays a year on average, while overseeing general dramaturgical work on the SDAC's more than a dozen productions per year. Yet when he started working for the SDAC in 1995, with a degree in sports medicine, he was just a drama enthusiast without any formal training and was assigned a job in the sales group. It was in that capacity he learned about how the type and quality of the drama might influence its ticket sales and began to write his own plays. His first play, *Last Winter*, a domestic drama for three characters about a new Shanghainese's marriage problem with a native Shanghainese wife, written in 1996, was produced by the SDAC after numerous revisions, to critical acclaim, winning a series of awards. With the appreciation and trust of Yang Shaolin, the SDAC's general manager, Yu went on to write more plays at a much faster pace, while his daytime job gradually moved from selling tickets to improving the dramaturgical quality of the SDAC's plays to generate more box-office income. It was mainly at the SDAC, and mainly with Yu's plays such as *Last Winter* and *Cappuccino Is Salty* and his followers' similar plays, that "white collar drama" emerged in Shanghai. This new type of drama with contemporary urban themes, of and for the newly formed group of university-educated, corporate or government-employed theatregoers, quickly became a national phenomenon.

A similar case can be found in Beijing. The National Theatre of China (NTC) is also the result of a merger, in this case in 2001, of the Central Experimental Theatre (founded in 1956) and the China Youth Art Theatre (CYT, founded in 1949). The CYT used to have an artistic office, similar to that of the SDAC. It was renamed the literary department of the NTC after the merger, then became the Center for Playwriting and Planning. The two names both seemed to be more focused on dramaturgical work in the Western sense, yet the real group still included many kinds of professionals such as playwrights, directors, designers, critics, editors, and some assistants. The major duties of the group looked very similar to those of the SDAC. In addition, it invited several outside translators and playwrights to be the NTC's dramaturgical advisors (*Juben Guwen*, literally advisors on plays) to recommend new plays. They included Hu Kaiqi, a former STA teacher now living in New York and specializing in translating such contemporary plays as *Copenhagen*, *Doubt*, and *Proof*, and Fan Yisong, an STA professor who has translated dozens of more commercial plays such as *Lend Me a Tenor* and *Popcorn*. The center, however, was abolished in 2010 when the NTC's new president, Zhou Zhiqiang, replaced the retiring Zhao Youliang. In lieu of the center, Zhou has been implementing his "producer-led approach" to produce more commercial plays to maximize ticket sales.[4]

This last case can be seen as the best explanation of why dramaturg is not an established profession in China, even less likely now than before; while dramaturgy, in its various meanings, is always practiced by many other theatre and non-theatre professionals.

Notes

1 I was a vice president of the STA until the fall of 2012. Though not directly involved in the production of *Opening of the World*, I was in the loop on all issues concerning this major STA production, funded by the Shanghai CCP Committee's Information Department.

2 Sun Huizhu, "On *Shows of Red Chamber Characters*," Shanghai Theatre, July 2010.

3 Unpublished document from the e-mail of May 20, 2013 from Xie Jingying, staff member of the SDAC's artistic office.

4 From an e-mail of May 27, 2013 from Luo Dajun, assistant to the NTC's president and former director for the literary department and Center for Playwriting and Planning.

13

Dramaturgy of separated elements in the experimental Japanese theatre

Eiichiro Hirata

From assimilation to separation

For the last two decades, there have been many attempts to integrate other theatre cultures and other art genres into modern Japanese theatre. These attempts to incorporate elements from different cultures, generally speaking, belong to "Hybrid Performance" in the sense of Richard Schechner.[1] For example, Western-oriented theatre groups stage an Ancient Greek tragedy in the form of Nô. Some directors, such as Yukio Ninagawa and Mansai Nomura, produce Shakespearean dramas in a kabuki or kyôgen style, while trying to create a performance which is different from a traditional psychorealistic drama. The directors from Europe, such as Jossi Wieler, stage a kabuki drama with Japanese non-kabuki actors, showcasing a mixture of realistic and stylistic gesture performance. Younger generations of directors and choreographers like Tomonori Kasai (from the theatre group HMP) and Un Yamada (from the dance company Co.YamadaUn) have been especially active in communicating with artists throughout the world and adopting elements of other cultures. Many of them in big cities like Tokyo, Kyoto, and Osaka, who have enjoyed many opportunities to see various kinds of guest performances from all over the world since the 1990s, have been eager to study theatre overseas. However, there seems to be plenty of room for improvements in this willingness to embrace otherness. The directors of modern Japanese theatre often have a tendency to assimilate the elements of other theatre cultures without deep consideration of the otherness which is incompatible with their own artistic concepts. The performances with this tendency are often just a mixture of the diverse theatrical elements organized around a simple concept. They are lacking in impact, which can only be made through intensive confrontations with the incompatible aspects of otherness.[2]

In order to work on otherness more intensely, it can be instructive to rethink the dramaturgical strategies of the production. The dramaturgy functions as "in between," which explores the theatrical elements' relationships arising from various combinations of texts, gestures, sounds, and time-space dimensions.[3] With the in-between-dramaturgy, the directors and the dramaturgs in Japan can investigate the relationships of diverse theatrical elements in every process of their hybrid theatre productions without assimilating them. They can make use of the differences, radically questioning and innovating their theatrical visions, while exploring the various combinations of different theatrical elements.

"The separation of elements" which Günther Heeg suggests with the help of Brecht's theory is effective as a starting point of this exploration. This concept dissects the combined theatrical elements like "language and voice" of a performer and "audio-visual" of the stage so that each element is individually exaggerated to make a strong impact on the audience.[4] This dissection should be so radical that "the self-evident order of perception, feeling and a way of thinking is collapsed"[5] and "new connections, new constellations of separated parts can be sought and found."[6] In the production process, from the separations/collapse to new connections many combinations of theatrical elements can be explored through the in-between-dramaturgy. This paper examines examples of this dramaturgy from two theatre groups, Marebito no kai and Chiten, who have practiced the separation of elements in their own ways.

The theatrical experience of distance and disconnection

The theatre group Marebito no kai, which was founded by a dramatist and director, Masataka Matsuda, in 2003 has broached the issues of catastrophes like the atomic bomb attacks on Hiroshima and Nagasaki, the nuclear accidents at Chernobyl and Fukushima, and conflicts in Palestine, often in a documentary form. Matsuda and the performers stayed at the sites of disasters for several months, researched documents about the themes, and interviewed the victims, their families and relatives. From these investigations, they created many small, fragmental episodes, which were shown in the form of small dramas, monologues, photo and film presentations.

What makes the documentary theatre of this group unique is a series of gaps between the catastrophe/the victims and its representations. In fact, the performers intentionally fail to say something about the traumatic event: they perform a comical gesture or are disturbed by a sound effect (for example, abrupt mute effects) when trying to refer to the catastrophe. Moreover, many performed episodes neither directly refer to the catastrophe nor even have anything in common with it. The audience notices the discrepancy between their expectation of documentary theatre and their experience of it. This discrepancy irritates the viewers, but it also brings them the opportunity to reconsider the question of how people should confront a catastrophe which has seemingly no direct impact on them. They may ask themselves whether they can imagine a catastrophe itself or may imagine something which is apparently very different from its reality.

In order to lead the audience from the initial disjointed experience to such diverse responses, the group works on the separation of the elements in their own way. They often disconnect text, gestures, spaces, and sounds from a context and let the audience perceive each of them separately, thus leaving something atmospheric, a vague impression about the event itself. However, this vague but suggestive impression can stir the imagination of the audience more strongly, leading them to think differently about the catastrophe in question.

The performance *Park City*[7] (in 2009 at Yamaguchi Center for Arts and Media, Biwako Hall Center for Performing Arts), which focuses on the remembrance of the atomic bomb in Hiroshima, is one of the best examples of the remarkable impact that the separated theatrical elements can produce. Not only Matsuda and the performers, but also a photographer, a video artist, and a sound artist researched the hypocenter of the blast, the memorial park with the river Otagawa, as well as the citizens and survivors of the affected city. In this production, the separation of the elements is best perceived in the visual and spatial dimensions. The audience sits about twenty meters higher than the stage and can barely see the performers in the dark, empty space; the performers' gestures and voices appear to be very small and distant. When a performer who seems to play the role of a postman sometimes rides a bicycle along the apron of the huge stage, it becomes much clearer how far the distance between the performers and the audience is. The photographer, sitting in the far distance, projects photos of the landscapes and the citizens on a screen on the upstage wall, which is ten meters back from the performers. The audience can also watch video documentaries of the city on a small monitor set beside each seat (often different videos on each monitor). While concentrating on the videos, the audience fails to observe the movements of the performers and the photos on the stage. The theme of Hiroshima is visually so separated that the perception of the audience is divided into the disconnected elements. Thus, the audience realizes that they cannot access the core of the catastrophe of Hiroshima or its remembrance.

Through various kinds of disconnections, the audience also notices that what they mostly perceive is the darkness and stillness which fills the distance between the separated elements in the theatrical space. From this distance, the movements and the voices of the performers can be seen, but soon they disappear into the darkness again. Thus, the spectators realize that although they try to find out something about the catastrophe, all they can see is something unclear and undefined. This situation forces them to rethink the catastrophe of Hiroshima since they are unable to access the core of the experience even if they try to learn something about the disastrous bomb explosion or the long-term suffering of the victims. This "something" is only a piece separated from numerous aspects of the trauma. The core – like the darkness in the distance of the performance – can never be clarified. The separation of the elements and the darkness in *Park City* allows the audience members to feel their uncertainty in the face of the catastrophe and to confront their perception of it; what we can get is only an indeterminate whole image of the disaster while losing many aspects of each element, which are often very different from the whole experience.

Interrupted narrations

The theatre group Chiten and the director Motoi Miura in Kyoto have worked on modern European and American dramas since 2001 and staged the texts of Shakespeare, Chekhov, Arthur Miller, Jon Fosse, and Elfriede Jelinek. Although they are very impressed by the European theatre style, they never stage their texts in a realist fashion as is customary in the conventional European theatre. Rather, they often separate narrations from the text: the performers interrupt their own narrations by changing their intonations, voices, and rhythms, setting caesurae and redundant accents or exaggerating articulation of words. Most of the time, their gestures have nothing to do with the intentions of a character or a narrator and in fact are often contradictory to these intentions.

The uniqueness of the Chiten performers is remarkable in two senses. First, the emphasis on the interruption itself makes the audience uncertain of interpretation. When a sentence or a phrase is interrupted, the meaning becomes suspended without leading to a certain interpretation. While the meanings, the intentions, and the identities of the character become indefinite, the interruption itself becomes emphasized. Second, the interruptions have so many variations that the presentation of the narrations also stands out in an extraordinary way. Most of the five performers of Chiten have worked together for over ten years, and they have a narrative technique full of diverse interruptions. The changing of intonation and voice, the shift of accent, the extension or cutting of a phrase, about-face of rhythm from too long to too short, etc. are all finely performed without indicating the psychological change of a character.

The contrast between both aspects of the interruption is remarkable in the performance *No Light*.[8] The text, which Austrian novelist and dramatist Elfriede Jelinek wrote on the occasion of the East Japan Earthquake on March 11, 2011, and the accidents of the nuclear power plant in Fukushima, is full of separated meanings and identities. The narrative subject in the text could be considered as the author herself, who wrote her impressions about the accidents mostly in surrealistic sentences, as a violinist who may be a member of an orchestra thinking of mourning for the dead in a concert, as a musical note which has its own voice, as a tsunami victim, as a rescuer, or even as a radioactive ray. They are so confusingly tangled that one discourse is contradicted by another and vice versa.

The performers and the chorus on the stage intensify these separations by many kinds of interruptions and abrupt divergences, which last throughout the whole two hours of the performance. Some punctuate the fragmented texts in a staccato rhythm, some set caesurae in the middle of a sentence. Some performers intervene in another performer's sentence only with a word, displacing the meanings. The chorus often disturbs the narrations with a warning siren. The contradictions in the text themselves are performed with the narrative interruptions. On the other hand, the interruptions have so much variety in rhythm that they create a musical resonance of the voices. For example, the staccato series performed by the actress Satoko Abe makes sounds like instrumental music. The presentation of the interrupted narrations has a great impact on the audience. Some viewers might regard the performance even as a kind of voice concert full of impressive musicality.

Between the interruption and its musicality, there is also a contradiction which confounds the perception of the audience. The former confuses, the latter attracts them. In the face of such insuperable contradictions, the audience might inevitably ask themselves what this extraordinary narrativity is all about. How, what, and what for can the performers tell the audience about a catastrophe? Can a theatrical presentation which has always something fictive about it tell us really something true? Throughout the performance, these questions are brought forth through the techniques of interrupted narrations which simultaneously confuse and allure the audience.

Pathos of the distance

The separation of the elements in both performances, *Park City* and *No Light*, confronts the audience with many questions about the relationship between the theatre presentation and the trauma. The dramaturgy of the separated elements in both performances does not seem to clearly indicate "new connections, new constellations of separated parts" which "can be sought and found" by the audience. However, this dramaturgy can give a hint towards rethinking a new connection. Because of the intensity of these contradictions, the dramaturgy of the separated elements can make the audience face those questions throughout the performance. Although the spectators remain torn in their perception and recognition, they can also persevere and maintain coherence in such a radically separated situation which they would usually avoid. The audience could question why they should be continually confronted with these contradictions without finding a reunification, thus prompting them to search for an extraordinary connection of the separated elements.

This specific combination between the separations and the possibility of a new connection is related to the "pathos of the distance," which Roland Barthes suggested for a "new lifestyle" in a utopian society. In the writing for lectures at the Collège de France (session of January 12, 1977), Barthes pointed out that the pathos

Figure 13.1 The stage and audience space of Park City, courtesy of Yamaguchi Center for Arts and Media. Photo © Ryuichi Maruo (YCAM)

Figure 13.2 Five performers and the chorus who show just their legs on the stage of *No Light*. Photo: Hisaki Matsumoto

of "living together" in society can be created just through opposite elements like "solitude with regular interruptions, the paradox, the contradiction, the aporia of bringing distances together."[9]

This kind of force can affect the audience member, who also struggles with the contradiction between the strong impact of distance on the stage and her/his willingness to reunify them in her/his mind. The dramaturgy of separated elements can thus transform her/his contradictory feelings into a force according to her/his own individuality. The collective force of each viewer can lead into a new connection. Experimental theatre artists in Japan who have strong passion to integrate the otherness of other cultures rely on the dramaturgy of separate elements in order to develop their own dramaturgy. The role of the dramaturg in this dramaturgical process is essential in developing deep and complex understanding of the separate cultures, theatrical traditions, and mediums.

Notes

1 Richard Schechner, *Performance Studies. An Introduction* (New York: Routledge, 2006), 304.
2 In Chapter 6 of my book *The Dramaturg*, I point out these problems and the possibilities that dramaturgical analysis can solve them, rethinking this attitude toward the aspects of otherness. In Eiichiro Hirata, *The Dramaturg: Toward Promoting the Theatre Arts*, (Japanese) (Tokyo: Sangensha Publisher, 2010), 216–18, 233.
3 As for the dramaturgical works as "in between": Cathy Turner and Synne K. Behrndt, *Dramaturgy and Performance* (New York: Palgrave Macmillan, 2008), 146–67.

4 Günther Heeg, "Transit Existence – a contemporaneidade do teatro, estratégias estéticas e o desejo da identidade transcultural," *Próximo Ato. Questoes da Teatralidade Contemporânea*, ed. by Fátima Saadi and Silvana Garcia (São Paulo: Itaú Cultural, 2008), 54.

5 Heeg, 56.

6 Heeg, 56.

7 *Park City* was performed from August 28–30, 2009 at Yamaguchi Center of Arts and Media and from October 24–25 at Biwako Hall Center for Performing Arts.

8 The performance *No Light* was performed by the group Chiten at the Tokyo Metropolitan Theatre from November 16–18, 2012.

9 Roland Barthes, *How to Live Together: Novelistic Simulations of Some Everyday Spaces*, translated by Kate Briggs (New York: Columbia University Press, 2012), 8.

14

Dramaturgy in Indian theatre

A closer view

Ketaki Datta

Dramaturgy in India is an age-old concept. In fact, *Natyasastra: Treatise on Ancient Indian Dramaturgy and Histrionics, Ascribed to Bharata Muni* is the most authentic book on Indian dramaturgy, a book of 36 chapters, dating back to the seventh or the eighth century. Discussions over authenticity of authorship still continue to this day. The original concept is said to have been composed by Lord Brahma (Lord of Creation, according to Hindu mythology) as mentioned in its first chapter; however, in the last chapter, the story claims that it was re-written or edited by Vatsya, Sandilya, Kohala, and Dattila, who are better famed as the descendants of Bharata. Bharata sent his descendants to earth to perform various *natyas* (plays) in King Nahusa's palace. They stayed, married, and even fathered children here on earth. And thus drama flourished.

Dramaturgy, however, traces back to third century B.C.E. prior to Panini making his literary presence known.[1] Panini referred to *Nata Sutras* or aphoristic guides for *natas* (actors) by two writers of his times: Silalin and Krsasv.[2] It took almost three-quarters of the nineteenth century to get the text as a whole. If we trace the background of the quest, we find that the West played a significant role in unearthing the text. In 1865, Fitz-Edward Hall found Chapters XVII–XXII and XXIV of *Natyasastra* and published them as an Appendix to *Dasarupaka*.[3] An English scholar of German origin, Hayman, wrote an article on them, which was later published in 1874. This article, in turn, inspired Paul Raynaud to publish a critical edition of Chapters XV, XVI, and XVIII, between 1880 and 1884.[4] Again in 1888, Chapter XXVIII was published in France. In 1896, K. P. Parab published a critical edition of quite a few chapters. Following Parab, in 1926, Gaekwad Oriental Series, Baroda brought out a critical edition of the first seven chapters only. Benaras and Nirnayasagar editions with different readings and footnotes followed. Gaekwad Oriental Series published eleven more chapters as Volume II; and finally, Volume III was published in 1954 covering Chapters XIX–XXVII.[5] Bharata talks at length about Brahma's creation of *Natyaveda*, which according to him was the "fifth" *veda* (in sanskrit, *veda* means "knowledge"), composed by Brahma culling words from *Rigveda*, musical cadence from *Samaveda*, makeup and postures from *Yajurveda*, and emotive base of performance from *Atharvaveda*. Bharata interestingly narrates how the demons suffered a pathetic discomfiture in the hands of the Gods. Even the *rakshashas* (demons) while witnessing their defeat on the stage rose up in arms in wrath and went straight to challenge the

Gods. Indra, the king of the Gods, quelled their rebellion with his flag pole (or *jarjaras*).

In *Natyasastra*, Bharata talks about the structure of the opera houses. He opines that the *Natyagrha* should be *tryasra* (triangular in shape) or *chaturasra* (either square or rectangular in shape). He suggests the theatre house to be *mattavarani* (literally, an intoxicated elephant, though here it means a "seat of honor") or *dwibhumi* (a two-planed structure). However, it is not clear whether Bharata aims at a "special seat" for Indra, the king of the Gods. It may be that, like a special seat on the back of an elephant, Bharata wishes to assign a "seat of honor" (a sort of royal box) to Lord Indra, the patron of theatre.

Bharata mentions the need of a *sthapaka* or *sutradhara* (the introducer), who through *sthapana* (prologue) would create a bridge between the audience and the play that was about to be staged. According to him, a *purvaranga* (prologue) should precede the real performance of the play (*natya*). The celebrated Sanskrit playwright, Bhasa, has followed this instruction verbatim. Again, he deviates from quite a few of Bharata's suggestions, like restricting the number of characters (Bhasa's plays contained a plethora of characters; hence, they were called *bahu-bhumika*) to the minimum and avoiding the hero's death on the stage.[6] As Bhasa flouts both these norms, it raises the hackles of many critics.

Kalidasa and Bhavabhuti, both great Sanskrit playwrights, follow Bharata's suggestions to the letter. Bharata suggests that dress and speech should conform to the regional usage of the spectators, and the actors and the producers should observe the local modes of speech and manners and conform to them. The playwright must also have a grasp of the speech and manners of the people of that region and should represent these in an entertaining way. Bharata in his *Natyasastra* makes it clear that *abhinaya* (acting) consists of *rasa* (flavors), *bhava* (emotions), and *sangita-nritya* (music and dance). This triune, according to Bharata, can only be instrumental to a successful performance on the stage. Music and dance, again, add meaning to the performance through the implementation of the two essential elements like *rasa* and *bhava*. Bharata talks at length about *rasa* and *bhava* in his treatise on Indian dramaturgy. According to Bharata, Brahma (Lord of Creation) himself enumerated eight *rasas* like *Sringara* (erotic), *Hasya* (humor), *Karuna* (compassion, pathos), *Raudra* (terror), *Adbhuta* (wonder, or magical), *Vira* (heroics), *Bhayanaka* (dread), *Bibhatsa* (disgust). While expatiating on the sources of these *rasas*, Bharata pinpoints only four basic passions: erotic (*Sringara*), heroic (*Vira*), terror (*Raudra*), and disgust (*Bibhatsa*). Tracing the formation of the flavors, Bharata even goes further to ascertain the birth of *Hasya* (humor) *rasa* from *Sringara* (erotic); *Karuna* *rasa* (compassion, pathos) from *Raudra* (terror); *Adbhuta* *rasa* (wonder or magical) from *Vira* (heroics); and *Bhayanaka* (dread) from *Bibhatsa* (disgust). Bharata associated shades of color particularly to these *rasas*: for example, the color for *Sringara* (erotic) is blue; for *Hasya* (humor) it is white; and in similar manner red is for *Raudra* (terror); *Karuna* (compassion, pathos) is represented by pigeon blue; *Vira* (heroics) by light yellow; *Adbhuta* (wonder, or magical) by yellow; *Bibhatsa* (disgust) by dark blue; and *Bhayanaka* (dread) by black. Even in *bhava* (emotions), Bharata clearly makes serious classifications, like *sthayin* (basic) and *sancari* (associated). Love, humor, compassion, horror, the heroic, fear, repulsion and wonder are the eight *sthayin* *bhavas*. Dejection, lassitude, suspicion, jealousy, infatuation, fatigue, laziness, helplessness, anxiety, confusion, reminiscence, boldness, bashfulness, fickleness, pleasure, excitement, sleep, frustration, pride, sorrow, impatience, forgetfulness, dream, awakening, intolerance, dissimulation, ferocity, desire, disease, insanity, death, fear, and surmise are the thirty-three *sancari* or *vyabhicari bhavas*. Even ecstatic emotions (*sattvika bhava*) carve a niche in Bharata's classifications. Thrill, feeling stunned, perspiration, faltering voice, convulsion, pallor, tears, breakdown – these are the eight *Sattvika bhavas* (or *anubhava*, intense emotions). Elaborating on the *rasas* and *bhavas*, Bharata firmly opines that, *abhinaya* (acting) stands mainly on the *rasas* and *bhavas*. Again, *abhinaya* is of three kinds: *vacika* (speech), *angika* (gesture), and *sattvika* (emotional reactions). From the multi-dimensional character of *natya*, Bharata segues on to the different levels of the contexts in which the play is produced and appreciated. Three levels as primarily pointed out by Bharata are sensuous presentation, empirical presentation, and the transcendental level. Sensuous presentation calls for impinging the sensations and images on the mind and thus points to an alternative world behind them. In the empirical-presentation level, entertainment engenders from the continuity of the spectacle with real life. Here, imagination, no doubt, plays an important role in making the spectators believe that they are witnessing the real-life situation on stage, and through the force of *anusandhana* (inquiry or search) they reach the *sthayi bhava*, which when fully matured becomes *rasa*. Thus, the transcendental level is reached in which the spectator feels that he himself is an impersonation of pure consciousness in and through feelings and images.

Bharata in his *Natyasastra* says that "drama is an imitation of the contemporary style of man." To be more precise, *natya* or drama was regarded by Bharata as some kind of imitation, be it speech, gesture, demeanors, appearance, attire, whatever was in vogue in contemporary society. Again, drama cannot be the blind imitation or just a visual documentary. Drama, in fact, wakes up its audience to a truth, which is hardly comprehended in the day-to-day reality. Thus, drama conforms to the norms of *dulce et utile* through the art of imitation.

In Greek plays, there is an emphasis on "action" and the result is in the nature of "catharsis," a sort of emotional purging. While according to Bharata, *bhava* in its numerous varieties must be taken primarily into account in a play. The effect of *bhava* in association with the mood or impression caused by this imitation gives birth to the total dramatic effect on the spectators, which ultimately is the *rasa*. Hence, compared to a Greek play on the stage, a Sanskrit play seems to be steeped in sentimental effusion, with a marked lack of "action" in it. Aristotle looks upon plot as the soul of a tragedy while Bharata takes plot as a body rather than the soul of a drama. In consonance with Aristotle's six parts of tragedy (as mentioned in Chapter VI of *Poetics*) like plot, character, thought, diction, melody, and spectacle, Bharata's *natya* comprises *vastu* (plot), *neta* (hero), *rasa* (flavor), *laksana* (signs and symptoms), *alamkara* (artistic frills), *nritya-sangita* (dance and music), and topping all *abhinaya* (acting).

While Aristotle talks about tragedy and comedy in his *Poetics*, Bharata emphasizes *nataka* (heroic play), *prakarana* (social play), and mostly comedy. Aristotle believes in the intervention of fate in a play, while Bharata mentions the presence of *purusartha*, or human values. To Bharata, a play leaves enough room to launch on a search for human values, not just blind fatalism. On the point of diction, however, both Aristotle (Chapters XX–XXII) and Bharata (*Vachika*) are of the same opinion; both think it is the base of stage-performance.[7]

In Sanskrit plays, especially in the plays of Kalidasa, Abhinavagupta, Dandin, and Bahmaha, poetry is used as the chief medium, endorsed by fourteenth-century critical works like *Bhavaprakasana, Natvadarpana, Srngaramanjari,* etc. Music and dance carve out a niche in the early *natakas* and *prahasanas.* Dramaturgy owes a lot to Kuttiyam performances in Kerala, which led on to Kathakali dance-forms, through intermediary forms of *Krsnattam* and *Ramanattam.* Indian mythology and even the protean society was represented through these forms. *Kathakali* performers use masks abundantly, just like the Nô actors in Japan; and unlike Kabuki, to convey emotions *Kathakali* depends heavily on eye-expressions.

In modern Indian drama, two names deserve special mention: Girish Karnad (1938–present) and Mahesh Dattani (1958–present). The former cashes in on the Indian myths and legends to fit into the *Yakshagana* mode of performance, while the latter concentrates more on dramaturgy motifs like use of symbols, multiple stage-levels, use of music and dance quite meaningfully. In this regard, Karnad's *Hayavadana* (1972) and *Nagamandala* (1988), and Dattani's *Tara* (1990) and *Bravely Fought the Queen* (1991) should be mentioned. Dattani's plays deal chiefly with the problems of middle-class urbanites. Let us take one play by each of these two dramatists of the modern era and discuss it from the dramaturgical point of view. Girish Karnad came to theatre with his love of the folk theatre and worked the folk dramaturgy into his well-written scripts. In *Hayavadana,* the story is adapted from *Kathasaritsagara*[8] and *Vetala Panchavimshati,*[9] while showing the influence of Thomas Mann's short story *The Transposed Heads,* which, in turn, draws from the same sources. Both stories tell about a newly married couple (Devadatta and Padmini) and a brother/friend (Kapila in Indian myths as well as Karnad's play or Nanda, the friend in Mann's story). The husband and brother/friend go to a temple and, in devotion, offer their heads to the deity, one after another. When the wife comes, she is horrified and decides to put an end to her life, but the deity appears to stop her and grants her wish of getting back both the deceased. She, mistakenly, mixes up the heads and torsos, and her husband's head is put on the body of her brother/his friend and vice-versa. Later, a child is born to the couple, the men decide upon a duel to the death, and the wife commits *Sati* (ancient Hindu women accompanied their husband to the funeral pyre), exonerating herself of this ignominy. The child is left in the lurch at the end. What is remarkable is that the stage props are in sync with the setting and moods of the characters; Girish Karnad follows Brecht and even the Nô plays of Japan in this regard. He prefers for his characters to put on masks. Again, in accordance with Bharata's *sutradhara,* he keeps a narrator (Bhagavata) on the stage. He uses a half curtain on the stage to reveal and conceal the transposed heads and even brings to life a subplot, in which horses' heads are displayed and concealed again.

Mahesh Dattani is a powerful, Sahitya Akademi Award–winning dramatist, who, in his *Bravely Fought the Queen,* shows varying social crises, such as a strained husband-wife relationship and sexual needs being fulfilled by the cook. His use of symbols through stage props, different stage-levels, and natural day-to-day dialogues keep the audience mesmerized.

Although Hindu dramaturgy has a long and illustrious history, in modern times, it is still a director's distant dream to have a dramaturg here on an Indian stage. The director has to play both the director's and the dramaturg's role for smooth-functioning of the play on stage. The noted Bengali playwright/director, Suman Mukhopadhyay, while asked about the role of a dramaturg, said, "Yes, we feel the need of a dramaturg with each passing day. It is not possible to do all things alone as a director." Another noted professor of Drama from Rabindra Bharati University, Dwijen Bandyopadhyay noted in a conversation, "These days when parallel productions are being run in different opera-houses in the city, the director obviously needs the help of a dramaturg. However, though new, the idea is gaining ground gradually."[10]

Notes

1 Panini was a scholar (born approximately 520 B.C.E.) whose notable work was *Astadhyayi* (or *Astaka*). In this work Panini distinguishes between the language of sacred texts.
2 *Sutras* generally mean rules, which become aphoristic. *Nata Sutras* are aphoristic guides for actors.
3 *FP Dasarupaka* or *Treatise on the Ten Forms of Drama*, one of the most important works on Hindu dramaturgy, was composed by Dhanamjaya, son of Vishnu, in Alalava, in the last quarter of the tenth century A.D., during the reign of Vakpatiraja II.
4 In Adya Rangacharya's annotated text, entitled *The Natyasastra*, Paul Reynaud is mentioned: Adya Rangacharya, *Natyasastra* (New Delhi, India: Munshiram Manoharlal Publishers, 2003).
5 Manmohan Ghosh, *Bharatamuni's Natyasastra* (Calcutta, India: Royal Asiatic Society of Bengal, 1951), 5–6,
6 Rangacharya, 25–78.
7 Rangacharya, 120–35; Joe Sachs, *Aristotle's Poetics* (London: Penguin Classics, 1997).
8 *Kathasaritsagara* is a famous eleventh century collection of Indian legends, fairy tales and folk tales in Sanskrit, as retold by the Shaivite (worshipper of Lord Shiva) Brahmin, Somadeva. The work was originally compiled for the entertainment of Queen Suryamati, wife of King Anantadeva of Kashmir. The principal tale is the story of the adventures of Naravahandatta, the son of King Udayana. Arshia Sattar, *Tales from the Kathasaritsagara* (London: Penguin Classics, 1997).
9 *Vetala Panchavimshati* (Twenty-five tales of Baital) is a collection of tales and legends, originally in Sanskrit, narrated by a supernatural. Cf. Richard F. Burton, *Vikram and the Vampire; or Tales of Hindu Devilry* (London: Longmans, Green, and Co., 1893).
10 Personal interview.

15

Dramaturgy in Australia and the case of *Avast* and *Doku Rai*

Peter Eckersall

Discussions of dramaturgy in theatre circles in Australia can register ambivalence to the apparent academicism of dramaturgy as a factor that might constrain the creative process and/or inhibit directorial and authorial voices. At the same time, a parallel trend shows the rise of dramaturgy in the interdisciplinary field of contemporary performance. Whereas only a small number of dramaturgs are employed in a full-time capacity in theatre companies, the number of dramaturgs working in devised-performance contexts has increased in the last decade, popularized by influences from European ideas of new dramaturgy and organizations such as Dramaturgies, as well as the Australia Council for the Arts pilot program of fellowships for dramaturgs that was funded for two years, 2005 and 2006.[1] This situation has also been aided by a curatorial approach to programming new work in venues such as Melbourne's Malthouse theatre and Arts House and Sydney's the Performance Space, and by a greater mobility among performing artists both geographically and in terms of their chosen mediums and practices. The current popularization of dramaturgs in contemporary performance has been aided by developments in theatre in the 1990s as well. Companies that were established in this era such as Marrugeku (artistic director Rachael Swain) and Not Yet It's Difficult (artistic director David Pledger) extensively used dramaturges; and indeed, I was the dramaturg for the NYID.[2]

There is a noticeable proliferation of forms and activities that are currently being described as dramaturgical. However, even when the work of dramaturgs has increased and we are seeing dramaturgs in a variety of contexts, such as that of play specialist, outside eye, co-deviser, researcher, and so on, there is no developed career path for dramaturges, and we are often working at the margins of contemporary performance. What dramaturgs are actually doing when they work on performances is also diverse, and there is no standard definition of the role of the dramaturg, a situation that is often seen as an advantage.

In the background to the development of dramaturgical theatre is a changing view of theatre and the arts that has seen mainstream support for the arts decline dramatically, and at the same time they are subjected to a regime of measures and efficiencies.[3] Dramaturgy has a slippery role to play here and might be seen among some producer organizations as a means of generating efficiency, ensuing relevance to key stake-holders and the timely development of creative work. We have also seen examples of interference on grounds decided in the bear pit of populist politics and media sensationalism. This has been evident especially in populist responses to art works depicting nudity, young bodies, anti-capitalist art works, and art that seeks to intrude into public spaces in non-authorized ways. The fact that such artistic production is often critiqued as being "out of touch with mainstream views," "elitist," or most tautologically "un-Australian" has become code for an abiding suspicion of art as a non-conformist activity in a conformist world. The implications for dramaturgy in this situation are both extremely interesting and complicated by dramaturgy's own inherent ambivalence as a creative practice.

A challenge for dramaturgs in Australian theatre is how to work with playwrights, directors, performers, and creative teams to make the theatre insistently about something more than a process of self-improvement, national cultural essentialism, and/or goodly consumer experience. The question then is how to make dramaturgy much more about the transformation of ideas and translate larger political questions into compelling representational, expressive modes of performance. How to foster a robust and critical theatre culture in a time of mass consumption? How to advocate for dramaturgy, not merely as a technical task but as a way of thinking about the function of theatre through its performative practices? We want to see more provocations for theatre where it might be seen as a place for expanded activity, one that would embrace ideas of theatre as a progressive community of artists and audiences who are active interpreters of culture and become agents of change. When talking about dramaturgy we might lessen the emphasis on structures of dramatic unity and production efficiencies and instead show dramatic forms as moments of rupture, surprise, anxiety, and violation. In this manner, we might come to think about theatre as a symbolic order in the larger task of reorienting cultural politics and community participation in an age of intensified management-control.

Black Lung Theatre's fragmented dramaturgy

Co-directors Thomas Henning and Thomas Wright established the Black Lung Theatre and Whaling Firm in 2006. Their first performance was *Avast: A Musical without Music*, a spiralling work, more loosely connected dramatic encounters than a completed story. Its anti-theatrical, dramaturgical "missingness" is shown in the focus on absence and in how Black Lung shatter the conventional ordering of staging, narrative, and dramatic intention. In place of convention, the work is hugely energetic, with chaotic sensibilities that overrun the stage.

Their "theatre/not theatre" dramaturgy of an elliptical form of story that is filled by uncanny moments of seemingly random connection might be compared to Tokyo's Chelfitsch, and the strong physicality of their performance and interest in exploring an aesthetics of amateurism compares to the Nature Theatre of Oklahoma. Black Lung has an uncanny, non sequitur dramaturgy that is literally turning the tables on the audience to display its naked immediacy and edgy destructive tendencies. Their careless style of presentation explores impossible situations and happenstance. They also have a deep interest in story and the mythic virtue of theatre; the chaos, in fact, reminds us of the power of theatrical reality and their work is developed with a rigor and consistency that is readable as an intentionally fragmented dramaturgical intervention.

Theatre director Chris Kohn, who saw *Avast*, wrote that:

> [t]he actors created an atmosphere of immediacy and real crisis ... of blurring actor/character distinctions in order to create a theatrical world that is utterly self-contained and immersive. It wasn't really "about" much, except for the experience of being there in the room with this thing that we had to deal with.[4]

The crucial point is the question of audiences responding to events in the small theatre. Both the immersion in the claustrophobic space and immediacy that Kohn describes make for discomforting viewing.[5] The audience cannot simply watch the performance but must "deal" with their presence as an audience, a presence that is expressly constructed as provoking the awareness of a breakdown in the spectator-performer relationship, thus challenging conventional expectations. The junkyard set spills out into the seats and the playing with roles pushes ideas of acting to a disturbingly visceral level of presentation. Black Lung is not metatheatre, but theatre where performativity undermines itself by showing moments of dramatic intensity, mixed with comedy, karaoke, and self-personification. Believing they will surpass gravity, their theatre sits out on the branch of the tree while cutting it from the trunk.

What Khon describes as "insanely face-paced, witty, artfully arrhythmic, metatheatrical – a breathtaking combination of precision and chaos" shows several dramaturgical features to do with this sense of interruption.[6] The arrhythmic speed is a disturbance that provokes questions about the meaning of a theatre intentionally left uncompleted. This in turn suggests a number of possibilities: a dramaturgy that leads one to think about theatre and its context more precisely. It points to a style of theatre that, in the act of falling apart, expresses a disbelief in the very sense of stability that theatre historically forecasts onto the audience. It rejects theatre that has a readable sense of mimesis and resolution. In short, Black Lung expresses a preference for precarity over certainty that is fostered in their characteristically tense and uncertain dramaturgy.

Precarious dramaturgy – "Dead Man, I Don't Believe You"

The initial prompt for making *Doku Rai* came from a meeting between Thomas Wright and the East Timorese actor Osme Gonsalves while working on Robert Connolly's film *Balibo* (2008), a film that dramatized the killing of five Australian journalists by the Indonesian military in East Timor in 1975. Plans for *Doku Rai* began to take shape following a further meeting with Darwin producer Alex Ben-Mayor. There is a complexity of circumstances that are important to the production, not least as the background is the fraught recent history of East Timor and Australia's part in this.

The fledgling nation has a long history of colonization and a complicated relationship with Australia. A Portuguese colony since the sixteenth century, it declared independence in 1975 and was then rapidly occupied by Indonesia and its Fretilin independence movement was violently suppressed. It was at this time that the five journalists were killed and yet there was no official reaction from the Australian authorities. Australia covertly supported the Indonesian invasion despite widespread opposition. National interest was deemed to be best served by placating Indonesia, with whom Australia had a sometimes difficult relationship during the autocratic, corrupt era of rule by the long-lived Suharto regime (1967–98). This was the situation until 1999 when, in the context of Suharto's departure, a referendum was held in East Timor on the question of independence. The outcome was overwhelming support for an East Timorese nation but again there were violent outbreaks from Indonesian-backed militia. This time an international peacekeeping force intervened. East Timor finally gained statehood on the May 20, 2002. The trauma of East Timor in Australian life has not been assuaged by the delayed intervention, however, and *Doku Rai* is the first theatre exchange between artists from these nations to tackle this troubled history.

Talking about an intense two-month development process of *Doku Rai* to journalist Andrew Furhmann, Wright described it as the "creation of a religion and the chronicle of its downfall."[7] The story concerns two brothers. One places a curse on the other, wanting him to die. Too late he then seeks to revoke the curse and the brother dies, only to come back to life. He is cursed by a *doku* that leaves him in limbo, haunting the living and unable to find resolution in death. Each time he is killed he revives, causing consternation and chaos. The living brother meanwhile descends into madness and the cycle of violence is unending. The story is told as a series of moments using music played by East Timorese band Galaxy, film projections, faux ritual, and dramatic dialogue. The stage design incorporates parts of the old hotel in Atauro and the staging is loose and energetic. People wander around the stage in a way that is suggestive of the village context of Atauro, where people and animals interrupted the rehearsal process. Time is slowed down and the audience are not sure when the performance begins and ends. Reviewing the performance at Melbourne's Arts House in August 2012 Cameron Woodhead noted that the interwoven dramatic structure was a way to span the different histories of the theatre groups: "*Doku Rai* unites myth and meta-theatrical playfulness, ritual and improvisation, music and multimedia to create a vivid communion of cultures ancient and modern."[8]

The focus on communion is important. *Doku Rai* was an experiment in intercultural dramaturgy. As Ben-Mayor notes: "In the show we started looking at … 'what does it mean when we talk about a cross-cultural collaboration?' … [Y]ou're bringing artists from two very different worlds together, what does that mean? How do you negotiate who does what?"[9] These are vexed questions seen in many contexts of Australian performance, where cultural differences are often present. *Doku Rai* was essentially an exercise in aesthetic interruption: using multiple languages and clashing performance styles the gaps in communication created the dramatic form and enabled a "communion" of contrasting styles/ideas of performance.

In the first version of *Doku Rai* (performed in Melbourne) Gareth Davies played an overwrought theatre director who interrupts the rehearsal process that was being staged as the performance. There is also an online film vignette that purports to show the making of *Doku Rai*.[10] The two media play off one another, with the film showing the artists in their Atauro surroundings, later reinterpreted in the theatrical setting. Davies is seen as a rake-thin, magisterial, suffering Sharman in a fit of artistic-malarial fever. His insistence that people respond to his vision, while around him they all do their best to ignore his ravings, captures a sense of how the jungle takes away Western decorum and defeats grandiose plans. He imagines having an animal sacrificed in the performance:

> If we could have a rooster in the production, we could cut its throat, cut its throat and let it run around and die, it'll take a while, then cut it into little pieces, cook it on a fire and then serve it to the audience … sorry, what was that … [11]

It is a trope from the lexicon of nineteenth-century colonial exploration that is being evoked. Davies's desire to make the story about his own neurosis parodies inter-cultural art. It is defeated by the repeating fiction of the *doku* and the piece remains in a state of wholly desired-for irresolution.

Doku Rai's mythic take on a man who can't die and whose fate is therefore to experience ongoing struggle and violence, enacts the experience of intercultural collaboration as one that is unresolved. It is a commentary on East Timor's history. Both play and history are evoked as detritus – an expression of something that remains after everything else has happened; even after the desire to kill someone is revoked the consequences of that initial decision will be played out no matter what. Taking the play to Adelaide in 2013 the script was reworked and the holy-mad director disappeared from the staging. The performance was developed in the context of a return of some internecine violence that briefly flared up again in July 2012.

Might this dramaturgical heart of darkness compare to another "gap" in East Timor-Australian relations and remain in the bounds of a productive discussion on dramaturgy? A notorious photograph from the prehistory of East Timor shows the foreign ministers of Australia and Indonesia celebrating the division of oil and gas resources while flying over the East Timor Gap in 1989. They drink champagne at a table covered with maps outlining their just-finalized claims on the resources below. The image is an, albeit unintended, exercise in gestus, a dramaturgy showing the two occupiers lording over East Timor space; the Australian grins at the camera with an untrustworthy demeanor (see Fig 15.1).

While the colonization of the East Timor Gap was abandoned after independence, the stench lingers. A new treaty has given a substantial allocation of resources to the East Timorese, "[b]ut the treaty precludes East Timor from pursuing claims against Australia for any other gas and oilfields in the Timor Sea."[12] Unsurprisingly, this is cause for resentment in East Timor: "People [in Timor] call Australians a word that means 'the man who comes to steal the fat of our land.'"[13] Real-politic lording over the geopolitical gap of East Timor contrasts with the theatrical "missingness" of "an irreducible non-satisfaction." The dramaturgy of this is symptomatic of the history of domination and colonialism's violent ruptures. By contrast, in *Doku Rai* we see a fruitful sense of giving and vulnerability in the theatrical process. We see gaps as moments to realise possibility, and we see a responsibility for dramaturgy and that is freely shared.

Figure 15.1 Australian Foreign Minister Gareth Evans and Indonesian Foreign Minister Ali Alatas, flying over the Timor Sea to celebrate signing the Timor Gap Treaty, a treaty that gives unfair treatment to East Timor, 1989. Photo: National Archives of Australia: A6180, 19/12/89/25

Notes

1 Dramaturgies aims to develop dramaturgical awareness in Australian theatre and holds workshops and symposia. See Peter Eckersall, Melanie Beddie, and Paul Monaghan (eds), *Dramaturgies: New Theatres for the 21st Century*, (Melbourne: The Dramaturgies Project, 2011).
2 Marrugeku and Not Yet It's Difficult company websites: www.marrugeku.com.au; and www.notyet.com.au, accessed June 6, 2013.
3 For recent commentary, see David Pledger, "Re-valuing the Artist in the New World Order," *Platform Paper* 36 (Currency House, 2013).
4 Chris Kohn, "The Sweet Breath of the Black Lung," *Real Time* RT 74 (August–September 2006): 43.
5 Cameron Woodhead, "Avast," *The Age* (May 11, 2006), available online at www.theage.com.au/news/arts-reviews/avast/2006/05/11/1146940651733.html, accessed May 12, 2013.
6 Kohn, 43.
7 Andrew Furhmann, "DOKU RAI (you, dead man, I don't believe you)," *Time Out* web listing, available online at www.au.timeout.com/melbourne/theatre/events/4430/doku-rai-you-dead-man-i-dont-believe-you.html, accessed May 13, 2013.
8 Cameron Woodhead, "Doku Rai," *The Age* (August 31, 2012), available online at www.theage.com.au/entertainment/theatre/doku-rai-20120830-253ax.html, accessed May 15, 2013.
9 Alex Ben-Mayor, *Grind Online* (August 21, 2012), available online at www.grindonline.com.au, accessed May 15, 2013.
10 See http://vimeo.com/47947594.
11 *Doku Rai*, production script, Melbourne.
12 Richard Barker, "New Timor Treaty 'a Failure'," *The Age* (April 21, 2007), available online at www.theage.com.au/news/investigations/new-timor-treaty-a-failure/2007/04/20/1176697092049.html, accessed May 14, 2013.
13 Cited in Lauren Jones, "'Doku Rai': A Personal Journey for Timor Artists," *Australia Network New*, available online at www.abc.net.au/news/2012-08-31/an-doku-rai-theatre-a-celebration-for-timor-australian-actors/4235568, accessed May 15, 2013.

16
Dramaturgies in/of South Africa

Marié-Heleen Coetzee and Allan Munro

The South African theatre and performance landscape is diverse, complex, and fractious, defined and described in multiple convergent and divergent ways. Within this landscape, the role, function, and position of the dramaturg mirror this diversity and complexity (and at times its fractiousness). In an attempt to trace the various dramaturgical trajectories at play in the South African theatre and performance domain, the context(s) produce or bring to the surface various discourses, both aesthetic and sociopolitical, that co-exist in an unresolved dialectical tension within the dramaturgical pursuit of "creating" South African theatre and performance. Within these discursive moments, the South African dramaturg "hovers," contributing in ways appropriate to a specific context, purpose, and task. In doing so, diverse and shifting loci of authority and hierarchies of discourse(s) interplay in/for the process(es) of creation. The function of the dramaturg within the South African context has become one of "discourse management,"[1] as the dramaturg operates in the slippages of discourse and the negotiation of authority in/through discursive spaces and strategies.

Historical context

There is a strong interface between aesthetic representations of life and the context in which and from which such representations arise. A cursory overview of the South African historical context – and the theatre(s) that arose from it – reveals the plethora of discourses at play. Matters that have dominated the South African landscape include the deep and trenchant impact of Western colonization within the (South) African trajectory, bringing with it the contesting discourses of race, culture, class, religion, identity, and language. This colonization process finds it markers in economic exploitation, labour abuse and oppression, territorial claims and counter-claims, identity markers through color and language, claims of Western "advancement" and African "underdevelopment," and interlocking and disparate strategies of resistance. Inevitably, such a vast tapestry or weave of domination, subordination, and rebellion brings with it the discourses that substantiate (and resist) such positions. Such discourses promulgate, support, embed, and "confirm" the ideological positions that are to be found in values, ethico-moral and legal positions, searches for normative perspectives, behavior, and therefore (inevitably) the aesthetic domain.

The history of South Africa is overwhelmingly dominated by discourses of oppression and resistance. The glimmerings of a sea change builds through the momentous 1950s to the 1980s and reaches its (supposed) culmination in the ratification of democracy, in the all-pervasive decisions that brought into being the new constitution of South Africa in 1994. Yet even here, the sea change brings new slippages and new discussion points as further engagements surface around gender, class, rights and responsibilities, retribution, reconciliation, and development and the role of dramaturgs and dramaturgy in this context.

Within this discursive topography Temple Hauptfleisch[2] attempts to chart the trajectories of performance in the South African landscape. He posits three strands of performance. One strand harkens back strongly to the Western "traditional" model of making theatre and performance, developing a "canon of excellence," where the exemplar is in Europe. The second strand draws on performance styles, demands, and practices that may be seen to be indigenous to South Africa in shape and purpose. The third strand cuts a swathe across both "traditions" offering a strong notion of hybridity or, to capture the complexity of this interface, theatre and performance that arises from the collision/collusion of cultures in a contested "third space."[3] To this we would add the burgeoning performance and dramaturgical demands of applied theatre as a fourth strand.

These four strands occupy much of our thinking around the role of the dramaturg, as they foster the embedment of the role and function of the dramaturg in the dynamics of each strand. Each strand suggests a purpose for performance, points to related discourses and discursive strategies, and fosters the migration of the locus of control over decisions made for inclusion and exclusion in the creative moment and product. We argue that in South Africa the role of the dramaturg engages with managing the interactions of context, purpose, strategies, and discourse selection (management).

Roles and functions of the dramaturg

In an attempt to demonstrate how these forces operate in South Africa, we posit a number of dynamics clustered around key purposes, discourses, and strategies in the theatre-making domain. First, one encounters the dramaturg as writer of plays or playwright[4] and the dramaturg as crafter and shaper of the storytelling, interpreting meaning and protecting the integrity of what the playwright is trying to achieve.[5] To a large extent this proceeds from a Western tradition in which this positioning of the dramaturg fosters the authorship and authority of the playwright.

Second, we suggest the director as dramaturg. In the South African context there is a strong conceptualization of the director as the locus of control in the creative process. This ranges from authorial centring in the directorial work of Marthinus Basson (in a strong Afrikaans and Western discursive position), includes the bulk of the writer/director work of Athol Fugard, and points toward the earlier work of Lara Foot Newton, amongst others. Fugard's work with Kani and Ntshona sees the beginnings of the concept of collective dramaturgy. In this instance, the theatre-making comes from a community and is generated for the community. Much of the early work of resistance (or protest) theatre came from the sharing of experiences of oppression and the dramatizing of these experiences coming from the collective. For example, the work of Workshop '71, the early work of Mbongeni Ngema, the Junction Avenue Theatre Company, and the work of Phyllis Klotz resonate in this category. In this domain the discourse of communal experience is supposedly democratically melded into the performance text. These texts predominantly aligned with political commitment. The idea of democratizing the creative process, the process-orientated approach to creation, and associated dramaturgy shifts the locus of control to the company/collective. In later years, a number of companies across genres follow some of the principles of this approach, albeit not for overt political agendas. The question remains, however, to what extent a locus of control can be dissolved or to what extent democracy in collective artistic processes is possible – especially in the light of historically exploitative practices capitalizing on black realities.

Tangential to this might be what we have rather clumsily labeled pseudo/quasi collective dramaturgy. In this case, the purpose of theatre-making is often intervention driven, as is the case in some applied theatre work. Fundamentally, a collective is developed whose shared purpose is to draw on the discourses of interventionist performance strategies and the discourses of the intervention "target" or even as a partnership with a community, to weave a performance event that will change, develop, and enhance that particular, purposively selected section of society. In this area the early work of DramAidE and Zakes Mda, for example, and a plethora of interventionist or educational companies come to the fore. Centrally, the role of the dramaturg (researching, structuring the material, gauging the purpose, and presenting the intervention) is shared within the collective. We argue that the "locus of control" may be in the hands of the commissioning interests or the partner facilitating the communicative or developmental process, rather than with what seemingly are "non-partisan" or developmental processes connected to the general understanding of applied drama/theatre.

Next, we suggest the community as dramaturg as observed in the indigenous rituals and performance practices that are embedded in a particular community – the dramaturg function of ordering, structuring, and directing the performance is embedded in the history and traditions of a community. These may range from religious practices to marriage, initiation rites, songs, and dances. These practices as communal texts open themselves up to further interrogation, as we argue that the locus of control may not only reside in symbolic or actual power position(s) within a community, but may reside in the hierarchy of cultural and historical discourses per se.

Finally, we must point out the presence of the autodramaturg. There has been a burgeoning of performances that draw on an individual's experiences of the world, and this "personal discourse tapestry" is used to develop the performance text. These performances range from personal experiences (the Truth and Reconciliation Commission gave rise to a number of these performances) to personal responses to events in the world (for example, much of the work of Pieter-Dirk Uys). In the case of autodramaturgy the "artist" is centrally located and therefore the authorship and authority (the locus of control) and the discourses accessed are personalized.

There are two artists operating in the performance domain that claim directly the role of dramaturg, namely Craig Higginson and Mark Fleishman, who attempt to place their positions within some of the domains suggested above. Broadly following a Western tradition of dramaturgy and focusing on English theatre, Higginson fuses dramaturgical trajectories as we have positioned them in this chapter. A playwright (including *The Girl in the Yellow Dress*, published in 2011) and the first literary manager in South Africa at the Market Theatre, he created the position for himself after having worked in theatre in the United Kingdom for a decade with dramaturgy and some dramaturgs.[6] For him, South Africa has no formalized tradition of dramaturgy outside that of the hybrid, and for him, inseparable playwright-director figure. He views a dramaturg as "someone who tries to help someone write the play they want to write but haven't yet fully realised."[7] With reference to his own work, he develops his plays via several drafts using readings and notes as reflective and developmental tools. In recent years, he prefers a more individual approach to playwriting. Ideally, when working with new playwrights, he would prefer to have a relationship with the playwright to work solely on what the playwright is trying to say and achieve.

Higginson is critical about the realities of South Africa's sociopolitical history (mapped out earlier in this chapter) where the politics of economic power and access to resources play a pivotal role in negotiating codes of dominance in terms of race, gender and sexuality, and language that could serve to foreground and reinforce the values and perspectives of a locus of control (conceptual, ideological, etc.). In Higginson's response, we encounter the tensions between the discourses suggested by the "expert" in theatrical construction and those of "nurturing" new material and new creators of that material. In this Bhabha's "third space" seems to appear – a space where the sets of discourses are allowed to engage to create a particular "product" (which, in the Higginson case, is the newly shaped and emerged written text) – and therefore the tensions between the "expertise" of the dramaturg, the "organic" reworking of the product in the third space, and making, or negotiating, decisions on what to insert and what to leave out in the new product emerge.

The ambiguities and peculiarities of the dramaturgies in/of South Africa, the elements of the relationship between the dramaturgical role as envisaged by Higginson, and the nature of an emerging text generated with assistance as Higginson suggests, point to a locus of control that resonates with a residual reference to a historical position (see earlier discussion of this point). Furthermore, this also suggests a seeming linearity to the process, starting with the development of the "written" text and then proceeding to performance. The "mutual text," therefore, draws on the memories, experiences, and discourses of both the writer and the dramaturg that are brought to the "creative third space." Inevitably, the consequences are (and must be) a negotiation of the locus of control over selections for insertion into the written text from moment to moment.

Mark Fleishman has garnered an international reputation as a theatre-maker who works in, from, and for communities.[8] (This is the work that we reference here, but he works in other domains as well). He has a specific interest in reflecting, commenting on, and "excavating" significant moments and locations in/from South Africa's sociopolitical landscape to make a new work for performance purposes – exploring discourses of memory. He acknowledges the centrality of his own authorship and authority in the making process. His working methods speak directly to many levels of the dramaturgical processes as outlined above. Fleishman presents a making process that engages with four strategies. He notes that the first, exploratory steps in the process have their origins in "archival exploration," both in terms of a concrete archive (museums, historical collections, and the like) and in geographical (and demographical) investigations. The very act of sifting through these investigations layered across time (and space) encourages a triggering of concerns, performabilities, or explanations of events for the dramaturg. We would argue here that the discourses of history are viewed through the discourse potentials of performance. In the first of these he enters the world of the archive, drawing on the recorded documents, the shards of history, the "voices" captured or resonating across time from the reports of the past. The second step takes him to the communities about which and from which the archives have "spoken," where he engages with that community and their experiences, stories, values, and, above all, memories. It would appear that the loci of control here are embedded in the "safety" of communality to reveal their archives and the freedom the community "grants" to reveal what may or may not be revealed. Furthermore, beyond the dramaturg himself, during this stage the possibility of selection or rejection of particular shards of archive for performance are not used as a locus of control but rather as an excavation of shared, overlapping, or contesting discourses. The third stage is attempting to explore and physicalize these experiences and significant memories, drawing on the discursive strategies of improvisation, theatricalization, and interaction. This stage provides the dramaturgical bridge between report and performance, between the telling and the presenting, between the story and the visceral. This stage, for us, fosters the move from the discursive moments of the past to the discourse of purposive performance.

The final stage seems authorial in nature as Fleishman "steps in" to ready the communal and community contributions for performance text. As such the dramaturgical authority of shaping, structuring, and directing are evident. In this, Fleishman draws on a large body of physical movement strategies available to his company. Although the direction of the "improvisations" is strategized by Fleishman, the content of what materializes or emerges does so from interactions with the shards of archive, memory, and community. The final product is steeped in the particularity of community or mediated interpretation thereof and the resonances of moving aesthetics. In this approach we posit that Fleishman as dramaturg seems at various stages to fulfil the roles of scribe to the community (thereby fostering the notion of community as dramaturg), facilitator to the community dramaturg as the community tells "their story" (either orally or through the archival resonances), and the individual member of the community, affirmed in the telling of his/her story (the auto-dramaturg). Finally, the production is prepared for the purpose of performance, and in this Fleishman appropriates the role of writer/"wrighter" as dramaturg and director as dramaturg, to harness the various discourse strands and contents for the demands of the performance. Here we would argue that Fleishman works at the limits of "discourse management."

In Higginson's and Fleishman's positions, tactics, and trajectories, as well as in the dramaturgical positions in notions of the collective and the applied, we see a range of current dramaturgical demands that play out in the South African theatre and performance landscapes. In the South African context the dramaturg (or the role or responsibilities of the dramaturg) negotiates between a plethora of discourses, purposes, texts, and contexts – focused or guided by the locus of control or authority who/that is determined by the same elements. This plays out on the macrocosmic level of the broad sweeps and discourses of the South African social and political landscapes, as well as that of South African theatre-making processes. Ideological and cultural positions slide across developmental and economics discourses and are influenced by an individual's idiosyncrasies. When the dramaturged tapestries of life and the possible dramaturgical interface with the potential tapestries of the theatrical moment interweave, we have a complex set of relationships where the locus of control in the decision-making process becomes all important, and the slippages between the different discourses "at play" become inevitable. We propose that the role of the dramaturg in South Africa is located not in the people operating in the theatre collective but in the power of discourse itself that manifests as dialectical and oscillatory in a "third space."

Notes

1 We use the term "discourse" in its broadest sense to articulate an ontology of dramaturgy. Discourse is a vehicle which makes it possible to map aesthetic, embodied, textual, historical, cultural, and sociopolitical "slippages" and the interstitial spaces between these that contest a fixed locus of control in the dramaturgical process and position.
2 Temple Hauptfleisch, *Theatre and Society in South Africa: Reflections in a Fractured Mirror* (Pretoria: Van Schaik, 1997), 29–45.
3 Homi K. Bhabha, *The Location of Culture* (New York: Routledge, 1994), 37.
4 The concept of writing is congruent with the notion of building, crafting, and making, thus eliding only the concept of the literary hinted at in the discourse of "writing." See Mark Fleishman, "A Genealogy of Playwriting in South Africa," keynote address to the GIPCA symposium, Directors and Directing: Playwrights, 2012, available online at www.academia. edu/ … /A_Genealogy_of_Playwrighting_in_South_Africa, accessed October 2, 2013.
5 Craig Higginson, interview, 2013.
6 Lara Foot Newton was appointed as resident director/dramaturg of the Baxter Theatre in 2005 before she became CEO in 2010.
7 Craig Higginson, interview, 2013.
8 The information from Fleishman contained in this section is drawn from Mark Fleishman, "A Genealogy of Playwrighting in South Africa"; and Mark Fleishman, "'For a little road it is not. For it's a great road; it is long': Performing Heritage for Development in the Cape" (2011), available online at www.slideshare.net/WAAE/mark-fleishman, accessed May 5, 2012.

Part II
DRAMATURGY IN THE AGE OF GLOBALIZATION

17

The dramaturg as globalist

Tom Sellar

Goethe famously declared in the early nineteenth century that an epoch of *Weltliteratur*, or world literature, was at hand – a development he thought could supplant, and eventually supersede, national traditions. In an 1827 interview the ur-dramaturg urged everyone in the sphere of letters to imagine this new era: "I therefore like to look about me in foreign nations, and advise everyone to do the same. National literature is now a rather unmeaning term; the epoch of world literature is at hand and everyone must strive to hasten its approach."[1] In the theatre, Goethe's anticipation of a dramaturgy embodying a worldly spirit led him to advocate for, among other things, the integration of Shakespearean dramatic structures into German-language plays. That extra-national innovation alone altered the DNA of German tragedy, which had acquired fixed traits over years of mutation within a monolinguistic tradition; eventually it opened the way for epic forms as radical as Brecht's.

Goethe's advocacy for world-consciousness may have transformed dramatic form at a literary level, but a *Welt* theatre practice has proven far slower to arrive, constrained by localized and material limitations of actors, audience, and architecture. His aspiration has persisted, however. Western attempts at formal syntheses have, of course, been made throughout modernity: from Artaud's appropriation of Balinese techniques and Brecht's interpolation of Beijing Opera physicality to Ariane Mnouchkine's Asian epics with France's Théâtre du Soleil or Peter Brook's integration of Persian storytelling into Western dramatic narrative. Several more recent examples, however, might prompt us to wonder if a new globalized dramaturgical practice is finally at hand. Is it possible that a performance equivalent of Goethe's *Weltliteratur* is perhaps only now, in an era of (post) globalization and digitization, coming to full fruition, made possible by changes even a cosmopolitan like Goethe could scarcely have imagined?

Jet travel, mobile electronic linkages, open markets, migration of peoples, and mass cultural production have worn down the already porous borders delineating national cultures. In the twenty-first century collaborations take place across continents with ease; productions deracinated from any national context tour the world, with ensembles drawn from multiple countries and backgrounds playing for audiences across the map. This expansive global dramaturgy is taking shape not in dramatic letters – as Goethe first wished – but in new collective practices that signal an important shift and evolution for dramaturgy.

Consider the example of *Ciudades Paralelas* (Parallel cities), a performance project conceived and curated in 2010 by the Argentinean director-dramaturg Lola Arias and Stefan Kaegi, a dramaturg-curator based in Berlin (best known as a member of the dramaturgs' collective Rimini Protokoll). *Ciudades Paralelas* originated as a dramaturgical initiative, seeking to investigate functional urban spaces, essential to the economies of cities but normally invisible to residents, through site-based performances. Arias and Kaegi invited eight artists to create original works offering audiences an immersive experience of these locations or otherwise calling attention to these architectural environments and their relationship with the public. The artists, selected from countries around the world, staged performances and spectacles in shopping malls, factory floors, libraries, halls of justice, hotel rooms, apartment buildings, rooftops, and train stations, among other sites. Their creations were remounted (with adjustments for local structures and audiences) in each of the world capitals where *Ciudades Paralelas* was presented: initially Berlin, Zurich, Warsaw, and Buenos Aires, and subsequently in additional presentations in Singapore, Calcutta, Delhi, and Utrecht, among other mountings.

Ciudades Paralelas demonstrates an expanded idea of dramaturgy at play in the twenty-first century, untethered from textual interpretation, dramatic repertory, and even from the production house. It is a practice synthesizing urban studies, global economics, politics, and architecture with traditional considerations of theatrical structure, design, and narrative. Arias and Kaegi did not function as directors or authors for this project, but defined the concept and shaped the project so that its constituent parts would have meaningful interplay. They calculated its effects for local audiences in consultation with residents and experts, while ensuring that each city's version would fulfill the mandate to research local architectures, economies, and experiences. Seen together, the various incarnations of the project offer a powerful glimpse of a global dramaturgy, one shaped with participants, collaborations, and publics around the world, probing questions shared by cities everywhere in the global economy. For Arias and Kaegi, however, platform comes before practice; a performance dramaturgy and structure emerges from, and after, the thematic contours have been imagined. For many reasons, this project might be seen as a blueprint for a twenty-first-century dramaturgy: its turn away from text; its decentered and flexible structure; its inclusion of multiple international collaborators and partners, linked by an online platform; its strategy for uncovering global resonances in local spaces.

Another example might be found in the initiatives of dramaturg and performance curator Matthias Lilienthal, currently based in Beirut and Berlin simultaneously. Lilienthal served as chief dramaturg of the Berliner Volksbühne under intendant Frank Castorf in the 1990s when that theatre responded with vigorous political and economic inquiries to the vast transformations of the city around it, following the collapse of state communism in 1990, questioning capitalism and the cultural and theatrical assumptions behind it. But Lilienthal's global practice flourished after he left the repertory institution to work, with fluidity, as dramaturg, curator, critical thinker, and programmer. Lilienthal has created, instigated, and nourished many of the most progressive developments in theatre and performance in the past three decades. These include his collaborations with the directors Christoph Marthaler and the late Christoph Schlingensief, as well as the collective Rimini Protokoll and many other artists who work regularly at the HAU, where he served as artistic director from 2003 until 2011, reinventing Berlin's former Hebbel Theater in three new locations to critical and popular acclaim, resulting in one of Europe's most exciting theatres. Lilienthal left HAU for Beirut, where he ran a postgraduate art project at Ashkal Alwan and helped to form a new performance festival in Cairo at a time of political transition.

From these global collaborations Lilienthal has theorized "an hysterical longing for reality"[2] in the contemporary theatre, and his commitment to that ethos has spawned nothing less than a new performance movement re-examining the documentary, asking what creates an engaged social encounter, and transforming public and private spheres to meet that longing. His projects have regularly transported audiences and artmakers across all kinds of borders, and he himself moves fluidly from Brooklyn to Beijing to Buenos Aires for meetings, workshops, and performances.

Two dramaturgy initiatives in particular demonstrate Lilienthal's commitment to using the world stage as a vehicle for social and political investigations, contemplating the real and further blurring boundaries between art and life. Since 2002 he has developed the X-Wohnungen (X-apartments) project, inviting spectator-participants into private residences in Caracas, Istanbul, Sao Paulo, Warsaw, and Johannesburg. The project stems from a conceptual framework developed by Lilienthal, and its implementation also results from a strategic institutional network he cultivated. Second, reflecting his ongoing preoccupation with the effects of globalization on societies on all sides of its economic coin, he created the framework for the producing festival he curated, Beyond Belonging – Migration, which has fostered a new critical dialogue around this crucial subject, enlarging the standard presenters' platform to put local communities, projects, and artists at the origin and center of this most global of conversations. Lilienthal's practice is dramaturgical in the broadest sense, shaped around advocacy, research, and investigations of a political economy and culture which links across national lines. He forms collaborations with artists in Beirut as easily as he does in Berlin; he initiates multinational projects dealing with questions that transcend national contexts and aesthetics.

These are examples of dramaturgs who became architects of global creations exploring globalized themes. Further afield, even from experimental theatre, are a growing number of performance-makers who have refashioned collaborative models to draw on the work of urbanists, NGOs, and activists in both local and global contexts. These "social practice" projects have profound implications for theatre-makers, for they are dematerialized, experience-centered social art projects rooted in collaborations and collaborative context. Consider City Council Meeting, for example, a performance piece created by Aaron Landsman and Mallory Catlett in 2012, which has been mounted in art spaces, former ballrooms, and schools in Houston's Third Ward, Queens and the Bronx, and Tempe, Arizona, among other locations. Viewers choose a role for themselves and re-enact actual municipal council deliberations from various US cities; they write personal statements and messages to their local representatives, which at some performances are read out loud by an actual local official. Depending on the performance site, other participants may include students from local junior high schools, a gospel choir, and additional members of community groups. Landsman and Catlett do not script the event so much as facilitate it with the participants from evening to evening and city to city. They function not as directors, not as authors or playwrights, but in another category that has a lot to do with dramaturgy: researching a given community's politics, economy, architecture, and community; selecting, conceiving, and shaping material; conceiving and responding to opportunities for collaboration. While *City Council Meeting* is ostensibly domestic in its themes – asking how democracy works, or is supposed to work, at the most local level – its model further asks how local meanings can be generated when they play off the notion of a "global" (in the sense of a universal or single system) template for public dialogue; how can you make the democratic process yours, here in your hometown, by performing it?

City Council Meeting is just one example from a rapidly expanding body of socially engaged art today that cannot easily be categorized as theatre, visual art, or activism. The notion of theatre production and artistic creation as a finished object is replaced with another proposition, in which theatre – including the performance event itself – is a continual process of social interaction and negotiation. As these disciplinary lines blur, making collaboration and participation defining elements rather than formal components, the dramaturg's role in facilitating communication among collaborators will only grow. The art critic and scholar Grant Kester noted in 2005 that this phenomenon was taking place largely outside arts institutions (although that is changing today) and was among the first to cite the global scope of its practitioners; this expansively collaborative dynamic has, he writes, "energized a younger generation of practitioners and collectives, such as Ala Plastica in Buenos Aires, Superflex in Denmark, Maurice O'Connell in Ireland, MuF in London, Huit Facettes in Senegal, Ne Pas Plier in Paris, and Temporary Services in Chicago, among many others."[3] Such collectives address the topics that define political and economic globalization: urban problems, community identity, economic systems, immigration, and local and universal cultural values.

Can the now venerable practice of dramaturgy adapt to aesthetic shifts like these, which alter the standard parameters of theatrical process? There is historical precedent for dramaturgy as an agent for change within the theatre. In the successive eras between Goethe and Instagram, the dramaturg has functioned as an essential conduit to theatrical traditions beyond the domestic. They have lobbied from their institutional perches – often in national organizations or theatres devoted primarily to a single linguistic or national tradition – and have advocated for new aesthetic ideas, labored for an expanded political awareness, and championed changes in the practice of theatre-making.

Indeed, without the dedication of certain individuals to specialized areas of international theatre research – whether as scholars, translators, critics, curators, producers, or institutional dramaturgs – it would be hard to imagine the introduction of key figures from world theatre into the repertory and into other national theatre cultures. Who knows when US theatre-makers would have heard of Thomas Bernhard or Elfriede Jelinek if Gitta Honegger had not translated their plays into English, directed and advised theatre productions, and authored biographies? A generation of essential Latin American dramatists – Mexico's Sabina Berman, Argentina's Griselda Gambaro, Brazil's Augusto Boal, Chile's Marco Antonio de la Parra – found introductions to North America via Joanne Pottlitzer's translations, teaching, and articles, and especially the nonprofit producing organization she founded in 1966, Theatre of Latin America.

The list could go on and on, showing individuals whose tastes, ideas, personalities, and perspectives serve as bridges across theatre cultures whose lines have, until recently, been drawn largely across national borders, with exceptions for countries sharing a common language such as Britain and America or Francophone or Spanish-speaking regions. But this nationalistic rigidity isn't necessarily intrinsic to theatre-making, and thus it can be altered; perhaps it merely reflects the theatre's historical emphasis on the drama as a literary text, with production elements subordinated. Dramaturgy formed as a practice for a theatre centered around creation and inter-pretation of dramatic texts, so naturally the profession's global aspirations have focused on reading (or reading about) foreign play texts, translating or commissioning transla-tions of classical and new dramas, championing foreign directors and other artists for production – making their case in print, in meetings, and in public forums.

Given the twenty-first century's wave of site-based, documentary, participatory, multidisciplinary performance created in a global context, this dimension of the dramaturg's métier will change correspondingly. While the field is still largely orientated to production houses and dramatic texts – classics and new plays – it would do well to acknowledge these models and consider how they might be applied or adopted to rapidly transforming performance forms.

In the era of digital media, theatre practitioners around the world find themselves interconnected as never before; productions, plays, and proposals circulate with fluidity, assisted by a globalized economy and its infrastructure; collaborations and partnerships form readily and regularly across national borders as a de-centered art world orientates itself to new opportunities and imperatives. International colla-boration is today a structural necessity rather than an isolated ideological or artistic gesture. The dramaturg, scholar, and critic must offer a practice informed by global currents, maintaining links to multiple theatre cultures as well as supplying expertise and context both at home and externally.

Performance, like the visual arts, is becoming increasingly interdisciplinary, requiring a facility in multiple media. Dramaturgical practice must begin to comprise a wider sphere of activity, including performance and socially engaged art; rather than emphasizing the refinement and translation of dramatic texts for the stage, it needs to place a premium on the structure and context of collaborations. It must consider the global makeup and dimensions of such projects, for the artists and for the public. Like all cultural custodians, dramaturgs will need to demonstrate an ability to think across and beyond national lines, reflecting an interdependent world of linked economies and regularly intersecting cultures.

Notes

1 Johann Peter Eckermann, *Conversations of Goethe* (1827), quoted in David Damrosch, *What Is World Literature?* (Princeton, NJ: Princeton University Press, 2003), 1.
2 Matthias Lilienthal, "Formats in Theater," presentation at Goethe Institut, New York (July 11, 2012).
3 Grant Kester, "Conversation Pieces: The Role of Dialogue in Socially-Engaged Art," available online at www.grantkester.net/resources/Conversation+Pieces_+The+Role+of+Dialogue+in+Socially-Engaged+Art.pdf, accessed October 13, 2013.

18

Freelance dramaturgs in the twenty-first century

Journalists, advocates, and curators

Anne Hamilton

With the way information is exchanged right now, it is very easy to engage with someone across town or across the world. News travels across the globe quickly, and it is the same with art. Theatre artists are becoming more international in the way that they engage with one another across continents, creating cultural movements which lead to transnational collaborations. As dramaturgs, we have always been developing plays, advocating for their widespread performance, and endeavoring to communicate cultural context. Now, we are doing it on a much larger scale. We use language and the practice of dramaturgy as a tool to help integrate productions, seasons, and international collaborations. Our dramaturgical lingua franca is an increasingly valuable asset in the global economy, as is our free-thinking spirit of creativity and diplomatic training. Our given assets are education, experience, and collaborative training.

In our fast-paced, "hyper-connected" global economy, as Thomas L. Friedman describes it, sometimes there are misunderstandings.[1] Thanks to our experience, dramaturgs should feel pretty much at home in this climate of multicultural inter-connectivity. As cultural liaisons with literary and performance training, we are poised to evolve into greater leaders as we assist others in navigating new employment and collaborative realities in the twenty-first century. But first, we would do well to build a new infrastructure of information sharing and archives. Three ways to build these bridges are by engaging our contacts and the world at large as journalists, advocates, and curators.

With the 2008 American financial industry collapse, our economic reality changed. Companies were downsized even more in favor of employing part-time workers and consultants. Many workers who would have expected to work for someone else for most of their lives began to consider self-employment. As a result of this trend, the office, or even the manufacturing plant, will not be a primary, long-term location for the worker of the future. It seems everyone is freelancing at some task, with many working at home stringing several part-time assignments together in an effort to create full-time income. "Indeed, statistics now show that about a third of journalists and creative workers are already independent, and that number is only going to increase."[2] Freelancing has become a global movement.

Due to these shifting employment parameters, new expectations and realities were met with invention, particularly in the form of more community-based workspaces all over the country. People are working at home and then meeting in a shared space to exchange ideas and opportunities. Union Square Ventures' Fred Wilson describes why co-working in the tech field, specifically, is a growing trend: "The main benefits of this kind of setup are camaraderie (small startups can be lonely), knowledge sharing, high energy, culture, and cost sharing."[3]

As creative artists, dramaturgs are used to contract-based work. We make our way through the world on a project-by-project basis and work on many projects at the same time. In a fortunate twist of fate, our mindset and professional abilities have placed us at the cutting edge of these new global employment trends. At this point in time, there is an unprecedented opportunity to focus our vision on the changing nature of employment norms and to evolve into theatre industry leaders using our education, passion, artistry, and assets. We need to take even more responsibility for our own actions, and futures, not rely on the theatre industry to offer us employment and projects.

We live in many communities. We cross boundaries all the time. I graduated from college with a bachelor's degree in English literature and spent a few years working in public relations, publishing, and as an administrative assistant in an architectural practice. I had been strongly influenced by watching my boss, Tom Joseph, manage his team of architects in a studio setting. He oversaw many design and construction projects simultaneously and gave his staff architects guidance on design problems. Professionals of varying skill levels collaborated to make sure the structure was completed properly. Even though I was an artist, I enjoyed learning about business, particularly working in finance. Thanks to my varied work experience, it felt natural to work as a freelancer when I finished my M.F.A. in Dramaturgy at Columbia University School of the Arts. I wanted to create theatrical projects, so I just kept working with playwrights and theatre companies on projects that came my way.

For many years, I also had a full-time corporate job. Because I was in New York City, it was easy to develop as a dramaturg while holding down a full-time job. I was committed to continuing education and admired the way architects, engineers, physicians, and attorneys, for instance, were in professions that required them to constantly learn and grow. It was natural to me, therefore, to set up a dramaturgy practice, name my company Hamilton Dramaturgy, and go about trying to serve my clients personally and thoroughly. I applied the design-studio business-practice model to dramaturgy.

I have had to constantly grow to keep up with the changing demands of a freelance business. I knew from my public relations background that besides offering high-quality services, keeping in touch with the public was very important. And fortunately, the technology innovations that have occurred over the past twenty years have made reaching the public as a dramaturg much easier than in past decades. Besides relying on word of mouth, I actively learned and took advantage of new technologies. The technology which seems primitive now, like email, listservs, websites, and cell phones, all came into use one by one. It is important to gain mastery of new technology to advance in the field of dramaturgy, especially when envisioning a personal impact and formulating programs and activities which will form the basis of my practice.

I had a sincere desire to be of service to the playwrights and directors I worked for and to help them in their careers beyond the projects on which we collaborated. I knew that serving as an arts journalist would accomplish this goal. As time went on, I created a series of publications and programs. My first was an e-newsletter named ScriptForward! I sent it to all my clients and invited the public to sign up through my website. Later, I was troubled by the lack of female theatre artists who were interviewed in documentaries and television shows, so I decided to create a public record of women talking about their artistic influences and processes. My first interview was with the playwright and librettist Quiara Alegría Hudes. We spoke about her early artistic influences and process. I turned the interview into a podcast called Hamilton Dramaturgy's TheatreNow! and posted it for free on the internet. Now the series is in its third season and serves as an oral history of the work of important theatre women, like Jennifer Tipton, Kate Valk, and Margo Jefferson.

I use my dramaturgical sensibility to write about topics which I feel are important to contemporary performing artists and writers. I have posted on my blogs many articles to advocate for the gender parity movement, particularly the efforts of Susan Jonas, Melody Brooks, and Julie Crosby, co-founders of the 50/50 in 2020 organization, and Ludovica Villar-Hauser's Works by Women meetup group. I also wrote about the Lilly Awards, which honor female artists every June around the time of the Tony Awards. By advocating for the groundbreaking work that others are doing, and providing accurate, articulate materials to the public, dramaturgs can help others understand what we do and what our artistic process entails. We can introduce new artists and topics to the global conversation rapidly and effectively. In this way, we can advocate for great theatre artists, cultural trends, and new works that we feel so passionately about, thereby magnifying our impact on the field.

What dramaturg among us does not have a few "dream" volumes of plays neatly organized by topic or genre in his or her head? Or a dream season, with an ideal set of collaborators? How about a new organization of like-minded artists or a professional program which would serve a meaningful, but neglected purpose? At the base of these projects is the desire to influence culture through skilled curatorship. It is an impulse which was so fatefully expressed by Lessing, the father of our profession, and it continues today.

Dramaturgs are curators and should increasingly view themselves as such. One of our basic functions is curating information. By selecting salient information to present, for instance, in actor's packets and program notes, we are influencing the opinions and artistic growth of both artists and the theatre-going public. This is a significant responsibility. When I think of all the artists with whom I've worked over the years, and the continued life of their plays after we have finished working, I realize that my impact, however small or great, can grow to have great consequences.

Two American artists exemplify my notion of being journalists, advocates, and curators. Although they don't identify as dramaturgs, both have mobilized their talents to influence public opinion in a global manner. First is Randy Gener, an editor, writer, critic, and artist living in New York City; he is the founder of the Culture of

One World, which is "a global media project devoted to foreign affairs, cultural diplomacy, international art projects and enterprise reporting in the public interest."[4] He travels frequently and publishes on the arts, culture, and politics in many media. Second is Jill Dolan, a Princeton professor who has created an award-winning blog called The Feminist Spectator. She writes that the blog, "ruminates on theatre, performance, film, and television, focusing on gender, sexuality, race, other identities and overlaps, and our common humanity. It addresses how the arts shape and reflect our lives; how they participate in civic conversations; and how they serve as a vehicle for social change and a platform for pleasure."[5] Models of cross-media influence like this are growing, and it is time for dramaturgs to actively lead these kinds of conversations.

The current state of technology is rapidly evolving and I don't know what new opportunities will present themselves in the next month or year, but I do know that actively searching out new trends and advancements, and then applying the innovations to traditional dramaturgical tasks is effective in creating a new role for dramaturgs as the pace of intercultural exchange intensifies. Whereas in past years one dramaturg might have had a "beat" or "territory" consisting of one city or region, now dramaturgs can move fluidly across geography and time zones by utilizing online technology, and traveling when necessary.

In the *New York Times* article "Need a Job? Invent It", Thomas Friedman writes, "My generation had it easy. We got to 'find' a job. But, more than ever, our kids will have to 'invent' a job ... Sure, the lucky ones will find their first job, but, given the pace of change today, even they will have to reinvent, re-engineer and reimagine that job much more often than their parents if they want to advance in it."[6] The more information is available, the more people will need to know how to put it to use. Dramaturgs possess the skills to help navigate the plethora of information. Others need someone smart to help them to navigate it. As dramaturgs, we need to position ourselves in the global economy by taking our professional identities to a new level of evolution and advancement. We are cross-cultural diplomats and can position ourselves as conduits at home and in international collaborations. We can do it in theatres and other contexts as well. In the theatrical process and in cultural communication, we serve as a buffer, providing a safe creative space in which to collaborate. We can professionalize our freelance working method in a way that makes us available as cultural, literary, historical, and theatrical diplomats.

How can we succeed in the twenty-first century? By imitating the successes in other sectors of the economy. In industry, the term "nesting" refers to the process of efficiently manufacturing parts from flat raw material. Dramaturgs can refine a process by which we efficiently create parts and products from our raw material – that is, we can use as much inexpensive or free technology as possible, to add our labor and influence to the global economy. We can "nest" by getting as much mileage as possible from as little raw material and effort as possible. This means sharing insight and case studies with one another, as well as archiving completed work, writing journal articles about our experiences, and advocating for the artists and causes we admire and support. We can create publishing companies and record playwrights reading their own work. We can introduce young audiences to a variety of contemporary plays and teach them to review performances in order to build their critical skills.

Economic collapse in America, which had worldwide repercussions, as well as the difficulties the European Union is experiencing, makes it clear six years later that the world is changing. The way that dramaturgs pursue their opportunities and their working relationships needs to evolve. This field is ahead of the curve while others are still catching up. There's a difference between the field of theatre and the field of dramaturgy. Freelance dramaturgs can lead the field of dramaturgy. And together we can lead the field of theatre. We have more resources than we think. We can see everyone's point of view. We have excellent training and collaborative skills. It's time to lead the field with our own conceived pieces and networks, to be producers, playwrights, directors, and actors, as part of our basic identity and mission.

In step with the trend of shared workspaces, we need to create freelance dramaturgical collectives all over the world, in which we share space and information. Individuals can practice their specialties while serving as a resource for professional theatre artists and the public. A workspace with room for readings and performances would double the efficiency of our mission. Perhaps we could share large workspaces or residences by offering residencies to artists and their theatre companies. Instead of working alone, freelance dramaturgs can begin to see themselves as community resources. A global freelance dramaturgy directory would facilitate this effort and would provide a means of contacting one another when we travel and work abroad. Extending an invitation is a gesture of goodwill. As artists, we are creators, not politicians or lawmakers, but we can go far in helping culture and artistry to advance.

Global dramaturgy in the twenty-first century will take advantage of parallel experiences by drawing on writings from people who speak many languages and may live in a country not of their own birth. We will continue to curate and create theatre pieces which talk about living with many languages, ethnicities, cultures, and religions. We will foster plays in which two or more languages are spoken. We will translate. We are the midwives who help birth other artists' ideas and stories, as well as the midwives of psychosocial and intellectual history. We are the diplomats who help complex, multi-lingual, multicultural artistic pieces find their way into the world. Of course, dramaturgs have been doing this for centuries. But our new global landscape requires more deliberate intention if we are to find our fullest expression as dramaturgs.

We will celebrate our experience and invite people in to share it. We will commission new works and create bodies of archives based on our own collaborations and interests. The new practice of twenty-first-century freelance dramaturgy consists of bringing the theatre artist's strengths to bear on the realities of global economic practice and the growth of international connections. As Tony Kushner writes in *Slavs! Thinking about the Longstanding Problems of Virtue and Happiness*, "Leap! Leap!" It's time to leap.

Notes

1 Thomas L. Friedman, "That Used to Be Us: A Crucial Time for America and the Role Education Must Play," lecture, Gonzaga University, Spokane, WA, September 4, 2012.
2 Shane Snow, "Solopreneurs, Freelancers Hoping for More Help from the Election Winner," *Washington Post*, November 6, 2012, available online at www.washingtonpost.

com/blogs/on-small-business/post/solopreneurs-freelancers-hoping-for-more-help-from-the-election-winner/2012/11/06/aa3c14d4–282e-11e2-b4e0–346287b7e56c_blog.html, accessed October 13, 2013.

3 Fred Wilson, "Coworking Spaces," *AVC musings of a VC in NYC,* entry posted September 2, 2010, available online at www.avc.com/a_vc/2010/09/coworking-spaces.html, accessed August 30, 2013.

4 "In the Culture of One World," available online at http://cultureofoneworld.org, accessed August 30, 2013.

5 "The Feminist Spectator," www.thefeministspectator.com, accessed August 30, 2013.

6 Thomas L. Friedman, "Need a Job? Invent It," *The New York Times,* March 30, 2013.

19

The National Theatre goes international

Global branding and the regions

Jens Peters

The year 2009 saw the launch of the National Theatre's digital broadcasting programme, NT Live. While previous live transmissions of theatre took place on TV or on the internet, NT Live with its reach of about 260 cinema screens in the UK and an additional 390 screens in over 25 countries worldwide marks the beginning of the live broadcast as a nationwide and indeed global large-scale event.[1] Digital broadcast of performances in cinemas had been pioneered by the Metropolitan Opera in New York in 2006, and it was followed by other international arts institutions. Nonetheless, the National Theatre in London was the first *theatre* to attempt the live cinema broadcast of its performances. Since 2009, NT Live has shown 29 productions to a global audience including spectators in the USA, Australia, South Africa, New Zealand, and Germany. The first two experimental broadcasts of NT Live, *Phèdre* and *All's Well that Ends Well*, were made possible by funding from Arts Council England and NESTA (National Endowment for Science, Technology and the Arts). For subsequent broadcasts, the National Theatre was able to attract the sponsorship of insurance company AVIVA. NT Live has clearly been a success in terms of audiences, and other theatre companies are following in its footsteps: the Royal Shakespeare Company will broadcast its production of *Richard II* "in more than 100 cinemas, overseas as well as in Britain."[2]

Audience surveys assembled after the first two NT Live broadcasts have demonstrated a strong positive reception of the program. It is not, as many people have feared, a stale and stilted imitation of theatre, but is able to create its own unique viewing experience and atmosphere. Since its beginning NT Live has attracted 1.5 million people,[3] amongst them a large section of lower income audience, thereby potentially acting as a gateway into theatre.[4] Moreover, performance rights were negotiated openly and fairly, a process that has resulted in benefitting not only the National Theatre, but the artists involved in the creation of the performance.[5] Given this success and the influence NT Live is likely to have on the development of digital broadcasts of theatre in the UK and elsewhere, it is crucial to pose some fundamental questions about the nature and implications of such a mediatization of theatre alongside the already present acknowledgement of its potentials in promoting theatre.

The National Theatre presents itself in NT Live as a global "brand," thereby participating in a global discourse geared towards an "event" culture in which aspects such as brand identity, interaction of the brand's different digital platforms, and the creation of an *impression* of authenticity take precedence over the artistic and experiential aspects of the performance itself. This tendency to present the live broadcast as a special event, often with implications of it being better or more con-venient than a theatre performance, could have serious long-term effects for the regional theatres in whose cities NT Live is shown. In order to assess the relationship between the National Theatre and the regional theatre, the position the former occupies with regard to the latter has to be scrutinized, since the "national" remit encapsulated in the name implies a specific role for the Royal National Theatre in the theatrical and cultural landscape of the whole country.

I was able to experience an NT Live "encore" (i.e. not live) screening of Nick Hytner's 2010 production of *Hamlet*, with Rory Kinnear in the title role, at the Cinemaxx Berlin Potsdamer Platz on November 7, 2013. At this screening of *Hamlet*, it was especially the contextual material shown before the actual performance that emphasized the strong branding of the event. The screening began with a slide show of images accompanied by the sound of muttering people, repeated twice. These images included rehearsal photos from *Hamlet*, advertisements for future NT Live broadcasts and National Theatre shows, some information on the National's history as well as references to NT Live's web presence (homepage, Facebook, Twitter, etc.). Afterwards, the TV broadcaster Emma Freud gave a short overview of the previous five productions of *Hamlet* that have been staged at the National and emphasized that this production had been "a total sell-out." The main part of the opening section was taken up by a behind-the-scenes video for *Hamlet*. This opened with a view of the National Theatre building seen from the Thames, accompanied by eerie music and lines from the play.

Afterwards, the director of the show, Nick Hytner (who was also the artistic director of the National), lead actors Rory Kinnear (Hamlet) and Ruth Negga (Ophelia), and Jerry Brotton (professor of Renaissance Studies at Queen Mary, University of London) and Shakespeare biographer Charles Nicholl discussed aspects of the play and its interpretation in this staging. The interviews were interspersed by videos from the dress rehearsal and from previous productions of Hamlet. Noticeably, the latter ones were taken from *films* and not from recordings of the five National Theatre productions mentioned by Emma Freud. Although this could have been due to the absence of such recordings, this decision seems to be motivated at least partly by the greater cultural prestige attached to these films. The current production was thereby positioned as the inheritor of a long tradition not only of what could be perceived as high-brow culture (Shakespeare, theatre) but also of the popular culture of films, and lead actor Rory Kinnear was aligned with star actors like Laurence Olivier and Kenneth Brannagh.

I have chosen to describe this additional content offered at the screening of *Hamlet* at some length instead of the screened performance since it illustrates most clearly how the National Theatre uses the live broadcasts to construct and strengthen its own brand identity. Its logo, building, and illustrious history featured prominently in all aspects of the opening section. The information provided often underlined aspects of scale (800 productions since the founding of the theatre), success (indicated by global transfers, which were specifically mentioned), and consistency (only five artistic directors since its founding). Together, this information helps to establish the National Theatre as both innovative and reliable – an important combination of attributes for any institution that wants to create a brand identity no longer mainly defined by its individual products. James Steichen has described a similar process for the broadcasts of the Metropolitan Opera in New York:

> The broadcasts work ultimately in service not of opera (or even the director or performance), but of the institution, and the original performance and its presenter gain even more cachet. Through this remediatization, the Met can capitalize on new forms of exhibition value and in turn reinvigorate the exchange value of its original product.[6]

Steichen here employs Walter Benjamin's concept of the "exhibition value" (Ausstellungswert), which Benjamin contrasts with the "cult value" (Kultwert) of the original (non-reproduced) art object. Whereas the latter underlines that an original art object has something auratic that remains unavailable to the spectator, the former privileges the aspect of intimacy through an impression of instant and ubiquitous availability.[7]

The NT Live broadcasts' aim to reach as large an audience as possible strongly emphasizes the exhibition value of its content. Its interaction with immediately available online content strengthens this association. Finally, the decision of the National Theatre to abandon the strict live principle and allow encore broadcasts is another step away from the cult value of the original theatre performance. Branding is an integral part of this emphasis on exhibition value. If the original performance has become incidental in attracting the audience, the institution trying to capitalize on the exhibition value has to establish a strong brand identity in order to create coherence for its various contents. It is therefore not surprising that

> 21.1 percent of cinemagoers said that their main reason for attending was to see a National Theatre production, greater than the 18.6 per cent saying that it was because they wanted to see Helen Mirren. This is testament to the strong "brand" value the National Theatre carries throughout the UK.[8]

The NESTA report evaluating the first season of the National Theatre has not only recognized this tendency towards branding, but signals its own predominantly economic rather than artistic perspective in praising this very feature: "NT Live presents the live transmission as more than a regular cinema screening: it is branded as a special event."[9] The presentation of the NT Live screenings as "events" is part of the National Theatre's branding strategy. The event is presented as both large and exclusive – compare for example the NT Live website, which advertises its "exclusive behind the scenes content."[10] NT Live's attempt to link exclusivity and scale certainly has an economic logic. Auslander explains how "live events have cultural value: being able to say that you were physically present at a particular event constitutes valuable symbolic capital."[11] The decision to broadcast plays no longer on TV, but in cinemas, is precisely motivated by this desire to create an event that bestows prestige on its visitors through the fact that it takes time and effort to attend.

But what impact does NT Live's tendency towards branding and event culture have on the British theatrical landscape? As a national theatre, the Royal National Theatre in London occupies a crucial position. With regard to the claim of being a "national" institution, Nadine Holdsworth has raised the question of "whether a single theatre, normally in a national capital, can legitimately claim to serve as a theatre of and for the nation as a whole."[12] NT Live clearly presents an attempt on the part of the National Theatre to legitimize this claim. David Sabel, head of the digital department at the National Theatre, has stated that one of the motivations for starting NT Live has been a desire to fulfill its obligations of providing theatre for the nation as a whole:

> The motivations were mission – making the National a truly national theatre. We do 22 to 25 productions every year. A few will tour but touring is expensive, not particularly environmentally friendly and there are so many places you can't go. But what if we could get cinema goers around the country to see the National Theatre's work?[13]

With its current distribution of about 260 screens in the UK, NT Live has obviously expanded the accessibility of the National Theatre, and Sabel's point of the logistic and environmental problems of touring is a strong argument in favor of live broadcasts. For the NESTA report, the impact has been entirely positive: "The findings also suggest that NT Live may have produced beneficial 'spillovers' for other theatres, such as those situated in localities where it was screened."[14] Other sources so far have corroborated this impression.[15] It is important – at this relatively early stage of live broadcasts – to remind ourselves also of the potentially problematic long-term impacts such a form of distribution could have on the regional theatres in Britain. The numbers presented in the audience survey conducted for the NESTA report allow an interpretation slightly different from the enthusiastic reception it receives in the report itself. While it is encouraging that 29.6 percent were "more likely to attend a play at another theatre in the future" even more (33.9 percent) were "more likely to attend a performance at the National Theatre in the future." Not surprisingly however, the largest majority (89.1 percent) was motivated to attend future broadcasts.[16] It becomes clear that while the possibility that NT Live can encourage people to explore live theatre is not negligible, it is far more likely to strengthen the brand identity of the National Theatre and to propagate its own format. Considering that a majority of the cinema audience already had some (68.9 percent) or detailed (27.2 percent) knowledge of theatre, the large percentage motivated to attend future broadcasts could indeed be interpreted as a drain away from theatre.

In this context, the emphasis on an exclusive brand and on event culture in NT Live is especially problematic. In underlining the special experience it provides, NT Live displays a development parallel to that of television drama:

> the goal of televised drama was not merely to convey a theatrical event to the viewer, but to recreate the theatrical experience for the home viewer through televisual discourse and, thus, to *replace* live performance.[17]

The NESTA report consistently draws on audience surveys to strengthen the impression that the experience of the live broadcast in many ways surpasses the experience of the theatre performance:

> Cinema audiences reported high levels of emotional engagement with the play, even compared with their peers at the theatre performance. Satisfaction levels ... were 15 per cent higher among cinema audiences than at the theatre.[18]

It does not consider how far categories other than absorption and emotional immersion could account for a *different* but equally valuable experience in the theatre.[19] Therefore NT Live, in spite of protestations to the contrary, could essentially end up positioning itself not as supplement in cooperation with regional theatre performances, but as their replacement, especially because they often lack the prestige the National Theatre is able to accumulate through star actors, directors, and expensive large-scale set designs.

In spite of these points of critique, NT Live's positive potential for the regional theatres lies in a different conception of what a national theatre can be: "a national theatre not only appears at designated national theatres but comprises a complex nexus of theatrical activity."[20] NT Live has already started the creation of such a nexus by showing productions from the Donmar Warehouse, Complicite (broadcast from Theatre Royal, Plymouth), and the Manchester International Festival. Especially the cooperation with the Manchester International Festival, which took place in 2013, is an important step away from a London-centric programing and towards a stronger cooperation with regional institutions. Since the National Theatre has expressed plans to broaden this cooperation, NT Live could present an opportunity to explore the positive aspects of its branding tendency in developing what currently is an institutional brand towards a national one that is truly representing "the best of British theatre."[21] As a broadcasting network for theatres across the UK, NT Live could more firmly assume a consciously supplementary function in promoting and enabling access to theatre.

Notes

1 Matt Trueman, "The Surprise Success of NT Live," *The Guardian*, June 9, 2013. The exact numbers of participating cinemas fluctuate with each specific broadcast.
2 Dominic Cavendish, "Should Live Theatre Be Shown in Cinema?" *The Telegraph*, October 30, 2013.
3 NT Live, http://ntlive.nationaltheatre.org.uk/about-us, accessed November 12, 2013.
4 "NT Live: Digital Broadcast of Theatre – Learning from the Pilot Season," NESTA report 2011, available online at www.nesta.org.uk/library/documents/NTLive_web.pdf, accessed November 12, 2013, 19 and 38.
5 "NT Live," 23.
6 James Steichen, "The Metropolitan Opera Goes Public: Peter Gelb and the Institutional Dramaturgy of the Met: 'Live in HD,'" *Music and the Moving Image*, 2.2 (Summer 2009): 24–30.
7 Walter Benjamin, *Das Kunstwert im Zeitalter seiner technischen Reproduzierbarkeit* (Frankfurt A.M.: Suhrkamp, 1963), 21–23.
8 "NT Live," 5.

9 "NT Live," 14.
10 NT Live, 'Behind the Scenes', available online at http://ntlive.nationaltheatre.org.uk/behind-the-scenes, accessed November 12, 2013.
11 Philip Auslander, *Liveness. Performance in a Mediatized Culture* (London and New York: Routledge, 1999), 57. For more information on the concept of symbolic capital, please refer to Pierre Bourdieu's *Distinction. A Social Critique of the Judgment of Taste* (London and New York: Routledge, 2010).
12 Nadine Holdsworth, *Theatre and Nation* (Basingstoke: Palgrave Macmillan, 2010), 34.
13 David Sabel quoted in Nancy Groves, "Arts Head: David Sabel, Head of Digital, National Theatre," *The Guardian*, April 10, 2012.
14 "NT Live," 6.
15 Compare, for example, Trueman.
16 "Beyond Live – Digital Innovation in the Performance Arts," NESTA research briefing, February 2010, available online at www.nesta.org.uk/library/documents/Beyond-Live-report.pdf, accessed November 12, 2013.
17 Auslander, 18–19.
18 "NT Live," 40.
19 Sarah Bay-Chang's article, "Theatre Squared: Theatre History in the Age of Media," *Theatre Topics*, 17.1 (March 2007): 37–50, offers a concise juxtaposition of the different presentational techniques of cinema and theatre.
20 Holdsworth, 8.
21 NT Live, 'About Us', available online at http://ntlive.nationaltheatre.org.uk/about-us, accessed November 12, 2013.

20

From alienation to identity

Transnational communication of Russian-Israeli theatre[1]

Miriam Yahil-Wax

"Them" and "Us"

In Israel, as in other places, there is no deep public awareness of how immigration has changed and continues to change the cultural landscape of the host nation, though international immigration has increased exponentially in the last couple of decades. In this context, the role of the dramaturg as transcultural liaison becomes essential for the global twenty-first-century theatre.

The Israeli imperative of integration is still based on the model of the "melting pot," which is antiquated and bears no relation to reality. This model sees the different nationalities as micro-containers of multicultural society and fixes the classification of "Israelis" (us) versus "New Comers" (them). It is left to the New Comers to combat the misconceptions of the majority society and make it realize the national order is already disrupted by immigration. Gesher Theatre differentiated itself equally from the standard of established multiculturalism (the immigration theatre niche) and from the narrow self-image of the host culture. In breaking away from the standards of cultural purity prescribed by their own nation and the host nation, Gesher created something new: a space of transnational communication.

Historically, Hebrew theatre began in Moscow in 1917 with idealistic Hebrew teachers, supported by Konstantin Stanislavsky, a firm believer in multicultural theatre. Their ensemble, Habima, was soon to become his single most success-ful multicultural project. After a world tour this Zionist company settled in Israel and the niche group became the national theatre. Sixty-three years later, when Gesher burst upon the Israeli scene (as part of the Jewish immigration from the crumbling USSR), Hebrew had come into its own. It was spoken not by immigrant enthusiasts with awe and an accent, but by third-generation native Israelis who had no problem 'reviving' it on a daily basis. Israeli theatre in 1991 had parted with the formerly dominant Russian tradition of the Habima ensemble. It had been dominated for years by local artists and foreign models imported from Western Europe and America. Financial pressures caused the dissolution of ensembles and artistic repertoire had to make room for commercial plays. Gesher landed in this vibrant, Hebrew, indigenous theatre, the eclectic product of the "melting pot" ideology.

Gesher – the company

Many of the Russian immigrants were actors. They did not expect to practice their profession, for language is the actor's main tool, and they did not know Hebrew nor expect ever to know it well enough for the stage. They dreamt of a niche theatre that would perform in Russian for their 1.5 million co-immigrants, and so Gesher was founded. No member of the ensemble spoke Hebrew, few were aware of their Jewish roots, fewer still had any knowledge of Zionism. Still, Gesher interacted inter-culturally with the Israeli audience, from the first performance of *Rosencrantz and Guildenstern Are Dead (ROS/GUIL)*. Out of courtesy to the local press, Gesher provided simultaneous translation into Hebrew. But why invite the local press at all? The Russian spectators couldn't read Hebrew newspapers.

Gesher was instinctively breaking away from the standards of cultural purity prescribed by their own culture and the host culture, and moving into a phase of transition. Being "outsiders" in transition, exiled from their native culture and not yet integrated in the new one, they were "liberated from normative demands … betwixt and between … In this gap between ordered worlds almost anything may happen,"[2] according to anthropologist Victor Turner. For the Israeli audience, on the other hand, watching *ROS/GUIL* with simultaneous translation was like making love with a surrogate, and love it most certainly was, at first sight, because theatre does not communicate through words alone. We were fascinated by a Russian staging of an English play whispered in our ears in Hebrew!

Host culture reception

The day after the opening, all the critics published rave reviews. The Israeli theatre world woke up to a new force pushing through it, aiming straight for the top. "Our" "national cultural order" had been changed overnight because "they" had broken out of the "multicultural niche." A few malcontents faulted the company for performing in Russian: Israel does not need cultural ghettos, Gesher should perform in Hebrew, they said. There it was again, the sad old melting pot. There were enough Russian spectators to keep the theatre going anyway, but limiting the audience would confine it to the multicultural niche, and Gesher had already created, inadvertently, a space of transnational communication. Gesher wanted to keep the Israeli audience that catapulted it from anonymity to fame overnight.

Gesher actors were lucky with the first show, but out of their native element and at a loss as to what to do next. It was clear that the theatre they made now could not be based on the Russian heritage alone; it must be a place for a new cultural construction. Gesher was subconsciously choosing transition, anti-structure, instead of structure and stability, making the existential choice to be "simultaneously members of … two or more groups whose social definitions and cultural norms are distinct from, and often opposed to, one another."[3]

Choosing the borderline

Within a year, after a second production in Russian which was as successful as the first, artistic director Y. Arye made the decision: Gesher will perform in Hebrew for the general Israeli public. Impossible, was my answer when he turned to me to realize this project of cultural translation with the company, no member of which spoke Hebrew. How will the actors manage intonation, timing, phrasing? Not to mention insurmountable obstacles like the Slavic accent, the Slavic lilt, musicality and rhythm of speech, which are the opposite of Hebrew.

I did my best to discourage Y. Arye from this experiment, afraid it would destroy Gesher. In a couple of years the actors would have learned Hebrew, then, maybe, we could try. I cited the historical example of Habima: "Your predecessors were Hebrew teachers first and actors second. Gesher actors are unable to even learn their lines."

"If the actors learn their lines in Hebrew," he challenged me, "will you work with them on the text?"

"Yes, alright, but let's conduct this experiment with the text of the second show, Jean-Claude Grumberg's *Dreyfus File*, not with the verbally sophisticated *ROS/GUIL*. Plus, the characters in Grumberg's play are Polish Jews, the Slavic accent won't be a problem."

Playing in Hebrew

Three weeks later I was invited to hear the result. Each actor was holding a notebook with the phonetic transcript of his/her part in Cyrillic letters. The Hebrew lines had been dictated to them phonetically, and they learned them from the transcripts. And, to my total amazement, they had succeeded in memorizing their parts in Hebrew. But they spoke like parrots. Worse. The accents were heavy, the phrasing and intonation pure Russian. Because each actor learned only his/her lines, they had no idea what their partner was saying, there was no dialogue, no action and reaction, no comic punch lines. My heart sank. With this they could not go on stage. Yet, if they succeeded in memorizing so much mechanically, perhaps I could teach them all of the above, also mechanically. It would be sheer cruelty to turn them down without giving it a try. Soon I realized that though I did not speak Russian, I did have a common language with those excellent actors, the language of theatre. And we had the performance in Russian to guide us: every actor knew what he/she was playing. The show already existed, it was "solved." For the first Hebrew performance we had a tiny audience of thirty spectators. A few minutes into the show I sighed with relief: communication happened. The audience laughed and cried in the right places.

The method

This became "the method," our method, which we invented together. A new play would be rehearsed in Russian. The directorial concept and acting issues would be tackled and resolved in the rehearsal room in Russian. It would have a first run in

Russian, then the performance would be re-done in Hebrew as described above. At the end of the double process we would have the same production in both languages, alternately performed by the same actors in the two different languages. The Russian version would be from three to five hours long. The Hebrew version would be cut to two and a half hours.

Mixed company: The Holocaust Project

The Holocaust Project marked the beginning of a new phase in Gesher's intercultural work. *Dreyfus File* was their first contact with a Jewish subject. *Adam Resurrected* was to be the second. It was an extraordinary endeavor. A group of "outsiders" decides to access, via an Israeli novel, a traumatic collective memory of Jews, which they barely were, having lost this part of their identity under Communism and the collective memory of Israelis, which they were hoping to become someday, but were not yet, and to broach a subject that Israeli theatre tends to avoid.

Adam Resurrected is the story of a German-Jew who was a clown and circus owner. Having survived the Holocaust and gone to Israel, Adam Stein goes in and out of mental institutions, haunted by the role of dog he played for the concentration camp commander to save his own life, by the loss of his wife and disappearance of his daughter. For Gesher's site-specific show a real circus tent was constructed, fully equipped, which served as both the metaphor and the unifying principle of the show. The audience and the performers were in it together. The plot was framed by Adam's mental present, and the action moved back and forth in time between the camp of his past and present-day Israel.

Adam Resurrected has toured major festivals, including Lincoln Center, but mainly, it has fulfilled Gesher's expectations: their particular cultural translation became a new 'script' for ritualized behavior, as well as a main feature of Israeli culture. And they succeeded in snatching both Jewish and Israeli identities for themselves from the daunting topic of the Holocaust.

Adam Resurrected began the Israeli chapter in the life of Gesher, *ROS/GUIL* in Hebrew expanded it to include Israeli actors. When the artistic director wanted to re-do *ROS/GUIL* in my Hebrew translation, I repeated my original objection: there is no way Russian speaking actors can master this particular oevre. After many heated debates, a casting solution was formed: the Russian actors will play all but the two leading roles. Their accent will be no problem in the parts of Players and Court, since the directorial concept satirizes the Soviet theatre and regime respectively in them. Native Hebrew speakers will play the two leads. Thus the verbal wit will work, and the clash between the two worlds of the play will be highlighted. The audience will also notice the metatheatrical parallel to Gesher's bicultural situation.

Rehearsing in Hebrew

Emboldened by the success of *ROS/GUIL* in Hebrew, the Artistic Director decided to take another leap and rehearse a play in Hebrew: Gorky's *The Lower Depths*. I thought it might be possible with this most Russian of plays, precisely because the Russian actors had studied this piece about the *misérables* of turn-of-the-century Russia and appeared in it many times. Instead of the traditional social-criticism approach, Arye wanted to direct *The Lower Depths* as a tragic parody about hopelessly naïve people, who play, drink, dream, and make merry, while their lives go to waste. This time I had to translate the play according to the given directorial concept, not a finished production.

This time the actors would be speaking their lines in Hebrew in rehearsal, and the text would be simultaneously translated back into Russian for the director. He would continue to give directions in Russian and discuss things with the dramaturg/translator in English! Surprisingly, this Babel, this multilingual reversed rehearsal process also worked. How? First, it turned out to be easier for the actors to work on Arye's original concept in translation. In Hebrew, they were less prone to fall back on the stereotypes of this famous play. A fascinating work process developed of dissecting the old clichés and reinventing the play in Hebrew, according to the new concept. The result was original, funny, and very moving. The decision to work on a show in Hebrew completed the shift towards the Israeli audience, which by then constituted the majority of Gesher spectators.

Shortly afterwards, other Israeli actors were invited to join the company. The process of negotiating the host culture begun by the immigrant artists was now being reversed: the host culture acknowledged the immigrant culture's artistic superiority and was prepared to assimilate it.

Village

Still, critics kept faulting Gesher for avoiding Israeli subjects, local plays. It was decided to commission a play for the first time from Israeli playwright J. Sobol. This very political writer proposed to Gesher the story of his childhood village in the pre-state years, during a curious time of World War II, when Europe was at war and the Middle East maintained peace and prosperity. It would be called *Village*. The Israeli actors' input in the rehearsal process turned it into an extended history lesson for their Russian colleagues, who were learning the history of the Zionist pioneers in Palestine while building their roles in the play. Multiculturalism in the plot extended beyond Jewish immigrants, to include the character of an Arab, an English officer, and Italian POWS. Each actor now trained with a separate language coach to overcome the Russian accent and acquire proper Arab, English, and Italian accents respectively.

The opening of *Village* coincided with Israel's 50th anniversary in 1998 and the Oslo Accords. Curiously, the peaceful coexistence in the Middle East of the play during the WWII years looked very much like what we were hoping to have as a result of the Oslo Accords 50 years later. The show was invited to festivals and theatres around the world, from London to New York, from Melbourne to Rome. It is still performed in repertoire in Israel.

Conclusion

By refusing to be packaged as a "national minority theatre," even as it rejected the notion of assimilation in the host culture, Gesher was able to carve out its own special artistic path. Embodying the "passage" of the entire Russian community and daring to play the "social drama" of "transition," they avoided being encapsulated and isolated in the multicultural niche, and drew the host culture into their space of transnational communication. Instead of falling into the well-worn patterns of the "immigrant experience," they made their "strangeness" the main attraction. Instead of being crushed by the obstacle of language, they turned multilingualism into a weapon, transforming the language problems into performance assets. Instead of being intimidated by the host culture, they used the interactive nature of theatre to seduce it. And so, finally, they were able to undergo a transformation of identity, without losing it in the process.

Notes

1 Reprinted with permission from Dr. MiriamYahil-Wax. The original article appeared in *Judaism: A Quarterly Journal of Jewish Life and Thought*, published by TAJC, Winter-Spring (March 24, 2004).
2 Victor W. Turner, *Dramas, Fields and Metaphors: Symbolic Actions in Human Society* (Ithaca, NY: Cornell University Press, 1974), 7–13.
3 Turner, 233.

21

Intercultural dramaturgy

Dramaturg as cultural liaison

Walter Byongsok Chon

They were all standing there beautifully, very funkily clad, in jeans and slinky tops and berets and their hair was all well done, and they all had AK-47s slung over their shoulders and very steely glares as they looked into the camera. I honestly had never seen such an image in my life: feminine, glamorous, intimidating, powerful, belligerent and African. I became completely enthralled. What stories rested behind those eyes. I knew at that moment, I had to endeavor to find out.

(Danai Gurira, Yale Repertory Theatre's program of *Eclipsed*)

Playwright Danai Gurira recalls her inspiration for *Eclipsed*, which was a photo of the Liberian female rebel fighters, including Black Diamond, in *The New York Times*. With that picture in mind, Danai went to Liberia in 2007 and interviewed several women who survived the 14-year-long civil war in the few ways possible for them: as soldiers, like Black Diamond; as "Peace Women," promoting peace and civic education; or as military "wives," who were really sex slaves and housekeepers. *Eclipsed* depicts the lives of five Liberian women at the end of the war, leading to the dethronement of the tyrant President Charles Taylor and the peace agreement among warring parties in August 2003.

Eclipsed, directed by Liesl Tommy, opened at the Yale Repertory Theatre in October 2009. As an M.F.A. student in the department of Dramaturgy and Dramatic Criticism at Yale School of Drama, I was entrusted with the task of serving as production dramaturg for this play. In the conservatory-meets-regional-theatre setting of the Yale Rep, a student dramaturg has to accomplish two primary objectives: to learn through practice; and to perform at the level of professional excellence, with duties including writing the program note, facilitating talks, and providing research in the rehearsal room. In this production, however, the unfamiliar topic of the play and the still lingering relevance of the depicted issues demanded of me, most of all, to expand the role of the dramaturg to cultural liaison.

During the last phase of the Liberian civil war in 2003, I was in my native country, South Korea, serving as an intelligence officer in the Navy. Coverage of Liberia was scarce in the South Korean media, and reports of the women during that period were more insufficient, if at all present. When I entered this project at the Yale Rep, I was a total stranger to the world of this play. What made me feel even stranger was the unexpected and coincidental similarity in the gender and ethnic configuration between the play and the rehearsal room: the play had only female characters, and the only male in the play, the commanding officer (CO), was an offstage character. The director, the playwright, the cast, and even the two stage managers were all female, and I, the dramaturg, was the only male in the rehearsal room. I could not bypass the question of ethnicity, either. With a play set in Liberia, a playwright born to Zimbabwean parents, a director from Cape Town, South Africa, and actors who were respectively from, or grew up in, the Republic of Haiti, Sierra Leone, and Nigeria, I became more conscious of my Korean nationality and more alert to the question, "How could I, as dramaturg, help the play come to life?"

Because of my gender and my actual military experience, I was immediately identified with the character of the CO at the beginning of the rehearsal. The CO is the master of his "wives." When he returns from a battle, he lines them up, calls one of them to bed, and rapes her. According to the script, we only see the chosen wife leave the stage and, after several moments, return and wash herself with a towel. This rape happens several times during the play. The CO never speaks a word or shows his face. Yet he is an overarching, oppressive presence who keeps his wives as property and treats them as sex slaves. The wives are numbered based on their length of time they spent with him. For wives "Number One" and "Number Three," the rape is a routine that they have grown to be nonchalant about. However, for the new wife "Number Four," it is devastating violence. For the CO himself, it is merely a release. He still shows them his kindness by bringing them wigs, dresses, and ornaments that he plundered from civilians. Frequently, the horrific deeds of the CO brought about questions from the actresses like "Why are men like that?" Even as a man who had served in the military, I could only provide my guesses. "You fight a war for 14 years, you just don't know what you're going to turn into," I had to tell them. Though the CO was not a character that developed onstage through the play, he was real to the women in the play, and he needed to be treated as such.

The play focuses on a specific moment in Liberia, and the characters are based on real people that Danai interviewed. Yet the world that Danai created was more than a portrait of the last couple of months before the end of the war. It was an imaginative and dramatic account, reflecting the Liberian culture and sentiment that had been formed through the country's long and complicated history. Getting in touch with the experience of the women in the play required an understanding of Liberia's politics, history, and culture. It was crucial to understand that the characters were living in a country that was related to America from its origin: Liberia was founded by freeborn African-Americans and freed US slaves in 1847, with the name meaning "land of liberty." The women in the play were torn and shattered by the long war, but they still lived with the awareness of their origin: the long bond with America and the longing for freedom. Acting, directing, and understanding these characters, therefore, required a complete embrace of Liberian culture and history as the characters felt it and lived it.

Authenticity was of utmost importance. The director, actors, and designers sought to create a portrait as true as possible. Telling these people's story as they lived it was the only way of providing our service to those who suffered during the war and are still suffering from its aftermath. My research for the creative team included the documented – that is, textual and contextual information – and live footages from video clips and documentaries. Because the background of the play's setting was as unfamiliar to the actors as it was to me, my constant presence in the rehearsal room became both a choice and a necessity. While I, as the dramaturg, was expected to be the literary expert, absorbing the world of the play so that we could access the sorrows and occasional joys of the characters in their dire situation was a journey we were embarking on together.

The dramaturgy packet that I distributed during table work included a wide array of information, including a glossary, Liberia's history and maps, excerpts from Danai's journal in Liberia, and news articles pertaining to the play's events. Still, new questions arose at every rehearsal regarding the specific reality that these characters belonged to. The characters needed an awareness of both the history and culture of Liberia as they had experienced it before the war and the ordeal of the 14-year-long war as they managed to survive it. Understanding the specifics of the script required precision. For example, the actors needed to understand that cassava was the most common and the only affordable food, because rice was too rare and expensive during the war. They also needed to be familiar with the superstitious inclination of the Liberian women, who believed in witches and the medicine man, a herbal doctor who prescribed juju, a magic charm that was believed to protect humans from bullets.

The documented research grew with every new question and gradually prepared the actors to access the characters intellectually. Yet bringing the characters to life required more than knowledge. We needed to see how these characters would speak, think, and act. As a stranger to Liberia myself, how could I have answered when actress Adepero Oduye asked if there was a Liberian etiquette of receiving food from an elder, like in her native Nigeria? Viewing filmed images of the way Liberians lived became a crucial course of our education. We devoted one day of rehearsal to watching two documentaries about the Liberian civil war, *Liberia: An Un-Civil War* (2005) and *Pray the Devil Back to Hell* (2008). By hearing the voices of the women who lost everything in the war and were hanging on to their lives by the minute, we could feel the devastation and despair. On the other hand, interview footage of Etweda Cooper, the head of the Liberian Women's Initiative, showed us how strong and heroic a woman could be in the midst of unimaginable conflict. Her face and voice revealed her determination for peace on any account. The most striking image in the documentaries was that of Black Diamond slapping and chastizing a white male soldier, twice her size. "Firm your jaw," she said, as she slapped him constantly, fixing him with her eyes and blocking his resistance with her other hand. She was fierce and fearless, yet calm and in control. This image turned out to be a strong inspiration for actress Zainab Jah, who portrayed a fierce soldier, nicknamed "Disgruntled," just like Black Diamond.

My relationship with the creative team remained active, as we all committed ourselves to exploring the depth and breadth of the world we were entrusted to create. Under Liesl Tommy's deft direction and due to the actors' dedication, which often brought tears to their eyes, the performance was coming into shape. For my next step, I began thinking about the audience. I could only assume that the patrons would be as unfamiliar with the women of Liberia's civil war as I was at the beginning of rehearsal. My program note was to invite the audience in to the world of the play.

Determining the content of the program note was a challenge. There was only limited space. Also, the program note was the only documented information I could provide for the audience. The audience needed to be educated just as the actors were. Moreover, as I learned in my research, the issues evoked in the play – human rights, especially women's rights, reparations for war victims, and bringing the war's perpetrators to justice – were still, in 2009, not fully resolved. In this respect, I envisioned the program to be a guide that would not only inform but also take the audience experience *beyond* the human drama and toward a higher political, cultural, and historical awareness.

The Yale Rep was gracious to grant me enough space for the program notes. I wrote seven short articles, starting with "Liberia: Tailoring (Then 'Taylor'ing) an African Democracy," a history of Liberia from its origin in 1821 to the 2005 election of Ellen Johnson-Sirleaf, the first female head of state in Africa. The second article, "Betsy Ross æ 7: A Flag for Liberia," was about the women who designed and hand-stitched the Liberian flag in 1847 and the symbolic meaning of the flag. The third article, "Liberian Women and Marriage," described the native practice of polygyny and revealed how the number of a man's wives measured his status and fortune, especially during the civil war, and how women were treated as war trophies and forced into sexual slavery. On Danai's request, I highlighted the sentence, "The UN estimated that approximately 70% of Liberian women had been the victims of sexual violence during the wars." "Liberian Women-At-Arms" introduced how women became soldiers and established themselves as a force to reckon with. Next, in "Path to Peace," I covered the topic of "Peace Women," and their actual role in ending the war. In "War and Peace: Liberia from 1979 to 2003," I provided a timeline, starting from the "Rice Riot" that instigated the military coup in 1979 to the end of the civil war, tracing, in more detail, the steps leading to the peace agreement. For the audience's better understanding of the language, I added "A Small Small Note on Dialect," where I explained the unique characteristics of Liberian English: sometimes, an "oh" sound is added to the ends of words or sentences, "I tink she a witch oh"; and a word might be repeated for emphasis, "I was small small."[1]

As a final touch to the program, I added links to organizations that are "continuing to promote peace in Liberia and further women's rights around the globe," including the United Nations Mission in Liberia, the United Nations Development Fund for Women, and the Women's International League for Peace and Freedom. In providing links to these organizations, the literary manager Amy Boratko and I considered getting brochures from these organizations for patrons to take home. However, we did not proceed with that. Neither the play nor the production asks anyone to take direct action. They simply present the lives of these five women caught in the transition from civil war to the next stage. We shared our hope that the impact of the production would go beyond the theatre, and believed that the contextual information about the play and names of organizations would harness the audience's compassion to make their own efforts for the peace movement.

The Yale Rep production of *Eclipsed* was very well received. *The New York Times* gave it a rave review, and it won the Connecticut Critics Circle Award for Outstanding Production of a Play. In terms of the American theatrical landscape, this production added to the list of productions that same year by African-American female playwrights, joining Lynn Nottage's *Ruined* (the Goodman Theatre/Manhattan Theatre Club) and Tracey Scott Wilson's *The Good Negro* (The Public Theatre).

In New Haven, in special educational discussions, *Eclipsed* raised awareness of a postcolonial African country and the plight of the women there. At pre- and post-show conversations, patrons asked about the current state of these *kinds* of women in Liberia; a few shared their own similar experiences; and several expressed hope that this play would reach wider demographics.

Seeing the potential humanitarian impact of the production confirmed my aspiration for the dramaturg's contribution to reach beyond the rehearsal room and continue after the closing of the production. Learning about Liberia and these phenomenal women, I realized I became part of a community of a different gender and nationality. While the cast members identified me as the CO in the beginning, by the end of the rehearsal, they gave me the nickname, "Wife Number Six." I suppose this meant I was integrated as part of the cast family. Though an outsider to the depicted world, I was, nevertheless, a necessary supporter and commentator who sought to help them navigate their onstage territory and leave a mark on their moment in history.

In navigating my own role as dramaturg in the rehearsal room and in the Yale Rep and New Haven community, I felt my role growing and I eventually performed as cultural liaison. My difference, a challenge in the beginning, gave me a new perspective on how the dramaturg could be instrumental in bridging the gap between cultures. In our global world of varying and often conflicting cultures, dramaturgs should have the courage to embrace and delve deep into the unfamiliar terrain. It is my hope that the dramaturg as cultural liaison can provide guidance in this multicultural world. Even as of 2014, the drama of the Liberian women portrayed in the play still continues. Yet their drama is no longer just their own. Their stage projects a landscape with broader awareness and more humane sensitivity.

Note

1 These quotations are from the script used for the Yale Rep production.

22

The dramaturgical bridge
Contextualizing foreignness in multilingual theatre

Debra Caplan

I begin rehearsal with a seemingly simple question: "Have you ever heard anyone speak Yiddish?" The actors nod their heads. Most are college students, while others are local community members who, for one reason or another, were attracted by the idea of performing in a Yiddish operetta. "From whom? What did it sound like?" "My grandmother spoke a little Yiddish and taught me a few idioms," offers one student. "I know *farklempt* from Saturday Night Live ... that's Yiddish, right?" ventures another. "I'm not sure," pipes up another, "I feel like I *should* know Yiddish because it's the language my great-grandparents spoke, and I know lots of random words, but I'm not sure if I've ever actually heard anyone speak it – as a real language." "Have you ever met anyone your age who speaks Yiddish? Your character's age?" I probe further. The room falls silent. Nobody has.

This was the first rehearsal for a bilingual production of Abraham Goldfaden's classic 1881 Yiddish operetta *Shulamis* at Harvard University, for which I was co-director, producer, and (unofficial) dramaturg. Unlike Goldfaden's nineteenth-century actors and spectators, who were primarily Ashkenazic Jews, most of our production team, performers, and audience members had never heard spoken Yiddish before, let alone seen a Yiddish play. Our actors did not share the common linguistic, historical, and cultural knowledge that enabled Goldfaden's performers to readily interpret the play without a mediator to guide them. In essence, the entire production was a dramaturgical undertaking. If we were going to bring this operetta out of the archives to reach our twenty-first-century audience, the actors were going to have to bridge the gap between their limited knowledge of Yiddish culture and the vibrant tradition represented in *Shulamis*.

Linguistic training and cultural knowledge-building became an integral part of our day-to-day rehearsal process. The actors met with professional Yiddish linguists and took notes on Yiddish inflection while watching films from the 1930s. They visited elderly Jewish residents at a senior center and listened as they related their memories of going to see Yiddish plays in their youth. There were assigned readings and group discussions. Part rehearsal process, part foreign language course, and part class on Jewish literature and culture, *Shulamis* was as much an educational project as a theatrical one. In order to understand their characters and the dialogue, the actors needed to enter into another world, a world that was as foreign to them as anything they had ever come across. As co-director and dramaturg, my primary job was to provide the actors and the production team with a way to access an Eastern European Jewish world that was intimately entwined with a particular body of religious, cultural, and linguistic knowledge. Only then, having fully entered the play ourselves, could we bring it to our audience as a vibrant contemporary piece rather than an archival relic.

The dramaturg working on a bi- or multilingual production faces a different set of tasks and challenges than on the monolingual stage. To what extent does the dramaturg's role overlap with that of the translator? How can the dramaturg support the production team in determining how best to contend with lines, dialogues, or scenes in a foreign language? How can a dramaturg prepare actors to understand and work with foreign language material?

These challenges are only exacerbated when the foreign language in question is, like Yiddish, more foreign than most. Actors working on a play that incorporates German, French, Spanish, Russian, or another "major" European language might reasonably be expected to have some familiarity with these languages: a sense of how the language sounds and a basic understanding of its literature and culture at minimum. Barring that, the production team would have a variety of external resources readily available that they could use to educate themselves: films, textbooks, audio tracks, language-learning software, dialect and accent guides, etc. With a lesser known language like Yiddish, however, the dramaturg must contextualize the world of the play starting virtually from scratch. He or she cannot rely upon the actors having any basic familiarity with the cultural or linguistic world of the play, nor point the production team to a ready array of resources for language learning and research. The dramaturg with specialized linguistic/cultural knowledge thus bears an extra-ordinary responsibility for shaping the performers' *perception* of the play, far more so than in a monolingual production where everyone enjoys more or less equal access to a raw body of textual material. In a production that employs a minority language, the linguistic barrier is indicative of the degree to which the actors and their audience are removed from the cultural world of the play. Dramaturgy in this context, then, is as much an act of interlingual and intercultural translation as it is a matter of contextualizing a particular drama.

In short, multilingual dramaturgy is the realm of theatre practice where cultures converse and collide. As such, the polyglossic dramaturg offers us a new way of thinking about what it is exactly that dramaturgs *do*. For in this sort of dramaturgy the precise role of the dramaturg may be more complicated, but it is also magnified. Dramaturgs have often been compared to midwives who bring the text of a play to life.[1] But for the dramaturg working on a polyglossic production, it would be more accurate to compare his or her role to that of an intercultural ambassador, whose job is to build pathways between cultures that are foreign to one another. In this context, the dramaturg's typical role – to represent and contextualize the world of the play – is heightened and magnified by the inaccessibility of the "foreign" linguistic atmosphere.

The dramaturg working on the macaronic stage thus requires a specialized toolkit that reflects the particular responsibilities and challenges of the multilingual milieu. Here are the guiding principles and tools of the multilingual dramaturg's craft as I see it. All of these principles are quintessential elements of standard dramaturgical practice as well, but are particularly salient within the context of a polyglossic production.

Dramaturgy is a mode of translation

Even when a translation of the non-English components is readily available, the dramaturg working on a multilingual production is constantly engaging in acts of translation, both *inter*lingual (from one language to another) and *intra*lingual (retranslating already translated terms and references to enhance comprehension). The dramaturg must thus negotiate between the demands of a variety of roles and must determine his or her relationship to any existing translation and/or any translator formally involved with the project. Just as the theatre translator must simultaneously consider the play's production and reception history alongside linguistic, historical, and cultural references in preparing the translation, so too must the dramaturg consider how best to convey (that is, translate) this network of allusions and semiotics into something that the performers – and, ultimately, spectators – can access.[2]

Strategize foreignness

As Barbara Thornbury has proposed, there are three primary strategies for dealing with "foreignness" in multilingual theatre. First, one can "advocate surrender" by granting performers and audiences permission to enjoy the production without fully understanding it. Alternatively, a production can take as its starting point that there are some things that do not require a translation. Finally, a production can resist the entire apparatus of translation and assert that true intercultural communication is not possible.[3]

While it is often the job of the director to *choose* how to negotiate with "foreignness" in the production, it is the dramaturg – as interpreter from one cultural world to another – who is primarily responsible for *implementing* the strategy. This aspect of the dramaturg's role must be understood by every member of the production team.

Cultivate awareness

Often in a multilingual production, the dramaturg is the sole member of the production team who can fully access the linguistic and cultural world of the play. The multilingual dramaturg thus must pay close attention to how his or her own presence, as a cultural ambassador of sorts, affects how this world is perceived. This often requires a delicate balancing act, where the dramaturg must carefully cultivate his or her reputation as an authentic and loyal translator, while also remaining conscious of the fact that bringing a play to life in a language that is not its own is an uphill battle.

Embrace the challenge

There are always an infinite number of ways that a play could be staged, but in the case of a multilingual production, questions of authenticity come into even sharper focus. There are, of course, an infinite number of ways to represent a foreign language and culture on stage. Should foreign words/concepts be translated or retained? What dialect should actors learn? Should there be supertitles or simultaneous translation devices to help the audience understand? Each of these tactics has its advantages and disadvantages, and each becomes part of the audience's experience of the play. When it comes to multilingual productions, as Thornbury has written of Japanese-language theatre productions in the United States, "there is no neutral stance: language ... inevitably calls attention to itself – and elicits a response."[4] No multilingual production can fully escape a lingering sense that there is artifice at play. But the best polyglossic productions embrace these challenges as creative fodder.

Understanding how dramaturgs work within a multilingual context is more relevant then ever, as the constant intercultural interactions of our globalized era have made polyglossic theatre increasingly prevalent around the world.[5] Reconsidering the role of the dramaturg in this context offers us a more nuanced way of understanding what dramaturgy is capable of in any production, multilingual or not.

Notes

1 Peter Hay, "American Dramaturgy: A Critical Re-Appraisal," *What Is Dramaturgy?*, ed. Burt Cardullo (New York: Peter Lang Publishing, 1995), 79. As Tamsen Wolff has demonstrated, dramaturgy has traditionally been "distressingly gendered." See Tamsen Wolff, "Women's Work: Gender and Dramaturgy," *Theatre Topics* 13.1 (March 2003): 103.
2 Anthony Meech, "Brecht's *The Threepenny Opera* for the National Theatre: A 3p Opera?" in *Staging and Performing Translation*, eds. Roger Baines, Cristina Marinetti, and Manuela Perteghella (New York: Palgrave Macmillan, 2011), 126.
3 Barbara E. Thornbury, "Negotiating the Foreign: Language, American Audiences, and Theatre from Japan," *Theatre Journal* 61.2 (May 2009): 250.
4 Thornbury, 250.
5 Marvin Carlson, *Speaking in Tongues: Languages at Play in the Theatre* (Ann Arbor: University of Michigan Press, 2009), 17.

23

Reading and (re)directing "racial scripts" on and beyond the stage

Faedra Chatard Carpenter

The Literary Managers and Dramaturgs of the Americas (LMDA)'s 2012 conference in Atlanta cast a determined spotlight on the issues of class and race. Notably, many of the conversations and events circulated around the issue of race as expressed through quantifiable representation. This observation is not a critique or condemnation. On the contrary, the need to consider race in terms of the inclusion or exclusion of raced bodies not only adheres to the spectacular worlds of theatre and performance, but it is a concern worthy of due and consistent attention. In deference to this practical truth, organized dialogues on race by theatre practitioners often ask us to consider the ways our institutional dramaturgy impacts the production and dissemination of racialized narratives. While issues of quantitative representation (a tangible presence in terms of season programming, artistic leadership, casting choices, and audience demographics) are important lines of inquiry, this essay aims to underscore how our storytelling and dramaturgical practices can also cultivate work with greater complexity and cultural sensitivity.

It is my contention that dramaturgs and directors should remain diligent in reflecting upon the ways that "racial projects" (that is, plays and performances that pointedly address the issue of race) are implicated and influenced by our *racial projects* – a sociological term coined by Michael Omi and Howard Winant. By remaining conscientious of the still-pervasive race-bias within our social (and literary) dramas, theatre practitioners are positioned to redirect the process and processing of both kinds of racial scripts, thereby nuancing public understandings of difference on and beyond the stage. Moreover, my hope is that the attention given to racial projects in this essay will provide a means for readers to think through myriad forms and issues related to staging "difference" within American theatre. This consideration of diversity and inclusion not only extends to the routinely acknowledged matrices of race, gender, sexuality, class, and (dis)ability, but it also encompasses the ever-increasing need to address regional, national, and international identities in the age of globalization.

Parsing the racial through-line: definitions, projects, and scripts

The critical race theorists Michael Omi and Howard Winant offer their readers a concise and useful working definition of *race*: "[R]ace is a concept which signifies and symbolizes social conflicts and interests by referring to different types of human bodies."[1] Acknowledging how this fundamental concept of race has been used to articulate and explain human difference in a number of contrasting ways, Omi and Winant also explicate how the idea of race powerfully impacts our social organizations and identificatory practices. To this end, they articulate how racial projects function to manufacture and promote ideologies that link social structures and cultural representations: "A racial project is simultaneously an interpretation, representation, or explanation of racial dynamics, and an effort to recognize and redistribute resources along particular racial lines."[2] This assertion helps to reveal why the notion of race – wholly dependent upon specific contexts and agendas – is such a slippery and capacious term. Moreover, it also speaks to how racial projects (that is, race-centric ideologies that foster material consequences) may be reinforced or undermined through both theatrical and metatheatrical means.

Building upon these understandings, it behooves us to take advantage of how dramaturgical research, artistic choices, and communal exchanges can be consciously utilized to construct and/or deconstruct racial narratives (as well as other narratives concerning human difference), while also highlighting how the world of theatre is positioned to disseminate or aggravate the socially inscribed roles animated in both life and art. To best illustrate this exploration, I turn to a specific case study: a recent production of Matthew Lopez's play *The Whipping Man* at Center Stage in Baltimore, MD. *The Whipping Man* – recognized by *American Theatre* magazine as one of the most produced plays during the 2011–12 theatre season – serves as a fruitful example with which to think through the processing and production of "racial scripts."

The Whipping Man, set in 1865 in Richmond, Virginia at the end of the Civil War, focuses on three self-identified Jews who, despite their dilapidated surroundings and meager resources, attempt to celebrate Passover, thereby commemorating the Jews' exodus from Egypt and deliverance from slavery. Strikingly, each man possesses intimate knowledge of forced servitude. While all three men know the travails of slavery through the study of their Judaic faith, they have also *experienced* slavery in divergent ways. Caleb, a severely wounded Confederate soldier and Sephardic Jew, is the former slave master of his two Black companions: John, a strong-minded young man; and Simon, an older, patriarchal figure.

When serving as the production dramaturg for Center Stage's production of *The Whipping Man*, I soon realized that Lopez's play offered a rich text with which to interrogate and destabilize familiar, racialized narratives. After all, *The Whipping Man* dramatizes a tale about Black Jews, thereby spotlighting a multi-faceted identity that is substantiated by "real-life" exemplars as well as historical facts. Moreover, the play itself – as a marketable product – resists convenient labeling. Written by a Puerto Rican playwright and featuring representations of African-American, Jewish-American, and Antebellum Southern culture, Lopez's drama troubles the categories that theatre practitioners often rely on when attempting to satisfy a particular demographic or community. The syncretic blend of experiences, perspectives, and ideologies embedded throughout the text defies the typical taxonomies that are all too often placed on dramatic literature (in other words, one would be cautioned against applying the singular label of a "Black play," a "Latino play," or a "Jewish Play" to *The Whipping Man*). These observations, however, reveal a certain truth: *The Whipping Man* is a distinctly *American* play that presents theatre practitioners with the opportunity (and perhaps the inspiration) to further dismantle boxes, transgress color lines, and cross borders.

Nevertheless, when fully considering the intricacies of *The Whipping Man*, Lopez's play proves itself to be both promising and problematic because even as it pointedly refashions familiar racial scripts, it simultaneously reinforces them. In dramatizing the presence of Black Jews in the Confederate South, the play aims to complicate expectations regarding the existence and construction of racial and religious identities. Yet, just as *The Whipping Man* examines under-explored aspects of American history and identities, the efficiency of the play's telling leaves the work especially susceptible to interpretive shortcuts and characterizations that fall into recognizable archetypes.[3]

Cognizant of the play's potential snares, Kwame Kwei-Armah (Center Stage's artistic director and the director of the production in question) pursued artistic choices that purposefully complicated the presentation of the play's narratives. While staying true to Lopez's script, Kwei-Armah capitalized on select moments, engaging in acts of disidentification by working "on and against dominant ideology" in order to "transform a cultural logic from within."[4] Pointedly working to disrupt assumptions gleaned by the available circumstances and characterizations, I would argue that it was Kwei-Armah's careful and conscientious direction that truly buttressed *The Whipping Man*'s potential to re-vision familiar tropes rather than substantiate them.

Kwei-Armah's intention to work on and against familiar racial scripts in *The Whipping Man* became apparent within our first dramaturgy meeting. When our conversation turned to the play's characters, we discussed how easy it would be for actors and audiences to conjure well-worn stereotypes. For example, when it came to the character of Simon, we recognized the potential for this older character to be read as exceedingly attentive, forgiving, and possibly even content with his circumstances – an embodied cliché of Harriet Beecher Stowe or Joel Chandler Harris proportions.[5] While the play's penultimate scene may obscure this possible reading, this eventual peek into Simon's complexity may come too late to be fully recognized.

In parsing through the play's characters and all the interpretive possibilities, it became clear that the production needed to make all of the characters' ideological tensions readily apparent. In service of this aim, a great deal of my dramaturgical research focused on uncovering and highlighting the dialectics and debates found *within* the play, as well as those pertinent to the time and cultures *signified* by the play. Among these lines of interest: the contested characterization of Abraham Lincoln. It is Simon, in fact, who speaks of meeting the recently assassinated Abraham Lincoln with seemingly unadulterated admiration – a sentiment that is somewhat challenged by John. However, in researching the play and reading past versions of the script, I was intrigued by the fact that earlier versions of *The Whipping Man* featured an extended debate between Simon and John, one that pointedly addressed whether Lincoln warranted African-American adulation. Buoyed by this discovery and further inspired by the director's own interest in Lincoln's debatable legacy, I used Abraham

Lincoln as an explanatory centerpiece for the ensemble's resource packets as well as for the theatre's lobby display.[6] Accordingly, Lincoln became a translatable symbol with which to understand the characters in *The Whipping Man*: a resonant example of complex viewpoints and conflicted narratives bound within one body.

While the production benefitted from in-depth conversations and dramaturgical material to help underscore *The Whipping Man's* latent complexities, Kwei-Armah also crafted moments within his production to endow the play with richer subtext. For example, in one scene the play's stage directions indicate that John (the younger black character) dramatically exits after delivering an emotionally charged diatribe to his former slave master. However, rather than removing John completely from the scene as suggested in the script, Kwei-Armah artfully directed John to exit "outside," allowing him to reappear through the set's living room windows. Maintaining the silence indicated in the script, Kwei-Armah then orchestrated Simon to follow John, at which point an inaudible, yet fiery, exchange ensued.

This brilliant "dumb-show" augmented the dramatic stakes and heightened the play's subtext, opening new ways for audience members to read the individual tenacity of Simon and John, as well as understand, more fully, the tensions and tenderness that undergirds their relationship. Moreover, this staged confrontation also consciously worked against potential misreadings of Simon by redirecting audience attention to identify the grit and strategy implicit in Kwei-Armah's vision of Simon.

For me, however, one of the most exceptional examples of Kwei-Armah's resistance to clichéd readings of race-related narratives was expressed through the use of a single, haunting image. The image was a fleeting projection of the oft referenced, but never embodied Sarah. Sarah, the daughter of Simon, is also Caleb's "lover" (of course, referencing her as such conjures welcomed debate: can a man *love* a woman he owns? Can a woman truly *love* her owner?). In accepting the complicated and sticky, however, Center Stage's production necessarily embraced the contention that Caleb believed that he loved Sarah (the quality and nature of that love, of course, is still a matter of dispute).

The inspired decision to include an image of Sarah was a design element of Kwei-Armah's own divining. Although the script never calls for this visage, its inclusion offered a powerful intervention in terms of common narratives. To remind audiences of Sarah's presence within the play's homosocial space – a space dominated by male energies and bodies – was to remind audiences, in an immediate and profoundly palpable way, of the women who were equally entangled (if not more so) in the machinations of a heterosexist and racist society. To my mind, however, the greatest significance attributed to this visual intervention was the image itself. The picture Kwei-Armah selected to portray Sarah was a simple photo of a notably dark-skinned Black woman. I recall being struck – and delighted – by this chosen image, for it was not until I saw it that I realized the ways in which it countered the vision of Sarah residing in the crevices of my own subconscious. I was immediately confronted with the realization that my Sarah – the Sarah of my imagination – bore the likes of a loaded stereotype: a light-skinned "house negro." Admittedly, I, too, had fallen into a trap of a faulty and over-popularized narrative, thereby unconsciously picturing Sarah as a woman whose visage conveniently conjured familiar tales of a "tragic mulatta." Such a vacuous and instantaneous conceit is not only painfully formulaic, but it belies the very complexities that I have long argued for others to understand and recognize, thus reminding me of the need to remain wary of the way racial scripts encroach upon even the most diligent of scholars, artists, and audiences.

We are all, in fact, susceptible to the assumption and perpetuation of racial scripts, a fact that was repeatedly brought to my attention during *The Whipping Man*'s run. Despite our most arduous and noble efforts, there were a number of post-show discussions that reminded me of why our endeavors to complicate the play's surface narratives – though not entirely effective – were necessary mediations. Case in point: the evening in which an audience member freely assigned a number of troubling, and implicitly race-tinged, attributes to the character of John. Among his matter-of-fact assessments was that John was distressingly "lazy."

John, a man who fiercely aspired to escape his forced servitude, a man who strategized to expand his mind despite the containment of his body – lazy? Damaged and addicted, perhaps, yes – but *lazy*? While I was startled by this patron's assertions, I was also aware of the decrepit racial scripts that undoubtedly shaped his perception of John. I quickly understood where this notion of laziness came from, and – more important – I knew what I needed to say to disrupt and reframe this voiced vision. I knew that, historically, the accusation of laziness was frequented upon enslaved Blacks who – in ways great and small – expressed resistance to their oppression. The account of the "lazy slave" was initially propagated by slave masters to characterize disobliging human chattel. Post-slavery, narratives of the "lazy *slave*" soon morphed into the "lazy *Black*", thereby becoming a defiling descriptor used to typify free Blacks with hopes to deny African-Americans full rights and active citizenship.

Suffice it to say, I certainly do not think the theatre patron understood the perilous nature of his chosen reading or its myriad manifestations. I do not believe he was conscious of the racial script he so readily adopted. And so, as a dramaturg and cultural mediator, I did not admonish him but rather opened the conversation to broaden conceptual possibilities. Given the opportunity to address this potential reading of John I took full advantage of the stage, passionately and enthusiastically re-directing the voiced perceptions by focusing on the historical, textual, and production elements that relinquished John from the annals of "laziness" and championed him as the epitome of a "righteous rebel."

Center Stage's production of *The Whipping Man* serves as an example of how an artistic ensemble may consciously intervene and redirect the processing of familiar racial scripts, both on and off the stage. Dramaturging *The Whipping Man* offered me innumerable opportunities to read, re-think, and re-direct a number of cultural tropes and, in the process, reminded me of the obligation that dramaturgically minded practitioners (directors, dramaturgs, designers, and actors) have to question even the most comfortable assumptions. This is particularly pressing in our age of globalization – a time that demands both sensitivity and fluency beyond both demographic and geographic borders. Dramaturgs are charged with taking the time to consider all valid possibilities rather than impetuously settling on the suspected, known, or overly anticipated. Such proactive interrogations not only aid in creating artful theatre productions, but they also empower our stories to intervene, adjust, and correct archaic and/or erroneous perceptions about human difference and social networks in everyday life.

Notes

1 Michael Omi and Howard Winant, *Racial Formation in the United States: From the 1960s to the 1990s* (New York: Routledge, 1994), 55.
2 Omi and Winant, 56.
3 The parsing and the articulation of these thoughts are deeply indebted to conversations with the resident dramaturg and associate artistic director of Center Stage, Gavin Witt.
4 For more on practices of "disidentification," see José Muñoz's *Disidentifications: Queers of Color and the Performance of Politics* (Minneapolis: University of Minnesota Press, 1999), 11.
5 Joel Chandler Harris, an Atlanta-based journalist and writer, was the creator of the "Uncle Remus" character initially popularized through a series in the *Atlanta Constitution Journal* in the late 1880s. Harriet Beecher Stowe created the "Uncle Tom" character that originated in the now-canonized *Uncle Tom's Cabin* (1852).
6 Of note is that Kwei-Armah's own interest in "the Lincoln debate" was evidenced by the fact that during auditions for Simon, he requested that actors play *against* the laudatory sentiments when they voiced Simon's lines concerning Lincoln. Unsurprisingly, the actor who best performed this exercise was offered the role of Simon.

24
Transcultural dramaturgy methods

Judith Rudakoff

When artistic engagement occurs without shared mythic or cultural references are there dramaturgical tools that can help bridge the intercultural gaps? With this question in mind, I developed and have applied transcultural methods and exercises that employ archetypal iconography and universally understood values as a way to initiate artistic exploration. These methods focus on the self as creative resource and on articulating relationships with and understanding home. Much of my recent investigative and developmental work in this area was made possible by *Common Plants: Cross Pollinations in Hybrid Reality*, a multidisciplinary, transcultural, research-creation project funded by Canada's Social Science and Humanities Research Council (SSHRC). I conceived and led this project as principle investigator from 2006–9. *Common Plants* cultivated the following dramaturgical principles:

- creative resources reside within the self;
- we must exercise our own voices, within our own context;
- to affect change, we must identify and articulate who we are, where we are, and how we relate to our landscape;
- we must engage with and speak to those outside of our context for our message to be heard;
- listening is as important as speaking;
- this project lives in a garden, where cross-pollination is vital to survival: art is the last line of defense in the war against cultural obliteration.

Common Plants engaged with groups of specifically located participants in geographically distant places, such as South Africa and Iqaluit, Nunavut in Canada's Far North, and then linked their development process and creative outcomes through a dedicated website. Many examples of the variety of work undertaken and evolved during *Common Plants* may be viewed in their entirety at www.yorku.ca/gardens.

During this project, participants could view each other's uploaded work, some of which had been created simultaneously in different locations, as well as interact on the website's Common Ground Forum,[1] to share observations, comment on each other's work, and document their own process. Some participants also posted regularly on personal blogs in the website's BLOGarden, often revealing personal and artistic discoveries made during the project.[2] The electronic component of *Common Plants* did not replace the immediate experience of place in performance with the virtual experience of the Internet. It sought ways to make use of both: valuing the sensory, concrete experiences and actions of people in local places while enabling them to interact and communicate across vast distances of electronic space. The virtual site also offered participants different perspectives on the familiar.

Common Plants aimed to offer participants "cross pollination": juxtaposing, inter-secting, inventing the individualized world of each performance, viewed through the artist participants' specific experiential and cultural filters in a hybrid, global context. Many participants from different geographical locations were, for example, overly dependent on Internet access, listened to the same popular American music, adopted the same fashion codes, spoke or texted on the same cellphones, and referred to the same contemporary iconography. They also shared a curiosity about the rest of the world and a need to know that their immediate concerns and daily challenges were not theirs alone. There was also a common need to discuss what home represented and how it was located, defined, and, in some cases, remembered from a distance imposed by time or space.

One of the exercises I dramaturged under the umbrella of *Common Plants* was *The Ashley Plays*, a series of cycles of untitled, short, original plays linked by a common theme and disseminated virtually. Between 2006 and 2008, groups of par-ticipants created independent cycles of Ashley plays that reflected their cultural and individual responses to core questions that were proposed to each participating group or individual: What is home? Is home a place? Is home a person? Where do you locate home? Engagement with these questions shaped the thematic through-line for all the plays in the cycles.

The *Common Plants* website provided a means of distributing these cycles and allowed participants from North America, Europe, Africa, and India to view each other's work and to discuss and reflect on their observations on the forum and in the blogs. The outcome was a greater understanding of similarity within difference and the common values, challenges, and concerns that were shared. By offering participants the distance and filter of the Ashley characters through which to speak, the telling of personal stories and reflections on home became less difficult, especially in a public arena.

Some of the plays in the various cycles were unconventional in form. While I have dramaturged many live, wholly performative Ashley cycles in other contexts, this transcultural *Common Plants* series included both cycles that were performative and others that were comprised of text, photography, and sometimes video. The use of the term "play" in the context of this exercise was non-traditional. This flexibility ensured that transmission of personal reflections on home was not hampered by unfamiliarity with theatrical form. Character voice, dramatic narrative, context, and action created dramatic containers for each offering regardless of the final presentation format.

The specific method for creating an Ashley cycle is fairly basic. Each play in an Ashley cycle requires the creation of the world of the play. To facilitate this process, a date is selected by participants and they are then responsible for researching the global, national, regional, and local context for that date. While all the information gathered does not have to appear in each individual play in the cycle, no facts can be contradicted. Each play in a cycle must be about a character named Ashley, who can be male, female, transgender, inanimate, or a genderless spirit. Because plays are linked thematically, not by linear narrative, the Ashley characters vary from play to play in each cycle. Ashley does not have to be present as a character in each play, but must be the focus of the plot. (When I first developed *The Ashley Plays*, I chose the name Ashley for this central character for several reasons: the name is non–gender specific; it is easy to pronounce in many languages; and it has equivalents in many cultures).

The Ashley character is inspired by a collaboratively created profile that participants in the cycle delineate. This set of provocative characteristics is intended to offer each play-making group within a cycle further inspiration for their individual play and their specific Ashley. As with the given circumstances, not all the character profile details have to be included in the creation of each individual Ashley, but no characteristics in the profile can be contradicted. When contributors to a cycle are not located in the same geographical place, the selection of the given circumstances and Ashley profile can be accomplished through e-mail communication.

Here is an example of an Ashley profile created this way for a cycle by a group that included participants who identified as being from the following countries (some of whom were living in Toronto, Canada): Cameroon, Jamaica, India, Iran, Iraq, Israel, and South Africa. This cycle was developed between July 26 and August 26, 2008. This entire cycle of plays can be viewed online at www.yorku.ca/gardens.[3]

Ashley is trying to figure out where or what home is.
Ashley rides a bicycle.
Ashley has a scar that is embarrassing.
Ashley feels transparent in the world at large.
Ashley has no electricity in her/his house.
Ashley loves to swim.
Ashley may or may not survive.
Ashley enjoys the four seasons, especially autumn.
Ashley once ran away.
Ashley is getting older but doesn't mind.
Ashley's home is burning.
Ashley has vivid, potent, and fantastical dreams.
Ashley is a survivor.
Ashley is anti-social.
Ashley keeps a collection.
Ashley has a secret obsession with stealing.
Ashley has spent time in another country.
Ashley has lost a dear relationship in the last three years.
Ashley is a hypocrite.

Because some of the participants in the international *Common Plants* Ashley cycles were not primarily writers or, in some cases, artists, the generation of text called for developmental dramaturgy exercises that did not require advanced skills or even prior evidence of writing talent. Further, I had to configure exercises that would be applicable simultaneously in a variety of cultures and situations. To this end, I used methods I call The Four Elements and Image Flash. The first method uses air, earth, water, and fire as templates for analyzing behavior, action, and characterization in plays, and also for stimulating the creation of narrative and character. This transcultural method is detailed in my essay entitled "The Four Elements: New Models for a Subversive Dramaturgy"[4] which explains:

> My distinctly non-scientific guides to The Four Elements ... have been developed from a multiplicity of sources, including empirical observation, orally transmitted, non-attributed neo-pagan teachings, the study of earth-based spiritual belief systems and mythological references from world cultures. These Element guides provide a starting point for individualized application: the key to this work is personalization and adaptation. The guides pertain both to the element itself and also place the element in particular power relationships with the other elements.[5]

The Image Flash method asks participants to focus on a remembered event or a visual cue (like a photograph) and quickly write a list of succinct images. By providing a catalog of images, this text-generating exercise results in a large amount of cues without expanding on the story of each specific image. The goal is for the Image Flash list to act as a creative menu for later use, when the image is ready to be mined and integrated into a work. Because the emphasis in this exercise is on chronicling rather than editing and revising, even participants who did not identify as writers found themselves exceeding personal expectation by generating evocative text fragments. Some participants in various Ashley cycles wrote Image Flash exercises in the voice of their Ashley character and later incorporated the images or stories inspired by the images into their individual play. In some cases, the Image Flash writing became part of the text of an Ashley play in a cycle.

During the creation of the July–August 2007 Ashley cycle, participants from five continents, over three time zones, discussed their process electronically. This global dramaturgy session on the Common Ground Forum among participants located in distant geographical sites offered perspective on the work as well as new opportunities for creative interplay. As in other cases of connection between groups from very different backgrounds during *Common Plants* exercises, participants found common concerns and challenges that allowed them to communicate and offered them an unanticipated sense of belonging to a community. Some of the topics discussed on the forum in relation to their Ashley plays were food, hair, heritage, danger and safety, racism, individual voice, and, of course, home.

Here is a sample post from the topic titled "Talking AS Ashley," in which participants in the July–August 2007 cycle wrote in the voice of their emerging Ashley character,

> Wrote a letter to her trying to explain why I did the things I did.
> Tried to make her understand who I was, where I'm coming from. Where MY HOME was.
> She instead, decided to make a joke about it.
> Made me look and feel like a fool.

There are stories about forgiving and forgiveness.
Forgiving fools
Foolish forgiving

Jackie Manyaapelo, Cape Town, South Africa
Posted: Mon Jul 16, 2007 8:14 am

Here is a sample of a post from the topic titled "Talking ABOUT Ashley," in which participants discussed their evolving collaboration,

> I keep getting this image of little ants digging tunnels and all of them meeting in one section where the tunnels merge. Just for a few moments of their busy day. Then they carry on in their own ways. The tunnel is forever altered though. It has a meeting place. They will likely never return all together to that meeting place – not all at the same time. But when they each return on their own they are reminded of those they met, the memories that they made, the stories that were shared.

Thank you all!!!
Heather Annis, Toronto, Ontario, Canada
Posted: Mon Jul 16, 2007 9:02 am

In the Common Ground Forum, during and after the creation of concurrent Ashley cycles, conversations emerged that showed transcultural bonding over the central questions about home. Here is a short exchange between Iranian-Canadian Sina Gilani and Mfundo Tshazibane (writing as "undo"), a Xhosa man from South Africa:

Untitled
Sina
Joined: 11 Jun 2007
Posts: 18
Posted: Tue Jun 12, 2007 9:36 pm

hi all.

my name is sina. i have two last names!!! Moyer, or P.Gilani.

i was born in Iran. i moved to england when i was 6. i came to canada 2 1/2 years ago. i've also lived in france, spain, china, and italy, but for short periods of time.

i think home is a really nice place, and i wish that i find one.
ps:i hate cockroaches!

– – – – – – – – –

HI this is Sina.

_____

sinethemba
undo
Joined: 10 Jul 2006
Posts: 20
Posted: Sat Jun 16, 2007 3:05 pm

Molweni,
Just thot i shud say one or two
things to Sina here. My brother,
One
You do have a home!
i grew up in township dat i don't
regard as my home but whether
i like it or not dat place did and
possibly still contributes to my concept of
home
but we'll talk about dat later.

two
i have a thing for names my friend
and i was looking at yours and thought
what could your name possibly be in my
language; Xhosa.

You can take that thought further and say
i was trying to bring you closer to home
or i was trying to find out how related i am
to you.

the word Si for us is WE in English and Na is
used in many different ways and one of
them is 'Nake nadibana?'
meaning, 'have YOU met?' and so forth.

However what i came up with is
Sinethemba
this name is given to boys and girls and it
means
'we have hope'.
Sine (we have)
Themba (hope).

thot i shud share dat with you.

– – – – – – – – –

Undo
'what is done can't be undone'.

156

Acknowledging their need to locate and retain home, working through the self as primary resource, sharing emotional memories and chronicling present challenges created a place without boundaries where everyone could claim citizenship and declare agency. The goals of the Ashley play cycles are to provide a collaboratively formed creative environment where the specificity of individual voice is strongly present. For participants in *Common Plants*, learning that people from distinct cultures shared questions, concerns, and challenges despite the overwhelming amount of differences between them was empowering.

Of course, generating the work was only part of this process. Responding to the work of geographically distant and culturally distinct co-creators through the online forum became part of the collaborative process, opening possibilities for knowledge transfer, engagement, and communication across a multitude of boundaries and borders. While difference was clearly tied to such influences as location, economic and social circumstances, the participants recognized sameness within that difference, which resulted in articulated feelings of community and belonging. The participants had established bridges between their worlds.

Notes

1 The Common Ground Forum host no longer exists, so the hundreds of pages of conversations are, unfortunately, no longer accessible online.
2 To view a sampling of the blogs, go to http://www.yorku.ca/gardens. Click on BLOGarden. Click on the icon for the blog you wish to view.
3 To view these plays, go to http://www.yorku.ca/gardens. Click on *The Ashley Plays*. Scroll through the list of available cycles and click on the icon for the specific cycle you wish to view. Follow the onscreen instructions to view individual plays in each cycle.
4 Judith Rudakoff, "The Four Elements: New Models for a Subversive Dramaturgy," *Theatre Topics* 13(1) (March 2003): 143–53.
5 Rudakoff, 144.

25

The dramaturgical process and global understanding

Robyn Quick

In *The Price of Empire* (1989), Senator J. William Fulbright describes his belief that international educational exchange will lead participants to "some feeling and understanding of other peoples' cultures – why they operate as they do, why they think as they do, why they react as they do – and of the differences among these cultures."[1] Fulbright saw great implications in this experience for the future of the world: "It is possible – not very probable, but possible – that people can find in themselves, through intercultural education, the ways and means of living together in peace."[2] The insight and empathy he sought, along with its potential to contribute to a more harmonious future for the planet, can also be cultivated in educational settings through the dramaturgical process. The dramaturg's questioning spirit, applied to the world of a play from a country other than one's own, can serve as a point of departure for a meaningful engagement with that culture.

I put this idea into practice in my position as a dramaturg and professor at Towson University in Baltimore, when I initiated and coordinated the New Russian Drama Project, a three-year venture to bring members of our community into conversation with Russian society through the study and production of contemporary Russian plays. As a Fulbright Senior Scholar in Moscow during the fall of 2011, I took the reverse journey and involved Russian students in a study of recent American plays that were being presented in Russian translation at professional theatres in that country. In both instances, we employed dramaturgical activities of textual analysis that opens up questions about the plays, research to help understand the context and specific cultural references utilized by each playwright, and audience engagement activities to help expand our understanding of the plays and their world.

The New Russian Drama Project was the result of a collaboration between Philip Arnoult's Center for International Theatre Development (CITD) and the Towson University Department of Theatre Arts from 2007–10.[3] Together with partners in both countries, we created and disseminated English-language translations of contemporary Russian plays, offered extensive coursework connected to the plays, produced a Russian season at the university, and hosted a conference to encourage production of the plays in professional US theatres.[4] The project focused on plays that were written in Russia by the first generation to reach adulthood since the fall of the Soviet Union.

Although quite varied in style and content, the plays frequently feature young characters, frank language, and contemporary social issues – characteristics that we thought would speak to the interests and sensibilities of college students in the United States. At the same time, we imagined the plays taking these young people on a journey into unfamiliar features of life in contemporary Russia. This idea was to prove effective in engaging Towson University students with Russian life and culture.

Our application of the dramaturgical process to new drama from Russia formed the basis of several different kinds of learning experiences throughout the project. Student actors, designers, technicians, and audience members engaged in a page-to-stage journey of ten plays through readings, workshops, and full productions. Coursework included, among others, the team-taught interdisciplinary Russian Theatre and Politics, which explored Russian cultural identity; a graduate dramaturgy seminar, which sought to help students understand the role of cultural differences in working with a translated text; and undergraduate production dramaturgy courses designed to give students practical experience in serving as dramaturgs on mainstage productions. In every case, our process began with script analysis.

Elinor Fuchs' fine suggestion, "before making judgments, we must ask questions,"[5] proved as useful to the process of understanding a play as it did to the journey toward cultural understanding. We employed strategies that encouraged questions, such as those found in Fuchs' article "EF's Visit to a Small Planet," in order to help students engage in dialogue with the play as a world moving in time and space. For example, students in a theatre history course reading Yury Klavdiev's Martial Arts (2007), translated by David M. White with Yury Urnov (2009), used Fuchs' questions to identify the specific ways in which the playwright employs space, sound, and action to create a theatrical reflection of violence in contemporary Russian drug culture. Klavdiev then juxtaposes this harsh world of gunfire, murder, and abusive language against the innocence of the children in the play who use magical thinking – along with an invented ritual and an incantation to the Queen of Spades – to create a space for themselves that is free of these evils. In classroom study, as well as in our production of the play, students' attraction to the vivid theatricality of the piece also piqued their curiosity about the society that inspired Klavdiev's writing.

In Russian Theatre and Politics, comparative analysis was particularly useful in serving the course goals.[6] Weekly journal entries designed to enrich class discussions required students to suggest how elements of the plays such as character, language, and action might correspond to aspects of Russian society and politics contemporary to the play. As a result, our conversation about Playing the Victim, written by the Presnyakov brothers (2003) and translated by Sasha Dugdale (2003), allowed us to consider how the attitudes toward various ethnicities expressed by characters in the play related to the class lecture by political science professor Alison McCartney on ethnic tensions in Russia. Similarly, the students were able to connect what they had learned about the difficult conditions of military life in Russia, particularly for lower ranking soldiers, to the physical and emotional experiences of the young private in The Moth by Pyotr Gladilin (2001), as translated by John Freedman (2003).

In several classes and rehearsals, groups of students, in collaboration with faculty artists, utilized a line-by-line questioning of the text (what Russian colleagues call a "close reading"). This activity helped students in our 2008 graduate seminar on translation to consider how the actions of characters in John Freedman's working translation of Olga Mukhina's *Flying* (2004) – from their visits to a café to their reactions to the domestic violence suffered by a friend – might resonate differently in both cultures. For our season's production of Yury Klavdiev's *The Polar Truth* (2006), translated by John Freedman (2008), dramaturgy students prepared questions prior to meeting with the cast for early rehearsals. The team of dramaturgs then took turns leading table-work discussions as the cast read the play aloud, and the group brought their individual questions to the collective. In many cases, director Joseph Ritsch determined that questions, such as those about the character relationships, should be further explored in rehearsal, so that a range of possibilities could be considered. In other cases, ideas raised during table work helped lead into contextual research, as students' questions about the play fed their curiosity about the world and their sense that fuller understanding of the play for readers, artists, and audiences would be enhanced by specific knowledge about contemporary Russia.

Dramaturgical research that emanates from questions about the world created by a playwright seems particularly well suited to help promote understanding of other people's cultures. In the case of *The Polar Truth,* issues raised during table work included a series of very specific inquiries about terms that were unfamiliar to the cast or were used in a surprising context. The dramaturgy students' research into items such as diseases, geographic locations, and recreational drug use were compiled in a glossary for the play. Our research on the project also extended beyond specific glossary entries to include the physical and social context in which the characters operate so that student actors could better understand their characters' choices and reactions to the events in the play. This information, compiled in a dramaturgical casebook, helped all involved in the production understand the relationship between these conditions and the physical and emotional suffering of the play's young Russians infected with HIV, who live in the Siberian city of Norilsk.

Our analysis and research not only helped bring the world of the plays to the artists working on our Russia season, but also to our audiences. We created resources and activities to help productions serve as a point of departure for audience members' engagement with contemporary Russian culture. Students crafted program notes, also posted on the project's website, to summarize their research and highlight specific glossary items. John Freedman's translation (2010) of Vyacheslav Durnenkov's *Frozen in Time* (2007), for example, depicts the impact of a new business venture on multiple generations in a small village. Program notes on capitalism, diverse generational experiences, and provincial towns in Russia were designed to expand the audience's understanding of the real tensions in Russian society that are manifest in the play as conflicts between characters who embrace the proposals of the urban businessmen and those who violently oppose their enterprise. We also held post-show discussions with experts who viewed Russian culture and society from a variety of disciplinary perspectives. For *Frozen in Time,* discussion leaders included a political science professor who reflected upon politics and economics in relationship to the play and professors raised in Russia who shared their thoughts on the various generational perspectives depicted in the performance. Through these conversations, we hoped to help audiences consider the relationship between what puzzled or intrigued them about the play and the society in which it was written.[7]

Our work at Towson University with Russian plays was followed by another project in the reverse direction. John Freedman, *Moscow Times* theatre critic and the Russian director of the New Russian Drama Project, working with Philip Arnoult and CITD initiated and curated the New American Plays for Russia project, sponsored by the Bilateral Presidential Commission of President Barack Obama and then-Russian-president Dmitry Medvedev. Freedman and his collaborators created Russian translations of seven contemporary American plays. These translations were then given readings at professional theatres across Russia. As with our work in the United States, cultural understanding was a major goal of the endeavor. Freedman hoped the project would provide Russians with "insight into the rich diversity of voices, viewpoints, beliefs and cultures that make up American society today."[8] Thanks to the Fulbright fellowship and an invitation to teach at the Russian State University for the Humanities, I was also able to apply the dramaturgical process to Freedman's goal in Russian university students' encounters with the project's American plays and with our culture.

In our collective process of exploring plays, the students and I often employed a beginning point provided by Geoff Proehl on the Dramaturgy Northwest website.[9] Proehl offers a structure for identifying our first responses to a play, in terms of its "strengths (+), challenges or problems (-), questions (?), cracks (/ – ways into the play)."[10] This starting point not only helped us to understand how specific elements of the play resonated for each person, but also to consider the relationship between our reactions to the play and our cultural contexts. It is perhaps no surprise that references to the story of Anna Karenina in our study of *Anna in the Tropics* by Nilo Cruz (2002) were ways into the play for many Russian students, but some had questions about the structures of class, power, and knowledge in the play's Cuban-American community. Fuchs' questions helped these students from a variety of disciplines to view a play as a world moving in time and space. Their theatrical observations also served to pique their interest in the aspects of American culture that informed each playwright's work. In our conversation with Annie Baker, who visited Moscow as part of the New American Plays for Russia project, students were particularly curious to learn how the specific character interactions and language patterns, including silences, that they had observed in her play *The Aliens* (2009) correlate to experiences in contemporary American society.

The students' questions about American culture in Suzan-Lori Parks' *Book of Grace* (2010) led to dramaturgical research projects with application outside the classroom. I had been invited to direct a staged reading of *Книга Грейс*, Yury Klavdiev's Russian-language adaptation of the play, at Moscow's Playwright and Director Center. I engaged the students as dramaturgs to conduct research and to present oral reports, which we videotaped and posted online.[11] Our overarching goal was to help bring the American world of the play to the world of the Russian artists and audiences. As with the student dramaturgs at Towson University, we prepared a glossary of specific terms that might be unfamiliar to Russians. One student researched items – from Kevlar to Camp David to Timothy McVeigh to the song "Deep in the Heart of Texas" – that appeared in the dialogue of the play. Another project involved an extensive study of the English word "grace" and its various resonances, something that would not be fully clear in Russian translation. Other reports helped to provide context for the history of Mexican immigration to the United States, describe the training and duties of a border guard, and analyze the writing style of Suzan-Lori Parks. In each case, we drew from our initial textual analysis and consistently worked to relate the research back to our evolving understanding of the play. By putting these reports online, we aimed to make them available simultaneously as resources for the actors to use in their work on the play and as opportunities for audience members to learn more about aspects of American culture reflected in the play.

Life in the modern world often brings us into brief and fragmented encounters with the cultures of countries other than our own. We are, perhaps, increasingly reminded of each others' existence. Yet the kind of insight and empathy that might indeed help us to live together in peace requires a deeper process of thoughtful and respectful inquiry – one that is integral to the work of the dramaturg. As we discovered in the collaboration at Towson University with political science majors, and the coursework in Russia with students from across the humanities, dramaturgical strategies can help students in any discipline find relationships between their studies of a country and the experiences of its citizens, as expressed through the vision of a playwright. These methods of analyzing a text, conducting relevant research into the world of the play, and creating audience-engagement activities present us with tremendous opportunities not only to enrich our work on stage, but also to involve our students, fellow artists, and audience members in a journey toward greater mutual understanding in our interconnected world.

Notes

1 J. William Fulbright, *The Price of Empire* (New York: Pantheon, 1989), 193–4.
2 Fulbright, 194.
3 CITD support for the project came from: the Trust for Mutual Understanding; CEC ARTSLINK; the New Drama Festival, Moscow and St. Petersburg; and The Golden Mask Festival. Towson University support came from: Council for International Exchange of Scholars, a division of the Institute of International Education; the Maryland Humanities Council; the Rosenberg Distinguished Artist Endowment; Towson University Faculty Development Research Committee; and the Literary Managers and Dramaturgs of the Americas.
4 More information about the project is available at www.newrussiandrama.org.
5 Elinor Fuchs, "EF's Visit to a Small Planet," *Theater* 34.2 (2004): 6. This essay is also reprinted in this book.
6 A fuller discussion of this course appeared in an article co-authored with Alison McCartney, entitled "A Case Study of Russian Theatre and Politics" in the 2009–10 issue of *Review: The Journal of Dramaturgy*.
7 For a discussion of insights gained in other aspects of the project, please see "Bringing New Russian Drama to the United States," co-authored with Yury Urnov, in the Spring 2011 issue of *Slavic and East European Performance*.
8 John Freedman, "New American Plays for Russia," last modified May 23, 2013, available online at http://johnfreedman.webs.com/americanplaysproject.htm.
9 See http://www2.ups.edu/professionalorgs/dramaturgy/.
10 Geoff Proehl, "Four Beginning Points," *Dramaturgy Northwest*, http://www2.ups.edu/pro fessionalorgs/dramaturgy/dramaturgy_northwest/understanding/fourpoints.htm, accessed May 13, 2013.
11 Reports can be found on our dramaturgical website *Книга Грейс/The Book of Grace* at https://sites.google.com/site/russianbookofgrace/.

26
European dramaturgy in the twenty-first century
A constant movement[1]

Marianne Van Kerkhoven

Where are we today? If we want to get closer to an answer to the question of how to define and actualize the notion of European dramaturgy, we have to focus on dealing with the actual relationship of the artist with this world, on the dialogue that is or could be held between the artwork and the audience, on the relationship between theatre-practice and its theoretical questioners, on the conversation we have to carry on with or about Europe, etc.

Since the decline of Communism there has been the overwhelming élan of the neoliberal political and economic forces that – supported by the superfast development of technology – have spread the modules of unrestrained production and consumption all over the globe. The growing attention today for the work of a thinker like Antonio Gramsci – for instance, his theory of hegemony – points to the rediscovery of the complex relationship in society between the economic basis and different political, social, and cultural superstructures and the determining influence of economic organization on culture and on the arts.

It seems that one of our first tasks is to examine how the economic foundation determines our daily work. Marketing philosophy has indeed become so powerful in our society that no social sector can escape it. Management philosophy has also left its mark on the functioning of theatres and companies. Even in Europe it has become more and more difficult to maintain the level of artistic budgets, although – compared with the United States – many theatre structures get the biggest part of their income from the support of authorities and therefore still dispose of a relative autonomy, autonomy necessary to be able to create and to take artistic risk. The fact that it is difficult to evaluate artistic matter by quantity is in this context one of our biggest weaknesses but also one of our biggest strengths.

One of the key notions in the organization of economic life today is this magic word *flexibility*. Workers must be able to function in often varying tasks. Labour is shifting from fixed-function labour to task-oriented labour. Speed, adaptability, short-term vision, superficial knowledge are today the qualities that managers expect from their workers. The building up of experience and the development of a genuine professional history has lost all value. In the United States and the United Kingdom interim employees are already the group of the working population that is growing fastest. They are not able to invest themselves in their work, not able to develop long-lasting social relations with their colleagues. Getting to know and to trust the people you are working with, developing an emotional relationship with your task as part of a bigger process – these are all qualities that in a creative process (such as in the theatre) play an important part. Artists are longing to research in depth; they need time to construct a language; they have a need to develop themselves in continuity.

Never have there been so many people in our society holding university degrees and never have the anti-intellectual reflexes been as strong as today. Instead of choosing the long and work-intensive way of searching, which possibly might bring some clearness to the complexity of society, time and again the choice is made for the fast, short-term vision, the easy simplification of reality, for clichés and slogans, which popular politicians of all kinds gratefully use. Quantity is more easily achieved than quality. To give more voices the opportunity to express themselves, more time and space is needed than just one voice.

Again, nobody – us included – is immune to this kind of phenomena. Do we not have to screen our own practice to see if these social influences are also present in what we do? What about the relationship between theory and practice in the arts, for instance, and more precisely the academization of the high schools involved in arts education. Although during my entire professional career I have always tried to bring theory and practice, art and science, closer to each other, I am very suspicious about this rapprochement that takes place in the high schools of arts. Artists suddenly longing to develop an academic career are questionable. The contrary phenomenon, academics suddenly feeling the need to create a performance are questionable as well. Is this careless handling of expertise the same as what happens with expertise, tradition, and craftsmanship in other sectors of society? The question is how we can get rid of these kinds of useless pressures in order to spend our energy on the real and permanent conversation between theory and practice that we urgently need? Perhaps today there are even more possibilities for art and science to meet. Very exciting things, for instance, are happening in the blending of scientific research and artistic innovation. Artists, mainly those who want to work with highly complex technological means, are looking for the help of scientific researchers in order to explore the possibilities of new media and technologies. Vice versa, scientific researchers – often as well-educated in arts as in technology – get caught by the charms of new media as a poetic force.

From these initiatives new ways of producing are emerging on the creative level. People with very different backgrounds, knowledge, and capacities are meeting each other in an intensive teamwork. In his book, *Internet et globalization esthétique*, the Italian philosopher and aestheticist Mario Costa speaks of a transition of the artistic personality into an aesthetic, epistemological researcher, or of teams consisting of technological artists and aesthetic technological researchers.[2] Science has reached the point at which it is discovering more and more keys to the secrets of life, the secrets of becoming. Does this also turn the existence and functions of art upside down? At least grammatical changes are already becoming visible in the language of scientists.

Science and art are two different cultures. In fact, by using the word *culture* we could say that in trying to live together these two cultures suffer under problems comparable to the different ethnic, religious, and political groups in our society. In society most often these problems are handled in two different, equally fast and simplistic ways. The two answers are either racism or compelled assimilation. Edward Said remarked about this: "I think that the real problem today is that there is no mediation between these two extremes. Either there is homogenization or there is xenophobia, but not in the sense of exchange."[3]

However fluctuating an identity is, however difficult it may be to define – what is peculiar to a group of people, to a culture – these identities, these difficulties do exist. We can throw stones at each other over the wall separating the two gardens, or we can be forced under control to bring down the wall and declare that all the gardens from now on are one single park. But other alternatives are possible.

Concerning Europe it's important to consider the whole of the continent, not only the west but also the east, the north, and the south, and to stay aware of the rest of the world. Europe has been a colonizer in the past, but there also exists a kind of culture-colonization and it has a tendency to continue its life long after colonization proper has come to an end. I hope that our Eurocentrism will not be the standard by which we will measure all things. I hope that artistic Europe will remember the possibility of whispering conversations through the leaves.

And to conclude: what about dramaturgy? However much the social power of theatre is limited, to question the political importance of theatre all the time also means to question its relationship with the audience. Many theatre-makers today are asking questions like "How and what do spectators see and hear? How do we develop strategies of perception?" By transgressing the borderlines between visual arts, dance, and theatre, installations and performances come into being in which the spectator alternatively is brought into a theatre or museum context, with an alternation between "looking at something" and "walking in something," an alternation between observation and immersion, between surrendering and attempting to understand. And in this way, the spectator can determine independently his own standpoint. Perhaps more important than the here-and-now character of the theatrical experience is today the consciousness of the spectator that, in or inside a performance, he can alternatively be alone, individualized, and together with other spectators. The dramaturgy emerging from this situation is a dramaturgy of perceiving, a dramaturgy of the spectator. What more about dramaturgy? Dramaturgy is for me learning how to handle complexity. It is feeding the ongoing conversation on the work; it is taking care of the reflexive potential as well as of the poetic force of the creation. Dramaturgy is building bridges; it is being responsible for the whole. Dramaturgy is above all a constant movement. Inside and outside.

Notes

1 The full version of this article was originally published in *Performance Research* 14(3), 7–11, adapted from the opening keynote at the conference European Dramaturgy in the Twenty-First Century, Frankfurt am Main, September 27–30, 2007.
2 Mario Costa, *Internet et globalisation esthétique* (Paris: L'Harmattan, 2003).
3 Daniel Barenboim, and Edward W. Said, *Parallels and Paradoxes: Explorations in Music and Society* (London: Bloomsbury, 2004), 152.

Part III
DRAMATURGY IN MOTION

Demolitions, definitions, and demarcations

27
Dramaturgy on shifting grounds[1]

Hans-Thies Lehmann and Patrick Primavesi

The current development of theatre and performance takes place in changing cultural landscapes, defined by new media technologies and new perceptional habits. Hybrids of theatre, dance, performance, installation, exhibition, film, and media art are gaining importance, often based on new production methods and institutions. Transdisciplinary theatre projects attract new audiences by deviating from the familiar interpretation of dramatic texts on stage. Thus contemporary dramaturgy is facing a challenge: to develop creative ideas in cooperation with authors and directors; to ensure the quality of theatrical work based on a fruitful communication process within the production team; to invent helpful concepts for season schedules and for cultural institutions in general; to enhance unconventional modes of exchange and discourse; to build up global networks and to use them effectively. Pragmatic tasks like management and public relations, promoting theatrical events in local and regional contexts are indispensable, but they can't replace artistic skills.

The aim of the international conference European Dramaturgy in the Twenty-first Century in Frankfurt am Main in September 2007 was to face and reflect on the ongoing changes in the dramaturgical practice and to ask for new concepts and strategies. Starting points for these discussions were some obvious tendencies that are significant for the current situation: that distinctions between theatre and performance are increasingly blurred; that the practice of postdramatic theatre demands new styles and competences of dramaturgy; that a constant dynamics of crossover and interdisciplinary art, of physical and choreographical theatre takes place that no longer necessarily needs dramatic texts to which a *drama*turgy in the traditional sense could be applied. In postdramatic theatre, performance art, and dance, the traditional hierarchy of theatrical elements has almost vanished: as the text is no longer the central and superior factor, all the other elements like space, light, sound, music, movement, and gesture tend to have an equal weight in the performance process. Therefore, new dramaturgical forms and skills are needed, in terms of a practice that no longer reinforces the subordination of all elements under one (usually the word, the symbolic order of language), but rather a dynamic balance to be obtained anew in each performance.

Media worlds

The shifting grounds that theatre institutions have to face are first of all the changing realities of a global media culture. This does by no means imply that theatre should adapt to media realities as the new norm. Rather, it will have to develop various strategies of playing with the difference and tension between live and recorded. Theatre tends nowadays towards creating "real" situations and to taking its starting point from the bodily experience of spaces. For some time now theatre has mingled with all kinds of artistic practices, including variety spectacles, musicals, mime, slapstick, and so forth. Operating within the larger framework of a culture of media and mediated performance, theatre is bound to an inter-mediality where the "inter" is decisive. Thus, theatre may open up and explore the "inter" as an artistic space – instead of trying only to copy media technologies or maintaining a defensive ontology of live "presence." Even in the experience of "now and here," the media, the structure of the double, the différance have always already intervened. Dramaturgy from this perspective does require a particular sensibility not only for social, cultural, and political contexts "outside" but also for the power relations within theatre institutions. Therefore the dramaturg should no longer be defined as the controlling power of the theatre. The dramaturg may instead become a negotiator for the freedom of theatrical experimentation and risk.

In the current media culture, dramaturgy needs to reflect upon and respond to altered ways of perception and participation, to rethink the position and the possible functions of the spectator. Media technologies also offer new dimensions for the self-reflection of theatre and performance, between repertoire and re-enactment, digital archive and physical memory. That does not mean that dramaturgy is forced to adapt to or to comply with each new technology. What is essential may rather be a new way of thinking about media, techné, technology as new possibilities to conceptualize spectating, viewing, witnessing, participating beyond the simple dichotomy of subject and object. The dramaturg is not supposed to function as an expert of technology but to think and act "with" it as an experimentalist. Who in the theatre is afraid of new media?

Dramaturgies of the body

In new kinds of dance, as in performance art and in physical theatre, the functions of the body are no longer subordinated to pre-existing structures and systems, stories or narratives. Dramaturgy may be helpful here not by filling the "gaps" but rather in doing the opposite: opening the one-way street of production and reception towards an open process, perhaps a shared and mutual productivity in the proliferation of movement. Increasingly important is also the influence of technical media on the appearance of the dancer/performer on stage, in terms of presence, intersubjectivity, and "interactivity." One of the basic questions, not only for dance dramaturgs, is how the theatrical situation (the copresence of performer and audience) and the role of the spectator (as voyeur, witness, and participant) are changed by the use of media technologies. Various dramaturgical methods and strategies are needed for the different questions raised by dance and choreography, but all of these questions share the awareness of an increasing desire for new corporealities and for unusual experiences of the body.

Images of the body are a dominant feature of mass media in neoliberal Western societies. The human body is praised as a value in itself, however manipulated, trained, gendered, and over-sexed, advertised as a product for consumption and abused as a battleground of ideologies, sacrificed for economic profit and for religious or political ideas of every kind. In the age of technical and scientific progress, the ideology of perfected bodies has its counterpart in the elaboration of more and more effective ways to destroy and extinguish the physical existence of whole populations. The very distinction between human beings and animals or machines, an essential precondition of humanist ethics and aesthetics, is radically questioned by the logic of technical progress itself. Dramaturgy in dance and performance art is therefore not confined to the narration of stories through elaborated movement. It may also work on structures of physical and spatial relations, among the performers and between them and the spectators. An important issue for dramaturgy here is the tension between different notions of choreography, dance, and movement that are no longer bound to the system of linguistic signs. They require their own "languages" as for instance the Improvisation Technologies by William Forsythe can show. Therefore dance dramaturgy is not at all marginal in relation to dramaturgical practice in theatre, opera, or ballet.

Politics of discourse/beyond interpretation

Since the times of Lessing, the notion of dramaturgy (not only in Germany) has been deeply rooted in the project of enlightenment, in the urge to educate the people and to build up the cultural identity of a nation. The development of a political theatre was based on this tradition, in the 1920s and 1930s (Brecht, Piscator, Eisenstein, Meyerhold et al.) and again in the 1960s and 1970s (Kantor, Weiss, Handke, Living Theatre, Boal et al.). After the decline of twentieth-century ideologies, the relation between performing arts and politics has changed too. In political theatre it has often been the role of dramaturgy to place a production in the framework of a social and political context, for instance, by giving some allusions to real events during the performance or by providing additional information in program notes.

In the last decades the urge to interpret and to explain the repertoire in light of a current perspective has often been questioned. The attitude in Susan Sontag's programmatic essay "Against Interpretation"[2] has since been adapted by many artists and dramaturgs who rather tend to let spectators themselves reflect upon their position than teach them lessons in politics. Thus the political and (in a broader sense) the critical potential of theatre and performance often depends on how the position of the spectator is defined or questioned. The function of theatre as a public sphere requires a dramaturgical discourse that is more ready to pose questions than to give answers and that is constantly reflecting its relation to political contexts without patronizing the audience or insisting on a particular interpretation. More important than the dramaturg is the dramaturgy, collective whenever possible.

Training

If dramatic writing loses its dominating influence on many kinds of theatrical practice, dramaturgy still remains indispensable for the whole field of the performing arts and also for the production of film and media, the organization of festivals and exhibitions etc. And yet the question remains open if and how a "profession" so manifold and difficult to define could be taught and trained. In times of rapid change, the dramaturg of the twenty-first century will need to be open-minded, ready to accept the job as a position on shifting grounds and to question the categories that used to define the art of theatre. Just as it is a quality of contemporary art not to be always easily recognizable as such, it is a quality of contemporary theatrical work often to trans-gress our traditional definitions. Successful dramaturgical practice within the theatre institutions of today demands a productive flexibility, a capacity to shift grounds oneself and to switch from an argument based in literary knowledge to an argument based in visual arts or in music, from choreography to document, from the strategy of presenting something in front of an audience to a strategy of communication.

Dramaturgy needs the development of a number of skills and competences – but among these skills is the capacity to renounce skills altogether, to be open and sensible to unexpected changes in the process of rehearsal and production. This does not mean faceless and faithless self-negation. The dramaturg has to learn that professionalism easily turns into normalization and routine. And that a sort of Heideggerian *Gelassenheit* may be an essential quality of dramaturgical practice – the calmness to let things happen without imposing one's own ready-made concepts on a work in progress. Working in site-specific forms of theatre and performance already requires a certain sensibility for space and context, but it can also be an inspiring way of learning and training dramaturgical practice, on shifting grounds.

Notes

1 This article is a reprint from *Performance Research* 14.3 (September 2009): 3–6.
2 Susan Sontag, *Against Interpretation* (New York: Picador, 1961), 3–14.

28

Dramaturgy as skill, function, and verb

Lawrence Switzky

Dramaturgy is a job perennially in search of a description. When the managers of the National Theatre of Hamburg hired G. E. Lessing in 1767, they envisioned him as an educator, a public relations coordinator, a playwright, an in-house critic, and the organizer of German national drama. Only a month after his appointment, Lessing was already writing to his brother, Karl, about the territorial squabbles at the theatre that would plague his two years as the first officially engaged dramaturg: "There is disagreement among the directorate, and no one knows who is cook and who is waiter."[1] In a memo to Laurence Olivier written nearly two centuries later, Kenneth Tynan, the "literary manager" at the English National Theatre, assembled a list of 13 tasks that he and his assistant performed to clarify their myriad duties for an uncomprehending board of directors, from "[t]ravelling to see plays, meet authors and directors, deliver speeches, take part in debates, in London and abroad" to "[p]reventing the Wrong plays from being chosen – as far as possible."[2]

What is continuous over two centuries is the ambition of the dramaturg's role, as well as the diffuseness, and often illegibility, of dramaturgical work in the eyes of the rest of a production staff. As much as dramaturgy consists of a series of specific duties or positions, the dramaturg also matters as a representative figure – of the social conditions that sponsor contemporary theatre more, perhaps, than the traditional division of labor in production. Many accounts of the dramaturg's calling are bifurcated between proficiency and disposition. Anne Cattaneo has described the dramaturg as "someone who keeps the whole in mind."[3] Mark Bly defines his "most significant activity as a production dramaturg in the rehearsal process" as "'I question.'"[4]

In this essay, I offer the terms skill, function, and verb, not as mutually exclusive ways of figuring the dramaturg, but as simultaneous and overlapping affordances of the dramaturg's position in the theatre. Any description of dramaturgical work requires an unusually flexible frame. Dramaturgy has a normative (or, as the case may be, counter-normative) dimension: institutions that maintain dramaturgs value the preservation of a designated non-specialist within the professionalized business of contemporary theatre. Philosopher Theodore Zeldin proposes that creativity is fuelled by conversation rather than specialization: "At the frontiers of knowledge, adventurous researchers have to be almost professional eavesdroppers, picking up ideas from the most unobvious sources."[5] By massaging the traffic between theory and practice, play and production, the dramaturg starts and listens to many conversations, but isn't confined to any one. Despite the anxiety that a fluid and elastic roster of tasks causes dramaturgs and their colleagues, the dramaturg's resistance to specialization is a part of the job: a symbolic reminder of theatre's enduring refusal to honor rigid distinctions between work and play, and knowing and doing.

Dramaturgy as skill

A skill is a specific practice that can be inventoried, but being "skilled" also indicates competence that has been developed through a prolonged engagement with a set of tasks and problems. My home country of Canada, for instance, defines skilled labor as at least "one year of continuous and paid ... work experience" in its instructions to immigrants.[6] The uninterrupted investment in a skilled task indicates that repetition and sustained attention are as important in gaining expertise as demonstrable success (in this case, payment implies competence).

In *The Craftsman*, sociologist Richard Sennett fleshes out this definition by arguing that skill is gained through practice, modulation, and self-criticism during the performance of a task, so that "the rhythm of solving and opening up occurs again and again."[7] The antiphonal relationship between detecting and resolving problems is most apparent to Sennett in architecture, where the disjuncture between "simulation and reality"[8] can cause serious trouble when a theoretical blueprint doesn't take into account the materiality of building materials or the interference of wind and heat. Drawing habits are corrected by tactile experiences on a building site, and the horizon of building techniques is supplemented by problem solving at the drafting table. Skilled craftsmen, in other words, are able to solve problems and in solving find new ones that allow for further, previously unimaginable precision.

Architecture and dramaturgy are readily analogous, of course, since dramaturgs are regularly involved with the architectonics of performance. As Cathy Turner and Synne K. Behrndt point out, a dramaturg's tasks regularly alternate between activities that resolve and those that open up: "'Dramaturging,' 'shaping the dramaturgy' or 'dramaturgical work' may all imply an engagement with the actual practical process of structuring the work, combined with the reflective analysis that accompanies such a process."[9] That "reflective analysis" is not only a skill, but is part of being generally "skilled" is the proposition behind dramaturgy-training programs. The Yale School of Drama's Dramaturgy and Dramatic Criticism degree mandates six terms of writing and criticism that inform more "practical" work like guiding rehearsals or formulating artistic policy.[10] The Applied Theatre Studies program at Giessen University in Germany recognizes the alternating systole and diastole of skillfulness by making every student a potential dramaturg: "The students (and faculty) investigate the foundations, basic functions and historical forms of theatre, at the same time experimenting with practical issues."[11]

Rather than conceiving the skill set of the dramaturg as outsourced contextual expertise or criticism from the outside, dramaturgy might also be described as the higher skillfulness that accompanies long-term, largely uninterrupted involvement with a project. During the 1992 production of Georg Büchner's play *Danton's Death* at the Alley Theatre in Houston, Texas, for example, director Robert Wilson was only intermittently present during rehearsals while he worked on other productions out of town. A team of actors and designers realized his "visual books" and sketches in his presence and his absence. The outcome of Wilson's work was the materialization of a vision. Dramaturg Christopher Baker's notes, however, which begin in preproduction and end by considering critical responses (including his own), are a record of skill. To read them is to track details over time and to see impediments ramify into creations. Early in the process, Baker observes in Wilson's drawings that "[i]n [scene] I-4, the prostitute, Marion, reclines on what looks like a white chaise; it is labeled 'A Marble Sofa.'"[12] Two months later, Baker records, with a mixture of alarm and excitement, "we continue to talk through the play using the model. Wilson makes adjustments on a few sketches. Some questions have already been answered ... and others come up (how and by whom will the marble sofa be constructed?)."[13] Three months later, Baker notes with satisfaction, "Sculptor Ben Woitena, who will make the marble sofa, begins to turn four thousand pounds of marble into Wilson's design."[14] This narrative of a single object in the long life of a production provides a small window into the dramaturg's skillfulness: the product of his sustained involvement with a production and his facility at shuttling between the drawing board and the building site.

Dramaturgy as function

In his memoirs, German playwright Carl Zuckmayer recalls his confusion when he met and worked with Bertolt Brecht in 1923: "Brecht needed listeners, even those who talked while he did or whom he asked questions while he was working. He immediately assimilated in his own way the useful part of what had been said. This type of collective work was totally foreign to me."[15] Zuckmayer's bewilderment stems from an encounter with an alien attitude towards artistic work – noisy, public, dialogic – but also from a disagreement about who counts as a theatrical worker. When Brecht established a dramaturgical collective at the Berliner Ensemble in 1949, he granted professional status to functions (taking notes, making observations, exploring contexts) that he considered necessary in production.

Mary Luckhurst takes Brecht as a major influence in her comprehensive history of the evolution of modern dramaturgy in England. She defines dramaturgy as a set of persistent "functions" that must be accomplished in "any public performance of a play by a company."[16] These functions predate the appointment of dramaturgs and may be carried on by anyone, no matter what their title is:

> The play must have been read and selected; unless perfectly crafted (rare indeed), it must also have been made stageworthy by cutting and/or rewriting; been cast; and, in some measure, rehearsed. Furthermore, if performed more than once, or subsequently revived, judgment about its artistic, ideological, popular and/or commercial appeals must have been exercised.[17]

Luckhurst's "functional" approach to dramaturgy evades shifts in – and uncertainties about – terminology in different times and places. But it also reinforces Zuckmayer's sense that only traditional preparatory and compositional tasks are labor, and therefore it seems to leave out functions that dramaturgs name as their most significant contributions, like questioning or responding to a production from a global perspective. Robert Brustein, for example, has claimed that the primary function of the dramaturg is to act as the "conscience of the theatre, reminding it of its original promise, when it threatens to relax into facile, slack, and easy paths."[18]

One way to think about the functions of the dramaturg is to examine the concept of a function more closely. In his essay "What Is an Author?" (1969), Michel Foucault proposes that an author is less a person than "a classificatory function" that "permits one to group together a certain number of texts, define them, differentiate them from and contrast them to others."[19] As a force that establishes boundaries, the "author function" becomes a way of delimiting the proliferation of meaning by excluding styles, forms, and ideas that do not fit within established ideas about a particular artist: the author "is a certain functional principle by which, in our culture, one limits, excludes, and chooses."[20] Samuel Taylor Coleridge did not, for instance, believe that Shakespeare would have written the porter scene in *Macbeth* because his version of Shakespeare-as-author would not have stooped to scatological comic relief.

Dramaturgy sits uneasily within this view of creative authorship as exclusion and limitation. Dramaturgs certainly are asked to perform functions associated with limiting, excluding, and choosing: selecting new scripts for possible future productions from a pile of submissions, for instance, as well as pruning productions during the rehearsal process. But many dramaturgical functions are likewise concerned with opening up a production and endorsing multiple simultaneous audience reactions to the same performance or exposing the latent fecundity of a specific word or detail. One example of this latter function is Peter Stein's 1976 production, *Shakespeare's Memory*, in which Stein made dramaturgical work the subject of a performance. Over two nights and seven hours, Stein's actors performed their research into the politics, science, and religion of the English Renaissance: "actors simultaneously did acrobatic acts, gave musical performances or lectured, harangued, and entertained a public which was free to wander from one attraction to the next."[21] The production was a profligate preparation for the company's eventual performance of *As You Like It*, a making visible of the strenuous labor and discussion that underlie a performance of a play but would typically remain invisibly tucked within it. While *Shakespeare's Memory* might be read as reducing a Shakespeare play to the penumbra of its historical influences, its riot of competing performances demonstrated the dramaturgical insistence on considering the multiple and contradictory contexts that are the cradle of any text. It is as though a collection of glosses had overtaken the play they were meant to illuminate. In this sense, the dramaturg's function of expanding the scope and implications of a production may not be economical in any sense, though, as Stein's actors demonstrated, it can be expansively productive – of material and inspiration.

Dramaturgy as verb

One of the most exciting recent developments in dramaturgical thinking is the widened ambit of dramaturgical doing. Maaike Bleeker, for instance, proposes that dramaturgy is a "mode of looking that implies an eye for the possibilities inherent in the ideas and the material, as well as an eye for their implications, their effects."[22] Bleeker not only delegates to designated dramaturgs the capacity to look for the relationships between a single production element and the synchronic and diachronic structures of a production. Directors and choreographers can assume a dramaturgical perspective as well. In this sense, dramaturgy is a position that empowers an action.

This essay has presented numerous accounts of what dramaturgs "do": from literary management to shaping rehearsals to guiding informed reception, but also interrupting, reminding, and, now, looking from several perspectives at once. It is difficult to quantify these latter actions or to reconcile them with work as it is typically conceived. In a study of the status of rehearsal as labor, Annemarie Matzke documents how the serious playfulness of preparing a production confounds even those social theorists who are willing to accept the transitory nature of a public performance as work. The freedom that is associated with playfulness – one might say looking with an eye for possibilities rather than foreclosures – introduces a categorical challenge to labor: "When one's work is playing, can it still be thought of as work?"[23]

The verbal qualities of dramaturgy emphasize its active nature, and by thinking of looking, questioning, and criticizing as actions that are as muscular as building a set or performing a role, we might reclaim the work of dramaturgy *as work*. Bleeker and Matzke, however, allow us to see that dramaturgy's weird productivity is not different in kind from the rogue labor that other theatre practitioners take on in relation to the world outside the theatre, in which play and work are placed in opposition. Yet the actions associated with broadened definitions of dramaturgy emphasize a particular quality that dramaturgs do not necessarily share with other theatre workers: their labor is not, and maybe should not be, specialized.

The dramaturg resists specialization at large, the better to facilitate thought between divisions of expertise. Hans-Thies Lehmann and Patrick Primavesi make the cognate argument that dramaturgy today "needs the development of a number of skills and competences – but among these skills is the capacity to renounce skills altogether."[24] I think this might be pushed even further. The dramaturg raises operations that cannot be assimilated as labor in the extra-theatrical world to the realm of professional activities. It is the dramaturg's calling to offer a kind of voluntary ignorance, an exuberant naiveté, in the face of inflexible competence and calcified knowledge.

Notes

1 Quoted in Mary Luckhurst, *Dramaturgy: A Revolution in Theatre* (Cambridge and New York: Cambridge University Press, 2006), 31.
2 Kenneth Tynan, letter of December 1, 1964, in *Kenneth Tynan: Letters*, ed. Kathleen Tynan (New York: Random House, 1994), 311–12.
3 Quoted in Cathy Turner and Synne K. Behrndt, *Dramaturgy and Performance* (Houndmills, New York: Palgrave Macmillan, 2008), 6.
4 Mark Bly, "Introduction" to *The Production Notebooks*, vol. 1, ed. Mark Bly (New York: Theatre Communications Group, 1996), xxiv.
5 Theodore Zeldin, *Conversation* (Mahwah, NJ: Hidden Spring, 2000), 54.

6 Citizenship and Immigration Canada, "Federal Skilled Workers," available online at http://www.cic.gc.ca/english/immigrate/skilled/apply-who.asp, accessed on May 5, 2013.

7 Richard Sennett, *The Craftsman* (New Haven, CT and London: Yale University Press, 2008), 38.

8 Sennett, 42.

9 Turner and Behrndt, 3.

10 Yale School of Drama, Dramaturgy and Dramatic Criticism, available online at http://drama.yale.edu/program/dramaturgy-and-dramatic-criticism, accessed on May 5, 2013.

11 Steve Earnest, "Justus Liebig Universität Giessen – A New Direction in German Theatre Training" (2002), available online at http://www.inst-uni-giessen.de/theater/en/institute/press/7, accessed on May 5, 2013.

12 Christopher Baker, *Danton's Death*, in Bly, 76.

13 Baker, in Bly, 79.

14 Baker, in Bly, 104.

15 Quoted in James K. Lyon, "Collective Productivity – Brecht and His Collaborators," *The Brecht Yearbook* 21, ed. Maarten van Dijk *et al.*, The International Brecht Society, (1996): 6.

16 Luckhurst, 11.

17 Luckhurst, 11.

18 Robert Brustein, "The Future of an Un-American Activity," *Dramaturgy in American Theater: A Source Book* (New York: Harcourt Brace, 1997), 36.

19 Michel Foucault, "What Is an Author?" *Aesthetics, Method, and Epistemology*, ed. James D. Faubion, trans. by Robert Hurley and others (New York: The New Press, 1998), 210.

20 Foucault, 221.

21 Wilhelm Hortmann, *Shakespeare on the German Stage: The Twentieth Century* (Cambridge: Cambridge University Press, 1998), 271.

22 Maaike Bleeker, "Dramaturgy as a Mode of Looking," *Women & Performance* 13.2 (2003): 166.

23 Annemarie Matzke, *Arbeit am Theater* (Bielefeld: transcript Verlag, 2012), 45. The translation is mine.

24 See Hans-Thies Lehmann and Patrick Primavesi, Chapter 27; taken from "Dramaturgy on Shifting Grounds," *Performance Research* 14.3 (2009): 6.

29

Interactual dramaturgy

Intention and affect in interdisciplinary performance

Bruce Barton

The expansion from text-based conventions and approaches to the diverse and multiplying sets of practices regularly referred to as "New Dramaturgies"[1] is a response to a broad range of intersecting yet rarely complementary factors. Multiple efforts, many of them comprising multiple perspectives, have attempted to articulate the scope, parameters, and significance of this development. In particular, recent (post 2009) issues focusing on dramaturgy from *Performance Research* and *Contemporary Theatre Review* have rallied an impressive range of reflections and manifestos related to this dramaturgical sea change. And while both issues include articles addressing more conventional text-based performance, the dominant impetus behind the drive to reimagine dramaturgical process relates to the transition from hierarchically organized theatre-making to collaborative performance creation – what is generally referred to as "devising" – with the attendant emphases on physicality and multiplicity (of source material, of form, of discipline, of medium) that accompanies this shift. A number of recently published volumes directly address the elusive dramaturgical implications of devising processes (see Barton; Govan, Nicholson and Normington; Mermikides and Smart; Milling and Heddon; Mederos Syssoyeva and Proudfit). The most articulate of these voices emphasize the inability to confidently or fully articulate these implications and the necessity to not merely entertain but actually engage with this explanatory shortfall as a strategic point of departure in any given dramaturgical process. As David Williams proposes, "Perhaps above all, the dramaturg asks how to be a *juggler of paradoxes* in an uncertain, unpredictable, and ultimately unmasterable terrain."[2]

For the past four years I have been engaged in a nationally funded research project on physical dramaturgies[3] that draws both on my own interdisciplinary background[4] and on my work for the past twenty-five years as a professional dramaturg. The research design involves extensive practice-based research and dramaturgical involvement with six Canadian performance troupes[5] and an intensive "Performance Lab" with participants drawn from a dozen additional Canadian devising companies.[6] Reflecting the contemporary embrace of heterogeneity in terms of dramaturgical practice, the emphasis lies distinctly on dramaturg*ies*, plural. More specifically, my focus is on the boundaries and barriers between dramaturgical perspectives – and on approaches for identifying, examining, exploiting, and/or overcoming these divisions. As such, the objective of the project is the formulation of theoretically complex yet practically utilitarian strategies for cross-discipline and cross-paradigm exchange and collaboration. The emphasis is, thus, not on standardized systems or normative techniques, but rather on the networked interrelationship of multiple, distinct (and thus differentiating) performance training and generation approaches.

A key component of the research has been the formulation and articulation of a sufficiently sophisticated and robust "lens" through which this complex intersection may be most productively engaged, experienced, and examined. In its earliest phases the project was inspired by, in effect, the inadequacy of the available conceptual frames.

> Many contemporary Canadian devisors combine dense, intertextual puzzles of found material – drawn from prose fiction, poetry, philosophy, history and the natural sciences – with adapted and original writing ... [H]owever ... [c]arrying and expressing the multiple versions of the work's many intentions in and through the implicit response, memory and decision-making of their performing bodies, the creator-performers clearly compose and collaborate *viscerally* and *corporeally* as well as verbally.
>
> One logical resort in this situation is to turn to theor(ies) of *performativity* to move the conversation beyond the insistent limitations of text-based discourse. ... Yet within virtually all understandings of performativity ... the inevitably "iterative" nature of expression results in a discursive determinism that similarly restricts compositional choice and agency.[7] ... [W]ithin performance contexts that purposely attempt to complicate conventional theatrical boundaries, a further shift in focus is required to shape dramaturgical strategies that foreground and exploit performativity's paradox of intentionality and iterative affect.[8]

In my attempt to move beyond this impasse I advocated for "dramaturgical strategies that treat *all* modes of expression (including textual expression) as interwoven *acts* of composition, in a manner related to J. L. Austin's *speech act*: a use of words that *does work*, that *has affect* (or, at least, which *attempts* to do so)."[9]

> In particular, what Austin calls "perlocutions" are examples of speech that "often, or even normally, produce certain consequential effects upon the feelings, thoughts, or actions of the audience, or of the speaker, or of other persons" (Austin 1962: 101). As G. J. Warnock points out, for Austin "whether or not I intended to produce such effects, they may be incorporated in the designation of 'what I did'" (Warnock 1989: 123), and, further, "the perlocutionary effect in question will very often be producible also in some completely non-verbal way."[10]

The significance of Austin's contribution can be measured by the roster of his subsequent interpreters, among which Judith Butler and Jacques Derrida are only the most prominent (and thus most often cited). Indeed, as Seigworth and Gregg have observed, the current fascination with one of Austin's key preoccupations – *affect* – has burdened the term with "a sweeping assortment of philosophical/psychological/physiological underpinnings, critical vocabularies, and ontological pathways, and, thus, [it] can be (and has been) turned toward all manner of political/pragmatic/performative ends."[11]

Perhaps the single most significant influence upon my emerging understanding of interactual dramaturgy lies in the recent scholarship of, and my ongoing exchange with, Pil Hansen. A Danish dramaturg and scholar, Hansen has been my primary collaborator on a series of creative projects and research-based inquiries over much of the past decade, and the effort to frame interactuality emerges directly out of our interaction. One of Hansen's primary contributions to date is the systematic integration of performance theory and cognitive science she terms "perceptual dramaturgy."[12] Perceptual dramaturgy acknowledges both the fundamental neuroplasticity of the human brain and the stubbornness of established "perceptual habits."[13] Drawing on a complex intersection of contemporary research focused on an understanding of human memory that Edelman and Tononi refer to as "the remembered present,"[14] perceptual dramaturgy builds upon the contemporary shift in the interpretation of memory from a "static storage" model to one based on the continuous – and continuously evolving – activation of learned neural patterning. As a complex set of strategies for identifying, engaging, and potentially expanding the perceptual competence of both practitioners and spectators, perceptual dramaturgy represents a paradigm shift in the application of cognitive science to performance creation and reception.

The incorporation of cognitive science into performance scholarship has been met with equal parts enthusiasm and alarm, the latter often taking the form of concerns related to universal or biological Darwinism, the omission of differentiating factors related to issues such as gender and culture, and – through the prioritization of brain function – the reinstatement of Cartesian duality. While these criticisms apply to very few of the more sophisticated current efforts to explore the potential of this intersection of science and art (and certainly not to perceptual dramaturgy), an explicit determination to directly counter these charges can be found in the integration of cognitive science and phenomenology referred to as *enactivism*.

Several key observations follow quickly upon a shift to the enactive paradigm (where one encounters the writing of Alva Noë, Francisco Varela, Daniel D. Hutto and Erik Myin, and Evan Thompson, and, with specific focus on theatre and performance, John Lutterbie and Philip Zarrilli, among others). First, for Thompson, "information is context-dependent and agent-relative; it belongs to the coupling of a system and its environment. What counts as information is determined by the history, structure, and needs of the system acting in its environment."[15] Of course, a primary motivation behind the enactive framing of perception is to break down the traditional yet enduring division between mind and body. For what Tim Ingold calls the "whole organism in its environment,"[16] perception is a *process in real time: a process, that is, of growth and development*,"[17] involving "the capabilities of action and perception of the whole organic being (indissolubly mind and body) situated in a richly structured environment."[18]

Yet an individual's ability to engage with her environment is neither arbitrary nor infinite. As Noë asserts, "*What we perceive* is determined by *what we do* (or what we know how to do); it is determined by what we are *ready* to do." Therefore, to perceive "is not merely to have sensations, or to receive sensory impressions, it is to have sensations that one understands."[19] The process of growth and development that involves the acquisition of perceptual skills is, in a sense, about learning to enact – to perform – a better understanding of one's environment.

In perhaps the simplest terms, an enactivist perspective holds that "[o]rganisms are not passive receivers of input from the environment, but are actors in the environment such that what they experience is shaped by how they act."[20] On a superficial level, this would seem to suggest a degree of agency and autonomy that runs in direct contradiction to the discursive constraints associated with Butlerian performativity. But an enactivist perspective (of which, of course, there are multiple variations) does not propose some form of unbridled free will, as much of the cognitive processing of an "organism" is implicit and intuitive – that is, unconscious and habitual. At all times, Varela *et al.* contend, "[s]ensimotor capacities are themselves embedded in a more encompassing biological, psychological and cultural context." Rather, "[b]y using the term action we mean to emphasize once again that sensory and motor processes, perception and action, are fundamentally inseparable in lived cognition."[21]

Moving these observations from conceptual underpinning to practical application within an interactual approach to dramaturgy requires an additional step, one that renders explicit the intersection of these generalized interpretations of perception, memory, and cognition with the interpersonal and more broadly contextual determinants of an individual's lived environment. For, as Christopher Jackman has noted, "[I]n devised performance, histories, structures, and needs are continually subject to renegotiation. Mutual agreement is not a condition of engagement."[22] As Hansen has observed, of particular utility in this respect is the heightened awareness of discursive frames that accompany *interdisciplinary* exchange and collaboration (Hansen and Barton 2009: 132). Fittingly, the dramaturgical strategies emerging out of the current research increasingly employ methodological perspectives from a broad range of disciplinary practices, including many non-performance-based and non-artistic forms.

Specifically, while the source of exponentially increased potential, the turn to interdisciplinarity is never only a liberating gesture. The performative nature of discipline, by definition, involves limitation as well as facilitation, and the expanded range of possibilities afforded by this orientation is inevitably accompanied by additional (and often highly durable) conventional frames and expectations. As such, dramaturgical awareness and practice that draws upon and proceeds through interdisciplinary sensitivity and exchange effectively enacts what Varela describes as "precisely that mixture of regularity and mutability, that combination of solidity and shifting sand, so typical of human experience when we look at it up close."[23]

Adopting an interdisciplinary lens arguably allows for the imagining of dramaturgical processes that both foregrounds and problematizes Butlerian performativity's emphasis on iteration and citation as the primary modes of (highly curtailed) individual and collective agency. In a spirited defense of interdisciplinary interpretive frameworks, Markus Hallensleben has suggested, "we create and constantly recreate and change our bodies by creating and producing our cultural space[,] we perform ourselves, we *do* our bodies, or in terms of performativity studies, we choreograph our bodies … The human body … *is* and *has* culture (quite literally) as a tool."[24] Further, however, when this orientation to interdisciplinarity is itself investigated through the insights

Figure 29.1 Kiran Friesen and Adam Paolozza in Vertical City's *YouTopia*, written and directed by Bruce Barton. Dramaturgy by Pil Hansen. Interdisciplinary performance combining theatre, aerial movement, puppetry, interactive media, and pole dancing (Toronto, 2013). Photo: Bruce Barton

afforded by perceptual dramaturgy and embodied cognition, the tools for comprehending the complex, reciprocal interplay of intention, attention, and affect are exponentially fortified.

An integrated engagement with this scholarship can open up avenues to common conceptual ground pertaining to the full range of acts and actions in interdisciplinary creation and performance contexts. By temporarily stratifying and then *reintegrating* our understanding(s) of the embodied mind's experience of sensory stimulus, current conceptualizations of perception, attention, and memory hold the potential to map the dynamics of affect with unprecedented precision. In the same gesture, traditional distinctions between specific disciplinary practices may be interrogated, if not entirely dismantled, thereby facilitating interdisciplinary exchange and collaboration with unprecedented effectiveness.

I am in the final design stages of the Performance Lab with my collaborators Pil Hansen (University of Toronto) and Steven Hill (Simon Fraser University). Via an online forum co-designed with and facilitated by Hansen, participants from a broad cross-section of training and disciplinary backgrounds are initially being asked to reflect upon their individual and collaborative practices with an unprecedented (and functionally artificial) degree of compartmentalization (training/creation/rehearsal/performance).

Then, in the lab proper, Hill and I will facilitate the exploration of diverse orientations towards common intentions, while multiple modes of observation and assessment will attempt to gauge the breadth of affect(s) generated by these processes. As previously noted, the objective is not a standardized dramaturgical system or method, but rather a heightened dramaturgical awareness of cross-paradigm criteria and priorities, coupled with flexible strategies for collaboration that respond to, exploit, and potentially enhance these elements.

Ultimately, then, *meaning* in this context is framed as a perpetual negotiation between intention and affect – a dense field of explicit signification and implicit experience that practitioners *and* spectators navigate consciously, intuitively, and instinctually. Put most directly, an interactual dramaturgical perspective invites creator-performers and audience members alike to recognize and work with what a performance is *doing*, rather than what it is trying to *be*.

Notes

1 Since the landmark European Dramaturgy in the Twenty-first Century conference in Frankfurt am Main (September 2007), a conspicuous surge of interest in the dramaturgy of non-dramatic performance has spawned multiple subsequent gatherings internationally around "New Dramaturgies" and influential special issues of the prominent British performance journals *Performance Research* 14.3 (2009) and *Contemporary Theatre Review* 20.2 (2010).

2 David Williams, "Geographies of Requiredness: Notes on the Dramaturg in Collaborative Devising," *Contemporary Theatre Review* 20.2 (2010): 197–202 (emphasis in original).

3 "'How the Doing Is Done': Canadian Physical Dramaturgies," funded by the Social Sciences and Humanities Research Council of Canada (SSHRC).

4 I hold separate bachelor's degrees in Literature and Visual Art, a master's degree in Drama, and a Ph.D. in Theatre and Cinema Studies.

5 Artistic Fraud of Newfoundland (St. John's, NF); Zuppa Theatre (Halifax, NS); Pigeons International (Montreal, QC); Theatre Gargantua (Toronto, ON); bluemouth inc. (Toronto, ON/New York, NY); Old Trout Puppet Workshop (Calgary, AB).

6 Representatives from member companies of Vancouver's Progress Lab, plus members of additional performance troupes from that city.

7 For a thorough discussion of this paradox, see James Loxley, *Performativity* (London and New York: Routledge, 2007), 97–147.

8 Bruce Barton, "'Stop Looking at Your Feet': bluemouth's *Dance Marathon* and Inter/Actual Dramaturgy," *Performance Research* 14.3 (2009): 18–20.

9 J. L. Austin, *How to Do Things with Words* (Cambridge, MA: Harvard Univerity Press, 1962), 101–8.

10 Barton, 20.

11 Gregory J. Seigworth, and Melissa Gregg, "An Inventory of Shivers," *The Affect Theory Reader*, eds. Melissa Gregg and Gregory J. Seigworth (Durham, NC and London: Duke University Press, 2010).

12 Fully articulated only in Danish as *Dramaturgy of Perception* at the present time, perceptual dramaturgy is given a briefer articulation in Pil Hansen, "Perceptual Dramaturgy: *Swimmer (68)*," *Journal of Dramatic Theory and Criticism* 25.2 (2011): 110.

13 Hansen, 110.

14 Gerald M. Edelman, *The Remembered Present: A Biological Theory of Consciousness* (New York: Basic Books, 1989), 110–11.

15 Evan Thompson, *Mind in Life: Biology, Phenomenology, and the Sciences of Mind* (Cambridge, MA: Belknap Press, 2008), 51–52.

16 Tim Ingold, *The Perception of the Environment: Essays on Livelihood, Dwelling and Skill* (New York and London: Routledge, 2000), 3.
17 Ingold, 19–20.
18 Ingold, 5.
19 Alva Noë, *Action in Perception* (Cambridge, MA: MIT Press, 2004), 33.
20 Edwin Hutchins, quoted in Marcio Roca, "Cognitive, Embodied or Enacted?: Contemporary Perspectives for HCI and Interaction," *Transtechnology Research: Reader 2011* (Plymouth, UK: Plymouth University Press, 2011), 4.
21 Francisco J. Varela, Evan Thompson, and Eleanor Rosch, *The Embodied Mind: Cognitive Science and Human Experience* (Cambridge, MA: The MIT Press, 1991), 173.
22 Christopher Jackman, *Disciplined Mind: Intuitive Cognition in Devised Performance* (unpublished Ph.D. dissertation, University of Toronto, 2013), 19.
23 Francisco J. Varela and Humberto R. Maturana, trans. Robert Paolucci, *The Tree of Knowledge: The Biological Roots of Understanding* (Boston, MA: Shambhala Pub, 1992), 241.
24 Markus Hallensleben, "Introduction: Performative Body Spaces," *Performative Body Spaces: Corporeal Topographies in Literature, Theatre, Dance, and the Visual Arts* (Amsterdam and New York: Rodopi, 2010), 16.

30

The expansion of the role of the dramaturg in contemporary collaborative performance

Sarah Sigal

In collaborative theatre-making in the UK, the role of dramaturg is a flexible one, often emerging as a necessary task that falls to someone present in the rehearsal room. The UK-based Dramaturgs' Network defines the dramaturg as "a member of the creative team dedicated to help[ing] the makers find their own artistic journey through the process to fulfil their artistic vision."[1] As British dramaturgy has gained a higher profile in the last ten years, its possibilities for collaborative creation have expanded. When Ben Power dramaturged Complicite's A Disappearing Number (2007), he worked alongside Artistic Director Simon McBurney to structure, devise, and script the production.[2] Synne K. Behrndt's work as a dramaturg on Fevered Sleep's An Infinite Line (2008) dealt not only with the text, but also the design and use of space in this site-specific performance. Companies such as Filter Theatre conceive of the dramaturg in ways that suit the project in question, the nature of the role emerging as a reflection of the company's process. Filter was established in 2001 by Oliver Dimsdale, Ferdy Roberts, and Tim Phillips to create work integrating text, design, projections, and soundscapes, employing a number of practitioners external to the company. In the case of Filter's first production Faster (2003), the role of dramaturg was shared by scripting writer Stephen Brown, director Guy Retallack, and producer Kate McGrath. To understand how these three dramaturgs emerged, we will separate the process into three stages, focusing on the development of the text: the first stage involving the production team without writers, dramaturged by McGrath; the second stage involving writers Oliver Wilkinson and Dawn King, dramaturged by McGrath and Retallack; and the third stage involving Brown, dramaturged by McGrath, Retallack, and Brown. This paper will analyze how the multiple-dramaturg model facilitated the complex collaborative process used to create Faster, and it will illuminate the possibilities for collaborative dramaturgy that have emerged within the UK in the past decade.

Stage one: dramaturgy without a writer

At the beginning of stage one, there was no designated writer or dramaturg, as Dimsdale, Roberts, and Phillips wanted to conduct a research-and-development week in order to devise a storyline and approach to staging before working with outside artists. *Faster* was adapted from James Gleick's book *Faster: The Acceleration of Just about Everything* (1999), which details the way in which human behavior has altered in response to the proliferation of new technologies. Filter then invited performers and director Retallack to join the project; their initial approach to collaboration was intended to give the three artistic directors authority over the process, while benefitting from the creative input of the commissioned practitioners.

In order to maintain a focus for the devising process and a structure for the emerging text, Filter relied on McGrath, who became the first dramaturg on the project. The performers developed a series of improvisations under Retallack's direction with the aim of creating a text for the scratch performance, edited by Phillips.[3] The company tried to find what Retallack called the "obvious scenes," but this process proved difficult because *Faster* does not provide a plot or characters that would lend themselves to a devising scenario.[4] Since Phillips had become increasingly involved with the sound design, McGrath became the dramaturg, playing a more important role in creating the text than Filter had anticipated. Retallack commented that McGrath's "input and dramaturgical structural overview were invaluable when it came to pulling together the different strands and elements," that "it was immensely useful to have someone who could come in with fresh eyes to make observations on structure, dynamics and communication."[5] It had become crucial for the company to have someone like McGrath involved in the project from the beginning, maintaining an outside perspective on the production's dramaturgy. Since there was no writer involved at this stage, Filter became reliant on McGrath to help shape a text in order to produce a scratch performance for other potential collaborators and funding bodies.

Although Retallack had McGrath's dramaturgical assistance on the text, the director performed the task of a kind of second dramaturg in terms of developing a narrative from the devising process. Filter's method of collaboration relied on the fine balance between the chaos of devising (which involved the input of performers and designers, in addition to the three artistic directors and Retallack) and the organization of McGrath's dramaturgy. Initially, Filter had wanted to devise the project for as long as possible without a scripting writer, as the three artistic directors were concerned that a text written by a single writer would not be able to realize the company's vision.[6] They acknowledged the conundrum that they did not have the skills to produce a text themselves, but at the same time, they wanted to retain as much control as possible over the scripting process; Retallack had to find a way of developing *Faster* with a certain amount of structure without taking too much control from Dimsdale, Roberts, and Phillips. The director said rehearsals often felt frustrating and non-productive for him, and his relationship with the actors was "chaotic."[7] This is unsurprising considering the fact that *Faster* was Filter's first production: the hierarchy was not entirely clear at this stage in the process and the devising process can be challenging for any company, even under the best of circumstances. Turner and Behrndt explain:

> A devising process might ... require, on the one hand, a search for structure, while on the other hand, the facilitation of possibilities. The need to keep the process open can make it seem chaotic because one idea might lead to an exploration of parallel stories or ideas which in turn lead to other ideas and before long the process is going down different, perhaps disparate avenues and paths.[8]

Filter wanted to devise as much material with the performers as possible, but had to allow for a certain amount of freedom within the process in order to do so, which Retallack found difficult: "I used to call it 'punk theatre' – that it was both chaotic and organized simultaneously ... It was always a bit of a struggle to ... find the direction that we were going in."[9] In order to develop "a piece with real meaning and depth," Retallack felt the company needed the organizing presence of a scripting writer.[10]

Stage two: two writers, two dramaturgs

After the first scratch performance, Filter hired writers Dawn King and Oliver Wilkinson to help them draft the second version of the text, despite the fact that neither writer had worked with Filter and they were inexperienced. What became problematic was that Dimsdale, Roberts, and Phillips considered themselves the authors of *Faster*, but as writers Wilkinson and King were given control of the script, which would ultimately dictate the production. Filter expected Wilkinson and King would script a text from the devising sessions directed by Retallack, editing the improvised scenes into a cohesive whole, despite the fact that they worked largely unsupervised. King commented that co-writing with another inexperienced writer, under the absented authority of the company, was difficult, involving a constant series of disagreements and compromises.[11]

At this stage, as a second dramaturg, Retallack had become the main point of contact between the writers and Filter. In addition to the lack of communication, the main problem was the bifurcated sphere of influence in generating material, in that Retallack was in charge of directing the devising process in the rehearsal room, while Wilkinson and King were in charge of creating the text, working separately. The writers were given Gleick's book to read, as well as access to Draft One of the text and the video of the first scratch performance, material they were expected to incorporate into Draft Two. The writers would come to rehearsals to see what the company had produced and try to incorporate the devised material, but most of the time they would bring in scenes they had written for the performers to develop with Retallack. In addition to the fact that King and Wilkinson were working independently from Retallack, it was unclear as to who was the ultimate guiding force within the process.[12] Dimsdale, Roberts, and Phillips grew frustrated when they felt the writers had become too independent of the devising process: "We kept sending stuff back to them going, this isn't what we want. We would be in the rehearsal room and they would be next door writing." Phillips also admitted, "It was our fault as well. ... [W]e hadn't explained to them how it was going to work in the first place."[13] Although Filter had a notion of the role they wanted the writers to perform, they were unable to articulate it clearly.

Stage three: three dramaturgs and a scripting writer

The company replaced Wilkinson and King with Stephen Brown, a more experienced writer who had the advantage of having seen previous scratch performances, videos of rehearsals, and previous drafts of the script. Filter learned that keeping King and Wilkinson at a distance from the rehearsal room resulted in a script that was separate from the devising process, so they helped Brown become an integral part of the process. Roberts explains that Brown was hired to "collate everything we'd done and to try and write something using all our ideas and our improvisations."[14] Brown estimated that he wrote a third of the script before rehearsals started and the rest over the next three weeks, scripting text by himself, but also in the rehearsal room watching improvisations and through discussions with the company. Brown explained that he "played around" with the material, adding in what he called "my particular obsessions" to the story, and then adjusted the rest with the help of the company, generating scenes collaboratively: "Some of it was fairly rapidly just taken up and put on its feet and played about with and tweaked a bit."[15] The assistance of McGrath and Retallack helped Brown gain an objective dramaturgical view of the text as he developed it.

With Brown, there were three dramaturgs who functioned not only in accordance with their primary roles within the production, but also in relation to each other, helping Brown integrate into the hierarchy of the production team. Even after it became clear that Brown's task would involve writing additional material to develop the existing script, his role continued to have a dramaturgical function as he shaped the material created before his arrival. Retallack maintained his role as director/dramaturg, liaising between Brown and the performers in order to work out script-related issues. McGrath also continued to play the role of dramaturg, liaising between Retallack and Brown, as well as between Brown and the performers. Brown noted that during the three-week rehearsal period, he met with Retallack and McGrath separately and together several times in order to keep track of how the drafts of the script were changing during rehearsal without interfering with the dynamic between the performers and director. Brown described McGrath as a "sounding board," that one of her strategies after a group meeting would be to summarize the key points of the meeting, "constantly kind of nudging and pushing."[16] Turner and Behrndt explain that "the dramaturg represents the audience within a rehearsal process, able to identify the potential gap between what is *intended* and what is likely to be *received* and to give the artist a perspective on what they are creating."[17] Alongside Retallack and Brown, McGrath functioned as a member of the production team who was able to watch rehearsals and read drafts of the script with the audience's perspective in mind. This three-layered approach to the dramaturgical process allowed Filter to maintain a balance between the organization of writing and dramaturgy and the chaos of devising throughout the third stage.

Conclusion: collaborative dramaturgy and the text

Faster demonstrates the way in which the dramaturg's role can be flexible enough to suit the needs of a production within a collaborative process in which company ethos, hierarchy, and politics of authorship problematize the collaborative creation of text. The process Filter had developed was one in which authorship was "filtered" through a process involving a group of people with specific roles at different points in the collaborative process.[18] As the scripting writer, Brown unified the improvisations, research, and previous drafts of the text in order to make the text more coherent. Retallack noted the company needed someone to "record" the different voices creating material for the production, but what Brown actually did was not simply record, but organize and augment those voices with written material.[19] Dimsdale, Roberts, and Phillips came to realize that in order to produce a cohesive script, they had to abdicate some control to Brown, who, in turn, developed the text carefully, referring to Retallack and McGrath for advice. The relationship between Brown and Filter functioned well because Brown was an experienced writer, had the dramaturgical support of McGrath and Retallack, and entered the project when much of the material had already been established. In order to adapt Faster in a way that satisfied the company, Brown created a narrative structure that allowed the company to experiment with the integration of sound design and staging conceits. Roberts admitted, "Without [Brown], we ... would have had a very devised script," that Brown was "integral" to the process.[20] The writer said that this task was a challenge, but "working with Filter made me feel much freer about location and about creating worlds rapidly," that the involvement of the performers pushed him to "think through 360 degrees" of the play.[21] Filter managed to work with Brown in a way that was mutually beneficial for both parties; they found a writer to work to their specifications and Brown found a company that could help him find new ways of working with text and performers.

As a result of Filter's collaborative approach to scripting and dramaturgy, the role of the dramaturg in Faster was shared by three practitioners already engaged in other roles on the project, overseeing the development of the production throughout different stages of the process. Brown served as both the scripting writer making independent contributions to the text, while also functioning as a dramaturg incorporating the scenes the company devised, unifying the work into a whole. Filter relied on Brown, Retallack, and McGrath as organizing presences in order to help shape and create material for the text, maintaining a balance between the chaos of creation and the order of dramaturgy.

Notes

1 Katalin Trencsényi, Dramaturgs' Network, available online at http://ee.dramaturgy.co.uk/index.php/site/comments/dramaturgy_and_the_dramaturg, accessed August 13, 2013.

2 On the British definition of the term "dramaturg," Power commented, "it's a good term because no one knows what it means and it can be flexible." Jane Edwardes, "Ben Power: Interview," *Time Out* (October 14, 2008), available online at http://www.timeout.com/london/theatre/ben-power-interview, accesed August 13, 2013.
3 Tim Phillips, personal interview, London, January 19, 2008.
4 Guy Retallack, personal interview, London, April 9, 2009.
5 Cathy Turner and Synne K. Behrndt, *Dramaturgy and Performance* (Basingstoke, New York: Palgrave Macmillan, 2008), 172.
6 "More often when you ... see plays, you just hear the writer's voice ... and no matter what they write, however brilliant, there's always going to be an element of them in ... every character." Ferdy Roberts, personal interview, London, July 31, 2008.
7 Retallack, personal interview.
8 Turner and Behrndt, 171.
9 Dawn King, personal interview, London, September 3, 2009.
10 King, personal interview.
11 King, personal interview.
12 "It was quite hard to figure out who was in charge ... and that's when we got into trouble.' King, personal interview.
13 Phillips, personal interview.
14 Roberts, personal interview.
15 Stephen Brown, personal interview, London, February 19, 2008.
16 Brown, personal interview.
17 Turner and Behrndt, 156.
18 Retallack, personal interview.
19 Retallack, personal interview.
20 Roberts, personal interview.
21 Brown, personal interview.

31
Who is the dramaturg in devised theatre?

Teresa Stankiewicz

Who takes the role of dramaturg in a devised work and what does that role encompass? Artists such as Eugenio Barba, Charles Mee, and Pina Bausch, along with companies such as SITI and Dell'Arte, are prime considerations for exploring this topic, as are universities that offer coursework in devising. The definition of devised theatre that I am using is a collaborative effort by a group that is involved in creating the script and staging, from inspiration to performance. In many devised theatre companies the director brings in the idea and guides the process for the entire ensemble. Scholars Tina Bicat and Chris Baldwin discuss this process in their book *Devised and Collaborative Theatre: A Practical Guide*. They also describe a different approach: "Often the company who work together regularly are so familiar with each other's creative process that no one really knows where the idea starts."[1] This type of devising project allows everyone and anyone to make proposals, there is no specific division of roles. In both cases, how does dramaturgy fit into a devising process? When we consider famous proponents of devising or dramaturgy we discover a variety of stances that include elements of similarity. In the devising process, is the role of dramaturg that of a production dramaturg or new play dramaturg? Is the role of dramaturg delegated, separated, combined, or converged, and does it matter?

Dramaturgs sometimes take on a separate role in devised theatre. As an example, one of the companies in the United States that uses devising as their primary process is the Saratoga International Theatre Institute (SITI) Company in New York.[2] Their collaborations generally begin with an idea from the director, Anne Bogart. She asks a question for the ensemble to explore such as "What is the relationship between the audience and the actor?" Work begins with research that includes bringing together stories, articles, and inspiration on the topic to be discussed before physical work begins. In the work *Cabin Pressure*, the company was in residence at the Actors Theatre of Louisville (ATL), where ATL dramaturgs spent several weeks on researching the actor to audience relationship.[3] The ATL dramaturgs were professionals who spent weeks "researching diverse theatrical styles and genres and any mention of the actor-audience relationship throughout theatre history."[4] In this case the dramaturgs were separate from the cast and their role was to provide historic and background research.

Continuing with the SITI process, sometimes the stage manager acts as dramaturg. Once preliminary research is completed, Bogart and company employ their Viewpoints technique to explore an idea physically through a nonverbal lens.[5] They use this physical exploration to block a scene before any specific text is added. Actors work instinctively to explore the topic and make discoveries. They work over days and weeks, reconsidering choices made and devising new ones. After they make physical choices they return to the text and research to add dialogue. The stage manager notes selections as they are made. In this instance, the stage manager becomes the dramaturg, taking notes as in new play development dramaturgy. The company also videotapes their work as part of the progress. Bogart guides the progress by making comments on the actors' choices and deciding which scene to consider next. Here, the video camera, the stage manager, and the director combine as new play dramaturgs, notating the process in order to guide the theatre-making and devising.

Another person who takes on the role of dramaturg in the SITI process is the sound designer, Darron West. He conducts his own research and then participates in the early discussions with the ensemble: "Those who observe SITI rehearsals sometimes define West's role as that of dramaturg, sometimes even codirector."[6] As dramaturg or codirector he adds his input after the ensemble has created the physical staging and the dialogue. At that time he brings music suggestions inspired by the actors' movement and selections of dialogue. He chooses sound cues to experiment with as rehearsals continue. With most devised works everyone in the ensemble is free to make comments and suggestions as rehearsals progress. This is true for SITI, and West offers critiques of the actors' choices the same way the actors review the music he has chosen. Together the ensemble makes the selections for the entire work. In the case of the SITI Company, actors, directors, and designers work as new play dramaturgs at different points in the devising process. They all participate in questioning choices for clarity and pulling the script together into a solid work.

Charles L. Mee is the only playwright listed as part of the SITI ensemble. His work generally consists of taking a historical text (often a Greek myth) and reinterpreting it. In this case the playwright creates a devised piece. Mee writes a text with the specific intention of directors and actors participating in the creation of the final performance. As stated by his daughter, who regularly directs his plays, "my father writes text for a performance in which what he has written will be a fraction of the total experience."[7] Mee writes plays in a collage style using text from many sources in the form of quotations, lines, and poetry. His approach to playwriting is a form of dramaturgy in that he is gathering information from a myriad of sources to provide inspiration and content for the play. Then he turns his play over to a director and expects her to interpret, insert, and enhance what he has written. This assumption or demand of collaboration is a form of devising, and in Mee's process the playwright is the dramaturg.[8]

Eugenio Barba uses a similar approach, except that Mee is a playwright and Barba is a director. In his book *On Directing and Dramaturgy: Burning the House*, Barba describes how he works with his ensemble to create a performance. He uses various texts for inspiration just as Mee does, which might include plays, poems, novels, religious texts, news stories, proverbs, a paradox, or a known quotation.[9] Barba has a notion that directing is a "dramaturgy of dramaturgies." He devises works by using impro-visation, movement, and vocal actions that his actors bring to rehearsal after they have processed their own dramaturgy. His actors research and improvise as part of their work before rehearsals begin. Then his actors recreate their improvisations in exact repetition. From these exercises he pulls the movement, speech, or expression that he wants to assimilate into the play. This type of devising embraces the director as auteur, who decides what will be incorporated in the piece, although the actors participate in the creation of the work. In this case the dramaturg is both the actor and the director, using elements of new play dramaturgy as well as production dramaturgy. Actors and the director separately research the topic (production dramaturgy), and the ensemble documents the creative process, making sure the play is contained in a framework that will engage the audience (new play dramaturgy).

Similar to SITI, Mee, and Barba, the Dell'Arte ensemble converges the production dramaturgy of research with new play dramaturgy. Together the ensemble plays the role of dramaturg. Dell'Arte uses traditional physical theatre forms to create original works by the ensemble.[10] One of the techniques the ensemble uses is "paper walls," as stated by member Joan Schirle, "we covered the studio walls with long sheets of paper, labeled 'theme,' 'intent,' 'characters,' 'scenes,' 'resources,' and so on."[11] The ensemble agrees on the idea, identifies themes, and then conducts field research as in production dramaturgy. In their work on *Slapstick* (1989–95) they wanted to explore gender tensions by performing classic slapstick. They used the paper walls to write down every slapstick routine they could think of as part of their devising. As they physically explored slapstick routines, a new theme of family violence arose which then changed their intent.[12] This is an example of how the ensemble plays the role of new play dramaturg: during the process of discovery a better theme and direction is identified and everyone agrees to follow it.

Pina Bausch used similar techniques in her work with Tanztheater. While she is generally referred to as a choreographer, her pieces go beyond dance and her artistic process can be considered a form of devising. Just as Barba asks his actors to conduct research and create improvisations that he then extrapolates for his plays, Bausch asks her dancers to explore their emotions and create movement combinations that she then weaves together for her works.[13] The idea for a piece originates with Bausch as director the same way it does for SITI and Barba. The performers of these companies then share what they have discovered for the director to choose for the final piece. The artists play the role of dramaturg and conduct the research for the exploration. The director plays the role of dramaturg in choosing the dialogue and movement to be used in the development of the piece. In these cases the role of dramaturg is not delegated or separated but combined and converged within the ensemble.

When devising is offered as part of university coursework, is the process of dramaturgy similar to the professional processes? In the college productions *Giving Voice* and *Voices from Hurt Street*, the students were led through a series of exercises in order to create the work. *Giving Voice* was devised as part of the Introduction to Performance Studies class that I taught at the University of Missouri. The idea was to have the students explore their identity with the question "Who am I?". In a series of exercises the students were asked to bring in poetry, short stories, and personal narratives that described who they were or what was important to them. Some of them also brought in songs and music. They all shared their assignments with each other in class, and I led the students through various exercises to show them ways of performing or interpreting the text. We used sounds, music, movement, original works, and borrowed works to create a final performance. The students were all dramaturgs for the piece in that they conducted their own research. Although I had final say as director, we all participated as new play dramaturgs in noting where there was confusion, which items worked well together, and what pieces we had to discard.[14] In *Voices from Hurt Street*, the professors, Brian Newbert (director) and Robert Miltner (dramaturg), from Kent State's Stark campus, spent a semester giving the students writing assignments on the topic of abuse. The idea for the class started after a student on campus had to deal with a case of sexual harassment. The students all chose subjects of their own that had to do with bullying, abuse, or social injustice. Many of them shared personal narratives and poetry born of their own experiences. Some shared stories they found based on their own research, inspired by their personal experiences with social injustice. In class they shared their writing with each other and critiqued one another just as a new play dramaturg might support a playwright. In the second semester the same students collaborated on choosing and staging the material.[15]

The role of the dramaturg depends on the situation and the people involved in the production. In devising, dramaturgs might be specifically assigned or in the form of true collaboration everyone might serve as dramaturg just as everyone serves equally as writer, musician, composer, actor, dancer, or in short creator-performer. It seems unimportant who plays the role of dramaturg as long as the dramaturgy is accomplished. Many times it is the process itself that is the most rewarding experience as sometimes a devised piece ends up not being stageworthy. The risk of spending time in collaboration that results in a tabled piece is a good reason to place more emphasis on the role of the dramaturg. When ensembles spend as much time as two years creating a performance, devising becomes an expensive proposition if the result is not successful. This is where the deliberate application of new play dramaturgy can assist; documenting the process with the idea that a performance-ready piece is essential may circumvent failure. Conversely, perhaps the dramaturgical work is to gather the results of the process to be used later in a different performance that is successful. Either way, dramaturgy is an essential part of devising, and it is not important whether the role of dramaturg is delegated or combined; what is vital is that dramaturgy be acknowledged and specifically applied to the process.

Notes

1 Tina Bicat and Chris Baldwin, eds., *Devised and Collaborative Theatre: A Practical Guide* (Marlborough, Wilshire: The Crowood Press, 2002), 8–9.
2 SITI Company, a New York City ensemble founded in 1992 by Anne Bogart and Tadashi Suzuki, places an emphasis on collaboration and international culture exchange.
3 Joan Herrington, "Breathing Common Air: The SITI Company Creates *Cabin Pressure*," *The Drama Review* 46.2 (Summer 2002): 127.
4 Herrington, 127.

5 Anne Bogart and Tina Landau, *The Viewpoints Book: A Practical Guide to Viewpoints and Composition* (New York: Theatre Communications Group, 2005).

6 Herrington, 134.

7 Erin B. Mee, "Shattered and Fucked Up and Full of Wreckage: The Words and Works of Charles L. Mee," *TDR: The Drama Review* 46.3 (2002): 85.

8 See www.charlesmee.org and www.siti.org, accessed December 22, 2012.

9 Eugenio Barba, *On Directing and Dramaturgy: Burning the House* (London: Routledge, 2010), 89.

10 "About Dell'Arte," Dell'Arte International, www.dellarte.com/dellarte.aspx?id=2, accessed December 22, 2012. Dell'Arte was founded by Carlo Mazzone-Clementi and Jane Hill in 1971 to bring physical training to the United States and develop actor-creators.

11 Joan Schirle, "Potholes in the Road to Devising," *Theatre Topics* 15.1 (2005): 93.

12 Schirle, 94.

13 *Pina*, directed by Wim Wenders (Germany, Neue Road Movies, 2011), DVD.

14 *Giving Voice* was performed in the Life and Literature Series at the University of Missouri at the Corner Playhouse in September 2011.

15 *Voices from Hurt Street* was directed by Brian Newberg and performed April 12–21, 2013. Newburg co-teaches the devising course with Robert Miltner at Kent State University at Stark. I interviewed them and observed one of their classes on November 6, 2012.

32

Finding our hyphenates
A new era for dramaturgs

Jessica Kaplow Applebaum

Over the past half century, devising theatre practices have been growing and developing into an established and recognized (though still ever evolving) set of performance-making methodologies. As we work our way into the twenty-first century, these modes of performance-making are receiving newfound attention, becoming popular and visible against the backdrop of, and even within, traditional performance practices. The visibility of these "alternative methods" of collaboration and creation demonstrate that performing is, in and of itself, an act of dramaturgy. This necessitates an evolution in our field: one that opens the space for the dramaturg to embody her practice and specify her own dramaturgical methodologies.

In the spring of 2012, the Prague Quadrennial held a symposium entitled "Devised Dramaturgy: A Shared Space." A central supposition that came out of the forum was the notion that the process of devising is continually shifting: it develops its methods and acquires its identity from the specific collaborators and conditions of each project. This supposition is not singular to devised work. Contemporary, postmodern, and post-dramatic performances also identify as genres that are contingent, self-reflexive, and open-ended. What we found together in the shared space of the symposium is that this idea, in particular, reveals an expanding practice of dramaturgy that encourages dramaturgs to perform their functions in new, more performative ways.

Tim Etchells, devisor, artistic director of Forced Entertainment, and keynote speaker at the symposium reminded us that when we define devised performance as the matter and material of a collaborative partnership that "starts and lives in and from performance,"[1] we highlight the fact that devising is a practice of discovery. It is a collective and present interrogation of a form, theme, question, subject, object, design element, or combination thereof, unfolding over place and time. Whatever stumbles forth first, be it the architecture of the space, the choreography of bodies, or a soundtrack of noise, every other element engaged in creation performs a response to the material being offered. The very interrogative weave of material and engagement demonstrates that devised performance is, in and of itself, an active dramaturgical process.

The juxtaposition of different media (dance, video installation, poetry, light) often seen within devised performance decentralizes the traditional "linear notion of theater."[2] Not only do language, image, environment, and movement all act upon each other, they act upon the very creation of each other. Shifting from a singular written text to the work of multiple performance texts, devised work prompts the dramaturg to participate and focus on what performance studies scholar, editor, and dramaturg Marin Blažević recognizes as "the changing potential of an act or event."[3] This space of potential (or creative chaos) moves the dramaturg to a productive fault line. Not only are we now looking at the potential of an action or an event, we are also aware that our responses and conversations about process dramatically influence that potential.

As devising inherently consists of actions of dramaturgy, the role of the dramaturg is expanded and performed by all practitioners, be they dancer-dramaturg, scenographer-dramaturg, director-dramaturg, and so on. This expansion challenges both practitioners and dramaturgs to rethink and redefine our methodologies. It compels us to ask the *fundamental* questions: if the role of the dramaturg is expanded to all practitioners, if the function of dramaturgy resides in shared process, where does that leave those of us who define ourselves primarily as dramaturgs? Are we no longer necessary in the creative/development process? Or could this be an opportunity to re-envision our practice and further enhance our field (or fields) of specialization?

For dramaturgs to be able to hone our awareness and to have clear and constructive relationships with the actions and events of the devising process, we must find the hyphenates to our dramaturgy. As a function of grammar, the hyphen is used to connect two words together as a compound. It is a simple, short dash of a line that, within the world of devised performance, functions as a bridge, endowing each dramaturg with further purpose and empowering her to embrace and further define the locative, temporal, and attributive role she performs throughout the development of a performance. Creating the bridge or connection to an additional craft, the dramaturg is able to recognize the creative portion of her identity, develop an embodied practice and frame her involvement within the creative process. The act of discovering and defining our hyphen illuminates the possibilities of our actions and organizes how we perform our role within the devising process. It allows dramaturgs to enter the space of creative thought along with our colleagues, physically generating material for performance. Let me take a moment to unpack this: what creative strategies might the articulation of the dramaturg-hyphenate bring forward?

Coming from a background in dance, I focus on the body of the actor. Working on a devised project in 2012, entitled *My Artichoke Heart*, I started highlighting gestures and bodily functions that came out of the performance score we were generating, so that we as a group could clarify where each moment in the performance resided. For example, one character – splintered in time – was embodied by more than one actor. I noticed that each of the actors' bodies interacted with breath in a different way: inviting or fighting the intake of oxygen changed depending on moments of pleasure or fear. After sharing this observation with the ensemble, the actors began to use breath as a collective, marking the beginning or end of particular moments. The method was a kind of choreography. By the end of our process a unique dramaturgy was added to the piece, one in which the actors physically manifested the structure of the play in and through their bodies. I began to envision the function of my work, articulating my role as dramaturg-choreographer.

Together with her co-hyphenates, the hyphenate-dramaturg interrogates the process of creation, defines the rules and conditions at work in the room, determines how the collective will make decisions for the final piece, *and also plays with her colleagues.* "Play, traced back to Lecoq's concept of *jeu*, refers to a state in which 'the performer is capable of spontaneous responses within preconceived rules, a flexibility that results from awareness of and connection to others.'"[4] It is a crucial function in the development of a devised work. Used as a method of exploration, play generates material through investigation, inquiry, and challenge, asking and answering questions through performance. In devising, the creative process of play resembles an infinite dramaturgical loop: trigger material, spontaneous creative reaction, evaluation of new material, spontaneous creative reaction, and so on. This loop starts by asking the practitioner-hyphenates to offer matter for the performance in some form: movement or language, architecture or light, sound or image. Then they must be able to engage, as Alison Oddey writes, "with the material in a personal and objective relationship at one and the same time."[5]

Play is also a critical component for the dramaturg-hyphenate. It allows her to discover the power and importance of spontaneity and advances the territories of her work. Whether through participation in a physical exercise, sharing creative thought, or perhaps making a sculpture from found objects in the room, the dramaturg's specific 'hyphen' articulates her strengths and willingness to play and enables her to have an embodied interaction with the process at hand. Perhaps even more crucial, the dramaturg can be the connective tissue of organized chaos in the devising process, following the thread of the performance when all others have lost it or providing disruption as needed to keep the dramaturgical loop from becoming stuck. In his book *On Directing and Dramaturgy: Burning the House*, Eugenio Barba writes, "creative thought is not linear, not univocal, not foreseeable."[6] From creative thought come "sudden disorientations which oblige [the practitioner] to reorganize [performance] in new ways, abandoning its protective shell and perforating anything inert."[7] It is a function of the dramaturg in devising to help with both the disorientation and the reorientation of the creative process.

Moreover, play opens up the space for the dramaturg to build upon attention: a primary component of all dramaturgical practices. Like scales for a musician or lines for an artist, attention is one of the building blocks with which dramaturgs perform their craft – except that, instead of notes, different forms of concentration mark attention. For instance, one can shift from the micro (interest in a subject or noticing a habit that repeats) to the macro (having an awareness of a group and possessing a consideration for the physical performance). Of course, the micro and the macro move and blend into each other throughout the devising process. It's not to imply that there is a hierarchy to attention (e.g. the physical performance). Rather, we engage acts of attention in different ways. As Anne Bogart writes in her book, *And Then, You Act: Making Art in an Unpredictable World*, "Attention is, after all, one of the few aspects of life that one can control."[8] That control is often found through an understanding of how and where we place our body in space and how we use that to hone our tools of listening and hearing. Finding and developing our hyphenate gives dramaturgs the ability to train and control our attention in a specific mode. From that training we strengthen our methodologies and our interactions with our colleagues and with the process of devising.

Devising embodies the dramaturg. Connecting to another form of practice the hyphen bridges the mind of the dramaturg to her body. Able to use her body, the dramaturg can hone in on the phenomenological qualities of a performance. Attuned to the feelings and consciousness of the performers and the design elements, she is able to "describe our 'situated experience'" as well as analyze the structure of a production.[9] The weave of these actions (honing in on feeling/analyzing structure) is something that Tim Etchells describes as "making shape of seconds."[10] This practice, this "doing time,"[11] is the application of pure/unfiltered dramaturgy. It is the heart from which the dramaturg should dare to work. In developing the creative portion of her identity, she will be enabled to develop an embodied practice, which will give her a clue as to where she wants to position herself in the room (while understanding there also might be a place she needs to be positioned as well).

In the genre of devised performance, form is no longer prescribed but discovered. So how do dramaturgs interrogate and investigate that? What tools do we use? Is a foundation in dramatic structure, even in its post-dramatic iterations, enough of a foundation for us to have as our primary tool of trade? What other tools do we need to develop to allow us to encounter and experience the varied languages from which to practice our craft in the devised world? What are the hyphenates that best suit our role as dramaturg while we venture forward into new forms of performance? And are they singular or multiple?

These questions keep us exploring who we are and how we work. They free us from the anxiety of trying to universalize the role of the dramaturg. Acknowledging that we draw on our own specificities, they encourage the dramaturg to enter a process ready to engage and perform with her fellow practitioners. As dance-dramaturg Bettina Milz suggests the dramaturg should dare to be the first to respond to the material offered, to "describe what he or she sees, to stumble, to jump in at the deep end, putting into words what you could hardly perceive, what is not yet named."[12] Far from being rendered obsolete, devised work gives both the dramaturg and her collaborators the opportunity to reinvigorate the traditional roles of the dramaturg. It demands, as it demands our devising-colleagues add the dramaturg to performer *et al.*, that we find the "hyphenate" to our dramaturgy: dramaturg-director, dramaturg-sculptor, dramaturg-theorist. The hyphenated dramaturg is more closely connected to the devising team, brought into the creative process instead of kept ringside. Together we become bodies who develop a collective method of playing, hone our abilities to focus and attend to the actions and materials of our collaborators. This then allows the dramaturg to augment a primary function of dramaturgy, which is care for the overall process and clarity of the work.

Notes

1 Tim Etchells, "In The Silences," paper presented at Devised Dramaturgy: A Shared Space. Symposium for the Makers, Prague, April 20–21, 2012.
2 Synne Behrndt, "Devising, Developing, Dramaturgy," moderator for Devised Dramaturgy: A Shared Space. Symposium for the Makers, Prague, April 20–21, 2012.
3 Marin Blažević, "Intro 2: Dramaturgy of Shift(s)(ing)," *Performance Research* 15.2 (June 2010): 9.
4 Jon Foley Sherman, "The Practice of Astonishment: Devising, Phenomenology, and Jacques Lecoq," *Theater Topics* 20.2 (2010): 89–99, 94.

5 Alison Oddey, *Devising Theatre: A Practical and Theoretical Handbook* (New York: Routledge, 2003), 154.
6 Eugenio Barba, *On Directing and Dramaturgy: Burning the House* (New York: Routledge, 2010), 84.
7 Barba, 84.
8 Anne Bogart, *And Then, You Act: Making Art in an Unpredictable World* (New York: Routledge, 2007), 52.
9 Simon Murray and John Keefe, *Physical Theatres: A Critical Introduction* (New York: Routledge, 2007), 26.
10 Tim Etchells, "Doing Time," *Performance Research – A Journal of Performing Arts* 14.3 (2009): 71–80, 76.
11 Etchells, 76.
12 Bettina Milz, "Conglomerates: Dance Dramaturgy and Dramaturgy of the Body," paper presented at the International Research Workshop-Dramaturgy as Applied Knowledge conference, Tel Aviv, May 27–9, 2008.

33

Dramaturgy as a way of looking into the spectator's aesthetic experience

Milan Zvada

The concept of *interactive dramaturgy* is an attempt to analyze how dramaturgy influences artists' approach to their work and relationship with the spectator. Dramaturgy implies certain philosophical and conceptual assumptions that have been ingrained in our minds while growing up in a particular culture, speaking a particular language. It has to do with the way we use words and understand them in relation to the extralinguistic reality. What words denote is very often a matter of social consensus and the historical experience of a certain community of "speakers." The same applies to an interactive approach to dramaturgy, which is not a literary science yet deals with text and words for its other qualities than a means to linear, narrative comprehension. Our application of this concept depends on the language of performance itself; text is only one of its many layers of audience reception.

In their book *Metaphors We Live By* (1980, 2003), George Lakoff and Mark Johnson exemplify how concepts influence our perception and understanding of the world and its phenomena. They claim that our communication through the use of language is essentially marked by concepts in the form of metaphors, even though we are not normally aware of it. Concepts can thus have an ontological status. They influence the way we think and act in relation to the outside world. They are "the simplest content of our thinking ... [mediating] between the mind and physical reality."[1] Concepts organize our experience, "they are systems of categories that give form to the data of sensation; they are points of view from which individuals, cultures or periods survey the passing scene."[2] As an example, Lakoff and Johnson take the phrase "argument is war" for a conceptual metaphor. They ask the reader to imagine "a culture where arguments are not viewed in terms of war, where no one wins or loses, where there is no sense of attacking or defending, gaining or losing ground. Imagine a culture where an argument is viewed as a dance, the participants are seen as performers, and the goal is to perform in a balanced and aesthetically pleasing way."[3] They continue by saying that in such a culture, everything would be different: viewing, experiencing as well as talking about these arguments. What's more, too, our "Western" perception and understanding would be different since "we would probably not view them [people from the different culture] as arguing at all: they would simply be doing something different. It would seem strange even to call what they were doing 'arguing.' Perhaps the most neutral way of describing this difference between their culture and ours would be to say that we have a discourse form structured in terms of battle and they have one structured in terms of dance."[4] In a way, metaphor is a principle of structuring our (world)views, which are in turn based on concepts.

In the context of dramaturgy and aesthetic experience, we may draw parallels to their process-oriented nature. They are not something fixed, they are not "states of being," yet they are intrinsically connected with ontology and the nature of the creative process. The impact of a performance on the spectator very much depends on his or her expectations, needs, and attitude towards the theatrical event, framed in a prevailing concept of the theatre. As concepts of theatre and dramaturgy differ from culture to culture, so does the experience of the spectator.

Re-inventing the concept of dramaturgy

Dramaturgy has been changing its context of use, both on stage and in academic life, depending on cultural and social habitat, and therefore it is open to interpretation, application, and further development. In some education systems and cultures, dramaturgy is not even articulated as a separate artistic subject or theoretical discipline. In other contexts, dramaturgy is part of directors' training, theory of theatre, or playwriting courses. It is obvious that the very concept is relative to its own particular theatre practice. Unlike acting or directing, dramaturgical work does not imply tangible results. To explain and justify what a dramaturg's concerns are, and how they can be implemented within theatre practice, is not as easy as understanding what an actor's job is. Nevertheless, "dramaturgy is a key function of the dramatic system, which is employed regardless of being associated with the dramaturgic profession or divided among other professions."[5] That is to say that even if there is no such person as a dramaturg, each theatre performance has one, usually embodied in the (artistic) director. Dramaturgy is inherent to every theatre production, and its steps can be traced within the structure, purpose, and other complexities of performance. Even an artistic statement such as "No dramaturgy!" implies dramaturgical purpose.

One-way and interactive dramaturgy

There is a formal distinction to be made between one-way and interactive dramaturgy. While one-way dramaturgy is preoccupied mainly with play text analysis, characters, adaptation, and semantic interpretations (referring to psychological and narrative theatre background), interactive dramaturgy deals with performance as a complex interactive process with an intended effect. Nevertheless, interactive dramaturgy too makes use of one-way dramaturgical methods as they ideally coexist in practice. In this context, so-called one-way dramaturgy signifies the dominant orientation of a dramaturg's (as well as a director's) efforts towards the artwork, taking it as "a world for, and in itself" – as a representation to be displayed, witnessed, and enjoyed "accordingly." On the other hand, in an interactive approach, a focus on the structural elements of performance is supplemented with a focus on the process. Interactive dramaturgy is concerned mainly with the fact that the theatrical world is being constructed gradually and purposefully to evoke certain kinds of responses in the audience, yet keeping its thematic, narrative, or psychological principles more or less integrated. Here, "the world on stage" is linked with the audience's world through an invisible thread of energies, which are constantly being exchanged and navigated. It is not a means to random contemplation but to profound experience. In such a world, space is filled with attention, concentration, and "being there" – due to the actor's intense sensibility, spatial awareness, and presence.[6]

In a one-way approach to dramaturgy, dramatic texts are the highest point of reference. It is their wordy interpretations that bother the minds of actors and spectators alike. In this case, the dramaturg is concerned mainly with character profiles, and motifs, following the principles of psychological necessity or probability. Such a working methodology is marked by the Aristotelian notion of the hero's fate, and it forms the basis of a realistic understanding of a character's behavior and actions. This type of dramaturgical approach presupposes the fact that "the essence of theatre is *dialogue*: words between people. Drama represents human beings *side by side*, one human being *with* another human being, and, of course, human beings *against* each other."[7] The goal of dramatic art resides in an attempt to overcome conflict situations, from which dramatic tension and storytelling arise.[8] Thus, it seems as if the process of overcoming these contradictions on stage – or its mere attempt to accomplish it, whether successfully or not – is the only thing at stake. Yet Artaud hinted that something other than dialogue might be at issue; he wondered how it is possible that in theatre, "everything which cannot be expressed in words or if you prefer, everything that is not contained in dialogue (dialogue itself viewed as a function of sound amplification on stage and the requirements of that sound) has been left in the background."[9] Although his question is a bit outdated, many theatre-makers still consider text, if using any, in terms of dialogue. Moreover, many actors in training still invest their energies in learning lines of dialogue by heart, taking words for what they appear to be at first sight, a means to denote object or meaning. How actors approach the written word is very much dependent on what they consider it to be, which in turn determines the spectators' mode of perception. In Artaud's words, "[a]bnormally shrunk, [actors'] throats are no longer organs but monstrous, talking abstractions."[10] That is to say, spoken words perceived as in everyday conversation (narrating story, character's opinions, etc.) only form one mode of their usage. In theatre, however, it is not enough only to "talk by talking." For, "[who] said [that] theatre was made to define a character, to resolve conflicts of a human emotional order, of a present-day, psychological nature such as those which monopolize current theatre?"[11]

In its broadest sense, *interactive dramaturgy* is not so much interested in text and dialogues as we know it but follows the notion of a "text" as understood in the theory of postdramatic theatre. Here, "the new theatre text (which for its part continually reflects its constitution as a linguistic construct) is to a large extent a 'no longer dramatic' theatre text ... [It] is considered only as one element, one layer, or as a 'material' of the scenic creation, not as its master."[12] The dramaturg's interactive approach is about making adjustments to one-way dramaturgy according to the evolving creative process with respect to the spectator. Strictly speaking, dialogue appeals to the intellect, not the senses, that's why it cannot be as effective as, for example, a combination of music, dance, and poetic imagery (using words as a means to trigger the imagination's latent powers). Similarly, for Artaud, "words do not necessarily mean everything, either in essence or because of their predetermined nature," because "they paralyze thought instead of fostering its development."[13] He calls for words to "be construed in an incantatory, truly magical sense, side by side with ... logical sense – not only for their meaning, but for their forms, their sensual radiation."[14] To divorce words from dialogue, one needs to become a secret lover of actions, gestures, and the voice. Words and actions must be redefined so that their potential to re-describe reality can be unleashed, and they can affect us more deeply than their consensual counterparts.

The dramaturg, working within the interactive approach, should have his or her answers to "why, and who for" a particular theatrical situation is being created. Not only in terms of relationships on stage between the characters (themselves) and other signs, but also between the staged piece and the spectator. Artaud's "specialist in objective, animated enchantment" would be a dramaturg who can think interactively for the sake of the spectator's aesthetic experience and not only for the conventional compactness of (re)presentation. The story or narrative framework should not work as a distracting factor but rather as an easy companion of the overall situation and its sensual impact on the spectator. Rational explanations should give way to intuition, immediacy of sound, and action on stage; at best, they should be imprinted on the situation itself. Hence, "[t]here is no question of abolishing speech in theatre but of changing its intended purpose, especially to lessen its status, to view it as something other than a way of guiding human nature to external ends, since our theatre is solely concerned with the way emotions and feelings conflict with one another or the way man is set against man in life."[15] That is to say, basic dramaturgic categories, conflict and dialogue as observed in life, should get rid of their traditional forms. Interactivity in theatre can be based on forces released from these new forms as a means to an end, which does not imply resolution, meaning, or story unfolded but spectator affected. It is about conflicts and tensions based on situational impulses rather than an exchange of words and dialogues in a pragmatic sense.

"The taste of experience savors its ingredients"

Two perspectives or roles from which a dramaturg can approach the creative process for the sake of interactivity are proposed. One concerns thought (dramaturg as philosopher), the other the spectator's experience (dramaturg as first spectator). Going back to conceptual metaphors, building performance can be seen as a process of growing the seed, and the spectator's experience as a process of tasting the fruits or as savoring the mixture of ingredients from the boiling pot, which is the stage. Speaking about interactivity, however, we must see beyond the dichotomized discourses on the nature of our sense perception, body, and mind. Perception is an active process, an exchange between particles. The perceived objects are not separated from us, nor does the term "aesthetic" refer to an added value of theatrical experience. Perception merges with sensation and feeling, the principle point is Heraclitean: "everything is motion (or change)."[16] It is a heightened, concentrated state of awareness and energy flow.

Interactivity implied in the role of dramaturg as philosopher concerns "thought in context." Here, the dramaturg is an ideologist who creates the theatre's profile (poetics) in terms of issues relevant to one's social/cultural habitat. Just like a philosopher, who wonders at perspectives, reflects, and questions the nature and causes of things, the dramaturg contemplates possible variations on stage in terms of their effects ("aesthetical") and follows the underlying principles that keep all aspects of the performance together (idea – sound – image). It is the dramaturg's constant questioning, and making the obvious problematic, which is the basic mode of his/her work. As the dramaturg watches the growing seed and facilitates the rehearsal, he literally becomes the first spectator. S/he does not substitute for the director yet makes up an impartial counterpart to the fact that the director is immersed, at times even lost, in his or her vision. In this way, the dramaturg is also an ideal spectator, who keeps a distance and does not need to be present at all rehearsals. A critical attitude can only be maintained by deliberate resignation from the production process.

The nature of aesthetic experience therefore depends on the level of the dramaturg's sensitivity, artistic providence, and awareness of the close connection between the senses and the intellect. Dramaturgy as practiced in rehearsals ("thinking") is thus a prerequisite for the nature of the spectator's experience ("feeling"), and yet these two cannot be dichotomized. That is to say, what is constantly at stake in theatre is the rupture and interdependence of these two aspects of one's experience; this rupture can take place by means of stimulating sensory perception always anew. This requires a turn to immediacy and sensuality, materializing thoughts and feelings through expressions which do not follow the principles of consensual reality as we talk. What is ultimately real for the spectator is the sensuous, experiential quality of the theatrical event itself, which is never an illusion as long as it bridges one's body and mind.

Notes

1 Nicholas Bunnin and Jiyuan Yu, *The Blackwell Dictionary of Western Philosophy* (Malden, MA and Oxford: Blackwell Publishing, 2004), 126.
2 Donald Davidson, "Inquires into Truth and Interpretation," in Bunnin and Yu, 128.
3 George Lakoff and Mark Johnson, *Metaphors We Live By* (London: University of Chicago Press, 2003), 5–6.
4 Lakoff and Johnson, 6.
5 Zdeněk Hořínek, *Úvod do praktické dramaturgie* (Introduction to Practical Dramaturgy), (Praha: Ústav pro kulturně výchovnou činnost v Praze, 1980), 5, translation mine.
6 In relation to the actor's work, Phillip Zarrilli identified a similar interactive approach by saying that "[t]he term 'dramaturgy' refers to how the actor's tasks are composed, structured, and shaped during the rehearsal period into a repeatable performance score that constitutes the fictive body available for the audience's experience in performance." In this way, "the overall dramaturgy, style, and tempo-rhythm … [of the production] are [all] shaped to create a specific experience for the audience." Phillip B. Zarrilli, *Psychophysical Acting: An Intercultural Approach after Stanislavski* (New York: Routledge, 2009), 113.

7 Hořínek, 9

8 Hořínek, 9.

9 Antonin Artaud, *Collected Works, Vol. IV* (Great Yarmouth, Norfolk: Galliard [Printer] Ltd, 1974), 25.

10 Artaud, 106.

11 Artaud, 28.

12 Hans-Thies Lehmann, *Postdramatic Theatre* (Abingdon and New York: Routledge, 2006), 17.

13 Artaud, 84.

14 Artaud, 96.

15 Artaud, 54.

16 Please note that "the word aisthesis as used by the Greeks … has the advantage of comprehending a large number of sensory and physiological experiences": F. Solmen, *Aisthesis in Aristotelian and Epicurean Thought*, Amsterdam: N. V. Noord-Hollandsche Uitgevers Maatschappij, 1961), 241. Ambiguity resides in using it as "perceiving" and "feeling," going back to Plato and pre-Socratic philosophers. At closer scrutiny, however, it will appear that making differences between "perceptions, sensations and feelings" is a result of the dualistic agenda of some ontological and epistemological discourses. There are concepts which avoid this dichotomy and objectivistic frameworks; in this interpretation, it is the concept of aesthetic experience.

34

Dramaturgy as training
A collaborative model at Shakespeare's Globe

Amy Kenny

At Shakespeare's Globe, the collaborative atmosphere of theatre is heightened by using a team of student dramaturgs for each production. Most theatre programs that allow this are geared towards students in dramaturgy and directing. Shakespeare's Globe (in partnership with King's College London) offers students this opportunity while completing coursework on the Shakespeare Studies M.A. in the English department. My differentiation here is that while performance M.A.s often offer some training for dramaturgs, those in English Literature usually do not. Before the season starts, select M.A. and Ph.D. students working at Shakespeare's Globe have the opportunity to answer dramaturgical questions from members of the company. Instead of assigning a specific dramaturg to each individual production, Shakespeare's Globe allows a team of five to six emerging academics to discuss the questions and responses together as a collective unit. In this article, I will use the collaborative model at Shakespeare's Globe as a case study to show how the dramaturg can be used as a function, instead of a job description, one that trains and hones students' research and information literacy skills for wider use. I will begin by describing the model used at Shakespeare's Globe and move on to discuss why this model is important in the changing nature of dramaturgy. It is my aim to demonstrate how the skills and expertise required of a dramaturg can be parlayed into a career elsewhere in the academic or theatrical world by exploring the unique model for dramaturgy in place at Shakespeare's Globe, pioneered by Farah Karim-Cooper, Head of Courses and Research. There have been two distinct periods of research at Shakespeare's Globe, one under the direction of Andrew Gurr, and another headed by Farah Karim-Cooper, which began in 2006. This article discusses the second and current phase of the Research Department, under Karim-Cooper's direction.

Dramaturgy at Shakespeare's Globe is collaborative, discursive, and, above all, academically rigorous. Postgraduates have the opportunity to respond to questions from actors and directors about Shakespeare's culture, characters, and canon by consulting a variety of primary and secondary sources and distilling the relevant information into a concise, accessible document delineating the response. Yet the dramaturgical model at Shakespeare's Globe provides researchers with much more than the excitement of seeing how their research manifests itself in performance. By the end of the rehearsal period, postgraduates learn to become more efficient and conscientious researchers because of the distinctive and practical demands the rehearsal process places on the dramaturg. In addition to this, interacting with actors and directors at this level trains postgraduates to write with precision for a broader readership, rather than purely an academic one. This training at the beginning of an academic or professional career is vital to the success of this model as well as to the student him/herself, as it equips the student with the ability to hone his/her research methodology and explain the information in a variety of circumstances. Instead of merely thinking about an academic argument with sourcing and a clear authorial tone, students at Shakespeare's Globe must consider the performative nature of the texts and contexts as well. The collaborative model equips the dramaturg with the ability to think about the information in diverse ways from an unbiased and more comprehensive standpoint than is often expected in academic papers.

Each person's individual research methodology and expertise culminates in a single document given to the company members containing primary and secondary sources, images, and assorted opinions about the given topic. The collaborative mindset is so ingrained in this theatre that information passed along to the theatre companies has usually had multiple hands in its creation, and no one entity is given credit for the creation or sourcing of the information. Instead of dealing with a single dramaturg or literary manager, the acting companies working at Shakespeare's Globe are offered knowledge and assistance from a team of students who must learn to work together. One of the benefits of this model is that students learn how to collaborate on a project with other academics with different research and writing practices. It is one thing to read and understand the contemporary sources from the early modern period, but quite another to be able to translate them into modern vernacular and circumstances, and speak knowledgably about their relationship to the text. The students acting as dramaturgs must learn this skill in the field, as it were, because the company is expecting them to act and respond to queries as dramaturgs.

Assigning the dramaturg's responsibilities to an ensemble of researchers not only mimics the company structure of theatres, but also improves the quality of conducted research and enhances the quality of responses given to actors and directors. This collaborative model disperses authority amongst a team of researchers instead of solely on one individual, requiring the dramaturgs to discuss research methodology and pedagogy with their peers and defend or define their practices. Not only does dramaturgy contain a more tangible outcome than other academic papers, it also insists upon an approachable and definitive response that can be performed onstage, which allows researchers to consider the practical implications and applications of their research.

A dramaturg must function in a multiplicity of academic and theatrical roles throughout any production, with literary specialist, theatre critic, and general researcher among them. Andrew James Hartley has argued elsewhere that "the dramaturg must therefore become a kind of translator, someone fluent – or close to fluent – in both languages, and thus able to move between the two respective cultures in ways producing the maximum number of productive options with the minimum amount of hostility."[1] The fact that he portrays the relationship between actor and scholar as speaking different languages is crucial to our understanding of the training that a dramaturg must receive in order to succeed in his/her role.

Dramaturgs must not only be experts on the play, context, and world for which it was written, but also masters of social relationships and dialogue as well. Dramaturgs at Shakespeare's Globe must mediate the ideological positions and theories from their academic training as M.A. or Ph.D. students with the practicalities and movements within the play from a practitioner's standpoint. This juggling act is something that most Ph.D. and M.A. students have not experienced. By integrating students into the mindset of a dramaturg for several large-scale productions, Shakespeare's Globe equips students with a unique skill set and training that is seldom offered elsewhere to M.A. or Ph.D. students.[2]

The students must learn where to find the material, how to sift through sources, and extrapolate the answers to questions from the company very rapidly. This task is easier said than done. Academia generally trains people to write an argument for a paper from the top down, meaning that once someone writes a thesis, s/he must find textual and contextual evidence to support that claim. Dramaturgy, however, requires the opposite methodology, because information must come directly out of a specific question. To find the needle in the haystack of all early modern sources to answer a single, often very specific question from a company member, requires a particular skill of weeding through sources quickly and efficiently. The needs of the theatre are immediate, and generally actors and directors cannot wait days for the answer to their question to be as thoroughly researched as most academics would prefer. Thus, a dramaturg must be proficient and resourceful with the sources and databases s/he consults. Shakespeare's Globe forces students to think in this manner, learning to quickly weed out any irrelevant information and apply any useful sources to the dramatic situation immediately.

The use of the dramaturgical model to further teaching practice in the classroom has already been argued elsewhere, with examples and situations outlining the importance of using the dramatic experience in one's pedagogical approach.[3] Yet Shakespeare's Globe allows for more than just dramaturgy to be adapted in the classroom; it enables a discursive environment that trains its students to speak the language of academic and practitioner while still maintaining rigorous research skills. Cary Mazer has argued that "there is no career in the professional theater that an undergraduate liberal-arts theater major better prepares a student for than professional dramaturgy."[4] Shakespeare's Globe ensures its students are given in-the-field training as dramaturgs to facilitate a more fruitful career in any field, not just academia. Instead of merely teaching dramaturgy to its students, Shakespeare's Globe offers a unique experience in conducting and producing dramaturgy while still in the early stages of a career as a way of preparing future members of the creative class to be more collaborative, well-rounded thinkers and contributors to any field.

A dramaturg's role is continuously evolving and mutating based on where s/he practices and the daily needs of the culture and company in which s/he is embedded. In fact, often a dramaturg is defined by what it is not, rather than what it is, because the function and use of a dramaturg in different theatres across the globe is as multi-faceted and unstable as the term itself.[5] Mary Luckhurst argues that the "meanings of the terms *literary manager* and *dramaturg* are relative and determined by the particular cultures and institutions in which individuals operate, but the functions remain."[6] The fluidity of this term means that regardless of who actually completes or compiles the dramaturgical support for a production – an actor, director, student, or specified literary manager – the practice of dramaturgy is an integral part of every production.

Regardless of where and how a dramaturg works, all dramaturgs share a common necessity to be fluent in both the academic and theatrical needs of a play. Shakespeare's Globe entrusts this role to M.A. and Ph.D. students who are only beginning their careers and learning proper research methodology and etiquette. The use of students in this often challenging role trains a new generation of theatre scholars and practitioners to think about a variety of contexts and meanings behind drama. Instead of merely developing their own readings of plays, these students must work towards the theatre company's reading of the play with efficiency and dedication. A dramaturg at Shakespeare's Globe must be willing to collaborate with a team of other researchers. By entrusting this role to emerging academics, Shakespeare's Globe trains them to think and research in a new light. Dramaturgy at Shakespeare's Globe is as much a research and pedagogical tool as a theatrical one.

The model of collaborative dramaturgy at Shakespeare's Globe can help us think about the ways in which dramaturgy can act as a training tool for students, regardless of their career goals or field. The ability to dramaturg for a production requires a unique skill set that is transferable to a variety of disciplines and fields.[7] The use of dramaturgy has been shown to be fruitful in a variety of disciplines, including political science, anthropology, philosophy, performance studies, as well as other art, science, and corporate areas requiring information literacy skills, teamwork, and collaborative research methods.[8] If students are given the opportunity to develop the kind of information literacy skills (efficiency and efficacy) that are necessary for the contemporary job market, as they are at Shakespeare's Globe, the nature of dramaturgy changes from a job description to a training tool. This model has emerged as a function for students at Shakespeare's Globe, but serves a much larger significance in the shifting field overall. If dramaturgy can be both useful for a theatre company and students removed from that theatre company, its possibilities are endless. Instead of teaching students how to be dramaturgs, the dramaturgy-training program at Shakespeare's Globe gives them versatile research knowledge that will endure long beyond the season and into their careers. Dramaturgy training can prepare a new generation of thinkers, regardless of their intended career path.

Notes

1 Andrew James Hartley, *The Shakespearean Dramaturg* (New York: Palgrave McMillan, 2005), 65.
2 Mary Baldwin College offers an opportunity for M.A. and M.F.A. students to act as dramaturgs in their program; however, most programs that allow this are geared towards students in dramaturgy and directing.
3 Ken Davis and William Hutchings, "Playing a New Role: The English Professor as Dramaturg," *College English* 46.6 (1984): 560–61; and Cary M. Mazer, "Dramaturgy in the Classroom: Teaching Undergraduate Students Not to Be Students," *Theater Topics* 13.1 (2003): 135–41.
4 Mazer, 135.
5 Hartley, 1. See also Art Borreca, "Dramaturgy in Two Senses: Towards a Theory and Some Working Principles of New Play Dramaturgy," in *What Is Dramaturgy?*, ed. Bert Cardullo (New York: Peter Lang Publishing, 1995), 157.

6 Mary Luckhurst, *Dramaturgy: A Revolution in Theatre* (New York: Cambridge University Press, 2006), 263.
7 Michael Mark Chemers, *Ghost Light: An Introductory Handbook for Dramaturgy* (Carbondale and Edwardsville: Southern Illinois University Press, 2010), 10.
8 Art Borreca, "Political Dramaturgy: A Dramaturg's (Re)View," *The Drama Review* 37(2) (1993): 57. Cathy Turner and Synne K. Behrndt, *Dramaturgy and Performance* (Houndmills: Palgrave Macmillan, 2008), 101–2.

35

The art of collaboration
On dramaturgy and directing

Anne Bogart and Jackson Gay

Anne Bogart

The choreographer Mary Overlie, the inventor of the Viewpoints, told me that early on she had considered calling the Viewpoints "Windows." I understood immediately. Look at a specific theatrical moment through the window of space. Look at the same moment through the window of shape. Look at the moment through the window of story or the window of time. The specific window through which we look determines how we look and what we are looking for defines our particular experience of the moment.

Mary's choice of the word "Windows" reminded me of the architecture of a peep show. In midtown Manhattan in the days before Times Square was transformed into a theme park, 42nd Street was littered with adult bookstores, topless bars, strip clubs, and peep shows. As part of research for a play about the seedy world of strip joints, I visited a peep show on the corner of Eighth Avenue and 42nd Street. I entered nervously into one of the booths that surrounded the circular performance space, put a quarter into a slot, and a window shade opened revealing a scantily clad woman on a raised platform in the middle of the circle of booths. I felt uncomfortable but also intrigued. I thought of the other people, probably men, each with very different intentions than mine, sitting in their own booths, with their own view of the woman's shape and movements. Perhaps the architecture of a peep show is a useful image in considering the way we approach different aspects of play development and also how we think about collaboration.

Each member of a collaborative team views the production from a separate booth and through a different window. There is a director window, a playwright window, a dramaturgical window, an actor window, a set design window, a lighting design window, a sound design window, a producer window, and so on. Each artist looks at the very same event through a vastly different lens. For the best results, every moment of the play is examined with clarity through all of the different windows. Each window demands different skills and abilities.

Perhaps it is helpful to imagine that there is no such person as a director, no such person as a dramaturg, no such person as an actor, playwright, or designer. Perhaps rather than specific people, think of these jobs as windows through which any member of the collaborative team can approach the shared effort. In thinking this way, the contributions of others may be less threatening.

For most of my life I have felt great passion for and interest in the profession of directing. I have studied and continue to study how to best look at a play through the lens, or window, of a director. But I do not feel threatened if someone else looks through my window. In fact, I know that at times it is essential to the process that I move away from my own window and look for a time through the dramaturgical window or the design window or the actor window. The views of the play through each window are radically different. And I know that it is also advantageous for my colleagues to do the same. Sound designer Darron West often steps into my proverbial booth, looks at the play through the director window, and makes useful observations. Actors are also welcome to step into my booth.

An actor spends his or her entire life training to meet a live audience. A playwright faces the predicament of the blank page and then forges into battle to make something out of nothing. As a director, I provide the litmus test for an actor's attempts at expression in rehearsal. I am the first audience. But this does not mean that from time to time the roles cannot be fluid. I do not have to identify with my role so inflexibly that I cannot step away from the director booth and allow another person to step in and look at the play from the director's point of view. In true collaboration, all of these lenses or windows are necessary in the realization of a play.

The Taoists say, "Be round on the outside and square on the inside," which means be generous, respectful, and civil on the outside but on the inside know exactly what you think and feel at all times. A director who spends time controlling the rehearsal in superficial ways, a director who is territorial and inflexible is not a strong director. To collaborate one needs a strong core and a supple and flexible exterior. Imagine steel wrapped in cotton. While it is true that the director is the person who makes the final decisions about how the play is put together, this aspect of control and power can be negotiated in various ways. If all of the collaborators genuinely feel the freedom to breathe and roam around, taking breaks from the relentless points of view of their own disciplines, they will ultimately contribute more and feel more ownership in the process and the project.

Jackson Gay

The artists you surround yourself with in a room have to be people you trust, not agree with all the time. For me this is especially essential for a successful relationship with a dramaturg. With all collaborators, this trust is important, but the relationship with a good dramaturg is much more intimate and personal. I think this is because a dramaturg's role in a process can be so hard to pin down or define and can change drastically from project to project. Ironically, it's because of the fluid, ambiguous nature of the dramaturg that I often find myself relying on them in a kind of artistic partnership. People often ask what a dramaturg does as if it's a mysterious secret, but I've found the best dramaturgs actually embrace that mystery and in doing so open themselves up to everything. I'm completely drawn to that mysterious aspect in my rehearsal room and find it strangely freeing.

The more experienced I've become as a director and as I grow older, the more guarded and private I've become in my life and in my work. It's hard to know who to let in. And in many situations, the dramaturg is the only member of your inner artistic team you've been assigned and not picked yourself. That can be scary. You have to speed date and get on the same page very quickly. Which brings me back to the importance of trust. I want someone I can talk to about things that are hard to put into words – a feeling or intuition, an image or a gesture. My best experiences have been with dramaturgs who aren't afraid to really talk about some existential truth, but are also able to say "Okay, enough already. The scene needs to be faster and funnier." It's through these conversations and, maybe most importantly, the questions that are asked that I'm able to understand something in a way that can be translated to the stage. Having someone who can help you place your work in a historical or cultural context, reminding you of things that have come before you and how the story you are trying to tell can resonate in the present is invaluable, but my ideal dramaturg is someone who embraces their place in the room, listens, laughs, questions, and challenges me to do what I said I wanted to do in the first place, someone who can see when everyone else has lost that ability from staring too long or out of fear and insecurity.

When I begin to work on a play I start with the dramaturgical work. I start by reading the play several times. I then read anything and everything I can find written on that play and its writer: all the reviews I can locate from past productions going back to the beginning of that play's life and any literary criticism on the play and the writer. I educate myself on the cultural and political happenings of the time period of the play and/or the time period in which the play was written. I try and read all the writer's work in an effort to get to know the writer in a deeper way. If it's a new play, I often read the play out loud with the writer. I find this an incredibly useful way to get to know the writer and how they hear their play. It is an instant clue to what the tone of the piece is meant to be. It also gives excellent opportunities to ask questions in the moment. In both new and classic plays, I search for their recurring obsessions and interests. I identify the play's themes and motifs, and through this exploration I determine how the play continues to excite and how it is relevant to our current times. This research and in-depth exploration further illuminates why I am doing this play at this particular moment and opens up a dialog with my collaborators in both the rehearsal room and later on the stage with our audience. In this way, I think research and thoughtful text analysis are gifts that keep on giving from the beginning of the process onwards. I believe in knowing where you come from, knowing where a play came from, and knowing who and what came before you. I don't want to skip over these things in an effort to make something "new." I feel a responsibility to join in the ongoing dialog with theatre artists and works of art from the sometimes distant past, and I know that whatever I create will be new simply because it will be coming through me in this moment in time.

When I get stuck or frustrated by my inability to really get at something in a play, I always go back to a dramaturgical exercise a teacher of mine, Liz Diamond, taught me. It's called an Action Breakdown and it demands that you remove yourself – your assumptions – and focus solely on what the characters actually do. What they say and what they do. Not what you want them to do or mean or what you in your director way want them to represent. Only what they actually do. You go through a scene and in a very simple way you bullet point each action that occurs. This includes dialog and non-verbal stage directions. This is done without comment and without your point of view on anything. It's simply a list of actions. When you have written down this list of actions (it is extremely time consuming) you most often are amazed by what you had missed in your reading of the text or how you had tried to make something happen that simply doesn't happen. It's easy for anyone to skip over basic things in an effort to get to the seemingly more exciting ideas you have about a moment in a play. The Action Breakdown forces me to go back to the text and let the text give me the answers I need to break through to something truly wonderful in my work.

The craft aside, I believe every artist working on a project has to have a deep and authentic connection to the work. I tend to be drawn to writing that in some way explores the human condition with its isolation, fear, and aspirations. I'm interested in what people are scared of, how they've failed or been disappointed, or how they've disappointed. What they've achieved, how they achieved it, and at what cost. Most importantly, I'm compelled by stories of the universal human desire to be seen and to be known by someone else.

When I first began directing, I found myself obsessed with German plays and directed many of them in quick succession. I directed plays by Brecht, Heiner Müller, Wedekind, and Kroetz. I was drawn to these plays because they were strange to me and unrecognizable. And they were hard. They took a lot of work to understand and make sense of in every way. I loved the challenge of them. I loved the text analysis required, but also the compassion and heart. I loved that something that seemed so far away from my own experience of the world (I grew up in small Texas towns) could speak to me in such a deep, specific, and profound way. When I moved to New York, it was clear from the word go that in order to have a life in the theatre here you needed to work on new plays. (Not surprisingly, there were few producers that were looking for Texas-born female directors of German classics). Regardless, the best new plays I have worked on have shared the same obsessions I responded to in my early work on the classics. They all share something big and mysterious about them, something that often cannot be explained with words and maybe never totally known. They require an intellectual rigor, but in the end it's the mystery of them that attracts me. I'm excited by plays that make you dream of the next time you get to work on them again.

In the end (or the beginning) when you get into the room with your collaborators, you have to have the courage to let all your research, intellectual understanding, and homework go. You have to be fearless to go somewhere you don't know and play around in there. All the preparation and work you did will be there regardless, and, if you trust that, you will set yourself up for discovering something you didn't necessarily know, but is right and honest.

36

Dramaturgy in action ... even if it's not as a dramaturg

Thomas A. Oldham

What are the employment prospects for job seekers with theatre training or a background in performing arts? Pretty good, actually. In recent years, researchers and journalists have addressed this topic, publishing studies and statistics analyzing the business acumen and marketability of artists. Providing ample evidence to silence naysayers, these studies give theatre-makers a plethora of reasons to be optimistic about their chances on the job market: the sheer number of artists succeeding in various businesses, including 15 percent of the Young Entrepreneurs' Organization;[1] the recent focus on "soft skills" like self-awareness, risk-taking, and playing well with others, which theatre practitioners possess in abundance;[2] and the assorted ways that theatre is utilized by everyone from business school students honing their soft skills through collaborative drama classes[3] to medical residents exploring empathy through theatrical techniques[4] and body language.[5] While steady employment is never guaranteed in any economy, it appears that employers appreciate and utilize the talents of theatre artists now more than ever. As I weighed my contribution to this volume on dramaturgy, I found that my personal experience with dramaturg colleagues provides a remarkable example of this subject. We are all intelligent, talented people who are highly employable, if I do say so myself.

This naturally prompts a question: What do we, as dramaturgs, do? Now, I am not attempting to generalize about the role of the dramaturg or to define dramaturgy in the abstract. That has been debated so often as to be cliché. The real question is: What are specific, real-life dramaturgs doing today, and are they making a career of it? In our information age, surely the hoariest definition of dramaturgy – historical research for production – is sorely outmoded. It is difficult to justify a salary for this position when Wikipedia is free. No, dramaturgy is an adaptable discipline and a skill set with myriad applications. The "dramaturgical sensibility" that Geoffrey S. Proehl cherishes reflects this adaptability: "Indeed, what I most like about sensibility is its inclusiveness: it signals a way of meeting the world that encompasses a range of responses."[6] My generation recognizes both the challenges and opportunities of our situation, taking steps to diversify our experience, challenge the definition of what dramaturgs do, and expand our notions of career success. Today, in addition to theatre, we work in marketing, education, research analysis, and corporate relations.

Since receiving our degrees, my colleagues and I have gone on to successful careers; none of us, however, earns a living as a full-time dramaturg, and few have even held the title of dramaturg in any professional capacity. We have not followed the typical career path of the American dramaturg, largely because there is no typical career path for an American dramaturg.

Surveying the diverse array of jobs held by the Columbia Dramaturgy class of 2007, I begin with myself. Since my writing is being included in a book on dramaturgy, I naturally have a vested interest in the field. I am, however, not working in professional theatre, but in academic theatre. Therefore, placing my colleagues on a continuum of dramaturg career options from traditional to unorthodox, I consider myself to be somewhere in the middle. As a teacher, I use my dramaturgical research proficiency and mastery of storytelling when I write my syllabi and in the ways I interact with my students in lectures and discussions. I organize information in accessible, meaningful structures. Another key aspect of my career, professional development in terms of writing and original research, also employs these skills. I have worked as a production dramaturg within my academic setting, collaborating on student plays, but the amount of time that I have devoted to that is dwarfed by my other duties. In short, my work has involved traditional skills of dramaturgy, but rarely as a dramaturg and never in professional theatre. As for the rest of my cohort, I will briefly detail their careers, beginning with the more traditional dramaturgs among us and proceeding to those no longer working in theatre as a profession at all. Nonetheless, all retain the highly practical skills we learned in our M.F.A. program.

First is Nancy Vitale, who has the largest number of credits as a dramaturg for conventional theatre companies. She is currently the producing artistic director for an up-and-coming nonprofit that has been produced at major venues and has garnered critical acclaim in its short life. For her company's premiere production, she served as dramaturg, doing meticulous research for a play containing complex cultural and geographical allusions. She also helped the production team negotiate the play's emotional and logical structure, assisting with revisions throughout the rehearsal period. Further, her leadership position within the larger company has often required her knowledge of the inner workings of nonprofit theatre and the development process: her proficiency in fundraising, marketing, and donor events helps to grow the company. Well-rounded dramaturgy curricula often include classes or internships covering some area of management, and when small theatre companies need managerial savoir faire, dramaturgs can provide it. Even though her duties with this company keep her busy, Nancy has branched out into a burgeoning market for dramaturgs: television. During her company's nascency, a reliable paycheck proved nonexistent, so she became an assistant at a major cable network. Lately, she has also "started writing and breaking out sit-com concepts."[7] Thus, for both practical and artistic reasons, she has expanded notions of dramaturgy to serial storytelling models in a different medium.

Samantha Chavis follows, with her traditional dramaturgical work of season planning and audience outreach. She is part administrator, part producer, part curator. She does not, however, work for any theatre company; she works for her city government, managing performing arts programming in the public park district. Her task is a multifaceted form of "matchmaking," fostering relationships between different performing artists, companies, and organizations within the city, "which then leads to some kind of partnership or rental dynamic" for both seasonal and year-round programs.[8] While our schooling prepared her with courses aimed at future artistic directors and development associates, Sam has found the most fruitful parts of her career were honed by the intangibles of studying dramaturgy. General aesthetic sensibility and practical organization are important, of course, but many of her responsibilities involve forming and nurturing partnerships. In the heavily colla- borative world of theatre, maintaining relationships with artists is vital to dramaturgical practice: dramaturgs inform and advise playwrights, directors, stage managers, pro- ducers, and actors working on individual projects and within artistic communities. What Sam most appreciates about her work is building relationships with her audiences, which in her case becomes a civic duty. She brings art to various localities, tapping into the polyvocality of city life and theatre as collaborative art form. Managing various logistical problems and developing a keen awareness of local aesthetics has enabled her to forge stronger bonds in her community.

Wei-ming Liu is the last of the more traditional dramaturgs from our class, though her career path has been anything but traditional. Originally from Taipei, she worked in American academia before returning to Taiwan and becoming a theatrical jack of all trades. Her multilingual abilities have led to translation work, but translation requires more than just mastery of language, especially in theatre. Having a sensibility for dialogue, dramaturgical structure, and theatrical viability is also necessary. Addi- tionally, she has worked in a "haze of festival planning and promo work" for multiple theatrical organizations, and her tasks include marketing, copyright negotiations (in multiple languages), programming, and outreach.[9] She manages a complex blend of text work, research, and development enabled by her study of dramaturgy. One of the more striking ways in which she uses her dramaturgical training has been in structural and thematic organization of a theatre festival itself: finding something akin to a play's through line. The integrity of a festival requires the same dramaturgical analysis as an individual play or the planning of a season. Good dramaturgy improves the sturdiness of all storytelling arcs, large and small. In addition to the multifaceted work that falls under the purview of this festival, she has curated dramaturgical materials in other venues, doing historical and literary research for informational purposes. Audience education is a constant part of her career, and she often prepares lectures and programming in both professional and academic settings.

If I place my academic work after Wei's in this dramaturgy continuum, then Brenna Hill comes after me; her role within a major arts organization is a less obvious use of dramaturgy. Even though it is not an artistic position per se, Brenna's work in corporate and foundation relations has its roots in her dramaturgical education. Our M.F.A curriculum included management and development training, such as researching and utilizing donor networks. Brenna is a master of these processes today, as she develops "intricate solicitation plans, exciting and professional program proposals, and accurate annual reports" for her company. She investigates resources and aggregates data, but her work also requires artistic sensibility and dramaturgical finesse. Communication and collaboration play vital roles in articulating the goals of the organization and in reaching the diverse groups who contribute to those goals. Brenna also credits her dramaturgical knowledge of narrative structure with helping her craft solicitation plans into "persuasive program proposals that fully communicate the need for and the benefits of" the company's work, much of which is tied to the educational portion of its mission.[10] Like the dramaturgs who work in marketing discussed below, attention-grabbing, informative, and clearly delineated writing is important. Then again, any dramaturg who has written a program note or given a curtain talk knows this well. Communication not only with the outside world but also within her own department hearkens back to the training that has been invaluable to her success.

The final two dramaturgs do not work in the arts as their primary source of income. Their careers are in fields that do not initially seem to be suitable opportunities for dramaturgs, yet upon closer examination it becomes obvious that they are well served by their dramaturgical skills. Courtney Todd works as a marketing manager for a luxury lighting and furniture designer. Naturally, she is responsible for a variety of advertising, including social media and different forms of creative collateral. Dramaturgical research plays a significant role in her job, because she is required to keep abreast of industry trends and tailor her message to a specific kind of audience: her company's customers. Not only must her marketing appeal to current customers, but she must build a base of new consumers constantly. Just as some dramaturgs help to grow subscriber bases, Courtney must do the same for her business. She draws a direct parallel between her job and our training: "As a dramaturg, you are the voice for the playwright. As a marketer you're the voice and ambassador for the brand. You have to know the brand inside and out as you do the play as a dramaturg."[11] Historical knowledge of the company's aesthetic and voice is of utmost importance for her, in order to maintain a consistent message among various creative inputs. Making complex art that reaches audiences in a coherent way is what a dramaturg does. Courtney does this as well, creating a marketing experience that her customers understand and appreciate.

As Courtney demonstrates, marketing is a form of dramaturgical storytelling; my final classmate confirms that in a managerial capacity. Melissa Parrish is a senior analyst for a large research firm, where she is a mobile marketing expert. Her job description at its most basic is to bring marketers and their customers closer together, much like a production dramaturg helps to bring together theatre-makers and audiences. Melissa uses analytical skills in almost every aspect of her work. She employs a form of textual analysis in cobbling together various sets of data from multiple sources (including her own research), finding usable structures and patterns within them, and relating this back to the marketers so they can reach their target audiences. Naturally, writing skills are important to her job; producing written material that is informative yet easily consumed by executive businesspeople is a key component of her productivity. She also takes a leadership role in special consultancy projects, collaborating with various corporate inputs and data to produce a workable, uniform strategy for their business needs. When a multitude of opinions and objectives need shaping into a coherent whole, it is a situation that she says "feels almost identical to production dramaturgy, except that I don't get to be there on opening night."[12] For Melissa, marketing is a form of storytelling, and her training as a dramaturg has sharpened her ability to help her customers tell their stories.

Although an increasing number of theatres around the country are employing dramaturgs on their staff, the position remains far less prevalent in America than in Europe. That does not mean, however, that students of dramaturgy are unemployable in this country. Far from it. The skills fostered by studying dramaturgy, whether through a graduate degree or by working closely with writers, directors, and other theatre practitioners, are remarkable in their versatility and almost universal applicability. This underscores the importance of dramaturgy (and arts education in general) to the professional world at large, at a time when educational programs are forced to justify themselves financially. Some writers have gone so far as to claim that the M.F.A. is "the new M.B.A.,"[13] and while that may sound extreme, it is clear that creativity, ability to handle criticism while engaging audiences, and comfort with ambiguity are just a few of the skills that are increasingly appreciated in today's economy.[14] Dramaturgs are clearly no exception to recent trends that prove theatre artists are marketable. The understanding of textual complexity, knowledge of historical context, and mastery of theoretical application – all of which are crucial to dramaturgy – also translate to myriad jobs inside and outside theatre. Or, to put it another way, "the idea of a dramaturgical sensibility is not limited to a job title."[15] All of my colleagues agree that we utilize dramaturgy every day, even if it's not as a dramaturg.

Notes

1 Kevin Daum, "Entrepreneurs: The Artists of the Business World," *Journal of Business Strategy* 26 (2005): 56, doi:10.1108/02756660510700546, accessed June 25, 2013.

2 Marci Alboher, "Sharpening the Soft Skills (Which Aren't Really Touchy-Feely)," *New York Times*, April 7, 2008, available online at www.nytimes.com/2008/04/07/business/smallbusiness/07shift.html, accessed June 25, 2013.

3 Alison Damast, "MBAs Acting Out," *BusinessWeek*, December 18, 2007, available online at www.businessweek.com/bschools/content/dec2007/bs20071218_281023.htm, accessed June 25, 2013.

4 Linda A. Deloney and C. James Graham, "*Wit*: Using Drama to Teach First-Year Medical Students about Empathy and Compassion," *Teaching and Learning in Medicine* 15 (2003): 250.

5 Alan Mozes, "Theater Classes Help Docs' Bedside Manners," *Washington Post*, September 7, 2007, available online at www.washingtonpost.com/wp-dyn/content/article/2007/09/07/AR2007090701277.html, accessed June 25, 2013.

6 Geoffrey S. Proehl, *Toward a Dramaturgical Sensibility: Landscape and Journey* (Madison, NJ: Fairleigh Dickinson University Press, 2008), 17.

7 Nancy Vitale, e-mail message to author, March 4, 2013.

8 Samantha Chavis, e-mail message to author, March 19, 2013.

9 Wei-ming Liu, e-mail message to author, December 17, 2012.

10 Brenna Hill, e-mail message to author, March 18, 2013.

11 Courtney Todd, e-mail message to author, March 30, 2013.

12 Melissa Parrish, e-mail message to author, March 7, 2013.

13 Katherine Bell, "The MFA Is the New MBA," *Harvard Business Review: HBR Blog Network*, April 14, 2008, available online at http://blogs.hbr.org/cs/2008/04/the_mfa_is_the_new_mba.html, accessed June 25, 2013.

14 Steven Tepper, "Is an MFA the New MBA?" *Fast Company*, March 28, 2013, available online at www.fastcompany.com/3007541/mfa-new-mba, accessed June 25, 2013.

15 Proehl, 21.

Part IV

DRAMATURGS AS ARTISTIC LEADERS AND VISIONARIES

Privileges and responsibilities of the office

37

Dramaturgs as artistic leaders

Gideon Lester

The dramaturg is potentially the artistic director's Good Angel – a corrective necessity in his dealings with Board members exhorting him to take the safe way, with managers asking him to toe the bottom line, with audiences proving unresponsive to challenging works, and even with reviewers displaying impatience with the laborious process of building a company or developing a playwright. As the humanist in the woodpile, it is the dramaturg who must act as the conscience of the theatre, reminding it of its original promise, when it threatens to relax into facile, slack and easy paths.

Robert Brustein[1]

Ever since Gotthold Lessing began working as an embedded critic in the Hamburg National Theatre, his self-defined task to make "recommendations for the improvement of the [German] theater,"[2] there has been a kind of utopian longing about the practice of dramaturgy. I remember my first professor at graduate school telling me that the role of the dramaturg was "to make theatre better" – a lofty-sounding task, though as a student I had no idea how to undertake it. Later, as I started working with the director Robert Woodruff when he took over from Robert Brustein as artistic director of the American Repertory Theatre, he told me that my job as his dramaturg and associate artistic director was to keep him brave. This vision of the dramaturg as the custodian of artistic integrity and bravery is compelling, if seldom easy to realize. Dramaturgy as practiced in the United States can sometimes seem like the phantasm of a theatre that is courageous and artistically complex, dreamed in an economic reality that is stacked against courage and complexity.

What might it take to enfranchise dramaturgs really to "make theatre better?" Rather than keeping them in supporting roles, perhaps the theatre world might begin by readying them to compete for leadership positions, that is, to become artistic directors, curators, programmers, creative producers, beyond the limitations of the institutional dramaturg's traditional function. This would entail an expansion of the definition of dramaturgy to include the articulation of a broadened institutional vision, so that the shaping and running of a theatre or cultural center itself becomes a dramaturgical practice.

It is not fantastical to imagine dramaturgs working as artistic leaders. A number of former dramaturgs are already heading American theatres, from Oskar Eustis, artistic director of the Public Theater, to Christian Parker, associate artistic director of the Atlantic Theater Company. Robert Brustein, founder of the Yale Repertory Theatre and American Repertory Theatre, was primarily a dramaturg in the wider sense – a scholar, a working critic, and a cultural commentator who shaped a new vision for artistically ambitious regional theatres based on what was then the European model.

If we look beyond regional and off-Broadway theatres to multi-arts centers and other, more idiosyncratic structures, we find that the borders between dramaturgy, curating, producing, and artistic direction are already blurred. Some of the most entrepreneurial performing arts organizations in the United States have leaders who operate on a dramaturg-curator-producer-programmer continuum, even if they don't consider their primary work to be dramaturgical. I find these outliers deeply inspiring when I consider the possibility of an enhanced definition of the dramaturgy of artistic leadership. Susan Feldman, for example, is the founder and artistic director of St. Ann's Warehouse, a multi-arts performance venue in Brooklyn that has effectively invented a new institutional model, incorporating elements drawn from both producing and presenting structures, and a financial system that blends aspects of the commercial and nonprofit theatre. Feldman does not refer to herself as a dramaturg, but her work is frequently dramaturgical in its scope. She gives notes to artists, writes copy for grants and programs, interacts directly with her audience in the lobby before and after performances, and directs all aspects of the artistic mission of her institution. Over the past twenty years she has created at St. Ann's the most daring, and frequently international, theatrical programs in New York City, and developed a large audience to support it. From the Polish director Grzegorz Jarzyna's vast, cinematic *Macbeth*, which Feldman sited under the Brooklyn Bridge, to Mabou Mines' semi-parodic adaptation of *A Dolls House*, which was developed at St. Ann's and toured the world for almost a decade, to Les Freres Corbusier's full-scale environmental reconstruction of an evangelical "hell house" play, no two projects are alike, and Feldman and her team develop new marketing and funding strategies and partnerships to support each of them.

To take an example from a quite different organization, Melanie Joseph, artistic producer of the peripatetic Foundry Theatre, which produces socially engaged, participatory, and site-specific theatre and performance in New York City, commissions guest artists to create productions that are always the expression of a strong political and social inquiry. She guides and contextualizes these productions with a strong curatorial hand, often working developmentally with her artists for months or years in an explicitly dramaturgical capacity. The company's recent projects have included an investigation of how we create values in society, a theatre festival reimagining community and social justice in New York City, and a performative bus tour through the South Bronx. All Foundry projects are born from dramaturgical research, and Joseph moves seamlessly between the roles of dramaturg/artistic collaborator and producer/artistic director. In Joseph's case as well as in Susan Feldman's, the "leadership" function (artistic programming, crafting the Foundry's interactions with the communities of audiences, media, and donors) and the "dramaturgical" function (helping artists to shape their projects) are inextricably connected, in both cases creating a unified expression of a singular institutional vision.

While there are still relatively few professional dramaturgs leading theatres in America, in Europe the phenomenon has long been commonplace, particularly, but not only, in festivals and interdisciplinary arts centers. Mathias Lilienthal, former dramaturg of the Berliner Volksbühne, later became for many years the outspoken and visionary director of the Hebbel am Ufer (HAU) theatre complex in Berlin; Florian Malzacher, a former critic and later artistic director of the Steirischer Herbst festival in Graz, is also a frequent dramaturg for the theatre collectives Rimini Protokoll and Nature Theater of Oklahoma; the independent curators Hannah Hertzig and Mårten Spångberg have run site-specific international festivals while maintaining their own substantial art practices; Sven Åge Birkeland, founder of the Teatergarasjen in Bergen, has provided a developmental base for experimental American artists who can't find funding at home: these are just a few of the most prominent and entre-preneurial dramaturg-curators who have shaped new models of cultural institutions, new modes of artistic production, new relationships with communities and audiences. In all these cases, the traditional developmental definition of dramaturgy has been expanded to include conceptual and thus institutional leadership, in a European milieu where institutions must display conceptual rigor to thrive.

Why should we enlarge the definition of dramaturgy to include practices of institu-tional leadership? Since the 1970s, when the director displaced the playwright to become the most influential figure in the hierarchy of American theatre, most institutions have hired directors to lead them. This makes good sense in a traditional model of pro-duction, where a playwright writes a script and delivers it to a director, who then rehearses it with a cast of actors for a certain number of weeks until the play opens for the public. This familiar structure has several advantages for theatre institutions: it is easy to budget, easy to schedule, and easily replicable, year after year. Each artist is hired to do a clearly defined job, as playwright, director, actor, or designer; and each project takes roughly the same time to rehearse, leading to a predictable production schedule and a reliable annual rhythm in which five or six productions are created each season. Under this system it is financially expedient for a director to head the theatre, since he or she can also direct two or three productions per year. (The development of the American dramaturg's function tended to align with these priorities, supporting the director's vision through research and artistic development).

Times have changed, however, and increasingly artists are challenging this historical model. Directors are no longer necessarily the primary artists, at least in the non-traditional sectors of the theatre and performance worlds. Ensemble-based and "devised" theatre have muddied the categories of playwright, director, and actor and replaced the three-week rehearsal process with development and research periods of several months, even years. The evolution of site-specific, socially engaged, and parti-cipatory modes of performance has dislodged the primacy of the dramatic text and created productions that may be difficult or impossible to fit into a regular season structure. Artists and collectives such as ERS, Big Art Group, Nature Theater of Oklahoma; writer-choreographer-director-performers Jack Ferver and Young Jean Lee; the conceptual director Annie Dorsen, who has opened a new field of computer theatre that she refers to as "algorithmic dramaturgy"; and socially engaged, colla-borative theatre-makers such as Michael John Garces and Aaron Landsman are working at the intersections of theatre and dance, film, video, performance, new technology, and visual art, developing new interdisciplinary practices that may look nothing like traditional theatre and might require equally innovative forms of financing and producing to support them.

These developments are changing the landscape of the twenty-first century American theatre, but institutions structured on the twentieth-century historical model, with a director at the helm, a fixed rehearsal period, and a season built around a predictable annual budget and schedule, may find it hard to respond to such innovation. In a healthy system, artistic creativity will shape the institutional structure, and not vice versa. In such a time of innovation, where theatres are being called upon to experiment artistically, administratively, and financially, it is wise to consider the "dramaturgy" of leadership and to conceive of dramaturgs as possible leaders, whether or not they retain that job description.

North American dramaturgs are, indeed, already trained to consider institutional structure from multiple perspectives. They work directly with many kinds of artists and therefore understand the artistic process flexibly; they are taught to communicate that process effectively to audiences, press, funding bodies, and administrators. They acquire a deep knowledge of theatrical history from which they could, potentially, imagine a theatre of the future. From their own production practice they know what works in our contemporary system and what might be improved. If we believe that our current institutions are imperfect, dramaturgs are, by training, in a strong position to identify what needs to be changed, and even to put that change into action.

At present training for institutional leadership in the American theatre is primarily offered by management programs, which naturally emphasize the financial and operational aspects of the business – marketing, development, commercial producing, and so on. There are no programs in *artistic* leadership, and the resulting asymmetry, where a theatre's managing director is likely to be a specifically trained professional but the artistic director is not, can tend to privilege administration and management over artistic innovation in a theatre's priorities. In our field there are no equivalents of the visual art world's numerous and highly regarded graduate departments in curatorial studies, where museum directors and curators are taught to imagine and implement new institutional models, new ways of supporting artists, and new ways of engaging with the public. (Two important exceptions have recently emerged. The creation two years ago of Wesleyan's Institute for Curatorial Practice in Performance, though primarily focused on performance art rather than theatre, is a promising and timely development. The Yale School of Drama will soon be launching a new track under the joint auspices of its Dramaturgy and Management departments, though it remains to be seen whether the pedagogical focus is on artistic direction or management).

There may be no graduate schools for artistic directors, but there are plenty for dramaturgs. The seeds of change are often planted by educational institutions, and I believe it would have a profound impact if two or three of the many M.F.A. dramaturgy programs that have proliferated in the United States in recent years were to expand their definition of dramaturgy to include artistic leadership. Such a shift would not require massive curricular innovation; some programs already teach theatre history, strategies for artistic development, collaboration, critical writing, and contemporary practice, to which might be added courses in leadership skills and entrepreneurism, curatorial and institutional case studies, fundraising and marketing. The greatest shift would be that of nomenclature and therefore self-definition; if students attend a program in artistic leadership as well as dramaturgy, then they will start to consider themselves possible leaders, and therefore in time they will *become* leaders.

Attitude is everything, and if dramaturgs continue to believe that they are fit only for service roles in literary offices and rehearsal rooms, nothing will change. They will remain the humanists in the woodpile, to use Robert Brustein's evocative phrase. But if our job is truly "to make theatre better" we owe it to that theatre to exit the woodpile and take over the woodshop.

Notes

1 Robert Brustein, "The Future of an un-American Activity," in *Dramaturgy in American Theater: A Source Book*, eds. Susan S. Jonas *et al.* (Stamford, CT: Cengage Learning, 1996), 36.
2 Gotthold Lessing, *Hamburg Dramaturgy: A New and Complete Translation*, trans. Wendy Arons and Sara Figal, available online at http://mediacommons.futureofthebook.org/mcpress/hamburg, accessed August 20, 2013.

38

Dramaturgical leadership and the politics of appeal in commercial theatre

Ken Cerniglia

In an early scene of Rick Elice's irreverent *Peter Pan* prequel, *Peter and the Starcatcher*, the precocious Molly Aster discovers three orphan boys in the bilge dungeon of the *Neverland*, a shabby merchant ship on an 1885 voyage from Portsmouth to the remote and dangerous isle of Rundoon. Upon her request for the leader, and without the consensus of his fellow orphans, the cocksure Prentiss declares that he's in charge. After a few more feeble assertions, including his claim that "The leader has to be a boy," Molly turns to the timid, tubby orphan: "Ever notice, Ted – the more you claim leadership the more it eludes you?" Appreciating the sly put-down, from a girl no less, Ted shoots Prentiss a sideways glare and anachronistically retorts, "Oh, snap!"[1]

Staged by Tony-winning veteran actor Roger Rees and rising-star director Alex Timbers, *Peter and the Starcatcher* was developed over five years by Disney Theatrical Productions (where I have now been employed for a decade) in successive collaboration with Williamstown Theatre Festival, La Jolla Playhouse, New York Theatre Workshop, and a partnership of Broadway producers. The play was Disney's best-reviewed project in *The New York Times*, surpassing even *The Lion King*.[2] It earned nine 2012 Tony nominations and took home five awards, including Best Scenic, Costume, Lighting, and Sound Design – a historic sweep. A darling of the New York theatre community, *Peter and the Starcatcher* became the longest-running play of the 2011–12 Broadway season, transferred off-Broadway due to continued demand, and booked a rare national tour, which launched in Denver to more critical acclaim in August 2013. But in the midst of this success, nobody besides industry insiders and scrupulous program readers knows that it is a Disney project.

Having taken Molly's keen observation to heart before *Peter and the Starcatcher* came to New York, Disney Theatrical's president and producer Thomas Schumacher made the prudent decision to keep "Disney" off the show's title and its leadership low-profile. Due to the power of the Disney brand and the huge target of sometimes unwarranted criticism that our theatrical ventures had become, at least in New York, it seemed better to let Disney's first play stand on its own and the Broadway credentials of its billed creators – Elice (*Jersey Boys*), Rees (*Nicholas Nickleby*), and Timbers (*Bloody Bloody Andrew Jackson*) – draw ticket buyers downtown to New York Theatre Workshop in the spring of 2011. The strategy paid off. Positive reviews and sold-out houses ultimately carried the project to Broadway the following spring.

Despite its status as a relative newcomer to commercial theatre, with *Beauty and the Beast* premiering in 1994 as an experiment, Disney Theatrical has now become one of the industry's most successful producers. Our shows, combined, regularly secure between 10 and 20 percent of the weekly Broadway box office, particularly during peak tourist seasons. *The Lion King*, which premiered in 1997 and won six Tony Awards, including two for director and costume designer Julie Taymor, became the highest-grossing Broadway show of all time in 2012, with over twenty global productions in eight languages to date. Only three of our eight Broadway ventures shuttered before recouping their initial investments, which is far below the 75 to 80 percent average commercial failure rate, but have since found profit in international and licensed productions. In just ten years, Disney's catalog of over twenty titles for adult and young performers at Music Theatre International has generated over 50,000 licensed productions worldwide. And Disney's partnership with Feld Entertainment brings the company's characters, stories, and songs to millions of spectators in over 80 countries each year through *Disney on Ice* and *Disney Live!* touring arena shows.[3]

So, why the far-reaching success? It would be easy to chalk it up to the deep, family-friendly movie catalog and incomparable distribution machinery of one of the world's largest entertainment companies. I will not deny that these elements provide a significant leg up for theatrical ventures – if they're good. However, I will argue that Disney's real, sustained success onstage stems from two essential elements: the core dramaturgical practice that leads creative development and the careful curation of appeal. Ever since the brothers Disney founded their namesake company in 1923, character and story have been at the center of every film, book, series, park, and play. Decades of refined "storyboarding" – a process by which animators and writers map out a film with drawings and words then act out the story for producers before pen ever hits celluloid (or now, before pixels illuminate computer screens) – have invited critical feedback and clarified themes and emotional through lines that might appeal to the widest possible audiences, not only in a specific place and time, but also for posterity. Although Schumacher and his producing partner Peter Schneider had worked many years in nonprofit and festival theatre before arriving at the Walt Disney Studios in the late 1980s, their time at Disney Feature Animation (now called Walt Disney Animation Studios) helped shape how they would lead commercial theatrical development when the opportunity presented itself just a few years later. Storytelling rigor would continue to be key.

One major difference between Disney Theatrical and other commercial theatre producers is that we develop all of our shows in-house with source material that the company already owns or acquires. Most shows come to Broadway after already establishing themselves as commercial hits elsewhere, usually London's West End or at a regional nonprofit theatre, where commercial producers may or may not be involved from an early stage. These shows' ticket sales must demonstrate potential to pay for weekly running costs *and* to pay back capitalization costs (underlying rights, rentals, developmental workshops, rehearsals, creative fees, etc.) with profits within a certain amount of time (usually 20 weeks for a play or a year for a musical) so that investors can eventually make money. Given that the vast majority of commercial theatre ventures *lose* money, there's often not much difference between nonprofit "donors" and commercial "investors." No matter the venue, rich people subsidize theatre tickets; on the rare occasion that a commercial show is a hit, the rich people get some of their money back. Disney works somewhat outside these two models, since we are responsible to stock shareholders. We use their money to capitalize projects. If the projects become profitable, Disney returns the money to the shareholders in the form of dividends; if not, the company writes off the losses. Of course, Disney Theatrical's annual profits funnel into the Walt Disney Studios, a major segment of the Walt Disney Company (which also comprises theme parks, media networks, consumer products, and digital interactive divisions), so it is difficult for the average shareholder to parse the theatrical contribution. However, our awareness of Disney's fiduciary responsibility to shareholders affects the projects we tackle. Unlike independent commercial theatre producers, who are able to take on projects based on personal passions regardless of financial outcome (especially the wealthy ones), we can only invest time and resources into theatrical projects that have a reasonable chance of turning a profit.

Thus we enter the debate over appeal. For whom will a given show be created? In Hollywood parlance, the "big hits" address four-quadrant home runs: children, adults, female, male. On Broadway, female adults often drive ticket sales.[4] What actually appeals to them and the friends and family they bring along is the $100,000 question (or more like $15 million for an average new musical). To illuminate, I present the case of *Newsies*, Disney's other recent unlikely hit, which picked up 2012 Tony Awards for Alan Menken and Jack Feldman (score) and Christopher Gattelli (choreography), along with six other nominations. Based on a 1992 musical film that was in turn based on the historical 1899 Newsboys' Strike, *Newsies* was never intended for Broadway. Directed by Kenny Ortega, who later helmed Disney's *High School Musical* mega-franchise, the film cost $15 million but only took in $3 million at the box office; however, on VHS and DVD it became a cult classic for an entire generation of musical theatre fans. The title was on the top of MTI's request list ever since Disney began licensing shows in 2004, but development on the stage musical, which could not seem to break free from certain of the movie's cartoony and convoluted elements, was in limbo until Harvey Fierstein serendipitously ran into Menken at the grocery store. When the composer lamented about *Newsies*, the veteran comic actor and book writer Fierstein, an unabashed fan of the movie, jumped at the opportunity to help out. With some streamlining and a few key character and plot changes, Fierstein's fresh contribution was able to put the project back on track and free up Menken and Feldman to write new songs and revise others.

Investing in our usual rigorous table work, we bent the script and score to a dramaturgically sound place. However, the developmental readings, which included fantastic new arrangements of fan favorites "Carrying the Banner," "Seize the Day," and "Santa Fe," revealed that something was not quite hitting the mark. This was a dance musical and we had yet to see it *move*. Although *Newsies* was aimed solely at the licensing catalog, Schumacher decided to invest in a one-off production with a top-notch creative team before we settled on the final version of the musical that would be done in high schools across the country. Paper Mill Playhouse in Millburn, New Jersey, stepped up to co-produce this pilot, and Jeff Calhoun, with whom we had developed and launched a successful stage version of *High School Musical*, agreed to direct. He and set designer Tobin Ost, along with projectionist Sven Ortel, created a modern unit set of three three-tiered swiveling towers that resembled fire escapes and could be decorated to evoke 1899 New York City. Gattelli, a former chorus dancer whose peers were in the movie, practically begged to choreograph. Filling out the creative team were veteran costume designer Jess Goldstein, lighting designer Jeff Croiter, and sound designer Ken Travis. The enthusiasm of the team quickly spilled over into auditions, with an unprecedented turnout of fine young dancers, including scores of working Broadway veterans who were willing to give up their steady jobs for a chance to be in this regional production of *Newsies*. Up-and-coming stars Jeremy Jordan and Kara Lindsay landed the lead roles of union leader Jack Kelly and reporter Katherine Plumber, Fierstein's conflation of two characters from the movie.

Although the young cast was enthusiastic beyond measure and took quickly to Gattelli's exuberant choreography in studio rehearsals, it was not until we got on stage at Paper Mill that we realized the potential of *Newsies* to go further than we had expected. Cast energy, exuberant dancing, impressive scenography, a soaring anthemic score, and a story of young striking workers that resonated with the 99 percent in the midst of the Occupy Wall Street movement created a whole that far surpassed the sum of its constituent parts. We had been bracing for negative responses from cult fans ("Fansies") since we had significantly altered the film's story, as well as critics, who came from New York City with pencils sharpened (especially with "Disney" over the title of this show). To our pleasant surprise, the disarming musical registered approval at almost every turn, and speculation about a Broadway transfer spread quickly.[5]

Back in New York, the Nederlander Organization approached Schumacher with an offer of the vacant Nederlander Theatre on 41st Street, which is in clear view of the Disney Theatrical offices atop the New Amsterdam Theatre across the street. Not wanting to promise theatregoers anything on the level of *The Lion King* or *Mary Poppins* in terms of spectacle, Schumacher agreed to bring *Newsies* to Broadway for an unprecedented (for us) limited run of 12 weeks the following spring. (Coincidentally, we had already agreed to let a consortium of producing partners transfer *Peter and the Starcatcher* to Broadway the same season, and opening nights ended up just two weeks apart. Lighting designer Jeff Croiter and I ended up doing a lot of shuttling between the Nederlander and the Brooks Atkinson Theatre on 47th Street, as we were working on both shows – admittedly, a good problem to have!)

With dates set, we went to work analyzing what worked at Paper Mill and what we could improve before Broadway. Everyone agreed that the cast, set, and score cornerstones checked broad "appeal" boxes, so we just needed to focus on some of the minor elements that could better support the show's highlights – what made people come and say "wow." Menken and Feldman went to work on new songs for the villain Joseph Pulitzer and the sympathetic burlesque star and theatre owner Medda Larkin. Ann-Margret had played the role in the film, and we had cast a fantastic actress, Helen Anker, in that vein for the Paper Mill production. However, on Broadway, Disney had become known for its diverse casting practices and even won a national award for its multiracial casting of *The Little Mermaid* in 2008. As good as the *Newsies* cast was, we realized that it was not visually reflecting the complexions of 1899 New York, much less those of today. A bit of research revealed that black entertainer Ada Overton Walker, wife of vaudeville star George Walker, was a rising influence in her own right at the turn of the twentieth century. She became the model for a reconceived Medda Larkin, whom African-American performer Capathia Jenkins ultimately played on Broadway. Diversity also broadened as we added three alumni from the television competition *So You Think You Can Dance* to the cast. Not only were they phenomenal dancers, but also their national exposure appealed to nontraditional ticket buyers. During a short re-rehearsal process, new songs were inserted, prudent script and score edits were incorporated, and new cast members were brought up to speed. We opened on March 29 to fairly positive reviews.[6]

But the show had already become a hit before opening night. *Newsies* cult mania, combined with very strong word of mouth from Paper Mill, went viral online. It led to ticket sales from all 50 states and exhaustion of inventory before first preview. Due to overwhelming demand, the run was extended ten weeks. Then, even before summer arrived, sales pressed the show into an open-ended run. Nobody saw this coming. Company management had to work quickly to extend contracts or find replacements for those who had already lined up other work after the initial contract date. Within 40 weeks, *Newsies* became Disney's quickest-recouping Broadway show.[7] While there are a few more dramaturgical tweaks I would love to make for the musical's next iteration (there always are), I fully recognize that *Newsies* is working – really working – in ways that transcend dramaturgy. Paying careful attention to appeal is absolutely essential for a shot at commercial success, and my job depends on shows that make money. We can have the most dramaturgically sound show on the boards, but if nobody wants to see it, what difference does it make? Examples abound of terrific theatre that could not find an audience to support a commercial run. In most of these cases, essential appeal was not identified or developed sufficiently for the market.

Our theatrical work is unusual within the Walt Disney Company. Unlike films or toys, our products are live and repeated, and as such can evolve over time. Since we have a dramaturgical forum at our core and multiple distribution options, we are able to go back to the drawing board on shows whose first iterations do not fully succeed. For example, we have created new versions of *Tarzan* and *The Little Mermaid*, which fell short on Broadway, that have found success in international and licensed productions. And even hit shows can get better. In 2009, we cut 12 minutes from *The Lion King* for the musical's premiere in Las Vegas and subsequently incorporated the successful cuts into productions around the world. Radically shorter versions of the show for young performers are being developed to join 15 other titles in our Broadway Junior collection, which we create to help inspire the next generation of theatre-makers.[8]

During their tearful farewell on the newly christened "Neverland" island, the already-growing-up Molly and the now-eternal boy Peter attempt to remember all the details of their awfully big adventure, even playfully swapping lines from one poignant exchange: "PETER: And you're the better leader. MOLLY: Really? PETER: No. (*They laugh, enjoying each other. Then it changes*)."[9] As we revisit and reshape familiar shows, new projects with new rules – like *Peter and the Starcatcher* and *Newsies* – reinvigorate the Disney Theatrical horizon and challenge us to become better leaders, especially when we (mistakenly) think that we have got it all figured out. Key dramaturgical questions of "why?", "why now?" and "for whom?" lead our constant pursuit of appeal to an ever-evolving demographic of theatregoers who desire high-quality family entertainment.

Notes

1 Rick Elice, *Peter and the Starcatcher: The Annotated Script of the Broadway Play* (New York: Disney Editions, 2012), 29.
2 *New York Times* chief theatre critic Ben Brantley raved about the play both at New York Theatre Workshop ("Peter Pan [the Early Years], with Bounding Main and All," March 9, 2011) and on Broadway at the Brooks Atkinson Theatre ("Effortless Flights of Fancy," April 15, 2012).
3 Since October 2008, when Disney Theatrical Group moved its headquarters to the "open office" environment of the renovated Rooftop Theatre above the New Amsterdam Theatre on 42nd Street, Schumacher has actively encouraged pragmatic transparency about our diversifying work, while avoiding unnecessary fanfare. See, for example, Gordon Cox, "Disney Theatrical Mixes It Up," *Variety*, March 17, 2012; and Patrick Healy, "Disney Shows in Development," *The New York Times*, June 20, 2013.
4 According to the Broadway League's 2011–12 demographics report, two-thirds of the Broadway audience is female: see www.broadwayleague.com/index.php?url_identifier=the-demographics-of-the-broadway-audience, accessed September 2, 2013.
5 Even *The New York Times* was welcoming to Disney's *Newsies* "out of town": David Rooney, "Newsboy Strike? Sing All About It," September 29, 2011.
6 Alas, once *Newsies* was on Broadway, Ben Brantley proved to be a less enthusiastic *New York Times* reviewer than Rooney ("Urchins with Punctuation," March 29, 2012).
7 For more details on this unusual project, see *Newsies: Stories of the Unlikely Broadway Hit*, ed. Ken Cerniglia (New York: Disney Editions, 2013).
8 Descriptions of all stage titles in the Disney catalog can be found at www.disneytheatrical licensing.com.
9 Elice, 149.

39

On dramaturgy and leadership

Vicki Stroich

Dramaturgy is a support function that offers great depth and focus to the creative process in the theatre. Dramaturgs embrace this role as the artist in the room who helps other artists tell stories and express their visions as potently as possible to an audience. In organizations, dramaturgs and literary managers help the artistic director realize a programming vision and connect the work deeply with an audience. "Artistic helper" was the short answer I gave at parties when someone asked me what I do and I saw in their eyes they only wanted a small-talk answer. If they asked a follow-up question, that is when I got into the great challenges and rewards of dramaturgy.

Recently, my work and understanding of what I contribute to an organization has shifted. I have been enjoying leadership roles; artistic directorships, executive directorships, and presidencies of international service organizations are not considered "helper" roles even if they are in support of a larger cause. I have spent quite a bit of time considering the question of leadership and dramaturgy and articulating why dramaturges are well suited for leadership roles. This articulation is extremely important not only in realizing my own professional goals moving ahead but also for my dramaturgical peers. We need to begin acknowledging and articulating the unique power and value of what we contribute and to see the leadership potential in our support role and our "dramaturgical sensibility," to borrow a phrase from Geoff Proehl.

What is leadership?

Leadership is the action of leading a group or organization towards fulfilling a shared vision or goal. In the basic terms of theatre employment and hierarchy, the roles that come to mind are artistic directorship, executive directorship, and other management level roles in organizations. It also extends to work on boards of directors. There are examples of dramaturgs who have taken on leadership roles, including Urjo Kareda (former artistic director, Tarragon Theatre, Toronto), Oskar Eustis (artistic director, the Public Theatre, New York), and André Bishop (artistic director, Lincoln Center Theatre, New York). Whether we are freelancing on a project or working in a literary office reading scripts, this definition can be applied in our day-to-day work as a way of reframing the way we think of our skills and articulating the intrinsic value of our work as dramaturgs.

I discussed dramaturgy and leadership for this chapter with Vanessa Porteous (artistic director, Alberta Theatre Projects, Calgary), Janet Allen (executive artistic director, Indiana Repertory Theatre, Indianapolis), and Ben Henderson (councilor Ward 8, City of Edmonton). This is a small sample and there are, of course, other dramaturgs in leadership roles, although the number of people who identify as dramaturgs in leadership positions in both Canada and the United States is smaller than that of directors in leadership positions.

Dramaturgical skills that are also leadership skills

Listening and research

The best dramaturgs are careful listeners and observers. They are also curious and efficient researchers, able to identify and pursue information that is most useful to a process or to a particular question. In leadership roles there is a lot of information and a great many perspectives to balance. One must weigh what happened in the past with what is needed in the present and consider how it affects the future. Leaders need to have a full view of the situation in order to determine a course of action. By taking on the role of witness in the room and actively listening to our collaborators, helping them articulate their goals for a project and their fears, we are very powerful because we hold a space for those varied perspectives. We then combine those present voices with an understanding of theatre history and the advances in performance studies to place the work we are doing on a continuum. In short, we view situations in the macro and know what questions to ask, what information to seek to inform our view of a project in much the same way that a leader does when confronted with a decision.

Interpretation, synthesis, and articulation

Our focus as dramaturgs is often on helping interpret a text. We take the information we have, based on the text in front of us, our research, and the visions of those around us; we then synthesize it and help our peers articulate what story is being told and why. This leads to a cohesive and potent piece of theatre or season of programming seen by diverse audiences. Leaders also interpret the information they have and synthesize it into a direction, a goal, or a vision that can be communicated and shared with others. It has been my dramaturgical ability to synthesize ideas and succinctly articulate what a large group is thinking or saying that has been one of my greatest assets in leadership situations. I have been complimented on my skills at interpretation, synthesis, and articulation by colleagues in other industries, including consultants who lead corporate seminars in strategic planning; whenever I receive one of those compliments I immediately think "that's dramaturgy."

Coming up with ideas, sharing information, stating opinions, identifying pros and cons are all valuable to a decision-making process, but a leader ultimately interprets all of these impulses from the group, synthesizes them and articulates a goal and course of action. As dramaturgs, we have strengths that we can activate in leadership positions in determining informed directions and actions. Vanessa Porteous, artistic director at Alberta Theatre Projects, describes the value of dramaturgical synthesis as "the ability to ask questions that lead to creative action. In running things you should be able to take the information you've gathered and come to action or help other people come to a course of action."

Vision

There is something about our search for meaning as dramaturgs, our quest to understand and unlock what a writer is looking to communicate about our world, our human condition, the need to laugh and cry that informs our skills as visionaries. We are not only interested in what is being said, but why it is being said and what lasting effect it should have on those that witness the work. We value vision.

Great leaders are able to inspire great work by sharing a strong vision and focusing people on the meaning and value of what they are striving for through their work. I was reminded of this recently during a natural disaster in my hometown Calgary, when our mayor, a great leader, was able to keep his staff and the whole city mindful and engaged in helping their neighbors by reminding everyone that volunteerism and generosity would create a shared momentum that would allow the city to recover and thrive in the short, mid and long term.

Ben Henderson, a dramaturg who has taken on a political leadership position as a councilor for the City of Edmonton, speaks about the value of presenting ideas in narrative. He hears many of his peers in politics, lobbying, and advocacy discussing the value of using narrative to influence people:

> As dramaturgs, we have skills in narrative. And meaning is best expressed through story. We are able to understand what makes people tick and find out what is important to them, match it with what is important to us and express where those values meet through story. It has been very useful in my work. Even knowing these skills exist and can be honed is an important advantage.

There is great value in supporting the vision of our peers, we need to remember that. When we want to express a vision and lead we also need to use the skills we have to imagine this vision and express it.

Planning and collaboration

Expressing a vision is not where leadership ends, of course. A leader who expresses a vision, sets a goal, makes an informed decision, or chooses a direction must then activate their team to take action towards the vision. As process engineers creating flexible models to fit different people and projects dramaturgs have strong planning skills. Our ability to navigate a range of personalities, work collaboratively with artists, and connect artist and management or artist and audience in service of a meaningful experience speaks to an inherent understanding of the value of teamwork.

Everyday dramaturgs exercise the creative and communicative skills that are sought after by executives in other industries. If dramaturgs wish to activate their skills to lead a group towards a shared goal the same way they focus their fellow artists and our audiences towards the meaning of a piece of theatre, they should be able to.

Constructive critique

Dramaturgs never rest in changing their perspective and taking a holistic view of a piece of theatre to assess its success at expressing itself to an audience. They don't take anything for granted and continue to ask questions of the team to refine the experience. In keeping the interpretation of the text, the story, the vision in mind they are able to offer thoughtful, constructive critique rather than personal criticism.

Great leaders also question the systems and processes that they and their teams are engaged in to assess how successful they are in reaching the shared vision or goal. They are not afraid to offer praise for what is working, and when something is not working they engage in the question of why and how it could work better. As dramaturgs we spend a lot of energy finding the right question that will unlock a stronger answer or direction. Dramaturgs are always engaged in this assessment process. Good leaders do that, too.

Renewal

When a goal is reached, a plan completed, great leaders celebrate with their teams and look to the horizon to see what new project, goal, or question inspires them next. In the theatre we are in a constant state of renewal. We dive into projects, work with new teams of people, and create something we know is ethereal; and we do it with passion, curiosity, and generosity. We work on varied timelines (weeks, months, years). We are always looking ahead.

And finally ... a balanced ego

What can someone who is in a support role offer in a leadership role? Respect for those that support them. This is probably one of the most valuable factors in effectively leading a group of people towards a vision. Dramaturgs come to leadership positions with that respect because we have chosen to support processes. Dramaturgs also come to leadership positions with a respect for the big picture. Indiana Repertory Theatre's Executive Artistic Director Janet Allen had to articulate a unique vision to the Indiana Rep Board of Directors when she applied for her artistic directorship. Directing was not a part of her application. Rather than discussing what art she could create at the company her focus was "What is the art we can curate for the community?" This vision was compelling to the board. In describing her style of leadership, Allen "leads by shepherding, leads by hiring, creating an environment conducive to the best work and encouraging from behind."

Leadership certainly requires a healthy ego, but it thrives with a balanced ego. "Ego" may not even be the best word. Perhaps "courage" is the word I am looking for.

Regardless of how one contributes to a project or a movement, the very act of contributing is an act of courage because you make an offer to a group and making offers requires some bravery. To step into a leadership role requires the courage to speak up and be held accountable. Dramaturgs have a view of the big picture and a respect for the support needed to fulfill a leader's vision. Combine that with the courage that it takes to lead and one has the balanced personality of a strong leader.

Porteous notes that dramaturgs value exploration and are often trained not to offer the solution first: "I got a lot of feedback when I started that this style of leadership was confusing for people, they didn't recognize my decision making. The exploration of ideas, consensus building and facilitation mislead people into thinking I wasn't making decisions." There may be assumptions about the nature of both dramaturgy and leadership that must be overcome.

Henderson discussed the notion of "personal capital" and how it can be difficult for dramaturgs to acquire the personal capital required to be perceived as a leader, because not taking credit for our contribution to our work is often inherent in the role. Porteous commented that "there are lots of issues of ego and power that you need to have resolved for yourself when you are leading people. Those of us in dramaturgy maybe don't have them resolved as much as we think we do." The personal courage and confidence that is required to step into a leadership role and be held accountable is something that we are all capable of; it is also something that we often discover when the project or the cause activates that courage within us.

In conclusion …

Not every dramaturg may want to take on a high-level leadership role. But every dramaturg should be aware of how our skill set can be applied to leadership and embrace how valuable these qualities are in leading. This understanding and articulation is a journey that will continue to evolve; others may take a different view of these skills and their application in certain situations. But the first step is to value what we do and begin to articulate that value for ourselves and others in order to be empowered in our roles, regardless of whether they support or lead a process.

40

Leadership advice to a dramaturgy student

Anne Cattaneo

I've been thinking about where dramaturgy was when I began my career in the 1970s and where things are now. I went to grad school at the Drama School at Yale in the then D.F.A. program for Dramatic Literature and Criticism. Dramaturgy was unknown. My entire experience with dramaturgy happened in my third and final year. It's odd that I have no memory of how I knew about the profession (though since I had lived in Germany and spoke German, perhaps somehow there I had heard of it?). I must have known something because I went to see the ever-accommodating dean, Howard Stein, and told him what little I knew and suggested that since Sean O'Casey's *Cock-a-Doodle Dandy*, directed by Bobby Lewis, was about to go into rehearsal (and is there a play whose exploration more calls out for a dramaturg?), perhaps I could try it out. Dean Stein called me back to his office a few days later, saying he'd spoken to Bobby and I should go see him outside the rehearsal room on their first day. I did so. I hope you know who Bobby Lewis was. I did and because I had been hired for my very, very first job in the theatre by Bill Ball at the American Conservatory Theater, I knew, let us say, the type – grand, great lineage and history, in Bobby's case The Group. I knew all this from the lowliest perspective, and I was of course scared to death. "Darling, Howard told me all about this and I'm thrilled. What a great idea! Why don't you run off to Sterling Library and find out everything about the play – and come back and see me on opening night!" That was the extent of my dramaturgy experience at Yale.

My work as a dramaturg has only happened in theatres, not in an academic environment. I have taught a little bit: I've taught theatre history to Juilliard's first-year acting students for many years, and I once tried to conceive what I thought was a pretty unique "essence of how to dramaturg" class, which I taught at Columbia for a semester in the 1980s. That syllabus and everything I have to tell you about the specifics of how I work as a dramaturg on classical and new plays is in the dramaturgy textbook *Dramaturgy in American Theater*, which was conceived and brought into being by the LMDA and is responsible for the creation of probably 75 percent of the dramaturgy programs in this country. I realize this classic textbook is almost 20 years old, but its collection of documents outlining the founding of our profession in the US alone makes it invaluable. Few people realize how long the history of our profession is here.

Today I would really have to think about how to prepare someone for this profession. And as I look around, it seems now that with the self-immolation of English departments into the ashes of critical theory (how many who would have been English majors in previous generations have fled to dramaturgy, or architecture even, as a result?), there is a flourishing environment training dramaturgs, with (compared to my early years) so many programs that now exist across the country. Up to now there have been two paths before you – one path in the theatre and one in the university. I can only reflect on the former. To me the difference seems simple: our job in the theatre includes creating an event that must interest a larger public; in a university setting, the public is contained and homogeneous. It may be that in the future, other paths will present themselves.

So where *did* I learn everything? From probably the two greatest dramaturgs (besides Brecht) of the twentieth century: Botho Strauss and Dieter Sturm, who worked with Peter Stein at the Schaubühne am Halleschen Ufer in Berlin in the 1970s and 1980s. I'm happy to pass on six short maxims – a summation of what I know – which I hope might spark some reflection.

1. Ours is a creative profession – one that requires as much creativity as acting, directing, and design. You have to be able to look at a text in an original way and know how to communicate your ideas to your collaborators. It's not a helping profession; if you want to help people, transfer your credits right now over to the medical school. It's not a job for an expert or an authority. On every successful project I have worked on there would have been someone easy to find who knew more than I do: Arnold Rampersad knew way more about Langston Hughes on *Mulebone*; for information on nineteenth-century Russia for *The Coast of Utopia*, I reached out to Tatyana Tolstaya or even the *Wars of the Roses*; when I was working on *Henry IV*, and I think I know a fair amount about Shakespeare, there were dozens of scholars to consult. But these experts didn't have my ideas about the stage and my insight and my relationship with artists. Thinking about a text as a director does, or as an actor does, is what we do – but from our point of view. Seeing material freshly and finding a way into it that no one has found before is something that takes time to practice and to get good at. It's the core of what we do. Original thinking among actors, directors, and designers is what we prize – it's the same for dramaturgs. How to get good at it?

2. Lateral relationships, a term I only recently became familiar with. It means, as you probably all already know, stay with your friends, work with them. I got my first job in the New York theatre as literary manager of the Phoenix Theatre when it was doing world premieres of new work by American and international writers (my very first day on the job was the second day of rehearsal of Wendy Wasserstein's *Uncommon Women and Others*) because I came into the interview with three full seasons of new play ideas, together with potential directors that the artistic director who hired me had never heard of. How did I find these? By going to the theatre *way* downtown, by talking with my friends, by recommending my friends. If you dream of leaving school and going directly to work at the Public Theatre, I hate to tell you, but you will be doing a lot of xeroxing. If you take a day job waitressing like every actor you went to school with, and you join a group of your friends making a new theatre company, perhaps outside New York City, you will be in the thick of things,

you will make art and your theatre will end up being invited to the Public – just like *Gatz* or *Good Person of Szechwan*.

Let's posit that our aim as artists is to memorialize our time on earth in a great play or plays that will go down in history and be performed in the future.

Our dream is to be a part of supporting and realizing the work of our Shakespeare, our Aeschylus, our Chekhov, our Brecht just as their and our careers begin. And please remember that we might be handed not *Mother Courage* or *Good Person* but *Baal*, Brecht's first play, a great but very, very new and difficult play. We would need to see the future Brecht in this play.

How to do this? How to understand this play? How to support this writer in the way that is best for *this* writer and his or her process? Is it true that no important theatre in history has ever begun by young artists penetrating existing institutions, but instead by young artists banding together to create new kinds of theatre with a new aesthetic – The Group Theatre, Steppenwolf, Joan Littlewood, the NEC, the Living Theatre, Joint Stock, SF Actors Workshop, the Moscow Art Theatre, Molière, the Lord Chamberlain's Men?

3. You will be able to chart your course to a successful career as a dramaturg in the theatre by your proximity to actors. If you know and love and spend time with actors you will be okay. If you don't, you won't. At the first meet and greet of a play, as your career advances, there should be more than one actor (and when you are as old as I am, hopefully they will be playing the leading roles) who will run across the room and hug you. Because they know that together you can take them higher. And you will know how to do that because you know them as a person. As an individual. I've never understood when people tell me dramaturgs pass out packets in rehearsal. How can anyone make use of cookie-cutter material when everyone is so different? Linda Winer did a nice talk with me for Women in Theatre after *Utopia* opened (which you can find on Youtube) and I mentioned the wildly different ways I worked with Jennifer Ehle, Brian O'Byrne, Ethan Hawke, Jason Butler Harner, Billy Crudup – and Stoppard actually. It's personal – that's what I learned from Botho and Dieter, who were masters of this. And the closer you live your life to that of an actor the easier it will be. *If* you're inside the gates of a theatre institution and they're outside, if you're secure and they're not, it's going to be harder.

4. Art is messy. Both Botho and Dieter were sought-after opinion writers for German literary journals and newspapers; and Botho once wrote a piece for the op-ed page of *Die Zeit* – our what? *New York Times* or *Wall Street Journal*, early on, so the late 1970s – comparing the rise of fundamentalist religious movements around the world to the rise of criticism and curating in the fine arts – how each sought to repress and control the richness and messiness of life and, in our world, the work of artists. Those who fit into an agenda or a religious code are rewarded, those who don't are banished, they can't even be understood. In life, they are sometimes killed. My message for you is "Watch out for any kind of theory, for any simplification. Watch out for things that have to fit in. Don't make structures where things have to fit in. Stretch *your* vision by looking to artists who aren't easy to understand. Who don't fit into any system or definition." Wouldn't you like to have been the first person to read and appreciate *Godot*? A play that looked like no play that ever existed?

5. Protect your work. I was president of the LMDA for three terms. It's the guild, the service organization that represents and protects our work. If you are going to work in the profession, you need to be a member. I got involved because I had created an evening of theatre called *Love's Fire*, a sequel of sorts to *Orchards*, which brought important writers together in evenings of short plays inspired by classic writers – Chekhov and Shakespeare. *Love's Fire* had a long and very successful national tour with the Acting Company. I think I personally did 20 or 30 interviews during that tour. It went to London to the Barbican, and then came to New York where it played at the Newman to excellent reviews. An important producer wanted to move it to Broadway, though with Hamish Linklater as our most famous actor, this was obviously only a pipe dream. But at that moment, had the move happened, it would have joined on Broadway *Angels in America*, dramaturg Oskar Eustis; *Rent*, dramaturg Lynn Thomson; *Having Our Say*, dramaturg Janice Paran; and *Bring in da Noise, Bring in da Funk*, dramaturg Shelby Jiggetts. When the musical was invented somebody started a union for chorus dancers. Who was going to watch out for those of us who played an even more integral part in creating these new works? If you succeed in your dreams, and I hope you do, you will be in a position to have to think about this – about your billing, about your financial participation – which, I promise you, will not be recognized by the commercial producers who sweep in after the work is done. You won't be happy when all your dear friends and collaborators are in London celebrating the opening of your show on the West End, cashing their $25,000 checks each week, and you are home in your apartment in Brooklyn. Jonathan Larson and Lynn Thomson each made $2000 from *Rent*. Its profits at the time of the *Rent* lawsuit, which she lost, including merchandise? One billion dollars. Anyone know who testified for Lynn, because they were familiar with the actual work of developing *Rent* during its time at NYTW? Craig Lucas and Tony Kushner.

6. What is our greatest asset? Positive thinking and encouragement – as any good director knows. If you do nothing else, say nothing else, know nothing else, if you do one thing only: speak up and say "You're wonderful! Try it! Have fun! Dig deep!"

41
Season planning
Challenges and opportunities

Edward Sobel

Most not-for-profit theatres in the United States operate on a subscription series season. Audiences buy a slate of plays (usually between three and seven) in advance at discounted prices. Benefits of this model are documented elsewhere, but include: greater financial stability and ability to plan based on known income; retention of audience rather than expensive acquisition of new; and cultivation of donors because of continued contact. Changes in the way we make and receive art have raised significant questions about the benefits and sustainability of the subscription model. In the face of greater competition for leisure and entertainment attention, and the shift from a passive recipient to self-curating and co-creative culture, it is incumbent upon artistic leaders to seize opportunities subscription-based seasons allow. If the model is beneficial but now endangered, what can one do as a dramaturg to help save and transform it?

Mission

Not-for-profit theatre companies operate under a formal mission statement, frequently written when they are incorporated as legal entities. Usually a few sentences long, mission statements can be generic or more specific. The idea is to succinctly articulate the reason why the company exists, and what purpose it serves. In theory, all programming, including season selection, supports, promotes, and reflects the mission of the company. Some theatres refer to their mission when planning the season. Frequently, one will also encounter terms like "brand" or "aesthetic," as in "Our brand is associated with family dramas" or our aesthetic is "less edgy."

Regardless of the stated mission, brand, or aesthetic of the company, two questions are worth asking: Why should we do this play? Why should we do this play now? The first of these is actually two questions (Why should we do *this* play? Why should *we* do this play?), asking for an articulation of the compelling reasons why this play demands to be done (relative to all the other possible plays one could do) and also why this particular theatre ought to do it. Answers vary widely: because we have an ongoing relationship with this playwright or with the director who is proposing we do the play; this play speaks to our audience's experiences in a new and interesting way; this play represents ideas or points of view we feel are important to raise; this play offers a superior quality of writing (language, storytelling, complexity of characters or ideas). The second question demands an articulation of the immediate need to do the play, as opposed to doing it some other time. Again, there are any number of answers: because the desirable artists are now available; the play speaks to issues that are of immediate concern; the play offers particular complements to other plays being produced.

Clear and succinct answers to these questions have enormous benefit. They help forge a link between the mission of the company and the actual programming, sometimes even more so than "Does this play fit our mission?" If the mission of the company is "to present stories that enliven the imagination," almost any play might fit the criteria. "Why this play?" demands specificity about how this play "enlivens the imagination" (for example, by dramatizing new solutions to a particular social problem). More importantly, the answers form the foundation of the argument for audiences to attend the play (or plays). To sustain the current model, theatres must make that argument forcefully.

Attending theatre is inconvenient. It is expensive, time consuming, requiring an investment of intellectual and social capital, happening at a specific place and time without flexibility or self-curation. Theatre companies must not only remove barriers, but also make a proactive case for why someone should set aside their laptop, get off the couch, and travel to and enter the building. This starts with a clear articulation of why the company is doing what it is doing, and what its value is. If audiences are to feel compelled to see a play, let alone a series of plays, they want to be assured it is important and relevant to their lives.

To theme or not to theme, that is the question

Planning a season is a curatorial function. This is distinct from a mission. It is the mission of an art museum to exhibit art. But what art to exhibit, and in what arrangement, is the exercise of curatorial responsibility. While many museums default to chronology, some of the most exciting exhibit work to create compelling connections in other ways. The newly relocated Barnes Foundation in Philadelphia is an apt, even extreme, example. There one can see ancient African masks next to a cubist portrait by Picasso.

Likewise, some theatre companies have sought to exercise their curatorial imperative – to view the season not as a random selection of plays driven exclusively by artistic whim, but as an opportunity to explore a particular issue or set of issues across a number of plays. One large regional theatre boldly announces choices with a catch phrase – a season of plays asking "What does it mean to be an American?" or a season examining "The Home Front." Providing an initial interpretative lens points audiences toward a relationship with the work that transcends the purely transactional. It also may provide a given audience member with a greater under-standing of the mission of the theatre. In turn, that may make him or her more forgiving of plays he or she doesn't like.

The process of "theming" a season can vary widely. A company may decide upon a theme and pick plays that fit it or select plays and attempt to find a theme that unites them. Most commonly, it is a dialogic process; plays the company feels compelled to do inform the theme, and the theme informs the plays being selected. Themes are often specific enough to allow for connections and conversation between plays, but not so narrow as to preclude alternatives or make the season a monotonic exercise.

But whether a company chooses to theme a season or not, or announce that theme or not, a dramaturg can play a role in creating a dialogue with and among audiences that allows for a deeper appreciation of the whole season. If a company produces *Mother Courage and Her Children* and *Glengarry Glen Ross* in the same season, it may be helpful to point audiences toward the complements and contrasts. Both are plays that struggle with questions about the relationship between morality and commerce, for example. One is a distinctly European creation, while the other distinctively American. One looks at a woman and the impact of business on her family, the other at men who are co-workers with a familial-like bond and code. Helping audiences make these connections, providing interpretative possibilities for them, adds ballast to the argument that an audience member should make the investment of subscribing, rather than just seeing one show in the season.

"We'll just do the Black play in February"

To represent a range of voices in a season is a matter of ethics. Is it not our moral obligation to tell the stories of people not generally afforded the platform of our stages? It is also a pragmatic necessity. The majority of ticket purchasers are women. Demographers tell us non-whites will represent the majority of the population in twenty or thirty years. Ignoring those two facts is not sound business planning. One hopes, given the cultural shifts about race, class, and gender that appear to be taking root, that this section will quickly prove irrelevant. Experience would predict otherwise. Many theatres persist in operating as if the act of making a play is sufficiently universal that it is not necessary to reflect the actual experiences of its audience or, if one wishes to grow, its potential audience.

Season planning need not, in fact probably ought not, be quota based. But it is important to acknowledge that universality is not a one-way street. If we hope that an African-American or Latina/o audience will be moved by *Hamlet*, why would we not believe that a white audience will be moved by a story from an African-American playwright based on Yoruba folk tales? It is often the institutional dramaturg's job to make these arguments and more importantly to be sufficiently familiar with a range of voices so that the default position in season planning is not exclusively the known universe of plays by white men. In the larger sense, increasing the range of voices is dependent upon authenticity and sustained commitment. Theatres that insist upon producing Lorraine Hansberry's *A Raisin in the Sun* in February as a claim to diversity are fooling no one. And while some intended audiences may attend out of interest, most empirical evidence shows they will not come back, let alone become a loyal subscriber base.

Practical idealism and priorities

The season-planning process is a bit like a political campaign: a mixture of lofty, passionate conversations about ideals, ambition, and big ideas which then runs headlong into the buzz saw of realities like budgets and scheduling. The trend over time has been for theatres to do plays with fewer characters, and very few plays with large casts. At professional theatres operating under agreements with the actors' union (Actors' Equity Association or AEA), the economics of season planning are partly driven by what is commonly known as "actor weeks," i.e. the total number of weeks one pays a salary to actors. If a theatre is producing a 4-character play with 3 weeks of rehearsal and a 5-week run, that play would have a total of 32 actor weeks: 4 actors at 8 weeks each. In practice, one also counts the AEA stage manager, who is paid for rehearsal and performance weeks as well as an additional preparation week. Therefore, a 4-character play equals a total of 41 "actor weeks." In the subscription model, a theatre budgets for a total number of actor weeks in a given season. So, if a theatre can afford a total of 250 actor weeks in a 5-play season, 40–50 or so actor weeks per play is about right. But if one wants to do a 7- or 8-character play, suddenly one has spent over 70 actor weeks on just one of the 5. That means another play would have to use only 25 actor weeks. Better go searching in that pile of terrific 2-character plays. These programming decisions happen in a larger financial context. For example, one could choose to privilege the number of bodies on stage over production values. If one were willing to spend less money on the set of a show, one might put that money toward actor weeks instead. But even those kinds of compromises are complicated. A large-cast show is likely to have greater production demands (unless actors are appearing nude, the larger the cast, the larger the costume budget, for example). Labor and material costs often make a "minimal" set not sufficiently less expensive than a non-minimal one.

The practicalities of season planning relate to other important artistic and mission-linked questions. For example, should one buy more actor weeks, or instead spend money to commission and workshop a new play, or extend the reach of educational programming to grow audiences for the future? Should one limit actor weeks in an effort to lower prices in order to allow access for audiences other than those who can traditionally afford tickets? The trend of choosing to limit cast-size can be unnerving. The gradual domestication of American drama, and the focus in our theatres on the internal and psychological rather than the social or political, while a reflection of American culture and interests, is also a consequence of economic choices under the current model. Dramaturgs can be advocates for the art, or at least help identify how economic realities are shaping the artistic content.

Balance/flow

Often in season-planning meetings, the term "balance" comes up. Usually that means someone in the room is afraid the season is not going to sell a sufficient number of tickets because there are no comedies under consideration. (Or occasionally, the opposite – the season, while entertaining and likely to be financially successful, does not sufficiently ask audiences to challenge themselves). On one level, those concerns are justified. Just as one may love going to a favorite Italian restaurant but not want every course to be pasta, so too an audience may love challenging, thought-provoking plays but not want all of them to be unremittingly desperate and hopeless.

However, concerns about balance can be overstated and often can be mitigated by "flow." A subscription-season audience is being asked to see a particular set of plays in a particular order. Order can be manipulated to better or worse effect. A DJ plays songs all night that keep people dancing, but not every song is the same – the mix of tunes contains variety, interesting juxtapositions, and touches intangible emotional qualities that make a satisfying experience. This is less about thematic juxtapositions, then about feel – things like the tone of play, its size and scale.

Sometimes order is dictated by pragmatic concerns such as artist availability or managing the demands on production or marketing staff. Sometimes conventional wisdom plays a role. For example, there is a common (if debatable) perception that in warm weather, audiences prefer lighter fare. Such notions can be misleading or, to put it more positively, present opportunities for "counter-programming." If every theatre in town is doing A Christmas Carol or It's a Wonderful Life during the holiday season, the daring theatre that instead produces the new dark comedy may find itself with an unexpected corner on the market.

Advocating for the new

Many theatres are hesitant to program new plays, believing that new work is "risky." While not entirely without merit, that argument masks a more fundamental truth. There is a good deal of careful empirical evidence[1] demonstrating that audiences are not afraid of new plays, nor are new plays inherently risky. What audiences fear are bad plays. If one were to say to an audience, "With all guaranteed certainty this new play is a great play," the overwhelming majority of audience members would quite happily, even eagerly attend. With Death of a Salesman, an audience knows they are getting a good play. With a brand-new play, there is no such guarantee. As a result, theatres attempt to find other ways to reassure audiences of the quality of a new play. Some build relationships between their audience and a particular playwright over time, producing work by that writer with sufficient frequency that audiences come to know and trust them. Others rely upon elements of their brand (quality of acting or production values, "name actors," "edginess") to give some assurance. Still others make "the new" and "innovation" a part of their brand itself. As with questions of diversity, an ongoing commitment reaps significant benefits. The more playwrights feel a theatre is a genuine home for new work, the more likely the best writers will want to have their work premiere there. If audiences have been educated about the new play process through repeated exposure, they will be more forgiving of failure and celebrate the institution as one dedicated to a larger project: not just producing plays, but moving the entire art forward.

Ultimately, season planning is an art. The balance of artistic ambition with practical realities is difficult, sometimes seemingly impossible to navigate. As with all art, experimentation is necessary, and sometimes failure is the result. But when seasons fail, and theatres fail, it ought to be for the right reasons. Good dramaturgs, regardless of their actual job title, work to ensure the season-planning process has integrity.

Note

1 For example, surveys conducted by the consulting firm Wolf Brown from 2008 to 2010 as part of work on audience segmentation and intrinsic impact at various theatres. Findings are not published.

42

The dramaturg's role in diversity and audience development

Julie Felise Dubiner

Who are we doing this for?

When we ask people to fork over their money on our schedule, and to sit in the dark for a couple of hours, what is our responsibility in considering them? We all have seen the precipitous decline of audiences at the mid- and large-sized regional theatres, and those that are still coming get older every year. Regional theatres continue to slide into irrelevancy in the cultural conversation of our communities. In the United States, racial and socioeconomic demographics have changed significantly since the dawn of the regional theatre movement. Each year it becomes harder and harder to justify the great swaths of resources the larger institutions swallow, when it is the smaller, community theatres that are actually essential in people's lives.

We pour our hearts into these productions, but we must not forget to think about what we want people to leave the theatre with. We must not be lazy or haphazard in knowing our current and potential audiences. In many cases, especially among large theatre's artistic staffs, you won't find many people who grew up in the town they're now working in, who are actually members of the communities in which they live, and many even have contempt and preconceptions about the people they live among but not with. Choosing plays often becomes a war between the stuff we do to keep *them* (the audience) happy and the art *we* (theatre staffs) do for our own sense of intellectualism or artiness. But let's think about them. Do we imagine *them* to be traditional upper-middle-class, white families? Do we think this is our only reliable target audience?

The big question: What is your theatre's mission? Does your work honor the mission? Do you believe in the mission? Do you believe the mission and the audience you want are aligned? If you don't respect your audience, why do you do this in the first place?

Why should anyone care what the dramaturg thinks?

As dramaturgs, we are trained to ask questions, and now is the time to ask the essential dramaturgical question, "Why this play now?" with greater urgency than ever before. We tend to focus pretty hard on new plays in the modern profession of dramaturgy. We take for granted that a new play is relevant simply because it is new, and so many classics are produced as passion projects, but theatres fail at asking hard questions of context and content. We must consider the world in which we are producing a play. We should try to anticipate aspects of classics and new work that are obviously cruel or unintentionally hurtful. As dramaturgical thinkers, it is our job to bring these points to the forefront of consideration in play and process development, season planning, and all aspects of production from conceptualization to design to performance to related events. We don't have to be overly earnest about it, and we don't have to avoid plays that are difficult, we just have to have the conversation. And dramaturgs should be leading that conversation.

Many theatres are making concerted efforts at audience development: to cultivate deeper relationships with existing audiences, and to try and reach new audiences. There is a synergy to be mined between marketing, education, literary, and development offices around the country, and many are moving in that direction. Sadly, some theatres cling to silos and rigid hierarchies, and it can be difficult for a dramaturg to find a place where these worlds come together. Those of us who are trained as dramaturgs need to have our influence reach beyond a literary office and into the areas where decisions are made about the long view.

The long view is that whether we are responding from an ethical impulse or a desire for survival, we need to keep striving towards creating institutions that are welcoming to artists and audiences. The larger institutions have a great responsibility in this, and it is the dramaturgical thinker's job to hold the institution's feet to the fire. We must open up our practices and break down embedded barriers. Theatre brings people together, to breathe in a room together, to share stories together, and to take in the world together.

The Oregon Shakespeare Festival as case study

The Oregon Shakespeare Festival (OSF) has taken a strange path by becoming a leader in diversity initiatives in the American theatre. To begin with, it's in Oregon, which even now in 2013 is the whitest state in the nation. Although Oregon became part of the Union in 1859 as a non-slave state and would support Abraham Lincoln and the North in the Civil War, it also entered with a caveat forbidding black Americans from settling here. The particular area where OSF makes its home, the Rogue Valley, was a stronghold of the Ku Klux Klan in the 1920s and 1930s. Even through the 1970s, "sundown" laws were in effect, meaning being black after dark in Ashland could get you thrown in jail. The non-white members of the acting company had to be escorted for their own safety through the town until more recently than you might imagine, and even in the last few years, there have been hate crimes in our area, some directed at members of the OSF company. That is a truth of the place we live and work in, which very much drives our own understanding of the need for diversity initiatives in our town, our country, and in theatre in general.

OSF was founded in 1935 by Angus Bowmer. What started as a 3-day, 2-play festival has grown into a multimillion dollar, 11-month, 11-play operation. In addition to the 11 plays, there are innumerable events and a free early evening performance (the Green Show) every night in the summer. Currently, the theatre employs about 500 people, including the largest repertory acting company in the nation. Upon restarting the festival after World War II, Angus Bowmer wrote a list of precepts:

1 The Oregon Shakespeare Festival should not be an exclusive watering place for the socially ambitious.
2 It should not be a platform for the exploitation of any single political, social, aesthetic, or religious thesis.
3 It should be a theater which presents its audience with a wide variety of theatrical experiences, including those provided by the world's great playwrights of all ages.

This list can be seen as the ur-diversity initiative. It set the tone for continued investment in diversity and inclusion at the festival. In 1991, the Diversity Council was formed, and in 1995, the council published the following statement:

> The Oregon Shakespeare Festival is committed to diversity in all areas of our work and all Festival Departments. This commitment is reflected in play selection, hiring, casting, marketing and public relations efforts, education and outreach programs, recruitment of volunteers, and the composition of the Boards of Directors.

The 1994–98 long-range plan included support for several programs aimed at diversifying the company and the audiences, and in 1997 a diversity consultant was brought in to meet with the staff and board. It was around this time that the various programs went from an attempt to move towards a "melting pot" model and instead moved more towards inclusion and the celebration of differences.

Bill Rauch became OSF's fifth artistic director in 2007 and immediately began building new diversity, inclusion, access, and audience development initiatives onto the fine work begun by his predecessors: Libby Appel, Henry Woronicz, Jerry Turner, and Angus Bowmer. Cynthia Rider became the executive director in 2012, following Paul Nicholson and William Patton. Rauch was a co-founder of Cornerstone Theater and its artistic director for 20 years before coming to Ashland. Cornerstone's mission is to bring theatre to underserved communities and to actively engage those communities in the creation and presentation of theatre. Alison Carey, with whom Rauch founded Cornerstone, was brought in to develop and implement American Revolutions: the United States History Cycle. American Revolutions is an ambitious program to commission up to 37 new plays about moments of change in American history with the goal of promoting re-evaluation of and continued conversation about our commonalities and differences on all levels – social, political, economic, ethnic, religious, etc. American Revolutions is one of four distinct commissioning programs, all of which have diversity and inclusion as part of their missions. At the time of writing, the majority of commissioned writers are women, and half are artists of color.

In 2008, Lue Douthit, the director of Literary Development and Dramaturgy at OSF began a series of meetings centered around the challenges and problems of the actors' experiences playing roles that are problematic – an African-American woman playing Mammy, an Asian-American playing a character speaking Pidgin English, and more. While there was no outright charge or evidence of intentional racism, the concerns for the company's well-being necessitated broader conversations. Over the rest of that season what started as a theatre topics lecture from Lue Douthit grew into a series of meetings and conversations about artistic representation, providing a safe place where anyone could come and talk about where a show or performance or concept "crossed the line" for them. The meetings continue here, and each year we try to face head-on the difficult questions brought up in classic plays, and the ramifications of our commitment to color-blind/color-conscious casting.

In addition to the Artistic Representation meetings, there are also standing meetings of the Audience Action Committee, the Inclusion Action Committee, and various affinity groups for company members along with allies groups, training as diversity conversation facilitators, all spear-headed by the Diversity and Inclusion Planning Committee (DIPC). Everyone who comes to interview for a senior-level position at OSF meets with DIPC as part of the hiring process.

In 2008, OSF released its Values Statement, and in 2010, we produced the Audience Development Manifesto, both of which are available to read on our website at www. osfashland.org. Inclusion is stated explicitly as a core value. The Audience Development Manifesto is, as far as I know, a unique document in American theatre. It lays out clearly how we value our current audience and also states explicitly what OSF wants and needs to do to cultivate future audiences. It touches on plans for increasing the socioeconomic, age, and racial and ethnic diversity of the theatre and for increasing access for audience members with disabilities. We return to these documents often as we plan events and the shows for the season.

Where are we now?

We are doing better than most theatres at keeping conversations about gender, sexuality, race, and class at the center of our lives at the theatre and in the season-planning process. For the last 20 years that process has also included Boarshead meetings. Boarshead started during Henry Woronicz's tenure as artistic director and has become an essential part of our selection process. About 60 company members from all corners of the company – marketing, production, development, artistic, education, front-of-house, everyone – get together several times over the 4 months before the artistic director chooses the season to present to the board. We are an advisory committee. The goal is to hear from the points of expertise of the people on the committee and also to get gut responses to the plays themselves. At OSF, we have a responsibility to our namesake playwright and commitments to our commissioned artists and the acting company, which is very diverse on all counts from race, gender and sexual orientation, ethnicity, religion, physical abilities and disabilities, and age. For the Boarshead to plan the 2015 season, we are presenting the plays to the committee without titles or authors' names in an experiment to see if reading the plays blind moderates our personal biases.

We also have a tremendous commitment to the audience that they will have variety to choose from in two or three theatres, depending on when they make their visit over the course of the season. As a destination theatre, most of the audience travels to us. Our local audience is only a small percentage of our ticket buyers. Most people come to the beautiful town of Ashland, see three or four plays, go hiking and rafting, and then head home. We are part of many families' summer traditions, loyal audiences who literally have been coming for generations. Over the last 40 years, most have embraced the exponential growth of the theatre, the inclusion of non-Shakespeare and world classics, and in the last few years, the incredible amount of new work we have commissioned and produced.

Especially through the new work, the number of artists of color writing and directing at OSF has gone up, but we struggle to approach equity. We struggle with questions of artistic representation and cultural authenticity nearly hourly as we try to strike a balance with the economic realities of running one of the largest theatre institutions in the country, in the whitest state in the union. Including the school groups we welcome every year, only about 10 percent of audiences are non-white.

Like many theatres, our ticket sales are driven by a majority of women purchasers, and we have done well here compared to many of our colleague theatres at hiring female directors, designers, and company members. However, we face the challenge of finding classics written by women and also the problem of how women are portrayed on our stages. We know that when the historical circumstances of women are honestly exposed, or when we find plays where women have been abused, eliminated, or reduced, we have to ask hard, thoughtful questions about representation and responsibility. In our current season (2013) two of the three world premieres are written by women, but we also found ourselves doing *A Streetcar Named Desire*, *My Fair Lady*, and *The Taming of the Shrew*, all running all year in the same theatre, three stories where women are brutalized in different ways. In our other theatres, women characters were not much better off. They are great plays and great productions, but as an aggregate, what will our audiences leave thinking about when it comes to women's lives and the issues and choices (or lack of choices) they face? We have tried to acknowledge the inherent misogyny of these plays head on through internal conversations among the company and the various diversity and inclusion committees, as well as through events organized by the education department for the audience.

We struggle to attract new audiences and a diverse audience. We struggle to reach non-wealthy audiences as well, as our tickets sales are built into the budget at a very high rate compared to non-repertory companies with shorter runs. This has led us to introduce dynamic pricing which drives up the single ticket cost, while the discounted tickets we have introduced to mitigate and honor the Audience Development Manifesto's imperative of attracting socio-economically diverse audiences are difficult to publicize.

The literary staff drives the Boarshead conversation in concert with the artistic director. We are building the list of plays that will be considered. We are conducting the search for writers to commission, and we serve the mission of diversity and inclusion. And we wonder if it is enough, and we carry that question into the next Boarshead process. We wonder as dramaturgs and promoters of dramaturgical thinking what more we can do.

43

Guthrie Theater's debt to women and diversity[1]

Marianne Combs

Guthrie Artistic Director Joe Dowling is struggling to protect his theatre's reputation after a week of outrage in the arts community over the Guthrie's new 2013–14 theatre season, which some have declared "a tragedy." When the Guthrie Theater announced its 50th Anniversary season, the absence of women and minorities among the playwrights and directors ignited a fierce debate in the Twin Cities arts community. Many who felt they have long been excluded from the Guthrie's main stage – and some who haven't – used the Guthrie's announcement to highlight what they called the flagship theatre's failure to embrace diverse audiences. Actress Heidi Berg was among them:

> To suggest that there just aren't talented women and people of color out there this season is appalling. It isn't as though the Guthrie's not hiring from a national and international pool of talent. While we are accustomed to being told there aren't enough local people qualified to fill positions in the Guthrie season, now we are to believe there aren't enough talented women and people of color in the WORLD.

The theatre's defenders rushed to say the Guthrie was only doing what it must do to fill seats and stay on budget.[2]

Given the region's increasingly diverse population – one the Guthrie will be pressed to cater to in coming years – the controversy might have led to a timely and thoughtful examination of the theatre's selection process. Guthrie Artistic Director Joe Dowling fumbled the opportunity, at first appearing to encourage a discussion on diversity and then – despite his protests to the contrary – taking the defensive. By the end of the week, he was openly hostile to the premise that the Guthrie does not present diverse works. When asked in a recent televised interview about charges that the season suffered from a lack of women, Dowling said, "This is a self-serving argument that doesn't hold water."

Underlying the artistic turmoil surrounding the Guthrie is a fundamental question: Does the theatre have any obligation to present the stories of women and people of color? And if so, to what extent? If not, at what cost, given the demographic changes transforming the nation and the Twin Cities?

In the next three decades, the seven-county Twin Cities metro area will see its minority population grow to more than 40 percent of the region, nearly double the current percentage, according to a recent report by the Metropolitan Council. Michelle Hensley, artistic director of Ten Thousand Things theatre company, and a board member of the national Theatre Communications Group, put it this way:

> Demographics are changing dramatically, and if the Guthrie doesn't start making enormous efforts to reach out and engage audiences beyond aging, wealthy white people, it will be struggling to sell seats. It is absolutely in the self-interest of the Guthrie to work hard to make its audiences more inclusive. And the way you get a more inclusive audience is for them to be able to see themselves, their stories and their perspectives on stage. Theater offers the possibility of stepping into another's shoes and seeing the world through his or her eyes. For too long we've had to look at the world through the eyes of white men.

Joe Dowling, in his own words

Joe Dowling's wide-ranging responses to criticism of the 50th season might appear to be the comments of a man who's still figuring out what the issue is and where he stands. But today's debate cannot come as a surprise to the man who was interviewed back in 2003 for a City Pages cover story titled "A Woman's Work Is Never Done." The entire focus of the story was the lack of women playwrights on the Guthrie stage. Here's an excerpt:

> [Dowling] readily admits that his record in the female-representation department is less than sparkling. "A lot of people sort of look at us and throw stones," he says. "And they're right to. I don't object to criticism, I don't object to the kind of inquiry [City Pages] is making, which is absolutely valid and right. Hands up," he says, raising his arms like a bank robber. "Caught. We don't do enough women. Yes. But I think the evidence is that we are shifting in the right direction."

When Dylan Hicks wrote his piece for the City Pages back in 2003, a survey of the past 10 seasons found that only 10 percent of the plays (7 out of 70) on Guthrie's stages were by women.

Today, a similar look back at the number of female playwrights in the Guthrie Theater's last 10 seasons, as listed on the theatre's own website, finds it staged 111 shows, 18 of which were written by women (that's counting 2 plays based on the novels of Charlotte Brontë and Jane Austen). That means that in the past decade, 16.2 percent of the plays were written by women. At this rate, women will make up 50 percent of the playwrights by the year 2036.

However, critics of the Guthrie will tell you that staging a play on the Wurtele Thrust Stage – which seats 1100 people – is not equal to staging a production in the Dowling Studio, which seats less than 200. And many of the works by women or playwrights of color are being relegated to the smaller space.

The difference a big building makes

When Joe Dowling celebrated the opening of the new Guthrie Theater on the Mississippi riverfront, he had this to say:

> I believe that the American resident theater movement, which was founded here in the Twin Cities with the birth of the Guthrie, now stretches from sea to shining sea in theaters all around the country. But it lacks a center … it lacks somewhere that can call itself a national center of theater art and theater education. And that is what we aim to become.

Dowling has got his wish. The Guthrie Theater is indeed a national center of theatre art and theatre education. And as such, the Guthrie is seen as a leader in its field. So what message is it sending to theatres across the country when it programs seasons that are dominated by white men, both as playwrights and in the director's chair?

Dowling alluded to the pressures of selling tickets when he told the *Star Tribune*, "It is a very stern task to direct on a stage of our size, and I am responsible to the board for the shows we produce" (point of clarification: the board does not approve the Guthrie's season, however it does approve the theatre's budget).

So is it impossible for large theatres to stage work by women, or playwrights of color, and still balance the budget? No, it's not impossible, according to Zan Sawyer-Dailey, associate director of the Actors Theatre of Louisville, which programs three different stages and also runs the national Humana Festival of new plays. She said her theatre makes a concerted effort to program seasons that feature a diverse array of plays.

> The community here is richly diverse – African American, Asian American, Hispanics, immigrants coming from Africa and Southeast Asia – and while they are not all a part of our audience, we are still aware that they are a part of our community and we want to make sure that they feel welcomed and embraced if they are able to come to the theater. And to that end we want to make sure that there are stories on stage about their experiences.

Sawyer-Dailey said it's not just good theatre, it's good business:

> Not because we're making a lot of money off these populations … we see it as good business because we're good citizens and that's what we want to be – good citizens to our community. It's just a responsibility, regardless of whether or not it's going to develop a new audience.

Sawyer-Dailey admits there are challenges involved in finding and scheduling diverse work, but she says finding female directors is not one of them:

> It's not difficult to find a female director. There are lots and lots of wonderful female directors out there, I think you just have to decide that you want to have them in your season, and find the one you want who best matches whatever projects you're interested in.

Public funding and a mission that includes diversity

In the last three years the Guthrie Theater has received more than $2.2 million from the Minnesota State Arts Board alone. But the arts board does not make reflecting a community's diversity a condition of funding. Many argue that the recipient of so much public support has an obligation to reflect the diversity of the community in which it lives. Twin Cities theatre director Ben Layne wrote in an open letter to Joe Dowling that the season announcement reflects a lack of recognition of the current climate:

> There is a real political war going on over Women's rights, right now, on the campaign trail and in the halls of federal and state houses of government. There is still racism alive and well and at the forefront of national news, due in part to the Trayvon Martin killing in Florida. The Guthrie is in a unique position to speak to these issues and more. As the old adage goes, "with great power comes great responsibility." That you doubled down on these choices in your comments to the *Star Tribune* last week and to TPT this weekend is troubling.

In fact the Guthrie Theater's own mission mentions diversity:

> The Guthrie Theater, founded in 1963, is an American center for theater performance, production, education and professional training. By presenting both classical literature and new work from diverse cultures, the Guthrie illuminates the common humanity connecting Minnesota to the peoples of the world.

The Guthrie does occasionally present work of diverse cultures, but not to the extent that critics would like. And often time "presenting" means giving one of its stages over to Penumbra Theatre or Mu Performing Arts, local theatre companies that specialize in telling the stories of specific cultures.

The Guthrie has also received funding from the National Endowment for the Arts. On two occasions it was awarded $20,000 for specific productions – *Burial at Thebes*, directed by the Guthrie's only resident female director, Marcela Lorca, and *M. Butterfly*, written by Asian-American David Henry Hwang. So even the Guthrie Theater recognizes that when applying for grants, diversity is key.

A self-fulfilling prophecy and a national problem

Many critics point to the Guthrie as the cause of its own problems. Bonnie Schock, one-time artistic director of the former Twin Cities theatre company Three Legged Race, said there are fewer "high profile" female and minority directors and playwrights because institutions of power and privilege such as the Guthrie are consistently failing to challenge the cultural assumptions that support that power and privilege.

It is the responsibility of our cultural institutions – particularly those that find themselves in the position of controlling a substantial piece of the region's resources – to use their position to lead. And leadership is hard. Leadership means investing in the future; it means intentionally creating opportunity for those who have historically been denied opportunity.

When asked about the pool of diverse and female playwrights available to major theatres, Jeremy Cohen, director of the Playwrights' Center in Minneapolis rattles off an impressive list of names.

We're now seeing the spotlight shine on such incredible talents as Quiara Alegria Hudes, Lynn Nottage, Sarah Ruhl, Marcus Gardley, Lydia Diamond, Amy Herzog, Qui Nguyen, Young Jean Lee, Tanya Saracho, Christina Anderson, Kate Fodor, Tanya Barfield, Annie Baker, Kia Corthron, Carson Kreitzer and Theresa Rebeck – with productions in NYC and around the country. And for the theatres around the country like Centerstage, Mixed Blood, Berkeley Rep, Ten Thousand Things, Victory Gardens, Children's Theatre Company, Cornerstone, and the countless others who are producing a truer and more accurate reflection not only of our country … but of the world … they will be the leaders we look to, that we take our children to for inspiration and reflection, and that offer us a visceral experience unlike any other.

According to Cohen currently more than 50 percent of the Playwrights' Center's core writers and fellows are women and/or playwrights/theatre artists of color.

Making theatre more inclusive is a national challenge, according to Teresa Eyring, the executive director of Theatre Communications Group, the national organization for American theatre.

Diversity is one of our core values; we believe that the theater field should be diverse and inclusive. What I say now and really believe is that the theater field should be striving to model the world we want to see, not reflecting the parts of the world around us that are lagging behind.

Eyring says a number of major theatres across the country need to be more inclusive, and she believes they are aware of the problem. She says the particular difficulties those institutions face are determined, in part, by the character of the institution itself and the community it resides in.

Notes

1 This article is reprinted from Minnesota Public Radio News online, April 24, 2012.
2 The Guthrie declined to make available members of the theatre's board, on the grounds that the board has no say in the theatre's season.

44

Reimagining the literary office
Designing a department that fulfills your purpose

Janine Sobeck

When I took over as literary manager at Arena Stage in the summer of 2008, the theatre was in a state of flux. Having recently moved out of its permanent home in southwest Washington, DC, in order to complete a major renovation, Arena was about to venture into uncharted waters with the upcoming launch of the ReStaged Festival. This ReStaged Festival was to be a two-year-long examination of Arena's mission, practices, and purpose that would determine the type of programming that, in fall 2010, would be taken back into the new building, Arena Stage at the Mead Center for American Theater.

As part of this examination, I was given the task of exploring the role, function, and possibilities of Arena's literary/dramaturgy office, as well as questioning the purpose, effectiveness, and worthiness of every action we currently performed. This act of questioning – in reality, the act of dramaturging the literary office – was a quest to find and adopt the best, most pertinent practices that would enable the Arena Stage literary office to function at a new level of efficiency and relevancy. In the end, we designed a literary office that was based on the current mission, needs, and purpose of Arena Stage. We also discovered that the act of questioning and then designing a department based on your own answers was a crucial step for every modern literary office in the regional theatre.

The mission

The first step in our process was to understand thoroughly the mission of the theatre. Together with then associate artistic director David Dower, I spent the next few months doing a close examination of Arena's mission statement and the brand new artistic strategy for the Mead Center. These foundational documents, which outlined the goals and priorities of the institution, provided the guide from which every practice could be measured.

The opening lines of the artistic strategy are as follows:

> This artistic strategy attempts to articulate the vision for the artistic life of Arena in [the Mead Center], a strategy that aims to capture the full potential of both the building and the moment to transform into a national center for the *production, presentation, development, and study of American theater.*

The 22-page document outlined the history of Arena Stage, providing great detail on what Arena had accomplished in the past, followed by discussion of where Arena was currently, and the vision of its future in the new building under these four "pillars" of production, presentation, development, and study. Each department was discussed, and there was a brief description of how the current programs fit into the new Arena Stage. With regards to the literary office, the document talked about where Arena would focus its season programming, the newly announced American Voices New Play Institute's Playwright Residencies, the audience enrichment programs, and our new play development activity (including commissions and workshops). Every single one of these programs needed to tie in with Arena's purpose of "transform[ing] into a national center for the *production, presentation, development, and study of American theater.*"

The examination

Once I had a firm grasp on the proposed mission and purpose of Arena Stage, the next step was to examine all of the programs and practices currently run by the literary office. The goal was to reveal which programs were still relevant according to the current focus of the institution and which practices needed to be changed, updated, or eliminated.

The first area of focus was our season programming. The literary manager was a part of the artistic team, which led season selection and was responsible for reading and evaluating all scripts that were in consideration, as well as helping to make sure that we were meeting our programming needs. From previous experience, as well as from the new artistic strategy, this is what I knew:

- Arena currently averaged 7–8 productions per year, and it was believed that this number would grow upon completion of the Mead Center;
- Arena's focus was on the presentation of American voices – past, present, and future;
- programming for the new Mead Center was going to focus on American musicals, first, second, and third productions by contemporary writers, American classics, contemporary American plays, and productions by outside companies.

With this knowledge, the first big question for the literary office was, How are we going to find these plays?

Due to the need of balancing its focus on "past, present, and future" voices, I knew that Arena was, on average, producing one or two new works per season. I also knew that we had a list of established musicals and classics that Arena was interested in or already planning on producing. This meant that the main question was, Where was Arena getting its new work?

The first, seemingly obvious, answer was through our script-submission policy. As is the case with many regional theatres, Arena's official script-submission policy was that we accepted all scripts submitted by an agent or a respected theatre artist (such as another artistic director or a director that Arena had worked with in the past).

Otherwise, a playwright could submit a query: a cover letter, resume, and 10-page sample. Unofficially, our policy was that we would read any script that was sent to our office, regardless of who sent it. This submission policy, which had been the same for as long as people could remember, resulted in Arena receiving anywhere from 600–1000 submissions per year, as well as countless queries. For every play and query received, a letter was sent back to the submitter confirming receipt; the play or query was given a specific priority level, and then it was sent to the reading pile. Eventually, it was read by myself, my intern, or by one of our script-reading volunteers. A script report was written (or in the case of a query, a judgment call was made) and based on the recommendation of the first reader, the script would either be taken into further consideration or a letter would be crafted explaining why we were passing on the project.

David and I decided that the effectiveness of the script-submission policy would be the first practice of the literary office to be scrutinized. The first question was, How did our current script-submission policy support the artistic vision of Arena Stage? The answer: it potentially allows us to introduce Arena to 'present' and 'future' American voices. The second question was, How effective was the submission policy in fulfilling its purpose? The answer came after a long examination.

The first step was to go through recent seasons and determine how many of our productions were a result of scripts that came through our submission policy. After going through the script log, we were startled to discover that while a very small number of the scripts had been chosen for our new play development series, there was not a single play in recent history that had come up through our open submission policy and into our season.

This led to the question of where were the plays coming from? Again, after looking back at the notes in our script log, we realized that all the new (including second and third productions) plays that had, in recent history, been produced at Arena were:

- plays we had scouted;
- playwrights we had reached out to because of our desire to work with them;
- through relationships we had with other theatre artists.

This led to the second question: did we believe that Arena was the place for new and undiscovered playwriting talent? Based on our recent production history and the goals of our artistic strategy, we could say that finding the new, hot, undiscovered playwright was not Arena's current purpose.

Which led to our third question: what changes did we know were coming with the Mead Center? Arena was getting ready to announce the creation of five playwright residencies, which included a commitment to produce one of their plays during their three-year residency. This dedication to the resident playwright's work was going to be a major source of our new works in upcoming seasons.

Once the major questions about our script-submission policy and our source of new plays had been examined and answered, the ideas of how we needed to revamp our policy began to flow. We knew that our current policy was ineffective – not only were we not producing the plays that were coming through the pile, it was taking an extreme amount of man hours in order to keep it going – hours that, with the other demands on the literary office, we did not have to spare.

As we continued to brainstorm ideas about how to revamp the submission policy, the next step was to hold a teleconference with three agents that we respected. During that phone call, we discussed many things about Arena's repurposing, including the current way we handled submissions: who was actually reading them, who was actually responding to them, and the way that we were working with the agents through our submission policy. This frank discussion had two basic outcomes. First, it supported many of the ideas and changes that we were discussing internally. Second, it revealed the agents' points of view about how they would like to work with Arena, including a desire for increased transparency about what the theatre was looking for and how we were choosing our plays.

After completing the conversation with the agents and looking over the information we had gathered, we realized that there was only one answer to the question of how efficient was our script-submission policy in assisting the literary office's purpose of supporting the artistic vision of Arena Stage.

It wasn't.

Based on our understanding of Arena's mission and purpose for the Mead Center, the demands on the literary office, and the examination of our submission policy's effectiveness, we concluded that the right answer for Arena was, for the moment, to close our submission policy.

What exactly did that mean? Knowing that it was a potentially controversial move, it was important that we explained both the reasoning and implications of the "closed" submission policy to both the agents and playwrights with whom we regularly worked. In our letter to agents and playwrights, we explained that:

> The re-birth of Arena Stage at the Mead Center for American Theater is providing us with an extraordinary amount of opportunities. One is the ability to codify our support of American Voices and pro-actively determine the artistic path to the Mead Center by advancing our normal season planning schedule into longer planning arcs. We're currently fully programmed through the opening season in the new building, fall of 2010. Another is the chance to re-examine the practices of our Literary Office in order to find better, deeply authentic ways to serve our community of playwrights.
>
> With the knowledge that our season roadmap is fairly concrete through the opening of the Mead Center in 2010, and the demands of restructuring the Literary Office, Arena Stage has decided to not accept any script submissions at this time. ...
>
> When Arena re-opens its script submission policy, you will receive a letter detailing a clear description of the type of work that Arena is interested in producing. We hope to open a clearer line of communication that will allow you to know specifically what Arena is looking for, and what scripts will be seriously considered. It is our hope that, through decreasing the number of scripts submitted that do not directly address our programming needs, we will be able to more effectively work with agents and playwrights in supporting our mission as the center for the production, presentation, development, and study of American Theatre.

Once the letters were sent, there was a period of anxiety as we waited for the reactions, as they would be crucial in helping us understand how effectively we were communicating our current situation and mission.

The responses that we did receive were, in the end, somewhat surprising. Some were simple acknowledgements of the change, stating that they would update their records. Some, despite several follow-up letters, simply ignored the request and continued to send us scripts. Others, however, wrote back and expressed appreciation for our open and honest explanation of our current situation and said that they looked forward to hearing from us the next time we had something to share.

The effect

It was this final response that spurred us on in our examination of the literary office's practices. With each practice that we examined, we asked the same foundational questions: How does it fit within our current vision as a theatre? and Is it effective? If, after close examination, the practice seemed both to support the artistic strategy and to work effectively, then it was left alone. If, however, it didn't – on either count – then new ideas were proposed that, through a process of trial and error, were either implemented or discarded in favor of a different idea. Many of these ideas led to large changes, some of which included:

- modifying the way we responded to the plays we read, including the decision to no longer give any sort of feedback in our rejection letters to avoid any unintentional institutional "dramaturging" of a play to which we were not committed;
- modifying our new play development program from a set five hours of rehearsal followed by a reading to a practice of working with each playwright to design a workshop/reading experience that would best serve the current developmental stage of the play;
- modifying the institutional policy of automatically assigning the institutional dramaturg (or the intern) to every show on the season to discussing with the playwright who he or she would like to bring onto the project;
- examining the role of the dramaturg in the rehearsal room;
- expanding the dramaturgical outreach from a single-page program note to an extensive behind-the-scenes website and, eventually, a four-page program spread.

The response

As I traveled to festivals, conferences, and other gatherings in the field, the topic of what was happening in the Arena Stage literary office began to spark interest. While some were merely curious, many members of the theatre community seemed to be nervous that the changes in our submission policy meant that Arena was starting a campaign to shut down the open-submission policy at every regional theatre. In speaking with many of my fellow colleagues, and striving to understand their fears, it became more and more apparent that the most important thing that had happened at Arena was not the actual closing of the submission policy but the very act of questioning, the process of "dramaturging" the literary office.

The questions that we asked, and the subsequent changes, created a stronger, more productive, and more useful literary office, one that completely aligned with the current mission and purpose of the theatre and that did not spend any valuable time or energy on unhelpful or unnecessary tasks. Because the examination was completely centered around Arena's mission and purpose, the answers and new solutions were unique to Arena. They were not, however, applicable to every literary office.

Instead of taking Arena's answers, it quickly became apparent that other theatres should, alternatively, take Arena's foundational questions and apply them to their individual institutions.

- How do the practices of your literary office support the vision and mission of your theatre?
- Are your current practices effective?

If every literary office within the regional theatre took the opportunity to embark on this journey of questions, of examining "why" their programs and practices are in place, it would be an invaluable step to ensuring that the literary offices nationwide are performing the precise practices needed to fulfill their unique purpose at their individual theatres.

45

The National New Play Network Collaborative Literary Office

New tools for old tricks

Jason Loewith and Gwydion Suilebhan

The National New Play Network (NNPN) is an alliance of more than 50 professional theatres across the country that champions the development, production, and continued life of new plays. Since its founding in 1998, the network has strived to pioneer, implement, and disseminate programs that revolutionize the way theatres collaborate to support new plays and playwrights. The NNPN's programs pull their strength from both formal and informal collaborative literary engagement among its members. Our flagship program, the Continued Life of New Plays Fund, generates Rolling World Premieres through inter-theatre script-sharing, active solicitation on the part of the NNPN staff, and the National Showcase of New Plays – itself a collaboratively sourced and selected new play event. And many of our other programs – Playwright Residencies, the M.F.A. Playwrights Workshop, and the annual NNPN commission – are similarly driven by collaborative dramaturgical efforts. Finally, the NNPN's longstanding monthly online literary chats and biannual in-person pitch sessions crowdsource the breadth of knowledge represented by our member theatres and frequently result in plays reaching production. Almost 80 percent of plays in the NNPN's showcase go on to production; more than a hundred scripts have found their way to the stage thanks to online literary chats; and more than 40 plays have received NNPN Rolling World Premieres thanks to this kind of crowdsourced literary engagement.

The network has been successful for many reasons, chief among them that its members share a common set of values about new plays and know each other (and each other's theatres) so very well. NNPN Core Member theatres are reimbursed for travel expenses to both the annual conference and National Showcase of New Plays, each of which is hosted by a different member. Over the course of many years, network artistic directors and literary managers have come to know the aesthetics, the spaces, the patron bases, the artist communities, and the personalities of their sister theatres.

That means a recommendation from one network artistic director to another automatically comes with bona fides, and those bona fides make that recommendation rise to the top of the ever-growing pile.

In the past three years, the NNPN has begun taking advantage of online technology to make this kind of inter-theatre script-sharing happen seamlessly. The Continued Life Alert is a quarterly email that lets member theatres know about scripts that are available for Rolling World Premieres. Alumni playwrights have been provided with a pipeline to member theatres for their new plays via our online reading rooms. (The network presumes that a playwright trusted enough to be produced by one member theatre can and should be considered by others). And the NNPN has created an online archive for all plays that have been produced as Rolling World Premieres, presented at its national showcases and the M.F.A. Playwrights Workshop, and commissioned by the network.

The NNPN began formalizing these three programs in 2012 into what it has called the Collaborative Literary Office: an Alumni Playwrights Council to provide access to member theatres for trusted playwrights, crowdsourced dramaturgy and literary management, and the office's centerpiece, the New Play Exchange. As the NNPN was designing this Collaborative Literary Office, network staff convened playwrights, producers, literary managers, and dramaturgs to brainstorm about whether there was a way to translate the network's crowdsourcing success to the broader field. Gwydion Suilebhan's influential HowlRound post about his envisioned "New Play Oracle" paved the way for new thinking about the old tricks NNPN had already mastered. That thinking turned into the New Play Exchange.

Working in close partnership with four organizations across the country, the NNPN will build and pilot an online tool, the New Play Exchange, to revolutionize the ways in which playwrights and theatres connect in the nonprofit arena. Combining a centralized script database, crowdsourced recommendations, and the interactivity of a social networking site, the New Play Exchange will change the way literary departments and playwrights function field-wide, ensuring that the right doors open to the right plays. Convenings with playwrights, theatre leaders, literary managers, and dramaturgs began in March 2013 to design the site's functions; website development began in September 2013, and the site will be piloted by the consortium partners and their constituencies through the end of 2014. The NNPN plans to open the New Play Exchange field-wide in 2015. A cornerstone grant of $110,000 from the Doris Duke Charitable Foundation was received in November 2012, and a three-year grant from the Andrew W. Mellon Foundation was received in July of 2013, $122,000 of which will go towards the New Play Exchange. Plans to complete funding the $300,000 project are moving forward rapidly.

Practitioners agree that this is a time of abundance: readings, workshops, development, festivals ... yet productions have not kept pace. So playwrights hurl themselves at the gates of opportunity, submitting multiple copies of the same script to dozens (or hundreds) of entities, all leading to a massive traffic jam. Meanwhile, the theatres most likely to take risks on as-yet-unheralded writers struggle to keep up with the onslaught. Many read and evaluate the same plays in a time-intensive process. Others simply privilege those "current winners" in the system – plays and writers that have already been anointed by favorable national press or the attention of flagship theatres – because they can't spare precious resources.

With the right technology, the New Play Exchange will enable a "long tail" to distribute success – for both playwrights and theatres – more broadly. Playwrights will send their plays through the right doors with a click of a button, while theatres crowdsource expertise to open their doors to the right plays. The result will be greater diversity in the production of new plays across the country, the creation of new and dynamic networks of playwrights and theatres, and more second, third, and fourth productions of plays by soon-to-be-heralded playwrights.

The New Play Exchange will be constructed on an extensive database of new plays, each tagged with critical metadata – everything from cast sizes and genres to subject matter keywords. Add a mechanism whereby users can champion their favorite new plays, then build in the appropriate search and filtering tools, and users will be able to find highly recommended scripts that meet precise criteria. And then suddenly, instead of just a database of scripts, the exchange will become the force that topples the current submission paradigm – in which thousands of playwrights submit their scripts independently to hundreds of theatres – in favor of a targeted search process. As Suilebhan explained on Howlround, this tool will "turn the noise (of 10,000 playwrights each churning out one new play a year) into a clear signal" so that theatres can access only those wavelengths that suit them and playwrights can broadcast their plays to the companies most eager to receive them.

The exchange will allow both readers and playwrights to access the same central database. Playwrights will create profile pages for themselves and for their work. Profiles for playwrights will include standard demographic data, as well as a variety of supporting material. Profiles for plays will include PDFs of scripts, synopses, sample pages, links to reviews, development histories, and other relevant background information. Theatres, literary managers, and dramaturgs will create reader profiles as well.

A script reader interested in reviewing the work of a specific playwright will be able to find it by several different means: by reviewing an alphabetical index of author names, for example, or by conducting a title or keyword search. Theatres looking for plays tackling specific subjects (environmental dramas, for example) or with certain cast sizes or ethnic profiles – just to name a few options – will be able to perform advanced, comprehensive searches. Plays and playwrights will be discoverable by multiple means. Readers will be able to either access scripts directly or contact playwrights (or their representatives) to request reading copies.

The anticipated power of the New Play Exchange will spring from crowdsourcing script recommendations: positive assessments authored by theatres, artistic staff members, literary managers, and dramaturgs. Recommendations will become part of a play's profile and displayed alongside search results. Readers will be able to recommend plays for specific individuals, furthermore, or for specific theatres. Scripts that earn the greatest number of recommendations will be displayed more prominently in search results.

Like a favorite bookstore, users will receive play recommendations from readers when they log on. Most importantly, users will be able to filter those recommendations according to who's giving them. For example, a user might only want to see aggregated recommendations for a script from literary managers. Or a user might aggregate those recommendations based on their "friends" list of trusted, mission-aligned readers:

- find the ten most-recommended, unproduced comedies by playwrights of color;
- find plays that feature the keywords "global warming";
- find the five most highly recommended dramas written since 2010.

And instantly, the user can download an appropriate script, contact the playwright, see the play's development path on the New Play Map, read about the playwright's other work, or view aggregated press reviews if it's already been produced. By privileging recommendations over ratings, furthermore, the exchange eliminates the potential for negative feedback going viral. Instead, it creates virtual networks of positivity surrounding promising plays and writers.

The exchange will be developed with a modern, open source web development framework that enables fast, cost-effective prototyping; access to many of the most creative programmers in the world; ease of integration for existing components; compatibility with complementary services like Facebook, Vimeo, and Twitter; and ready deployment to devices like tablets and smart phones. Project development will be staged to match the emerging understanding of the most compelling value points for the pilot playwrights and theatres. Like all modern technology, too, the exchange will continually evolve: the ability to constantly make the most of new ideas will be a key to its long-term success.

The NNPN has succeeded because it has created its own "network of positivity" in which good new plays and playwrights meet theatres they have yet to encounter and find artistic homes. Each of its member theatres has its own network, furthermore, that the others access, and the NNPN facilitates that access through its various programs. By bringing aboard Chicago Dramatists, the LMDA, Playwrights Foundation, and the Playwrights' Center, the NNPN will broaden those "networks of positivity." The consortium partners were chosen because:

1 They represent extremely important geographic communities in the new play sector.
2 They each serve a meaningfully sized group of pre-vetted "Resident" or "Core" writers.
3 Their writers are well-respected by the NNPN's members (and vice versa).
4 The NNPN has pre-existing relationships with each of them, both formal and informal.

The NNPN reached out to the Literary Managers and Dramaturgs of the Americas because they bring a committed group of new play readers who want to ensure good scripts and good theatres find each other. On reaching out to the LMDA, the NNPN learned that the organization was just beginning to pilot crowdsourced script-sharing on its own, fortuitous timing. Their online Script Exchange is an informal and rough-hewn model to be followed.

The NNPN began developing the strategy for the New Play Exchange in earnest at a gathering of literary managers in the fall of 2011, which led staff to abandon the original idea of a "Centralized Literary Management Office" in favor of crowdsourcing the knowledge base that member theatres represent. After the publication of Suilebhan's "Oracle" article in February 2012, the NNPN gathered a group of DC-area playwrights, dramaturgs, and literary managers with both Suilebhan and Vijay Mathew (of the New Play Map) to talk about the contours of this online model. It was at this meeting that the idea of including new play development organizations arose. (It's worth noting that Suilebhan had been working for a year with the Playwrights' Center in Minneapolis to revamp the members area of its website to better represent playwrights to the world).

From there, after a period of intense conversations with the NNPN's Literary Committee, Suilebhan and Mathew produced a two-year timeline (to include a longer pilot period than the New Play Map) and identified potential partners for a consortium. The partners were contacted to assess their interest, and the NNPN's board was consulted. With the help of consultants, the NNPN drafted a budget and timeline for the back-end coding and front-end design. The DDCF grant was approved for work beginning in January 2013.

Since March 2013, a Core Development Committee culled from the consortium partners has led the design process. In time, each partner will host a local gathering in which playwrights, producers, and dramaturgs will meet with the entire committee to address vital questions:

- How can the Exchange best serve your needs?
- How can we ensure that it becomes the most essential item on your desktop?
- What kind of recommendation system will both protect playwrights and provide useful information to theatres?

The NNPN envisions a tight schedule – relying on a launch-and-iterate approach – to the development and testing of an initial prototype, expecting that the initial system will likely go through multiple development cycles to provide the optimal platform and services over time. Upon launch of the beta in early 2014, the consortium partners will actively and frequently encourage the tool's use among their constituents, with the aim of making it a constant desktop fixture. Only resident playwrights at the new play development organizations, LMDA members, and NNPN member theatres and alumni playwrights will use the exchange during the pilot year.

Finally, the committee and the NNPN will convene during the pilot year to strategize how best to open the New Play Exchange to the entire field in 2015, at which point there will be no tiered access or entry barriers. In the long term, the NNPN envisions a stand-alone site, governed by its own board of playwrights, producers, and dramaturgs. Imagine an inexpensive online tool, accessible to every new play professional, through which the right plays are matched to the right theatres. Imagine theatres in communities across the country meeting new playwrights, kicking off their careers, mounting productions full of diverse voices, and encouraging a new generation of theatre-lovers embracing the rewards of artistic risk. That's what the New Play Exchange will engender.

Part V

DRAMATURG AS MEDIATOR AND CONTEXT MANAGER

Transculturalism, translation, adaptation, and contextualization

46

A view from the bridge

The dramaturg's role when working on a play in translation[1]

Katalin Trencsényi

When talking about translation, the United Kingdom has the lowest rate of published works in translation within the EU, estimated at only around 2–6 percent of annual books published, including fiction and non-fiction. (Compare this number with statistics from the rest of Europe: Germany, 12.4 percent; Spain, 24–8 percent; France, 15–27 percent; and Turkey, 40 percent).[2] Literary translations in Britain make up around a fifth of this very low figure – a fraction.[3]

Plays in translation commonly appear on the British stage as readings rather than full productions. Only a limited number of theatres regularly invest in commissioning a new translation and take the risk of producing foreign plays and keeping them on their repertoire. The most notable of these companies are: the Gate Theatre, the Young Vic Theatre, the Arcola Theatre, the Royal Court Theatre, and the National Theatre in London.

Browsing through the British theatres' repertoire, it shows that plays in translation are more often than not well-known classics (Euripides) or modern classics (Ibsen, Chekhov). Contemporary plays in translation on the stage are rare. However, there are some exceptions, mainly presented at festivals: for instance, Company of Angels' bi-annual Theatre Café Festival aims to show contemporary theatre for young people; and the recently established, but growing CASA Festival focuses on Latin–American plays (and performances).

The different paradigms of translation for the stage

When a theatre decides to produce a play in translation, one of the first decisions it has to make is whether to use an existing translation (if available) or commission a new one. If an existing translation is going to be used, it is often the dramaturg's responsibility to hunt down the translations, read them all, and discuss them with the artistic director (or the director of the show) in order to choose which best suits the production in mind. Once the translation has been selected, it still needs to be prepared (perhaps refreshed and edited) for the production. The dramaturgical work here is very similar to the script-preparation process when working on classics or modern classics. It is a traditional dramaturgical task.

If a theatre decides to commission a new translation, it has two main paradigms to choose from, each of them resulting in a different working method. One is to commission a translator or playwright (fluent in both the source language and the target language) who is able to create a literary translation of the original that works well on the stage. The other is to commission first a literal translator (who speaks the source language) and then a playwright (who speaks the target language). The playwright using the (annotated) literal translation then creates a playscript (a version or an adaptation) of the original work. The result of the former way of working is usually considered as translation proper, whereas in the latter process the final product is usually called a "version." In order to make this latter process succeed, the person who makes the literal translation and the version-maker need to have access to each other, so the version-maker can make informed choices. In an ideal case they are also in touch with the original author of the play as well.

There is a third method that can accompany either of the two paradigms: the collaborative translation process. In the translation process, practical development periods are built in (readings, workshops with actors, etc.) in order to ensure the evolving translation is suitable for the stage. The process is very similar to the collaborative new drama development processes. It is often led by the director of the production with the translator(s) present.[4]

Practices at the Royal Court and at the National Theatre

At the Royal Court Theatre, plays in translation (proper) are usually part of the theatre's biannual International Playwrights' Season. Since 1993 the theatre has regularly given a taster of its extensive international work by producing readings and short plays from all the countries where its play development work takes place (Brazil, Cuba, Mexico, France, Germany, Spain, Russia, Nigeria, Syria, and the Nordic countries). Many of the plays developed through the theatre's international residency program have been presented as full productions at the Royal Court.[5] On average the theatre produces one or two productions of contemporary plays in translation (usually for the theatre's smaller, upstairs stage), while several others are read as part of a festival or focused event of some kind.

At the National Theatre in 2010, out of its 20 premieres, 2 were as a result of some sort of translation process. Both were "new versions" of classics: *Danton's Death* by Büchner "in a new version by Howard Brenton";[6] and *The White Guard* by Bulgakov in a new version by Andrew Upton. The literal translators were not acknowledged on the theatre's website.[7] It is worth noting that both plays were written in languages (German, Russian) for which translators or playwright-translators could have been found. Instead of commissioning a translation proper, the National Theatre chose the route of working from a literal translation process, showing that this choice is not happening out of necessity but is part of the theatre's artistic policy. Sebastian Born, literary manager of the theatre, explains:

> The reason that we do it mostly this way is because ultimately we feel that we want to create a play that would work for a production here. That the actors will feel they can speak the dialogue, and that there isn't a sense that what we are presenting is an alien artefact.[8]

Whilst Born is aware of the challenges that working from a literal translation can pose, he is primarily concerned with the theatre's audience, who mainly go there for "meaningful entertainment."[9] Although it is not an explicit aim, often the familiar name of the version-maker (the playwright who creates the playscript from the literal translation) can serve as bait to bring in an audience to see a play written by a dramatist who is unfamiliar in Britain. In Born's opinion, a good translation has to perform a balancing act: "preserve the otherness where the play comes from, but on the other hand not create a barrier for the English audience."[10] Accessibility, audience engagement, and performability are the main criteria for Born of a good translation.

Notably, for Christopher Campbell, literary manager at the Royal Court Theatre, performability is the key criterion for a good translation:

> The simple answer to it is: a translation that you can produce in your theatre, that's a good translation. Everything else for me is secondary to that, and that's partly because of the position I occupy, that my primary responsibility is to put plays on the stage in the theatre. Of course, there are more complex ways of answering the question: carrying as much as possible of the meaning, the sense, the significance of the original work; making it sound as if it was written in the language in which it is performed – it is often a virtue, not always – sometimes there is a value in strangeness. Successfully communicating something of the original intention, for the audience of the translation, I think that has to be the secondary answer. But the primary answer undoubtedly is: a good translation is a playscript I can produce.[11]

One of the main criteria of performability, according to Campbell, is the translation's speakability: "It has to have an interest in the language, but it has to sit convincingly in the mouth of an English actor. Very often there are simply too many words in the English translation, or it doesn't sound credible."[12] By credibility Campbell means that it creates a world within which the words on stage sound valid "from an English mouth."[13]

It is worth noting here that these criteria can be also problematic, as Patrice Pavis warns: "once it degenerates into a norm of 'playing well' or verisimilitude. The danger of banalization lurking under cover of the text that 'speaks well' (*bien en bouche*) lies in wait for the mise-en-scène."[14] These criteria best serve only one particular type of theatre, the realistic–naturalistic, and seem to be almost meaningless when trying to employ them in postdramatic theatre or non-naturalistic directing styles. So perhaps it is wiser to look further than speakability and establish what Pavis suggests: "what is much more important than the simple criterion of the 'well-spoken' is the convincing adequacy of speech and gesture, which we may call the *language-body.*"[15]

Pavis brings into play another important criterion of translation for the stage, which Penny Black, translator, emphasizes as well: the economy of the dramatic text (as opposed to, for instance, the descriptive qualities of the prose):

> It has to be what people say and it has to be concise. ... When you work on a theatre translation, you're working on a piece of theatre collaboration. You know what your job is, and you hand it on to somebody else who does his job on it. ... The reason academic translations don't work [on the stage] is because they're explaining the text and the context at the same time. Whereas a good theatre translator knows that this is an actor's job and that you have to leave space for the subtext – for the actors to do their work. ... I think a good theatre translation is about always paring down as opposed to talking up.[16]

Performability is a difficult term to define theoretically. To make matters more complicated, it is sometimes connected to the play's marketability.[17] However, it is not a term we can ignore. The live nature of the theatre performance means that the audience is an immediate witness, with no facility during the event to stop, pause, rewind, or just ask for some more explanation. The action on stage has to be clear enough for the audience to grasp meaning, intentions, emotions, subtext, etc., and to evoke their active participation in the event. If that is lost, it is lost forever. Although the Royal Court and the National Theatre have similar aims (performability of the translation), there is a difference in the way they set out to achieve this.

Campbell emphasizes that it is the Royal Court's artistic policy not to work from literals, but to commission translators:

> Here at the Royal Court we do not employ literal translators. It is our policy not to do that because we are encouraging translators to engage with the language directly. We use a wider range of people, and we are less demanding.[18]

Campbell reassures his interviewer that "less demanding" does not mean compromising the quality of the translation, but that as the Royal Court is primarily producing new works, a certain level of "rawness" is acceptable, and the theatre's audience is aware of this: "Here we have a slightly rougher aesthetic."[19] As a translator and dramaturg who is highly experienced in various translation processes, Campbell is aware of the possibilities a literal translation can offer. He knows it provides a greater choice of plays available; he knows that a fruitful conversation between the two playwrights and the literal translator can enrich the work greatly. But he is also aware of the method's constraints: "It inherently devalues the work of the so-called literal translator."[20] He is also aware that in order to enable this three-way conversation, a theatre needs resources – it is not a cheap process. Therefore Campbell argues for translation proper, that gives a "more direct connection with the original, and you also have, if you like, a purer version."[21]

In contrast, Born emphasizes that the National prefers to work with playwrights because, in his opinion, only they can enable a translation to work on the stage. In an ideal case, the playwright is a fluent speaker of the original language. Unfortunately this is rare, although there are excellent exceptions (for instance, Michael Frayn). "For us it's about: are there translators who have what we feel are the skills of a playwright? You can argue that some translators do, some don't. We tend to go the literal translation–playwright route,"[22] says Born. Campbell, who previously worked for the National Theatre, is aware of this argument. In his opinion, one of the reasons for this preference lies in the nature of British theatre – that it is (compared to theatre in continental Europe) logo-centric: "In British theatre, words spoken on stage have a supreme value. It is to do with the feeling we have that the words on the stage would not be adequate unless they are written by a playwright."[23] The ideal scenario for Campbell would be to use a playwright-translator, who speaks the source language:

> The advantage of a playwright translation is that you have the creative ima-
> gination there and the play is being filtered through directly. And that can
> give rise to wonderful things. It very often happens that the play will sound
> like a play by the playwright, but that's because that was what attracted him
> to the play in the first place.[24]

Both theatres, then, have notably similar values. Each literary manager ranks the highest ideal as translation proper by a playwright, who speaks the source language; compared with the other possibilities of translation proper by a non-playwright translator, and translation via a literal and a version-maker playwright.

The same aims (performability, speakability) and values (to have a playwright-translator), however, lead to two very different translation approaches. The National Theatre compromises the direct contact with the original for a playwright's voice; whereas the Royal Court retains that and would rather sacrifice the skills a playwright may offer (for the process). During both processes very strong dramaturgical work can be detected.

The dramaturg's role in the process

Throughout the five distinct stages of the work, the dramaturg performs different roles. In Stage 1: dramaturgical choices, the dramaturg is instrumental in choosing the parties best suited (play, director, translator) for the project. In Stage 2: creating a script in the target language, the dramaturg functions as a communicator and a person who facilitates the work. Stage 3: creating the playtext (the director's copy) is part of the intersemiotic translation, whereby traditional script-based dramaturgical work can be observed, often combined with dramaturgical work that is used in new drama development. In Stage 4: pre-rehearsal dramaturgy, production dramaturgical roles can be observed, which may continue in the last phase of the work, Stage 5: rehearsals.

In the work based on a literal translation, the dramaturgical work shifts between the literary manager, playwright-adapter, and the director. In the translation proper process it is shared between the director, translator, and the dramaturg. Campbell finds the dramaturg's role essential in the translation process:

> I think a dramaturg is highly desirable for the translation process. As a match-maker in the first place: picking the right translator is hugely important; there is a strong analogy with this and with casting actors. It is important to have someone there who values the original play, who understands what the translation can or cannot deliver.[25]

Campbell summarizes the facilitative aspect of the dramaturg's role:

> It is always *communication*; it is to do with being able to facilitate communication between the original writer, translator and director. In an ideal world the dramaturg is at the centre of that triangle, and making sure that the work is entirely collaborative, and each of the three people feels that they have made the largest contribution.[26]

To conclude, throughout the various dramaturgical tasks a dramaturg performs in a translation process, there is a strong, underlying role that is concerned with communication, facilitation, and acting as a mediator.

Notes

1 A longer version of this essay, including detailed case studies from the Royal Court and the National Theatre, can be found in Katalin Trencsényi, *Dramaturgy in the Making* (London: Methuen Drama, 2014).
2 Arash Hejazi, "Last Call for a New Blood: The Disinterest of UK and US publishers towards Books in Translation and Its Implications," *Garnet on Publishing* 4 (April 2011), available online at http://blog.garnetpublishing.co.uk/2011/04/04/last-call-for-a-new-blood-the-disinterest-of-uk-and-us-publishers-towards-books-in-translation-and-its-implications, accessed September 8, 2013.
3 Gunilla Anderman, *Europe on Stage – Translation and Theatre* (London: Oberon Books, 2005), 15.
4 This practice is documented in Katalin Trencsényi, "Labours of Love: Interview with Penny Black on Translation for the Stage by Katalin Trencsényi," *Journal of Adaptation in Film & Performance* 4.2 (2011): 189–200.
5 "International Productions at the Royal Court," available online at www.royalcourttheatre.com/playwriting/international-playwriting/international-productions, accessed March 24, 2013.
6 As advertised in the National Theatre's program.
7 Source: the National Theatre's website: www.nationaltheatre.org.uk. The online information on *The White Guard* is no longer available.
8 Sebastian Born, interview with Katalin Trencsényi, London, March 14, 2011.
9 Born, interview.
10 Born, interview.
11 Christopher Campbell, interview with Katalin Trencsényi, London, January 27, 2011.
12 Campbell, interview.
13 Campbell, interview.
14 Patrice Pavis, *Theatre at the Crossroads of Culture* (London and New York: Routledge, 1992).
15 Pavis, 143.

16 Penny Black in Trencsényi, 192–3.
17 Cf. Clare Finburgh, "The Politics of Translating Contemporary French Theatre: How 'Linguistic Translation' Becomes 'Stage Translation,'" in Roger Baines, Christina Marinetti, and Manuela Perteghella, eds, *Staging and Performing Translation: Text and Theatre Practice* (Basingstoke, New York: Palgrave Macmillan, 2011), 232.
18 Campbell, interview.
19 Campbell, interview.
20 Campbell, interview.
21 Campbell, interview.
22 Born, interview.
23 Campbell, interview.
24 Campbell, interview.
25 Christopher Campbell, interview with Katalin Trencsényi, London, 27 January 2011.
26 Ibid.

47

Lost in translation[1]

Gitta Honegger

During my tenure at Yale I frequently noticed students in the drama school's library leafing through issues of *Theater heute*. Without knowledge of German, the students would look at the impressive production photographs without any awareness of the plays or their complex social, political, and cultural circumstances. Studious imitations of these illustrations abounded in their productions, regardless of the play in question.

Unfortunately, Marvin Carlson, distinguished professor of theatre at the City University of New York, seems to have taken a similar approach. Under the umbrella of director-dominated *Regietheater* (director's theatre), he surveys the works of ten directors from three generations in *Theatre Is More Beautiful than War*.[2] All burst on to the scene as representatives of *Regietheater*, an approach to staging based on a thorough dramaturgical interrogation of text and context, both historically and in its relationship to the present, in which the director – in intense collaboration with a team of dramaturgs and designers – asserts unique authority as quasi-co-author of the text in performance. Unfortunately for the sake of American theatre's absorption of German dramaturgy, Carlson pays no critical attention to the processes of such collaborations, which would contextualize and support his choice of directors. Instead, the criteria of selection bring to mind David Letterman's "Top Ten."

Much could be said about every one of the directors on Carlson's list. However, by dint of sad coincidence, Peter Zadek's death on July 30, 2009, just one month before the publication of Carlson's book, gives us reason to highlight its shortcomings. The author's narrow view of the director's provocations to postwar Germany is representative of his overall approach. Born in Berlin, Zadek emigrated with his parents to London at the age of seven, in 1934. Because he spent his formative years in England and began his theatrical career there, he was shaped by Anglo-Saxon skepticism of Teutonic self-importance, *Weltschmerz*, and pathos. Perhaps his greatest gift to German theatre (he began to direct in Germany in 1958) was his love of the music hall, revues, "lowbrow," and even the "boulevards" – mainstream entertainments much maligned by trendsetting German critics (and Marvin Carlson). Zadek infused these styles into his now legendary productions of modern classics from Anton Chekhov, Henrik Ibsen, and Frank Wedekind to Brendan Behan; *Der Spiegel* praised him by saying he was no "smartshit" (*Klugscheißer*). Instead, Zadek asked the simplest childlike questions: "Why do people hug each other? Why do they clobber each other to death? Why is Ibsen's Nora so dense? Why is Hamlet always in a bad mood? And what makes (Wedekind's) Lulu so hot? And why on earth do we all make theater all the time?"[3]

None of this energy, or its brilliant intellectual foundation, comes through in Carlson's perfunctory account. In a numbingly repetitive manner, he introduces the titles of each and every play directed by his subjects, from their breakthrough production, which was generally the one promoted by *Theater heute*, to the pinnacle of fashionable stardom validated exclusively – at least in Carlson's variation of Broadway's hit/flop sentencing – by an invitation to the Berlin Theatertreffen: the annual jury-selected showcase of notable productions from the German-language theatre. With no further reminder or information as to what these various new plays are about, Carlson skips to a few flashy details of the set and staging, without analysis of the given text and its dramaturgical underpinnings. The problem with this approach is that German theatre without dramaturgy is like a Broadway musical without music. As Andrzej Wirth recently reminded the diverse participants of a panel discussion at Berlin's Rotes Rathaus: "There are two words which cannot be translated into English: 'Dramaturg' and 'Intendant.'" The formulaic approach and extensive list-making provides no context for deeper understanding, let alone critical examination of contemporary German theatre, which cannot be reduced to the Berlin Theatertreffen.

In his exclusive and uncritical focus on the Theatertreffen, Carlson falls victim to our event culture, a hit parade of "winners" that reduces to losers the unnamed works not selected (often for political reasons – after all, the Theatertreffen was a direct result of the construction of the Berlin Wall; having lost its political footing after the *Wende*, the festival has been redefining its purpose and goals ever since). Most problematically – particularly for students for whom this book will be the first introduction to German theatre – Carlson presents the "winners" completely out of the context of their theatrical homes and the rich diversity of seasons at repertory companies in Austria, Germany, and Switzerland. No attention is paid to the dramaturgy of season planning, the choice of plays and artists (including Carlson's "top ten") at theatres across German-speaking Europe, how works speak to each other, interact with their communities, and address regional as well as global concerns – in short, everything that goes into what Carlson so much admires about the range and depth of "German theatre."

While American students have cheerfully learned to get around Germany with one four-word sentence – "Noch ein Bier bitte" – their Berlin-bound theatre counterparts too often rely on just a couple of individual words, cited here with numbing repetition: "Theatertreffen," "*Theater heute*," "Heiner" (as in Müller), "Freie" (not Freya as in Wagner, but as in University), "Erika" (Fischer-Lichte, not Munk), and, for good measure, "Bob" (as in Wilson), whose enormous influence on German mise-en-scène in the late twentieth century Carlson surprisingly ignores. While students seem not to mind at all eight-hour drinking binges made possible by their knowledge of German, their theatre teachers' experiences in Peter Stein's much-discussed eight-hour production of *Wallenstein* were not as happy (no references to *Theater heute*, Theatertreffen, or Heiner). Ignorance of the German language did not prevent Ivy League theatre experts from instantly voicing their irritation (too many words, no exciting stage effects) about this deliberately text-oriented, finely tuned if fastidious production of a complex historical trilogy that examines, in difficult poetic language, issues of European identity, religious strife, territorial wars, and claims to power that are of particular relevance to the united Germany and its position within the expanding European Union. One professor, for example, wondered how she, like most Americans, hated the production, while Germans apparently found it quite meaningful.

Under the circumstances, Carlson's quote, however misspelled and grammatically bungled, from an article on Peter Stein in the *Neue Zürcher Zeitung*, comes as a welcome if unintended comic relief: "Der Stein Zeit ist forbei,"[4] suggesting another one of Max Bialystock's and Leo Bloom's Broadway hits. Carlson's command of German is, however, much better than that of his Berlin fellow-travelers, allowing him to translate from *Theater heute* and other sources. Therefore, the curious mistranslation of a crucial statement by the late Peter Zadek is all the more troubling.

A headline in the July 1990 issue of *Theater heute* reads, "Ich möchte lieber Verbrecher als Opfer sein" (I'd rather be a perpetrator than a victim),[5] a reference to the German Jewish director's reinterpretation of Shylock as a reflection of Israel's aggressively assertive self-defense. Thus Carlson's mistranslation, "I would also rather be a rebel than a scapegoat,"[6] raises all the more serious issues.[7] Though Carlson rightly acknowledges the controversial director's unique importance to postwar German theatre, he fails to understand, or perhaps consciously tries to soften, not to say dumb down, the full cultural/political significance of Zadek's polemical contrariness.

In his 1990 interview with *Theater heute* the famously confrontational director talked at length about his now legendary 1988 production of *The Merchant of Venice* at the Vienna Burgtheater. In that staging Shylock, as played by Gert Voss, was a sophisticated Wall Street–type banker of the Reagan era, as savvy, suave, and cut-throat as his yuppie corporate clients. According to Carlson, Zadek "suggested that both as an artist and as a Jew he no longer wished to portray the Jew as sacrifice or scapegoat but rather as rebel."[8] Carlson concludes his brief summary of the complex, nuanced interview with his (mis)translation of the direct quote from the director: "That is the caption of this Shylock: 'Rather a rebel (*Verbrecher*, perpetrator) than a scapegoat.' And in fact I agree with this. I would also rather be a rebel than a scapegoat. Not only as a Jew. Also as an artist. Completely. At all times."[9] The substitution of *rebel* for *perpetrator* allows the professor to avoid the term *victim* as the opposite to perpetrator in contemporary legal terminology (as would befit Zadek's staging of *The Merchant of Venice*). Instead, he inserts the more poetic biblical meaning of *Opfer* as "sacrifice," in conjunction with "scapegoat" (*Sündenbock*) and its reference, both in English and German, to "the goat upon whose head are symbolically placed the sins of the people after which he is sent into the wilderness in the biblical ceremony of Yom Kippur."[10]

The use of "sacrifice" for *Opfer* (though possibly justified in a Freudian analysis of Zadek's ambivalence) misses the point in the context of the social and political realities of the time both of the production in 1988 and of the interview two years later. Zadek's *Merchant* was part of the Vienna Burgtheater's season dedicated to the commemoration of the fiftieth anniversary of Austria's *Anschluß* to Hitler's Reich. It played in repertory with Claus Peymann's legendary production of Thomas Bernhard's *Heldenplatz* and with two productions by George Tabori: the latter's own tragic cabaret of the absurd *Mein Kampf* about Hitler plagiarizing Herzl's original draft of the infamous text, and his staging of *Othello*, with Gert Voss as the moor in black make-up that rubbed off on the other actors in the course of the performance, thus highlighting "otherness" as a construct of the dominant culture's imagination. The importance of Tabori – who gets no mention in the book – to German-language theatre cannot be overstated. His interventionist dramaturgy in Vienna from the late 1980s, both as a director at the Burgtheater and as legendary intendant of his provocative theatre Der Kreis (1986–90) sped up and helped focus Vienna's long overdue examination of Austria's participation in the Holocaust. A Hungarian Jew, long-term US émigré (in the West Coast circle around Brecht and as a writer/director in New York) he eventually gained international recognition in Germany and Austria, most prominently at Peymann's theatres in Bochum, Vienna, and Berlin.

Curiously, Carlson concludes that in Zadek's *Merchant* "the Jewish question disappeared entirely from the play, to be replaced by a modern capitalist lust for financial gain." One can't help wondering who – or rather what image or stereotype – would qualify for Carlson's notion of "the Jewish question." Had he spent some time in Vienna with an ear for the nuances and subtext of local idiom, he might have been surprised how brilliantly the production captured the subtler negotiations of "the Jewish question" in so-called polite society, which are much more insidious than the loud blatant manifestations of anti-Semitism that get instant media attention. As Zadek cogently suggests, it is much easier to be nice to the victim than to the perpetrator.

Interestingly, Zadek's conversation with *Theater heute* took place two years after the opening of *Merchant*, while Zadek was in rehearsal for Chekhov's *Ivanov*, also at the Burgtheater. Quite clearly – and contrary to Carlson's claim – "anti-Semitism" continued to be very much an issue in the director's take on the play, albeit not in a "pathetic sort of way" and therefore all the more true to Chekhov's – and Viennese – society. Carlson characteristically describes the set – that is, only at the opening moment when "the curtain rose, revealing a stage totally empty of scenery, open to the theatre's rear wall, with only a single chair at the center and the rather unkempt figure of Voss, as Ivanov, reading a book."[11] A one-sentence, rather bland quote from *Theater heute* ("A richly detailed, innovative look at mankind, tempered with sympathy but also frankly exposing the lack of a stable foundation"[12]) does not convey the production's subtle dramaturgy, which included the use of chairs. These were added or taken off throughout the performance, always forming a straight line facing the audience. Carlson's information that "the evening began with a musician before a closed curtain, playing traditional Russian music on a balalaika,"[13] gives the wrong impression of the music serving as a cliché mood piece. Instead, it put the audience in a listening mode, which was further encouraged by the quasi-orchestral configuration of chairs with the actors as players of the textual score. As in a concert, the houselights stayed on throughout the production (a fact not mentioned by Carlson). Thus the text's musicality was highlighted. However, rather than letting the spectators indulge in melancholic reverie, it made them *hellhörig* in the most literal meaning of the German term – that is, "bright of hearing." What came to the surface, bright and clear, was a sort of salon anti-Semitism, which continues to be quietly tolerated by the public at large – as suggested by the seated actors facing the lit spectators. It was also no coincidence that *Merchant*, *Heldenplatz*, and *Othello* remained in rotating repertory with *Ivanov*, as part of an ongoing discourse about the "Jewish issue" in Vienna – not really a "German" city.

Through the (in every sense) exclusive lens of *Theater heute* Carlson claims that Zadek's provocative production of Marlowe's *The Jew of Malta* "delighted" Burgtheater audiences "on the whole" – although, he asserts, "some critics argued that Zadek's love of music-hall entertainment had not only robbed the play of any general political message but in fact had allowed its basic anti-Semitism to pass unchallenged, perhaps even celebrated."[14] In his astute critique Michael Billington correctly notes that "the point Zadek's production makes is that Barabas's amoral individualism has to be seen in the context of a society where Jews are routinely stereotyped, plundered, persecuted. In the end, what Barabas sacrifices most tragically is his sense of community. For all its occasional flashiness – a group of bikini-clad whores singing *Hey, Big Spender* – this production offers a radical reappraisal of the play by daring to take it seriously. It also confronts a Viennese audience with powerful images from its collective memory."[15] Carlson's cavalier dismissal of Zadek's staging ignores the remarkable choice of 2004 Nobel laureate Elfriede Jelinek for the translation/adaptation. Anyone even vaguely familiar with Jelinek's deconstructions of language, let alone her scathing criticism of Austria, would take into account her contribution to the provocative re-examination of Marlowe's text in the context of the position of Jews in contemporary Austria.

I have discussed the chapter on Zadek at length here because it exemplifies the book's major problem, which also indicates what is wrong with our contemporary festival culture. Organized and packaged festival presentations of theatre productions turn them into mediatized events. Productions appear on display, as in an exclusive fashion show, but completely cut off from the specific social/cultural contexts that shape local audiences and the theatre's interaction with its immediate community.

The intensity of Zadek's argument and the controversies surrounding his productions are a perfect example of the intense interactions of German-language theatre artists with their times, which of course have a long tradition, as do the fierce questioning and subversions of that same tradition (which drives the younger generation of directors in Carlson's "top ten"). It is summed up succinctly by the pre-eminent theatre critic and scholar Günther Rühle in his book *Theater in unserer Zeit*:

> Theater history quickly becomes a listing of names and dates. What is missing is the eye for the processes occurring in the theater, for the entire active field of impulses, effects and retro-active effects, of antagonisms, the power of strategies, the systems of images, the withholding of images, of altered material, the connection between political processes in society and work in the theatre – the eye for these aspects is not very pronounced. This is why they are deprived almost completely of observation and analysis.[16]

Postscript: The productions discussed above first ran at Vienna's Burgtheater during the 1989/90 season and remained in the repertory for several years. Peter Zadek's comments with regard to *The Merchant of Venice* refer directly to the political situation in Israel at that time and in the context of the Austrians' commemoration of the fiftieth year of the *Anschluß* to Hitler's Reich. It would be intriguing to speculate if and how he would have changed his argument and portrayal of Shylock after 9/11 and the worldwide economic crisis. As this volume focuses on the scope and depth of dramaturgical thinking and practices, which includes translation, Peter Zadek's productions still represent challenging models for dramaturgy in practice. Sadly, Professor Carlson's disregard for the complex dramaturgical underpinnings of those productions and of the politics of language and culture embodied in translation reflects the widespread and continued neglect, if not disrespect, within the US academic and theatre communities for both traditional and innovative dramaturgy and the new practical and theoretical challenges of translation in a global festival culture.

Notes

1 A full version of this article was published in *Theater* 40.3 (2010): 116–127.
2 Marvin Carlson, *Theatre Is More Beautiful than War* (Iowa City: University of Iowa Press, 2009).
3 All translations by the author unless otherwise noted: see www.guardian.co.uk/stage/ theatre blog/2009/aug/03/peter-zadek-director-german-theatre; www.spiegel.de/kultur/gesellschaft/ 0,1518,druck-639370,00.html; and www.faz.net/s/Rub4D7EDEFA6BB3438E 85981C05ED 63D788/Doc~E, acessed August 12, 2009.
4 Carlson, 195. Also see Christiane Pohle, "Der Stein-Zeit ist vorbei," *Neue Zürcher Zeitung*, May 17, 1998, 17.
5 Olivier Ortolani, "Ich möchte lieber Verbrecher als Opfer sein," *Theater heute* 7 (July 1990): 22.
6 Carlson, 38.
7 Ortolani, 23.
8 Ortolani, 23.
9 Ortolani, 23.
10 Definition of "scapegoat," www.merriam-webster.com/dictionary/scapegoat.
11 Henning Rischbieter, "Der wahre Zauber," *Theater Heute* 7 (July 1990): 19–21.
12 Rischbieter, 20.
13 Rischbieter, 20.
14 Michael Billington, "Theatre of the Repressed," available online at www.theguardian.com/ culture/2002/jan/19/artsfeatures, accessed January 30, 2002.
15 Billington.
16 Rühle, Günther, *Theater in unserer Zeit* (Frankfurt Main: Suhrkamp, 1976), 175.A.

48

The dissemination of theatrical translation

Adam Versényi

Why do we translate? Why do theatrical translation? Why is theatrical translation a dramaturgical endeavor? The answers to these questions are both simple and complex, bridging as they do concepts global, local, and epistemological. At the most basic level we translate to know words in another language, to gain cultural understanding, and by opposition to learn something about ourselves. Theatre, with its multimodal structure encompassing word, image, and physical presence, is in a unique position to contribute to this acquisition of knowledge. As Gershon Shaked puts it,

> We become familiar with foreign cultures through plays because in the process of reading or viewing them we must interpret and translate materials, patterns of behavior, and images of the world which are alien and incomprehensible in order to expand our world and familiarize ourselves with the unknown.[1]

As dramaturgs we are concerned with how meaning is conveyed in performance in all of its facets. Theatrical translation is, therefore, inherently a dramaturgical enterprise and increasingly urgent given the asymmetrical and inequitable production of knowledge and information due to globalization.[2] Theatrical translation is a powerful tool for facilitating the global exchange of cultural production. It increases our ability to know.

In her foreword to *Translating through History* (2012) Judith Woodsworth writes, "A weaving together of different strands, drawing on diverse stores of evidence, history is a creative, interpretive act, to some extent an act of imagination. Not unlike translation, in other words."[3] Not unlike dramaturgy. Translators and dramaturgs both seek to provide textured cultural, social, political, and imaginative contexts that are compelling and comprehensible to their respective audiences. *Translating through History* focuses upon the translator, "the agent rather than the product or process."[4] In 2005, I began to conceive of a new journal that would be an agent for the promotion of the production of theatrical translation, a place for the publication of theatrical translations from any language into English, and a site for discussion of the theory and practice of theatrical translation. In 2007, I took the plunge and created *The Mercurian: A Theatrical Translation Review* distributing it electronically to a moderated listserv of subscribers. While numerous places to publish translated prose and poetry existed and there was a growing body of journals oriented towards translation studies, the possibilities for publication of theatrical translation, aside from occasional opportunities in more specialized journals or as excerpts in more broadly conceived periodicals, were limited. Since the demise of *Modern International Drama* in 1996 there was no journal focused solely on theatrical translation. *The Mercurian* was created to fill that gap.[5]

In his book *Translation and Identity* (2006), Michael Cronin suggests that the ancient Greek figure of Diogenes is pertinent to a "contemporary understanding of the relationship between translation, society, and culture."[6] It was Diogenes who first used the term "citizen of the world" to describe someone not bound to a city-state, but belonging instead to a cosmopolitan community of shared mental compatibility. While this might suggest a flattening out of cultural difference in which we all ultimately share the same core values and ideas, Diogenes frames the cosmopolitan, as Cronin puts it, "primarily as a *practice* or a *competence*."[7] Such an approach to cross-cultural exploration opens up "the possibility of thinking about translation as a way not only of thinking but of being and acting in the world."[8] As the Turkish author and translator Sema Kaygusuz puts it, "all progress in this world [is the] result of people traveling and discovering each other,"[9] becoming cosmopolitan.

If we think of it as a *practice* or a *competence* then completing the translation of a text is only the beginning of the process by which the translator's examination of art in one cultural context allows that art to regain its original force from the force of its audience's attention in another cultural context. In the same way that theatrical collaborators must approach a text for performance on its own terms, rather than impose themselves upon it, so also must the theatrical translator challenge audiences and collaborators to approach the translation on its own terms rather than to expect immediate accessibility or familiarity. Translation is not only about what we do with other languages, as theatre is not only about the performance text; both translation and theatre are also, fundamentally, about how we experience and think about ourselves.

The translator's role is that of an intercultural informant, bridging cultures through the medium of translation, yet caught in the nexus between them. The translator is constantly in motion, dancing back and forth between cultural and theatrical languages, attempting to comprehend how meaning is generated in performance. Theatrical translation is inherently an epistemological endeavor. What we are investigating as translators is the origin, nature, methods, and limits of human knowledge across the globe. The translator's examination of artistic creativity in one cultural context allows that artistic product to regain its original force from the force of its audience's attention in another cultural context. As the translator sorts through a multitude of possibilities for each performative moment, registering each nuance, not fixing meaning but allowing it to float, the mechanics of translation create a space between cultures, a conduit for conversation and comprehension as opposed to the concrete complacency that comes from defining the object of study. To translate a play or performance piece faithfully, then, is to imbue oneself with the theatrical process itself: to imagine, and imaginatively discard, a range of potential performances for each moment;

to rehearse and reassess, to reassemble and redress; to explore the space Beckett describes in *Texts for Nothing* as "a road ... between parting dreams."[10]

The theatrical translator seeks to enact the representation of both text and texture in the theatrical language he or she employs: a language capable of carrying collaborators along on a journey through a foreign culture and thereby inspiring them to the creation of intercultural solutions for performance in their own culture. Epistemologically, the inherent liminality involved in translation is akin to Henry Giroux's "border pedagogy" in which culture is not viewed as "monolithic or unchanging, but as a shifting sphere of multiple and heterogeneous borders where different histories, languages, experiences, and voices intermingle amid diverse relations of power and privilege."[11] Translation is a two-way street. It opens the road between cultures and it charts the myriad byways between.

Since its inception in 2007 the masthead of *The Mercurian* has carried the following:

> *The Mercurian* is named for Mercury who, if he had known it, was/is the patron god of theatrical translators, those intrepid souls possessed of eloquence, feats of skill, messengers not between gods but between cultures, traders in images, nimble and dexterous linguistic thieves. Like the metal mercury, theatrical translators are capable of absorbing other metals, forming amalgams. As in ancient chemistry, the Mercurian is one of the five elementary "principles" of which all material substances are compounded, otherwise known as "spirit". The theatrical translator is sprightly, lively, potentially volatile, sometimes inconstant, witty, an ideal guide or conductor on the road.
>
> *The Mercurian* publishes translations of plays and performance pieces from any language into English. *The Mercurian* also welcomes theoretical pieces about theatrical translation, rants, manifestos, and position papers pertaining to translation for the theatre, as well as production histories of theatrical translations.

To date *The Mercurian* has published three and a half volumes of fourteen issues containing forty-three translations of plays from ten different languages and nineteen different countries. Languages translated from include French, Spanish, Serbian, German, Polish, Ukrainian, Japanese, Russian, Italian, Greek, and Hebrew. The countries represented are France, Peru, Spain, Ivory Coast, Congo, Serbia, Argentina, Germany, Poland, Haiti, Ukraine, Puerto Rico, Japan, Mexico, Cuba, Russia, Italy, Greece, and Israel. These translations have comprised both classical and contemporary works. *The Mercurian* has published articles on Arabic plays in translation on the Israeli Hebrew stage; on translating Latin American plays for a German audience; on bringing Ancient Greek plays to contemporary audiences; on staging identity through art; on staging the works of the twentieth-century Argentine avant-garde novelist and playwright Roberto Arlt; and on the role that translation has played in the creation of contemporary theatre in Sri Lanka. *The Mercurian* has published a piece by US dramaturg Michael Evans, who has lived and worked in Norway for over twenty years, "Credo: 18 Thoughts on Translating for the Theatre"; a number of short papers from a roundtable, "Translation into Production," that I co-organized for the Association for Theatre in Higher Education's annual conference; and book reviews including one on a collection of contemporary Finnish plays in translation and another on the implications for theatrical translation of David Bellos' book, *Is That a Fish in Your Ear?: Translation and the Meaning of Everything*. Three years ago I constituted an advisory board for the journal and raised its status to a peer-reviewed publication. The advisory board has given me invaluable assistance and the overall quality of the journal has improved. Clearly, there was and continues to be a need for a publishing outlet for theatrical translation. The vast majority of submissions *The Mercurian* receives are play translations, and, were I to accept them all, I currently have a backlog of submissions large enough to fill several issues. Submissions of theoretical articles about the practice of theatrical translation have not been as robust as I would like, provocations like Michael Evans' "Credo" are rare, and production histories of theatrical translation non-existent. Most importantly, publication in the journal does not seem to have moved these translations to production.

To remedy that lack in April 2012, *The Mercurian*, in collaboration with the Department of Dramatic Art and The Process Series at UNC–Chapel Hill, and Theater Studies and the Embodied Performance Research Colloquium at Duke University, convened Theatrical Translation as Creative Process: A Conference Festival. A group of 23 international participants spent 4 days together discussing the process of theatrical translation and viewing staged readings of 4 plays previously published in *The Mercurian* with the translators in attendance. Each staged reading was followed by a conversation between the translator and the conference participants about his or her process in translating the work and how it had worked in performance. Two of those conversations have now been published in *The Mercurian*.

One of the ideas to emerge from the conference festival was a conviction that new translations, whether of classical or contemporary work, should be treated the same way as new plays and developed accordingly. In August 2013 a convening of parties interested in establishing a New Works in Translation Network took place in Washington, DC. We have taken as inspiration the National New Play Network in the US. The NNPN is a network of small and medium-sized theatres throughout the United States with a central clearing house that solicits new plays. Several of those new plays are selected each year and sent to the network's constituent theatres, who are invited to commit to producing one of those plays in a Rolling World Premiere, wherein a single play is produced by several theatres across the country during a single season. The theatres share production costs and the playwright tests the work with different artistic sensibilities in different communities.

The New Works in Translation Network plans to connect individuals and institutions interested in producing new works in translation. The NWTN seeks to include theatres, universities, and colleges who could use new works in translation as part of their educational mission in a number of ways, cultural exchange organizations such as the Goethe Institut and the Japan Society, national embassies that do some performances of works in translation on an ad hoc basis already, as well as other institutions, organizations, and individuals that have yet to appear on our radar screen.

Unlike the European model, where an essential role for the literary departments in theatres is translating plays from different languages, works in translation, with the exception of Ibsen, Chekhov, and Molière, have formed a minute part of the theatrical landscape in the US.[12] Partially, this is a function of language and geography. We are a vast country, with a monolingual bias. While there have always existed bilingual US citizens, the dominant culture has insisted upon English as primary and has painted exploration of other cultures as unnecessary. Despite our immigrant roots, approximately two-thirds of US citizens do not possess a passport. In 2012 out of a total population of 313,900,000 citizens only 113,431,943 held a US passport.[13] Until the recession in 2008, North Carolina, where I live, experienced a decade of 400 percent annual increase in its Latino population. Yet, except for isolated pockets, this explosion has not led to increased bilingual education or bicultural programming. In 25 years of researching and teaching Latin American and US Latino theatre and performance I have found this to be the case nationwide. As playwright and translator Caridad Svich has written, "bilingualism and biculturism engenders not only a double view of society and one's place in it but also an outside perspective on one's own identity within the cultures of which one is a part," yet "celebrations of 'Latinidad' while certainly valid, [beg] for a homogenized view of Latinos, reinforcing old world taboos and structures, whether the old world in each individual case [is] Mexico, Cuba, Puerto Rico or elsewhere."[14] Ethnicity can also become a trap whereby a Latino/a (or Polish, Nigerian, or Japanese) writer who confounds uninformed notions of cultural norms is rejected as not conforming to the reader's expectations of ethnicity. Artistic directors have told me that my translations of an Argentine playwright's work were "not Latin American enough."

Over the past few years, presenting organizations have increasingly programmed "international" events and festivals, such as the BAM Festival, the Carolina Performing Arts Series here at UNC, TeatroStageFest in NY, or, before that, the Festival Latino at the Public, Under the Radar in both NY and at RedCat in LA. Such programming brings a wide variety of theatre to audiences that would never see it otherwise, but engagement with the work and the artists who create it tends to be scatter-shot, several performances lacking context and then the road show moves on. In this respect theatrical performance becomes another byproduct of an increasingly globalized culture, where easy air travel, and hastily assembled translated supertitles, create the impression that artistic creation is easily malleable and seamlessly transferable from one context to another. In the age of social media we take translation for granted.

The near hegemonic sway of English as a global language militates against Diogenes' version of cosmopolitanism. The decision not to translate illustrates as much a way of being and acting in the world as the decision to translate, and English speakers from different cultural contexts may speak the same words though not the same language. To refuse the necessity of translating oneself across the cultural divide is also an epistemological choice. The epistemic nature of translation, however – its constant avoidance of closure to engage with the contingent and its privileging of the journey rather than the destination reached – provides a potential counterweight to the homogenizing effects of globalization. *The Mercurian* and the nascent translation network are attempts to break through such biases and, by providing greater access to theatrical practice from around the world, engender greater cosmopolitanism, in Diogenes' sense, through translation.

Notes

1 Gershon Shaked, "The Play: Gateway to Cultural Dialogue," in *The Play Out of Context: Transferring Plays from Culture to Culture*, eds. Hanna Scolnicov and Peter Holland (Cambridge: Cambridge University Press, 1989), 18.

2 *Words, Images and Performances in Translation*, eds. Rita Wilson and Brigid Maher, Continuum Studies in Translation (London: Continuum, 2012), 1.

3 *Translators through History*, eds. Jean Delisle and Judith Woodsworth (Amsterdam: John Benjamins Publishing Company, 2012), xiii.

4 Delisle and Woodsworth, xiv.

5 See *translation*, *Latin American Theatre Review*, *Gestos*, *two lines presses*, *Asymptote*, *The Brooklyn Rail*, among others. *Modern International Drama* was published from 1967–96.

6 Michael Cronin, *Translation and Identity* (London: Routledge, 2006), 7.

7 Cronin, 10, emphases in the original.

8 Cronin, 10.

9 Sema Kaygusuz, "Literature Does Not Stop at National Borders," *The Guardian*, February 27, 2013.

10 Samuel Beckett, *Stories and Texts for Nothing* (London: Calder & Boyars, 1974), 57.

11 Henry Giroux, *Border Crossings: Cultural Workers and the Politics of Education* (New York: Routledge, 1992), 32.

12 A review of the 2013–14 seasons of the 72 LORT theatres in the country shows that beyond productions of Chekhov, Ibsen, and Molière (with only one production listed for each of them), our nation's major theatres will do one production apiece of works in translation by Schiller, Eduardo De Filippo, Brecht, Marivaux, Sternheim, Beaumarchais, and Goldoni, with two productions of Dario Fo, and one each for the contemporary playwrights Guillermo Calderón and Wajdi Mouwad.

13 http://travel.state.gov/passport/ppi/stats/stats_890.html, accessed October 4, 2013.

14 Caridad Svich, "Out of the Fringe: In Defense of Beauty (An Introduction)," in *Out of the Fringe: Contemporary Latina/Latino Theatre and Performance*, eds. Caridad Svich and María Teresa Marrero (New York: Theatre Communications Group, 2000), xi, xv.

49

Literary adaptation for the stage
A primer for adaptation dramaturgs

Jane Barnette

In theatre and performance studies, adaptation usually implies revising, devising, or interpreting a previously written text for the stage. Scholarly and practical considerations about the implications of adaptation in recent years have proliferated; as Thomas Leitch asserts, "After years of being stuck in the backwaters of the academy, adaptation studies is on the move."[1] And yet, as he acknowledges, "the field is still haunted by the notion that adaptations ought to be faithful to their ostensible sourcetexts."[2] Most of this scholarship in adaptation studies addresses cinematic adaptations, however; if the stage is considered at all, it is typically referenced as a step in the evolutionary path toward the film version. This is a remarkable omission, especially if we accept Maya Roth's claim that "[t]here is no theatre without some act of translation and adaptation."[3] When the stage is considered in adaptation scholarship, writers usually reflect on the process they followed in adapting and/or directing the production, with strikingly infrequent references to dramaturgy at all. While exceptions to this pattern certainly exist, few scholars (or practitioners) have considered the important intersection (or even intervention) of dramaturgy into adaptation studies. Vincent Murphy's 2013 book, *Page to Stage: The Craft of Adaptation* barely mentions dramaturgy (or contextual research, for that matter) at all; instead, Murphy creates a step-by-step guide for novice adapters of literature for the stage, with a cursory reference to the dramaturg as one of many potential collaborators in this process.[4]

The questions and possibilities surrounding adaptation demand dramaturgical reflection, since the craft of dramaturgy shares compelling characteristics with that of adaptation. Like adaptation, dramaturgy has been a notoriously difficult thing to define, in part because "we use the same word for process and product" in both fields.[5] With regard to process, the similarities between the two actions of adapting and dramaturging hinge in varying degrees on their source text: in the case of literary adaptation for the stage, this is the literature upon which the stage version is based; in the case of dramaturgy, this is whatever script the production team has chosen to perform. Thus, dramaturgs' work (also understood as both process and product) can be assessed in relation to the evaluator's prior knowledge, expectations, and/or assumptions of the source text and their ability to communicate the necessary aspects

of this script (however wrought) to their audience. As for the dramaturgical product –
perhaps in the form of program notes, a study guide, a website, and/or a lobby
display – it is virtually impossible to evaluate any of these possibilities without
considering the source text as a major criterion. The same can be said of adaptation,
of course, with one major exception: whereas in adaptation fidelity to the source text
tends to be expected (even demanded), in dramaturgy our loyalty shifts from the
script to either the playwright or the director.

Frequently dramaturgs are categorized as either production dramaturgs or new
play dramaturgs: the former typically work with published or previously produced
plays, while the latter help to develop new work. A production dramaturg thus
works to communicate, clarify, and refine the director's vision for his particular
staging of a play; a new play dramaturg communicates, clarifies, and refines the
playwright's vision through the script development process. If we consider these
categories as points on a continuum rather than silos, we can begin to see the
significance of analyzing the process/product of dramaturgy for the adaptation of
literature for the stage, as this sort of dramaturgy moves between both points,
creating a more holistic understanding of both stage adaptation and dramaturgy
itself.

On the continuum of new play and production dramaturgy, adaptation dramaturgy falls somewhere between the two, in part because it requires the skills and
approaches typically associated with both. The process of adaptation dramaturgy can
be summarized in three steps: the development of the script, contextual research,
and audience outreach. These steps are not necessarily sequential; often they occur
simultaneously, or even in different orders for different projects. It is worth noting
that while audience outreach is part of every dramaturg's responsibility, script
development is typically the province of new play dramaturgs, while production
dramaturgs focus primarily on contextual research.

In the context that assumes a traditional leadership role for the director, the
dramaturg works as part of the production team rather than as co-creator of the
project. (There are other models of collective creation, including the work of
Lookingglass, Rude Mechs, and Tectonic Theater Project, to name a few). In a conventional production setting, an early task for any dramaturg is to read and analyze
the play; for an adaptation dramaturg, the first step, before reading and analyzing the
source text, is to meet with the adapter and/or director to discuss her vision for
staging this project. The same questions apply (Why this play/project now/here?),
but in this case the answers to these questions become an essential tool in focusing
that crucial first read of the text upon which the production will be based. In my
work with Georgia Shakespeare's adaptation of Homer's *Odyssey*, for example,
I knew from the outset that the director/primary adapter, Richard Garner, wanted
his adaptation to speak to contemporary veterans returning home from Iraq or
Afghanistan.[6] From the larger epic tale, he wanted to select scenes/moments that
highlighted the recovery process from soldier to civilian; this changed the way I
(re)read the epic, as well as the feedback I would offer on his early drafts. Our early
conversations considered questions of selection: which scenes would best illustrate
this vision (while also being most attractive for putting onstage)? A related set of
selection questions centered around the source texts themselves: first, which

translation/s of the epic would we consider our baseline? and then, which previous stage adaptations would inspire us?

Here we are reminded of the "palimpsestuous" complexity of adaptations. This evocative term, coined by Scottish scholar-artist Michael Alexander, refers to the ways the source text continues to haunt any adaptation of it, leading to both "pleasure and frustration" due to "the familiarity bred through repetition and memory."[7] Like a palimpsest, the residue or trace of previous writing/staging is inescapable when adapting literature; for adaptation dramaturgs, a review of the history of previous versions is one of the most critical contributions we can make to the overall process, especially in the early stages of script development. And yet it can also be over-whelming, especially when the source text is as classic as a Homeric epic. This is why knowing the director's vision is crucial to our ability to parse the possibilities, keeping in mind that often dramaturgy – like adaptation itself – can be "a code word ... for elimination,"[8] just as adaptation is often called a "surgical art."[9] The selectivity (or surgery) continues throughout the adaptation dramaturgy process, but the dramaturg's power to recommend exclusion is strongest in the script development phase.

Once the basis for the adaptation is established, the script development phase follows the path of new play dramaturgy, generally speaking: we provide feedback on written drafts (by recommending cuts or rearrangements as well as providing alternate lines or suggesting different verbiage) in an editorial capacity, followed by offering further feedback after hearing (a) reading/s of the polished script. In some cases, as occurred with the development process for John Gentile's adaptation of W.B. Yeats's *Red Hanrahan* at Kennesaw State University, the reading takes place months before the production is cast.[10] In others, as was the case with my drama-turgy for Garner's *Odyssey*, this reading is the first day of table work for the rehearsal process, and I have the opportunity to hear the script read by the actors who will perform it. Both scenarios have their obvious advantages; since adaptation drama-turgs rarely have a say in how the script development process will transpire, what is significant is that we attend these read-throughs, so that we can make the vital switch from readers to listeners.

This change in our form of reception – listening rather than reading – is worthy of further reflection, as it intersects with several key concerns within adaptation studies overall. According to Linda Hutcheon, whose book *A Theory of Adaptation*, now in its second edition, helped to jumpstart the revitalization of adaptation studies, "with the move to the mode of showing, as in film and stage adaptations, we are caught in an unrelenting, forward-driving story."[11] She contrasts the interactive reception of reading, wherein we can choose to skip ahead or pause to reflect on the meanings of words, with that of spectatorship, arguing that with the latter we are mostly passive receivers of what we see, rather than imaginers based on what we read. I would also add two stage-based distinctions: 1) the aural reception of staged readings; and 2) the storytelling basis of narrative theatre. In both cases, imagination is ignited rather than quelled, although the listener cannot fully interact with the text as she might with a novel or a videogame. With this caveat in mind, the significance of attending early readings of the script for adaptation dramaturgs becomes paramount: it is at this stage that we can offer feedback regarding the images, associations, and memories that hearing the adaptation inspires.

The next step in adaptation dramaturgy is the contextual research and analysis. Once again, the director's vision for the stage production is paramount in filtering the possible approaches to this hunting/gathering phase; indeed, especially when the director is also the adapter, they will have dedicated substantial energy and time to this phase before choosing (how) to adapt the material in the first place. That said, there are some basic categories of material for (any) dramaturgical research that are useful to consider in this step. Among these, common starting places for adaptation dramaturgs include: production history (Who has adapted this text before and how was it critically received?); common interpretative approaches to the source author (How do scholars tend to analyze Homer? What does current research tell us about Yeats, and how might that differ from how he was understood half a century ago?); and milieu research, for both the original setting and especially the time/space of production at hand. Ideally, adaptation dramaturgs will recruit both the actors and the designers in their milieu research, as these questions regarding the world of the play will influence how the actors perform their roles as well as how the designers sculpt the material reality of the production.

In some cases, this phase of work can become what D. J. Hopkins has called a "counter-text," a repository of research that informs the process but usually can only be glimpsed "through the cracks and around the edges" of the production itself.[12] At its fullest expression, such counter-texts represent the work of a co-creator involved in a collaborative project, instead of the more traditional hierarchy of theatre practice. And yet, even within the *gesamtkunstwerk* model (wherein the director's vision guides all production decisions), a conundrum persists along the lines of how Erik Ehn envisions dramaturgical co-creation.[13] For example, during my dramaturgy for John Gentile's adaptation of the Brothers Grimm stories, *Dark Forest*, I supplemented historical research with feminist analyses and revisions of fairy tales.[14] While in this case a spectator would be hard-pressed to find any evidence of feminist tactics in the performances, my counter-text was decipherable through our audience outreach materials.

The final step of adaptation dramaturgy – audience outreach – marks the shift from process to product and thus represents the most visible phase of the dramaturg's contributions. Although some audience-outreach approaches remain more process-oriented (e.g. talkbacks or pre-performance discussions; class visits or curricular assignments, etc.), tangible kinds of outreach, like program notes, lobby displays, and study guides, are equally important. Outreach at KSU also includes a "companion website" for the production, wherein all these materials reside.[15] Including these materials on the internet does not replace their usual format (that is, dramaturg's notes are still included in paper programs, etc.); rather, the adaptation websites make dramaturgical outreach accessible beyond the scope of our actual audience, both in terms of who we reach and when the materials are read. Moreover, since the possibilities for what can be included on these websites are virtually infinite, using them for adaptation outreach is creatively rewarding. When preparing such a website, the dramaturg should consult with the public relations or marketing professionals affiliated with the institution, since each situation differs with regard to web design and maintenance protocol.

Although dramaturgical websites are fairly common for production and new play dramaturgy, they are an essential part of the adaptation dramaturg's outreach. Not only do they provide resources for future adaptations of the same source text, but they also address one of the key modes of engagement that we otherwise lose in the transfer of literature from page to stage: the ability to interact with the material. Especially since each spectator will have a different relationship with the source text – for some, the stage adaptation may even be their first encounter with it; for others, the original text or author/s may be an area of expertise – the interactivity of web-based dramaturgy allows spectators to choose their own path. In addition, websites cultivate the palimpsestuous nature of adaptation, since references to other adaptations, translations, or versions of the source text can be embedded or hyperlinked to the site. For example, our website for KSU's 2008 production of *Moby-Dick* includes references to the 2004 staged reading that adapter/director John Gentile held, the award-winning 2009 trilingual version he adapted for the International Theatre Festival in Morocco, and the 2013 site-specific professional mounting of the 2008 script in Atlanta.[16] In addition to these possible areas of exploration, by browsing this dramaturgical website, a spectator can also choose to learn about Melville studies or Gentile's production concept of staging the numinous, and so on.

The pervasiveness of literary adaptations for the stage shows no sign of waning soon; indeed, "there is an obvious financial appeal to adaptation," especially during times of economic uncertainty.[17] Therefore, adaptation should be a substantial part of dramaturgical training, and scholars of dramaturgy would be wise to pay close attention to the developments in adaptation studies. Dramaturgs have critical insight into the craft of adaptation, in part because our practice in both fields shares fascinating overlaps, but also because dramaturgy is the very lifeblood of adaptation.

Notes

1 Thomas Leitch, "Adaptation Studies at a Crossroads," *Adaptation: The Journal of Literature on Screen Studies* 1 (2008): 63.
2 Leitch, 64.
3 Maya E. Roth, "Introduction," in *International Dramaturgy: Translation and Transformations in the Theatre of Timberlake Wertenbaker*, eds. Maya E. Roth and Sara Freeman (Brussels: Peter Lang, 2008), 25.
4 Vincent Murphy, *Page to Stage: The Craft of Adaptation* (Ann Arbor: University of Michigan Press, 2013).
5 Linda Hutcheon, with Siobhan O'Flynn, *A Theory of Adaptation*, 2nd ed. (London: Routledge, 2013), 15.
6 Richard Garner, *The Odyssey: A Journey Home* (Atlanta: Georgia Shakespeare, 2010).
7 Quoted in Hutcheon, 6, 21.
8 Kirk Lynn, and Shawn Sides, "Collective Dramaturgy: A Co-consideration of the Dramaturgical Role in Collaborative Creation," *Theatre Topics* 13.1 (2003): 112.
9 H. Porter Abbott, *The Cambridge Introduction to Narrative* (Cambridge: Cambridge University Press, 2002), 108.
10 John Gentile, *Red Hanrahan: Stories by W. B. Yeats* (Kennesaw, GA: Kennesaw State University Department of Theatre and Performance Studies, 2013).
11 Hutcheon, 23.
12 D. J. Hopkins, "Research, Counter-text, Performance: Reconsidering the (Textual) Authority of the Dramaturg," *Theatre Topics* 13.1 (2003): 12.
13 Hopkins, 4–5.

14 John Gentile, *Dark Forest: Tales and Poems from the Brothers Grimm* (Kennesaw, GA: Kennesaw State University Department of Theatre and Performance Studies, 2011).

15 For examples of these "companion websites," see www.kennesaw.edu/theatre/dramaturgy Sites.sthml.

16 John Gentile, *Moby-Dick* (Kennesaw, GA: Kennesaw State University Department of Theatre and Performance Studies, 2008).

17 Hutcheon, 5.

50

Intermingling literary and theatrical conventions

Tomasz Wiśniewski

Among numerous interests of dramaturgy, intense performativity of literature, on the one hand, and possible textual aspirations of a stage event, on the other, may be considered – in times when artistic autonomy of theatre is taken for granted – particularly stimulating. There is no danger now that literature and literary studies aspire to subordinate theatre and the whole range of theatre studies, dramaturgy included. Distinct as they are, literary and theatre studies are, to a certain degree, interconnected and may be, in particular aspects, mutually instructive. Literature, in its entire variety, has remained one of the major inspirations for theatre; even when treated instrumentally, or deconstructed, literature institutes a point of (negative) reference for a theatrical event. There is, of course, a group of performances which deliberately ignore all possible allusions to the literary, the textual, and the written, but this group is not the subject of the present research.

It is frequently stressed that dramaturgy, and the profession of dramaturg, is spread between a text, or texts, and the stage.[1] Although the function of the discipline is usually seen as directed towards the stage (echoing the cliché dictum "from page to stage"), we certainly should not forget about the contrary tendency. First, the theatrical work of actors and directors results, at times, in substantial changes introduced to the post-production editions of previously published plays. Second, playwrights confront their scripts with the practicalities of stage craftsmanship in the process of writing, i.e. before publication; and, finally, the playtext itself may be a textual reflection of a collective theatrical work, as is the case in devised theatre. These illustrative examples give credence to the statement that dramaturgy – as the discipline spread between the domain of texts and that of theatre – is not a one-dimensional enterprise of adapting textual material to the requirements of theatre. It also encompasses those processes which adjust theatrical material to the needs of the written.

There is one substantial consequence of assuming such a perspective. The primacy of the mediatory role of dramaturgy reveals the ethical dimension of the discipline. By stimulating varied processes of meaning transformation, dramaturgy participates in transposing the singularity of a literary experience (i.e. reading) to the domain of theatre; or, vice versa, it aims at "translating" the singularity of theatrical experience into the specific "language" of literary drama. Both processes are endowed with huge communicative responsibility as they put at risk intrinsic qualities of what may be best named, with the help of a term adapted from translation studies, the "source material."

When discussing similar issues, Derek Attridge states that

> a responsible response to an inventive work of art ... is one that brings it into being anew by allowing it, in a performance of its singularity for me, for my place and time, to refigure the ways in which I, and my culture, think and feel.[2]

In many ways, dramaturgy is the art of exploring the singularity of the communicative act in one medium so as to transpose it to another (literature used for theatrical purposes or theatrical practice put in literary context). In this process of innovative transformation of meanings, the position of a mediator is exposed and endowed with a crucial role: the dramaturg is supposed to "responsibly respond" and "bring it anew" so as to remind the theatrical audience of their specific communicative position. (It works in a parallel way in the case of readers of drama).

The question arises how all this works in practice.

Generally speaking, when dealing with contemporary playtexts, readers tend not to bother with nuances of their linguistic materiality. Playtexts are usually seen as scripts for theatrical performances and not complete literary "artifacts." Dramatic literature is highly underestimated. Yet some of the best work of dramaturgy is yet to come in the domain of written drama, which is to be observed also in the case of such theatre-based companies as Complicite.

Complicite's published plays are usually treated as textual accounts documenting certain versions of "constantly shifting and moving"[3] "compositional pieces"[4] which originated in theatre. Yet, functioning as textual adaptations of their stage predecessors, Complicite's playtexts generate new meanings, incite original aesthetic experiences, and challenge some of the implications set by performances. This is to say that even in the case of playtexts published by Complicite, we are faced with artistically independent entities. Unlike fleeting performances, playtexts are accessible at any time and in any place; they are capable of reaching those who did not have the chance to see the play in the theatre; and, finally, in spite of the collective origins of a devised performance, playtexts based on such performances are endowed with a certain degree of textual authorization. Hence, the inherent qualities of a written text provide structures which reshape the semantics of a devised play. Trivial as it is, the statement that a theatre performance is one thing and a playtext another bears interesting aesthetic consequences and gives additional prominence to the work of the dramaturg, the one who is – in this case – responsible for adapting theatrical conventions to the textual specificity of dramatic literature.

Such adaptation usually requires substantial changes in methods of segmentation. Unlike in the theatre, the division of a playtext into smaller compositional units can be achieved by neither visual nor acoustic stage signals but only by their linguistic descriptions. This is to say that in dramatic literature even the most rudimentary theatrical delimitators (such as a curtain) acquire linguistic materiality (the word "curtain" is necessary to depict an image of a curtain and, thus, announce the beginning of the action). As basic elements of stage directions, words describing visual and acoustic signals become involved in relations with other linguistic signals and are subordinated to strictly literary regulations.

The playtext of *The Street of Crocodiles* is Simon McBurney and Mark Wheatley's textual adaptation of a performance "based on the stories by Bruno Schulz"[5] and devised by Complicite. Unlike in the theatre, the composition of the published play reveals superimposed senses that facilitate its interpretation. The play is divided into four parts, which are embedded in the clearly biographical framework of the "Prologue" and the "Epilogue." The play's intertextual context is communicated by naming each part with a phrase originating in Bruno Schulz's narratives: "Part One: Act of Remembrance," "Part Two: The Age of Genius," "Part Three: The Republic of Dreams," and "Part Four: The Act of Destruction." What is more, each part is further divided into episodes, which are not only named but also contain appropriate quotations from a variety of letters and Schulz's narratives. It is worth stressing that these citations are an exclusively textual phenomenon and they were not presented during the performance. As this example illustrates, the very nature of a published play provides means for endowing its segmentation with superimposed textual meanings. This, in turn, shapes the reader's further interpretative procedures in a way that is independent of the procedures fixed by the original theatrical production. In other words, in the mediating process of adapting the devised play for the page, McBurney and Wheatley "responsibly responded" to the Complicite's "inventive" performance and attempted to "bring it anew" in the context of dramatic literature.

In their "Note on the script," McBurney and Wheatley underline the complexity of the hermeneutic process in which *The Street of Crocodiles* is involved. After all, its textual version is an adaptation of a theatrical performance based on Bruno Schulz's narratives and biography, which means that the playtext is seen as a dramatic response to a theatrical response to a narrative work of art:

> So, this book is more the record of a process than a text for performance; a map rather than a play. A play is a place which demands to be inhabited; both origin and destination, linked by a clearly determined path. A map indicates the landscape, suggests a multitude of directions, but does not dictate which one you should take. A map, however beautiful, is a guide not a site. If you wish to visit the site yourself, pick up Schulz's books. And travel.[6]

By drawing our attention to the tertiary character of their text on the one hand and to the true artistry of the original on the other, McBurney and Wheatley not only give prominence to the singularity of an aesthetic experience (as if to say, "this is our reading of Schulz, check what's yours"), but also complete what George Steiner calls the "reiterative stage" of a hermeneutic process. They restore communicative balance. They compensate for what they have taken away from the original.[7]

In this way, McBurney and Wheatley express one of the central ethical concerns of the discipline in question. As the art of mediation, dramaturgy incessantly disrupts the balance between literature and theatre and it does so in more or less radical ways. So far I have used the example of *The Street of Crocodiles* to illustrate shifts in the semantics of segmentation in the course of authorial adaptation of a theatrical performance to the structures of dramatic literature, but it is true that the reverse process is nowadays more frequently associated with the discipline of dramaturgy.

Adaptation of literary conventions and structures to theatrical purposes may result in equal shifts in the semantics of segmentation. In Complicite's production of *Endgame* by Samuel Beckett, for example, the opening and ending scenes were embedded in ambient music, which blurred the demarcation line of theatrical semiosis. By subtly contemplating the transgression of the boundaries of the performance, Complicite lay much emphasis on the framework. Given the fact that the final visual image (the light coming on Clov from the right window) was one of the few added elements in this otherwise text-bound performance, the framework (hence, the segmentation) acquires a significant role as a theatrical commentary – "a responsible response" – to the playtext. A more radical transformation of compositional principles may be observed in the play based on John Berger's long short story and entitled *The Three Lives of Lucie Cabrol*, in which Complicite substitutes the three original parts with just two, and substantially reduces the third posthumous "life" of Lucie. Unlike Beckett's *Endgame*, where the promotion of the frame underlined the company's subtle commentary on Beckett's play (i.e. blurring the boundaries between the fictional and the external; introducing – with the ray of light – a notion of disturbing hope to the final tableau), in *The Three Lives of Lucie Cabrol* the transformation of the overall segmentation lays emphasis on the process of selecting the literary material when it is adapted to theatrical purposes. Whereas the former provides an innovative response to the original piece, the latter exposes one of the essential features of dramaturgy when it deals with adapting narrative texts for stage.

The example of Complicite has illustrated that even in the case of a strictly theatre-based company, dramaturgy encompasses a range of processes that mediate between literature and theatre. As the dynamic history of the term proves, dramaturgy operates in both directions and is equally prominent when adapting literature for theatre and when theatrical conventions are transcribed for the objectives of dramatic literature. In one way or another, the role of dramaturgy exhibits an ethical dimension as the decisions undertaken by a dramaturg are burdened with much hermeneutic responsibility. As elsewhere, it is not an easy task to give justice to the transformed original.

Notes

1 An extensive and multifaceted debate on these relations was presented in *Notatnik Teatralny* 58–9 (2010).
2 Derek Attridge, *The Singularity of Literature* (London: Routledge, 2004), 125.
3 Complicite, *Plays 1: The Street of Crocodiles, The Three Lives of Lucie Cabrol, Mnemonic* (London: Methuen Drama, 2004), xi.
4 Complicite, x.
5 Complicite, 6.
6 Complicite, 6.
7 For a more detailed discussion of Steiner's understanding of a hermeneutic process, see George Steiner, "Translation as conditio humana," in *Übersetzung Translation Traduction*, eds. Harald Kittel *et al.* (Berlin: Walter de Gruyter, 2007), 1–10.

51
Research strategies in dramaturgical practice

Matt DiCintio

> But how many of us, for instance, have observed the original Swan drawing since it was discovered in 1888 or visited Dulwich College in south London to observe the painting of Edward Alleyn?[1]

The historian Thomas Postlewait poses this question as he explores the value of iconography in early modern English theatre history. Of first-hand experience with primary sources, Postlewait concludes, "Very few of us can claim such diligence in our research methods."[2] I use Postlewait's question and answer as a basis for evaluating the role of research in the practice of production dramaturgy. While Postlewait is justly concerned with thoroughness and precision in writing history, I suggest that thoroughness in dramaturgical practice consists less in accuracy than in overcoming physical and figurative boundaries. Research is a creative process. To consider it as such is to understand more fully the role a dramaturg plays in contemporary theatre.

Dramaturgs have been considered an integral part of productions for a generation, as directors, actors, and playwrights emerge in the field and from training programs with significant experience working with them. Dramaturgy is "an integral part of the gestalt of the production," as the actual work of a dramaturg informs the direction, acting, and design and disappears inside them.[3] Our understanding of how that disappearing act takes place has changed radically since the regional theatre boom gave rise to the American dramaturg and traditional Lessing-inspired models. In that paradigm, a dramaturg impartially aggregates supposedly pertinent data to put in service of other parties. Henk Borgdorff refers to such outcome-oriented research as "the articulation of the unreflective, non-conceptual content in aesthetic experiences, enacted in creative practices and embodied in artistic products."[4] Contemporary dramaturgy ought instead to be considered as indeed reflective and conceptual, just as creative as it is informative.

Approaching research as a creative act destabilizes conventional notions of production dramaturgy: written, visual, and aural documentation of given circumstances conducted prior to rehearsals. In service of subverting that prototype, Lenora Inez Brown refers to a quest for "atypical triggers."[5] Judith Rudakoff, in exploring "new models for a subversive dramaturgy," believes such triggers can stem from "a multiplicity of sources, including empirical observation, orally transmitted, non-attributed neo-pagan teachings, the study of earth-based spiritual belief systems and mythological references from world cultures."[6] D. J. Hopkins goes so far as to develop a "counter-text" in the dramaturgical process: "an alternative space of authority in performance, an alternative center of gravity that exerts influence over the trajectory of the production process."[7] The counter-text is meant to echo "R&D divisions providing the resources that incite or fuel production,"[8] rather than merely "generate source material that remains secondary to the primary authority of the text."[9] Research, like the act of artistic production of which dramaturgy is a part, is not a finite resource. As Royston Coppenger asks of research, "The word implies the hunt for something hidden, important information that has somehow been misplaced. To look again. But what are we really looking for?"[10] I ask additionally: Where are we looking for it?

I traveled to conduct research for two productions for which I served as dramaturg: A Streetcar Named Desire for the University of Richmond and an adaptation by Simon Bent of John Irving's A Prayer for Owen Meany for PlayMakers Repertory. For Streetcar I traveled to New Orleans and Laurel and Moon Lake in Mississippi. The poetic and geographic liberties Williams took in composing his plays have been well documented. While Elysian Fields, the Moon Lake Casino, a St. Louis fire escape, and a Georgia plantation house were indeed real places, the actual (and in many cases continual) presence of these locations often bears little resemblance to their avatars in A Streetcar Named Desire, The Glass Menagerie, and Cat on a Hot Tin Roof.[11] The restaurant on the shores of Moon Lake (now called Uncle Henry's Place) is still open for dinner. On a visit one can imagine Blanche DuBois, Alan Grey, and company having a (nearly) grand time, but for the fact that Moon Lake is in Northern Mississippi, near Williams's birthplace in Clarksdale, and not in Southern Mississippi, near Blanche's Belle Reve home in Laurel.

For Owen Meany I traveled to Phillips Exeter Academy in Exeter, New Hampshire, the model for the school and city of Gravesend in the novel and adaptation. In much of his work, from The World According to Garp to In One Person, Irving relies extensively on his own experiences as a native of Exeter and student at Phillips Exeter to create the world of his novels. The descriptions of Gravesend often correspond identically to the real geographies of the school and town on which they are based. In New Hampshire and in the South, I tracked fictional and real geographies, their differences and their similarities. More important than showing my own Polaroids and my own marked-up maps, I shared in the rehearsal halls the experience of being in those places, creating detailed and first-hand descriptions of, if not walking in their shoes, at least sharing their sidewalks. I experienced the trip between Exeter's locker rooms and the gymnasium where Owen and John practice their fateful basketball play. I experienced the trip from the Greyhound bus station to the French Quarter (even in a modern car and notwithstanding modern traffic, it would have been quite a haul for Blanche once she had arrived from Laurel). Having traveled, I was able to treat "artistic research as a form of knowledge production"[12] and join the actors and directors in the act of creation.

Several key aspects of these particular plays certainly made their settings attractive destinations: they were written in a naturalistic mode during an identifiable time period, within an identifiable setting. However, models of research that are so applicable to historicized modes are now often displaced in favor of more particular processes. Even 20 years ago Paul Castagno identified a "new dramaturgy" in works by Constance Congdon, Len Jenkin, Eric Overmyer, and Mac Wellman, which "liberates language from realistic conventions such as exposition with its demands for 'filling in' past events and offstage actions. As the need for motivational development becomes superfluous, character psychology and historicity are erased or rendered insignificant."[13] (Today, it is easy to see that dramaturgy at work in plays by Erik Ehn and Young Jean Lee, for instance). Plays written in the "new dramaturgy" emerge as more diverse and continue to find greater traction in mainstream theatres. The same is true of plays created by devising and plays intended for audience inter-action. These all present challenges to the conventional role of a dramaturg and the function of research.

In recalling Jill Dolan's "utopian performatives" – plays that consist of "socially committed moral values of active and engaged democracy and the protection and implementation of universal human rights"[14] – Michelle Prendergast notes, "Our socially committed work in process drama/applied theater operates as publics *or* counterpublics, performances *or* counterperformances in reassertion with *or* opposi-tion to dominant cultural publics and performances."[15] Although Prendergast writes specifically of a new philosophy in theatre education, which "may counter prevailing sociopolitical problems of passive spectatorship and its attendant apathy,"[16] her references to "counterpublics" and "counterperformances" recall Hopkins's develop-ment of a "counter-text." The aim is not to proffer historically accurate documents for occasional consultation. The aim is to incite curiosity, aesthetic inspiration, social change. Eugenio Barba refers to artistic discipline and technique as "the practice of a voluntary and lucid disorientation in the search for new points of orientation."[17] Little wonder Castagno refers to Overmyer's "Terra Incognita" as a destination for the creative team.[18]

I stop short of issuing a clarion call for all dramaturgs to travel for each production they research. That could be difficult for Overmyer's *On the Verge*, not to mention *Henry V* or *Tartuffe*. I also stop short of calling for such travel even when the dramaturg suspects real geography and the play's setting may be at odds enough to offer meaningful opportunities for developing the production's themes. The resources of time and funding are obvious obstacles to such journeys. Still, how many of us have considered the limits of our research and the limits of the possibilities we then offer to our colleagues and audiences? Have we considered a trip to Terra Incognita?

In recognizing first our methodologies of research and then the limits of those methodologies, we ought also to recognize ways of expanding our fields of vision, perhaps literally. "The articulation of the world we live in is what we may call the realism of artistic research."[19] In this sense, a dramaturg's research constitutes the clearest mimetic act of a production, however historical or unnaturalistic, against which audiences formulate views of the play they are producing or watching. The production ultimately situates itself within the dramaturg's body of work, and that relationship is indeed most productive when it is most complete – however far a dramaturg needs to go. A dramaturg may even fall in love with long distances and skip the light fantastic out of town.

Notes

1 Thomas Postlewait, "Eyewitness to History: Visual Evidence for Theater in Early Modern England," *The Oxford Handbook of Early Modern Theatre*, ed. Richard Sutton (Oxford and New York: Oxford University Press, 2009), 580.
2 Postlewait, 580.
3 Travis Preston and Royston Coppenger, "The Way We Work," *Dramaturgy in American Theater: A Source Book*, eds. Susan Jonas, Geoffrey S. Proehl, and Michael Lupu (Fort Worth, TX: Harcourt Brace College, 1997), 170.
4 Henk Borgdorff, "The Production of Knowledge in Artistic Research," *The Routledge Companion to Research in the Arts*, eds. Michael Biggs and Henrik Karlsson (London and New York: Routledge, 2011), 47.
5 Lenora Inez Brown, "Active Dramaturgy: Using Research to Inspire Creative Thought," *Playing with Theory in Theatre Practice*, eds. Megan Altrutz, Julia Listengarten, M. Van Duyn Wood (Houndmills, Basingstoke: Palgrave Macmillan, 2011), 118.
6 Judith Rudakoff, "The Four Elements: New Models for a Subversive Dramaturgy," *Theatre Topics* 13.1 (2013): 144, doi:10.1353/tt.2003.0018.
7 D. J. Hopkins, "Research, Counter-text, Performance: Reconsidering the (Textual) Authority of the Dramaturg," *Theatre Topics* 13.1 (2003): 2, doi:10.1353/tt.2003.0008.
8 Hopkins, 4.
9 Hopkins, 3.
10 Preston and Coppenger, 172.
11 Lyle Leverich, throughout *Tom: The Unknown Tennessee Williams*, traces the development and transformation of Williams's real and invented geographies for many of his works through 1945 (New York: Crown, 1995). *The Tennessee Williams Encyclopedia*, ed. Philip C. Kolin, also documents these (Westport, CT: Greenwood Press, 2004).
12 Borgdorff, 44.
13 Paul C. Castagno, "Informing the New Dramaturgy: Critical Theory to Creative Process," *Theatre Topics* 3.1 (1993): 37, doi:10.1353/tt.2010.0065.
14 Monica Prendergast, "Utopian Performatives and the Social Imaginary: Toward a New Philosophy of Drama/Theater Education," *Journal of Aesthetic Education* 45.1 (2011): 59, doi:10.1353/jae.2011.0008.
15 Prendergast, 69. Original emphasis.
16 Prendergast, 63.
17 Eugenio Barba, "The Deep Order Called Turbulence: The Three Faces of Dramaturgy," trans. Judy Barba, *TDR* 44.4 (2000): 56. Available online at www.jstor.org/stable/1146862.
18 Castagno, 34.
19 Borgdorff, 61.

52

Dramaturg as context manager

A phenomenological and political practice

Graça P. Corrêa

Dramaturgy implies a keen perception, an extensively sought orientation, and a steadfast purpose in the process of interpreting and creating an artwork. Dramaturgs love *texts*, and texts are everywhere: not relegated to written or verbal words, they exist as you walk, as you gaze, as you breathe. Within the premise that texts are compositions of signs in every form – as Jacques Derrida proclaims, "all is text and all is writing [*écriture*]"[1] – dramaturgy may be seen as what animates the text; it is the *spirit* of the text. Dramaturgy is also a political practice. Dramaturg-director Bertolt Brecht was concerned with producing a political theatre that would galvanize historical consciousness and ignite social change; he therefore broke away from mimetic representation and provoked spectating awareness through distancing/estranging effects and other "epic" techniques.[2] Brecht's political aesthetics, however, is inseparable from a specific historical context, namely the need to discontinue the dramatic illusion produced by well-made naturalistic drama that tended to elicit passive empathy from the audience. Following Augusto Boal, who claims that "all theatre is necessarily political,"[3] I consider that playtexts may produce oppositional political effects in many forms and through different techniques, without being committed to conveying a prescriptive political message. In effect, a contemporary political dramaturgy should address the micropolitics of power or the ways normative values and institutionalized modes of production permeate personal relationships and individual desires.

In a dramaturgical encounter we aesthetically engage with a text by experiencing its material qualities and letting it interact with our own lived body and imagination. That is why, dramaturgically speaking, the same play can be viewed differently by separate individuals and at distinct times, since it is a compositional score of ideas, sensations, and emotions that is open to new configurations through an interaction with the individual imaginative activity of dramaturgs, directors, designers, and actors. By implying a subjective engagement with an object-text, dramaturgy is also a phenomenological practice. Inspired by the writings of French philosophers Maurice Merleau-Ponty and Gaston Bachelard, phenomenology foregrounds the non-linguistic material aspects of both drama and performance, calling attention to space, bodily configuration, kinesthetic patterns, handling and presence of objects, light and darkness, sound and silence, temporalities, and other interconnected sensory effects. A phenomenological-dramaturgical approach is useful in bringing sensory material into rehearsals, so as to "carry over" to the stage the cultural, conceptual, and imaginary worlds of the play through a dynamic language that is specifically theatrical.[4]

Dramaturgical practice varies with the dramaturg's own epochal context, since it should endow the spectators of a particular production with knowledge and ability to speculate about the interrelationship between the performance-text and the world in which they live. In *Performing Drama*, Vanden Heuvel asks for the return of an ethical and political function of art, "an art directly related to the polis."[5] In my professional practice as a dramaturg, I have always been concerned with theatre as a forum for the exchange of ideas and as a public art that can actively engage in social transformation.

Dramaturgy inevitably has political dimensions because theatre, by the very fact of being publicly performed, is not an "autonomous" art dissociated from social reality. Theatre produces political effects whenever it produces a gesture towards an event/ situation. These may be effects of political compliance with normative morality and ideology or effects of wonder, perplexity, revolt, and opposition. As philosopher Theodor Adorno suggests, political art "is not intended to generate ameliorative measures" but instead "to work at the level of fundamental attitudes."[6] Following the tradition initiated in the 1760s in Germany by Lessing, the dramaturg performs "an approach to staging based on a thorough dramaturgical interrogation of text and context, both historically and in its relationship to the present."[7] The dramaturg is thus a decision-maker of what to highlight in a playtext so as to make it topical or relevant for contemporary times. Consequently, dramaturgical practice is not exempt from ideology (in the sense of production of meanings and ideas) or from embracing select theories/perspectives.

French theatre theorist and practitioner Bernard Dort wrote that dramaturgy is a state of mind (*un état d'esprit*) extensive to all participants in a theatre production and should not remain the job of a specialist.[8] Although dramaturgical awareness should indeed concern all theatre performers and mediators, I propose that dramaturgical practice can advantageously be assigned to a specialist. In this sense I follow the suggestion put forward by Joachim Tenschert (a long-standing dramaturg at the Berliner Ensemble) that the dramaturg is par excellence the theorist in a theatre collective and a key collaborator of the director, designers, actors, executive producers, stage managers, and marketing agents.[9] The fact that dramaturgy is a phenomenological and political endeavor may perhaps be elucidated by sharing a few of my professional experiences as a dramaturg and by discussing how they varied according to the *text* in question. In most theatre companies in Portugal, the need for dramaturgy as a resident practice assigned to one or more specialists is rarely acknowledged. Nonetheless, I was invited in 1990 by director Carlos Fernando to become resident dramaturg of GTH-Teatro da Graça, in Lisbon, immediately after I graduated in theatre at Escola Superior de Teatro e Cinema. During the five years of my dramaturgical work at GTH, the repertoire was organized into seasonal cycles, namely of North-American drama (Tennessee Williams, Edward Albee, Paul Selig), of Russian works (Ivan Turgenev, Anton Chekhov, Maxim Gorki, and Aleksandr Galin), and of Scandinavian plays (Henrik Ibsen and August Strindberg). This enabled us to explore cultural contexts in depth, to write up extensive didactic programs, and produce related activities (exhibitions, poetry readings, music recitals) that enriched the audience's reception of the text.

Although any playtext evokes a singular world and must be approached specifically, there are basic tools and methodological procedures of dramaturgical analysis that may be applied to most scripts. As dramaturg Karen Jean Martinson states, the first impressions from the first reading of a play should always be kept present, since "[t]his first moment is all about affect – how does the play impact me on an emotional, impressionistic level?"[10] I consider this initial intimate moment with the text to be deeply phenomenological, for it is an embodied perceptual experience of an object that speaks to my mind-body and connects to the way I live in my own existential and social habitat. During this first reading the dramaturg should note down how the play interacts with other texts that come to mind – be it drama, fiction, philosophy, poetry, dance, paintings, sculptures, or films – and retain them as potential evocative materials in the scripting of its performance.

When dealing with a foreign-language play, the choice of its translation or version becomes crucial. From my experience as resident dramaturg at GTH-Teatro da Graça, I recall two instances of flawed and censored versions that we managed to avoid. The first occurred when we were preparing a production of Maxim Gorki's *Vassa Geleznova* (1910); as the company's dramaturg, I started analyzing the play from an English translation, while director Elisa Lisboa was translating it from the French. Shortly before the beginning of rehearsals, and because we were working on a tight schedule, I helped type Elisa's translation and was amazed to discover that in our Portuguese translation there were no references to the 1905 Revolution in Russia, a violently repressed social upheaval that dramaturgically structures Gorki's play. Apparently the French translator had eliminated all such references and focused merely on the play's domestic plot, thereby turning it into a lighter "apolitical" drama. Two years later, when we were producing *The Pelican* (1907) by August Strindberg, we also came across several different versions of the play, including a Spanish one that replaced the final devastating fire, in which both house and family members burn, with a happy ending. In both cases we revised our translations and had them examined by Portuguese readers of Russian and Swedish. Matters of translation are thus at the heart of dramaturgical practice.

On other occasions, however, the dramaturg must adapt the play, by adding, editing, and subtracting scenes and roles, so as to make the performance's concept clearer and feasible, provided there is authorization from the playwright. When at GTH we produced Brian Friel's *Fathers and Sons* (1987), a brilliant adaptation of a very complex Russian novel by Turgenev, we saw the need to modify a scene in which the revolutionary proletarian Bazarov confessed his infatuation for Anna, a conservative landowner. In Turgenev's book the episode makes us realize Bazarov's micropolitical dilemma of feeling attracted to someone ideologically opposed to him; in contrast, Friel's love scene appeared flimsy and, unlike the rest of his adaptation, dramaturgically astray from the novel.

In a production of Arthur Schnitzler's *La Ronde* (1897) presented in 1996 at the Emerson Stage Festival in Boston, I introduced a young contemporary heterosexual couple between scenes. Although their outward appearance and physical behavior was utterly androgynous, in typical mid-1990s fashion, their dialogue (written by Colleen Shea) revealed the same fears, power games, and deceit as the couples of Schnitzler's splendorous but decadent turn-of-the-century Vienna. This dramaturgical strategy encouraged the audience to question present-day notions of love, sex, and gender, instead of viewing the play as a tale of bygone sexual mores. In a similar vein, when I produced Christopher Hampton's *Savages* (1973) at CCB in 2003, as dramaturg-director I found that one actor alone could represent the collective of twenty or more Amazonian Indians of the play. Since characters Alan West and Carlos Esquerdo illustrate and even typify two opposing political, ethical, and ecological viewpoints on the Amazonian question, namely a "developed country" attitude and a "developing country" stance, the choice of having a sole actor represent the Amazonian tribe actually accentuated the dramaturgical "triangular configuration" of *Savages*.[11]

In order to edit a play, however, the dramaturg has to study its text in depth so as to arrive – together with the director, designers, and actors – at a concept or production of meaning/s for its performance. Michel Bataillon proposes that any dramaturgical investigation of a playtext consists of an external analysis and an internal analysis.[12] By external analysis he means research into the author's biography and oeuvre, the work's historical and social context, critical studies on the play, and its production history, if any. I would add to this a research of intertexts, or of other texts, fragments and citations that relate to the work. An internal analysis of the play consists of a thorough analysis of its dramatic structure, including a survey of its images, symbols, similes, metaphors, recurrent verbs, characters, geography, and spatial, temporal and kinesthetic patterns.

Such investigation makes up the dramaturgical notebook, which additionally to the annotated script (divided into scenes, sub-scenes, and beats) and other intertexts often contains analytical lists, tables, charts, and graphs of lines of speech per character, of onstage presence per scene, of spatial and temporal settings, and so on. In some cases, especially upon approaching an historical drama (such as Peter Shaffer's *The Royal Hunt of the Sun*, 1964) or a documentary drama (Moisés Kaufman's *Gross Indecency*, 1997), I had to do extensive research on actual historic figures, namely the Inca rulers and Spanish invaders of Peru during the early sixteenth century and the many celebrities who took part in Oscar Wilde's trials.

Dramaturgical practice involves an analytical and critical engagement throughout the various stages of a play's production. Within such a permanently evolving relation between playtext and performance-text, the dramaturg must regularly attend rehearsals, to ensure that the concept is manifest to the audience. For the adaptation of Marguerite Duras's screenplay *Hiroshima mon amour* (1959) at the National Theatre stage, in 1998, the production became framed with other texts, namely paintings and poems inspired by "The Hiroshima Murals" of Iri Maruki and Toshiko Akamatsu, a Japanese couple who traveled to the devastated city just three days after the atomic bomb was dropped. The horrors they witnessed and expressed provided a much-needed contextual landscape to our play, which, like the film, consisted of brief interactions between the two lovers. Such texts not only offered awareness of the carnage and destruction that ensued after the bombings, but also echoed the ongoing wars of the late 1990s, where a similarly unethical use of advanced technological weaponry was taking place.

Without dramaturgical awareness, playtexts risk being used not for their own material qualities and the world that emanates from them, but as pretexts for extraneous motives, connotations, and effects. Yet, as Brecht well perceived, the same story can be told in varied ways, and for that very reason he insisted on the dramaturgical significance of the notion of *fable*, which does not equate simply to the play's plot, but rather expresses a perspective and assessment, indicating not just *what* happens but also *why* and *how* it happens. In our day, as normative ideology subtly permeates the most intimate levels of our individual existences through mainstream media controlled by a few conglomerates, a dramaturgically informed political theatre is crucial to preventing the decline in diversity of perspectives, as well as the censorship of vital issues.

Notes

1 Jacques Derrida, *Of Grammatology*, trans. Gayatri Spivak (Baltimore, MD: John Hopkins University Press, 1976), 158.
2 John Willett, *Brecht on Theatre: The Development of an Aesthetic* (New York: Hill & Wang, 1994).
3 Augusto Boal, *The Theatre of the Oppressed* (London: Pluto Press, 2000), xxiii.
4 Graça P. Corrêa, "Translation and Dramaturgy as Phenomenological Practices: Harold Pinter's *The Hothouse* in Lisbon, Portugal," IFTR 52nd annual conference, Lisboa, July 2009.
5 Michael Vanden Heuvel, *Performing Drama/Dramatizing Performance: Alternative Theater and the Dramatic Text* (Ann Harbor: University of Michigan Press, 1993), 62–3.
6 Theodor Adorno, "Commitment," in *The Essential Frankfurt Reader*, eds. Andrew Arato and Eike Gebhardt (New York: The Continuum Publishing Company, 1982), 304.
7 See Chapter 47; also, Gitta Honegger, "Lost in Translation," *Theater* 40.3 (2010): 117.
8 Bernard Dort, "L'État d'Esprit Dramaturgique," *Théâtre/Public* 67 (1986): 8.
9 Joachim Tenschert, "Qu'est-ce qu'un dramaturge?," *Théâtre populaire* 38 (1960): 43.
10 Lisa Arnold and Karen Jean Martinson, "Dramaturgs Like to Talk: A Production Dramaturg and an Installation Dramaturg Discuss Their Approaches to Making Art," *Review: The Journal of Dramaturgy* 19.2 (2009): 14.
11 Graça P. Corrêa, "Ecocritical Translation in Christopher Hampton's *Savages*," *Journal of Adaptation in Film & Performance* 4.3 (2011): 284.
12 Michel Bataillon, "Les finances de la dramaturgie," *Travail Théâtral* VII (1972): 53.

53

New play explorations in the twenty-first century[1]

Mark Bly

In the spring of 2002 a graduate student in the Yale School of Drama's Playwriting Program wrote a play that featured a Soho-hip party where the festive, poetic spirit of Immanuel Kant, Frank O'Hara, e.e. cummings, and Gertrude Stein collided impishly. I scheduled the new play for a reading in my Drama 47 class, a six-semester advanced course for the graduate Playwriting students. Before launching into what happened to the play, perhaps a word about my approach to working on new plays in Drama 47 would be beneficial.

First, prior to my arrival in 1992 the course was populated primarily by playwrights. This reinforced their sense of isolation in the school and the impression that a knowledge of their process was not deemed to be an integral part of the other students' training. For example, the dramaturgy students lacked any formal practical training beyond reading plays in dramatic literature courses. This lack of any ongoing training in a class such as Drama 47 meant that the Dramaturgy students were assigned to dramaturg a single New Play Workshop each year without training and without any on-line mentoring about the process of working on a new play. This attitude toward the new play process is regrettably all too pervasive in the United States' theatre today. I was eager to help change this practice from my narrow perch at Yale. Now, for over a decade, the yearlong class is composed of nearly 50 students who are derived from the Acting, Directing, Dramaturgy, Playwriting, and occasionally the Design Programs. The rhythm of the class schedule is simple: in the first class each semester, two new scripts are rehearsed with two different companies selected by the playwright, director, and me; in the second and third classes we then do a concert reading of each play followed by an animated conversation with all 50 students led by me. This cycle is repeated throughout the course of the year, generating over 20 readings and discussions.

Second, instead of viewing the plays as an invalid that we diagnose and then volunteer prescriptive commentary about, we offer descriptive commentary focusing on the play's inherent strengths and the laws that govern the world of the play.

At the beginning of the school year, during the first class, I frequently share an observation by Elinor Fuchs from her essay, "EF's Visit to a Small Planet: Some Questions to Ask a Play." In the essay, Fuchs offers a strategy for approaching a new play that concentrates on asking questions about the world of the play rather than merely offering a one-dimensional perspective or interpretation:

> A play is not a flat work of literature, not a description in poetry of another world but it is in itself another world passing before you in Time and Space ... The stage world never obeys the same rules as ours, because in its world, nothing else is possible besides what is there: no one else lives there, no other geography is available, no alternatives can be taken.[2]

Fuchs's approach is an invaluable one, for it amplifies rather than reduces our perspectives on a new play or on a classic for that matter. As a dramaturg, I had used a similar method in my stage work for years but encountering Fuchs's words in the early 1990s helped to focus my approach to teaching. If we approach a play as if it were a new world, we should encounter it free of assumptions. We cannot expect it to behave the way we are used to, nor should we dramaturgically "terraform" it. If we try to make it conform to how we believe a play should "work," we may lose the possibility of a new creation or new form evolving out of it.

So, in Drama 47 rehearsals and in the post-reading discussions, we focus on a wide spectrum of questions that we ask the playwright and other students. After the reading, the playwright and I ask a series of questions of the other class members, which we have carefully formulated in a tutorial. These questions focus the discussion and are designed to help the playwright get feedback on those dramaturgical issues that will enable the writer to move forward to the next draft. Invariably, I direct the discussion in such a way that other key questions are also focused upon. First, I ask the playwright at the center of this event, what was the spark that led to the play's genesis? What was the play's starting point? Second, we ask questions of the playwright helping to locate the her or his intentions in all areas of dramaturgical/theatrical discourse. Third, we try to help the playwright by measuring our impressions of the new play against her or his original intentions. Fourth, what are the rules or laws that govern the play's world? What is unique about it? Fifth, what are the play's strengths? How can the playwright continue to develop the play so that the strengths are enhanced and not hacked away or diluted in future drafts? Finally, sixth, did you find what María Irene Fornés calls "a charge of some understanding" in the play? Either as an actor or listener?

But in the spring of 2002 when we rehearsed the Drama 47 play, something else happened when what I came to call a "Flatlanders" perspective emerged rather than the approach described above. On the rehearsal day, the actors, director, dramaturg, and perhaps even I (in the midst of 19-hour days for previews for a Yale Repertory Theatre production) did not immediately demonstrate the openness, patience, and curiosity for the new world that the play required. As we rehearsed the play, many of those present grew impatient with the play's alleged inaccessibility. A scene would be read and the actors would fight the scene's rhythms, insisting on motivational pauses where there were none. They tried to make sense of their characters from a one-dimensional perspective, leveling off any enigmatic psychic or rhythmic terrain by "terraforming" it according to their specifications or what they needed to make their characters live. The playwright emerged from the rehearsal frustrated and bewildered. I was unhappy about the rehearsal too, but I felt that was of little comfort to the playwright in the moment.

Then, several days before the actual reading was to take place in the class, I encountered serendipitously a poem that awakened me to how close-minded and unfaithful to the class's first principles we had been in the previous week's rehearsal. So, on the day of the reading, I opened the class by reading a 16-line poem by the contemporary United States poet laureate, Billy Collins. It was a poem that I felt merited hearing before we moved into the reading and discussion at hand:

"Introduction to Poetry"
I ask them to take a poem
and hold it up to the light
like a color slide
or press an ear against its hive.
I say drop a mouse into a poem
and watch him probe his way out,
or walk inside the poem's room
and feel the wall for a light switch.
I want them to water-ski
across the surface of a poem
waving at the author's name on the shore.
But all they want to do
is tie the poem to a chair with rope
and torture a confession out of it.
They begin beating it with a hose
to find out what it really means.[3]

Billy Collins

After reading the poem in Drama 47, I gently reminded everyone, including myself, that as artists:

We need to resist prematurely turning a harsh light on a work of art or an artist.
We need to believe that under the right light or conditions a poem or play will reveal its many hues and not merely a single one.
We need to understand that listening to the invisible buzzing in a hive may teach us far more than poking a hole in the hive with a stick.
We must learn to accept that sometimes we may not find the "light switch" immediately; but that will be alright, for if we stay in the room long enough our eyes may adjust to the darkness and objects that were invisible before will be revealed gradually to us with all of their blemishes and all of their glories.

Everyone in the class heard the poem and listened to my cautionary words. The play was read, and our observations after the reading were modulated, respectful but filled with curiosity for the new world before us.

Still, too often playwrights in this country are thought of as dramaturgically challenged "savants" who have not a clue about the source of their work or what they have created. The playwright is all too frequently viewed as a theatrical "Rain Man" or "Rain Woman" whose understanding is limited, a "matchstick" reality (for those who have seen the film), knowing nothing about human behavior or the world.

It is also commonplace for theatre artists to see a play as essentially a "blueprint for action." In part that is true certainly, but in the plays that matter there is ultimately something much richer, more textured present. It is a world of signs and symbols – deep myth that is in touch with not only the visible world but a hidden, invisible realm as well. The "blueprint for action" approach depends upon a shared knowledge of known signs and symbols: a "blueprint" that knows or can anticipate the end of an artistic journey or series of playwriting gestures. But the playwrights who continue to haunt us write plays that struggle with questions; they have not merely created a legible behavioral answer or furnished us with a "dramaturgical kit" for understanding reality. These artists intuit the invisible forces, the seemingly chaotic patterns of energy alive in our universe, ones that must be rediscovered or retranslated for each emerging, thriving, or dying culture. We all nod knowingly when we talk about myth and symbols, citing the explorations of Joseph Campbell, George Lucas, and J. R. R. Tolkien as our guides. But sometimes they are not enough. When students or playwrights at a formative stage opine that they wish they knew where their plays were going and that they cannot possibly continue, let alone finish their explorations, I find myself challenging them and comforting them with a passage from Annie Dillard's closing words of her prose work *For the Time Being*:

> In Highland New Guinea, now Papua New Guinea, a British district officer named James Taylor contacted a mountain village, above three thousand feet, whose tribe had never seen any trace of the outside world. It was the 1930s. He described the courage of one villager. One day, on the airstrip hacked from the mountain near his village, this man cut vines and lashed himself to the fuselage of Taylor's airplane shortly before it took off. He explained calmly to his loved ones that, no matter what happened to him, he had to see where it came from.[4]

In keeping with Fuchs's strategy, we all need to re-imagine ourselves as explorers and to encounter these theatrical worlds fearlessly with a love of the invisible, the unknown, and hopefully with the same courage and curiosity demonstrated by the intrepid Highland New Guinea villager. Perhaps we all, mentor, student, artist, and audience member alike would do well to recall and embrace what T. S. Eliot once asserted:

> Except in directions in which we can go too far there is no interest in going at all; and only those who will risk going too far can possibly find out just how far to go.[5]

Notes

1 This article is reprinted from *Theatre Topics*, 13.1 (March 2003): 19–23.
2 Elinor Fuchs, "E.F.'s Visit to a Small Planet: Some Questions to Ask a Play," *Theatre* 34.2 (2004): 5–9.
3 Billy Collins, "Introduction to Poetry," *Sailing Alone around the Room* (New York: Random House, 2001), 16.
4 Annie Dillard, *For the Time Being* (New York: Alfred A. Knopf, 1999), 204.
5 T. S. Eliot, "Preface" to *Transit of Venus* by Harry Crosby (Paris: Black Sun Press, 1931), 62.

54

Thinking like an actor
A guide for the production dramaturg

Andrew Ian Carlson

To meaningfully communicate with actors, production dramaturgs have to become fluent in multiple performance pedagogies. In the contemporary theatrical marketplace, actors are trained in a variety of styles, including Viewpoints, commedia, period movement, Suzuki, and Stanislavski. In each production context, dramaturgs respond to the needs of their collaborators; the Suzuki-influenced *King Lear*, for instance, may require a dramaturg more proficient in physical vocabulary than in rhetorical devices. While knowledge of various acting training methods develops a versatile dramaturg, this essay focuses on the unique miscommunications between the intellectually minded production dramaturg and the impulse-driven Stanislavski actor. By speaking to Stanislavski actors in their own language, dramaturgs are empowered to translate potentially anecdotal historical research into visceral given circumstances that motivate playable action.

Stanislavski-trained actors are taught to question the usefulness of intellectual approaches to theatre. Actress Uta Hagen, for instance, writes in her famous text on acting technique, *Respect for Acting*, that "to act is to do, not to think."[1] Director and educator Bill Ball advises young directors in *A Sense of Direction* that "talking, theorizing, and intellectualizing must be reduced to an absolute minimum" in the rehearsal room because "[i]t misleads the actors into thinking that they can make points by using their intellects. Never allow an actor to engage you in intellectuality ... most discussion is fruitless."[2] In the often-used acting training textbook *Practical Handbook for the Actor*, the authors advise their students, "if you take the time to intellectualize what is happening in any way, the impulse will be lost and your attention will be thrown back onto yourself."[3] In *On Acting*, Sanford Meisner criticizes a student for being a "thinker" and advises his class to avoid "working from your head."[4] The now received notion underpinning these comments is that the actor should not over-think or intellectualize character, but play actions in pursuit of goals. The idea is commonly taught in university classrooms, repeated in professional rehearsal halls, and codified in theatre textbooks. Common aphorisms of the theatre normalize the dichotomy between the mind and the art. Actors criticize their own work by saying that they were "in their heads." Acting is not planned, but is "reacting," effective when spontaneously felt "in the moment." Indeed, it is by *not* thinking that actors "live truthfully in imaginary circumstances."[5]

Most dramaturgs are aware of the potentially contentious relationship between the mind and the art and, more specifically, between the scholar and the actor. The liminal position of the production dramaturg as intellectual and artist has been well explored since dramaturgy became part of the American theatre lexicon. Andrew Hartley writes in *The Shakespearean Dramaturg*, for example, that "literary academia and practical theatre are particularly different and, at least sometimes, proud of and adamant in their difference," stating that "it is a critical commonplace to say that theatre practitioners are generally wary of theory."[6] Though few dramaturgs still understand themselves to be textual guardians, the scholar/artist divide continues to create communication barriers in the rehearsal hall. Because the dramaturg is often (perhaps mistakenly) shorthanded as the intellectual presence in the room, trained in theatre history and theory, practitioners can be disposed to think that dramaturgical contributions are not the real raw material of the acting process. For actors, there is a perceived danger in basing performance on ideas or literary character analysis because it has the potential to throw them into their heads. Because of this, a dramaturg who is trained to guard the text from artists, or who details historical context without understanding its practical application, is generally not going to be effective in an environment that focuses on what "works."

To begin to bridge these communication gaps, dramaturgs can learn the core concepts of the Stanislavski system. Though terms vary among teachers, Stanislavski-based acting training consistently focuses on objectives, actions, points of view, and given circumstances. Actors pursue their objectives, or needs, with "playable" verbs that answer this fundamental acting question: What do I want from the person I am speaking with, and how am I going to get it? Playable verbs answer the "how" of the question by engaging actors in ongoing actions, such as attacking, intimidating, seducing, and mocking. Stanislavski actors are thus trained to see their characters as using actions to affect a change in their partners. This notion stands in contrast to the idea that characters should be seen as *being* something such as evil, good, angry, or happy. Actors develop a specific "point of view" of the people they speak with through an understanding of the "given circumstances." Given circumstances come from textual and historical understandings of the character's situation, by answering the questions, Who am I? What am I doing? When and where is the scene happening? and Why do I do what I do? The "point of view" is articulated by determining what characters think of others. For example, actors may see another character as "my salvation" or "my worst enemy" in a given play, scene, or moment. Point of view, actions, and objectives are not intellectual formations, but viscerally inspiring language that motivates the actor.

In the rehearsal process, actors clarify their choices by making them personally meaningful and specific. Stanislavski states, "to make something particular, as opposed to generalizing or to keep general, is an essential for everything in acting from identification of the character right down to the tiniest physical object you come in contact with."[7] He comments that phrases like "in general" or "approximately" are words that "do not belong in art."[8] Common rehearsal notes from directors focus on encouraging actors to be more specific about what they want the other character to do. Bill Ball says, "the only real reason a director is needed in rehearsal is to perform the following function: persistently to draw the actor to a more meaningful and appropriate choice of objectives, and then to persuade the actor to lend his full commitment to those objectives."[9] Though most directors do not state their function so bluntly, the practice of clarifying characters' needs guides many rehearsal processes. Despite the fact that actors are trained to pursue objectives, many will rely on playing an idea, quality, or mood of the character. When this occurs, Stanislavski-trained directors will challenge actors to refocus on their character's needs. Ball writes that "actors tend to run like pigs in a barnyard to avoid pinning down the objectives. Frequently they will throw up a barrage of adjectives."[10] From this perspective "adjectives" belong to the world of intellect; they are unplayable ideas that inhibit active pursuit of human needs.

Indeed, according to Stanislavski, characters do not exist as ontological formations that represent ideas or adjectives, but as human beings fighting for something specific. In *An Actor Prepares*, Stanislavski gives an example of this reframing: "in Goldoni's *La Locandiera* we made the mistake of using 'I wish to be a misogynist,' and we found that the play refused to yield either humour or action ... I changed to 'I wish to do my courting on the sly' and immediately the play came to life."[11] Stanislavski illustrates this principle elsewhere in his text:

> if you tell an actor that his role is full of psychological action, tragic depths, he will immediately begin to control himself, exaggerate his passion, 'tear it to tatters' dig around in his soul, and do violence to his feelings. But if you give him some simple physical problem to solve and wrap it up in interesting, affecting conditions, he will set about carrying it out without alarming himself or even thinking too deeply whether what he is doing will result in psychology, tragedy or drama.[12]

In this system, actors avoid playing the generalized quality of an idea by solving practical problems in pursuit of a goal.

These principles of actor process are not easily activated with intellectual analysis. Beginning dramaturgs will rightly consult historical articles, literary analysis, and character descriptions to contextualize the work, but if the analysis is not translated into active language, it will not influence process. For instance, many have argued that the character Edmund from *King Lear* is a classic Shakespearean villain who represents evil. Shakespearean scholar Harley Granville-Barker describes him as a wicked, "ignoble scoundrel."[13] Yet "ignoble," wicked, and scoundrel, are not "playable actions" because they are qualities that comment on character from an outsider perspective. They turn the actor into a storyteller who is responsible for sharing the character with the audience; Stanislavski-based training encourages actors to make the character's case from the inside. The job of the actor is not to figure out what Edmund *is* or what he represents in the universe of humanity, but what he *wants*. For the actor playing him, Edmund is not an angry villain, but a human being who wants to change his circumstances. As Robert Benedetti writes, emotion should not motivate the actor: "you don't create an emotion and then do things because of that emotion; rather, you do things in order to fulfill a need, and emotion naturally results from that doing."[14] In Edmund's soliloquies, he has many options in his "doing." He may want to mock, inspire, ridicule, reason with, or entertain in an effort to make the audience agree with, despise, or celebrate him. Because actions are connected to specifically defined relationships decided within a production context, there is no "correct" action to play. What is essential for Stanislavski-trained actors is that the language is spoken to advance a human need, not to present an emotional quality.

This approach has implications for the way dramaturgs take rehearsal notes for actors and directors. Dramaturgical notes that focus on analysis from an outside perspective, such as "Edmund seemed too angry" or "Edmund needs to be more villainous," are not going to intersect with actor process. However, if notes or questions can be framed in the language of objectives, specificity, point of view, and given circumstances, the dramaturg participates as a fluent practitioner. For instance, dramaturgs sensitive to instances when actors are being driven more by emotions than objectives provide vital information for directors. If a moment is not working in a production, the language of Stanislavski gives dramaturgs some basic questions to uncover what is unclear: What is it that you want from the person you are speaking with? Why do you need it *right now*? What is your point of view of her? What is the ideal response she would give you? Do you get it? By asking these questions, dramaturgs can help directors track the clarity of the production.

In addition, the actor-sensitive dramaturg can make distinctions between intellectual and active given circumstances. To be a resource for actors, dramaturgs can frame history as context that places pressure on characters to act. A dramaturg working on *King Lear* may research the role of the bastard in the Jacobean class structure and family, detail the rules of inheritance, or explain how Edmund embodies a new Renaissance worldview. Yet for this information to matter to artistic collaborators, it requires another level of translation. If history and textual analysis are framed as active given circumstances, as visceral forces that determine the stakes of a moment, they clarify what characters need in the specific world of the play. From this perspective, Edmund has a very strong case for doing what he does. Edmund's father, Gloucester, has just joked about having sex with Edmund's mother in front of a high-ranking person he has just met. Shakespeare's language is actually more sexually frank: there was "much sport" at "Edmund's making." The importance of class position in Jacobean England raises the psychological stakes of the slight. Once again, Edmund is publically negated. Unlike his brother, Edmund has been sent away for nine years and he is told he "will away again." The conditions of the new world of Renaissance individualism are only important because they give Edmund the reasoned language to transcend his deprivation. He does not have to accept the old world of his father Gloucester, who represents "the excellent foppery" of an increasingly irrelevant and superstitious generation. The Stanislavski-trained Edmund is motivated to act: he deceives his father and brother not because he is the classic Jacobean villain, but because he has been deprived of his land and deserves better. He has to do it now – there is urgency to the need – because he will be sent away again soon. The given circumstances thus make Edmund *do* something, not *exist* as something.

Ultimately, successful production dramaturgy is not defined by text packets, contextual knowledge, or rehearsal presentations, but by the moments of collaborative communication. It exists in the minds of the actors, designers, directors, playwrights, and audience members who make use of information to deepen the artistic journey.

To reach the Stanislavski-trained actor, this means that the dramaturg must know how to identify lack of psychological clarity and translate the given circumstances into specific, urgent, and playable needs. If dramaturgs can do this, they challenge the divide between the mind and the art by making the intellect a source of practical artistic contribution.

Notes

1 Uta Hagen, *Respect for Acting* (New York: Macmillan, 1973), 67.
2 William Ball, *A Sense of Direction* (New York: Drama Book Publishers, 1984), 55.
3 Melissa Bruder, Lee Michael Cohn, Madeleine Olnek, Nathaniel Pollack, Robert Previto, and Scott Zigler, *A Practical Handbook for the Actor* (New York: Vintage Books, 1986), 43.
4 Sanford Meisner and Dennis Longwell, *On Acting* (New York: Vintage Books, 1987), 41.
5 Meisner, 15.
6 Andrew Hartley, *The Shakespearean Dramaturg: A Theoretical and Practical Guide* (New York: Palgrave Macmillan, 2005), 1.
7 Constantin Stanislavski, *An Actor Prepares*, trans. Elizabeth Reynolds Hapgood (New York: Theatre Arts Books, 1936), 44.
8 Stanislavski, 54.
9 Ball, 81–2.
10 Ball, 83.
11 Stanislavski, 258.
12 Stanislavski, 141.
13 Harley Granville-Barker, *Prefaces to Shakespeare, Volume II* (1945; New Delhi: Atlantic Publishers & Distributors, 2006), 56.
14 Robert Benedetti, *The Actor in You: Sixteen Simple Steps to Understand the Art of Acting*, third edition (Boston: Pearson Education, 2006), 20.

55

The youth respondent method

New work development of Theatre for Young Audiences

Kristin Leahey

In her article *The Once and Future Audience: Dramaturgy and Children's Theatre*, Suzan Zeder writes, "Dramaturgs in increasing numbers find themselves coming out of the library and rehearsal hall and into the classroom."[1] More and more dramaturgs, in addition to writers, directors, and educators, many of whom have a particular interest in Theatre for Young Audiences (TYA), have immersed themselves in classrooms working directly with students in the development of plays and musicals through a process I describe as the youth respondent method: artists and/or producers involve children and/or young adults through planned theatre activities or discussions, with the objective of answering specific questions about the development of the work and collect feedback to improve the text or further the production. This pluralistic practice grants agency to the target audience, while informing the creators of the possibilities of the play and answering challenging questions regarding the developing piece. The spring 2008 Adventure Stage Chicago (ASC), in association with the Chicago Humanities Festival, produced the world premiere of noted playwright José Cruz González's play *The Blue House* for young audiences. Cruz González extensively employed the youth respondent method in this play's early development.

The ASC falls under the auspices of the Northwestern Settlement House and performs on the Vittum stage, a 299-seat proscenium house. The company creates stories about its Chicago community to serve Chicago audiences with work such as *The Blue House*. The play's protagonist, Maricela, is a 13-year-old girl living in the present-day Chicago neighborhood of Pilsen, located on the lower west side of the city. Ghosts lead Maricela to an abandoned lot where they died a century before in a fire at the Blue House. The play explores the history of Pilsen as a port for immigrants: people of Slavic decent arriving in the US during the late nineteenth century and undocumented Mexican families in the twenty-first century. Before working with youth, who helped generate ideas for the play, Cruz González selected the Pilsen community to focus on, created a female protagonist who traced her history in relation to that of her neighborhood, and desired to address the clash of the ever-changing populations of the past and present in Chicago. Cruz González collaborated with middle-school students to create the structure for the narrative and much of the detail for his new work. ASC Director and Artistic Director Tom Arvetis and the writer partnered with Betsy Quinn, a drama education specialist and teacher at Evanston's Haven Middle School, to work on generating ideas and feedback for *The Blue House* with her middle-school students.[2]

While attending the 2006 Bonderman National Youth Theatre Playwriting Development Workshop and Symposium, Quinn and Cruz González participated in a number of new play development workshops where artistic teams solicited feedback from children. Inspired by the immersion, they decided to employ a variation of the method with Quinn's students for Cruz González's commission. The participating students represented the target audience age of 10 years old and older. Cruz González and Quinn, with the assistance of 18 Northwestern creative drama undergraduate students, created a list of questions about the play. Instead of directly asking the 140 youth participants these questions, they explored possible answers with the students through drama exercises and play. This was Cruz González's first experience of obtaining feedback from youth via creative drama, a process-centered form of drama in which participants are guided by a leader to imagine, enact, and reflect upon the human experience.

During the three Saturday mornings dedicated to the program, the participants devised possibilities to tell the story of the fictional Blue House and its characters. For the first week – working in four classrooms – they imagined they played together in an empty lot, which eventually became the piece's setting and where the Blue House formerly resided. From discussions and the participants portraying characters during in-role exercises, the idea emerged that a developer (who recently bought the lot) planned to build condos in the area, thus furthering the gentrification of Pilsen. The youth made the decision that this sale would erase the history of the location, which helped the writer find the play's conflict.

During the second week, Quinn and Cruz González removed themselves from the drama in order to observe and take more notes. In the participants' creative play, objects came to life to warn the children of the ghosts in the space. For instance, the students imagined a music box that suddenly began to play to warn the characters of danger. This music box, including the various ideas about setting, character, and plot, emerged from the process drama, and eventually found their way into *The Blue House*. In an interview Cruz González said, "This world is interactive and moving and it's so amazing to watch it. You learn so much by what it is doing."[3] For the third Saturday, Cruz González again involved himself in the drama and asked the participants questions, which they responded to in-role. Also, the facilitators playing the character Ms. Betnorakate allowed children to ask them questions, which Cruz González recorded. For instance, he asked the question, "How do the little girl and the ghost communicate with each other?" Quinn asked a student to portray "Maricela" and one of the college students to portray the ghost who communicated with the girl. Within a few exchanges of impromptu dialogue, the "Maricela" said, "The ghost is writing in my diary." They both began to pretend to write in the diary together. This pivotal moment helped Cruz González to define the rules of ghosts in the play. In an interview, the writer said of the children's assistance, "Those were probably some of the most powerful, articulate, insightful and deep discussions I've ever had with anyone."[4] The group informed the play by cohesively working together through drama exercises. In an interview, Quinn described the pride and the empowerment the children felt seeing their ideas realized onstage a year later when they all attended the production.[5] Both the writer and teacher believed in the effectiveness of the collaboration, and would repeat it for the development of other new plays. Cruz González embraced a process where he created with the audience at the work's inception.

The architecture of playmaking is changing in that theatres, artists, educators, and youth work together on a more equal plane where many voices are considered. The lack of time, tightened budgets, and a focus on traditional curriculums makes these immersions challenging for schools and theatres. However, they often illuminate the work and prove invaluable to the involved participants' education and cognitive and emotional growth. They inform the writer about the possibility of his play serving the target audience. Cruz González's engagement with Quinn's students to write *The Blue House* is an example of what I label as the youth respondent method.

The method is a process by which playwrights and dramaturgs involve participants through planned theatre activities or discussions with the aspiration of attaining invaluable information about the play during its development stages. Considering a continuum that places creative dramatics and children's theatre at its poles, the youth respondent method demonstrates a merger of the two genres. Master teacher, scholar, and writer of *Creative Drama in the Classroom and Beyond*, Nellie McCaslin defines creative dramatics as "informal drama that is created by participants."[6] She believes the term is interchangeable with playmaking. As examples of creative drama McCaslin offers story creation and the exploration and development of ideas and feelings through dramatic enactment.[7] These processes are also inherent to the youth respondent method. Children's theatre scholars Jed H. Davis and Mary Jane Evans' text, *Theatre, Children and Youth*, describes "children's theatre" as an all-encompassing form of theatre designed for audiences ranging in age from early childhood to adolescence. The term Theatre for Young Audiences (TYA) represents both theatre for children (ages 12 and below) and theatre for youth (ages 12 and older).[8] Because TYA focuses on the product and creative dramatics on the process, many scholars believed the fields oppositional. In *Theatre for Children*, forerunner in American children's theatre Winifred Ward describes the practices of Peter Slade, drama advisor to the Birmingham Educational Committee and leading drama teacher primarily working in the 1950s. He believed that creative drama and children's theatre competed with, rather than complimented, each other.[9] Davis and Evans, in agreement that the two fields should not dramatically overlap, writes, "Creative dramatics and children's theatre should be treated as separate – though mutually complimentary – phases of a total children's drama program."[10] Without undermining the goals of either of these disciplines, the youth respondent method relies upon the merger of creative drama techniques and those of TYA in the act of including the audience in the creation process, in turn maintaining the respective focuses on process and product. Sometimes the process lends itself to discovering specific moments of the play, while at other times answering global questions about it. In the scenario of *The Blue House*, the entire play grew and changed as a result of this practice. The method complicates a traditional power dynamic in which the audience strictly receives the theatrical event as spectators; instead they contribute to the creation process. For artists, this nontraditional method to create work focuses on collaboration instead of artists creating in isolation. As a result of this method, the audience becomes a stronger voice within the production. Youth serve as active producers, who no longer are the next generation of artists and future spectators but the "it" generation of artists and audiences. Throughout the play development process, playwrights create with the guidance of directors and dramaturgs. In creating for young audiences, another collaborator is joining the development discussion: the audience.

The dramaturg often serves as the interlocutor and is particularly necessary in a process in which the questions of the playwright are being translated with a diverse group of contributors and artists. Having the ability to communicate these questions through a process drama and recognize what responses are potentially useful to the development process are essential to the effectiveness of the method and an ability inherent to one's dramaturgical toolbox. The dramaturg can easily integrate into the drama or withdraw to become an observer without disrupting the process. Also, if the dramaturg is not participating as the creative drama facilitator, the dramaturg can be another eyewitness.

From this direct contact, artists learn about the youths' perspective on their work. In scholar and playwright David Woods' 1999 publication *Theatre for Children: A Guide to Writing, Adapting, Directing, and Acting*, he contends that TYA professionals appear too easily satisfied with informally acquiring feedback from teachers and occasionally soliciting answers from children leaving the theatre to determine audiences' responses to their work. He writes, "It seems, through many of these efforts, an assessment of a kind of general effectiveness has been sought, but we have too often been satisfied with less specific outcomes of the process."[11] The youth respondent method greatly values and is reliant on this assessment and the thoroughness of the process. Many questions about how to archive this process remain and have so historically. Charlotte Chorpenning's 1954 publication *Twenty-One Years with Children's Theatre* documents her work as educational theatre director at the Goodman School of Drama. In 1931, Chorpenning began writing and directing plays for the children's theatre branch. For over 21 years, she entertained young audiences with her adaptations of fairytales, fables, and classic children's literature. By her death in 1955, she doubled the canon of children's theatre plays. She describes her experiences, processes, and the children's theatre tropes associated with many of her most successful productions, such as *Jack and the Beanstalk*, and experiences teaching at Northwestern while developing work. This narrative, filled with the details of the teacher-director-artist's work, illuminates the first example of the youth respondent method. Unfortunately, many of the specific details of her studies she decides not to include in her monograph, which is ostensibly more autobiographical in nature. But the overall, general themes and feminist pedagogical ideas of the text prove indispensable in analyzing the youth respondent method. Chorpenning dedicates a chapter to "How I Used What the Children Taught Me." She writes, "The general principles of plays for children and for adults are the same."[12] Instead of making assumptive generalizations about the youth audience, she spoke to youths individually about the work she created for them and continued to improve it with their suggestions. Little, if any, of her data from these studies remains, though Chorpenning made an indelible impact on progressing the play development process by incorporating the young audience's reception during the preview and production process.

The endemic challenges of contemporary theatre are not limited to certain subjectivities of theatre, including TYA. Development processes for professional theatre for both adult and child audiences share many of the same issues. Some of these include: a lack of producing enough high-quality work, a lack of time and resources, and a lack of full and diverse audiences. Perhaps, as Woods argues, "If the children's theatres of this country, by presenting only superior plays, can develop in the boys and girls who will be the adult audiences of tomorrow, a more discriminating taste in drama than their parents have, they will have made a distinct contribution to American life."[13] Placing a greater emphasis on producing work of better quality for all young audiences will cultivate not only the next generation of artists but audiences. Besides improving the quality of work and telling new stories, the field needs to embrace new modes of communication and development to reach these audiences, such as audience engagement, web-communication, and social media.

The child is another essential collaborator in creating this tool and determining how their generation can make a better future through the practice and art of theatre. The youth respondent method strengthens TYA plays while it gives children the agency to learn, exchange ideas, and address subjects that are important to them. It is a model that can easily transfer to many different types of plays, not strictly for young audiences, and the dramaturg can be instrumental in this immersion.

Notes

1 Suzan Zeder, "The Once and Future Audience: Dramaturgy and Children's Theatre," *Dramaturgy in American Theater: A Source Book*, eds. Susan Jonas, Geoff Proehl, and Michael Lupu (Fort Worth, TX: Harcourt Brace and Company, 1997), 447.
2 Tom Arvetis, personal interview, October 13, 2011.
3 José Cruz González, personal interview, July 10, 2011.
4 Cruz González, interview.
5 Betsy Quinn, personal interview, October 25, 2011.
6 Nellie McCaslin, ed. *Children and Drama* (New York: D. McKay Co., 1975), 8.
7 McCaslin, 8.
8 Jed H. Davis and Mary Jane Evans, *Theatre, Children, and Youth* (New Orleans: Anchorage Press, 1982), 40.
9 Winifred Ward, *Theatre for Children* (Anchorage, KY: The Children's Theatre Press, 1958), 26.
10 Davis and Evans, 19.
11 David Wood with Janet Grant, *Theatre for Children: A Guide to Writing, Adapting, Directing, and Acting* (New York: Faber and Faber, 1997), 47.
12 Charlotte Chorpenning, *Twenty-One Years with Children's Theatre* (Anchorage, KY: The Children's Theatre Press, 1954), 49.
13 Wood, 81.

Part VI
DRAMATURGY AMONG OTHER ARTS
Interdisciplinarity, transdisciplinarity, and transvergence

56
Complex *in-betweenness* of dramaturgy and performance studies

Marin Blažević

This essay should be read as a prolegomenon. It presents an attempt to identify the locus and focus of dramaturgy, emphasize its shifts within the *postdramatic paradigm*, and correlate dramaturgy with performance studies as their neglected yet sisterly meta-/inter-/post-discipline.

Dramaturgy is nowadays apprehended and applied in at least two conflicting ways. From one standpoint, actions should be taken towards the disciplinary establishment of dramaturgy as a sort of artistic management in-between production and reception of theatrical representation. When, for example, advocating the authority of a dramatic text or facilitating the director's authorship or supporting the setup of roles in a theatrical transaction that reflects a clear division of domains and disciplines, dramaturgs are considerably contributing to the building up, maintenance, and adjusted operation of the normative machine of the theatrical institution and the social arrangements it is representing and fostering. There are, nonetheless, those that contest such conformity and grant dramaturgy with resistant stance.

Owing to the reputed vagueness of their operative modes and efficacy range, hence their ambivalent authorial function and reach, dramaturgs and dramaturgy may become the agent and agency that the institution tames, controls, and directs with considerable difficulty. The inability or strategic unwillingness to constitute dramaturgy as a discipline and to institutionalize its practice as authorial or executive activity enables dramaturgs to question and divert authority regimes and protocols, thus challenging relations in established social situations. The particular artistic, social, and political responsibilities of a dramaturg rest on her volition and competence to cope with the decisive role of dramaturgy in charging performance with a critique of the power status (assigned to the director, choreographer, or playwright) and structures (of representational mechanisms, institutional frames, and protocols, societal hierarchies, etc.). In these times, however, such a counter-role is ascribed to dramaturgy on the account of its professed interdisciplinarity and manifold tactics rather than a formed ideological *gestus*.

Whereas most of the recent revisions of dramaturgy grant it expanded capacity by adding disciplines, competences, theories, attitudes, methodologies, and tasks to its domain, I tend to widen the breadth of dramaturgy by initially reducing its definition to the core concept and potentiality of *drama*, but *drama* conceived as *action*, not a play or dramatic text. Derived from the classical Greek verb *drán* (to do, to act; and, in a broader semantic scope, to execute, to effect, to work, even to perform) *drama* translates as a deed, an act, and an *action*. The notion and motion of *action* are the locus and focus of dramaturgical thinking and doing in theatre, but also in cultural performances altogether. In varying degrees *action* is implied in all the other manifestations and comprehensions of dramaturgy, such as the composition, construction, strategy, devising, mediation, moderation, collaboration, feedback, etc.

Resting on the structuralist understanding of the dramatic situation, dramatic action can be defined as a chain of situations that unfolds due to the recurring process of their formations and transformations induced by the interventions in the structure of a situation. Such understanding, however, can be extended to comprehend situations and actions beyond the realm of the dramatic. Ergo, dramaturgy could be brought into play as an activity that re/structures the constellation of functions (forces, interests, desires, objects) and orchestrates the interaction of factors or doers (characters, actors, performers, persons outside the theatrical frame, social groups, milieus, ideas, etc.) in a particular situation (whether it is a representational, performative, aesthetic, social, or political situation). Dramaturgy is the actualization of the potential of a single act or a more complex event – an act being the cause of, or caused by, the occurrence of the event – to alter the structure of a situation, thus animating the action.

When looking for a key to understanding dramaturgy, Eugenio Barba finds it in "its etymology: *drama-ergon*, the work of the actions. Or rather: the way the actor's actions enter into work,"[1] the action itself later being defined as an activity contingent upon the potential of reactivity or as "any change, however minute, which consciously or subliminally affects the spectator's attention, their understanding, sensibility and kinaesthetic sense."[2] Action is not only effecting the (trans)formation process in-between the particular situations, but also affecting the state of minds and bodies involved in the process (even when the process is only latent or false or failing).

The initial conceptual reduction of dramaturgy to action is a prerequisite for the extension of its breadth. The locus and focus of dramaturgy are shifting through and across the transformative situation/state-act-change sequence that generates the action and is composed by the action. Besides the various disciplines, methods, and functions that current discussions are adding to dramaturgy, the critical extension should include the performance of the action, that is, the way the action performs, and a shift or a change that the action could induce. The performative potential, actualization, and effect of the action/change/dramaturgy (misfire and inaction included) constitute the whole field and flow of theatrical as well as other cultural performances, their somatic as well as semiotic scope: from semantic investments and narrative strings to emotion memory and kinesthetic empathy; from vocal expression to spatial intervention; from organic experience to political attitude; within as well as beyond the dramatic text/fiction/situation/conflict and its enactment. Moreover, the performance, operation, dynamics, the *work*, or, in one word, the *action* of an action, always implies and mostly incites a re-*action*. A specific dramaturgical re-action, however, would be the one that is not reduced to the mere proceeding of (re)actions and continuation of the action-sequence (situation/state-act-change). Dramaturgical re-action assumes reflection.

Such a reflective reaction to the action is not performed only by the spectators or observers (including the experts) outside of the theatrical event. This *meta-action* is grafted already on to the act of acting. According to the director and theoretician Branko Gavella, the most prominent representative of modernism in Croatian theatre, "the whole essence of the problem of acting lies precisely in the ... vertiginous goal to be at the same time the onlooker and the one looked at." Initiated by "theoretical considerations" reponsive to "organic experiences,"[3] the internalized spectatorship pervades the performance of acting. Brechtian *organon*, on the other hand, requires externalization of the duality of *spect-acting* in the act/performance of acting, prompted by the *estrangement effect* for the purpose of critical (dialectical) thinking. In both cases acting is conceived as a sort of embodied dramaturgy – the actual execution of the action and synchronous analytical flexure over that action.

Dramaturgy is, therefore, the *work of* and the work (interpretive, analytical, critical, theoretical) *on* and *over* (before, after, and during) the action. Situation, function, factor/doer, act/event, and action itself are observed, reflected, questioned, correlated, analyzed, evaluated and – at the same time – activated by dramaturgy in the process of composing a story, devising or conducting a performance (from happening and dance to concert and opera), creating and criticizing social relations, constituting institutions, and, inversely, deconstructing them. Moreover, dramaturgy gives special consideration to the contextual conditions and implications – political, ideological, and cultural – of an action. Marianne Van Kerkhoven stated: "Dramaturgy is for me learning to handle complexity."[4] Let me add: first and foremost, it is the *complexity* of *in-betweenness* – theory and practice, critical reflection and embodiment, knowledge exploration and production on one side and artistic inspiration and execution on the other.

In the framework of the *postdramatic paradigm*, instituted by Hans-Thies Lehmann,[5] dramaturgy attains additional complexity. Theoretical (self)reflection, analytical (self) observation, critical (self)questioning – all aspects of the common dramaturgical approach – are often viewed as a reaction or anticipation at a safe and thus notorious distance from the risk of immediate and actual embodiment, ideologized and mystified presupposition of the sublime aesthetic experience and artistic expressivity supposedly *becoming present* in the performance. As we know, however, the autoreferential function could be integrated into the structure of the work itself by meta-theatrical/performative multiplication or folding of the planes of representation/performance, illusion/reality, fiction/factuality. Furthermore, *postdramatic* dramaturgy experiments with the modes of insertion of theoretical, analytical, and critical thinking into the overall system and even the bodies of performance. Performed (autoreferential) exploration of correlations and complementarity of expression and reflection, of affect and concept, could now inform the whole process of production, presentation, and reception of a performance, transforming the theoretical, analytical, critical *meta*-position into a dynamic, complex, and often dramatic – *meta*-in the *inter*-action. Such a shift enhances the competence and intensifies the performance of dramaturgy in questioning the constellation and activity of subjects and bodies in the representational/performative situation. Accordingly, dramaturgy could take up the challenge of experiment with the organization and politics of social relations that are not determined by the hierarchic arrangements of authorities and distribution of power which maintain oppressive or simply inert regimes of functions and disciplines.

Further *broadening* of the action *spectrum*, to paraphrase Richard Schechner's dictum, allows for extension of the reach of dramaturgy beyond performing arts: from everyday life (as it was already pioneered in Goffman's dramaturgical approach to *presentation of self*) to reality shows, from sports to political rituals, from social networking to wars. However, more intriguing than the shared *broad spectrum*, it is the interaction and interweaving of theory and practice, scholarly creation, artistic research, and embodied critical thinking, as well as the testing of political strategies and social efficacy of performance, that bring the resistant and especially *postdramatic* dramaturgy in the proximity to performance studies, and the other way around, notwithstanding the prevalent mutual ignorance.[6]

One of the key challenges in conceptualization, constitution, and consolidation of performance studies has been the integration of "studying performance and doing performance."[7] The founders of performance studies called for "an active inter-change between … art form and knowledge formation."[8] Performance studies should accept the "inter"[9] and embrace the "collaborative agenda" as "an ethic of reciprocity and exchange" intended to "refuse and supersede … the division of labor between theory and practice, abstraction and embodiment."[10] Consequently, the performance studies project might "act *on* or act *against* strictly ordered or settled hierarchies of ideas, organizations, or people"[11] and bring about a transformation of normative social arrangements.

One cannot help wondering, what is keeping performance studies away from the resistant dramaturgy, and even the dramaturgy that entered upon the *postdramatic* stage, thus reaching a turning point in the emancipation of performance studies itself?[12] Could it be that such a curious bypassing is not only due to the fact that (until recently) predominantly "US/UK PS"[13] was somehow misrecognizing drama-turgy as a mix of secondary practices confined to dramatic theatre, such as literary management, production facilitation, and textual transformations (adaptation, trans-lation, and other alterations), a misconception which still prevails in the US and UK context? Or, the reason might be found in the danger that dramaturgy could distract from the (self)perception that performance studies has in fact sorted out its territorial disagreements with theatre and drama/literary studies in the hallways of academia? Could it be that performance studies is avoiding dramaturgy since it keeps reminding drama, theatre, and performance studies of the mutual origin of their objects of study in the semantic scope of the old Greek notions of *drán* and *drama*?

Despite divergent histories, many of their present convergences – of ideas, metho-dologies, and strategies, institutional as well as oppositional – affirm the assumption of the corresponding practices and discourses that have developed in relatively distinct cultural environments. I am inclined to suggest that the role of the Continental European resistant and especially *postdramatic* dramaturgy has been – some way and partway – played by performance studies in the US/UK context, and vice versa. I am not arguing that the two are acting as (mutual) doubles. Rather, they seem to inhabit the same (liminal?) zone, function and strategy of *in-betweenness*, of resisting disciplinary constraints and operating in the *inter* of aesthetic performance, academic research, and sometimes even activism, thus introducing "a postdiscipline of inclusions,"[14] which is a capacity that performance studies tends to ascribe exclusively to itself. Predictably, such exclusivity is strategic as it usually goes with the ambition to secure inclusion in the institutional (re)arrangements of power combined with symbolic (and related financial) capital, which is primarily deposited in, disposable at, and managed by the universities and associated businesses in knowledge production and distribution. Shannon Jackson in *Professing Performance* reminds us that "the language of subversion," which marks the performance of performance studies, "co-exists uneasily next to the language of institutionalization." She rightfully warns, "such a contradiction is not peculiar to performance studies. ... It replicates the paradoxes, privileges and conventions of resistant humanism."[15] There is indeed a widespread feeling in the circles of *postdramatic* dramaturgs that performance studies is hopelessly trapped in this *contradiction* and effectively follows the call of academia, though the dispute remains tacit as there are no publications by respective dramaturgs, at least not to my knowledge, that elaborate on the issue.

Nevertheless, the persistence of the resistance *gestus* that still actuates performance studies remains compelling. Despite its immersion in institutional structures and protocols, performance studies – becoming less UK/US and more international – resists abandoning the self-critical attitude and liminal latitude, even when they are turned into the vehicles of normativity. Ideally, the paradoxical mechanism of the "liminal norm" (coined by McKenzie[16]) keeps performance studies in a permanent state of crisis, iteration of promises, and expectations of a *liminal* action that could, despite the burden of normativity, lead to a distinctively dramaturgical event. The uneasiness of the liminal norm contradiction indicates awareness of the identity rift and alternatives to the permanent trouble: either maneuvering within the system or else performing an act, a shift towards the change. What an archetypal dramatic situation!

> That there are difficulties in the relationship between object and process, text and performance, structure and play (...) becomes especially apparent when an agent or subject appears to have trouble negotiating between the name of the act and the practice. This trouble is especially visible in *Hamlet* ... [17]

In the final fragment of this prolegomenon I would like to propose the next chapter in discussion, on the reading of Alice Rayner's book *To Act, To Do, To Perform: Drama and the Phenomenology of Action* as fundamental to both the *postdramatic* dramaturgy and performance studies, notwithstanding the trouble that her argument builds on the theory and analysis of drama.

Notes

1 Eugenio Barba, *On Directing and Dramaturgy* (London and New York: Routledge, 2010), 8.
2 Barba, 106.
3 Branco Gavella, *Teorija glume* (Theory of acting), eds. Nikola Batušić and Marin Blažević (Zagreb: Akcija, 2005), 140.

4 Marianne Van Kerkhoven, "European Dramaturgy in the 21st Century: A Constant Movement," *Performance Research* 14. 3 (2009), 11.

5 Hans-Thies Lehmann, *Postdramatic Theatre*, trans. Karen Jürs-Munby (London and New York: Routledge, 2007), 24.

6 There are some exceptions, such as the Centre for Performance Research and *Performance Research* journal, both conducted by Richard Gough, and the Performance Studies international conferences in Zagreb and Utrecht, in 2009 and 2011, organized by teams of researchers that had previously been more closely affiliated with *postdramatic* dramaturgy than performance studies.

7 Richard Schechner, *Performance Studies: An Introduction* (London and New York: Routledge, 2002), 1.

8 Barbara Kirshenblatt-Gimblett, "Performance Studies," *The Performance Studies Reader*, ed. Henry Bial (London and New York, Routledge, 2007), 48.

9 Schechner, 19.

10 Dwight Conquergood, "Performance Studies at Northwestern" and "The Five Areas of Performance Studies," in Schechner, 18.

11 Schechner, 3.

12 There was no place for dramaturgy in the contents or index of Schechner's *Performance Studies: An Introduction* (2002); and the notion features in only 1 of 42 chapters, unsurprisingly Barba's, collected in *The Performance Studies Reader* (2007) by Henry Bial. On the other hand, although Schechner does play a role in Lehmann's argument, there is no explicit reference to performance studies in his dramaturgical analysis and poetics of *Postdramatic Theatre* (2006). A modest progress can be noted in the *Performance Research* issue "On Dramaturgy" (2009) – performance studies is mentioned in a couple of contributions (Barton, Kelleher, Radosavljević).

13 J. McKenzie, H. Roms, C. J. Wan-Ling Wee, eds., *Contesting Performance: Emerging Sites of Research* (New York: Palgrave Macmillan, 2009), 7.

14 Kirshenblatt-Gimblett, 43.

15 Shannon Jackson, *Professing Performance* (Cambridge: Cambridge University Press, 2004), 30.

16 Jon McKenzie, *Perform or Else: From Discipline to Performance* (London and New York: Routledge, 2001), 40–53.

17 Alice Rayner, *To Act, To Do, To Perform: Drama and the Phenomenology of Action* (Ann Arbor: University of Michigan Press, 1994), 5.

57

The dramaturg(ies) of puppetry and visual theatre[1]

Dassia N. Posner

As a dramaturg, when I have created visual resources for productions with live actors, puppets, or both, my approach has typically been to find images inspired by a dramatic text or by the story a director, puppeteer, or company hopes to tell. Some are illustrative and give needed answers to practical questions. Others are conceptual, creating open-ended potential signifiers for elusive signified ideas or emotions. These conceptual images are not always captured literally in a production, but might make their way into how an actor holds her body at a particular moment, which materials are used to construct a puppet, or how a scene's rhythmic structure and mise-en-scène are shaped.

Recently, however, I have moved away from the idea that visual dramaturgy is necessarily connected to story, character, or metaphor, and have begun exploring other ways the dramaturg can, in both puppetry and in other kinds of visual performance, support alternate "systems of meaning."[2] In this essay I will explore this expanded definition of visual dramaturgy as it relates to puppetry and visual theatre, examining in particular what Sumarsam has described as things that are "peripheral to the story, but essential to the performance"[3] in order to track how the visual elements of theatre create unique trajectories of meaning that interweave with text or story.

Inspired by Sharon Carnicke's explanation of Stanislavsky's notion of a production's through line as akin to a rope woven out of multiple, individual "lines,"[4] I view the theatrical event as consisting not of a single through line, but of many. One is the narrative as it unfolds as a result of the interplay of multiple "strands": words, characters, sounds, or images. Another is the artist's conversation with the audience about how and why s/he constructs meaning with a particular theatrical grammar for a specific production. A third is something more ineffable, something related to what Basil Jones has called the "*ur*-narrative of life" in puppet theatre,[5] which I expand to also characterize the fragile thread of belief that is birthed and nurtured by audience and artist over the course of a production, something that, in the puppet theatre in particular, is woven out of things like breath, gaze, surprise, and expectation.

Visual narrative, in my proposed definition, is comprised of images that support, interpret, contrast with, or otherwise interact directly with text or story. Visual meta-narrative is the visual grammar the artist uses to engage in self-reflexive theatrical dialogue with the audience about the performance itself and its aesthetic values. Lastly, visual ur-narrative encompasses visual elements of performance that exist independently of plot or spoken text, but that generate a distinctive through line of emotive and visceral audience response. These three unique narrative strands support distinct, interweaving, simultaneous systems of theatrical meaning that together produce a polyphonic rather than simple melodic theatrical experience for an audience.

In order to explore the profound significance of the latter two, visual meta-narrative and visual ur-narrative, I will briefly analyze two well-known productions that use puppetry in innovative ways, *The Lion King* (1997) and *War Horse* (2007), investigating how each develops these alternate visual dramaturgies. Both have been instrumental in bringing puppets to the attention of mainstream theatregoers and are therefore often talked about in conjunction with one another. Both juxtapose puppets and live actors, use spoken and sung dialogue, and have a plot-driven dramatic structure. However, the visual grammars of these two productions are conceived very differently: while each tells a linear story, *The Lion King* actively interweaves this narrative with meta-narrative, while *War Horse's* greatest innovation lies in its development of the puppet's ur-narrative. I hope to illuminate new approaches for analyzing puppetry and visual theatre productions by investigating how.

Meta-narrative and *The Lion King*

In *The Lion King,* director-designer Julie Taymor and co-designer Michael Curry condensed the metaphorical and emotional content of the musical into specific, precise images or "ideographs." Herbert Blau, who pioneered this term, defined the ideograph as "the stage image or tableau that symbolically visualizes the distinctive world of a play."[6] As applied to the performer, this echoes what Soviet actor Solomon Mikhoels called a "gesture leitmotif."[7] It also tallies with many puppeteers' understanding of the puppet as a repository of visual dramaturgy; the puppet *is* character and *contains* story even before it is set in motion. Taymor's understanding of the ideograph also encompasses condensed, concentrated visual metaphors more broadly defined; she states, "An ideograph is an essence, an abstraction. It's boiling it right down to the most essential two, three brush strokes."[8] Many of Taymor's ideographs visually capture *The Lion King's* verbal themes, the most obvious being the recurrent use of circles in the design, inspired by the song "The Circle of Life," from the rising of the sun that begins and ends the play, to the spiraling movement of Pride Rock as it enters the stage, to the circular leaping of gazelles.[9]

Taymor's additional aim was to converse theatrically with *The Lion King's* audiences about her artistic thought process. She did not want the production to be simply a theatrical illustration of the Disney film, but an overt dialogue with the story; she held that "[t]he meaning comes in the telling, not in the story itself."[10] One way she sought to provoke this dialogue was to significantly rewrite Disney's original to include material that celebrates African culture. She also placed a great deal of emphasis on non-verbal dialogue with an audience as a form of theatrical structure, creating a visual dialectic between, in Richard Schechner's words, "the mask character and the mask itself."[11] This meta-narrative is depicted in the persistent

Figure 57.1 The Lion King. Directed by Julie Taymor (2007). Image used by permission of the Walt Disney Company. Photo © Brinkhoff /Mögenburg

simultaneous presence of and equal emphasis on both puppeteer and puppet. It is implemented through fully exposing the puppets' mechanics, so that the puppets move seemingly by magic even while the audience sees how the magic works. Thus the swaying safari grass is worn on the heads of fully exposed dancers, and the masks are designed to seemingly magically move away to reveal the actors' faces behind them.

Taymor calls these intersections between the production's narrative and meta-narrative the "'double event' of *The Lion King*," adding, "[i]t's not just the story that's being told. It's *how* it's being told."[12] The design of the *Lion King* puppets is focused on productively capturing, in Paul Piris's words, the "co-presence" of puppet and puppeteer[13] – essence of giraffe-with-puppeteer, essence of lion-with-puppeteer – rather than on focusing our attention on how an inert puppet lion is imbued with life. In Taymor and Curry's visual vocabulary, there is no need for the puppet to create the illusion of reality, but instead for it to make visible the process of creation. Significantly, the audience never forgets that the puppeteers are perpetually present or that there are masks atop the actors' heads. Although puppet theatre is inherently self-reflexive – it is always a performance of the creation of a performance – Taymor's production is every bit as much about defining theatre as an interactive visual conversation with an audience as it is about Disney's story of a young lion who comes of age.

Ur-narrative and *War Horse*

In *War Horse*, the puppet represents a fragile life that is upheld in the omnipresent face of death. This metaphor is not inspired by the story of *War Horse*, even if it is set during the Great War, but, for Handspring Puppet Company's Basil Jones and Adrian Kohler, it is central to the function of all theatrical puppets: every puppet performance is, to some degree, a performance of the *ur*-narrative of life. According to Jones, "A puppet is by its very nature dead, whereas an actor is by her very nature alive. The puppet's work, then … is to strive towards life. This struggle … is literally in the hands of the puppeteer and need have no connection to the script-writer or the director."[14] As puppeteers and spectators together create and sustain this life from the moment a puppet first begins to move, they also create and sustain something else: a fragile thread of conscious belief. As Jones muses, "when we go into a theater and the lights go down, and we … are shown objects – i.e., puppets – that are brought to life, I think it ignites a smouldering coal of ancient belief in us – that there is life in stones, in rivers, in objects, in wood."[15] This belief is irresistibly personified in Handspring's horse puppets, but it is also a fundamental part of the theatrical experience, where the fantasy of the audience is similarly conceived, birthed, and nurtured.

In *War Horse*, Jones and Kohler develop the "performance of life" (and therefore also the nurturing of belief) as an independent narrative that interacts and contrasts with spoken text. Jones writes: "The puppet's Ur-narrative is something quite different to, and more fundamental, than storytelling. It is the quest for life itself."[16] The *ur*-narrative of the production's horses allows the audience to participate in something miraculous. The more obviously dead the puppet looks, based on the materials of which it is contructed, the greater the wonder of its life; hence Hand-spring's puppets are made of undisguised, obviously inert materials such as cane or wood, but are designed to be absolutely lifelike in their movement.

Figure 57.2 The cast of *War Horse* at the New London Theatre. Puppets by Handspring Puppet Company. Photo: Brinkhoff Mögenburg

Jones suggests that it is the interweaving of a puppet's macromovement and micromovement that produces what I call visual narrative and visual *ur*-narrative. For him, macromovement "engages with the script and the choreography," while micromovement – moments of stillness or breathing – is "a performance of the Ur-narrative."[17] It is these micromovements with which he is most concerned, these moments during which the most distant spectator in the theatre perceives the puppet's almost imperceptible breathing as life. Frequently, while the spectators are able to sense that gentle undulation of breath, they forget entirely about the humans who generate the breath and cease to see the puppeteers.

Significantly, spectators also sometimes become so focused on *War Horse*'s visual *ur*-narrative that they become literally unable to hear the spoken dialogue. Jones notes, "Often we hear the comment: 'lovely puppets, pity about the text.' Most often this remark is made not because the text is poor, but because it is hard to ... *hear* or apprehend the text when one becomes fully engaged with ... this more profound level of performance."[18] Thus, while *The Lion King* uses visual narrative and meta-narrative to condense language, theme, character, and artistic point of view into images, *War Horse* creates a visual *ur*-narrative of life that is independent of – and sometimes even erases – spoken language. Hence Jones's claim that "the work of the puppet ... can be seen implicitly as a rebellion against the word."[19]

Tracking visual narratives

In the visual meta-narrative of *The Lion King* and the visual *ur*-narrative of *War Horse*, the audience is embraced as a co-creator of visual meaning and is made a participant in a celebration of belief (rather than a suspension of disbelief). The conscious juxtaposition of contrasting, simultaneous narratives within a single production creates a productive environment for the generation of this belief. These discrete yet interweaving strands of visual narrative create what Bert States has called "binocular vision,"[20] allowing the audience to peer into a performance through multiple lenses simultaneously. The awareness that this parallel vision exists is not new; it is the tension that lies at the heart of Diderot's *Paradoxe sur le comédien* and is the foundation of Meyerhold's entire theatrical poetics.[21] But although, as Joe Roach has observed, "[t]heatrical performance is the simultaneous experience of mutually exclusive possibilities: truth and illusion, presence and absence, face and mask,"[22] we remain, to date, more adept at analyzing the *stories* those illusions and faces tell than we are at investigating the productive tensions of theatre's "mutually exclusive possibilities."

Robert Scanlan's plot-bead play-analysis technique, cogently outlined by Shelley Orr,[23] is an invaluable way to chart patterns of recurrent themes, metaphors, and events in a dramatic text. I suggest that it can also be used effectively to trace the interweavings of multiple visual narratives. Among the many things that may be valuable to track in conjunction with one another are rhythm, tempo, and dynamics; moments of self-referentiality and the frequency, density, and nature of their occurrence; different levels of movement (micro, macro, stillness, breathing);

the dramaturgies of material objects in performance; the architecture of suspense and surprise; tensions and juxtapositions between the phenomenological and the symbolic; and, especially in the puppet theatre, the interplay between liveness and objectness. Attending to such things can shift how a dramaturg or director imagines conceptual visual research and understands the visual elements of a production. Visual materials that deal with simultaneity, self-referentiality, rhythm, or the agency of objects can carry different meanings but equal value to those that capture a historical moment or evoke an elusive emotion.

Chikamatsu Monzaemon famously said in a conversation about bunraku that "art is something which lies in the slender margin between the real and the unreal."[24] Every production inevitably grapples on some level with the interplay of these elements; however, many contemporary theatre artists are choosing to make the process of grappling itself central to the structure of performance. Delineating and analyzing the distinct visual narratives that reside in Chikamatsu's productively liminal space can help us to articulate the ways in which this interplay works.

Notes

1 I presented earlier versions of this essay on a visual dramaturgy panel at ATHE (2012) and at Playwriting, Puppets, and Dramaturgy: A Symposium (2013) at the Ballard Institute and Museum of Puppetry. Sincere thanks to the participants of both for their comments and suggestions.

2 Michael Mark Chemers, *Ghost Light: An Introductory Handbook for Dramaturgy* (Carbondale: Southern Illinois University Press, 2010), 73.

3 Sumarsam, respondent comments, Playwriting, Puppets, and Dramaturgy: A Symposium, Ballard Institute and Museum of Puppetry, March 9, 2013.

4 Sharon Marie Carnicke, *Stanislavsky in Focus: An Acting Master for the Twenty-First Century,* 2nd ed. (Abingdon and New York: Routledge, 2009), 2.

5 Basil Jones, "Puppetry and Authorship," in Jane Taylor, ed., *Handspring Puppet Company* (Johannesburg: David Krut, 2009), 255.

6 Jonathan Bate, "Lecter meets Lear," *Weekend Australian* (September 9, 2000) R2.

7 Jeffrey Veidlinger, "The Moscow State Yiddish Theatre as a Cultural and Political Phenomenon," in Jonathan Frankel, ed., *Dark Times, Dire Decisions: Jews and Communism* (Oxford: Oxford University Press, 2005), 89.

8 Richard Schechner and Julie Taymor, "Julie Taymor: From Jacques Lecoq to *The Lion King*: An Interview," *TDR* 43.3 (Autumn 1999): 38.

9 Schechner and Taymor, 42.

10 Schechner and Taymor, 51.

11 Schechner and Taymor, 36.

12 Schechner and Taymor, 43.

13 For Piris, "Co-presence inherently supposes that the performer creates a character through the puppet but also appears as another character whose presence next to the puppet has a dramaturgical meaning." Paul Piris, "The Co-presence of the Performer and the Puppet in Solo Performance," *Puppetry International* 33 (Spring/Summer 2013): 22. I expand this definition to include puppeteers who appear as deliberately undisguised performers.

14 Jones, 254.

15 Basil Jones and Adrian Kohler, "The Magical Life of Objects," *Lincoln Center Review* 55 (Spring 2011): 12.

16 Jones, 255.

17 Jones, 257.

18 Jones, 256.

19 Jones, 268.
20 Bert O. States, *Great Reckonings in Little Rooms: On the Phenomenology of the Theater* (Berkeley: University of California Press, 1985), 8.
21 See especially Vsevelod Meyerhold, "The Fairground Booth," in Edward Braun, trans. and ed., *Meyerhold on Theatre* (New York: Hill and Wang, 1969), 119–42.
22 Joseph Roach, "It," *Theatre Journal* 56.4 (December 2004): 559.
23 Shelley Orr, "Teaching Play Analysis: How a Key Dramaturgical Skill Can Foster Critical Approaches," *Theatre Topics* 13.1 (March 2003): 153–58.
24 Hozumi Ikan in Donald Keene, ed. and trans., "Chikamatsu on the Art of the Puppet Stage [from Naniwa Miyage] by Hozumi Ikan," *Anthology of Japanese Literature, From the Earliest Era to the Mid-Nineteenth Century* (New York: Grove Press, 1994), 389.

58

A method for musical theatre dramaturgy

Brian D. Valencia

The role of a dramaturg on a musical project – one in development, in production, or in scholarly analysis – is a perennial problem. If a dramaturg is not a trained musician, the musical components of "musical theatre" can seem arcane or intimidating, prompting the dramaturg to skirt them altogether. If a composer and lyricist are suspicious of input from those they perceive to be uninitiated in the mysteries of their craft, the dramaturg can be deliberately sidelined from the discussion of musical ideas. Or, if the creators of a musical project attempt to avoid the taint of what they judge to be a bourgeois Broadway style, they may argue that theirs is not a conventional musical and that its musical material is, therefore, intentionally *un*conventional and ought to be left alone. The result in any case is the same: the songs are left to fend for themselves as the dramaturg limits focus to the play's more familiar, non-musical terrain, dramaturging it as he or she would dramaturg a non-musical play. Yet musical and non-musical plays are not the same and cannot be approached as if they were.

Besides the specialized personnel and additional rehearsal time music and song can require of a musical production, music and song often impose unique structural and theatrical demands on a dramatic text, many of which stem from temporal considerations. A musical score fixes theatrical timing in ways that are difficult to amend and almost impossible to halt without sabotaging a piece's musical and dramatic momentum. Stage activity and characters' emotional discoveries cannot be allowed to unfurl in their own time; rhythm and tempo dictate when and at what pace both explicit and implicit action occur. Because musical numbers occupy considerable stage time, the spoken book scenes must accomplish their work with a super efficiency unknown to most non-musical plays. They do this by relinquishing to the songs much of the development of character and theme typically found in a play's dialogue, making the musical's book look and feel comparatively abbreviated.

In exchange, music and song considerably expand the range of expressive possibilities conventionally available to realistic spoken drama. They can complicate and sometimes confuse the boundary between subtlety and exuberance. They can jolt the hierarchical balance among the theatre's always-already shifting relationships among multimedia elements, thus suddenly altering tone. They can excite or subvert expectations, amplifying a musical's ability either to penetrate or else to alienate its audience. And by augmenting the suspension of disbelief – facilitated, as the late Scott McMillin posited, by the modal separation of the musical numbers' suspended, ruminative "lyric time" from the progressive, expository time of the book[1] – music and song can rather handily make the implicit explicit ("I Don't Know How to Love Him" from *Jesus Christ Superstar*) and the hypothetical immediate ("If I Loved You" from *Carousel*); they can stop or accelerate narrative (the "Tick Tock" ballet from *Company*, in the latter case) and effortlessly welcome magic or fantasy ("Come Spirit, Come Charm" from *The Secret Garden*). The list of functional possibilities hardly stops here.

When musical theatre practitioners do acknowledge such manifold possibilities for a song, they almost always do so tacitly, relegating them to secondary or tertiary importance, as they are anathema to the contemporary American musical theatre's dogged commitment to "emotional truth" and the outmoded dictate that good theatre music will do one of two, and only two, things: "forward the plot" or "illuminate character." Limiting musical functionality to these two narrative-based alternatives ignores the fundamental polymodal fabric of musical theatre, stunts the theatrical imagination, and results in replicative productions in which putative realism often exists uncomfortably alongside the musical's inherently non-realistic conventions.

Much of this attitude is rooted in the faulty "integration" model of the form, which persists as the supposed zenith of dramaturgical responsibility for musicals. In actuality more a salable brand than an artistic method, integration was touted by Rodgers and Hammerstein as the capital achievement of their 1943 musical *Oklahoma!*, the work still looked to as the exemplar of it. In his autobiography, composer Richard Rodgers describes his long-held "theory" of the integrated musical show – in an attempt to set it apart from the musical comedies of the early twentieth century, with their stock plots and hodgepodge scores – as one in which all of the elements dovetail with each other, there is "nothing extraneous or foreign," and, though the work of many hands, the result gives "the impression of having been created by one." "In a great musical," he writes, "the orchestrations sound the way the costumes look,"[2] and it was on this platform of purported homogeneity that he and his librettist collaborator Oscar Hammerstein II informally but effectively marketed most of their musical plays that followed.

In the absence of a systematic definition of *integration*, the term has come to mean the aspiration to seamless transitions from spoken book scenes into musical numbers and then back again, and the assurance of a logical cause-and-effect relationship between the dialogue and the songs over the full arc of a musical's plot. It is the second, though, and not the first part of this working definition that Rodgers and Hammerstein really set up in *Oklahoma!*, and this, perhaps more than anything, is the significant artistic achievement of that work. In his 1949 essay "Notes on Lyrics," Hammerstein explains that the innovations of *Oklahoma!* were born of "a conflict of dramaturgy and showmanship," in which the dramaturgy won out.[3] The writers rejected the then-expected inclusion of the flashy opening chorus, non-sequitur specialty numbers, and extraneous comic subplots not in the high-minded name of integration, but because their project – the musical adaptation of the somewhat sober play *Green Grow the Lilacs* – did not support them.

The lesson here is that Rodgers and Hammerstein avoided conformity to a dramaturgical model that did not suit their projects and found unprecedented success in measuring out their own bespoke distances between their musical books and scores. For them, these distances are indeed fairly short. For other successful musicals since, they have been sometimes shorter (*Les Misérables*, for example, which arguably has no book), sometimes longer (*Spring Awakening*, for instance, a kind of concert–play, in which the book and songs are purposely separated by more than a century's worth of discrepancies in diction, tone, and style). Undertones of the Wagnerian *Gesamtkunstwerk* lurk suspiciously beneath the notion of a "seamless transition" between dialogue and music, as though, by tethering itself however tenuously back to Bayreuth, the American musical might claim highbrow continental parentage and, therefore, heightened artistic legitimacy. Because of the inherent polymodality of musical theatre, however, there will always be felt, both semiotically and phenomenologically, McMillin's evocative "crackle of difference"[4] between the book and the songs – or, when there is no book, between the recitative and the songs, or between one song and the next.

In musical scripts, song lyrics are typically indented, organized into block stanzas, and appear in all caps. Additionally, materials licensed from Music Theatre International, whose catalog contains over 300 titles (including the works of Stephen Sondheim, Stephen Schwartz, and Disney Theatricals), indicate musical cues via horizontal black bars across the page, marking the start of each new number. Even in two dimensions, these formatting indications foreground the musical numbers against the rest of the musical's text, inviting our special attention. In performance, of course, musical numbers are foregrounded even further. Highlighted via instrumental accompaniment, the piling up of singing voices into unison and harmonic textures, measured repetition of musical and lyrical phrases, changes in lighting, and large-scale synchronized movement, dance, and other spectacular effects, the songs point to themselves as moments of keen theatrical interest against the somewhat flatter armature of the book that holds them in place. As if this were not enough, the titles of the songs (and who sings them) almost always appear in the playbill amid a listing of numbered scenes. It must be acknowledged, then, that there are intrinsic forces in musical theatre working at virtually every level – from the page to the stage to the printed program – to maintain perceptible seams between the book and the songs. Once we allow ourselves to recognize that they are not made of the same elastic dramatic material, we can free ourselves from the futile burden of attempting to integrate the two, whether in development, in production, or in analysis. But if seamless integration is no longer the ideal, and musical numbers extend distinctive dramaturgical exigencies separate from those of the book, how should a dramaturg go about grappling with musical theatre?

Rather than evaluating musical numbers by gauging their conformity to the old functional expectations, the dramaturg might instead ask a series of open-ended, exploratory questions about the intent, execution, and effect of each number. This method allows for each musical moment to be engaged on its own terms and, furthermore, generates a treasury of possible artistic choices, from which the most exciting can be selected and tested as part of the creative or analytic process.

Some Questions to Ask a Song:

1 Who is singing?
2 Why does the character sing?

> To introduce himself to other characters onstage, or simply to the audience.
> To communicate directly with the audience.
> To impart otherwise-secret knowledge to the audience.
> To pass the time, or to make time pass.
> To stop the show!
> To punctuate an entrance or an exit.
> To establish sympathy with or antipathy to other characters or ideas in the play.
> To expedite the exposition.
> To provide thematic reinforcement.
> To make the unsaid explicit.
> To cover a scene or costume change.
> To offer textural variety.
> To ironize – or otherwise defamiliarize – the situation.
> To facilitate magic or fantasy.
> To evoke something that has happened offstage.
> Because she is so [fill in the blank] she cannot merely speak.
> Because the plot calls for a song, or it has been suggested that someone sing.
> Because he is in disguise and singing helps to effect his alternate identity.
> Because the actress in the role is a star, and, therefore, her fans expect her to sing.
> Because no entertainment in that century was complete without music.
> Because the music adds needed [fill in the blank] to the text.
> Because he is beginning or ending a scene or act, when it is customary to hear a song.
> Because the writer(s) thought it would be amusing to parody a well-known song.[5]

3 What has just happened before the song starts? What happens immediately following?
4 What happens over the course of the song? Is the song an opportunity to advance the drama ("forward the action"), or is it more of a dramatic resting place?
5 How much a part *of* or a digression *from* the dramatic action or situation are the song's music and lyrics?
6 What internal or external artistic and cultural cues govern or influence the musical flavor of the song (meter, mode, melodic contour, harmonic palette, etc.)? Does the music reprise any previously heard material?
7 What staging does the song require or invite? Does it call for dance or other spectacle?
8 What does the song provide that mere spoken dialogue would not?
9 How might the song's placement (e.g. opening number, act-one finale, eleven-o'clock slot) affect its role in the drama? Its reception?
10 Dramatically speaking, what are the relationships among the text, action, vocal line, and musical accompaniment?
11 Theatrically speaking, what are the relationships among the singer, the musicians accompanying her, and the audience?

12 Do you see any autobiographical glimmers of the writer(s) in the song? What might these say about the play, and what might these say about the writer(s)?

13 Do you see any glimmers of the play's own cultural moment reflected in the song? What might these say about the play, and what might these say about the times?

14 Does the performer provide a credible performance of character? If not, how does this affect the song's reception?

15 What is the desired effect of the song on the audience? On the page and in performance, what effect *does* it have on the audience?

The seemingly banal question "Why does the character sing?" stands to yield several illuminating functional possibilities once the specter of integration has been dispelled. The sampling of potential responses to this question above represents not only narrative concerns but performative concerns as well, which, when combined with one another, assume the capacity to imbue song with a color and complexity the standard characterological analysis cannot match. Due consideration of all relevant possibilities for this and for all such questions is not only responsible dramaturgy, it is also a catalyst for shaking off stale clichés carried over by tradition from one production to the next (the costly yet frequently clumsy flying sequences of *Peter Pan*, for one example among many) and instituting in their places fresh, unexpected solutions. Re-examination of *why* a song occurs may very well lead to re-examination of *how* it occurs.

Applicable as they are to the extant repertoire, these kinds of questions can also be of terrific assistance to works in progress where the dramaturg can guide a creative team through the slating of hypothetical answers for a given song spot, and the songwriters can then extrapolate backward from these answers in order to shape the desired musical number. The clearer the outline of the germinal song at the beginning of the songwriting process, as determined by the contextual circumstances of the drama, the greater the likelihood that the resulting song will achieve all that the moment demands of it. As a check of this, the same questions may be asked again of the completed number. If the answers this time stray too far from their original targets, musical or lyrical rewrites may be called for; on the other hand, the writers could decide they have stumbled upon promising ideas they had not previously considered and re-chart their course in light of these happy discoveries.

The substantial benefit of this method is that it presupposes nothing of the works it probes, requiring only that they contain discrete musical moments that can be interrogated independently. It may be brought to *Hair* as effectively as it may be brought to *Hello, Dolly!* since it seeks to identify and dissect the foregrounded work of the score and its unique functional relationship with the book, without insisting that the one ought to be wholly elided into the other. When responses to such series of questions are collected for every musical number over the course of a theatrical score, a data map of this relationship emerges. Because this map is purposely descriptive and impartial, however, critical assessment of it can come only through comparison with a given project's goals. For example: in a musical two-hander, the writer intends for Jamie's songs to propel narrative time forward, whereas Cathy's songs should repel it backward. Does its map suggest the score achieves this?

In another show, several of the numbers are meant to be performances of musical routines from the fictive Weismann's Follies, not personal expressions of characters' individualized selves. Does the map for the production at hand make this clear?

From the first calls to integrate the musical theatre, its music and song have been instructed what they *should* accomplish instead of encouraging frontier exploration of what they *might* accomplish. This has by no means pre-empted the occasional departure from the integrated model in both writing and production, but it has discouraged the establishment of a mode of analysis equipped not only to tolerate but also to value the essential fissures between disparate formal elements, and to examine the disruptive, as well as the conventionally non-disruptive, contributions of musical numbers to a dramatic text. By rejecting adherence to any one particular agenda, the ecumenical method for musical theatre dramaturgy proposed here offers an analytic framework capable of tackling even the most peculiar of musical theatre pieces, while supporting the continued expansion of creative and intellectual experimentation within the form.

Notes

1 Scott McMillin, *The Musical as Drama* (Princeton, NJ: Princeton University Press, 2006), 6–9.
2 Richard Rodgers, *Musical Stages: An Autobiography*, 2nd ed. (Cambridge, MA: Da Capo, 2002), 227.
3 Oscar Hammerstein II, "Notes on Lyrics" in *Lyrics* (Milwaukee, WI: Hal Leonard, 1985), 8.
4 McMillin, 2.
5 Sample responses adapted and expanded from Elizabeth Hale Winkler, *The Function of Song in Contemporary British Drama* (Newark, NJ: University of Delaware Press, 1990), 30–34.

59

Borderless dramaturgy in dance theatre

Vessela S. Warner

Within the array of contemporary dramaturgies, developmental dramaturgy for physical and experimental theatre has been the most elusive subject of examination. As hybrid genres push the boundaries of rehearsal and performance, attracting collective devising and limitless possibilities of multidisciplinary art forms, the target and scope of dramaturgy often dissolve into the process of theatre-making and conceptualization, among other production needs. Such "borderless" dramaturgy, discussed in this chapter, involved the author's dramaturgical work for the experimental performance of *Ecocentric* by Overground Physical Theatre Company, which premiered at Manhattan Movement & Arts Center June 21–22, 2012. The production experience outlined the challenges and opportunities of constructing a complex and multisensory performance that drew on the genre of dance theatre (*Tanztheater*): a postmodern fusion of dance, speaking, singing, props, set, and costume, developed by Pina Bausch at Wuppertal Dance Company in the 1970s. Rooted in the aesthetics of German Expressionism, Rudolf Steiner's eurythmics, and modern ballet, *Tanztheater* was also inspired by the 1960s American avant-garde theatre. With its non-hierarchical composition that blends dramatic text, choreography, and art, dance theatre sets specific dramaturgical goals in aiding the dialog among text, stage, and audiences. The main developmental aspects of dramaturgy include a rather subtle orchestration of performative signs, instead of the establishment of a firm dramatic composition, and transpositions of poetic and "sacred" meanings in the text and stage imagery, instead of their validation through storytelling or within a larger historical-theoretical discourse. In the polyphonic structure of *Ecocentric*, that "subtle dramaturgy" engaged a deeper investigation as well as limitless interpretations of the subjects of nature and ecology.

Established in 2000 in New York City, Overground Physical Theatre Company has produced over forty full-length shows under the artistic leadership of director-choreographer and creator of the original works, Antonia Katrandjieva. Accepting the mission of social engagement, also noticeable in Pina Bausch's work, the company is an experimental laboratory for hybrid forms of performance, which raises awareness of various political, cultural, and global processes in the world. Overground's multi-ethnic cast has performed at many prominent dance and experimental-theatre venues in New York City, including Brooklyn Academy of Music, Dance Theatre Workshop, La MaMa Experimental Theatre Company, and Judson Memorial Church, among others. With *Ecocentric*, the company attempted to articulate a holistic view of humankind and nurture self-understanding in a material and spiritual world. The plot of the original play is structured as a series of loosely connected dialogical and monologic scenes featuring nine contemporary women – residents of the apartment complex Terra Condos – who struggle with their phobias and addictions as a result of living in a consumerist, egocentric, and techno-s(t)imulated world. Guided by a mysterious garbage lady, Penelope, and a singing elevator, El'Eve, the characters travel through real and imaginary spaces, and embody various ancient and modern archetypes in a ritualistic reinstatement of humans' broken connection with nature. *Ecocentric* employs allegory, fantasy, and postmodern irony in articulating the notion of mankind's homecoming to Mother Earth.

Dramaturgical orchestration: text transpositions and sacred rests

In experimental and multidisciplinary performance, the dramatic text struggles to keep the leading role in the semantic production of stage signs. Its function could be twofold: centripetal, creating references to and reflections on reality, and/or centrifugal, achieving meaning through deconstruction and poetic ambiguity. In the dance-theatre structure of *Ecocentric*, language naturally remained the leading agent of storytelling, depicting whimsical, grotesque, and symbolic situations, such as the auction of the Earth's organs, a ping-pong match at the Stock Exchange, a psychiatric therapy session, a cartoonish political campaign with empty presidential promises, and a series of shopaholics' and cyberholics' confessions. Consequently, mundane activities were estranged and ritualized in order to emphasize the political, techno-logical, and psychological extremities in modern life. The dramaturg's role in devel-oping the script, therefore, consisted of balancing the text's informative qualities and poetic minimalism in order to secure points of reference in the dramatic action as well as in the abstract content of postmodern dance. To use Eugenio Barba's theory of the "three dramaturgies," the first task in the script development involved the "*narrative dramaturgy*, which interweaves events and characters, informing the spectators on the meaning of what they are watching."[1] In *Ecocentric*, narrative dramaturgy expanded to include the video-storyboard featuring a montage of pro-jected images: from realistic spaces to symbolic representations, to text projections inspired by epic theatre.

Although the situations and characters in the performance purposefully referred to modern-day clichés, the dramatic text nevertheless aimed at composing them into a poetic form that is inseparable from the rhythmic and musical structure of the whole piece. Eventually, the text incorporated heterogeneous speeches, rhymes, oxymoronic figures, and linguistic paradoxes written in haiku verses. For instance, the character of the bald-headed hairstylist Oxymora introduced herself in wordplay: "My nature is contradictory. Why? Because I like small crowds, and most of the time I am clearly misunderstood. ... Last month I blew up $5,000 on a reincarnation seminar. I figured: hey, we only live once!"[2] Penelope's "chant" in the scene

"ConsumERA" exemplified a rhythmic pattern, which generated the parody of a ritual in the Hair Dance:

> Garnier shampoo
> With nutrients ...
> We take it home with oil.
> To clean the soil with oil ... ,
> Oil for beatification
> Oil for manipulation
> Oil nation ...
> Oil salvation.[3]

In the attempt to construct an image of a heterogeneous and transcultural planet, the verbal score of *Ecocentric* also incorporated the multilingual speeches of the cast members in the scene "Braiding Memories," which featured the characters' self-searching and remembrance. The actresses, members of the multicultural cast, began to deliver their childhood memories in English, but continued in their native tongues, weaving overlapping voices that spoke in eight foreign languages into an intricate soundscape. The dramaturgical composition of this and other scenes, similar in their musical complexity, ultimately turned into a dramaturgical orchestration of language patterns that alliterated and expressed, rather than depicted, various conflicting states: inner self vs. public image, technical world vs. nature, and modern habits vs. archaic rituals. In *Ecocentric*, as Barba notices for physical theatre in general, the narrative dramaturgy yielded to the *"organic or dynamic dramaturgy,* which is the composition of the rhythms and dynamisms affecting the spectators on a nervous, sensorial and sensual level."[4] The musicalization of the dramatic text complemented the musical score and framed the choreography, seamlessly connecting the dramatic action with the abstracted emotion, energy, and subconscious impulses in the dancing parts.

In the production of *Ecocentric*, dance served a role similar to that of the ancient Greek chorus: to summarize the episodes as well as poetically reflect on the emotions each scene evoked. Building on the literary structure and figures of speech, movement and choreography completed what Barba identifies as the most elusive *"dramaturgy of changing states,* when the entirety of what [is shown] manages to evoke something totally different, similar to when a song develops another sound line through the harmonics."[5] In *Ecocentric*, such dramaturgy of transient and transposed images produced a constant flux of stage signs, spatial voids (or "rests") in particular, which eschewed historical and cultural specifics and determined a mythological – simultaneously contemporary and archaic as well as close and distant – vision of the Earth. Similar to this function of dance-theatre dramaturgy is the capacity of non-realist drama "to activate a particular quotient of energy, a form of active and holistic knowing, qualitatively different from 'normal' discrete subject/object cognition."[6] Consequently, the dramaturgical focus moved from the characters and action to the creation of multiple referential sites, like in the scene "Gaia on Sale," where the auctioned continents were introduced as Gaia's dismembered and polluted body: "Eyes of the Earth. Origin: The Americas. Sold only as a set. We can sell at $95,000, now at

$100,000, rising to $120,000, $130,000. You wish to try one more, sir? Fair warning. SOLD!"[7] Whether presented in verbal-visual paradoxes or inconsequential, surrealist transitions, the "changing states" in *Ecocentric* behaved similarly to the production of existential and religious subtexts in theatre of the absurd and, onstage, to the ascetic and imaginative staging of "poor theatre" (Jerzy Grotowski) and "holy theatre" (Peter Brook). The *chronotope* in such sacred theatre is characterized by a "sense of flowing" and a "sense of doubleness," in the words of Franc Chamberlain, or as Ralph Yarrow puts it, a "moment when I seem to move outside known configurations."[8] The effect of that liminal and sacred spatiality in the dramaturgy of *Ecocentric* allowed postmodern form and ancient ritual to create a contemporary "eco mystery."

The content of form in dance theatre

The dramatic action in *Ecocentric* followed a spiral composition, which was generally constructed as a sequence of dramatic scenes featuring the contemporary female character-types and folklore-based dance numbers revealing ahistoric female archetypes. This duality of representations is intrinsic for dance theatre and was already encoded in Pina Bausch's productions, which simultaneously underlined the "history of the body" as well as the "mythical body of human totality" in "the confrontation between archaic and absolutely current material within one piece."[9] The dramaturgical role in finding a new idiom for the Earth consisted of tapping into that formalistic quality of *Tanztheater* while also reinstating the double image of body/nature within the conglomerate of other genres and media already included in Overground's postmodern performance: ethno-contemporary dance and singing, multimedia, ritualistic theatre, theatre of images, and epic theatre. Shunning excessive theorization, the dramaturgical research portfolio accounted for the styles and forms involved in Overground's aesthetics in order to identify possible ways by which they could initiate "accidental" analogies between performance and nature as well as stimulate an even broader "ecomimesis," or "nature writing," on stage.[10] By mediating the actor's body, the various aesthetic forms additionally elaborated on the central image of Gaia/Earth, ultimately constructing it in the multidimensional trinity dancer-character-archetype, which encompassed physical/natural, cultural/mimetic, and prehistoric/syncretic identities, respectively. Eventually, the human body itself – its physical presence, cultural variety, and sacred memory – brought up the most complex representation of the Earth as a natural abode, a diversified globe, and a cosmic temple. By observing, guiding, and encouraging the interplay of these three controlling images in the performance, the dramaturg continued to distinguish, channel, and embellish the ecomimesis originating in the fluidity of the dance-story and the polyphonic language of performance, focusing on one of the most important transpositions of meanings in experimental theatre: from the formalistic combination and/or displacement of styles to the content of the final, "received" in the audience text.

In *Ecocentric*, the multiplicity of stage signs freed the literary text from its cultural referentiality, allowing the performance to transcend any didactic, reductionist, politicized, or essentialized concepts of ecology and nature. Procedurally, this deconstructive-reconstructive dramaturgy was similar to that of non-realist play, where the "dramaturg must embrace confusion [and work] to discover the happy accident, the pattern, the meaning in the ink blot."[11] Making a step further into postmodern and postdramatic theatre, the dramaturg also discovered various trans-positions of the subject of nature in the eclectic and "confused" form of Over-ground's performance. The company's "total theatre" aesthetics served as a mirror and a soundboard, rather than a transparent intermediary code, of the story/concept. It determined informative binaries of nature-made and man-made creations by contrasting the live and the mediated via video body of the actor, the real stage props and digital objects, the music sung onstage and the one played in audio recordings, as well as the spoken and written/projected text. Dance and dramatic action further complicated the nature-man relation, as they conveyed the inter-connectedness of archaic (mythological and ritualistic) and contemporary (technological, postmodern) spaces, envisioned as the "vertical" (temporal) and "horizontal" (spatial) axes of existence in some projected images (photo). Ultimately, the dichotomies of natural-artificial and archaic-modern qualities constructed a holistic image of physically and historically evolving Earth. The image of Gaia encompassed the perceptions of our planet as a living cosmic body and as a technologically and multiculturally mani-fested globe. The "Eco-manifesto," written by the dramaturg and published in the production program, reiterated this intricate duplicity and prompted the audiences to actively look for analogs and clues to the meaning of "ecocentrism" on all semantic levels:

> To be "ecocentric" is:
> to awake the sensory experiences of the world from the time before one's social confirmation and conformity;
> to cherish the sacredness of childhood: playing, imagining, naming, learning, feeling, and expressing;
> to develop an ear for the "music" of all languages – human as well as nature's – in order to avoid another Babylonian discord;
> to tune into the rhythm of the universe and recognize the planetary presence and holiness of humankind;
> to tend to our land like we tend to our bodies; to cultivate our bodies like we cultivate our land;
> to speak of nature and humanity in a new, original, contemporary, and expressive language.[12]

In the hybrid of dance theatre and multidisciplinary performance in general, dramaturgy builds on the language of music by guiding the interflow and transposition of artistic languages: the rhythm of the text introduces the rhythm of dance, and, by analogy, dance assumes the referentiality of poetic speech, informing the subject of performance. Drawing on the variety of aesthetic techniques, such dramaturgy orchestrates a limitless production of meaning, paradoxically devising-while-determining the synergy of radically heterogeneous stage signs. Freed of learned protocols and analytical restraints, the borderless dramaturgy of dance theatre struggles to achieve infinite opportunities for meaning-making by activating dynamic transpositions of symbols,

Figure 59.1 Ecocentric by Overground Physical Theatre Company, Manhattan Movement and
Arts Center, 2012

images, and rhythmic patterns. It sanctions a non-hierarchical yet artistically cohesive
structure of performance that thrives on unanticipated polyphonic inflections and
liminal spaces ("rests") typical of ritualistic, holistic, and sacred theatre.

Notes

1 Eugenio Barba and Judy Barba, "The Deep Order Called Turbulence: The Three Faces of
Dramaturgy," *TDR* 44.4 (Winter, 2000): 60.
2 Antonia Katrandjieva and Vessela S. Warner, *Ecocentric*, unpublished script, 2012.
3 Katrandjieva and Warner.
4 Quoted in Bruce Barton, "Navigating Turbulence: The Dramaturg in Physical Theatre,"
Theatre Topics, 15.1 (2005).
5 Barba, 60.
6 Ralph Yarrow, Franc Chamberlain, William S. Haney II, Carl Lavery, and Peter Malekin,
Sacred Theatre, ed. Ralph Yarrow (Bristol and Chicago: Intellect, 2007), 16–17.
7 Katrandjieva and Warner.
8 Yarrow *et al.*, 16.
9 Kay Kirchman, "The Totality of the Body: An Essay on Pina Bausch's Aesthetic," *The Pina
Bausch Sourcebook: The Making of Tanztheater*, ed. Royd Climenhaga (London and New
York: Routledge, 2013), 295.
10 Timothy Morton, *Ecology without Nature: Rethinking Environmental Aesthetics* (Cambridge
and London: Harvard University Press, 2007), 8.
11 Tori Haring-Smith, "Dramaturging Non-Realism: Creating a New Vocabulary," *Theatre
Topics* 13.1 (2003): 52.
12 Vessela S. Warner, "Program Notes," *Ecocentric*, Overground Physical Theatre Company,
Manhattan Movement & Arts Center, New York, June 21–22, 2012, n. p.

60

The role of the dramaturg in the creation of new opera works[1]

Andrew Eggert

The successful development of new work for the opera stage is a complex and often elusive process. Ask anyone who has contributed to the making of a new opera, and they will tell you there is no single formula that works every time. Composers, librettists, directors, designers, and producers who collaborate on new work must always reinvent the process to suit the unique musical and dramatic needs of the piece they are creating. Increasingly, composers and producers have called on the knowledge and experience of a dramaturg – a knowledgeable theatre practioner – to help give direction to the creative process. Whether one of the central members of the creative team (for example the director) or a freelance consultant, the dramaturg can be anyone who helps guide development by serving as advocate for the piece and catalyst for collaboration, as well as editor and sounding board for the authors.

Some opera companies in North America regularly employ dramaturgs to work on new productions of established operas in the repertory. The dramaturg provides research on the historical and cultural context of the opera, helps in the translation or interpretation of words and music, and works with the director to find ways to transform a classic score into an original stage production. The development of new work is different, since the creators are engaged in an ongoing conversation about how to shape a work in progress. But in both cases the ultimate role of the dramaturg remains the same: to focus on the big picture, to think about the overall structure of the work, and to make suggestions that will improve how the piece comes to life on stage.

"The dramaturg can ask the questions that no one else has asked because they are immersed in the process in a very particular way," said Brian Quirt, former president of the Literary Managers and Dramaturgs of the Americas (LMDA), a service organization with over 500 members from a variety of theatrical and literary backgrounds. "Dramaturgs are different [from the other collaborators] in that their responsibility isn't to a single aspect of the creation. Whether dealing with text on the page, a musical played at the piano or in action on the stage in front of you, the dramaturg is there to respond to the ideas that are being expressed and to help find the next step in the process." Quirt works actively as a dramaturg in theatre, dance, and opera, and he values the creative energy generated by collaboration across the disciplines. "It's great that we can begin a conversation between people who do this work in the opera world and the theater world," said Quirt. "The work is similar – we're both telling stories – but the tools that we use can be somewhat different ... It's the kind of crossover that can be particularly rich and productive."

Composer Jake Heggie has built close collaborative relationships with artists who have extensive experience in the theatre world, including stage directors and playwrights. For Heggie, it is important to have the entire creative team on board from the beginning of the process of writing a new opera, since each collaborator brings a different perspective on how to unlock the theatricality of the story. "As the composer, working from my perspective, you spend so much time alone, and it's dangerous if you get too close to the show in the wrong way," said Heggie. "You fall in love with one version of it, or you fall in love with one character, and you want to make sure that everyone gets their due. The dramaturg or director gives me perspective in the same way that the conductor gives me perspective on the score."

In the case of the opera *Dead Man Walking*, the director Joe Mantello took on the role of dramaturg during development by asking questions that Heggie and librettist Terrence McNally had not considered, which led to further revisions to the structure of the first act. These changes addressed both large and small aspects of the storytelling, including what Heggie calls the "emotional thread" of the characters – how the background of their individual lives is told and connected to the dramatic action onstage. Other more detailed changes suggested by Mantello were geared toward the goal of clarity for the audience on many levels: making sure the individual words of the libretto would be understood and that the original set and costume designs would support the dramatic and musical arc of the story. Heggie likes to use workshops to assess the dramaturgical effectiveness of his operas and to open up a dialogue that includes his creative collaborators and the singers who will interpret the opera's characters. His latest opera, *Three Decembers*, premiered as *Last Acts* at Houston Grand Opera in February 2008, directed by Leonard Foglia. The opera, with a libretto by Gene Scheer adapted from a play by McNally, was given a full workshop in December 2007 by San Francisco Opera in preparation for the world premiere production.[2] For Heggie, the workshop was an important final opportunity to confirm that, in his words, "the journey of the piece was clear and balanced among the three characters."

Workshops can also be important during earlier stages in the genesis of a new work. James Leverett, who teaches dramaturgy and dramatic literature at the Yale School of Drama and the Columbia School of the Arts, has participated in a series of five development workshops with the composer Philip Glass and the director JoAnne Akalaitis, who are creating a new music-theatre piece, *The Bacchae*, adapted from the ancient Greek play by Euripides. The work was co-commissioned by Stanford University and the Public Theatre/New York Shakespeare Festival and is a hybrid of spoken theatre and opera. The creators have used the workshops to look at one particular aspect of the storytelling: the role of the chorus and the many functions it serves in the stage production. Leverett sees the workshop as an important time to refine the piece and increase its chances of reaching its intended audience. "One of the things that a dramaturg does is to serve as a kind of first audience as the work is coming into being, and that includes the work as it is being written," said Leverett. "We often have to work in such curtailed circumstances – in terms of time and financial resources – that if you have this process by which a director and composer can have an ongoing sounding board, you are actually increasing the work's likelihood of success on the stage." In the series of workshops for *The Bacchae*, Leverett has played an active dramaturgical role from the very beginning. He has supported the creators in the process of setting the text of the large chorus scenes to music, and his feedback has led to cuts and word changes in the translation. Because these text changes have been made on the spot, Glass has been able to respond by recomposing the music in small ways that accommodate the text and "[m]ake it sharper and sharper," as Leverett said.

Important dramaturgical contributions can be made before composition even begins. The Canadian stage director and dramaturg Kelly Robinson has developed a specific type of workshop that he uses in the early stages of opera development to help composers and librettists reach consensus on the direction and meaning of the story they want to tell. Robinson will lead a workshop of actors who speak the text of the libretto. "With a group of actors, you can immediately change the interpretations, so the composer has a chance to actually hear the text spoken with intention by experts who can quickly change their approach. It becomes a very useful roundtable discussion about meanings," said Robinson. He has conducted many such workshops at the Banff Centre in order to help composer-librettist teams deal with the dramatic reality of the spoken text before the first note of music has been composed.

In Germany, where extensive workshops of new operas are less common than in North America, some composers collaborate with freelance dramaturgs. The German composer Christian Jost has worked with the American dramaturg Minou Arjomand on several opera projects, including *The Arabian Night* and *Hamlet*. For Jost, the collaborative relationship can be very personal, both an intellectual and emotional extension of his own creative work as a composer. "The process of creation is an intimate moment, so talking about it has to do with trust and the thoughts of the other person as well," said Jost. "It is like performing chamber music: You think similarly and you feel similarly, and in the best case you have in the opposite person an extension of your own thoughts." Jost writes his own librettos or adapts existing texts, so his collaborations with Arjomand have focused on the range of source material and sometimes on the structure of the dramatic action. Arjomand has also assisted Jost in working out the unique compositional challenges of adapting sources from both German and English. "Christian and I are similar, and we work so well together because we can appreciate the importance of sitting down and spending time with the book," said Arjomand. Together they have worked on a range of source material, from texts by the German Romantic poet Friedrich Hölderlin for the choral opera *Angst* to the writings of filmmaker Woody Allen for the one-act chamber opera *Death Knocks*.

Many North American opera producers are seeking to give composers, directors, and dramaturgs adequate time for experimentation and discussion. Music-Theatre Group (MTG) is an organization dedicated specifically to supporting new works from the early stages of commission through development to fully staged productions. Producing Director Diane Wondisford emphasizes that no two works have the same needs and that creative teams must be given the necessary time and space before the work is rushed into rehearsal. "It's an exploration," said Wondisford, who considers dramaturgy an important part of her role as creative producer. "We're asking the 'who, what, when, where, why' questions about the material for the first time. One has to be acute and rigorous in the process, and it requires that all of the collaborators share the discoveries each step of the way." In fostering new work, Wondisford has also shown a commitment to bringing together creative teams of composers and writers who do not write primarily for the music-theatre with experienced stage directors who assume the role of dramaturg during the development process. This was the case for the team behind the jazz-opera *Running Man*, the first of several stage collaborations for stage director Diane Paulus, the jazz composer Diedre Murray, and the poet Cornelius Eady.

Music-Theatre Group and the MIT Media Lab developed a new opera entitled *Death and the Powers*, which had its world premiere in Monaco before going on a world tour, including performances at the American Repertory Theater, Chicago Opera Theater, and the Dallas Opera. Composer Tod Machover enlisted former US poet laureate Robert Pinsky to write the libretto. The collaborative team also includes Randy Weiner, who co-authored the story with Pinsky, director Paulus, production designer Alex McDowell, and a team of robot, content, and technology designers from the MIT Media Lab. The project employs cutting-edge music and stage technology to tell the story of one man's life and his attempt to overcome death. Even for an opera that is so avant-garde in musical language and stage technology, much of the dramaturgical inspiration behind the structure of *Death and the Powers* came from working with theatrical texts of the past, in particular the plays *Oedipus at Colonus* and *King Lear*. "There are very few operas, even the great masterpieces, that are wholly original," said Paulus. "I am a great believer that when you are making something new, you are also looking back at older models and stories. The hidden dramaturg in the room is the great theatrical literature of the past that you look at and consult." Paulus emphasizes that the top priority in development is working out the right structure for the piece as a whole – the spine underneath the words, music, and production technology. The creators of *Death and the Powers* drew upon these classic plays to help forge complex relationships between characters. From the structure of *Oedipus at Colonus*, the team found a model for their meditation on death; and *King Lear* provided additional material for the way that the final chapter of life can bring out tensions within a family. Ultimately, the team found their own original perspective on these central themes, but only after a long period of experimentation in which these models provided important dramaturgical inspiration.

The future holds much potential for new directions in the creation and development of new works, especially with collaborations at the institutional level between opera and theatre producers. The Metropolitan Opera and Lincoln Center Theater are charting new territory in their partnership to co-commission new works. By working together, the organizations hope to provide more resources and flexibility to composers and playwrights working in various musical and dramatic styles. The collaboration was an initiative of the Met general manager, Peter Gelb, and is being managed by the company dramaturg, Paul Cremo. André Bishop, artistic director of Lincoln Center Theater, sees the partnership between companies – the first sustained collaboration of its kind between two constituents of Lincoln Center – as a joining of forces from which both sides stand to gain. From his extensive experience fostering new plays and musicals, Bishop hopes the new project will give operas more time to develop, even after they have been through an initial round of workshops. He cited the example of the Broadway musical, which traditionally has several weeks or even months of previews and out-of-town tryouts when the creators can make final changes before the official opening. "Part of the problem with new works in the opera world is that there isn't a lot of rehearsal time," said Bishop. "For something new there has got to be more time." The first collaboration to reach the stage of the Metropolitan Opera was composer Nico Muhly's *Two Boys*, with a libretto by Craig Lucas and directed by Bartlett Sher, in the 2013–14 season.

Cremo hopes the long-term support will give creative artists greater opportunity to experiment and refine their work both musically and theatrically. The proximity of the two organizations as neighbors at Lincoln Center will facilitate an ongoing development process that combines the best of both worlds. "We're inventing something new here, to bring together both the theater-based model and the opera-based model," said Cremo. "Opera boils down to essential emotions that are visceral, and the goal of new work is finding the most sophisticated way to focus those emotions both dramatically and musically."

Whether on the intimate scale of a two-person collaboration or for large-scale projects that bring together the resources of several arts organizations, the dramaturg can be both an active collaborator and a creative inspiration in helping to foster new work of lasting importance.

Notes

1 This article is reprinted from *Opera America Magazine*, April 1, 2008.
2 The opera was commissioned by HGO in association with San Francisco Opera and Cal Performances.

61
Dramaturgy and film

Gerry Potter

Since I first added film and television to my work in theatre, over ten years ago, there has never been a time when the dramaturgical skills I've learned in the theatre have not been of profound and immediate use. If we define dramaturgy as a broad set of activities that may include researching, pattern-finding and structuring, questioning, and reflecting in order to help artists do their best work, as well as creatively educating the public about works of dramatic art, then film dramaturgy has long been and still is widely employed. Since the night in 1896 when the Lumière brothers, in one of the first films projected for the public, terrified Parisian audiences with that steamy train entering a station, the above activities have been much prized and practiced in the motion picture world.[1] Yet the term "dramaturgy" is seldom used in film and the official title "film dramaturg" doesn't exist. There are both genuine differences and unnecessary barriers between the media of film and theatre. Superficial differences include those of terminology, deeper differences, those of professional practice and of medium, including the live vs. recorded and projected or screened nature of the performance. A few barriers to the free flow of artists and ideas persist, like an invisible curtain, propped up by oversimplified assumptions about the respective media. There is a need for greater understanding between those working in theatre and film and for more opportunities for dramaturgs and other artists to move between worlds. These opportunities, once created, will in turn release the immense potential for sharing ideas and for new synergies. As new digital media are developed there will also be chances to jointly explore their dramaturgical possibilities. On both sides of the curtain, we have much to learn from each other.

If a theatre dramaturg were to explore the world of film, the first type of dramaturgical practice encountered in the motion picture world might be research. As it is in theatrical dramaturgy, research is a primary activity for screenwriters, directors, actors, designers, cinematographers, editors, composers, and craft departments in motion pictures. For one of the best examples of the role of this research, our theatre dramaturg might watch the special features on the *Lord of the Rings*, extended edition (2006).[2] Here the extraordinary extent of the dramaturgical research applied to Tolkien and his works, to medieval armor, ways of creating scale, special and visual effects, visual character design, and more can be discovered.

In the film world, as in theatre, artists and craft departments research print sources such as books and newspapers. Film artists especially value visual sources such as paintings, photography, and earlier films, in order to plan the visual style of a film. This planned look will in turn determine length of shots, format of film or video, camera choice, camera rigs, lenses and filters, studio vs. location shots, live action vs. computer graphics, editing styles and rhythms, as well as lighting, sets, and costumes. All these choices affect the meaning and impact of a film and need to be informed by effective research.

A second skill film dramaturgy employs is the ability to find and help create structure. Film directors need pattern recognition, structuring, and story-shaping skills in order to make shooting and editing choices. These skills are essential because the footage captured, even in fiction film, rarely conforms precisely to what the screenwriter wrote or imagined, yet it must be shot, cut, and re-arranged in an artful way. The dramaturgy of editing, in particular, is rarely appreciated by the general public, but, as Orson Welles observed, "the whole eloquence of cinema is that it's achieved in the editing room."[3] The need for these skills grows geometrically when editing the massive amounts of unscripted footage shot in documentaries. Well-known US theatre dramaturg Morgan Jenness believes documentary film editing is a "natural fit" for theatre dramaturgs and has worked as a dramaturgical/edit advisor with Josh Fox on his documentary films *Memorial Day* (2008), *Gasland* (2010), and *Gasland 2* (2013).[4] Jenness also describes a conversation she had with renowned documentary filmmaker Frederick Wiseman: "Fred Wiseman advised me to become a film editor – which he said was really dramaturgy."[5]

A feeling for structure is, of course, useful in the dramaturgy of new works. New screenplay dramaturgy, referred to simply as script consulting, and usually involving "development," plays a leading role in the film industry. In Canada some well-known script consultants and story editors are Amnon Buchbinder, Tom Shoebridge, Scot Morison, and former theatre director and dramaturg Ken Chubb. In the US, major screenwriting consultants and teachers who have written books and digital guides include Syd Field, Robert McKee, John Truby, Michael Hague, Chris Vogler, and theatre director/professor Linda Seger. Though they don't call their work dramaturgy, these film dramaturgs have exerted considerable influence on screenwriting and both the film and television industries.

These screenwriting teachers and script consultants are often more prescriptive than theatre dramaturgs, actively promoting the use of classic story structure. Field, McKee, Seger, and Hague, as well as Chubb in Canada, follow in the Aristotelian tradition, highlighting the importance of high-stakes conflict, both inner and external.[6] While all of these dramaturgs also encourage screenwriters to work on characterization, theme, and visual storytelling, their focus is on dramatic action and story. Field is known for breaking down screenplay structure into a "three-act paradigm," with an approximate percentage of screen time allocated for each act; he claims to borrow this structure from theatre. As in the theatrical tradition of the well-made play, once taught by George Pierce Baker and others, most of these film dramaturgs champion the redemptive melodrama. In this model an engaging but slightly flawed central character commits to a soul-testing conflict against powerful forces of opposition and changes profoundly through the struggle and the choices and discoveries made.

A few film dramaturgs take a different approach. As author of *The Writer's Journey: Mythic Structure for Writers* (2007), Chris Vogler, like George Lucas in the *Star Wars* films, has been deeply influenced by cultural anthropologist Joseph Campbell's writings about myth. Vogler concentrates on the journey or mythic quest structure and encourages screenwriters to make creative use of archetypal characters. Like Vogler, John Truby is interested in archetypal story structures, but he also proposes a 22-step "organic structure" and suggests Field's three-act paradigm is too mechanical. Truby's analysis emphasizes the moral dimensions of characters' actions. Originally inspired by the work of Northrop Frye, the title of Truby's book, *The Anatomy of Story* (2007), owes something to Frye's famous *Anatomy of Criticism* (1957). For an even less orthodox dramaturgical voice, we might look to Ken Dancyger and Jeff Rush's book, *Alternative Scriptwriting: Successfully Breaking the Rules* (2007), which explores several alternatives to the three-act structure.

The film world also encompasses not-for-profit development centers. US film has centers such as Sundance, and Canadian film has Praxis, Canadian Film Centre, and National Screen Institute, among others. Each supports the development of screenplays in different ways, but most use group workshops, testing works in readings by actors and discussions with other screenwriters, directors, and script consultants, all serving as unofficial dramaturgs.

The development phase of a new script is often more formalized in film than in theatre. Hollywood studios and production companies make extensive use of development departments to read and recommend scripts and to work with writers. The successive phases of evolution of a script are often contracted separately, proceeding from options to treatments, then successive drafts, so that the producer can drop the contract after any phase. Production companies, particularly in television, may ask writers for interim products such as log lines, a sentence or two describing the central character's journey through a story; step outlines, a scene-by-scene description of the main action; beat sheets, similar but broken down by dramatic action rather than scene; and treatments, an evocative prose description of the dramatic action, with little or no dialogue. Because of the huge cost of producing, these companies are extremely careful about what they are investing in and will stop funding a project quickly if, at any phase, they feel it will not be commercially successful. Of course, dramaturgy informs the selection of film scripts and writers, the guiding of the development process, and even the decision-making on whether scripts, in each successive phase, will be funded to the next phase.

We should also consider the dramaturgy practiced in filmmakers' and videomakers' co-operatives, such as the Alabama Filmmakers Co-operative in the US or FAVA (Film and Video Arts Society – Alberta) in Canada. Through their courses, workshops, inexpensive access to equipment, and ready supply of expertise and fellow filmmakers, these centers make it possible for many screenwriters and filmmakers to learn their art form and to create artist-driven works of film, video, and digital media art. Through encouragement, supportive questioning, and critiquing of one another's work, co-op members practice film dramaturgy.

The role of dramaturg as educator and developer of audiences is practiced in many forms and at many levels of the film world. Hollywood marketing departments, for example, employ a certain amount of dramaturgy in the process of making trailers and seeking out the right audience for a work. However, a more comprehensive audience education is pursued in the not-for-profit area. Film festivals now operate in almost every major city in North America and Europe. These festivals, along with film societies such as Metro Cinema in Edmonton and cinematheques, such as Cinémathèque Québécoise in Montreal, led by dramaturg-curators, help to promote dialogue between the public and filmmakers and assist audiences in understanding film as a changing art form.

It is clear that there are myriad types of dramaturgy practiced in film. But why don't dramaturgs move more easily between these two worlds? As noted earlier, one barrier to communication is terminology. In film and television, dramaturgs may be called researchers, script consultants, story editors, script editors, programmers, curators, head writers, show runners, or, occasionally, executive producers. Some of these different titles represent different responsibilities, while others simply arise from a different vocabulary.

A greater obstacle to exchange between the two media lies in stereotypes held by many in each medium about the other. These are a few of the simplistic differences sometimes cited, often expressed as binaries, between the two media: film is visual/ theatre is verbal; film and television are commercial/theatre is for a rarefied art audience; film is realistic/theatre is stylized; film is formulaic/theatre is organic and innovative in form. While it is true that fictional narrative film is a recorded and screened art and theatre a live one, and that film has the technical capacity to create and manipulate visual information in a more fluid and complex manner, there are few other real differences. Yet oversimplifications abound, even among critics and scholars. As scholar Robert Knopf notes, "most scholar-critics who favor the strict division between theatre and film define cinema on the basis of its silent roots, as image with sound added, and theatre as 'plays', language-strong … But either definition is descriptive of the majority practice, not the inherent qualities of each."[7]

Better communication and understanding may eventually break these stereotypes down. As Knopf points out, this understanding needs to arise from a differentiation between common practice in a medium and that medium's actual qualities, potentials, and limitations. Once we've separated conventions from inherent qualities, we can begin to see both genuine differences between these two media and their commonalities. Such clarity may arise as more artists, producers, and technicians expand their field of work to the other medium or co-operate on the increasing number of inter-disciplinary works. Finally, and counter-intuitively, more cross-media exchange between practitioners of these two well-established art forms may result from the evolution of new digital technology.

Several aspects of this technological evolution may be of special interest to dramaturgs. One is the increasing demand, arising partly from social networking's popularity, for interactivity with user/audience members. We now have the technology to allow this interaction in digitally created and displayed dramatic stories and in cross-platform auxiliary web material frequently created to complement these stories. We might note that the dominant digital entertainment medium using inter-activity is the computer/video gaming industry, which is now economically larger than the film industry. Gaming companies, long-dominated by computer programmers, increasingly recognize a need for richer stories, fuller characters, and more dramatic and complex narrative structures, and are calling on dramaturgs and playwrights to help. For example, one prominent gaming company, Bioware, creators of the award-winning *Baldur's Gate* and *Mass Effect* games, now employs both a dramaturg-playwright and a dramaturg-screenwriter to work on character development. Other recent technological changes include the increasing use of 3-D formats in film and television and the expanding range of modes of delivery of dramatic material, as more people experience films, television, and web series through the internet on laptops, tablets, and smart phones. Because live theatre involves both interactivity with an audience and expression in three dimensions, all these digital developments raise the question: who better to assist screen producers and gaming companies in exploring these areas than theatre artists and, especially, dramaturgs?

For those theatre dramaturgs interested in expanding into film, gaming, or cross-platform work, we might consider a few strategies. A necessary first step would be to get filmmaking experience, working on actual productions. Second, a potential film dramaturg needs to develop an understanding of cinematic storytelling, by watching films and studying film history. Next, a dramaturg moving into film should renew an acquaintance with classic story structures, techniques, and tools. Finally, film dramaturgs need a basic understanding of the technologies of film, video, gaming, and new digital forms of screen drama.

To summarize: dramaturgy is alive, well, and much practiced in the film medium, in the areas of research, script consulting, editing, and audience education. There remain a few barriers to the free flow of personnel from one medium to the other, particularly for those who see themselves as theatre dramaturgs or, alternatively, screenplay consultants. Yet, if we can dispel the stereotypes and mistaken assumptions, it is clear that more dramaturgs working solely in either film or theatre will pass through the invisible curtain and, in doing so, bring enormous skill, knowledge, and creativity to their sister medium and to new media, yet to be invented.

Notes

1 *Arrival of a Train at La Ciotat*, directed by Auguste and Louis Lumière, 1895, Paris, Société Lumière.
2 *The Lord of the Rings*, special extended edition, directed by Peter Jackson (2003; Los Angeles: New Line Home Entertainment, 2006), DVD.
3 Orson Welles, quoted in Michael Ondaatje, *The Conversations* (Toronto: Vintage Canada, 2002), 194.
4 Morgan Jenness, a renowned US dramaturg, was presented in 2003 with an Obie Award Special Citation for Longtime Support of Playwrights.
5 Morgan Jenness, e-mail message to author, May 16, 2013.
6 Michael Tierno's book, *Aristotle's Poetics for Screenwriters* (New York: Hyperion, 2002) is a good quick guide to Aristotle's observations about drama, as they might be applied to film.
7 Robert Knopf, *Theatre and Film: a Comparative Anthology* (New Haven, CT: Yale University Press, 2005), 15.

62

Phronesis for robots

(Re)covering dramaturgy as an interdiscipline

Michael Chemers

What is digital media, and what role does dramaturgy play in it?[1]

Dramaturgy has an unexpectedly central role to play in artificial systems of various kinds and a unique potential to unite disciplines (including mechanical engineering, sociology, psychology, cultural studies, aesthetics, and performance) long held to be discrete. The nature of theatrical performance is changing radically due to the prevalence of new technologies, and theatre must adapt to and indeed predict the coming of those machines that now seem impossible but in five or ten years will be yawn-provokingly commonplace. Addressing the questions of how new technologies might collude with dramaturgy is becoming more urgent with each passing product launch. The answers, as might be expected, are complex, offering not so much an easy solution as a difficult process. Perhaps less predictably, many of the answers to this futuristic problem lie in the distant past. Once again we must ask the omnipresent question: "What exactly IS a dramaturg?"

Phronesis is one of five "intellectual virtues" that Aristotle discusses in Book 6 of his 350 BCE moral handbook *Nichomachean Ethics*.[2] The other virtues are: art, which Aristotle describes as a "capacity to make" (sec. 4) according to rational principles; "scientific wisdom" (sec. 3), which is knowledge derived from the rational contemplation of first principles; "philosophical wisdom," which is knowledge of things that are "remarkable, admirable, difficult, and divine, but useless" (sec. 7); and "intuitive reason," which is the ability to grasp first principles without training (sec. 6). *Phronesis* is "practical wisdom," which includes everything one must know in order to live a good and harmonious life. In section 5, Aristotle writes that *phronesis* is a rational deliberative quality that is employed to advance the greater good for oneself and one's society in general. It is a mediator between the universal and the particular. It seeks truth and knowledge not for their own sake, as philosophy does, nor to solve some scientific problem, but specifically for the creation and maintenance of happiness and harmony for humanity. It may employ scientific, artistic, or philosophical wisdom to bring this about, but it is neither science, nor art, nor philosophy in and of itself.

I have argued[3] that it is productive to view dramaturgy as such an endeavor of *phronesis*, rather than as an art or a science. The goal of the dramaturg is to employ knowledge gleaned from study and critical engagement in the creation of works of aesthetic power, and that power is best used when it is devoted to a particular end: the cultivation of the understanding of human suffering in the audience. On this, the luminary dramaturgs of history seem to be in full accord; Aristotle in his *Poetics* writes of the importance of Tragedy to solicit *eleos*, a term which he defines in his book *Rhetoric* as "a kind of pain in the case of an apparent destructive or painful harm *in one not deserving to encounter it*, which one might expect oneself, or one of one's own, to suffer, and this when it seems near."[4] Horace in his *Ars Poetica*, Bharata Muni in his *Natyasastra*, Hrosvitha, Boilieu, Beaumarchais, and Lessing all argue the same – the greatest asset and the highest aspiration of theatre is the fostering of understanding of the suffering of others. The emphasis is on *understanding* of human suffering more than on any specific fellow feeling: empathy, perhaps, rather than sympathy.

Ancient empathy, then, ought to be our guiding principle as we move forward into the digital future. *Phronesis* is the trait of bridge-builders, not only bridges of empathy between people but of collaboration between disciplines. Lessing's mightiest contribution to theatre art was to re-define the theatre as a method of inquiry into matters of conscience and social justice, and dramaturgy plays a critical role in that. As we in the last two centuries united dramatic aesthetics with emerging trends in psychology, sociology, and political science, now we are challenged to build bridges to mechanical engineering, computer science, game design, and digital imaging.

What, then, exactly is digital media? The term refers to a wide range of cultural products that have been enabled by the explosive development of computing technologies. Initially we might imagine video games, online entertainment like "webisodes," and collaborative web projects like Wikipedia and the Internet Classics Archive. But that is just the tip of the digital iceberg; digital media must also include interactive films, digital literature, and, perhaps most strikingly, artificial intelligence and social robotics.

Noah Wardrip-Fruin has argued convincingly that the prevalence of new works of art that are predicated on the use of advanced computational process requires the development of a new, broader critical apparatus. Any apparatus employed to evaluate digital media most productively must be conceived more widely than those we usually employ for criticism of traditional literary or performance art. For one thing, evaluation of digital media must include analysis not merely of the cultural product itself but the sociological effects of the performance on its audience; although this is certainly not a new idea in theatre scholarship, the potential real-world members of a digital "audience" represent a very wide spectrum not only of individuals but also of social contexts.[5]

Wardrip-Fruin notes further that digital media is capable of, indeed takes particular delight in, modeling circumstances that are not possible in the world of real physics:

> For example, in my own collaborative work I take advantage of processes supporting room-sized virtual reality displays in order to create the illusions of words (from short fictions about memory) peeling loose from paragraphs, flocking around the audience, and flying back (or breaking apart) when hit by an audience member's hand. The exact details of this experience are different every time, but it always unfolds within parameters determined by authored

processes, and we can see authorial expression in these processes as surely as in those meant to invoke elements of the everyday world.[6]

Artists working in digital media come up with new ways of using this technology every day, and it seems that digital media regularly provokes astonishing new ways of shattering our preconceived notions about what separates now and then, here and there, self and other, the past and the future.

Certainly, then, there is much that is new and exciting about digital media's use of cutting-edge technology, focus on interactivity, and polymorphousness, but since digital media leans strongly towards performance events which are undoubtedly "authored," which is to say *scripted* by a single authorial figure or a collaborating group, we may entertain the notion that digital media is not, in fact, a new form of artistic expression but merely the most recent flavor of something very ancient. If this is true, then the application of dramaturgical principles and practices to digital media products is perhaps not so much of a stretch. Dramaturgical thought remains central to the process of dramatic storytelling no matter what the medium may be.

There is one key trend in digital media, however, that demands a fresh perspective. Authorship of digital media leans significantly, and increasingly, towards a management of *narrative systems* rather than the plotting of single narrative arcs. Wardrip-Fruin calls these "author-crafted processes."[7]

Although uncommon, this condition too is not unknown to theatre history. We might bookend the discussion by considering the outdoor festivals of the middle ages, when a patron could wander through a given town watching the short plays that described the great moments of biblical history in any particular order; and on the other end we would look to the experimental theatre of the 1970s, when such authors as Fornés and Gambaro cultivated an "open" narrative in plays like *Fefu and Her Friends* and *Information for Foreigners*. The tradition continues with the 2011 production of Punchdrunk theatre's *Sleep No More* in which the audience is free to wander through simultaneous interactive stagings to create a unique narrative arc. But such a choose-your-own-adventure structure is rather more the rule for digital media products than the exception. Most digital media attempts to generate a Borgesian "Garden of Forking Paths" that the user can explore, and this is a metaphor that I have elsewhere[8] relied upon to discuss the *process* of theatre-making itself, which is repetitive (even ritualistic), redundant, multidimensional, contradictory (even paradoxical), full of strange surprises, and in desperate need of a skilled navigator.

Perhaps we might at this point describe an old concept in a new way by coining the phrase *systemic dramaturgy*, in this case using "dramaturgy" in the sense of the aesthetic architecture of the piece. A systemic dramaturgy would take into account that the goal of the author(s) is to define the characteristics and parameters of a web of possible interactions in which the audience itself is the protagonist, making the critical choices that define the nature of the character and the arc of the narrative experience.

What would a systemic dramaturgy look like? I propose a scheme:

1 Operational logics: A term I borrow from Wardrip-Fruin,[9] operational logics refers to the interaction of the ingredients of the system and the predictable

patterns that emerge from that interaction. At a basic level, it has to do with the way in which space and matter are represented virtually – how two objects might "touch," for instance, or how a robot might indicate that it is listening or thinking – but it also governs the psychological relationship between the system and the user as well as the physical. The revelation of story elements throughout the interaction is critical to all of these relationships; the story both controls the parameters of interactions and guides the user to a successful interactive experience. Questions of operational logics, then, are ultimately aesthetic questions and require aesthetic philosophy as profoundly as they require computer programming.

2   Systemic dramatic action: Action, the raw material playwrights employ to map plot, character, given circumstances, conflict, theatricality, aesthetics, and theme, is as intrinsic to digital media as it is to theatre. A systemic dramaturgy starts with an understanding of theatrical action as a tool for storytelling, and new media is often dependent on its storytelling for success. This appears to be the case not only for games and interactive videos but also for robots and other autonomous intelligences; should they have their own stories to tell, the possibilities for increasing an empathic connection with the user are magnified.

3   Systemic dramaturgical structure: In many forms of new media, the audience is also the protagonist, capable of making his or her own choices. Since choices compose character, and since character is integral to plot, many traditional writers are uncertain how to proceed when the protagonist is a free agent. One of the great challenges presented to new media developers is the creation of a meaningful story in the absence of such control. Critical to effective storytelling in digital media is a deep understanding of how dramatic stories unfold, how to make use of (or even invent) new storytelling techniques that are adapted to the operational logics of the piece, and a broad understanding of audience response theory and psychology.

4   Collaborative scripting: As in devised and documentary theatre,[10] the script for a digital media event does not exist a priori to the production process. Usually, game developers work in concert to develop a script as they build the operational parameters of a game, perhaps starting only with a story or a setting. Roboticists develop personalities and backstories for robotic characters as they build the robots themselves. An individual writer is rare; even in cases when there is only one writer rather than a team, he or she operates in close collaboration with the designers. Here the dramaturg's skills of script development, asking critical questions, and general navigation of the collaborative process become central to a successful outcome.

5   Theatrical integration of design: Like a theatrical event, digital media products employ visuals and sound, often including costume, set, lighting, music, sound effects, and all the other trappings of live performance. Someone on the production team needs to be thinking about all the ways in which these elements work with the plot and development of character to support the play's overall themes and aesthetic goals.

6   The Eliza effect: Game developers know "Eliza" as an early example of a simulated personality. Eliza was a computer program designed to mimic a therapist; an algorithm alone dictated her responses (which consisted mainly of reparsing the

statements of the user), but people who interacted with the program insisted that Eliza was an independent intelligence with her own motives and an intrinsic psychotherapeutic wisdom. As it happens, humans are quite prone to perceive computer intelligences as possessing far greater depth, complexity, and emotional content than they possibly could. I have argued that this susceptibility is due to an evolutionary imperative towards empathy that is manifested in all sorts of interactions between humans and nonhumans.[11] It is such cognitive dissonance that theatre artists from all ages have sought to foster; it, or something like it, is what Coleridge called "suspension of disbelief." It is that suspension that makes the empathic work of performance possible. Again, the dramaturg is on familiar ground in fostering a sustained Eliza engagement.

When digital media events employ effective dramaturgy, the results are noticeable. A 2008 review of the video game *Grand Theft Auto IV* noted a significant change from the earlier iterations of the franchise: the introduction of some level of empathy for the victims of the user's digital rampage. This is a change in the dramaturgy of the video game, owing to increased depth of plot and character, and the reviewer calls this dramaturgical change "legit."[12] There is at least a whiff of Tragedy about it, that ancient tool for the cultivation of compassion, for virtual lives corrupted and cut short, to be sure; but we might ask whether Oedipus and Agamemnon are not similarly virtual, made more of information and idea than substance, whose stories give us the opportunity to experience vicariously the thrill of deviance and the horror of the punishment that follows – an experience that, dramaturgs have argued for centuries, makes us better people in the real world.

There is a role, a grand role, for dramaturgy to play in digital media, but like everything else dramaturgs undertake, as we plan out this role we must take a measured approach and remember that our struggle towards *phronesis* is neither an art nor a science, but a bridge between them.

Notes

1 With gratitude to colleagues who were generous with their time and knowledge on this piece: James Harding, Robin Kirk, Michael Matteas, Jane Pinckard, Aaron Reed, Adam Versenyí, and Noah Wardrip-Fruin.

2 Aristotle, "Nicomachean Ethics by Aristotle," *The Internet Classics Archive*, 2009, available online at http://classics.mit.edu/Aristotle/nicomachaen.html, accessed March 26, 2013. Originally published as *Nicomachean Ethics*, trans. W. D. Ross (Lexington, KY: World Library Classics, 2009).

3 Michael Chemers, *Ghost Light: An Introductory Handbook for Dramaturgy* (Carbondale: Southern Illinois University Press, 2009), 5–6, 11, 13, 123.

4 This from his *Rhetoric* 2.8, 1385b13–16, trans. David Konstan and Stavroula Kiritsi in "From Pity to Sympathy: Tragic Emotions across the Ages," *Athens Dialogues*, 2012, available online at http://athensdialogues.chs.harvard.edu/cgi-bin/WebObjects/athensdialogues.woa/wa/dist?dis=46, accessed March 18, 2013, italics mine.

5 Noah Wardrip-Fruin, *Expressive Processing* (Cambridge, MA: MIT Press, 2009), 2.

6 Wardrip-Fruin, 4.

7 Wardrip-Fruin, 3–4.

8 In Chemers, *Ghost Light*, 7–9. Pursuing the notion of the Garden of Forking Paths as a new media metaphor, see N. Monfort, "Introduction to *The Garden of Forking Paths*," *The New*

Media Reader, eds. Noah Wardruip-Fruin and Nick Monfort (Cambridge, MA: MIT Press, 2003), 29. See also in the same volume Lev Manovich, "New Media from Borges to HTML," 13–25.

9 Wardrip-Fruin, 13–14.

10 See Chemers, *Ghost Light*, 133–40.

11 Michael Chemers, "Like unto a Lively Thing: Social Robots and Theatre History," *Performance and Technology*, ed. Kara Reilly (Basingstoke: Palgrave Macmillan, 2013).

12 Hillary Goldstein, "Grand Theft Auto IV: Special Edition Review," *IGN*, April 29, 2008, available online at http://www.ign.com/articles/2008/04/29/grand-theft-auto-iv-special-edition-review?page=1, accessed August 13, 2013.

63

Dramaturgical design of the narrative in digital games[1]

Klaus P. Jantke

Dramaturgy is the design of emotional experience. For digital games that are intended to tell a story, game design includes anticipation of the players' experiences, which will lead to excitement, fascination, thrill, perhaps to immersion and flow. What players will experience takes place over time. Events that happen are linearly ordered and those that may potentially happen form a partially ordered space, the game's story space. Dramaturgical game design is the anticipation of varying experiences and their thoughtful arrangement in a partially ordered space of events that players may possibly experience when playing the game. The approach particularly applies to those digital games that bear the potentials of telling a story.

Motivation and introduction

Game dramaturgy is the design of emotional experience that will take place when humans engage in game playing. By its very nature, dramaturgical design takes place prior to game playing. In game design, one anticipates the potential future experiences of human players who will engage in playing the game currently under development. Planning – whether deductive, inductive, abductive, or in any other algorithmic way – means to foresee the timely order of events which will possibly happen in the future. From a structural perspective, planning means the setup of a partially ordered space of potential events. From the same structural perspective, game playing means finding some way through this story space. "Fundamentally, stories are sequences of events, each of which involves some form of action."[2] The crucial occurrence of time in storytelling is the order in which events happen.

The art of dramaturgical design is to construct the story space in such a way, according to the authors' intentions, that players going along such a way experience the game play as exciting, fascinating, frightening, or amusing, for example. The present chapter introduces *inductive plan generation* into the practice of dramaturgical design for digital games. This perspective is new to games design investigations. *Story space* and *storyboarding* are key prerequisite concepts.

The ambitious task of anticipating human game-playing behavior is well described by Andrew Stern, who claims that "the first wish that most players, developers and researchers originally feel when first encountering and considering interactive story, is the implicit promise to the player to be able to directly affect the plot of the story, taking it in whatever direction they wish."[3] Although every individual story that unfolds during game play appears as a linear sequence of events, the game design must foresee a potentially large variety of arrangements of actions in time. Potentially occurring events form a partially ordered space which may be visualized as a usually rather complex directed graph.

Now that we have a fundamental idea of what time in storytelling games might be – a partial order as long as events are only prepared to possibly happen and a linear order as soon as game play takes place – we may go and exploit time for dramaturgical design.[4] The present research relies on Jesper Juul's seminal work,[5] which reflects the structural clarity of Chatman's earlier investigations,[6] but the deeper insights into time as elaborated by Sir Arthur Eddington[7] are also taken seriously. Time – so to speak – does not exist; it is an abstraction.[8]

Time in digital games

Which time concepts do we need when dealing with digital games that bear the potentials of telling a story? It depends. Studies on the effects of motion pictures – seen as a precursor to the present field of interest – range from an artistic perspective[9] to neurophysiology.[10] It seems that for digital games comparable investigations do not yet exist. The Xbox 360 game BRAID has been praised in the media for its innovative treatment of time. BRAID is mostly a Jump 'n' Run game. There are numerous opportunities for the player to lose her virtual life. The new quality of game playing in BRAID is that the player has the possibility to turn back the wheel of time. But what does this mean precisely? The answer is complicated by the fact that the possibilities of manipulating the game time change with increasing levels. It seems that the concepts of controlling time are becoming more and more sophisticated. To say it here in advance, this is not really the case. More complex time manipulation options are followed by those that are simpler. It obviously needs some scientific conceptualization to make the essentials of the game explicit. In another game, SHADOW OF DESTINY, it is the player's task to change the past such that a murder she just experienced does not take place the next moment when the same critical point of virtual game world time is passed again. One of the occurring patterns is that the murder has a precondition, which has been established earlier in time. For illustration, a murderer hiding behind a tree depends on the tree to hide behind and, thus, depends on the earlier action of planting the tree.

All the dramaturgy rests upon the ordering of events – the key concept of time in SHADOW OF DESTINY, in BRAID, and in a large number of other high-quality digital games. In the simplest cases, there is a clearly distinguished set of actions that may be performed when playing the games. Those actions may be performed by a single player, by several players, or by the digital game, i.e. by a computer system. What is taken into account depends on the scientific interest driving our investigations.

In another game, THE SECRET FILES: TUNGUSKA, a point and click adventure, players have to solve a large number of varying problems which all follow the same pattern. There are four main actions to be performed in every one of these cases: preparation, trapping, response, solution. Everything begins with some "preparation" to find out how to set a snare for the player's adversary (called "trapping"). The "response" is the adversary's reaction or the reaction of other virtual characters to the player's activity, which leads to a "solution" to the current problem. The player always has to investigate the situation carefully to find out what to do. In one case, putting a cigarette in the right place; in another case, manipulating a newspaper works as a trap. The ordering of activities according to the game mechanics, which, hopefully, reflects an entertaining dramaturgical design, leads to the concept of a story space.

Stories are partially ordered spaces of events. Stories evolve over time during game playing when new events are entering the story space and new relations of time dependence are becoming known. This is a crucial point for understanding what it means to experience a story when playing a digital game. In sophisticated games, it may happen that there are events recognized by one player, but overlooked by another. Those players, necessarily, experience different stories even when performing completely identical sequences of actions. This does not necessarily provide events in a chronological order with regard to time in the virtual world.

Here is an illustration. In a criminal story, you – your avatar – may talk to some virtual character who tells you about a murder that happened sometime earlier in the virtual game time of the virtual world. From the one perspective, there are two events: the talk and the murder. From the other perspective, if you are not interested in recording and investigating events such as talks, you may confine yourself to the consideration of just one event: the murder. It is an obviously interesting and often very important question to decide what shall be seen as an event and taken into account and what not. However, this fundamental question is not further discussed here. Instead, we focus on the issue of time. In the present example, the murder is an event that took place in the past. The event has to be inserted into the totality of events recognized so far. It might easily happen that it is not completely clear how this new event relates to several others that have entered the story space earlier. Formally speaking, the story space becomes only partially ordered. In other words, although game playing is seen as being linear, the story does not evolve linearly because events come up in an unordered manner. In fact, the way in which (knowledge about) events come(s) up is an issue of dramaturgy.[11] Dramaturgical design deals, very abstractly speaking, with the arrangement of game playing activities which allow for an appealing evolution of story spaces.

The JOSTLE & GORGE case

Let's take the game JOSTLE[12] as a basis to investigate issues of dramaturgical design. The practical goal is to develop a digital game. One of the game's purposes is to illustrate game intelligence. Children have been introduced to the game and have been enabled to control the NPC (non-player characters) intelligence. In such a way, the game may be demystified and children may enjoy the power of being in control of complex IT processes – a step towards media and technology competence.

Based on JOSTLE, another educational game, GORGE,[13] has been developed. In this game, the process of dramaturgical design proceeds as follows:

1 Think about what effects or affects you are aiming for.
2 Design the general ideas of a digital game in which the effects you are interested in might possibly show.
3 Choose terms to formalize sequences of game play.
4 Determine sequences of interaction, i.e. game play, likely to support the envisaged goal.
5 Develop some qualitative game idea possible for allowing those sequences.
6 Design a related game mechanics such that the target sequences of interaction you are focusing on occur when playing the game.

The following enumeration of practical application steps refers to the process model of dramaturgical design:

1 Players shall be forced to decide between friendly and aggressive behaviors. The behavior players shall be quite easy to identify such that human players may naturally experience different characters and respond accordingly. We want them, roughly speaking, to love or hate their playmates.

For the purpose of research and experimentation, the design should be as simple as possible.

2 The key idea is that of a "gorge" interrupting a game track. Players cannot pass a gorge unless another player willing to take sacrifices has stepped into the gorge before.
3 Every player is controlling several characters. The game proceeds in turns. A player roles a dice and chooses one of her characters to be moved forward as many steps as the dice shows.

Dichotomy of storyboarding and planning

The peculiarity of inductive plan generation – in contrast to deductive planning – is the absence of any concept such as executability. In conventional deductive planning, one may (logically) prove the executability of a plan being generated. In contrast, in dynamic environments conditions may change during plan execution such that after a certain number of actions have been performed, it turns out that the remaining part of the plan is infeasible.

Future dramaturgical design will take benefit from the inductive perspective at anticipated behavior. The dynamics of advanced digital games that are able to tell a variety of stories will lead to more dynamic variation of planned behaviors. Nowadays, storyboarding is mostly conventional. In the future, advanced storyboarding will become inductive plan generation introducing more dynamics into the story spaces.

Storyboard interpretation technology

Story spaces seen as partially ordered sets of events provide the essential information for implementing digital games that bear the potential of telling a story. Thus, story spaces are storyboards of a bunch of diverging and possibly partially converging sequences of actions performed by human players and by the digital game system. Storyboards are thoroughly digital including all necessary assets such as cut scenes, audio, digital objects including 3D objects, pictures, text, and the like stored in an RDF database. The most recent innovation is named Storyboard Interpretation Technology. In a digital game implemented accordingly, the storyboard is sitting outside the game in a database. During game play, the game is running, so to speak, along the storyboard and reading what to do. The potential is enormous. One may simply change the storyboard in the database to allow for varying game play. In educational settings, one may try out varying pedagogical patterns. Best effects and affects may be explored by experimenting with variations of digital storyboards interpreted by the game engine.

Notes

1 This article is an excerpt from a longer paper entitled "Dramaturgical Design of the Narrative in Digital Games: AI Planning of Conflicts in Non-Linear Spaces of Time," which was presented at the 2009 IEEE Symposium on Computational Intelligence and Games. Reprinted with the permission of the author.

2 D. Thue, V. Bulitko, and M. Spetch, "Making Stories Player-Specific: Delayed Authoring in Interactive Storytelling," in *Interactive Storytelling*, U. Spierling and N. Szilas, eds. (Paris: Springer Verlag, 2008): 230–41.

3 A. Stern, "Embracing the Combinatorial Explosion: A Brief Prescription for Interactive Story R&D," in *Interactive Storytelling*, U. Spierling and N. Szilas, eds. (Paris: Springer Verlag, 2008): 1–5.

4 K. P. Jantke, "A Closer Look at Time in Digital Games," *Erzählformen im Computerspiel: Zur Medienmorphologie digitaler Spiele*, J. Sorg and J. Venus, eds. transcript, 2009.

5 J. Juul, "Introduction to Game Time," in *First Person. New Media as Story, Performance and Game*, N. Wardrip-Fruin and P. Harrigan, eds. (Boston: MIT Press, 2003), 131–42.

6 S. Chatman, *Story and Discourse: Narrative Structure in Fiction and Film* (Ithaca, NY: Cornell University Press, 1978).

7 A. Eddington, *Time Space and Gravity* (1920).

8 E. Mach, *Die Mechanik in ihrer Entwickelung, historisch-kritisch dargestellt*, 6th ed., (Leipzig: F. A. Brockhaus, 1908).

9 A. Hitchcock, *Hitchcock on Hitchcock: Selected Writings and Interviews* (rpt; Berkeley: University of California Press, 1997).

10 U. Hasson, O. Landesman, B. Knappmeyer, I. Vallines, N. Rubin, and D. J. Heeger, "Neurocinematics: The Neuroscience of Film," *Projections* 2.1 (2008): 1–26.

11 Hitchcock.

12 K. P. Jantke, "Jostle 2007," TUI IfMK, Diskussionsbeiträge, February 2007.

13 Klaus P. Jantke. The Gorge approach. Digital game control and play for playfully developing technology competence. In José Cordeiro, Boris Shishkov, Alexander Verbraeck, and Markus Helfert, eds, *CSEDU 2010. 2nd International Conference on Computer Supported Education, Proc., Vol. 1*, Valencia, Spain, April 7–10, 2010, pages 411–14. INSTICC, 2010.

64

New media dramaturgy

Peter Eckersall, Helena Grehan, and Edward Scheer

We coined the term new media dramaturgy (NMD) to investigate the transformations underway in live performance in relation to and in response to new media and vice versa. New media constitutes a turn to visuality, intermediality, and dialectical moves between performance and installation arts that show these expressions embodied or visualized in live and virtual performance spaces. We are interested in how these expressions might be understood compositionally and dramaturgically. This is a field of performance that is situated inbetween theatre, dance, music, and visual arts. In this project we engage with a range of works by artists and companies such as: dumb type, the iCinema project, Back to Back Theatre, Kris Verdonck and A Two Dogs Company, Kornél Mundruczó, and Hotel Modern. New media dramaturgy is a concept linking dramaturgical innovations in the globally distributed field of contemporary theatre with theories and practices in media/visual arts.

We focus on the key word *dramaturgy*. Understood as a transformational, interstitial, and translation practice, dramaturgy bridges ideas and their compositional and embodied enactment. We understand what Eckersall has called "an expanded dramaturgy"[1] to be one that in the production of art is always showing expressions of the idea or trace of its process, something that performs a relation between idea/concept/statement and form/enunciation/reception. Thus it is a dialectical process of creativity that is also practical and based in an understanding of performance as a process of and in work.

Interactivity is a key concern of NMD. This is not, however, a superficial idea such as audiences "interacting" in the development of performance by choosing story arcs using screens or pushing buttons in the theatre in realtime. Nor do we mean experiments using visual-screen headgear and interactive software to create a more porous sense of space and time in theatrical form (although this is a more fruitful area of investigation than the push-button theatre, above). Instead, as Rosie Klich and Ed Scheer argue, contemporary performance uses new media as a means of aesthetic innovation. It is what they call "a training regime for the exploration of contemporary perspectives" on "AV and information technologies."[2] New media is a potentially destabilizing force in their summation but so is live performance – "they are continually reframing and colonising each other."[3] NMD is not about worrying about the status of the live in performance – or about the virtualization of theatre. Rather, questions of destabilization, colonization, informational economy, and affective and ethical understandings of communication are considered as NMD material. It is about the technologies and techniques of new media in relation to the dramaturgical function of translating ideas into practice and compositional awareness. It is a nexus between context, content, form, and audience, what Marianne Van Kerkhoven calls "listening to the bloody machine" of theatre[4] or, as Yukiko Shikata describes in relation to dumb type's work, media performance as "image machine."[5]

In effect, NMD is the name we use to designate both the *composition* of this kind of performance in and through new media art works, and its *effects on an audience*.

To participate, to respond: rethinking spectatorship and new media dramaturgy

> "In a world where everyone can air their views to everyone we are faced not with mass empowerment but with an endless stream of egos levelled to banality."[6]

Claire Bishop argues that in the current media-saturated landscape there is a merging of spectacle and participation, and this merging engenders a new proximity that "necessitates" the need to sustain the "tension between artistic and social critiques." She explains that as participation has progressed through the twentieth century it has changed and morphed in "each historical moment." And that until recently the audience enjoyed "its subordination to strange experiences devised for them by an artist," but we are now in a situation where each audience member is "encouraged to be a co-producer of work."[7] While her focus is on "participatory" art and ours is on NMD our concerns are similar. One key question that animates this project is what does it mean to respond within the landscape of new media (performance) work, what job can or does the spectator do? Given that the works we focus on in this are often concerned with or negotiate relationships or situations where technology and the body operate in a process of exchange and where the technological elements are integral to the work's meaning, our role is also to wonder about or explore how this alters the involvement of the spectator, be they participants who are, to follow Bishop's schema, willing to be subordinated or those seeking an involvement.

NMD changes everything for the spectator. The landscapes of production and reception are unrecognizable in the sense that the use of space and the demands on our attention as spectators are radically different than they have been up until now. Time spans merge through filmic and live performance; spaces both virtual and real (or both virtual and performative) are negotiated; performers can become phantasmagoric – both present and absent, live and mediatized; things (stories, bodies, screens) are remediated; machines, robots, soundscapes, and tools operate within or often control the performance landscape. As a result the act of responding changes and it must.

For example, if we are situated in a media-saturated world, how does work that employs media as integral to its dramaturgy do this in a way that still allows the work to affect the spectator – ethically, bodily, emotionally, and at the same time to avoid cannibalizing itself? There are of course many answers to this question.

A work can become a sensorium where the spectator is enveloped and overwhelmed by sound image and vision/footage – where the pain of engaging becomes a determining factor – should one leave or risk losing an eardrum? What kind of state is this performance attempting to induce? And how does the visceral experience or the physical pain endured relate to something beyond its impact on a single body?

NMD work can be unsettling or alienating in its attempts to prick the ethical consciousness of the spectator, as in the production *Hard to Be a God* by Kornél Mundruczó in which a concern with sex trafficking and political inertia animates the performance. Spectators are confronted with performers as garment workers and sex slaves who are projected via live film feed being brutalized in a seatainer on set, only to emerge with gaping (fake) bloody wounds and break into Burt Bacharach numbers (such as "What the World Needs Now Is Love") with their oppressors. Spectators are in effect forced to become voyeurs watching this shaky hand-held footage of violation and abuse and eventually witnessing a murder – they are implicated. They leave the space with questions about consumption, spectacle media saturation and participation looming large, but they also leave potentially furious, unsettled, or at least confused. There are also works, such as Hotel Modern's *KAMP*, in which the eye of the spectator/participant is drawn between projections of puppets in a concentration camp and the actual camp mapped out on the floor of the performance space – where the footage of these puppets/figurines (plasticine people) at work sweeping, cleaning, and then being hanged, electrocuted, and gassed provokes spectators to imagine these known stories anew – the work's dramaturgy through the filmic representation and manipulation of plastic figures that we watch and see (on screen and on stage as they are moved around) – both rehumanizes the figure of the victim and makes a visceral or bodily claim on the spectator to respond.

These are just some examples of the ways in which NMD performances operate to involve the spectator and to tread the fine line between participation and unsettlement. In effect these works create what Viktor Shklovsky was seeking in 1917 when he argued that art's "technique" is to "to make forms difficult, to increase the difficulty and length of perception because the process of perception is an aesthetic end in itself and must be prolonged."[8] NMD works are difficult. From some of the examples discussed here we can see that the difficulties experienced by spectators are manifold. They range from the sense of an eardrum on the verge of explosion and a question about the limits of endurance to the realization that plasticine figures beautifully curated through horror can remind one at a profound and emotional level of the figure of the human. All of these examples impact on the spectator bodily, viscerally, and meta-politically. What happens is that through the combination of formal, aesthetic, and political elements – through an "expanded (new media) dramaturgy – such works break through the shell of information overload in a media-saturated society to create a disturbance or, as Shklovsky would term it, to "increase the difficulty and length of perception." As a result of the combination of an important question or provocation at the heart of each work, its use of media or technology in some form, and its dramaturgical realization, NMD works demand attention, interaction, or response from the spectator as participant. Ultimately these works open up the space of responsibility where the spectator as participant must think about where or how they might mobilize their response, but where not responding becomes increasingly difficult or indeed impossible – there is no space to hide.[9]

NMD and the image machine

NMD describes a performative space which has become an "image machine" as in Shikata's description of dumb type's mediated scenography. The term *image machine* denotes the extent to which such spaces have become populated with digital projections, animated with digital light shows and sound scapes, and more generally mediated. A consequence of this focus is that screen-based installation environments for performance must also be considered in the production, description, and analysis of the "image machine" of contemporary performance culture. It is no accident that a number of key dumb type performance works such as *S/N* (1994) and *OR* (1997) were remediated as installation works. *Lovers* (1994) was produced as a collaboration between dumb type co-founder Furuhashi Teiji and Tokyo's Canon ArtLab. It involves timed slide projections on to the walls and floor of a cubic space. Here the bodies of the company's dancers approach the viewer with arms wide open before falling back out of reach, like the dancers in *S/N* on which it is based, performing the unattainable virtual body and also the ghost of Furuhashi.

In the *OR* installation, commissioned by the Tokyo ICC, the cybernetic experience is pushed and amplified into the body of the spectator, who stands above a row of flat life-size screens placed on the floor while images of the dancers appear and disappear, still and silent, like beautiful corpses on a mortuary slab. The image machine of these pieces focuses on the intimacy of the encounter with death and disappearance, and on the many ways we are completely reliant on technology to manage the interface between life and death. This refocusing is an effect of the dramaturgy of the installations, the way the spatial and intermedial composition translates the idea of the impermanence and fragility of life at the threshold into an affective encounter between the image and the viewer.

Such works also refocus the problem faced by many theatre-makers that the most intensely embodied experiences are best conveyed virtually or, to put it another way, that media art provides a way to more fully experience an event at the level of the body. This mutual intensification is what Scheer has called "performative media." This term refers to "media that in their mode of production and reception involve meaningful gestures, symbolic acts and significant behaviours on behalf of human actors."[10] NMD is a way of analyzing performative media in just this sense, by proceeding with the understanding that the body/technology nexus in performance functions to amplify not to negate bodily and affective experience or, to put it another way, that the interaction between live forms and mediated experiences re-intensifies both (media and performance).

This type of work clearly raises questions about the limits of live performance, since the only live component here is the spectator and the remixing of the elements of the recorded performances. This dislocation of the familiar roles assigned to viewers and performers is not an evolutionary sideshow in aesthetic terms; it is for media artist Jeffrey Shaw the core of contemporary art practice as he understands it. Shaw describes a kind of "euphoric dislocation" arising from the perceived friction that occurs when our bodily senses start rubbing up against our projections and fantasies: "Representation is and always was the domain of both our embodied and disembodied yearnings."[11] Spaces such as the Advanced Visual and Interactive Environment (AVIE), a 360-degree immersive screen-based projection space developed by Shaw and the iCinema project, located at UNSW in Sydney, Australia, are designed as much for performative media as for more generic immersive screen-based experiments. The new media artist and director of iCinema, Dennis Del Favero, describes the AVIE as a "theatrical space."[12] For example, in developing his most recent work for the AVIE, entitled *Scenario* (2011) Del Favero's dramaturgy took an explicitly new media turn.

On a visit to the ZKM Center for Art and Media in Karlsruhe, Germany, Del Favero witnessed a video performance of Samuel Beckett's *Quadrant* that was more a study in mathematical choreography than a theatre work, and saw its potential for further investigation with non-human performers. He saw in Beckett's attempt to designate the performance through geometric arrangements a prototype for a media performance in the AVIE and took the idea to Maurice Pagnucco from the Centre for Autonomous Systems at UNSW, where mechatronics (smart robotics) and AI research is undertaken. Del Favero was interested in using robotic language in a theatrical setting and worked collaboratively with mechatronics technicians and programmers to develop the virtual performers in *Scenario*.[13] The video performance of Beckett's *Quadrant* thereby became the base performance text to enable the iCinema project to aesthetically re-conceptualize "the relationship between spatialisation and group consciousness"[14] in *Scenario* in which motion-captured virtual performers work with the live spectators to carry out certain tasks and perform a kind of rescue in which the figure of a gigantic lost child is brought back to life.

This kind of work simply maps in art the movement of social space into mediated environments, but it also engages in a complex dramaturgy of response. The audience members in *Scenario* are followed by their virtual counterparts, who read their behavior in subtle ways to bring about the rescue, a denouement which is not guaranteed. The failure of the "operation" results in a catastrophic outcome in which the child figure is doomed to wander in the virtual forest while ash falls apocalyptically from the sky. This NMD work promotes a group behavior that acts ethically to restitute our collective lifeworld, not in any glib sense of the participatory art movements Bishop critiques in her book, but in the sense she suggests at the end, when she talks about the value of works which "elicit perverse, disturbing and pleasurable experiences that enlarge our capacity to imagine the world and our relation anew."[15] Such works she argues require a "mediating third term – an object, image, story, film, even a spectacle – that permits this experience to have a purchase on the public imaginary."[16] Perhaps the "third term" for NMD is the spectacle of performative media, used to translate the idea of the ethical into an experience designed to critique the alienation inscribed and produced by Guy Debord's "society of the spectacle."[17]

Notes

1 Peter Eckersall, "Towards an Expanded Dramaturgical Practice: A Report on The Dramaturgy and Cultural Intervention Project," *Theatre Research International* 31.3 (2006): 283–97.

2 Rosemary Klich and Edward Scheer, *Multimedia Performance* (Basingstoke: Palgrave Macmillan, 2011), 1–2.

3 Klich and Scheer, 3.

4 Marianne Van Kerkhoven and Anoek Nuyens, *Listen to the Bloody Machine: Creating Kris Verdonck's "End"* (Utrecht: Utrecht School of the Arts, 2012).

5 Yukiko Shikata, "White-Out Dumb Type's Image Machine," *Art Asia Pacific* 27 (2000): 45.

6 Claire Bishop, *Artificial Hells: Participatory Art and the Politics of Spectatorship* (New York: Verso, 2012), 277.

7 Bishop, 277.

8 Viktor Shklovsky, "Art as Technique" (1917), reprinted in *Modern Criticism and Theory*, ed. David Lodge (London: Longman, 1988), 131.

9 For a more detailed discussion of responsibility (following Emmanuel Levinas), see Helena Grehan, *Performance, Ethics and Spectatorship in a Global Age* (Basingstoke: Palgrave Macmillan, 2009).

10 Edward Scheer, *Scenario* (Sydney and Karlsruhe: UNSW Press and ZKM Center for Art and Media, 2011), 36.

11 Mark Hansen, *New Philosophy for New Media* (Cambridge, MA and London: MIT Press, 2006), 90.

12 iCinema, http://www.icinema.unsw.edu.au/.

13 Scheer, 27.

14 Scheer, 28.

15 Bishop, 284.

16 Bishop, 284.

17 Guy Debord, (1967/1994) *The Society of the Spectacle*, trans. Donald Nicholson-Smith (New York: Zone Books, 1967/1994).

65

The science of dramaturgy and the dramaturgy of science

Jules Odendahl-James

The failure to communicate

Science. Dramaturgy. Two terms that enjoy opposite disparities in public comprehension. Everyone has a basic concept of what scientists do and what science is; almost no one has the faintest idea what dramaturgs do or what dramaturgy is. Within their discursive frameworks another complicated term emerges as a site of potential generation and complex disagreement: experimentation. Contrasting views of experimentation are a fundamental stumbling block when theatre and science meet on a collaborative field of inquiry beyond the mechanics of illustrative representation. For the theatre, experimentation implies a freedom from constraint, an engineered chaos that frequently refuses conventional narrative content and construction. Experimental theatre often exposes its mechanics to an audience. It can invoke a sense of frivolity or serious urgency but much critical and audience reception remains conflicted over the "success" of the communication. For the uninitiated, such pieces may seem intentionally and frustratingly unintelligible.

Scientific experimentation might also be considered as engineering and measuring chaos but one where the disciplinary legibility of the process and results are scrupulously ordered and transparent to other practitioners. Experiments are an investigation of aspects of the unknown through known means and measures. They are an effort to illuminate an answer or specific next steps in a processional inquiry. In its most successful exercise a scientific experiment leads to the confirmation and/or discovery of material facts and forms.

Since dramaturgy "concerns the relationship between the subject matter and its framing," a dramaturg's role in experimental performance can be to cast audience confusion as a feature instead of a failure by placing an artist's work in a disciplinary and historical context.[1] In some sense the science of dramaturgy or the codification of dramaturgical analysis into "accumulated techniques that all theatrical artists employ or do" connects experimentation across disciplinary domains. In *Ghostlight:*

An Introductory Handbook for Dramaturgy, Michael Chemers offers a step-by-step outline of dramaturgical process that closely mirrors steps enacted in a scientific experiment:

> [D]etermine what the aesthetic architecture of a piece of dramatic literature actually is (analysis). Discover everything needed to transform that inert script into a living piece of theater (research). Apply that knowledge in a way that makes sense to a living audience at this time in this place (practical application).[2]

Similarly, in *The Play of Nature: Experimentation as Performance*, philosopher of science Robert Crease invokes theatrical practice to illuminate a "comprehensive philosophical discussion about the nature of experimentation" within scientific discourse. For Crease, the performative aspects of experimentation are too often dismissed: "experimentation involves bringing something materially into being through skillfully created actions, along with theoretical investigation of ideal forms."[3] The artistry central to creation is one reason why a theatrical analogy is so productive for Crease's vision: "Experimental work is not just the implementation of theory. It has its own distinctive kind of knowledge, its own distinctive kind of achievements, and its own distinctive kinds of risks."[4]

What are the parameters of experimentation for science and theatre disciplines that direct, restrict, and/or illuminate their interdisciplinary collaborations given the different understandings of experimentation within each larger discourse? How can dramaturgy prepare scientific collaborators and audiences for the reception and transformation of experimental performance in ways that encourage all parties to consider the productive power of communication failures to catalyze further inquiry and creation?

Seeing the *Forest* and the trees

How to Build a Forest (hereafter *Forest*) is an immersive performance conceived, created, and performed by PearlDamour (Obie Award–winning duo, director Katie Pearl and playwright Lisa D'Amour), New Orleans–based visual artist, Shawn Hall, and a company of professional performers.[5] Initially inspired by the loss of trees felled by Hurricane Katrina on Louisiana property owned by D'Amour's family, the 2010 BP oil disaster and extensive ecological trauma on the Gulf Coast amplified the artists' exploration of collective labor and sustainability. The piece does not illustrate environmental science data and avoids over-messaging about legislative policy; instead it embeds a logic of connectivity between the natural world and human effects on the environment in a decidedly artificial ecosystem that fills the stage space over the course of six hours. Then, for the final two hours of the piece, the human "builders" increase pace and intensity as they dismantle the once lush *Forest* comprised of fabric, wire, string/rope, counterweights, and assorted craft and art materials (see Figure 65.1).

Figure 65.1 *How to Build a Forest*, conceived, created, and performed by PearlDamour (director Katie Pearl and playwright Lisa D'Amour), designed by Shawn Hall. Image from the October 19, 2012 performance of *How to Build a Forest* at Duke University's Page Auditorium. They have been building for 6 hours and 11 minutes. Photo: Jules Odendahl-James

During the deconstruction individual performers read snippets of text. For example:

Time is relative.
I mean what if at the same time
I could feel time like a 3 year old feels it
And time like my grandmother feels it
And time like an oak tree feels it
And time like a piece of coal feels it.
A piece of coal does not feel time.
How do you know?
There is a name for that kind of irritating
Unanswerable question
If we could feel time in that way
Maybe we would act differently
We'd understand how NOW relates to THEN.[6]

Every element in *Forest* embraces the notion of "tree time," one of the five "core values" that govern the piece's creation and performance. In this rubric, chronological time does not deny the movement of a conventional clock; however, it demands recognition that "'human time' is just one way of perceiving time" and that *Forest* is going to "take the long view, the patient view."[7] In order to convey an embodied sense of the scale and impact of an ecological landscape on human experience, the *Forest* builders, participating audience members, and volunteer interlocutors must attend to the minutiae and the immensity of the *Forest* without speed or pretense.

Volunteer participants facilitate this consciously constructed opportunity for communion. "Rangers," dressed in outfits similar to those of the performing builders, greet audience members, explain the protocols of entering the stage space, and distribute the one explanatory text booklet that maps the origin of the *Forest's* fabricated objects. "Breathers" enter the performance space for two 20-minute intervals in the initial build, literally breathing a layer of human sound into the found and created, natural and industrial, atonal and antiphonal soundscape.

"Speakers" make up the final group of volunteers; four to six individuals activated over the course of the six-hour initial build at times initiated by specific changes in the *Forest* architecture. They enter the house at a leisurely, unobtrusive pace and sit amongst the viewing audience (itself sometimes as few as four people) and intone their text in ways that overlap but resist the synchronicity of a choral ode. In rehearsal, D'Amour and Pearl cautioned all volunteers that there is "no pretending" in the *Forest*. Text is one of many sensual layers. It does not provide the piece's ultimate "message."

An education in experimentation

Forest arrived at Duke University after 12 months of planning and preparation by the Franklin Humanities Institute working group, EPA[2]: Environment, Performance, Arts: Engagement, People, Action, which I co-convened with two colleagues in the Nicholas School of the Environment. The artists were in residence for two weeks, concluding with three performances.[8] To access the effectiveness of our outreach, education, and engagement work, Dr. Christine Erlien, my primary collaborator in the Nicholas School, and I collected feedback from the elementary and secondary teachers who attended *Forest* with their classes and from the college faculty, students, and local volunteers who participated in the performances either as participants or required attendance and response from their students.[9]

In general, K–12 teachers spoke positively about the opportunity to talk with the artists in advance of the show and to have the support of university science and theatre communities when building lesson plans based on the artists' approach and performance's content.[10] Since *Forest* offers an abstract and immersive performance in contrast to a well-made play, pre-performance workshops with secondary school teachers helped them prepare students for how to engage the work on its own terms, particularly the artist's aforementioned core values.

Forest translates larger concepts such as sustainability, ecology, and climate change into its own performance language. The artists use materials that are safe and suitable for a theatre space (for example, flame-retardant fabrics). As a result, *Forest's* palate is decidedly man-made. Its connection to sustainability is not dependent upon the reuse/recycling of materials, as is often anticipated in the phrase "environmental performance." Instead the connection between material and origin is a lineage illustrated in the show's field guide (see Figure 65.2), which tracks the objects back to nature (ironically, often back to petroleum).

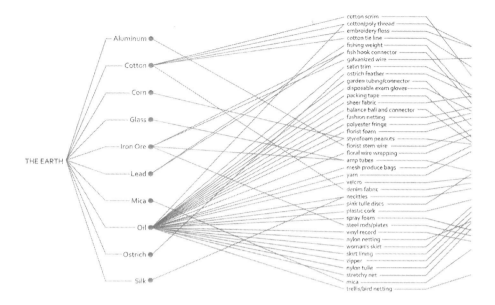

Figure 65.2 Detail from *How To Build a Forest* Field Guide. Design Angela Driscoll (2011)

This variation on a scientific field guide offered instructors one model of constructing and communicating performance. One group of high school students constructed their own rainforests out of scrap/found objects, which they tracked to different locations/ rooms at their school. Another class measured local tree growth over a period of weeks and collected supporting data about the growth processes of forests with students brainstorming throughout their research ways to best communicate their findings beyond typical charts and graphs.[11] Their feedback illustrated how pre-show preparation allowed secondary school students to anticipate *Forest*'s atypical parameters as both a piece of theatre and an examination of environmental practices. A dramaturgical perspective made the piece's intermingling of performance and science visible and largely understandable.

University students were more difficult to sway regarding both *Forest*'s environmental-science connection and its theatrical form. There were particularly divergent opinions in response to our question of whether the performance "communicates effectively."[12] Some respondents felt the lack of explanation meant that key subtleties in the work went unnoticed by the "general public." Others felt "artistic expression" was a problematic approach to communication. They wondered why there was no program note, formal post-performance discussion, or the construction of internal dialogue and cues to identify "a story."[13]

When asked about the process of using art or theatre to communicate scientific topics, a majority of these students responded with ambivalence. There were enthusiastic supporters ("I think it's an awesome idea!") and those who felt it was easier for "non-science people [to] understand" or "engage" a scientific topic such as climate change or environmental management through artwork or performance as opposed to having them "read scientific articles." Others were less convinced. "Useful but risky," was one unelaborated response. "It is new but only communicates to a specific audience (art enthusiast)," asserted another. Still another noted that both (visual) art and science material require a practiced eye to decipher effectively:

[Visual communication] can be effective if done properly – think infographics, for example. An art installation, on the other hand, might make science more accessible to a different audience but it is equally challenging to understand to the ordinary viewer as a series of scientific equations.[14]

Provisional findings

After reviewing the questionnaire responses, discussing the project with my theatre and science colleagues, and embarking on another science + humanities collaboration, I want to offer three core values of science dramaturgy as it relates to interdisciplinary experimentation and communication. First, authority must be shared in a collaborative investigation of phenomena. Science cannot provide the data or "facts" and theatre the illustrative dynamic to convey said facts to an audience. Collaborators must agree that each discipline provides different means to organize experience. Our truths are *not* self-evident either to each other or to our audiences. It is largely accepted that science operates in the realm of numbers and molecules, while theatre operates in the realm of physical expression and feeling. Both realms are essential to insightful communication. The subject of collaborative investigation should determine the interaction among and between those realms and an audience. Interestingly, in our *Forest* outreach efforts we found that disciplinary lines remain permeable in elementary and secondary classrooms in ways that might allow "grown-up" theatre artists and scientists to venture into each other's worlds and create performative experiments that reach into the very heart of knowledge construction.

Second, collaborating disciplines must expand their parameters of experimentation. Pieces like *Forest* that stretch or question linear time, magnify scale and setting beyond expected proportions, and eschew dialogue among three-dimensional characters require even theatre-savvy audiences to find alternative mechanisms of identification and experience. If the primary goal is the communication of fundamental concepts that will increase knowledge and promote activism on key issues, it is easy to see the benefits of conventional modes of storytelling; however, this should not mean that realism is the only construct of value.

The last point is a slight mutation of *Forest*'s "no pretending" requirement. My science major students and science colleagues have described an unease with what they perceived to be theatre's core mechanic of make believe. Conversely, my theatre students often resist the notion that there are performative aspects embedded in scientific inquiry (beyond the doctor-patient dynamic of medical treatment). A highly constructed world, however, does not equal a false world. A process in which the human actor becomes just one small part of a larger field does not necessarily negate embodied epistemologies. An abstract, even indefinable experience can produce a useful, even significant reaction in an attendee. Foregrounding the theoretical background and/or mechanical processes of a scientific experiment rather than the interpersonal struggles of the scientists who create it allows audiences to engage material realities without putting themselves at the center of the drama, obscuring the phenomena. While this approach might fail to communicate a specific, detailed message, one might gain invaluable insight into fallibility, uncertainty, and creativity.

Notes

1 C. Turner and S. Behrndt, *Dramaturgy and Performance* (New York: Palgrave Macmillan, 2008), 25.
2 M. Chemers, *Ghostlight: An Introductory Handbook for Dramaturgy* (Carbondale, IL: Southern Illinois University Press, 2010), 3.
3 R. Crease, *The Play of Nature: Experimentation of Performance* (Bloomington, IN: Indiana University Press, 1993), 109.
4 Crease, 116.
5 *Forest* was originally commissioned by The Kitchen Center for Video, Music, Performance, Dance, Film and Literature (NYC) and was developed with generous support from the Creative Capital Foundation, the MAP Fund (a program of Creative Capital, supported by the Doris Duke Charitable Foundation), the Ogden Museum of Southern Art, Appalachian State University, the Moore Family Fund for the Arts of the Minneapolis Foundation, and many individual donors.
6 L. D'Amour, unpublished text from *Forest* performance at Duke University, 2012.
7 L. D'Amour, K. Pearl, S. Hall, *"How to Build a Forest* Background Information for Duke University"* (2012), 1–2.
8 *Forest* was performed at Page Auditorium, Duke University campus October 19–21, 2013, funded in part by a Visiting Artist Grant from the Council for the Arts, Office of the Provost, Duke University, support from the Department of Theater Studies and the Nicholas School for the Environment, and a grant from South Arts in partnership with the National Endowment for the Arts and the North Carolina Arts Council.
9 For an anecdotal account of audience reception of *Forest*'s performances at Duke, see "The Psychology of the Audience," a series of blog postings by J. Mosser on Howlround.com, November 15–December 13, 2012, available online at http://www.howlround.com/tags/psychology-audience-series, accessed December 15, 2012.
10 During the summer of 2012, Christine Erlien facilitated a Skype session including secondary school teachers, Shawn Hall, and Katie Pearl to discuss strategies for building lesson plans around *Forest* attendance. This group included visual art, theatre, and science instructors from elementary, middle, and high schools across Durham, NC. We also collaborated with Duke's Sustainability Office and Duke's Environmental Leadership (DEL) Project, in partnership with the Coca-Cola Foundation, to construct specific on-campus K–12 programing and activities.
11 C. Erlien and J. Odendahl-James, "Assessing the Impact of an Art/Science Project, *How to Build a Forest*," survey (Duke University, November 2012).
12 Erlien and Odendahl-James.
13 Erlien and Odendahl-James.
14 Erlien and Odendahl-James.

Part VII

DRAMATURG AS SYSTEMS ANALYST

Dramaturgy of postdramatic structures

66

Postdramatic dramaturgy

Gad Kaynar

This article sets out to explore some basic tenets of postdramatic dramaturgy as theorized and practiced mainly in the German-speaking countries. It is based on interviews with some 30 dramaturgs from the German-speaking region, conducted between 2003 and 2013 in the context of two ISF (Israeli Science Foundation) researches. The emphasis on German dramaturgy rests on two foundations: a) that practical dramaturgy has been created and developed in the German-speaking region for over 250 years and has always – especially since the 1980s – served as the realm of extreme experimentation; b) that consequently the contemporary German-speaking theatre offers the optimal case study for exploring the notion and practice of postdramatic dramaturgy.[1]

Postdramatic theatre: the moments of the performance

In order to explore what is meant by postdramatic dramaturgy, we must first and foremost clarify what is meant by postdramatic theatre. Hans-Thies Lehmann defines "postdramatic theatre" as in a nutshell:

> [a] repulsive, controversial attitude of the new theatre to the dramatic tradition, in other words … an abundance of "concrete negations" of the dramatic that began in the historical avant-garde and in the neo avant-garde of the 1950s.[2]

The most conspicuous features of postdramatic aesthetics and dramaturgy, in the wake of Richard Schechner's formative performance theory and Lehmann's derivative observations in his signature work *Postdramatisches Theater*,[3] comprise inter alia: the transition from a verbally predominant, narrative, and sequentially structured poetics to a performance-oriented aesthetics, distinguished by plotless, characterless, deconstructed, and fragmentary theatrical texts. These texts highlight the performers' corporeal and concrete stage presence, as well as what Patrick Primavesi defines as "the moment of the performance itself" rather than the traditional coherent and cohesive representation or presentation of a fictional world, plot, and characters.[4] For instance, the German director Michael Thalheimer commented on his own dramaturgical interpretation of Friedrich Schiller's *Kabale und Liebe* (Intrigues and love), which reduced the volume of the classical text and instead accentuated the actors' bodily articulation, thus annunciating his critique of capitalism as subversion of the natural and the genuine, that "[t]he body speaks its own words ... since it often says the opposite of what it puts into words."[5] The postdramatic idiom is also distinguished by questioning the very nature of theatre and perception. Whereas dramatic theatre is often concerned with the referential import of the play and its stage realization, treating constituents such as plot, character, theatrical language, style, genre, etc., as mere vehicles for transporting the message to a passive spectator, postdramatic theatre focuses on the self-sufficient and self-referential form and process, practicing a semantics and rhetoric of form proper which conjoins both performers and spectators as active participants. The dramaturgy of Smarthouse 1+2, an anti-globalization and anti-consumerist cult show by René Polesch (2003), is based in part on an "auction." The well-educated German adolescents come to the stage, "buy" a subversive slogan, vehemently shout it at their accompanying parents, and then meekly return to their seats. The act of "selling" and "buying" the anti-commercial slogans and then hurling them at the audience as if they were commercials ironically constitutes both a rebellious gesture and a reification of the sophisticated methods through which capitalist society suppresses revolt by turning it into a marketable commodity.[6] A distinct trait of postdramatic performance resides accordingly in the encroachment of the liminal borders between fiction and reality, actor and role, parole and langue, verbal and visual dramaturgy, trying through highly theatrical means to refute the exclusive ascription of theatricality to declared performative events.[7] Similarly, postdramatic performance defies and intermingles "purist" definitions of artistic fields, including performance genres such as "high" and "low" drama, burlesque, stand-up, poetry reciting, classical and pop music, and dance. Moreover, a specific genre of postdramatic eclectic and interrelated attributes, such as that of the "Rimini Protokoll" collective, tries to breach the established dramatic theatre's politics of excluding reality per se from the stage and to empower "everyday specialists" to relate their biographical stories, what Jacques Rancière defines as "re-devising the territory of the communal."[8]

Furthermore, postdramatic theatre replaces venues associated with bourgeois culinary theatre by spatial configurations that challenge the diachronic, evolutionary conventions of plot structuring in the dramatic theatre, as well as habitual norms of audience reception. This kind of enterprise, which is usually invested with political import, also tends to prefer environments least associated with established performance activities, such as the invitation proffered by the late radical German theatre-maker, Christoph Schlingensief, to four million unemployed Germans in 2000 to bathe in the Wolfgangsee in order to swamp the prime minister's holiday resort. The rationale underlying the aesthetics and dramaturgy of postdramatic theatre is quintessentially summarized by Lehmann: "Everything depends on the capability to find theatre where it is usually not perceived."[9]

Postdramatic dramaturgy, or the dramaturg as text

As emerges from the above, in the postdramatic era the closed traditional approaches of textual dramaturgy are challenged by the conceptually open-ended and autogenic dramaturgy of the self, or of the dramaturg, as text. Consequently, one of the major respects in which the dramaturgy of postdramatic theatre differs from the dramaturgy of dramatic theatre relates to the notion of "applied dramaturgy." Dramaturgical conceptions in the dramaturgy of dramatic theatre (or dramatic dramaturgy) usually are subject to apparently irrelevant extra-aesthetic constraints – phenomenological, sociological, institutional, cultural, political, etc. – that interplay with the work's predominantly immanent interpretation. Quite often they modify the final pattern, effect, and meaning of the production more than any "purely artistic" deliberations. The dramaturgical choice of repertoire and its interpretation for performance in a public, "dramatic" theatre might, in many cases, be primarily "circumstantial" (mainly accounting for the contextual performance conditions) rather than play or text oriented. However, these relations must not necessarily be understood as binary and dialectic since the terms "play or text oriented" and "circumstantial" are relative and interpolative. In postdramatic theatre and performance art, "applied dramaturgy" experiences a relative reversal: instead of considering the external contexts, the dramaturg's concern is predominantly self-referential and reflexive, attuned to what one might call the dramaturg's subjective space. Devising methods and multimedia, (primarily) non-textual orientations background dramaturgical consideration of the "objective" circumstances of conventional reality and highlight instead the dramaturg's subjectively interpreted "contextual circumstances," i.e. environment, biography, memory, and ideology, sustained by her or his direct involvement in the rehearsals/conception process as actor and co-director.

Carl Hegemann – the veteran ex-dramaturg of the Volksbühne in East Berlin – provides us with a simple, yet striking demonstration of the contrast between dramatic and postdramatic dramaturgical procedures. In his lecture at the International Research Workshop, "Dramaturgy as Applied Knowledge: From Theory to Practice and Back" (Tel Aviv University 2008), Hegemann, enacting the director, drew a rectangular form on the blackboard, representing a show in rehearsal, and asked us, the listeners who enacted the dramaturgs, to mention anything of which this form reminded us (coffin? shoe box? cigarette box?). He then contended that whereas in the dramatic theatre it is the director who would most likely raise these associations in the context of presenting his or her stage conception to the dramaturg, the situation in devising processes that pertain to the non-representative postdramatic aesthetics is reversed: the dramaturg, as the hermeneutic agent resorting to free, arbitrary associations, interprets for the director throughout rehearsals what he or she considers that the director has done – not meant, just done – as the dramaturg perceives it. This contextual interpretation, based on the dramaturg's subjective space, fuels in turn further developments in the performance script, with the dramaturg thus becoming a kind of "co-director."

So it can consequently be maintained that in the postdramatic devising production, in which the performance text emerges out of the rehearsal process, or in text-based postdramatic productions, in which the dramaturg rewrites the play or curates the collage- structured scenario, the dramaturg becomes an equally privileged partner of the director, and the difference between their functions is blurred and potentially inverted. For instance, the dramaturg Stefanie Carp, while working with Christoph Marthaler at the Zürich Schauspielhaus, presented herself to me, like some of her colleagues, as a "projector," one who translates the caprices of her artistic director's mise-en-scène into her own metatexts.[10] The traditional tectonic approaches of textual dramaturgy are thus challenged by the non-diegetic, a-tectonic, self-referential, and autogenic dramaturgy of the self or of the dramaturg as text and context.

A typical example of this dramaturgical strategy might be discerned in the evident correlation between the mental biography and ideological standpoints of Jens Hillje, the former chief dramaturg of the Berlin Schaubühne – anchored in the anti-capitalist sentiments of the German intelligentsia after the Wall – and his dramaturgical work. Hillje told me how his performative juvenile rebellion against his native conservative Bavarian environment – asserted in his subsequent dramaturgical predilection for the "brutal" British "in yer face" drama – caused a confrontation with the writer-director Falk Richter over the dramaturg's apparently arbitrary interpretation of Chekhov's *The Seagull*. Reading the play in his neo-Marxist terms, Hillje regarded the piece neither as a comedy about a stagnated decadent society nor about love-seeking couples, but as a cold, unsentimental analysis of society as a conglomerate of manipulative, exploiting opportunists. He contended, in insurrection against his own philistine origins and in disregard of the play's obvious givens, that "each of the characters strives towards personal gain, either social status, financial success or creative material. No one is interested in Love per se, in pure feelings."[11]

The widespread trend in mid-European theatre in the last two decades to read the classics not merely in sociopolitical and cultural terms, but predominantly in accordance with the dramaturg's ghosted biography, memory, and ideology seems also to mark a tendency towards a revised attitude to the implied spectators. The latter are provoked into becoming enraged spect-actors, as they are exposed to violent verbal, sensory, and visceral rhetoric as a protest against a smug and commoditized reality-convention. This dramaturgical approach asserted itself in manifest infidelity to the classical text, in an attempt to shatter the barriers between the fictional (play), theatrical (stage), and real (audience) spaces, as well as in redefining the relations between actor, character, theatre visitor, and spectator. It culminated in the collaboration between dramaturg and philosopher Carl Hegemann, mentioned above, and that other enfant terrible of the German theatre, Frank Castorf, while working together at the experimental Volksbühne in East Berlin for almost twenty years. In a series of iconoclastic, deconstructed, and New Media–sustained postdramatic dramaturgical adaptations of Russian, German, and American literary and dramatic masterpieces, Castorf as director and Hegemann as dramaturg displaced the diachronic narrative, the fictional structure of the original works by drawing on the implied spectator's phenomenological reality-convention after Germany's reunification as seen through their idiosyncratic East German perspective. Thus they deliberately infuriated the spectators by thwarting their canonical preconceptions about the deconstructed classical texts, turning these into "disembodied," "hollow" vehicles for political discourse and imposing on the addressees a synchronous consciousness space common for them, for the productions' creators and performers alike, consisting of ironic longing for the socialist past and criticism of the consumerist present.

A striking implementation of this approach can be seen in the metatheatrical, hybrid dramaturgy, containing foreign text implantations, through which Hegemann and Castorf converted Tennessee Williams's realistic-psychological *A Streetcar*

Named Desire into their own self-referential nostalgic satire, renamed *Endstation Amerika* (Endstation America, 2000), on non-adjusting East European and East German hardcore communists. Stanley Kowalski in this production is neither the dramatic character nor its famous Marlon Brando image, but someone much closer to the actor: an elderly, anti-heroic, down-and-out German-Polish type from the streets of cosmopolitan Berlin, presenting himself as an ex-member of Solidarność who, through the devising mediation of the dramaturg, delivers nostalgic tirades about his friendship with Lech Wałęsa. When he gets angry at the new circumstances, he very slowly and deliberately breaks plates in a ceremonial fashion so that splinters fly into the spectators' faces as if in order to impel the eruption of the real. The originally Southern belle Blanche Dubois becomes a communist German Democratic Republic freak, whose neurotic and fervent nostalgia for her proletarian past asserts itself ironically in goosestep marching to the sound of an imaginary Soviet military band. In both and in many other similar stimuli, the seams between actor and role, theatre visitor and spectator are torn open, and the dramaturgical/theatrical processing turns from an objective mimesis of a detached dramatic metaphor into an ultra-subjective, neo-expressionist materialization of the psyche and collective consciousness of the dramaturg as con/text.

In summary: when interviewing Carl Hegemann, he commented, recalling Heiner Müller, that "[t]heatre is the model for the fundamental tension between determinism and liberty, between impotence and omnipotence. It keeps us alive because it shows us what will annihilate us."[12] If we apply this observation to the dramaturg as text, then one might say that in postdramatic theatre and its derivatives, the dramaturgs, whoever fulfils this function (be it professional dramaturgs or directors, actors, designers, etc.), are the icons of the stage art. They are the catalysts of the absolute freedom and apocalyptic anarchy that concomitantly underlie the constitution of the performance event. They incite, legitimize, and embody the artistic and existential chaos of the creative process. They are also, however, the ones that guard it, this deconstructed process, against total deconstruction and destruction. They constitute the factor that, in a sense, fixates the fixation-resistant, open-ended process, determines its borders, and turns it into a performance that safeguards existence since, in Heiner Müller's words, "Das Schöne bedeutet das mögliche Ende der Schrecken" (The beautiful signifies the possible end of the horrors).[13]

Notes

1 See e.g. M. Luckhurst, *Dramaturgy: A Revolution in Theatre* (Cambridge: Cambridge University Press, 2006), 9; J. Schechter, "In the Beginning There Was Lessing. Then Brecht, Müller, and Other Dramaturgs," in S. Jonas, G. S. Proehl, and M. Lupu, eds., *Dramaturgy in American Theater: A Source Book* (Fort Worth, TX: Harcourt Brace College, 1997), 16–24; M. Esslin, "The Role of the Dramaturg in European Theater," in B. Cardullo, ed., *What Is Dramaturgy?* (New York: Peter Lang, 1995), 43.

2 Hans-Thies Lehmann, "Wie politisch ist Postdramatisches Theater?" in Jan Deck and Angelika Sieburg, eds., *Politisch Theater Machen: Neue Artikulationen des Politischen in den darstellenden Künsten* (Bielefeld: Transcript, 2011), 34.

3 Hans-Thies Lehmann, *Postdramatisches Theater* (Frankfurt am Main: Verlag der Autoren, 1999). The references are taken from the English translation by K. Jürs-Munby, *Postdramatic Theatre* (London and New York: Routledge, 2006).

4 P. Primavesi, "Theater/Politik – Kontexte und Beziehungen," in Deck and Sieburg, 49.

5 M. Merschmeier, "Die Stunden der Wahrheit," *Theater heute* 38. 2 (February 1997): 8.

6 G. Kaynar, "German Theatre, Summer 2003: Journey Impressions," *Teatron* 12 (2004): 31.

7 See J.-L. Nancy, *Singulär plural sein* (Berlin: Diaphanes, 2005), 20.

8 J. Rancière, *Das Unbehagen in der Ästhetik* (Wien: Passagen, 2007), 32. See also F. Malzacher, "The Scripted Realities of Rimini Protokoll," in Carol Martin, ed., *Dramaturgy of the Real on the World Stage* (London: Palgrave Macmillan, 2010), 80–87.

9 Lehmann, 31.

10 S. Carp, interview with G. Kaynar, Zurich, June 2003.

11 J. Hillje, interview with G. Kaynar, Berlin, February 2005.

12 C. Hegemann, interview with G. Kaynar, Tel Aviv 2008.

13 H. Müller, *Material: Texte und Kommentare* (Leipzig: Reclam, 1990), 19.

67
Teaching deconstructively[1]

Barbara Johnson

Teaching literature is teaching how to read. How to notice things in a text that a speed-reading culture is trained to disregard, overcome, edit out, or explain away; how to read what the language is doing, not guess what the author was thinking; how to take in evidence from a page, not seek a reality to substitute for it.[2]

Deconstruction has sometimes been seen as a terroristic belief in meaninglessness. It is commonly opposed to humanism, which is then an imperialistic belief in meaningfulness. Another way to distinguish between the two is to say that deconstruction is a reading strategy that carefully follows both the meanings and the suspensions and displacements of meaning in a text, while humanism is a strategy to stop reading when the text stops saying what it ought to have said. Deconstruction, then, has a lot to teach teachers of literature to the extent that they see themselves as teachers of reading.

What, then, is a deconstructive reading, and how can its strategies be translated into classroom procedures? Deconstruction is not a form of textual vandalism or generalized skepticism designed to prove that meaning is impossible. Rather, it is a careful teasing out of the conflicting forces of signification that are at work within the text itself. If anything is destroyed in a deconstructive reading, it is not meaning per se but the claim to unequivocal domination of one mode of signifying over another. This implies that a text signifies in more than one way, that it can signify something more, something less, or something other than it claims to, or that it signifies to different degrees of explicitness, effectiveness, or coherence. A deconstructive reading makes evident the ways in which a text works out its complex disagreements with itself. As Paul de Man puts it:

> The deconstruction is not something we have added to the text but it constituted the text in the first place. A literary text simultaneously asserts and denies the authority of its own rhetorical mode, and by reading the text as we did we were only trying to come closer to being as rigorous a reader as the author had to be in order to write the [text] in the first place.[3]

Because deconstruction is first and foremost a way of paying attention to what a text is doing – *how* it means not just *what* it means – it can lend itself very easily to an open-discussion format in a literature seminar. And because it enables students to respond to what is there before them on the page, it can teach them how to work out the logic of a reading on their own rather than passively deferring to the authority of superior learning. What kinds of signifying conflict, then, are articulated in, and constitutive of, the literary text? And what sorts of reading do they demand?

Ambiguous words

Derrida's readings often focus on a double-edged word as a condensed articulation of conflicting levels of assertion in a text. In Plato's *Phaedrus*, for example, the word *pharmakon* can mean both "remedy" and "poison."[4] In referring to writing itself as a *pharmakon*, Plato is therefore not making a simple value judgment. Yet translators, by choosing to render the word sometimes by "remedy" and sometimes by "poison," have consistently decided what in Plato remains undecidable, and thus have influenced the course of the history of readings of Plato. When one recalls the means of Socrates' death, one can see that the undecidability between poison and remedy is not a trivial matter. Far from posing confined, local interpretative problems, ambiguities can stand as the hinge of an entire discourse.

Undecidable syntax

One of the most condensed examples of syntax as the locus of a suspension of the text's claim structures between two often incompatible possibilities is the rhetorical question. As Paul de Man suggests, a reading of Yeat's poem "Among School Children" is drastically changed if one admits the possibility that its terminal question – "How can we know the dancer from the dance?" – is *not* rhetorical.[5] Or the question with which Baudelaire ends his celebration of a woman's hair in "La Chevelure" – "Are you not the gourd from which I drink the wine of memory?" – suspends the energy of the poem not only between self and other but between the success and the failure of the attempt to rewrite the other as a container for the self.

Incompatibilities between what a text says and what it does

An obvious example would be the figure known as *praeteritio*, in which a text elaborates itself by detailing at length what it says it will *not* speak about. Variants upon this structure pervade all literature, as when an author devotes much more space to what he wants to eliminate than to what he wants to instate, or when a text in one way or another protests too much. A simple example of the discrepancy between saying and doing occurs in the last line of Archibald MacLeish's "Ars Poetica": "A poem should not mean but be." The line itself does not obey its own prescription: it means – *intends* being – rather than simply being, thus revealing that it is more complicated than it first appears to be for a poem to assert what the relations between meaning and being are.

Incompatibilities between the literal and the figurative

In Lamartine's poem "L'Isolement," the speaker, who is lamenting the death of his beloved, cries, "There is nothing in common between the earth and me." He then goes on, "I am like the withered leaf." In a poem that is entirely devoted to the question of the mode of aliveness of one whose heart is in another world, this suspended stance between earthliness and unearthliness reveals that the problem of mourning has something to do with the opposition between the figural and the literal, and vice versa.

Incompatibilities between explicitly foregrounded assertions and illustrative examples or less explicitly asserted supporting material

Derrida points this out in the discrepancy between Saussure's explicit assertion that linguistics should study speech, not writing, and his repeated recourse to linguistic properties that are derivable from writing, not speech. A literary example can be found in Wordsworth's "Intimations Ode." The poem begins by asserting the fact of loss:

> There was a time when meadow, grove, and stream,
> The earth, and every common sight,
> To me did seem
> Apparelled in celestial light,
> The glory and the freshness of a dream.
> It is not now as it hath been of yore; –
> Turn wheresoe'er I may,
> By night or day,
> The things which I have seen I now can see no more.

This sense of loss expands mythically, phylogenetically, and ontogenetically to include the common experience of all mankind:

> Our birth is but a sleep and a forgetting;
> The Soul that rises with us, our life's Star,
> Hath had elsewhere its setting,
> And cometh from afar:
> Not in entire forgetfulness,
> And not in utter nakedness,
> But trailing clouds of glory do we come
> From God, who is our home:
> Heaven lies about us in our infancy!
> Shades of the prison-house begin to close
> Upon the growing Boy,
> But he beholds the light, and whence it flows,
> He sees it in his joy;

...
At length the Man perceives it die away,
And fade into the light of common day.

But in the supporting invocation to the little child, Wordsworth cuts the ground out
from under this narrative of loss:

... Thou little Child, yet glorious in the might
Of heaven-born freedom on thy being's height,
Why with such earnest pains dost though provoke
The years to bring the inevitable yoke,
Thus blindly with thy blessedness at strife?

The little child, the seer of the light, here turns out to be blind to his very ability to
see. The experience of blessed sight, the loss of which Wordsworth began by
lamenting, seems never to have existed in the first place as a lived experience. The
loss of *something* is a story retrospectively told in order to explain the *sense* of loss.
What we have lost by the end of the poem is precisely loss itself.

Obscurity

A student's first encounter with the work of a poet such as Mallarmé can be profoundly
disconcerting. If one attempts to smooth over the difficulties and make the poem add
up to a meaning, the student might well ask, "Ce n'est donc que ca? – Why couldn't
he have said it in plain, comprehensible language?" One would have to answer that
"it" isn't something his language is *saying* but something his language is *doing*.

A look at the sonnet "La chevelure vol d'une flamme à l'extrême occident de
désirs" reveals that although one can't make sense of it, it contains an interesting
collection of highly charged images and concepts: man and woman, life and death,
doubt and joy, truth and mockery, tenderness and defamation, nakedness and jewelry,
outward exploits and inner fires, weather, geography, and education. The entire
complexity of the world seems to be condensed down to a microchip. This is what
Mallarmé called "simplifying the world." But the text itself is far from simple.

What happens in reading Mallarmé is that one talks one's way into the poem by
describing the specificity of one's difficulties. Rather than remain stuck before an
obstacle or paralyzed before a forking path, the reader must say, "My reading is
blocked here because I can't tell whether this is theft or flight, literal or figurative,
noun or verb, statement or question, masculine or feminine, and so forth. But that
uncertainty may be precisely what the poem is talking about." The reader can then
track down each thread of all possibilities and ask the significance of their coexistence.
Eventually, the narrating of one's frustrations and difficulties begins to fill in for, and
to partake of, the missing thematic coherence in the poem. The poem is not *about*
something *separate* from the activity required to decipher it. Simplification, doubt,
distance, and desire are all acted out by the reading process as well as stated in
the poem.

With Mallarmé, in other words, the student can learn to see the *search* for meaning as being illuminating and meaningful in itself. One's struggles with ambiguity and obscurity cease to be obstacles to reading: they become the very *experience* of reading. Meaning is not something "out there" or "in there" to be run after or dug up. It inhabits the very activity of the search. And what better training for "living as and where we live" (as Stevens puts it) than to learn to direct our attention to what we experience *now* rather than to those answers that lie somewhere up the road; to take indecision, frustration, and ambivalence, not as mere obstacles and incapacities, but as the very richness and instructiveness of the reading process? This is what Mallarmé's poetry has to teach, not by *telling* us this, but by making us go through it, interminably, for ourselves.

Fictional self-interpretation

Sometimes the challenge posed by a text is not excessive obscurity but, rather, some form of excessive clarity. Many literary texts appear to commend upon themselves, to solve the enigmas they set up. A common student response to texts in which such self-interpretations are explicit is to protest that the author has taken all the fun away by doing the work the reader ought to do. Deconstruction, with its insistence on interpretation itself as a fiction-making activity, enables one to read such metalinguistic moments as allegories of reading, as comments on the interpretive process itself, in a sort of inside-out version of the involvement the student engages in with Mallarmé.

I would like to conclude with a somewhat more extended version of what can come out of a discussion of textual self-interpretation. For this, I will comment on two inversely symmetrical thematizations of textuality itself: Nathaniel Hawthorne's "The Minister's Black Veil," in which a character named Reverend Hooper mysteriously and without warning dons a piece of black crepe, which he refuses to remove even on his deathbed; and Hans Christian Andersen's "The Emperor's New Clothes," in which two imposters weave nonexistent clothes for the emperor, telling him that their cloth has the property of being invisible to those who are either simpletons or unfit for their offices. The denial of literality takes place, in both stories, in an intersubjective context in which meaning is tied to a figure of authority.

The emperor's subjects thus veil from themselves the literality of the invisibility of what they see, while members of the minister's congregation, projecting their own concealments behind the veil, are blind to the possibility that nothing is being concealed – or that concealment is what is being revealed. Both stories dramatize the intrusion – indeed, the inescapability – of allegorical structures in the conduct of "real" life. Socialization is training in allegorical interpretation. But an allegory that reveals that the act of reading consists in a blindness both to literality and to the fact that one is allegorically denying literality puts *us* in a difficult position. If the blindness of the emperor's subjects and of the minister's parishioners is a forgetting of literality through the act of reading *themselves* into the text, then aren't we, by reading the texts as allegories of reading, suffering from the same blindness to the second degree? Yet could we have chosen to read literally? Or is the act of reading always, in a sense, an act of resistance to the letter.

At the beginning of this paper I define deconstruction as a reading strategy that carefully follows both the meanings and the suspensions and displacements of meaning in a text, while humanism was a strategy to stop reading when the text stops saying what it ought to have said. What the deconstructive reading of Hawthorne and Andersen has shown, however, is that no matter how rigorously a deconstructor might follow the letter of the text, the text will end up showing the reading process as a *resistance* to the letter. The deconstructor thus comes face to face with her own humanism. This is small comfort, of course, since the text has shown humanism to consist in the blindness of self-projection. But then, in the final analysis, it is perhaps precisely as an apprenticeship in the repeated and inescapable oscillation between humanism and deconstruction that literature works its most rigorous and inexhaustible seductions.

Notes

1 Reprinted from *Writing and Reading Differently*, eds. G. Douglas Atkins and Michael L. Johnson (Lawrence: University Press of Kansas, 1985), 140–48.
2 This is not meant to imply that nothing should be read outside the text at hand, or that a text is unconnected to any discourse outside itself. The "inside" of the text is no more a "given" than the "outside," and what is inside the text is not necessarily accessible to the reader without philological, historical, biographical, etc., research. But it does imply that history, philology, biography, the "spirit of the age," and the "material conditions of production" are not less problematic – or less textual and interpretively constructed – than the literary text they would come to explain. Training in reading must also be training in evaluating the relevance and authority of external resources as well as internal ones.
3 Paul de Man, *Allegories of Reading* (New Haven, CT: Yale University Press, 1979), 17.
4 See Derrida, "Plato's Pharmacy," in *Dissemination* (Chicago: University of Chicago Press, 1981).
5 In the opening essay of de Man.

68

EF's visit to a small planet: Some questions to ask a play[1]

Elinor Fuchs

The following walk through dramatic structure is a teaching tool. For the past several years I have used it at the Yale School of Drama as an entry to Reading Theater, a critical writing course for students in the M.F.A. Dramaturgy program.

The questions below are in part designed to forestall the immediate (and crippling) leap to character and normative psychology that underwrites much dramatic criticism. Aside from that corrective bias, the approach offered here is not a "system" intended to replace other approaches to play analysis; I often use it together with Aristotle's unparalleled insight into plot structure. Rather, it could be thought of as a template for the critical imagination.

In a fine article on *Hedda Gabler*, Philip E. Larson described the nature of "a genuine performance criticism." If criticism "is unwilling to rest content with the evaluation of ephemera," he wrote, "[it] must attempt to describe a potential object, one that neither the dramatist, the critics, nor the reader has ever seen, or will see."[2] These questions are intended to light up some of the dark matter in dramatic worlds, to illuminate the potentialities Larson points to. No matter what answers come, the very act of questioning makes an essential contribution to the enterprise of criticism.

Elinor Fuchs

We must make the assumption that in the world of the play there are no accidents. Nothing occurs "by chance," not even chance. In that case, nothing in the play is without significance. Correspondingly, the play asks us to focus upon it a total awareness, to bring our attention and curiosity without the censorship of selective interpretation, "good taste," or "correct form." Before making judgments, we must ask questions. This is the deepest meaning of the idea, often-repeated but little understood, that the study of art shows us how to live.

The world of the play: first things first

A play is not a flat work of literature, not a description in poetry of another world, but is in itself another world passing before you in time and space. Language is only one part of this world. Those who think too exclusively in terms of language find it hard to read plays. When you "see" this other world, when you experience its space-time dynamics, its architectonics, then you can figure out the role of language in it.

If too tight a focus on language makes it hard to read plays, too tight a focus on character creates the opposite problem: it makes the reading too easy. To look at dramatic structures narrowly in terms of characters risks unproblematically collapsing this strange world into our own world. The stage world never obeys the same rules as ours, because in its world, nothing else is possible besides what is there: no one else lives there; no other geography is available; no alternative actions can be taken.

To see this entire world, do this literally: mold the play into a medium-sized ball, set it before you in the middle distance, and squint your eyes. Make the ball small enough that you can see the entire planet, not so small that you lose detail, and not so large that detail overwhelms the whole.

Before you is the "world of the play." Still squinting, ask about the space, What is space like on this planet? Interior or exterior, built or natural? Is space here confined or wide open? Do you see a long passage with many "stations"? Do you see a landscape of valleys and mountains? Sea and land? Are we on an island? In a cave? In a desert or a jungle? On a country road?

Now ask about the time. How does time behave on this planet? Does "time stand still"? Is time frantic and staccato on this planet? Is it leisurely, easy-going time? How is time marked on this planet? By clock? By the sun? By the sound of footsteps? What kind of time are we in? Cyclical time? Eternal time? Linear time? What kind of line? One day? One lifetime?

Ask about the climate on this planet. Do we have storms? Eclipses of the sun and moon? Do we have extreme heat? Paralyzing cold? Is the environment on this planet lush and abundant, sere and life-denying, airless and suffocating? What is the seasonal "feel" of this world? Autumnal? Wintry?

What is the mood on this planet? Jolly? Serious? Sad? Ironic? Sepulchral? The mood is not just a question of plot (comedies are "happy," etc.), "tone" also contributes to mood. What is the tone of this planet? Delicate or coarse? Cerebral or passionate? Restrained or violent? How are mood and tone created on this planet? Through music? Light, sound, color, shape? What shapes? Curves? Angles?

Remember, you can't just decide the planet is wintry or dark because you think it would look more interesting in snow or smog, at least not yet. Make sure you're alert to what's there; there should be actual evidence on the planet for what you report.

You're not done. In most dramatic worlds there are hidden, or at least unseen, spaces. Ask questions about them as well. What are their characteristics of space, time, tone, and mood? How do they relate to the represented world, the world you can see?

Finally, while you're looking at this planet, listen to its "music." Every dramatic world will have, or suggest, characteristic sounds – of mourning, celebration, children's patter, incantation. It will alternate sounds of human and landscape, or sound and silence. Listen for the pattern of the sound.

The social world of the play: a closer look

You are still not ready to examine the beings who inhabit this world. Before you inquire into their individual traits and motives, there are other things you need to know.

Keep squinting at the planet. Is this a public world, or private? What are its class rules? Aristocratic? Popular? Mixed?

In what kinds of patterns do the figures on this planet arrange themselves? Do you see groups in action, isolated individuals, both? Is there a single central figure, surrounded by a group? Are figures matched off in conflicting pairs? Are you seeing (and feeling) the tension of interlocking triangles?

How do figures appear on this planet? Are they inward or two-dimensional? Subtle? Exaggerated? Are they like puppets? Like clowns? Like you? (Are you sure?)

How do figures dress on this planet? In rags, in gowns, in cardboard cutouts? Like us? (Are you sure?)

How do figures interact? By fighting? Reasoned discussion?

Who or what has power, or indeed agency, on this planet? Humans? Animals? Things? The landscape? How is it achieved? Over whom is it exercised? To what ends is it exercised?

What are the language habits on this planet? Verse or prose, dialogue or monologue, certainly. But also, what kinds of language predominate – of thoughts or of feelings? And what kinds of feelings? Is language colorful or flat, clipped or flowing, metaphorical or logical? Exuberant or deliberate? And what about silences?

What changes?

You have gotten a feel for this world. Now look at it dynamically, because it moves in time. Within the "rules" of its operation, nothing stays the same. What changes in this world?

Look at the first image. Now look at the last. Then locate some striking image near the center of the play (the empty box in Kyd's *The Spanish Tragedy* is a good example). To give an account of destiny on this planet range over these three markers. Why was it essential to pass through the gate of the central image to get from the first to the last?

What changes in the landscape of this world? Does it move from inside to outside? From valleys to mountains? From town to wilderness?

What changes in time? Does time move from dusk to night? Night to dawn? Morning to midnight? Through four seasons of a year? Through the stages of a human life? Or the stages of eternal life, from Creation to Last Judgment?

What changes in language? In tone, mood, dress?

All of the changes you discover will of course contribute to and reflect on character, but each trajectory should be seen as a signifying system on its own.

What changes in the action? Have we moved from confusion to wedding (the basic plot of romantic comedy)? From threat to peaceful celebration (the basic plot of [traditional] tragicomedy)? From threat to disaster (the basic plot of tragedy)? From suffering to rebirth (the plot of the Passion play)? From threat to dual outcome, suffering for evil persons and vindication for good (the basic plot of melodrama)?

What doesn't change? Is there a stable or fixed point in this world? An absolute reality? God? The grave?

Squint one last time. Putting together space, time, the natural world, and the social world, elements that change and those that don't, you are discovering the "myth." Plays are full of archetypal places – castles, gardens, forests, roads, islands, green worlds, dream worlds, storms, night scenes, and on and on. If the play starts in a palace, goes on to a moonlit forest, and returns to the palace the next day or night (which is it? Day or night?), what does that progression tell you? How is the final palace scene conditioned by the night journey into the forest? Is the world of the play at the end of the play a transformed world? Or is it the same world returned to "normal," with minor adjustments? Worlds stand or fall on your answer.

Don't forget yourself

Seeking what changes, don't forget to ask what changes in you, the imaginer of worlds. Ask, what has this world demanded of me? Does it ask me for pity and fear? Does it ask me to reason? To physically participate in the action on the stage? Does it ask me to interact with other spectators? To leave the theatre and take political action? To search my ethical being to the core? Maybe this world means only to entertain me, why not? But how does it make this intention known?

Theatrical mirrors

Important as these internal systems are, dramatic worlds don't just speak to and within themselves; they also speak to each other. How many performances are signaling to you from inside this world? How many echoes of other dramatic worlds do they suggest? How do these additional layers of theatricality comment on what you have already discovered?

The character fits the pattern

Only now are you really ready to examine the figures who inhabit this world. Every assumption you make about a character must reflect the conditions of its world, including the way psychology functions in that world. You can arrive at the most interesting version of any question about character by first exploring the features of her theatrical planet. Characters mean only as they inhabit, enact, fulfill, engage a succession of sites, actions, and objects under a specific set of conditions. They are constituents of a complex artistic pattern. Find the pattern first!

Warning: Don't permit yourself to construct a pattern that omits "singularities," puzzling events, objects, figures, or scenes that "do not fit." Remember, there is nothing in the world of a play by accident. The puzzles may hold the key. Assume that the dramatic world is entirely conscious, determinate, limited. Give an account of that world that attempts to consider the role of every element in that world – visual, aural, temporal, tonal, figural. Become curious as each element is revealed as a player in the play. Be someone who is aroused to meaning.

Of course you can construct meaning in this world in many different ways. Construct it in the most inclusive way you can. There will still be more to see.

Notes

1 Reprinted from *Theater* 34.2 (2004): 5–9.
2 Philip E. Larson, "French Farce Conventions and the Mythic Story Pattern in *Hedda Gabler*: A Performance Criticism," in Daniel Haakonsen, ed., *Contemporary Approaches to Ibsen, Vol. 5: Reports from the Fifth International Ibsen Seminar, Munich 1983* (Oslo: Universitetsforlaget AS, 1983/4), 202.

69

Dramaturging non-realism
Creating a new vocabulary[1]

Tori Haring-Smith

Non-realism is not simply the absence of realism, nor is it the opposite of realism. It is a form in itself. There are, of course, many kinds of non-realism as well as mixtures of realism and non-realism, forming a rich spectrum of theatrical styles ranging from the classical realism of Ibsen through the visual and verbal poetry of *Death of a Salesman* to the dream pieces of Aishah Rahman and Anne Bogart's experimental extravaganza *No Plays, No Poetry*. If directors and dramaturgs only share the language of realism, then they will be tempted to impose realist expectations on all scripts, thereby diluting the richness of any non-realist elements and limiting the production's meaning-making apparatus.

Features of non-realism

To create a vocabulary for non-realism, we should strive to define the features of the style, expressed through the form, which can be manipulated to make meaning. At the heart of a modern realist text is character. In realism, we analyze characters in terms of intentions or desires. Realist characters are expected to display some kind of explicit or implicit consistency; their actions and their feelings must be linked in understandable ways. They conform to the rules of modern psychology. Their past is visible through their present. Their social status shapes their attitudes. We describe the richness of linked psychology and action as subtext and text. Without a rich subtext, communicated clearly to the audience, we say that a character is thin or flat. Dramaturgs working with realist productions typically ask questions like "Will the subtext be clear to the audience?" and "Is the connection between action and feeling sufficiently clear?"

Non-realism, on the other hand, is inhabited by figures, not characters. Spectators see glimpses of human figures, not full, three-dimensional depictions of characters. In María Irene Fornés's *Abingdon Square*, a glazier appears in a brief scene and drinks water from a flower vase. He is never seen again, and yet his presence haunts the play. Figures like this one lack subtext but may be motivated instead by historical necessity or by happenstance. Their action must be taken at face value and may well be inexplicable in conventional terms. In Caryl Churchill's *Heart's Desire*, Brian and Alice repeat the action of waiting for Susy, each repetition providing a different attitude and relationship, any and all of which might be true at any one time. Figures lack the fixed boundaries required of a character. For example, Adrienne Kennedy creates figures like "She who is Clara Passmore who is the Virgin Mary who is the Bastard who is the Owl" in *Owl Answers*. Whereas dramaturgs want spectators to seek the truth of realist characters, they want spectators to appreciate the multiple and sometimes apparently contradictory truths of figures like Kennedy's She. This web of social, disconnected notions, not a coherent individual need, lies behind the character's urge to write. Understanding this symbolism would make a character in a realist production too self-conscious, but failing to do so in non-realism would undermine the collective meaning-making that actors in non-realism perform.

Because characters in realist scripts have related texts and subtexts, the language of these scripts is usually rational and referential. Characters speak or take action (a physical form of language) that explains their thoughts and feelings. Because non-realist figures act in ways that escape familiar conventions and do not conform to the myths of modern psychology, they usually do not use conventional, referential language to explain themselves. In non-realist texts, the language is often more abstract, non-referential. Churchill dissolves language into pure sound without recognizable words at the end of *Blue Kettle*, and in her *Mouthful of Birds*, some figures can only dance their unconventional and apparently irrational feelings. Anne Bogart's *Going, Going, Gone* creates meaning by juxtaposing the physical blocking of Albee's disintegrating marriage from *Who's Afraid of Virginia Woolf?* with dialogue consisting solely of scattered passages from scientific discourse on chaos theory.

In working with realist texts, a dramaturg's research clarifies the meaning of the text for the character who is speaking. In working on Suzan-Lori Parks's *The America Play*, a dramaturg would want to help the director and cast explore the "forefather" as referring to the faux father, the foe-father, and the fo'father, not in terms of individual psychology but in terms of socially constructed resonances within the play world. A dramaturg working with *Going, Going, Gone* would not ask why a character voices a given statement about chaos theory at a particular point, but rather would want to help the actor brainstorm about the resonance of chaos theory with the movement and character relationships being gestured toward at that moment in the production.

Just as realist characters conform to the conventions of modern psychology, so, too, the plots of realist texts respect the laws of physics as we have codified them. The stories are linear. They may include flashbacks or loops, but the audience can and must construct a timeline in order for the play to "make sense." Non-realist scripts, on the other hand, operate more associatively, often sidestepping cause and effect as irrelevant or inexplicable. Eelka Lampe sees Bogart's work as "a complex interactional system rather than a linear action-reaction sequence."[2]

María Irene Fornés's *Fefu and Her Friends* avoids linearity by staging actions simultaneously in different rooms of Fefu's house. In this world, cause and effect are unhinged; the cause and effect relationship between a gun being fired and a person being shot is disrupted. Why is Julia paralyzed? We don't know. We don't even know if she really is paralyzed since she walks across a room at one point. However, that walk could be imaginary or real or (in Fefu's world) both. Transitions can occur coincidentally and/or without explanation. Bells mark the transitions in Parks's *The Death of the Last Black Man in the Whole Entire World*, moving us from location to location, subject to subject. The contrast between this random movement and the constant references to historical narrative creates meaning by calling conventional historical narrative into question. If there is a physics or a psychology at work, it is that of dreams. Dramaturgs working on realist scripts construct elaborate timelines. Those working on non-realist scripts are more likely to construct associative webs of meaning or cover the walls of a rehearsal hall with collages of visual images to explore a play's structure.

As with the physics of time, so with the physical manifestation of the playworld in the set. Realist sets are illustrative – they present the world as calm, sane people perceive it. Spectators peer through the fourth wall to see rooms or landscapes they recognize. Directors and designers reach out to new audiences when they move beyond the commonplace depiction of middle-class homes and set plays in the gritty streets of modern America. In non-realism, however, the set is rarely illustrative. Like the script, it may be fragmented, allowing the audience to see many different places at once. Non-realist designs work as metaphor rather than illustration. Production dramaturgs working with non-realist scripts need to interrogate not the realistic clues the set provides, but its symbolic role within the production. In a realist production, a dramaturg would want the bed to be sufficiently ornate or tacky to illuminate the personality of the characters who own it. But in *David's Red-Haired Death*, the dramaturg would want the bed to look sufficiently surreal to take on symbolic and universal overtones. The dramaturg would want spectators to consider the color pink not as a reflection of individual character traits, but as a socially constructed expression of gender.

The presence of consistent characters explaining their desires through rational language in a linear plot surrounded by a concrete setting contributes to creating a sense of psychological, physical, and thematic coherence in realist plays. All elements of the play focus on a central story that illuminates a unifying issue or theme, crystallized in the resolution of a bi-polar conflict. Rather than relying upon a bi-polar conflict to highlight meaning, non-realism depicts opposing values through a web of contrasts or dissonances. Meaning in these productions is rarely unified but instead fluctuates; it is often undefined, multiple, and transformative. JoAnne Akalaitis maintains that "chaos, not conflict, is the essence of drama."[3] The contrasts may be tonal (the alien's scientific objectivity and the human angst of Constance Congdon's *Tales of the Lost Formicans*), linguistic (George's philosophical argument in Tom Stoppard's *Jumpers* and his wife's cries for help), or imagistic (the movie version of "Indian Love Song" overlaid with the Spiderwoman trio singing the same song in *Sun, Moon, and Feather*). The contrasts among these elements are capable of creating meaning by resisting resolution not, as in realist conflict, by forcing the spectator to choose sides. Audiences still experience coherence in these performances; it is, however, the coherence of tone, mood, or image.

Many non-realist scripts situate their meaning(s) in gaps like these between characters, events, and visual elements. As Bogart argues, for non-realist texts, "truth … exists in the space between opposites."[4] She describes the meaning in *Going, Going, Gone* as existing between the words and the action, "in their shifting collisions and sudden harmonies."[5] The coherence of non-realism allows for multiple and unstated meanings, glimpsed through the gaps in the text because it is elastic, fluid, a "dizzying multiplicity."[6] To illuminate meaning in non-realism, dramaturgs do not trace a narrative or mine a character's depths, but rather identify complex patterns of action, image, and language. They must encourage the spectator to see both what is present on the stage and also what is absent, unsaid.

Rehearsing and staging non-realism

Because non-realism follows a different kind of logic and creates meaning in a different way than realism does, working with non-realist productions changes the dramaturg's role in the rehearsal process. Dramaturgs working with non-realism must cultivate more playfulness in their own questioning. They must open up meaning, not secure it. They must point to the gaps in the text not as holes to be filled in, but as sites of meaning that escape simple representation through language or image. They become less the source of answers and more the source of questions. As the advocate for the script and the liaison both between the director and the actors and between the stage and the house, the dramaturg must be cognizant of, and prepared to support, the new processes of exploring meaning in non-realism.

Realism requires very little of spectators. Because, in its purest form, realism invokes the fourth wall, spectators sit outside the world, watching it passively as observers, voyeurs. But to engage with non-realism, spectators need to become active participants in meaning-making. Because non-realism focuses on the gaps between events and avoids explaining the motivations of its characters in rational terms, the spectators must consciously connect the dots. To assist spectators in understanding the expectations inherent in this kind of work, dramaturgs need to write clear and useful program notes, create appropriate lobby displays, educate the press, and often hold post-play discussions.

Non-realism is also unfamiliar to many American-trained actors. In fourth-wall realism, actors become their characters, bringing all of their human three-dimensionality to the fictional world. They map out the characters' lives, probing their unstated motives, constructing personal histories to explain present actions. They must be able to get "inside" a character, connecting to the character through a shared understanding of psychology. In non-realism, however, the actor can remain outside of the character in a way that reminds many actors and directors of Brecht, who wanted actors to demonstrate his characters, not become them, to tell the characters' stories to the audience rather than embody them. To help actors work in this new way, Bogart often asks them to assume a persona before exploring their characters. This "fictive identity" distances the performers from the characters, allowing them to engage in performed or ritualized behavior rather than trying to duplicate "natural" behavior.[7]

In exploring how characters can be constructed on the basis of ritualized gesture, actors may wish to shift roles in rehearsal, mirroring one another to highlight defining movements and moments. Dramaturgs can assist in this process by collecting photographs and videotapes of people in similar roles so that actors can study their physical life. Watching actors rehearse a non-realist script, dramaturgs should not ask questions like,"Do I believe his character? Do I understand her?" but rather "What is the story we're telling? What is the purpose of this scene in that story?" These kinds of questions will help actors focus on the entire tapestry that is the production as well as on their individual roles.

Finally, working on non-realism often changes the relationship between the dramaturg and the other theatre artists, including the director. When working with realism to illuminate a central meaning through a coherent plot and rational characters, most American directors work hierarchically. Finding a focus for the script and mapping out the trajectory of its plot can be done from a single point of view and then clearly communicated through the blocking, the design, and the action of the play. In the associative, transformative world of non-realism, however, most directors must work more collaboratively. Multiple points of view may be embraced in the script, and they should also be embraced in the rehearsal process. In a SITI Company rehearsal, "It is sometimes difficult to identify the director. Although Bogart's is the final voice, all those present have what is usually considered to be directorial input."

Just as the director must learn to embrace multiplicity in non-realism, so, too, the dramaturg must embrace confusion. The dramaturg for non-realism works to discover the happy accident, the pattern, the meaning in the ink blot. Doing this not only involves the kind of textual and library research that is familiar to most production dramaturgs, but also invites the dramaturg to talk with folks, to encourage public or private explorations of associations with the text. If the director is fluent in non-realism, the dramaturg can be guided by him or her. If, however, the director is less familiar with the expectations of non-realism, the dramaturg may want to help the director consider rehearsal techniques that will open the text rather than close it down, that will create figures and not require fully developed characters, and that will make everyone comfortable in an achronological, alogical, open-ended world.

Conclusion

Because non-realism as a form resists simplicity and coherence, it is particularly attractive to playwrights who feel that their worldview is not shared by the popular media and conventional representations of human life. If the playwright is dreaming the possible, the dramaturg must not convert that dream to an apprehension of commonly constructed reality. If the world of the play is incoherent, we must not present it as coherent. Converting a non-realist script to a realist one is to change the language of the piece, to distort its method of meaning-making. Subtlety is lost. Meaning is conventionalized. The spectator is not invited into the undefined world of the margin, but rather welcomed into a world that is little different from the familiar world of the mainstream.

Table 69.1 Comparing realism and non-realism: summary of terms

Realism	Non-realism
Character	Figure
Texts and subtexts	Texts and contexts
Referential language	Abstract and dissolving language
Linearity	Associative images
Conflict (often bi-polar)	Contrast and dissonance (often web-like)
Illustrative set	Demonstrative set
Psychological/physical/thematic coherence	Mood/tone/image resonance
Meaning grows from focused thematic coherence	Meaning exists in intentional gaps
Spectator who observes	Spectator who constructs
Actor becomes character	Actor tells the character's story
Hierarchical directorial process	Collaborative directing process
Dramaturg answers questions	Dramaturg asks questions

Notes

1 This article is reprinted with permission from Tori Haring-Smith, "Dramaturging Non-Realism: Creating a New Vocabulary," *Theatre Topics* 13.1 (2003): 45–54.
2 Eelka Lampe, "From the Battle to the Gift: The Directing of Anne Bogart," *The Drama Review* 36.1 (1992): 30.
3 Deborah Saivetz, "An Event in Space: The Integration of Acting and Design in the Theatre of JoAnne Akalaitis," *The Drama Review* 42.2 (1998): 151.
4 Anne Bogart, *A Director Prepares* (London: Routledge, 2001), 56.
5 Anne Bogart, "*Going, Going, Gone* (An Article)," in Michael Bigelow Dixon and Liz Engelman, eds., *Humana Festival '96: The Complete Plays* (Lyme, NH: Smith and Kraus, 1996), 43.
6 Susan Carlson, "Cannibalizing and Carnivalizing: Reviving Aphra Behn's *The Rover*," *Theatre Journal* 47 (1995): 518.
7 Lampe, 35, 39.

70

On dramaturgy in contemporary dance and choreography

Sandra Noeth

> There is more force in a question than in an answer.
>> Thesis on the Political Agency of Networks

> There are more non-relations than relations.
>> Thesis on Unbinding Problems and Absolving Complexity

These working theses as well as the following inserted in this text have been formulated by and are borrowed from architect and urban designer Adrian Lahoud.[1] Although taken out of their original context, they seem to address some crucial concerns and ideas related to practices and concepts of dramaturgy in contemporary dance and choreography: questions of structure and composition, of networks and relationality, of singularities and methodological concerns, of intention, intuition, agency; questions that address the very headlessness of any artistic process as well as experiences of movements of the disquieting.[2]

How to build a universe that *does* fall apart two days later?[3]

At the basis of the following notes lies an expanded notion of choreography which integrates its historically grown medial hybridity (i.e. its constitutive exchanges with music, theatre, painting, sculpture, architecture, scenography, media technologies, etc.), moving back and forth between everyday actions and organization, documentation and art work, live event and institutional representation. Rather than distinguishing choreography from other arts, I propose a space-time structure, formative principles, and a dynamic and perception-oriented dialogue that speaks *in* and *with* choreography and that implies transcending and breaking the limits of the art form. This involves an opening of a physical and movement-based practice to other disciplines, to writing and thinking, to the social and political, i.e. to elements and dynamics of moving and being moved in culture, society, and political life.

Historically linked to structuring, valuing, and giving form to artistic and creative processes, the concept of dramaturgy in choreography has been toppled anew over the last years, not least of all by a confident and self-reflexive community of artists. Both in reaction to and as a consequence of a "world in search of," they have created room for collaboration in self-organized research and exchange processes and re-appropriated concrete as well as imaginary spaces that have emerged between the definition of roles, division of labor, and economic processes of distribution. Consequently, artists have been dealing with more "open" ideas of œuvre and interpretation, worked on collective and ongoing practices of creating and educating, or situated their choreographic work in or in relation to concrete social events and spaces, and thereby have also been challenging concepts of order and disorder, of parting and participating. Hence, in a large number of contemporary choreographic creation and production processes, form, content, and idea of movement are inter-connected. The intertwining and combinatory nature of research, conception, training, production, and dissemination in a performance not only has an effect on the shifting positions and demands that artists themselves have to manage, but also reduce the need for a distinction of dramaturgical discourse from choreographic practice.

In the course of these developments, a practical as well as methodological re-formulation of dramaturgy (its concepts, operating elements, and terminology) seems clearly needed: a re-formulation that gives less priority to questions of structure or form in the sense of notation or repertory in order to engage in tracing the balance and equilibrium of the singular elements of choreography, the responsibility of all parties involved, and the shifts and the changes created in their relationships. I therefore propose to think about dramaturgy less as a task than as a potentially shared *function* within a process. As an often shared practice of understanding, perspectivating, and tracing our positioning and repositioning in artistic but also in social or political terms. As a practice that exercises resistance to too easy images and forward-oriented logics and that addresses strategies and processes of responsiveness, hesitation, and affirmation in our actions and encounters. As a practice that is not limited to the work's entrance in front of a public. As a practice that does not belong to anyone.

Much more, dramaturgy designates a space of negotiation that works on under-standing how different, multi-layered materials and elements are attached to one another – how they act, react, and interact, within and outside the process. It means more than binding together separate elements or achieving consensus. It is much more the attempt to integrate the vague, the not-yet-attained, misunderstandings and paradoxical movements as well as the monstrosity of all artistic work. This means observation, analysis, and the precision of intentions and intuitions, as well as the re-evaluation of the (individual and collective, artistic, institutional, and political) prerequisites of our work, experiences, and agendas.

It means dealing with our politics of decision and our protocols of encounter.

Dé-position: on the body's individual and collective capacity for action

> We learn most about something at the moment of its collapse.
>
> Thesis on Failure

The political dimension of any system is its blind spots.

Thesis on Blind Spots

I approach choreography as a space of (conditional) hospitality,[4] as a territory in which by working on different options and perspectives, languages and influences, rules and obligations our responsibility for our decisions becomes crucial. The question of the body's agency is therefore central when thinking about dramaturgy: What is the body's capacity to resist, to react, to respond to a moment of time, to affect and to be affected? How do dramaturgical and choreographic practices and analyses operate in a "deregulated world" today, having to handle disturbing and disorienting experiences, the unknown, concurrent worlds, whose connections and correlations, resonances and counterpoints, paradoxes and ambivalences must continuously be re-integrated in life and work? What might be the physical, political techniques for a dancer to gain agency? How does dance participate in mobilizing and making visible a social, a collective body? What kind of (public, urban) space, and what kind of time do moving bodies shape, mobilize, and choreograph?

I propose to think about agency as a *dramaturgical dimension*, i.e. how and why do things *work*? And not only what do they *mean*? Thereby, addressing the body's agency as a very condition for choreography to potentially perform politically is based on the assumption that "the world" is not given nor stable, but emerging as social, political, etc., texture creating knowledge, meaning, and action embodied in art works and practices.[5] Agency consequently is not limited to the reproduction or representation of existing structures, but upcoming as a relation between bodies. It cannot be reduced to intentionality or a neo-liberal form of productivity but operates in a mode of listening: a potentially critical attitude which strengthens the responsive quality of choreographic and dramaturgical work and implies an ethical dimension of the aesthetic. Not as an external system of judgement and evaluation, but as one that considers the Other not outside but always already part of us, already going *through* us. Concretely, this also implies to rework and extend the traditionally elaborated elements of dramaturgy (e.g. time, space, sound, movement, etc.) through political, social, as well as non-Westernized concerns.

Dramaturgical research consequently encompasses processes and strategies of participation, of in- and exclusion, of closeness and distance, of trust and confidence, of affiliation and preservation; it encompasses widening our corpus and resources, the way we move and how we speak about movement, bodies, and art. This perspective addresses the body in its contemporary environments through issues of vulnerability and violence, practices of harm, colonized, racialized, poor, gendered bodies, issues of care and safeness, and of mobility as potentially dramaturgical questions.

Scale is a mode of problem posing. It refers to the binding of near and far, strong and weak, small and large. It is always conflated, always paradoxical.

Thesis on Scale as Problematic

In choreographic terms, the French *déposition* offers a possible and perhaps helpful description to illustrate the responsive and continually actualizing quality of dramaturgical practice: basically it means a binding, oral testimony before court, which authorizes the subject as a civic and legal subject. If we spin a bit further along the word's etymology, it describes a movement which makes leaving one's own position (*dé-position*) a prerequisite for being able to take a standpoint and thus making testimony possible at all. The decisive factor here is the responsivity of one's own act, which by the step aside, by moving away from it but simultaneously staying connected, marks one's position regarding the other, and which through the interplay of response and responsibility, in the moment of mobilization sets one's own thinking and doing in motion. Besides its illustrativeness, the idea of *dé-position* also puts the problem of positioning and classification at the focus of investigation of the dramaturgical. Instead of understanding dramaturgy as a forward-oriented movement of inscription or notation of bodies in motion, we have to seek a starting position again and again in order to disclose the premises of our artistic and theoretical concepts, our thoughts and words, our expectations and preferences, as well as the prerequisites of our encounter, to view our own position anew, to review it and make it visible. The issue is a continuous reassessment of our own predilections and aversions, experiences and expectations, of our own terms on which our acting and doing are founded. However, in this process of re-positioning it falls short of the mark to content ourselves with affirming the standpoints taken in the sense of fixation and standstill. Rather, the metaphor, the movement of *dé-position* proposes to try to understand how our own voice, which always has been an address and required a response, how this voice, which seems so personal and individual to us, cannot be separated from that which it shares and imparts. And how this voice (in which several voices have always formulated themselves) connects with the other in a movement of address.

Weaving: dramaturgy as a practice of agonal dialogue

An object is only as strong as the network it is installed within.

Thesis on Reality and Endurance

The problem conditions the part, the part conditions the problem.

Thesis of Reciprocity

Dramaturgy means weaving a choreography of ideas, a protocol of being-together. In the process, the focus lies not primarily on the identification of authorship, chronologies, or a succession of scenes, images, phrases, and ideas, not on the creation of an imitable scheme or the production of a certain form; it is also not primarily about "right" or "wrong" and the prevention of mistakes. On the contrary, in each process the question arises anew, how the different formative elements and valid principles and tools are to be handled.

A dramaturg's material is hence unstable. And it is precisely this moment of insecurity which sets the body, the voices in motion over and over again. This is not about advocating too quickly or too simply designed, comfortable images and readings or false promises of flexibility and hybridity. Instead, I seek to define dramaturgy as a mode of thinking, as a tool without a fixed a priori in which failure, in which "what escapes" is an immanent component. To work and think dramaturgically means opening up a divided, usually temporary space of negotiation and the creation and reflection of the evolving act of tracking the diverse traces of what is emerging.

It does not mean *not* making decisions.

It is much rather about the shouldering of responsibility with respect to the politics of decision-making. This concept of dramaturgy maintains a strong relationship to the outside. It writes a protocol of encounters, which develops in the shared period of time, in the contributed vocabulary of the situation. Dramaturgy means thinking about these traces of delegating and sharing, about how information is generated, produced, communicated, rejected, reapplied, and finally brought onto the stage; in this respect it is not about communication or mediation and not about the representation of a prefabricated status, but about the contemplation of strategies and processes of community and participation. Dramaturgy is concerned with the emerging and the moment of emergence, with the precision of intentions and the formulation of questions, and also with the means to draw closer to each other in this process and in terms of an emancipated friendship, to become vulnerable, but also tangible. Dramaturgy enters another, shared body, organizes processes between intentionality and non-intentionality, between contradicting movements, bodies, and relationships. We are looking here at a practical concept of responsibility for one's own work, but also for the interaction of all participating elements and the temporary community of artists and audiences.

The relationship between dramaturgy and choreography is a friendly one. Dramaturgy is not aimed at suppressing choreography or forcing it into a specific, dance-technical aesthetic or virtuous form. It is a monster – phantasmal, an analysis that in its survey of the conditions and conditionality of encounters accepts and addresses the instability of life and of art as given. Thus, dramaturgy is maybe exactly about ever anew building and constructing worlds that *do* fall apart two days later. About a practice of an agonal dialogue that needs the fragility and the composed in our position in order to be able to connect and to construct with one another. About a texture, that can only be approached by questions:

- What is the *material* of dramaturgy – its bodies, movement techniques, texts, languages, media, atmospheres and feelings, expectations, and needs? How do they intervene, communicate and contradict, seduce and exclude each other?
- What does the art work want to engage with? Is it about the definition of an interest (formal, personal, political, economic, etc.) or about a theoretical or methodological inquiry? Or is it about a much more vague desire, a question, an intuitiveness?
- What and who does the art work address and want to get in touch with?
- What are the structural and logistic decisions during a working phase? What are e.g. the timely parameters of it: durational aspects, restrictions, limitations, references to the past, the present, or the future? How does the contemporaneity of a dance or a performance unfold? What are the personal, collective, and institutional prerequisites of the process? How can they be reflected upon? What are the strategies of collaboration, (co-)authorship, co-habitation? How should feedback be organized; and which voices are to be heard, in which way? How does the process of decision-making take place? How much control, how much coincidence is needed or

allowed? How do knowledge and non-knowledge meet and articulate in the process? What is the relation in between bodies on stage and bodies in urban space?

- What are the conditions of the space – its dimensions, its codes and historical backgrounds, its ways of dealing with conventions and memories?
- What are the audiences' concrete as well as imaginary spaces? How is the relationship amongst the public, artists, and civil society conceptualized and realized? What are the values and the strategies of valuing immanent to the work and its reception?

Notes

1 Adrian Lahoud, "Thesis on Failure," unpublished document. See *Post-Traumatic Urbanism: Architectural Design*, eds. Charles Rice, Adrian Lahoud, and Anthony Burke (September/October 2010).

2 See Gilles Deleuze, "Nothing Is More Disquieting than the Ceaseless Movement of that which Appears to Be Motionless," *Pourparlers (1972–1990)* (Paris: Editions de Minuit, 2003).

3 See Philip K. Dick's speech, "How to Build a Universe that Doesn't Fall Apart Two Days Later" (1978).

4 See Jacques Derrida, *Of Hospitality*, trans. Rachel Bowlby (Stanford, CA: Stanford University Press, 2000).

5 See Sandra Noeth, "Protocols of Encounter. On Dance Dramaturgy," *Emerging Bodies. The Performance of Worldmaking in Dance and Choreography*, eds. Sandra Noeth and Gabriele Klein (Bielefeld: Transcript-Verlag, 2011), 247–56.

71

Research, counter-text, performance

Keywords for reconsidering the (textual) authority of the dramaturg[1]

D. J. Hopkins

Counter-text

Counter-text describes the results of a period of independent dramaturgical research and development, and the contribution this material makes to a theatrical production. The counter-text need not be a "text" in the sense of a written or spoken script, nor take the form of "another" play, nor offer anything like narrative or characterization. The meaning of "text" in this context is the now-familiar usage given the word by Barthes: text as "a methodological field."[2] But, "Barthes's understated précis of 'text' fails to capture the sense of far-reaching interconnectedness and conceptual referentiality that has come to be associated with his use of the word."[3] For the dramaturg, this understanding of "text" confers on the research process the substance of an accumulation of meaning and referentiality, and situates dramaturgical practice within a wider cultural discourse.

Whatever its medium or message, the counter-text presents an alternative site of authority in performance, an alternative center of gravity that exerts influence over the trajectory of a production process. The possible relationships a counter-text may have with a pre-existing script, and the textual practice by which a dramaturg develops a counter-text, are the subjects of this essay. I will begin with a reconsideration of "research" and then draw some conclusions about dramaturgical research and counter-textual practice.

The protocols of research

A traditional understanding of the dramaturg's contribution to the production focuses on "historical research" to be used "once rehearsals begin."[4] This understanding of dramaturgy locates research in a tertiary position: after the director's initial selection of and approach to a play, and after the designers' conception of the physical space, then the dramaturg can serve the belated function of providing the actors with characterological data of limited impact on the overall production. In this traditional view of dramaturgical practice, notions of personal and intellectual etiquette are often used to limit the scope of a dramaturg's contribution. The dramaturg should provide "relevant historical, cultural, social or other pertinent background of the play," along with "relevant biographical information concerning the playwright."[5] The word "relevant" imposes a boundary on dramaturgical practice: only that which is "relevant" should be included in the dramaturg's "protocol." Though this latter word, in general, refers to a dramaturg's "pre-production study of a play," the idea of "protocol" connotes strictly defined comportment; and indeed there are definite expectations of "decorum ... governing the conduct" of a dramaturg.[6] For the traditional dramaturg, behavior as well as research must be carefully regulated.

However, some approaches to dramaturgy refuse to rule out creativity in favor of "relevance" and selfless service to text and director. Instead of protocol, Mark Bly uses the term "casebook." More than merely a nominal change in the word used to describe the container for the dramaturg's research, this conceptual adjustment transforms research into "a tool for exploration, rather than a prescriptive, formulistic guide to staging a particular play."[7] Bly is perhaps the most famous exponent of a more open approach to research and practice, though he is seconded by many, including Royston Coppenger, whose dramaturgical credo insists that "it is vital to treat the play primarily as a catalyst for one's own imagination and a vehicle for personal expression."[8] But even the most creative, individual, intuitive approaches to dramaturgical work, like Gregory Gunter's extraordinarily valuable practice of "imaging," generate source material that remains secondary to the primary authority of a text. And even those experimental projects that lead to the most exciting results in production, like Norman Frisch's work with the Wooster Group, often relegate the dramaturg to a curatorial function: in Frisch's words, the "traffic cop" who applies structure to the disorderly desires of other collaborators.[9] And the creative limitations of the field are often compounded in the case of historic research: "exploration" and "personal expression" count as limited consolation for thankless hours of bookish drudgery spent in the library, sifting through antique reference texts and decades of critical essays for "relevant" information.

The library can be an unhelpful place to locate the dramaturg, an exclusionary site away from the rehearsal room and the work of making theatre, but it can be a great place to go if you want to start some trouble.

In many ways, the dramaturgical method I describe here is about starting trouble. Though the method is research-oriented, the principal model for research in this vein is not taken from theatre scholarship but from architecture. Rem Koolhaas and his firm, the Office of Metropolitan Architecture (OMA), initiate all their design projects with an extensive period of research. For Koolhaas, this approach to architecture emerged as a "radical solution to the difficulty of getting projects built: don't even try."[10] The research projects produced by OMA are often intuitive, free-form "investigations" of the basic assumptions behind a given project. Many of these investigations are collected in S, M, L, XL, a book that Koolhaas developed in the early 1990s as an outlet for his theoretical ideas and as a way to document OMA's many rejected proposals and unbuilt structures.

One example of a remarkable rejected proposal is the OMA design for a massive ferry station in the North Sea. The OMA project for the Zeebrugge Sea Terminal pursued the question of "authentic" construction. The research and investigation concluded that the authentic is the result of process, not product. This conclusion was integrated into the conception of the terminal by way of an overtly theatrical proposal. Koolhaas explains:

> We proposed that a crew of just 24 Belgians begin the building ... and simply grow old with the construction. The minimal progress that the building would make [from the passengers' perspective], in the interval of different rides on the ships, would be a strong part of the building's appeal, while after 40 or 50 years, the Belgian construction workers, by then old men, would finally reach the top. The price of this option was that construction was very slow, but the end product would be a completely authentic and real building.[11]

Not surprisingly, Koolhaas was propelled into the architectural limelight on the strength of his conceptual prowess more than for OMA's few completed projects.

Today, however, OMA is overwhelmed with commissions, as cities and companies around the world vie for a Koolhaas to call their own. Prada's New York City flagship store and the new Seattle Public Library are only the most prominent of examples. OMA's idea-driven approach has been so successful that Koolhaas has created a spin-off. The research part of the process is now performed by a new arm of the company: AMO, a nominal inversion that wittily reflects Koolhaas's "love" for the raw ideation of the research process.

Following the international success of S, M, L, XL, Koolhaas's ideas about architecture and urban space have continued to appear in print. A relationship between Koolhaas and Harvard University led to the formation of the Harvard Design School Project on the City, the unwieldy name for a research program led by Koolhaas. The Project on the City has already produced a series of massive and fascinating books written according to principles of "hybrid authorship" in which a number of authors bring an eclectic range of approaches to bear on a single topic.[12] Koolhaas's project has addressed subjects as wide-ranging as the global city, urban legends, and shopping.

The vitality and productivity of Koolhaas and his cohorts, and the fanfare with which their work is received, stand in contrast to the labors of many production dramaturgs, for whom the job of research is all too infrequently endowed with a sense of creative investigation. On those occasions when dramaturgical research rises above the status of bookish drudgery, it still frequently occupies a marginal position in relation to other elements of a production, and can at times feel like the mere superfluous support of that which is already self-evident in the text. Unlike the research phase of a Koolhaas project, the literary offices of regional theatres are not structured to serve as the R&D divisions providing the resources that incite or fuel production. Given the extraordinary (if recent) success of OMA/AMO and the celebrity status accorded Koolhaas and his architecture, learning to privilege research and conceptual development may be one of many lessons which North American theatre can take from this field.

The 2002 conference of the Literary Managers and Dramaturgs of the Americas took new play development as its theme. One of the most common functions of a dramaturg in a professional/institutional theatre setting is to provide support for the development of new plays; and in the convention-bound setting of regional theatre production, this support often takes the form of critical input calculated to clarify, simplify, and, all too often, homogenize a new play. In the context of such conventional dramaturgical practices, the library and research become the tools of mere information-gathering – pronunciations, definitions, watered-down history. But while this approach is conventionalized by common practice, this is not the only way that dramaturgs have approached new plays, nor the only way to apply research to new play development.

With the theme of the 2002 conference in mind, keynote speaker Erik Ehn gave the following pronouncement about dramaturgy: "The best thing a dramaturg can do is co-create, to create a conundrum as problematic as the play itself."[13] Ehn's model of dramaturgical co-creation challenges conventional dramaturgical practice on two points. First, this model seeks to position the dramaturg at one remove from the playwright. The dramaturg would not, in this model, hover over the writer, serving as a project manager who decides when a script is suitably polished and ready for production. A degree of creative independence for the playwright is secured by distancing the playwright from one of the conventional roles of the dramaturg. Second, this model offers enormous creative independence to the dramaturg as well. Eschewing the restrictions of conventional literary management, the task of co-creation challenges the dramaturg to creatively engage in the production process to a degree that matches the engagement of the other collaborators in the "hybrid authorship" of the theatre: playwright, director, designers, actors.

Under Ehn's model, research would be understood in the way that it is understood by Koolhaas and AMO: not the drive to "solve" or "explain" problems or conflicts in the text, but instead the drive toward independent development of an equal and opposite idea. Ehn has another way of thinking about such a conundrum: the dramaturg "creates a space that neither the writer nor director are able to enter; and to which they are both attracted. Revision/invention is a byproduct of thwarted yearning."[14] This conundrum, this space of attraction, is the counter-text. Counter-textual research and development need not be limited to the merely "relevant"; the dramaturgical counter-text is, by definition, irrelevant: it is not confined to references in a script, nor bound by any proprietary notion that only a writer or director should be considered an "author" of a production. Under a system of co-creative dramaturgy, "decorum" would be replaced by audacity.

Creative use of the dramaturg in theatrical production is not without precedent, but Ehn's challenge to dramaturgs puts into words a radical proposition at odds with the most common assumptions about dramaturgy. Rather than contributing to a text in the service of production, the dramaturg's contribution could be independent, serving not as a corollary but as a supplement to the text. Research should trouble the production, not simplify it, and dramaturgy should create complications alongside, parallel to, and in conjunction with the playwright's text. In the case of co-creative dramaturgy, the dramaturg's contribution to production would be conceptual work that may have no direct relation to the playwright's script, that may precede, and even exceed, the playwright's text.

The co-creative model posed by Ehn and the example set by Koolhaas *et al.* offer challenging models for dramaturgical practice. The effect of this approach in production is captured by Koolhaas, who, in describing the relationship between research and practice in his projects, said, "We want to see if we can combine with two focuses and generate a third one ... A literal thing where a skin becomes a volume."[15]

Hybrid authorship

My interest in counter-text coincides with my interest in the comparable (though much more refined) approach of Koolhaas and company. Both of these approaches to the process of research suggest ways of disrupting the boundaries commonly placed on the contributions that the dramaturg can make to a production. And by subverting the limitations on conduct and contribution prescribed by the "protocol" paradigm, counter-textual dramaturgy can develop unexpected, useful products in performance: the results of the organized pursuit of something else.

While portions of the preceding account take the form of a critique of conventional dramaturgical practice, I recognize that there are no conventional dramaturgs. The counter-textual model advanced here is not meant to be prescriptive or exclusionary; rather, it extends and articulates existing currents in contemporary dramaturgy, and offers an alternative to conventional approaches to production dramaturgy and dramaturgical research. Counter-textual practice broadens the opportunities available to the individual dramaturg for creative and conceptual contribution to performance, and expands the potential for hybrid authorship in theatrical production.

Notes

1 This article was reprinted with permission and is composed of excerpts from "Research, Counter-text, Performance: Reconsidering the (Textual) Authority of the Dramaturg," a full-length article that first appeared in *Theatre Topics* 13.1 (March 2003): 1–17. An early version of this article was presented at the 1998 ATHE conference in San Antonio, Texas. My thanks to panel chair Tori Haring-Smith and my fellow panelists. For subsequent support, thanks to DD Kugler, Michele Volansky, Erik Ehn, Geoffrey Proehl, and Shelley Orr.
2 Roland Barthes, "From Work to Text," *Image–Music–Text*, trans. Stephen Heath (New York: Hill and Wang, 1977), 157.
3 D. J. Hopkins and Bryan Reynolds, "The Making of Authorships," *Shakespeare after Mass Media*, ed. Richard Burt (London: Palgrave, 2002), 275.
4 Anne Cattaneo, "Dramaturgy: An Overview," in *Dramaturgy in American Theater: A Sourcebook*, eds. Susan Jonas, Geoff Proehl, and Michael Lupu (Fort Worth, TX: Harcourt Brace, 1997), 9.
5 Leon Katz, "The Complete Dramaturg," in Jonas, Proehl, and Lupu, 115.
6 Katz, 115–16.
7 Mark Bly, "Bristling with Multiple Possibilities," in Jonas, Proehl, and Lupu, 50.
8 Royston Coppenger and Travis Preston, "The Way We Work," in Jonas, Proehl, and Lupu, 173.
9 Norman Frisch and Marianne Weems, "Dramaturgy on the Road to Immortality: Inside the Wooster Group," in Jonas, Proehl, and Lupu, 190.

10 Arthur Lubow, "The Architect's Architect in the Architect's Time," *The New York Times Magazine*, July 9, 2000, 35.

11 Rem Koolhaas, *Conversations with Students*, ed. Sanford Kwinter (Houston, TX: Rice School of Architecture; New York: Princeton Architectural Press, 1996), 27.

12 Rem Koolhaas, OMA, and Bruce Mau, *S, M, L, XL* (New York: Monacelli Press, 1995), xxii.

13 Erik Ehn, "Stuffing for This Pillow: Dreamaturgy Recalled" [sic], keynote address, Literary Managers and Dramaturgs of the Americas Annual Conference, Simon Fraser University, Vancouver, June 12, 2002.

14 Erik Ehn, e-mail to the author, July 8, 2002.

15 Lubow, 35.

72

The bead diagram
A protean tool for script analysis

Shelley Orr

Eugenio Barba, in his article "The Deep Order Called Turbulence: The Three Faces of Dramaturgy," likens the process of working on a theatrical production to navigating a route between Scylla and Charybdis:

> On the one hand there is Scylla, representing the risk of straightening out the route, thus transforming the intricacy of the many paths into one direct line running in the right direction. Everything then becomes clear, even though it does not correspond to our experience. Within the reality of work, creativity is like a stormy sky. It is perceived as disorientation, doubt, frustration, discomfort. ... On the other hand, there is Charybdis, with the risk of speaking only of storms and forgetting about the geometry of the compass and the sextant, which make the route possible. It is the risk of becoming anecdote or confession.[1]

Barba's metaphor underscores both the dangers and the necessity of these two opposing forces. The productive tension Barba describes is one of avoiding, on the one hand, making everything so clear and easy for the audience to apprehend that what is represented loses its immediacy and relevance to lived experience and, on the other, making the work so specific and idiosyncratic that it has relevance only to its creators. How can you successfully navigate this route? With tools that help theatrical collaborators track patterns in their work without squelching creative forces. The bead diagram can be used to reveal patterns in a script or a performance and aid creators in shaping theatrical pieces, both those that use unconventional structures and those that follow established tradition. A particular strength of the bead diagram is that it reflects the priorities of the person who applies it, so it is possible to reveal existing patterns without forcing the play into a particular structure.

Suzan-Lori Parks notes in her essay "Elements of Style" that "[p]laywrights are often encouraged to write 2-act plays with traditional linear narratives. Those kinds of plays are fine, but we should understand that the form is not merely a docile passive vessel, but an active participant in the play which ultimately inhabits it."[2] She points out that conventional structures emerge from particular cultural moments. As such, structures bear the marks of a society's views on representation and the relationship between the stage and the street. Most methods of play analysis are predicated on a conventional, linear, Aristotelian structure. Ironically, plays that do *not* follow traditional structures can present more challenges (even just in their novelty) and could be regarded as being more in need of tools and methods of analysis. The bead diagram's flexibility allows you to analyze plays with many different kinds of structures.

Greg Gunter introduced the diagram to me in the mid 1990s in a graduate course at the University of California, San Diego. At that time Gunter was the dramaturg at La Jolla Playhouse. He learned the technique at Harvard University from Professor Robert Scanlan in his Production Dramaturgy seminar. My version of the diagram expands on Scanlan's focus on plot events and allows the user to track many different elements in a script or a production. I have used this diagramming technique in my work as a professional dramaturg and taught it to my students in script analysis classes for the past 12 years. The bead diagram is the tool that my students tell me they return to again and again in their own work, due in large part to the fact that it can be adapted to suit the needs of most scripts. The bead diagram's flexibility can keep the goals of the particular production in view, while at the same time the diagram can help you see aspects of the script from new angles and develop new perspectives on what seems so familiar. The bead diagram can be helpful both in the pre-rehearsal phase (or in the classroom setting), when you are trying to prepare as much as possible for the design process and the cast's participation; and it can also be helpful *during* rehearsal, when collaborators may feel they have lost their way in the whirlwind of rehearsal, with all the various collaborating voices seemingly speaking at once.

With a bead diagram, you can focus on a discrete section of a script (one act or scene) and select small icons – the "beads" – that stand in for elements that recur, such as plot events, themes, blocking, bits of dialogue, or sound cues. Anything that recurs in a script or a production can be tracked with a bead diagram. It is best to limit your diagram to around five or six elements (and consequently, five or six icons). The first step is to prioritize what you will be looking for: Will you focus on aspects related to the shifting allegiance of a particular character? Or on specific onstage action? Or on more practical aspects of production, such as entrances/exits or sound effects/music cues? The central decision of which elements to track is where the diagram reflects the interests and priorities of the person creating the diagram.

You should take great care in selecting the icons. If you make each icon distinct and immediately recognizable as representative of the element you are tracking, your diagram is most effective. "Representative" means that if you want to note a bit of action in your diagram – for example, the queen signing documents – you might use an icon that looks like a paper with a pen, or if you want to note where characters are confessing their love for one another, you might use a heart. The icon is then immediately recognizable when you are looking at the diagram as a whole. These icons are put in the order that they happen in the script or the production. The goal is to produce a diagram that fills one page and can be apprehended in a glance. Often it is best to choose a manageable section of the play, though this technique can be used to track selected elements in an entire play. Even having a diagram of each scene on one page can be helpful to get a "bird's eye view" of the script. The bead diagram is especially helpful at identifying patterns. Perhaps you notice from the bead diagram that signing papers is part of the beginning and the end of a scene, but does not take place during the middle. Or you might find that discussions of love happen more frequently than anything else in the scene. These aspects may not have been clear while reading the play or watching a scene in rehearsal. When we read or watch, we often focus on character or on dialogue and may not recognize other patterns at work. The bead diagram can make these patterns evident, as it zeroes in on the frequency and placement of particular elements.

The bead diagram highlights your own interpretation of the play. The individualized, tailored aspect of the diagram also limits the findings of the tool. The beads that one person chooses to track may be entirely different from those of another, and yet both diagrams could be useful in providing particular information about a script. The flexibility of the diagram is a great advantage, but, of course, it can be a challenge to appropriately identify and prioritize the elements to track.

Here is the step-by-step guideline for creating a bead diagram. This example comes with suggestions pertinent to Doug Wright's play *I Am My Own Wife*.

1 Prioritize elements. You choose what you will track throughout the section of the play that you are diagramming. Re-read the section and make note of what stands out to you. Your priorities may change as you work on the diagram; perhaps you start out tracking one thing and notice that something else is more prominent. It is very difficult to diagram everything, even for just one scene of the play. You need to be *selective* in what you will focus on. I suggest limiting the number of symbols to five or six.

2 Choose symbols that are clear and have something to do with what you are tracking, so that when you look at the diagram as a whole, you quickly get a sense of what is happening. Often the most simple and easily recognizable symbol is the best choice. If you have to explain your symbol, it is likely not the right one.

3 Look carefully at your section of the play and start diagramming. Your diagram should not quite fill one sheet of paper (one-sided). Try to be comprehensive, but also make your diagram simple and clear enough to be useful.

4 You can diagram across the page or down, whichever you feel helps make your diagram most clear.

5 Some of the categories of plot events that pertain to the play's themes that you might want to trace include: Charlotte's description of her antiques, Charlotte's memories, or Doug's process of uncovering information. German history in the twentieth century also figures prominently in the play. One of the real challenges with this script is the way it handles time. How can you make it clear *when* a moment is happening on your diagram?

Please include the following elements with your diagram:

1 A title that gives a sense of the focus of your diagram.

2 A key to the symbols you use in your diagram. You may put your key on the back of your sheet if you do not have room on the front. The key should make clear what each symbol stands for in the play.

3 A brief one- or two-paragraph statement detailing what your diagram helped you to see about the play. Perhaps you noticed something about the structure or the prominence of a theme or a bit of important staging that had not been clear to you when you read the play.

Note that you will likely need to do more than one draft of your diagram. You may use color in your symbols, if that seems helpful. Try to be thorough, but stick to the limit on the number of elements you are tracking: remember that this is intended to give a focused view of particular aspects of the play and is not an exercise in being complete or comprehensive. See Figures 72.1 and 72.2 for examples of how the diagram might look. Two of my former students created the diagrams in the figures, both for Eugene Scribe's well-made play *The Glass of Water*.

Some of the innovations and variations that people have used in their diagrams include: adding the initials of the characters who are involved in each bead; adding brief phrases indicating what is happening in each bead; adding a ban sign over a symbol or inverting it. This last technique has the salutary effect of doubling that symbol while still respecting the limit. Some have used clip art while others have hand-drawn their icons. I ask my students to work independently on their diagrams and then gather in groups, with four or five students all diagramming the same scene of the play. I have yet to see more than one or two symbols repeated in the five diagrams on the same scene. Often, each of the diagrams adds a helpful piece of information to our consideration of the scene. Scribe's play may well have one of the most familiar structures in all of dramatic literature, but using the bead diagram often reveals new information.

The bead diagram is highly useful in analyzing scripts that feature non-traditional structures. Because the diagram helps track the script in a moment-by-moment way,

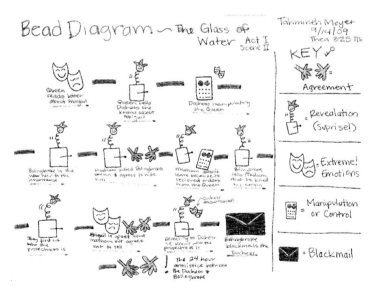

Figure 72.1 An example of a bead diagram created by Tahmineh Moyer. She focused on Act I, Scene ii of Scribe's *The Glass of Water*. The clear, clever symbols make this diagram highly useful

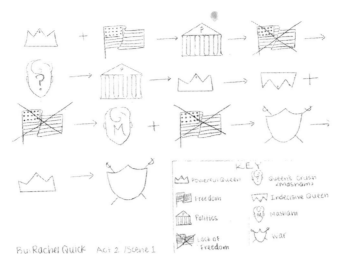

Figure 72.2 An example of a bead diagram created by Rachel Quick. She focused on Act II, Scene i of Scribe's *The Glass of Water*. Inverting the queen's crown at times and using a flag with a ban symbol over it effectively doubles those symbols without causing confusion

it can show patterns at work that may not correspond to traditional or familiar structures or may be lost in a reading. In my script analysis and dramaturgy classes, I ask students to use the diagram with Suzan-Lori Parks's *The America Play* and Doug Wright's *I Am My Own Wife*. I encourage students to modify the diagram as they see fit. For example, students have taken the principles at work in a plot bead diagram and created a sound bead diagram, charting the occurrences of the gunshot (and its echoes) in *The America Play* or tracking the use of particular selections of music called for in *I Am My Own Wife*. Noting the lines that surround the gunshot or the music can provide more information about the plays than charting plot events. While sound or music cues may not be as significant in other plays, modifying the tool to identify patterns related to the sonic element could be most appropriate for these plays. Once students have experienced modifying the tool, they often begin to fashion new ways to reflect the elements that they prioritize in the play. In rehearsal and performance, bead diagrams can be used to track the way that the stage space is used, or when particular colors appear on stage. Diagrams can be used to track repetitions of bits of text, segments of music, or even select choreography and blocking. I encourage those using the bead diagram to create hybrids of the diagrams to best track what they consider to be a high priority in a script or a production. I have been continually impressed with the myriad ways in which this diagram provides a fresh vantage point to theatrical collaborators.

Notes

1 Eugenio Barba, "The Deep Order Called Turbulence: The Three Faces of Dramaturgy," *The Drama Review* 44.4 (Winter 2000): 58.
2 Suzan-Lori Parks, *The America Play and Other Works* (New York: Theatre Communications Group, 1995), 8.

73

Method for a new dramaturgy of digital performance

Jodie McNeilly

New dramaturgy is a development upon the rich history of dramaturgical practice established within the theatre. Rather than breaking with tradition it experiments with the tradition's fundamental principles in contexts outside of theatre. Marianne van Kerkhoven describes new dramaturgy as the practice of looking at the "internal structure of a production," while Elinor Fuchs sees it as examining "the organic structures of the performance."[1] The taking up of dramaturgical practice in the production of non-text based performance and art events has motivated theatre artists to understand the cohesion of their work in light of these fundamental principles and sensibilities. New dramaturgy is a movement away from prioritizing the play text towards the democratic inclusion of the visual, physical, spatial, sonic, and virtual. Resistance to linear, plot-driven narratives with neat character arcs is historically found in the deconstructive and reconstructive strategies of performance makers labeled as postdramatic and throughout twentieth-century avant-garde theatre.[2] With the help of new technologies, interactions between the visual, physical, spatial, sonic, and virtual in performance have taken on further structural complexity for the maker and audience. These events induce a range of hybrid experiences for the audience member that involves the body's entire *sensorium*.[3] Dealing with a rich layering of non-textual elements, the question of *how* to approach performance-making that is hybrid in nature becomes paramount.

Dramaturgy is a fundamental practice to postdramatic contemporary performance forms. Dance, as the embodiment of gesture and movement, combined with the use of digital technologies within live performance and interactive installations can now with this expanded conception of dramaturgy benefit from a dramaturgical approach. I propose a model of dramaturgy for a performance practice where moving bodies interact in complex ways with digital technologies (hereon called digital dance).

Dramaturgy and digital dance

Dramaturgy considers the internal structure of a production; it is a synthesizing process: a "weave" or "weaving together" of elements.[4] A dramaturg will identify patterns, rhythms, and structural qualities, and attempt to make sense of these layers through description. They will intuit the link, the bridge, and the inner logic between elements, and consider their transitions: what, where and how these interstitial movements occur. The dramaturgical context is a process of interpretation whereby the dramaturg looks at ways in which meaning is and can be created.

In *Dramaturgy and Performance*, Cathy Turner suggests that "[t]he impact of new technologies on theatre, while remaining unpredictable is likely to be of increasing significance, suggesting new dramaturgies."[5] She points to the prolific dearth in dramaturgical strategies for performance-makers in theatre, dance, and media arts working with ever increasing new technologies. My primary concern here is to address the lack of strategies facing dance-makers. Digital dance performances create fluid spaces of interactivity amongst performers, audience, and a range of technologies both digital and analogue. They are interactions between live bodies in movement with media that enable the visual or sonic representation of bodies or objects in two dimensions to be streamed in real time ("at the same time") or in play back as digital doubles: televisual, projected, or holographic in form. Performers may enable visual or sonic outputs through wearable technologies, or be performed by avatars in second-life and mediated through other social networking technologies like webcam devices for telematic distal presentations.

A digital dance event may originate within the research and development of an interactive system, rather than strictly a choreographic genesis. In this case, it becomes a question of what can the technology do in the presence of a live moving body. Take for example the Melbourne-based company Chunky Move's production *GLOW* (2007), choreographed by Gideon Orbazanek in collaboration with programmer Frieder Weiss. Here we have a solo dance performance, lit overhead by a single data projector, and viewed from above by the audience from a square-shaped mezzanine balcony. A camera tracking system films the dancer overhead and feeds this into the computer as real-time data. Graphical representations are generated as projected output. The projections are pre-determined visualizations, but rely upon the movement and position of the dancer to trigger the system. The overall interaction between dancer and system is the symbiotic result of the dancer responding visually and spatially to the generation of graphics, while simultaneously the output of graphics is determined by these movement choices. Despite set choreographic choices, no two performances are exactly the same.

From this technical description it is possible to draw attention to three provisional aspects for dramaturgical focus:

1 structure and internal logic;
2 spatio-temporal dimensions;
3 interactions: the relationship between elements.

From these three aspects we can ask:

1 Who within the collaboration between choreographer, programmer, designer, and performer is making decisions about the structure and internal logic of the digital event? What are the processes? How is a meaningful coherency achieved

between the different layers of concern, such as system function, conception, choreographic vocabulary, performer capabilities, etc.?

2 How is the relationship between three-dimensional bodies and two-dimensional representations formulated in space and time? There is nothing more frustrating than seeing a dancer placed in front of a screen without regard – a consequence of ignoring the relationships and conversions that occur between two and three dimensions in audience reception.

3 Interaction is key to live, digital performance events. How can we develop a model that takes all the known quantities of interaction into account while anticipating an emerging horizon of possible encounters and meanings?

Phenomenology and dramaturgy

A phenomenologist illuminates the structure of things by paying attention in a particular kind of way. It is a unique mode of study that inquires into the *constitution* of things as they appear in the world: how things in the world take on sense. It "is a type of reflective attentiveness ... that occurs within experiencing itself," a practice where "one describes the experience of the thing [object, mental act, relation] as it is given within the very process of experiencing the matter."[6] How do the constituted relations between bodies and media take on sense, and what are the structural dimensions of our experience?

Description in a phenomenological sense is not empirical. Rather, phenomenological understanding is sought through a particular kind of dispositioning of the self, "and by doing so, we dispose ourselves to being struck in whichever way" by the phenomena to which we are turned.[7] Dramaturg Hildegard De Vuyst notes that the dramaturg becomes a mirror by reflecting the work: she/he "does not aim to give her opinion," but describes.[8] If this is the case, what kinds of reflections are evident, or even possible, in digital dramaturgy? Phenomenology works in much the same way as traditional dramaturgy: both share an interest in the essential structure of – in the case of phenomenology – the thing in itself, and for dramaturgy, the production or performance. Phenomenology identifies structures through specific processes of disclosure, while dramaturgy is open to varying processes conducted by a dramaturg to identify, create, and construct a coherent structure.

The Poetics of Reception Project: a method for digital dramaturgy

The following method emphasizes audience receptivity as fundamental to an aesthetic understanding of any digital performance event. It is a framework for mediating access, documenting and distilling experiences. The Poetics of Reception Project involves workshops for ascertaining the structure of audience experiences through a phenomenological approach to watching, writing, and textual analysis. The workshops engage a small group of up to eight participants attending a live dance performance using digital technologies; they produce descriptive texts (experiential data) that are further analyzed through eidetic procedures. All facets of the workshops follow the techniques of a phenomenological and attentional reduction. In brief, a reduction (or Husserlian *epoché*) involves a double movement of opening upon phenomena and our experiencing with embodied attention, while simultaneously bracketing and suspending any presuppositions, preformed opinion, or prejudicial judgments that may close down the experience. A method of textual analysis is employed to disclose the essential aspects of each individual's account across the writing tasks and different groups. This process is known within phenomenology as the *imaginative variation* procedure of *eidetic analysis*. In this context, *imaginative variation* is a manual process of sifting through various textual accounts to see what remains invariant once all differences are taken into account. The eidetic reduction in Husserl is the distilling of the *eidos* or essence, which is the essential structure of a thing. There are several stages to my Poetics method, starting with a line-by-line transcription of participants' texts. I then sift through the transcribed texts and look for connections, patterns, and the repetition of linguistic motifs; compare and contrast to ascertain points of convergence and difference; identify any bodily felt or imaginative insights; make distinctions and elaborate upon emergent themes. Phenomenological practice in this vein points us analogically to the script dramaturg, who forensically attends to the words in a playtext looking for points of connection between meanings and possible actions. The final stage is philosophical elaboration, where interpretation discloses the essential and meaningful structures within intersubjective experiences, deepening our understanding about the relationship between bodies, media, systems, and audience. The dramaturgy results from this hermeneutic massage of phenomenological data, a movement that clarifies and produces a multiplicity of essential relations to eventually be fed back into the making.

Textual analysis for a digital dramaturgy

Here is one small sample of text to demonstrate how analysis proceeds:[9]
Participant One (P1) writes:

> The Helix ... The H the skeleton of technology – taking over the Body of senses – sliding into the second skin pop out of the physical form

P1 refers to a moment where a digitally projected double emerges out of the corporeal performer and stands identical at their side in an encounter of Digital Other. After a few moments, the performer takes a sideways step and moves back into their holographic presence. The live dancer's movements are recorded, then projected as a three-dimensional holographic image, creating a "second skin" for inhabitation by the physical dancer. The world of this 'other' comes alive through the movement of the dancer in real time.[10]

The writer (P1) suggests a "taking over" or possession of the senses by the technology. The light creates a spiralling form: a skeleton producing a second skin. The description suggests three entities forming a triadic structure: first is the spiralling technology, an acting force; the second is a projected form that has "popped out of" the three-dimensional third form, the performer body. It is a paradoxical possession.

The physical body enters the projected form, unlike possessions where the possessor enters the possessed. The projection fits like a glove. The corporeal performer now moves as a function of the video projection, their senses overtaken. A body once autonomous in its having-been-ness, now prized and popped from its original sense-laden existence. The performer is futurally oriented toward a body without senses.

Focusing upon the interactive encounter "digital touch" above (and in the text not appearing here), five statements can be deduced:[11]

1 A distinct triadic relationship between a 'corporeal self,' 'digital other,' and the 'technology' enables the interaction.
2 The digital double experienced as other effects imaginings of a different world to create curiosity.
3 A power 'over' the corporeal by the digital. Corporeal embodiment serving and/ or created by the technology.
4 The verisimilitude of a corporeal body in its three-dimensional presence for the spectator is questioned because of the technology: doubting corporeal presence.
5 A perceptual disjuncture between the unity and logic of visual perception in experience and one's ineffable feeling states, which are sensorially pleasurable, surprising and/or unbelievable.

These five statements (combined with extrapolations from other participants' accounts) form the procedure for a digital dramaturgy. Reducing these five statements further, I can reconsider the configuration of bodies and media where the perceptual possibilities are greatest, where disbelief and/or the imagination are engaged. For example, in points 2 and 4, the spectators imagined other worlds precisely with this juxtaposition between a physical body stepping into the digital projection and then standing by its side. A dramaturg working with this method could consider 'otherwise' cases: alternative configurations of the body moving with media. For instance, if the holographic double were flown in from the roof, or slowly formed from a point in space and positioned elsewhere on the stage, different relations and meanings would be constituted. The moment where the dancer steps into their holographic image was poetically elaborated differently in the writings of the phenomenology group. And yet, in the accounts analyzed, possession and power were common themes used to describe the relationship between the performer and their projected other. Was this the original intention of the makers? Arguably, if the meanings sought had little to do with possession or power, then their intentions were not realized in reception, suggesting a failure in the work's dramaturgy. By and large, a phenomenological dramaturgy may prevent a problematic disjuncture between the work's intended meanings and its mise-en-scène; its makers from stressing the non-essential aspects of an interaction; and ultimately, the creative process from becoming myopic and imbalanced such that it is either too technological or too choreographic in its vision.

Who is the dramaturg in the application of this method? Phenomenology is more successful when there is a rich variance of intersubjective experiences. A small group of phenomenologically trained dramaturgs reporting to the key creatives (choreographer, interaction designer *et al.*) would be an ideal scenario. Alternatively, a group of phenomenologists or trained spectator-analysts outside of the creative process could then inform the dramaturg of their findings. The question of *when* the method should be applied is relatively open. The role of the dramaturg is always context determined. Digital dramaturgy could work back from the performance event or contiguously alongside and simultaneously with the production process. For instance, if following scenario one, a phenomenological analysis of the interactive encounter 'digital touch' would be an apposite starting point for the dramaturg to build an arsenal of devices for ensuring successful experiences of digital touch. Interaction design, system design and set-up, choreography/blocking, scenic creation (visual and audio), and thematic development are areas constituting a digital performance event, and could be individual points of focus for a digital dramaturgy. Digital doubling scenarios using projection technologies, or a piece intending to impart the themes of power and possession through interaction, would be able to draw upon previous analyses of like performances. A digital dramaturg would be constantly storing this information whilst iteratively refining their strategies. A phenomenology group working at the phenomenological and attentional reduction phase would be open to a range of phenomena and directed toward explicit dramaturgical concerns. During the stages of reduction and textual analysis, the dramaturgical emphasis could be on any phenomena, relational or otherwise. By and large, if the dramaturgy requires something other than understanding the structure of an interaction like digital touch, then one's phenomenological regard can be reoriented towards that very relation.

The second scenario would take place during creative development and rehearsal of a production. In this case, the group phenomenologists would need to work on the fly to provide immediate feedback while the performance is being constructed. If the practices of an artist or company are understood from the outside in academic contexts as a set of meaningful assumptions, or reified into a working model from processes of documentation, how is information fed back to the maker? By adopting a specific type of phenomenology as dramaturgical practice, the digital dance-maker is provided the opportunity to understand at a structural level the given and potential relationships between all the production elements. The maker will understand these relationships from the structures identified in the writings of those trained spectator/analysts. With this information, the performance-maker can then weave the internal structure and aesthetics of the performance based on experiential suggestions that are visual, spatial, aural, kinaesthetic, emotive, temporal, and imagined.

Dramaturgy is akin to phenomenological practice. Indeed, where a practitioner working under the broader conception of new dramaturgy opens up material – as Norman Frisch describes – to "expose the plumbing, the wiring, the termites, the invisible world that existed inside the walls of the structure," they are phenomenologically engaged with their world.[12]

Notes

1 Cathy Turner and Synne Behrndt, *Dramaturgy and Performance* (Basingstoke and New York: Palgrave Macmillan, 2008), 17.
2 See Hans-Thies Lehmann, *Postdramatic Theatre* (London and New York: Routledge, 2006).
3 See Caroline A. Jones, *Sensorium: Embodied Experience, Technology and Contemporary Art* (Cambridge, MA: MIT Press, 2006).

4 Eugenio Barba, "The Nature of Dramaturgy: Describing Actions at Work," *New Theatre Quarterly* 1.1 (1985): 75–8.

5 See Turner and Behrndt, 17.

6 Anthony J. Steinbock, *Phenomenology and Mysticism* (Bloomington and Indianapolis: Indiana University Press, 2007), 3.

7 Steinbock, 4.

8 See Turner and Behrndt, 157.

9 Text from Participant One, group 2, Poetics of Reception phenomenology workshop, Sydney, August 8, 2007, *Érection*: company: Compagnie Dernière Minute, Théâtre National de Toulouse, France; concept, choreographer, interprétation, video: Pierre Rigal; conception/art production: Aurélien Bory; sound creation/music: Sylvain Chaveau, Joan Cambon, Arca; program: Future Tense; curation: Mikhail Baryshnikov; venue: the Playhouse, Sydney Opera House; program: Adventures 07; season: August 1–11.

10 The digital other in this performance is an example of digital doubling. Steve Dixon categorizes the digital double into four different types: reflection; alter ego; spiritual emanation; and manipulable mannequin. Steve Dixon, *Digital Performance: A History of New Media in Theater, Dance, Performance Art, and Installation* (London and Cambridge, MA: the MIT Press, 2007), 241–70.

11 During the Poetics of Reception project, six interactive encounters were identified over several case studies: (1) digital touch; (2) moving with digital other; (3) hybridity; (4) transmorphism; (5) environment and new worlds; and (6) expressing the inner.

12 Turner and Behrndt, 151.

74

Drametrics

What dramaturgs should learn from mathematicians

Magda Romanska

The relationship between math and music has long been known and analyzed. We know that a well-structured musical composition is like a well-structured mathematical formula. The mathematician and violinist James Stewart argues that mathematics, like music, is concerned with structure, "the way mathematical objects fit together and relate to each other."[1] The same can be said of art: from classical realist paintings and sculptures to the most abstract works of Picasso, Kandinsky, Malevich, Mondrian, and Pollock, each composition follows a carefully arranged structural order with colors, shapes, patterns, and empty space consciously complementing, supplementing, and juxtaposing one another. Like music and art, literature too has a long-standing relationship with mathematics. Drawing on the relationship between math, art, and music, in his 2012 *New Yorker* article Alexander Nazaryan attempts to trace implicit similarities between mathematicians and fiction writers. Like mathematicians, fiction writers create patterns that follow a well-defined structural order, from the meta levels (the sequence of chapters and paragraphs) to the sublevels of sentences, words, and syllables. Nazaryan quotes Ernest Hemingway, who is said to have written in 1945 to his colleague Maxwell Perkins: "The laws of prose writing are as immutable as those of flight, of mathematics, of physics."[2] From Hemingway to J. K. Rowling, fiction writers are known to draw elaborate diagrams for their novels, structuring the organization of their stories on the basis of mathematical formulas.

The close affinity between math and poetry has also long been known to poets and literary theorists. As it is based on meter that defines the rhythmic structure of each verse, poetry is nothing more than the linguistic equivalent of a complicated mathematical pattern; it's a highly intricate, word-based math game. Let's take our basic iambic pentameter, one of the most often used meters in English poetry, a form favored by William Shakespeare, John Donne, and John Keats. Iambic pentameter has ten syllables per line that alternate unstressed and stressed beats. They are arranged in five pairs following a clear mathematical pattern: "1 2 1 2 3 4 3 4 5 6 5 6 7 7." In *Four Riddles*, Lewis Carroll uses the iambic pentameter quadratic $x^2 + 7x + 53 = 11/3$ in one of his riddles. Other poetic forms, the octave, for example, follow a different rhyming scheme that looks like "1 2 1 1 1 2 2 1." In addition to the mathematical arrangement of their lines, the overall structures of poems follow mathematical formulas. A villanelle, for example, has six stanzas, with three lines in the first five stanzas and four in the last.

Most recently, mathematicians, humanists, social and computer scientists have come together to devise algorithms that would explain such diverse phenomena as the progression of history and the development of language. Kevin Slavin, an MIT professor and a designer of large-scale, real-world games, argues in his popular TED Talk that algorithms guide our world.[3] Likewise, the Harvard mathematician Jean-Baptiste Michel, for example, argues that there is a mathematical pattern to the evolution of the English language and that math can explain certain historical forces, including wars. Michel suggests that mathematics can be used to predict future events and perhaps even to prevent calamities. For Michel, the huge databases we're currently amassing thanks to the digital revolution will allow us to process unimaginable amounts of data, which will reveal mathematical patterns in every sphere of life.[4] This is where science and digital humanities are coming together.

But what about drama and theatre? The idea that theatre is guided by the same rules of mathematics appears both absurd and absolutely logical. If all other art forms work according to the same rules, why shouldn't theatre? Indeed, although the relationship between math and dramatic structure has never been explicitly explored, math has always been implicitly present in the development of Western drama and dramatic theory. In 1863, the German novelist and playwright Gustav Freytag published *Die Technik des Dramas* (Technique of the drama), in which he outlined a geometric pattern of dramatic structure in classic Greek tragedy. With (a) introduction, (b) rise, (c) climax, (d) return or fall, and (e) catastrophe, Freytag's triangle outlines the basic flow of dramatic action:

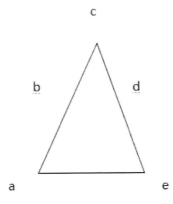

Figure 74.1 Freytag's triangle

Although it doesn't provide any actual numbers, Freytag's triangle quite closely resembles the golden triangle, in which the ratio a:b is equivalent to the golden ratio *Phi*, $\varphi = 1.61803398875$.

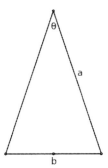

Figure 74.2 Golden triangle

In the golden ratio formula, a + b is to a as a is to b, and is equal to φ:

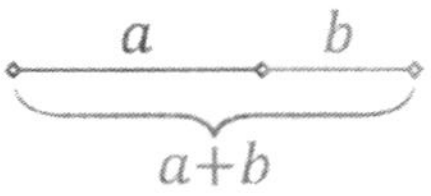

Figure 74.3 Golden ratio formula

$$\frac{a + b}{a} = \frac{a}{b} \equiv \varphi$$

Figure 74.4 Golden ratio formula

Freytag's triangle is based on the classic Aristotelian model of dramatic structure. Aristotle, like many ancients, was as proficient in math as he was in dramatic theory. Aristotle's *Poetics*, a book of dramatic theory, has been a guidebook for both playwrights and dramaturgs for centuries. Aristotle's model of the dramatic arc, as described in *Poetics*, has been traditionally illustrated by dramatic theorists like this:

Conflict Climax

Rising Action Falling Action/Resolution/Dénouement

Figure 74.5 Aristotle's model of the dramatic arc

In music, many compositions are based on the golden ratio, including some of Chopin's most famous études and nocturnes. Likewise, in art, classical and modern paintings are built around the golden ratio formula. In fact, in the visual arts and architecture, the golden triangle and golden ratio have been a standard of design, most famously perfected in Leonardo da Vinci's works.[5]

But what about theatre? Since (dramatic) theatre is a two-tiered art form based on text and its performance, the space (number of pages) and time (the duration of the performance) continuum and the correlation between the two doesn't lend itself to easy geometrical calculations in the same way that visual art and music do. Theatre artists – actors, directors, stage managers, designers and choreographers – have an innate understanding of the importance of time (timing) and space (blocking). When we do consciously calculate the time/space continuum of dramatic structure, not surprisingly, we find that like in music and in visual art, in drama the best well-made plays – from Sophocles' *Oedipus the King* to Ibsen's *A Doll's House* – follow the same mathematical formula, timing their climactic moments at or around the vicinity of the golden point.

Let's see how it works in Ibsen's classic, *A Doll's House*, a play about Nora, a housewife who decides to leave her husband, Torvald. Early in the opening of the play, we learn that in the past Nora falsified her father's signature to borrow some money to save Torvald's life. Krogstad, an employee in the bank that Torvald runs, attempts to blackmail her with the document she signed; he asks her to intercede on his behalf with Torvald, who intends to fire him. When the matter comes to light, Torvald, rather than appreciating the fact that she saved his life, even if it meant she had to break the law, disowns Nora, which prompts her to leave him. With a script that's 101 pages long, the moment of conflict – Nora trying to convince Torvald not to fire Krogstad – falls on pages 38 and 39, with the golden point falling mathematically on page 38.57856. Likewise, the climactic moment – the conversation between Nora and Krogstad and his dropping off the fateful envelope in her mailbox – falls precisely on pages 62 and 63. The golden point falls mathematically on page 62.42143. The geometric breakdown of the play then looks something like this:

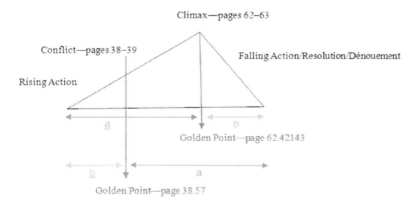

Figure 74.6 Script diagram of *A Doll's House*

The golden ratio formula of *A Doll's House* script of 101 pages would look like this:

$$62.42143 + 38.57856 / 62.42143 = 62.42143 / 38.57856 = 1.61803398875$$

Regardless of how we format the script, barring some major formatting disfigurations, even when the placement of the two golden points changes, the formula remains the same.

Can we then try to revise Aristotle's model of dramatic structure to consider the placement of conflict and climactic scenes to fall within the vicinity of the two golden points on the spatial continuum of the script? If we do so, Aristotle's dramatic arc looks more like two golden triangles:

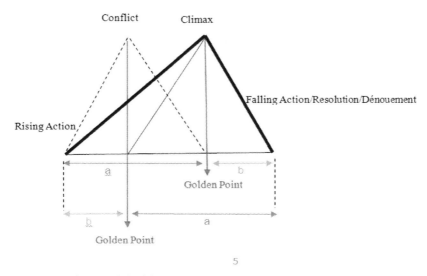

Conflict   Climax

Falling Action/Resolution/Dénouement

Rising Action

a   b
Golden Point

b   a

Golden Point

5

Figure 74.7 Aristotelian model of dramatic structure

Interestingly enough, the dramatic structure that constructs the best well-made plays similarly constructs the best well-made movies. In fact, in cinema, the dramatic arc of the narration follows the mathematical formula of the golden ratio almost to a T. Drama theory scholars as well as film scriptwriters have long known that the narrative arc of the best movies closely follows the Aristotelian model. In his book *Aristotle's Poetics for Screenwriters* (2002), Michael Tierno advises aspiring screenwriters that Aristotle's *Poetics* "can't tell you everything about writing an immortal screenplay, but it's a great place to start."[6] To test our thesis that mathematical rules guide cinematic conventions in the same way that they guide dramatic conventions, let's use some basic observations about film structure made by Christopher Keane, a legendary screenwriting teacher. Keane notes that the average well-made film script is roughly 120 pages long and that it can be broken into three acts, with act I being 30 pages long, act II, 60 pages, and act III, 30 pages again. Plot Point I (interchangeably referred to as an incident, crisis, or subclimax) falls approximately on pages 25 to 30, and Plot Point II (also referred to as the second reversal) falls approximately on pages 75 to 80. The so-called first reversal falls on page 45. Applying the golden ratio formula to Keane's observations, we see that Plot Point II falls exactly at the golden point of 74.16407. Furthermore, applying the golden ratio model to the first subsections of the plot, we see that Plot Point I typically falls at 28.647450, that is, between pages 25 and 30 (act I ends on page 30). Other screenwriting teachers have also noted that the first reversal generally takes place on page 45. Taking into consideration the symmetry of the two reversals and two plot points, our mathematical movie diagram would look like this:

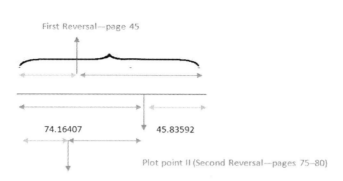

Figure 74.8 The diagram of Christopher Keane's film plot structure model

The overarching structure follows the golden ratio model, as well as the sub-elements of the dramatic structure resembling the golden ratio model of Fibonacci's spiral. The same mathematical calculations apply to the time dimension of well-made films. With a typical 90-minute movie, Plot Point II falls roughly around the 55th minute of the film, while Plot Point I falls roughly around the 21st minute of the film. The first reversal should take place around the 34th minute of the film. Test it with some old-time classic Hollywood movies or even the most recent Oscar winners.

The golden ratio calculations work all fine and dandy in classical art, architecture, and perhaps in the classical dramatic structure, but when it comes to modern abstract art, at first we feel like we cannot discern any patterns at all. Although it's hard to believe that Picasso, or Jackson Pollock, follows any structure, the modern art works, just like their predecessors, are tightly guided by mathematical proportions.

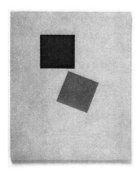

Figure 74.9 Kazimir Malevich, *Suprematist Composition* (Red Square and Black Square) (1915)

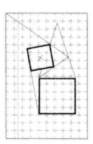

Figure 74.10 Diagram showing the relation of the golden triangle to the structure of painting (reprinted from John Milner's *Kazimir Malevich & the Art of Geometry*)

One example is Malevich's *Suprematist Composition*, which appears at first glance to be nothing but a random arrangement of two squares. Only when we look more carefully do we realize how painstakingly careful Malevich's composition is, how many hours of mathematical calculations it required for it to follow all of its golden ratios and golden triangles.

But are the same mathematical patterns that are present in abstract art also present in contemporary postmodern drama? Elinor Fuchs argues that modern works of drama, even such seemingly plotless ones as Beckett's *Waiting for Godot*, follow the Aristotelian model of the dramatic arc.[7] If *Waiting for Godot* follows the Aristotelian model, it must also follow some kind of mathematical formula, right? Even if – as in modern art – it is not readily discernible. Beckett's existential story *Waiting for Godot* is the tale of two tramps, Didi and Gogo, who wait for Godot, who (spoiler alert!) never arrives. There are basically three kinds of scenes in the play: 1) the scenes in which Didi and Gogo wait for Godot; 2) the scenes where the Boy comes to tell them that Godot won't come; and 3) the scenes where two wandering tramps, Pozzo and Lucky, pass by Didi and Gogo's waiting area. Nothing else happens – ever.

Like Malevich's two squares in *Suprematist Composition*, the two acts of the play remain in a mathematical relationship with each other through the two inter-connected subplots. The entrances of Pozzo and Lucky are the two structural pillars on which the two acts of the play are built. They also are paced according to strict adherence to the rules of the golden ratio. If in the case of *A Doll's House* we can argue that our choice of climactic moments can be arbitrary, in the case of *Waiting for Godot* the placement of entrances and exits is not. In the 98 single-spaced pages of the script, Pozzo and Lucky enter on page 16 and exit on page 42 of act I. In act II, they enter on page 75 (page 25 of act II) and exit on page 91 (page 41 of act II). In both instances, their entrances fall at the golden point relative to their exits:

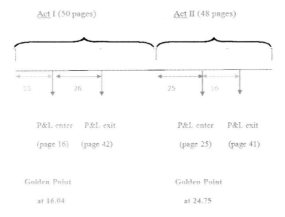

Figure 74.11 Script diagram of Beckett's *Waiting for Godot*

Likewise, the entrances and exits of the Boy provide the connecting arc between the two acts. In act I, the Boy enters on page 43; his entrance is a sign of hope for

Didi and Gogo that Godot will come. The Boy's second and final exit on page 94 (page 44 of act II) dashes their hopes indefinitely; there is no doubt that Godot will never come. The golden point between these two markers falls precisely on Pozzo and Lucky's second entrance, thus connecting the two subplots.

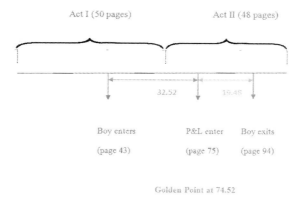

Figure 74.12 Script diagram of Beckett's *Waiting for Godot*

Perhaps it is a combination of conscious work and some innate sense of balance, symmetry, and composition that drives the great artists to create works that somehow fit into the mysterious golden ratio design that seems to govern all other natural phenomena.

If the mathematical structure of *Waiting for Godot*, however, doesn't seem too explicit, Beckett's other plays, in fact, have a deliberate and very explicit mathematical formulas. One of them is the well-known *Quad*, a 1981 television play, in which four actors dressed in distinctly colored robes (blue, red, white, and yellow) silently walk in sync around the square stage in well-defined patterns: "*Quad* has a musical structure. It is a kind of canon or catch – a mysterious square dance. Four hooded figures move along the sides of the square. Each has his own particular itinerary. A pattern emerges and collisions are just avoided."[8] The geometric diagram for the play drawn by Beckett accompanied the first publication of the play in 1984.[9]

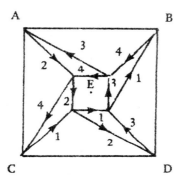

Figure 74.13 Diagram of Beckett's *Quad* (1981). Reprinted from Samuel Beckett, *Collected Shorter Plays of Samuel Beckett* (London: Faber and Faber, 1984)

Beckett's *Quad* is perhaps the extreme example of geometry as applied to theatre, but in our increasingly fragmented and abstract postdramatic theatrical universe, where the traditional Aristotelian model no longer always fits, how are we to think about dramatic structure? What new rules and principles can guide the dramaturgy of postdramatic theatrical works? Robert Wilson is known to use mathematical formulas for his pieces, including *Einstein on the Beach*, which is structured according to pre-determined sequences. More and more contemporary theatre artists are turning to computer science and mathematics to design their performances. One of the most famous is Anne Dorsen, an Obie-winning director and writer, who uses algorithms to create theatre works, a practice she calls "algorithmic theatre." Dorsen's first piece of algorithmic theatre, *Hello, Hi There* (2010), was a "conversation" between two computers, which were programmed by "inputting a huge dataset of possible language/responses and then creating a natural language processing algorithm that allowed the two computers to respond to one another."[10] The computers replicated Michel Foucault and Noam Chomsky's 1971 debate about the eternal issue of nature/nurture. In *A Piece of Work*, Dorsen creates a literal "hamletmachine" by "using a far more complicated algorithmic modality for fragmenting and assembling the text of *Hamlet*. In this piece, light, sound, and text [are] all controlled by probabilistic algorithms called hidden Markov models. The hidden Markov model we are all probably most familiar with is T9 texting; your phone will guess which word you might be spelling based on what letters you have already typed and the frequency."[11] Thanks to Markov's model, the audience of Dorsen's take on *Hamlet* experiences a new version of the play each time it is performed.

Likewise, Ruth Little, a dramaturg and the winner of the 2012 Kenneth Tynan Award, uses chaos theory in the creation of newly devised works. Little writes: "I'm interested in dramaturgical dialogue that goes beyond linear determinism – the orderly predictable world of classical physics and Aristotelian dramaturgical models – to an understanding of non-linear dynamics and living systems. In fact, the majority of natural phenomena are non-linear, and energy is replacing matter as a fundamental feature of reality. We need to shift the register of our thinking to gain new perspectives on our own experience."[12] Employing chaos theory, Little is able to channel the serendipitous energy of the rehearsal room into non-linear theatrical narratives.

In my own play, *Opheliamachine*, which premiered at the City Garage in LA in 2013, I use simple mathematical formulas to arrange seemingly random scenes. Their order and sequencing creates dramatic structure which is not Aristotelian, but which none-theless creates its own meanings.[13] Such Drametrics, a combination of mathematics and dramaturgy, will become more and more prominent, as both theatre artists and scientists try to make sense of the world, and as our globalized, fragmented reception of reality renders the traditional Aristotelian storytelling obsolete. The new meanings will emerge out of surrealist yet premeditated arrangements of concepts, images, and ideas.

Notes

1 Katharine Merow, "Mathematics and Music," Mathematical Association of America, n.d., available online at www.maa.org/meetings/calendar-events/mathematics-and-music, accessed October 12, 2012.

2 Alexander Nazaryan, "Why Writers Should Learn Math," *The New Yorker*, November 2, 2012, available online at www.newyorker.com/online/blogs/books/2012/11/writers-should-learn-math.html, accessed November 6, 2012.

3 Kevin Slavin, "How Algorithms Shape Our World," YouTube video, 15:22, from a July 2011 TED Talk, posted by "TED," July 21, 2011, available online at www.youtube.com/watch?v=TDaFwnOiKVE, accessed October 6, 2012.

4 Jean-Baptiste Michel, "The Mathematics of History," TED video, 4:26, from a February 2012 TED Talk, posted in May 2012, available online at www.ted.com/talks/jean_baptiste_michel_the_mathematics_of_history.html, accessed October 12, 2012.

5 For more connections between da Vinci's art and math, see Bülent Atalay's *Math and the Mona Lisa: The Art and Science of Leonardo da Vinci* (New York: Harper Perennial, 2006).

6 Michael Tierno, *Aristotle's Poetics for Screenwriters: Storytelling Secrets from the Greatest Mind in Western Civilization* (New York: Hyperion, 2002).

7 Elinor Fuchs, "Waiting for Recognition: An Aristotle for 'Non-Aristotelian' Drama," *Modern Drama* 50.4 (2007): 532–44.

8 Synopsis from *Radio Times*, quoted in database entry for "Quad," British Film Institute, available online at http://ftvdb.bfi.org.uk/sift/title/326964, accessed October 30, 2012.

9 Samuel Beckett, *Collected Shorter Plays of Samuel Beckett* (London: Faber and Faber, 1984), 293.

10 Annie Dorsen, *A Piece of Work* (Formerly False Peach), digital program for February 21–4 performance, On the Boards, 4, available online at www.ontheboards.org/sites/default/files/dorsen_digital_NEW_title.pdf, accessed November 12, 2013.

11 Ibid.

12 "Ruth Little's Thoughts on Dramaturgy," available online at http://ee.dramaturgy.co.uk/index.php/site/comments/ruth_littles_thoughts_on_dramaturgy, accessed October 12, 2012.

13 Magda Romanska, *Opheliamachine*, City Garage Theatre, available online at www.citygarage.org/opheliamachine, accessed November 20, 2013.

75

Parallel-text analysis and practical dramaturgies[1]

Toby Malone

Compilation of prompt books, performance texts, and rehearsal scripts is an active process. Scripts evolve, develop, contract, and expand during rehearsal and performance, and for many dramaturgs pre-production script compilation both looks ahead to the script's future while acknowledging past productions and dramaturgical innovation. Literary critic Gérard Genette evocatively suggests that "the object of poetics is not the text but ... its textual links with other texts"[2]: usefully, comparative analysis of extant texts, including manuscripts, drafts, prompt books, and ephemera, is one key to a dramaturg's preparation. For classical dramaturgs, familiarity with past textual approaches – both iconic and local interpretations that might exist in an audience's memory – offers the opportunity to learn from and speak to past adaptations. Further afield, textual benefits lie in historical comparison, which highlights the breadth of the great variety of copy-texts (both primary sources and re-edited editions) that might be considered in script compilation. Comparison of prompt books and staged texts can be a logistically elusive process, given that performance-reflective editions, when available, are difficult to manually contrast. This paper draws attention to the dramaturgical efficacy of digital parallel-text analysis, a textual approach which has heretofore rarely included working scripts.

As a working dramaturg, I find great practical, applicable use in understanding historical treatments of texts I develop, which includes primary texts and editions, but also extends to performance- and publication-based cuts, additions, and alterations, in productions both local to me and further afield. Comparative textual analysis is traditionally undertaken piecemeal through archival searching for uncollated fragmentary evidence. Disorganization is a particular inconvenience for the practical dramaturg: incomplete data can compromise the efficacy of script collation. Not all development requires precedent for classical dramaturgs, but as Laurie E. Osborne notes, "it is comparison, not origins, which authorizes any text."[3] Quite simply, it is the juxtaposition of dramaturgical and artistic choices which illuminates any performance edition far beyond singular analysis. To address this functionality gap, I turned to and adapted a long-standing technique of data comparison, called *parallel-text analysis*. As a process, parallel-text presentation of scripts has its origins in Shakespeare studies – pioneered with P. A. Daniel's 1874 facsimile comparison of *Romeo and Juliet*[4] – as a means of comparing quarto (Q) and folio (F) editions of a single play. Ever since, scholars have applied parallel-text fundamentals to test theories, compare published versions, and "translate" texts into modern English, as simplified learning tools. This technique uses the parallel placement of Q-F texts to demonstrate correlations and departures between versions, to illuminate changes made by first-generation scribes, typesetters, and performers. Parallel-texts offer convenience, clarity, and readability for textual questions often difficult to quantify singly, including chronology, provenance, influence, and departures.

Despite the establishment of Q-F parallel-text analysis, the technique has untapped potential as a dramaturgical tool: without the logistical difficulties of manual comparison, parallel-text analysis can be used to compare changes made in performance, will offer insight into structure, and may even be applied to multiple drafts of a single script, to root out chronology of changes. This paper demonstrates my constructive technique, and concludes with a brief set of examples to show the insight on text cutting, character analysis, doubling, staging, and design that such analysis can offer. This analysis is a comprehensive entry into the textual and structural questions arising from both classical, repeatable scripts and postmodern, devised works, in which dramaturgical detail may fluctuate through a creation process and benefit from progressive tracking. While this structural work is a possibility of the parallel-text system, this paper will focus on treatments of Shakespearean texts.

Edition creation

The most time-consuming element of parallel-text comparison is compilation. When tasked with a Shakespearean cut, I begin with arranging Q-F copy-texts in spreadsheets. This allows for consistent cross-platform comparison, where one cell corresponds to a single line of text. The consistent structure of Shakespeare's writing means there are never more than ten words in a verse line (sometimes more for prose), so cells are not overly extended. Q-F copy-texts are laid out chronologically, left to right (Figure 75.1).

Q1 - 1603	Q2 - 1604	F - 1623
Ham. O that this too much grieu'd and salted flesh Would melt to nothing, or that the vniuersall Globe of heauen would turne al to a Chaos!	**Ham.** O that this too too sallied flesh would melt, Thaw and resolue it selfe into a dewe,	**Ham.** Oh, that this too too solid flesh would melt, Thaw, and resolue itself into a dew,
	Or that the euerlasting had not fixt	Or that the Everlasting had not fix'd
	His cannon gainst seale slaughter, ô God, God,	His canon 'gainst self-slaughter. O God! O God!
	How wary, stale, flat, and vnprofitable	How weary, stale, flat, and unprofitable
	Seeme to me all the vses of this world?	Seems to me all the uses of this world!
	Fie on't, ah fie, tis an vnweeded garden	Fie on't! Oh, fie, fie; 'tis an unweeded garden
	That growes to seede, things rancke and grose in nature,	That grows to seed; things rank and gross in nature
	Possesse it meerely that it should come thus	Possess it meerly. That it should come to this!
O God, within two months; no not two. married,	But two months dead, nay not so much, not two,	But two months dead - nay, not so much, not two -
	So excellent a King, that was to this	So excellent a king, that was to this
	Hiperion to a satire, so louing to my mother	Hyperion to a satyr; so loving to my mother
	That he might not beteeme the winds of heauen	That he might not beteen the winds of heaven
	Visite her face too roughly, heauen and earth	Visit her face too roughly. Heaven and earth,
	Must I remember, why she should hang on him	Must I remember? Why, she would hang on him
	As if increase of appetite had growne	As if increase of appetite had grown
	By what it fed on, and yet within a month,	By what it fed on; and yet within a month -
	Let me not thinke on't, frailty thy name is woman	Let me not think on't - frailty, thy name is woman -
	A little month or ere those shooes were old	A little month, or ere those shoes were old
	With which she followed my poore fathers bodie	With which she followed my poor father's body,
	Like Niobe all teares, why she	Like Niobe, all tears - why, she, even she -
	O God, a beast that wants discourse of reason	O Heaven! A beast that wants discourse of reason
Mine vncle: O let me not thinke of it,	Would haue mourn'd longer, married with my Vncle,	Would have mourn'd longer - married with mine uncle,

Figure 75.1 Parallel primary texts

I strongly believe in the importance of primary copy-texts, as opposed to editorially conflated 'paperback' editions, wherein textual choices are pre-moderated and are nearly always aimed at scholars rather than performers. By working from a Q-F platform, the dramaturg must consider alternatives and textual variances on their own merits. I begin the process by obtaining textually rendered first-generation scripts from the peer-reviewed Internet Shakespeare Editions website.[5] This resource avoids the editorial dilemmas in texts such as the Moby/MIT/Open Source Shakespeare[6] – a text based on the 1864 public domain Globe Edition, which has similar editorial issues to paperback copy-texts.

Once copy-texts are established, prompt books may be added, which help supplement and inform the overall cut. These are recreated by copying and reinserting the F column to the right. The edition is then created by deleting cuts and adjusting textual variances (Figure 75.2).

When lines are moved or interpolated, new lines are inserted into the tables to accommodate them; when lines are cut or altered, this is reflected in the body of the text (as demonstrated in the blank spaces in Figure 75.2). Like a sculptor, the task here is to chip the performance text away from the copy-text. Once every textual detail has been included, a utilitarian, easy-analysis version of the script remains. This process is then repeated, as many times as necessary. Once the desired performance texts have been incorporated, an additional column is added for the new cut, based on the findings of the previous texts.

Obviously, this is not a quick-stop system for textual analysis. It is a rigorous, exacting process which requires patience and an analytical eye. The transcription of texts, formatting, standardization, and alignment takes the bulk of the required time, but I can fully format a multiple Q-F edition (prior to adding performance texts) in a single work day. The addition of any individual script will take anywhere from several hours to many more than that, depending on the condition of the prompt book. For

Q2 - 1604	F - 1623	Trafalgar Hamlet - Smith 2004
Ham. O that this too too sallied flesh would melt,	**Ham.** Oh, that this too too solid flesh would melt,	**Hamlet:** Oh, that this too too solid flesh would melt,
Thaw and resolue it selfe into a dewe,	Thaw, and resolve itself into a dew,	Thaw, and resolve itself into a dew,
Or that the euerlasting had not fixt	Or that the Everlasting had not fix'd	Or that the Everlasting had not fix'd
His cannon gainst seale slaughter, ô God, God,	His canon 'gainst self-slaughter, O God! O God!	His canon 'gainst self-slaughter. O God! O God!
How wary, stale, flat, and vnprofitable	How weary, stale, flat, and unprofitable	How weary, stale, flat, and unprofitable
Seeme to me all the vses of this world?	Seems to me all the uses of this world!	Seems to me all the uses of this world!
Fie on't, ah fie, tis an vnweeded garden	Fie on't! Oh, fie, fie; 'tis an unweeded garden	
That growes to seede, things rancke and grose in nature,	That grows to seed, things rank and gross in nature	
Possesse it meerely that it should come thus	Possess it merely. That it should come to this!	That it should come to this!
But two months dead, nay not so much, not two,	But two months dead - nay, not so much, not two -	But two months dead - nay, not so much, not two -
So excellent a King, that was to this	So excellent a king, that was to this	So excellent a king, that was to this
Hiperion to a satire, so louing to my mother,	Hyperion to a satyr, so loving to my mother	Hyperion to a satyr, so loving to my mother
That he might not beleeme the winds of heauen	That he might not beleem the winds of heaven	That he might not beleem the winds of heaven
Visite her face too roughly, heauen and earth	Visit her face too roughly. Heaven and earth,	Visit her face too roughly
Must I remember, why she should hang on him	Must I remember? Why, she would hang on him	
As if increase of appetite had growne	As if increase of appetite had grown	
By what it fed on, and yet within a month,	By what it fed on; and yet within a month -	and yet within a month -
Let me not thinke on't, frailty thy name is woman	Let me not think on't - frailty, thy name is woman -	Let me not think on't - frailty, thy name is woman -
A little month or ere those shooes were old	A little month, or ere those shoes were old	
With which she followed my poore fathers bodie	With which she followed my poor father's body	
Like Niobe all teares, why she	Like Niobe, all tears - why, she, even she -	why, she, even she -
O God, a beast that wants discourse of reason	O Heaven! A beast that wants discourse of reason	O Heaven! A beast that wants discourse of reason
Would haue mourn'd longer, married with my Vncle,	Would have mourn'd longer - married with mine uncle,	Would have mourn'd longer - married with mine uncle,
My fathers brother, but no more like my father	My father's brother - but no more like my father	My father's brother - but no more like my father
Then I to Hercules, within a month,	Than I to Hercules. Within a month,	Than I to Hercules.
Ere yet the salt of most vnrighteous teares,	Ere yet the salt of most unrighteous tears	
Had left the flushing in her gauled eyes,	Had left the flushing of her galled eyes,	
She married, ô most wicked speede; to post	She married - O, most wicked speed! To post	O, most wicked speed! To post
With such dexteritie to incestious sheets.	With such dexterity to incestuous sheets!	With such dexterity to incestuous sheets!
It is not, nor it cannot come to good,	It is not, nor it cannot come to good	It is not, nor it cannot come to good
But breake my hart, for I must hold my tongue.	But break, my heart, for I must hold my tongue.	But break, my heart, for I must hold my tongue.

Figure 75.2 Insertion of performance text

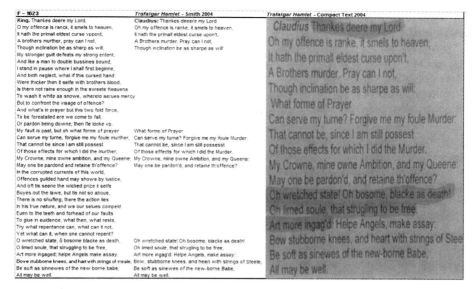

Figure 75.3 Driftwood compact performance script

example, the Driftwood Theatre prompt book in Figure 75.3 (far right) excises all unneeded text, meaning that analysis of the cuts is not as simple as noting what has been stricken out. By presenting this script in the parallel-text format, we can see exactly what has been removed. Often, blank space is the most telling factor of all: absence speaks volumes.

The primary advantages of this rigorous process are manifold. Compilation of copy-texts and performance editions in this manner is a greater engagement than the editorial process, and begets a structural and material comprehension unavailable in single texts. The "sculptural" process of cuts, particularly through a third or fourth performance text, offers patterns of changes, alterations, and instances of influence in the most opaque available manner. This structural intimacy feeds into the cutting process, by offering perspectives on precedents and innovations, and extends to the creation of glossaries, notes, readings, and textual/performance histories. As a system of analysis, the parallel-text apparatus is surprisingly efficacious in what it offers. The reading eye is drawn to white space, and when text is removed from excised points, the edition's construction is clearly exposed. Furthermore, when significant textual variance is noted, I color-fill to flag impacted cells, meaning that skim-reading yields material.

Case study: *Hamlet* in Toronto

Over the past decade, the artistically diverse Toronto (Ontario) area has hosted multiple adaptations of *Hamlet*, with companies ranging from large festivals to co-operative groups. Each approach has been markedly different, including a one-man touring *Hamlet* (*Hamlet (Solo)*, Raoul Bhaneja, touring, 2000–present[7]);

a site-specific promenade production in a converted castle (*Trafalgar Hamlet*, Drift-wood Theatre Group, Whitby, ON, 2003[8]); two large-scale "traditional" stagings at the Stratford Festival (Joseph Ziegler, 2000;[9] Adrian Noble, 2008[10]); two minimalist versions at middle-level theatre companies in Toronto (Soulpepper Theatre, 2004–5;[11] Necessary Angel Theatre, 2008–9[12]); an outdoor production staged in a park tent (Resurgence Theatre Company, Newmarket, ON, 2010[13]); and a digitally enabled, truncated adaptation simulcast on the internet (*Hamlet Live*, Kyle McDonald, Toronto, 2012[14]). For the purpose of visualizing this paper's examples, I collected and codified prompt books from each of these productions to demonstrate the efficacy of the system. I use these *Hamlet* productions as illustrative of the parallel-text system in relation to geographically linked productions, not as definitive examples of this play.

Hamlet is a useful case study, though this process is easily applied to any classical text. The perceived fixity of Shakespeare's words is problematic, given the historical changeability of text from production to production and performance to performance, and the significant differences between published Q-F texts. The performance-edition phenomenon of the eighteenth century – in a time when specific actor-managers' texts shifted, evolved, and were regularly published – demonstrates that textual fixity is a fiction. Even keeping in mind that each prompt book or performance edition represents the state of a palimpsestic script at a single point in a single production (usually the final version), the comparison of prompt books offers compelling insight. Every textual cut is different and depends heavily on the production's venue, personnel, and artistic vision. Acknowledgement of past innovation is not an imprimatur for text larceny, as understanding how other artists skirted previous problematic dramaturgical moments is informative.

Each Toronto *Hamlet* offered distinct textual and performative approaches: there was moderate evidence that these versions were influenced by one another, although it is reasonable to assume that there was further crossover with artists in a close-knit community. The point of analysis is not necessarily to identify patterns and trends – often the very lack of confluence is remarkable in itself – but the process of contrasting multiple texts offers insight into the structural nature of the adaptation. Variances will emerge as adaptations are logged: changes in text, reassigned speeches, omitted lines, interpolated material, and solutions to staging concerns intrinsically impact the overall cut. Each approach offers a strong, medium-based take on a canonized central core text – one staged so often that it can be difficult to differentiate between emendations without the proper apparatus.

For example, a cut may point to a production's technical focus: Kyle McDonald's *Hamlet Live* was designed specifically to be live-streamed on the internet while playing before a physical audience, which offered the technological necessity of dramaturgical innovation. The text was treated with the medium in mind (Figure 75.4), with an interpolated scene staged high above the platform, on silks, showing Gertrude's murder of Ophelia (with the stage direction inserted into the body of the document); this was immediately followed by a textual alteration which brought Hamlet's letter to a video projection. Unnecessary characters were omitted, a solution to the conveyance of Hamlet's missive is neatly offered, and Gertrude's later account of her presence at Ophelia's death is highly problematized.

Q2 - 1604	F - 1623	HAMLET LIVE - McDonald 2012
		Enter Ophelia, mad. She swings on the silks, and is joined by Gertrude, who stabs her. Exeunt. Enter Horatio.
Enter Horatio and others	*Enter Horatio, with an Attendant.*	
Hora. VVhat are they that would speake with me?	**Hora.** What are they that would speake with me?	Horatio: What are they that would speak with me?
Gent. Sea-faring men sir, they say they haue Letters for you.	**Ser.** Saylors sir, they say they haue Letters for you.	
Hor. Let them come in.	**Hor.** Let them come in.	
I doe not know from what part of the world	I do not know from what part of the world	
I should be greeted, if not from Lord Hamlet.	I should be greeted, if not from Lord Hamlet	
Enter Saylers.	*Enter Saylor*	*Show Hamlet, projected on a screen.*
Say. God blesse you sir.	**Say.** God blesse you Sir.	
Hora. Let him blesse thee to	**Hor.** Let him blesse thee too.	
Say. A shall sir and please him, there's a Letter for you sir, it came	**Say.** Hee shall sir, and't please him. There's a Letter	
frõ th'Embassador that was bound for England, if your name be Ho-	for you Sir: it comes from th' Ambassadours that was	
ratio, as I am let to know it is	bound for England, if your name be Horatio, as I am let	
	to know it is	
	Reades the Letter	
Hor. Horatio, when thou shalt haue ouer-lookt this, giue these fel-	HOratio, When thou shalt haue ouerlook'd this, giue these	Hamlet: Horatio,
lowes some meanes to the King, they haue Letters for him: Ere wee	Fellowes some meanes to the King. They haue Letters	ere we were two days old at sea, a pirate of very
were two daies old at Sea, a Pyrat of very warlike appointment gaue	for him. Ere we were two dayes old at Sea, a Pyrate of very	warlike appointment gave us chase. Finding ourselves too
vs chase, finding our selues too slow of saile, wee put on a compelled	Warlicke appointment gaue vs Chace. Finding our selues too	slow of sail, we put on a compelled valour, and in the grapple, I
valour, and in the grapple I boorded them, on the instant they got	slow of Saile, we put on a compelled Valour: In the Grapple, I	boarded them. On the instant they got clear of our ship, so
cleare of our shyp, so I alone became they prisoner, they haue dealt	boorded them. On the instant they got cleare of our Shippe, so	I alone became their prisoners. They have dealt with me like
with me like theeues of mercie, but they knew what they did, I am to	I alone became their Prisoner. They haue dealt with mee, like	thieves of mercy.
doe a turne for them, let the King haue the Letters I haue sent, and	Theeues of Mercy; but they knew what they did, I am to doe	
repayre thou to me with as much speede as thou wouldest flie death,	a good turne for them. Let the King haue the Letters I haue	Repair thou to me with as much speed as thou wouldest
I haue wordes to speake in thine eare will make thee dumbe, yet are	sent, and repaire thou to me with as much hast as thou wouldest	fly death. I have words to speak in thine ear will make thee
they much too light for the bord of the matter, these good fellowes	flye death. I haue words to speake in your eare, will make thee	dumb, yet are they much too light for the bore of the matter.
will bring thee where I am, Rosencraus and Guyldensterne hold their	dumbe, yet are they much too light for the bore of the matter.	These good fellows will bring thee where I am. Rosencrantz
course for England, of them I haue much to tell thee, farewell.	These good Felowes will bring thee where I am. Rosincrance	and Guildenstern hold their course for England. Of them
So that thou knowest thine Hamlet.	and Guildensterne, hold their course for England. Of them	I have much to tell thee. Farewell.
	I haue much to tell thee, Farewell	He that thou knowest thine.
	He that thou knowest thine.	Hamlet
	Hamlet.	
Hor. Come I will you way for these your letters,	Come, I will giue you way for these your Letters,	
And doo't the speedier that you may direct me	And doo't the speedier, that you may direct me	
To him from whom you brought them.	To him from whom you brought them	

Figure 75.4 Hamlet Live technology edits

Similarly, Raoul Bhaneja's one-man *Hamlet (Solo)* was forced to account for logistical concerns. The actor performed a text based on the Arden edition, only cut when the stage action was unable to be clearly conveyed with a single actor modulating voices and physicality. In the play's final moments, Bhaneja duels with himself before dying four times (Hamlet, Laertes, Claudius, Gertrude) and saves his most poetic death for the last (Figure 75.5). This textual choice means that the lines immediately following Hamlet's death (excepting Horatio's iconic farewell) are, by necessity, removed.

Q2 - 1604	F - 1623	HAMLET (SOLO) - Bhaneja 2000-present
Ham. I am dead Horatio, wretched Queene adiew.	**Ham.** I am dead Horatio, wretched Queene adiew.	**Hamlet:** I am dead, Horatio. Wretched Queen, adieu.
You that lookes pale, and tremble at this chance.	You that looke pale, and tremble at this chance.	You that look pale and tremble at this chance,
That are but mutes, or audience to this act,	That are but Mutes or audience to this acte:	That are but mutes or audience to this act,
Had I but time, as this fell sergeant Death	Had I but time (as this fell Sergeant death	Had I but time - as this fell sergeant, Death,
Is strict in his arrest, ô I could tell you,	Is strick'd in his Arrest) oh I could tell you	Is strict in his arrest - O, I could tell you -
But let it be; Horatio I am dead,	But let it be: Horatio, I am dead,	But let it be. Horatio, I am dead,
Thou liuest, report me and my cause a right	Thou liu'st, report me and my causes right	Thou liv'st. Report me and my causes right
To the vnsatisfied.	To the vnsatisfied.	To the unsatisfied.
Hor. Neuer beleeue it,	**Hor.** Neuer beleeue it.	
I am more an anticke Romaine then a Dane,	I am more an Antike Roman then a Dane	
Heere's yet some liquer left.	Heere's yet some Liquor left.	
Ham. As th'art a man	**Ham.** As th'art a man, giue me the Cup	
Giue me the cup, let goe, by heauen Ile hate,	Let go, by Heauen Ile haue't	
O god Horatio, what a wounded name	Oh good Horatio, what a wounded name,	O god Horatio, what a wounded name
Things standing thus vnknowne, shall I leaue behind me?	(Things standing thus vnknowne) shall I liue behinde me.	
If thou did'st euer hold me in thy hart,	If thou did'st euer hold me in thy heart,	
Absent thee from felicity a while,	Absent thee from felicitie a while,	
And in this harsh world drawe thy breath in paine	And in this harsh world draw thy breath in paine,	And in this harsh world draw thy breath in pain
A march a farre off		
To tell my story. what warlike noise is this?	To tell my Storie.	To tell my story.
	March afarre off, and shout within.	
	What warlike noyse is this?	
Enter Osricke	*Enter Osricke*	
Osr. Young Fortenbrasse with conquest come from Pola	**Osr.** Yong Fortinbras, with conquest come frõ Poland	
To th'embassadors of England giues this warlike volly.	To th' Ambassadors of England giues rhis warlike volly	
Ham. O I die Horatio.	**Ham.** O I dye Horatio.	O, I die, Horatio.
The potent poyson quite ore-crowes my spirit,	The potent poyson quite ore-crowes my spirit,	The potent poison quite o'ercrows my spirit.
I cannot liue to heare the newes from England,	I cannot liue to heare the Newes from England,	
But I doe prophecie th'election lights	But I do prophesie th'election lights	
On Fortinbrasse, he has my dying voyce,	On Fortinbras, he ha's my dying voyce,	
So tell him, with th'occurrants more and lesse	So tell him with the occurrents more and lesse,	
Which haue solicited, the rest is silence	Which haue solicited. The rest is silence. O, o, o, o.	The rest is silence. O, O, O, O. *Dies*
	Dyes	Now cracks a noble heart.
Hora. Now cracks a noble hart, good night sweete Princ	**Hora.** Now cracke a Noble heart.	Good night, sweet prince,
	Goodnight sweet Prince,	And flights of angels sing thee to thy rest.
And flights of Angels sing thee to thy rest.	And flights of Angels sing thee to thy rest,	
Why dooes the drum come hether?	Why do's the Drumme come hither?	

Figure 75.5 Hamlet (Solo) finale

While this choice was clearly informed by the logistical challenges of having a single actor play multiple roles, it also offers an option for an expedient play-ending cut. While not shown in Figure 75.5, the comparison process means that contrasting this style of finale with those of the other productions yields a striking result.

Finally, two adaptations of the play (Joseph Ziegler, 2000; Adrian Noble, 2008) at the Stratford Festival, along with Resurgence Theatre's 2010 outdoor production represent a large-company festival mentality which influences the way the text is emended. For the Stratford Festival (Canada's national Shakespeare festival and the largest theatre of its kind on the continent), large budgets allow for opportunities like presenting *Hamlet* lightly cut. Resurgence's outdoor production had very strong links to the Stratford productions, in part because a well-known Stratford actor, Graham Abbey (Laertes in the 2000 Stratford production) played the title role for Resurgence. Furthermore, Resurgence's artistic director, Lee Samuel Wilson, has worked at Stratford himself and was mentored by former artistic director Robin Phillips. Textual alterations were informed by links to previous *Hamlet* productions, including one actor, David Ferry, undertaking his fifth *Hamlet* production. Links between productions are often surmised or considered, but the parallel-text system clarifies these connections beyond doubt, demonstrating structural and textual links obscured in singular prompt books. As can be noted (Figure 75.6), precedent and textual agreement is clear in parallel.

Further applications

While the parallel-text system is of greatest use as a means of analysis and text construction, its practical uses are just being established. In late 2012, Glasgow's Bell Rock Company commissioned a new edition of *Hamlet* – staged as *Hamlet (Variorum)* – based on the line structure of the first Quarto, with text exclusively from the First Folio.[15] Similarly, in early 2013, I was commissioned to construct Shakespeare's *Richard III* with a structural adherence to Shakespeare's source, the anonymous *True Tragedy of*

F - 1623	Hamlet (Stratford) - Noble 2008	Hamlet (Resurgence) - Wilson 2010
Qu. What shall I do?	**Ger.** What shall I do?	**Ger.** What shall I do?
Ham. Not this by no meanes that I bid you do:	**Ham.** Not this, by no means, that I bid you do:	**Ham.** Not this, by no means, that I bid you do:
Let the blunt King tempt you againe to bed.	Let the blunt King tempt you again to bed.	Let the blunt King tempt you again to bed,
Pinch Wanton on your cheeke, call you his Mouse,	Pinch wanton on your cheek, call you his mouse,	Pinch wanton on your cheek, call you his mouse,
And let him for a paire of reechie kisses,	And let him, for a pair of reechy kisses,	And let him, for a pair of reechy kisses,
Or padling in your necke with his damn'd Fingers,	Or paddling in your neck with his damn'd fingers,	Or paddling in your neck with his damn'd fingers,
Make you to rauell all this matter out.	Make you to ravel all this matter out	Make you to ravel all this matter out
That I essentially am not in madnesse,	That I essentially am not in madness,	That I essentially am not in madness,
But made in craft. 'Twere good you let him know,	But mad in craft.	But mad in craft.
For who that's but a Queene, faire, sober, wise,		
Would from a Paddocke, from a Bat, a Gibbe,		
Such deere concernings hide, Who would do so,		
No in despight of Sense and Secrecie,		
Vnpegge the Basket on the houses top:		
Let the Birds flye, and like the famous Ape		
To try Conclusions in the Basket, creepe		
And breake your owne necke downe.		
Qu. Be thou assur'd, if words be made of breath,	**Ger.** Be thou assur'd, if words be made of breath,	**Ger.** Be thou assur'd, if words be made of breath,
And breath of life: I haue no life to breath	And breath of life, I have no life to breathe	And breath of life, I have no life to breathe
What thou hast saide to me.	What thou hast said to me.	What thou hast said to me.
Ham. I must to England, you know that?	**Ham.** I must to England, you know that?	**Ham.** I must to England, you know that?
Qu. Alacke I had forgot: 'Tis so concluded on.	**Ger.** Alack, I had forgot. 'Tis so concluded on.	**Ger.** Alack, I had forgot. 'Tis so concluded on.

Figure 75.6 Stratford and Resurgence text agreement

Q1 - 1603	F - 1623	Hamlet [Variorum] - Malone 2012
	Ham. I so, God buy'ye: Now I am alone.	
Ham. Why what a dunghill idiote slaue am I?	Oh what a Rogue and Pesant slaue am I?	Ham. Why, what a dunghill idiot slave --
		No! What a rogue and peasant slave am I
Why these Players here draw water from eyes:	Is it not monstrous that this Player heere,	Why, these players here draw water from eyes,
	But in a Fixion, in a dreame of Passion,	
	Could force his soule so to his whole conceit,	
	That from her working, all his visage warm'd;	
	Teares in his eyes, distraction in's Aspect,	
	A broken voyce, and his whole Function suiting	
	With Formes, to his Conceit? And all for nothing?	
For Hecuba, why what is Hecuba to him, or he to Hecuba?	For Hecuba?	For Hecuba!
	What's Hecuba to him, or he to Hecuba,	What's Hecuba to him, or he to Hecuba,
What would he do and if he had my losse?	That he should weepe for her? What would he doe,	That he should weep for her? What would he do
His father murdred, and a Crowne bereft him,	Had he the Motiue and the Cue for passion	Had he the motive and the cue for passion
He would turne all his teares to droppes of blood,	That I haue? He would drowne the Stage with teares,	That I have? He would
	And cleaue the generall eare with horrid speech:	cleave the general ear with horrid speech;
Amaze the standers by with his laments,	Make mad the guilty, and apale the free,	Make mad the guilty, and appal the free,
Strike more then wonder in the iudiciall eares,	Confound the ignorant, and amaze indeed,	Confound the ignorant, and amaze indeed
Confound the ignorant, and make mute the wise,	The very faculty of Eyes and Eares. Yet I,	The very faculty of eyes and ears. Yet I,
Indeede his passion would be generall.	A dull and muddy-metled Rascall, peake	A dull and muddy-mettled rascal, peak
Yet I like to an asse and Iohn a Dreames,	Like Iohn a-dreames, vnpregnant of my cause.	Like John-a-dreams, unpregnant of my cause,
Hauing my father murdred by a villaine,		Having my father murd'red by a villain,
Stand still, and let it passe, why sure I am a coward:		Stand still and let it pass: why sure, I am a coward?
	And can say nothing: No, not for a King,	
	Vpon whose property, and most deere life,	
	A damn'd defeate was made. Am I a Coward?	
	Who calles me Villaine? breakes my pate a-crosse?	Who
Who pluckes me by the beard, or twites my nose,	Pluckes off my Beard, and blowes it in my face?	Plucks off my beard, and blows it in my face,
Giue's me the lie i'th throate downe to the lungs,	Tweakes me by'th'Nose? giues me the Lye i'th'Throate,	Tweaks me by'th'nose, gives me the lie i'th'throat
Sure I should take it, or else I haue no gall,	As deepe as to the Lungs? Who does me this?	As deep as to the lungs - who does me this?
	Ha? Why I should take it: for it cannot be,	
	But I am Pigeon-Liuer'd, and lacke Gall	
	To make Oppression bitter, or ere this,	
Or by this I should a fatted all the region kites	I should haue fatted all the Region Kites	Or by this I should 'a fatted all the region kites
With his slaues offell, this damned villaine,	With this Slaues Offall, bloudy: a Bawdy villaine,	With this slave's offall, this damned villain:
Treacherous, bawdy, murderous villaine:	Remorselesse, Treacherous, Letcherous, kindles villaine!	Remorseless, treacherous, lecherous, kindless villain!
	Oh Vengeance!	O, vengeance!

Figure 75.7 Building a new *Hamlet*

Richard III.[16] Both of these contracts – while unusual in their emphasis on early modern performing text structure – were undertaken through the parallel-text process. After arranging the editions in the parallel-text format, structural consistency became very apparent, meaning that the *Hamlet* text (performed in both Glasgow and Toronto) was a simple matter of line transference (Figure 75.7). While there was a measure of work to be done after the initial transfer, this process benefited immeasurably from the expedient parallel process.

Obviously, the parallel-text system has extensive scholarly and research-based implications: practical dramaturgy is only a single outlet, but has proven crucial to my pre-production script preparation process. It is time-consuming, but offers an intimacy with multiple script iterations that single texts will not provide, and gives excellent structural indicators that inform future emendations. This system has applications to any dramatic edition and offers insight into any multi-faceted iteration of a performing text: it is critical to my dramaturgical process, and I continue to refine, formalize, and embellish as necessity arises.

Notes

1 My gratitude to the following individuals who very kindly provided access to their *Hamlet* prompt books: D. Jeremy Smith, Lee Samuel Wilson, Kyle McDonald, Raoul Bhaneja, and Nora Polley at the Stratford Festival Archives.
2 Gérard Genette, *Palimpsests: Literature in the Second Degree*, trans. Channa Newman and Claude Doubinsky (Lincoln: University of Nebraska Press, 1997), ix.
3 Laurie E. Osborne, "Rethinking the Performance Editions: Theatrical and Textual Productions of Shakespeare," in *Shakespeare, Theory and Performance*, ed. James Bulman, (London: Routledge, 1996), 172.

4 P. A. Daniel, *Romeo and Juliet* (facsimile; London: Trubner, 1874).
5 Internet Shakespeare Editions, available online at http://internetshakespeare.uvic.ca/index.html.
6 Moby/MIT/Open Source Shakespeare, available online at http://shakespeare.mit.edu/.
7 Raoul Bhaneja (adapter), *Hamlet (Solo)*, Hope and Hell Theatre Company, touring, 2000–present.
8 D. Jeremy Smith (adapter and director), *Trafalgar Hamlet*, Driftwood Theatre Group, Trafalgar Castle School, Whitby, ON, 2003.
9 Joseph Ziegler (director), *Hamlet*, Stratford Shakespeaere Festival, Festival Theatre, Stratford, ON, 2000.
10 Adrian Noble (adapter and director), *Hamlet*, Stratford Shakespeare Festival, Festival Theatre, Stratford, ON, 2008.
11 Joseph Zielger (director), *Hamlet*, Soulpepper Theatre, Harbourfront Centre, Toronto, 2004–5.
12 Graham McLaren (director), *Necessary Angel's Hamlet*, Necessary Angel, Buddies in Bad Times Theatre/Harbourfront Centre, Toronto, 2008–9.
13 Lee Samuel Wilson (adapter and director), *Hamlet*, Resurgence Theatre, Fairy Lake, Newmarket, ON, 2010.
14 Kyle McDonald (adapter), *Hamlet Live*, Hamlet Live Theatre, Annex Theatre, Toronto, 2012.
15 Toby Malone (adapter), *Hamlet (Variorum)*, Glasgow City Free Church, Scotland; Glen Morris Studio, Toronto, 2012.
16 Toby Malone (adapter), *Richard III*, University of Waterloo, ON, 2013.

Part VIII

DRAMATURG AS PUBLIC RELATIONS MANAGER

Immersions, talkbacks, lobby displays, and
social networks

76
Dramaturgy and the immersive theatre experience

Catherine Bouko

The concept of immersive theatre is today growing in success, be it with artists – such as international avant-garde for commercial success such as *Then She Fell* by Third Rail Project (2012, New York) – or indeed with researchers. This explains why the journalist Mark Lawson has stated, "On a bad day at the Edinburgh or Manchester festivals, there were times when a critic felt dizzy nostalgia at the sight of a seat or a script."[1] The term *immersion* designates a multitude of different practices in various disciplinary fields: naturally cinema and video games, but equally theatre, installation art, performance, dance, and the fine arts. Due to the broad use of the concept of immersion, it is becoming increasingly metaphorical, even opaque and contradictory. In this context, to what extent does the notion of immersion constitute a paradigm, best able to take into account a certain dramaturgical specificity? What criteria constitute the necessary conditions for a paradigm of immersion, applicable to different theatrical forms?

Theatrical immersion: two facets and three degrees

Given the variations of physical and dramaturgical proximity and environmental penetration, our model of immersive theatre is centered upon three steps. This can be summed up in the following manner:

1 physical integration vs. breaking down frontality;
2 sensory and dramaturgical immersion;
   a placing the immersant at the center of an environment, between simulation and representation;
   b the immersant's dramaturgical integration, first-person dramaturgy;
3 immersion and spatiotemporal indeterminacy.

Each step represents a specific anchorage of the fluctuation between the real and the imaginary. Once the first stage is reached, the boundaries between the real and the imaginary are physically disturbed; the fluctuation between the real and the imaginary is no longer structured by physical separation. At this stage, it cannot yet be called immersion. Another level of fluctuation is achieved once the second stage is reached: the immersant is sensorially and physically plunged into an imaginary world.

The third step takes the form of absolute immersion, whereby the immersant experiences confusion between the real and the imaginary universe, even at the level of his approach to the existence of his body in the space: the body scheme can be manipulated; the ability to situate one's body in a space can be impeded. The immersion achieved in this third stage is such that even when the immersant stops cooperating, he is unable to distinguish between the real and imaginary worlds, his approach to his own body being hampered. It is hardly worth stating that such moments of immersion are temporary and very difficult to attain.

These three stages align to a certain extent with those suggested for video games by Emily Brown and Paul Cairns,[2] who identify "engagement," "engrossment," and "total immersion." The second and third steps previously identified echo the two methods of operation for illusion singled out by Grau with regards to virtual space.[3] The first level coincides with the classical mechanism of illusion, by which the participant consciously chooses to play along with the artificial world. The second level becomes apparent once the suggestive effects are intensified, temporarily preventing differentiation between virtual and real spaces. In this article, we will concentrate on the second step, which is at the heart of the immersive theatre experience.

Step 1: physical integration vs. breaking down frontality

Many theatrical practices described as immersive theatre cannot really be aligned with immersive theatre *stricto sensu*. Indeed, it is not enough just to break the frontal division between the stage and the audience in order to achieve immersion. Gareth White appears to support this idea when he states,

> "Immersive theater," then, is an inviting but faulty term to use to describe the phenomena it currently designates. Immersive theatre often surrounds audience members, makes use of cleverly structured interiors and ingenious invitations for them to explore, addresses their bodily presence in the environment and its effect on sense making, and teases them with the suggestion of further depths just possibly within reach. But it has no strong claim to creating either fictional or imaginative interiors in any way that is different in kind than in more conventionally structured audience arrangements.[4]

Breaking down frontality is only the first step to immersive, physical integration.

Step 2a: sensory immersion vs. sensory vertigo

Dominic Arsenault and Martin Picard have identified three types of sensory immersion: visceral, contemplative, and kinaesthetic.[5] These three variations can be combined in one and the same immersive experience. The sensory appeal offered to spectators does not necessarily make it an immersive experience. Mark Reaney's theatre, which is often described as an immersive experience, poses exactly this issue. His work on three-dimensional projections marked the digital theatre of the 1990s. In *Wings* (1996), Reaney turns to head-mounted displays with the aim of immerging the spectator in a partially virtual environment. These screen-glasses, placed as close as possible to the spectator's eyes, thus prevent any perception of distance from the piece. This technology allows the actor's presence on stage to be combined with a real-time projection of three-dimensional images. Nevertheless, this cannot really be considered as sensory immersion in a virtual environment; indeed, these three-dimensional images always fulfill a representative role, with some of them devoid of all desire for mimetic immersion.

Work on immersion generally underlines the central role of corporal appeal in creating an acute sense of being. For example, Josephine Machon[6] concentrates on the visceral dimensions of immersive performance; Sarah Rubidge[7] evokes the fact that certain installations appeal to what Paul Rodway calls the "intimate senses (the haptic, the kinaesthetic, the visceral, the proprioceptive)"; Frances Dyson[8] demonstrates how the work of Char Davies (particularly her famous installation *Osmose*, 1995) frees itself from a Western, dualistic view of the world, in that she offers the experience of being dominated through breathing and balance rather than through sight; the British company Punchdrunk aims for participants to "become most aware of *being* in the moment."[9]

Far from being a side effect whose purpose could be summarized as breaking the spectator's classical appeal, the immersant's sensory appeal constitutes an experience which places his body at the heart of the dramaturgy. The immersant's body experiences first hand the fluctuation between what is real and what is imaginary. In numerous immersive performances, the perceptive confusion caused by illness acts as a starting point to explore our perceptive processes and identity construction. In the Belgian company Crew's performances, the participant is plunged into a modified perception of character via a head-mounted display. The feeling of immersion essentially comes from the 360-degree vision which the display allows; the image which is projected in front of the participant's eyes follows every movement of his head. These images mix pre-recorded sequences with scenes produced with performers in real time, around the participant. One such example is in *Eux* (Crew, 2008), where the spectator takes on the role of a patient suffering from agnosia (a loss of recognition). Kurt Vanhoutte *et al.*[10] have analyzed how such performances transform performance space into a "transitional space" in which it becomes difficult to discern the barrier between the immediate universe and the mediatized universe.

Step 2b: dramaturgical immersion vs. dramatic identification

The stake involved in immersive theatre is in trying to achieve that delicate dramaturgical balance, which consists of linking the way in which the immersant is guided with the freedom which must be allowed him in order to appropriate the piece. Ryan[11] warns against the "myth of the Holodeck," whereby interactive narratives would allow the participant to become a character in the same way as those in novels or plays. Ryan emphasizes the fact that only certain plots can come close to this myth.

In the case of immersive theatre, we cannot talk about interactivity *stricto sensus*, in spite of its extensive use and fashionable state. Steve Dixon emphasizes how many displays referred to as interactive are merely *reactive*.[12] The researcher identifies four levels of interactivity: navigation, participation, conversation, and collaboration. The variability which each immersant brings to the interactive experience increases as we pass from one level to the next. Above all, immersive theatre seems to develop strategies for navigation and participation; sequences which provoke true conversation and/or collaboration are rare. Performers will react to the immersant's dealings following a predetermined framework, in an almost identical manner for each one.

The power of many immersive plays is the way in which they exploit first-person dramaturgy centered on the exploration by a character suffering from perceptive confusion. The character embodies auto-reflexive actions: he observes the world and tries to understand how his perceptions have been modified by illness. This display allows for the achievement of a particular "internal-exploratory interactivity."[13] The enacted dimension of the dramaturgy is limited but nevertheless indispensable to the way in which the plot plays out. Immersive plays are based on constant give and take between narrative coherence and the immersant's exploratory freedom.

Crew's plays preserve the fluctuation between the real and the imaginary. In particular, this is made possible by the way in which the immersant is addressed. At the beginning of *Eux*, a male voice calls the immersant by his first name, at the same time as it is shown on a screen. The participant is invited to embody a character yet his personal identity is nevertheless taken into account. In immersive theatre, the pronoun "you" is frequently employed when addressing the immersant. Jeremy Douglass has shown how games use the second person to encourage an effect of identification or immersion in the first person.[14] As in the digital fictions analyzed

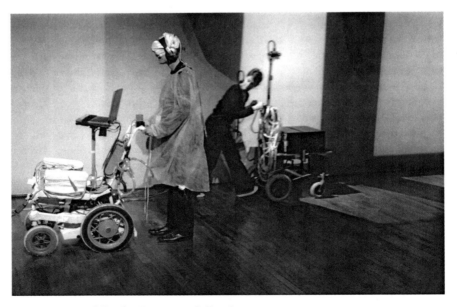

Figure 76.1 Crew and *Eux* by Eric Joris. © Eric Joris

by Alice Bell and Astrid Ensslin, immersive theatre "employ[s] the textual 'you', mostly by combining actualized and fictionalized address with doubly deictic 'you', in order to blur the boundaries between game and fiction while simultaneously subverting the subjective, uncritical behavior and attitudes exhibited by readers/players [immersants]."[15]

Immersive fluctuations between the real and the imaginary

Dramatic immersion distinguishes itself from literary immersion by the tangibility of the world into which the individual is plunged, as opposed to the world of literature into which the reader is absorbed. For Ryan, the latter produces an imaginary relationship with a literary world, which leads the addressee to metaphorically plunge into the tale.[16] Richard Gerrig links literary immersion with the concept of "transportation," through which a reader of fiction distances himself from his immediate physical environment in order to "lose" himself in the story.[17] Marie-Laure Ryan's suggested depiction of immersive theatre only takes into account the spectator's identification processes.[18] The spectators (represented by the white spots plunged into the black background) remain removed from the action being played out by the actors (black spots) and maintain their role as observers. Here, immersion is simply synonymous of mental projection into the work.

Immersive theatre places the participant at the heart of a work. All the same, it abandons the exclusive search for physical and mental transportation in order to place the subject in a specifically theatrical entredeux, between adherence and denial. Rather than a difficulty to be hidden, the medium's visibility is exploited and lodges itself at the heart of this theatrical language: at particular moments, the immersant may be absorbed to the point of substituting the environment for every-day reality; the medium appears transparent and the created world seems to be offered without any intermediary. At other times, he becomes aware of the artificial nature of the world into which he is plunged and adopts a position external to the work. It is precisely this game of coming and going which constructs and decon-structs physical and mental immersion and which constitutes the specificity of immersive theatre.

Matthew Causey reminds us, "the theatre has always been virtual, a space of illusory immediacy."[19] In her study on video games, Elena Gorfinkel brings to mind the fact that immersion is not a characteristic but rather an *effect* which a work may produce on the participant.[20] It is important to make this distinction as she explains, in part, to what extent it is impossible to establish a strict dichotomy between immersion and critical distance. According to Oliver Grau, it is not a question of "one or the other"; the relationship between immersion and critical distance depends on numerous parameters, including the participant's temperament.[21] Indeed, the parti-cipant's immersion is dependent on his willingness. No matter how immersive a piece may aim to be, it will always be possible to maintain one's critical distance, thereby negating the immersion. No piece can guarantee immersion; thus our model depends not on particular pieces but rather on immersive strategies which are employed and which can be encountered in a variety of works.

Assuming that immersive fluctuation is at the heart of all theatrical practices, we have seen to what extent it can take on an immersive specificity, which nourishes a multitude of dramaturgical explorations. For these dramaturgs, immersion makes it possible to forge an *authentic* type of relationship with the spectator. The passage from the notion of *site-specific* or *site-sympathetic* to the notion of *immersive* theatre, as in the case of Punchdrunk, highlights the change of focus from the dramaturgical space to the experience encountered by the spectator – an experience that aims to be *empowering*. The extreme care exercised in Punchdrunk's scenography illustrates it:

> In terms of empowering the audience, those sensual details give the audience the chance to really become part of it. You can open the drawer, you can root around, see the pen that wrote that letter, smell the ink, just so that it intoxicates them, they become part of it and it has greater impact. A lot of it's to do with ... that extra sense and the power of the imagination, its smells, things that haunt you and flavour the experience.[22]

Beyond the writing of a dramaturgy that manipulates the boundaries between the real and the imaginary, the dramaturg now often plays a role in *accompanying* this embodied dramaturgical experience. Many immersive performances, such as the ones created by Crew, offer the spectator the possibility of attending the experience lived by the other spectators, in order to uncover the dramaturgical and technical tools.

Notes

1 Mark Lawson, "How I Learned to Love Immersive Theatre," *The Guardian*, September 25, 2012.
2 Emily Brown and Paul Cairns, "A Grounded Investigation of Game Immersion," *CHI 2004 Proceedings* (New York: ACM Press, 2004), 1297–1300.
3 Oliver Grau, *Virtual Art. From Illusion to Immersion* (Cambridge, MA: MIT Press, 2003), 17.
4 Gareth White, "On Immersive Theatre," *Theatre Research International* 37.3 (2012): 233.
5 Dominic Arsenault and Martin Picard, "Le jeu vidéo entre dépendance et plaisir immersif: les trois formes d'immersion vidéoludique," paper presented at the symposium Le jeu vidéo: un phénomène social massivement pratiqué?, 75th congress of the ACFAS, Université du Québec à Trois-Rivières, 2007, 5.
6 Josephine Machon, *Immersive Theatres: Intimacy and Immediacy in Contemporary Performance* (Basingstoke: Palgrave MacMillan, 2013).
7 Sarah Rubidge, "Sensuous Geographies and Other Installations: Interfacing the Body and Technology," in *Performance and Technology: Practices of Virtual Embodiment and Interactivity*, eds. Susan Broadhurst and Josephine Machon (Basingstoke: Palgrave MacMillan, 2006), 113.
8 Frances Dyson, *Sounding New Media. Immersion and Embodiment in the Arts and Culture* (Ewing: University of California Press, 2009).
9 Josephine Machon, "Felix Barrett in Discussion with Josephine Machon," 2007, available online at http://people.brunel.ac.uk/bst/vol0701/felixbarrett/home.html, accessed January 4, 2013.
10 Nele Wynants, Kurt Vanhoutte and Philippe Bekaert, "Being Inside the Image. Heightening the Sense of Presence in a Video Captured Environment through Artistic Means: The Case of CREW," in *Presence 2008: Proceedings of the 11th International Workshop on Presence in Padova*, eds. Anna Spagnolli and Luciano Gamberini (Padova: Libraria Universitaria Padova, 2008), 159–62.

11 Marie-Laure Ryan, "Beyond Myth and Metaphor: Narrative in Digital Media," *Poetics Today* 23.4 (2002): 581–609.
12 Steve Dixon, *Digital Performance* (Cambridge, MA: MIT Press, 2007), 563.
13 Ryan, "Beyond Myth and Metaphor," 601.
14 Jeremy Douglass, quoted in Steve Benford and Gabriella Giannachi, *Performing Mixed Reality* (Cambridge, MA: MIT Press, 2011), 207.
15 Alice Bell and Astrid Ensslin, "'I know what it was. You know what it was': Second-Person Narration in Hypertext Fiction," *Narrative* 19.3 (2011): 318.
16 Marie-Laure Ryan, *Narrative as Virtual Reality: Immersion and Interactivity in Literature and Electronic Music* (Baltimore, MD: John Hopkins University Press, 2001), 14.
17 Richard Gerrig, quoted in Marie-Laure Ryan, "Immersion vs. Interactivity: Virtual Reality and Literary Theory," *Substance* 28.2 (1999): 116.
18 Ryan, *Narrative as Virtual Reality*, 299.
19 Matthew Causey, *Theatre and Performance in Digital Culture* (London: Routledge, 2009), 15.
20 Elena Gorfinkel, quoted in Arsenault and Picard.
21 Grau, 13.
22 Felix Barrett, quoted in Machon.

77

Barrack-dramaturgy and the captive audience

András Visky

The theatre is a device for the construction of truths.

Alain Badiou[1]

In the year of the turn of the millennium, I took part in the filming of a documentary about my father as the assistant to the director and the conversation partner of my father in the film. In 1958, he had been sentenced to 22 years in prison as a criminal in the show trials that were leveled primarily at dissident intellectuals in Romania under the Communist terror. After the political changes of 1989, he came to the center of public attention as a living memory of the near past. During the making of the documentary, I proposed taking my father back to the prison where he had spent most of his time as an inmate, to evoke the everyday situations of confinement in his former cell. I was familiar with the dark stories of my father's torture and humiliation. However, when we entered the prison and were shut into a cell for the duration of the filming, I confronted an unthinkable reality. Knowledge of a verbal nature, all linguistic experience, was transformed in a moment into an *avant la lettre* experience of my body. The penetrating smell of confinement that a prisoner carries with him far into his civilian years as his aromatic aura; the speech, similar to barking, that is louder than the norm; the acoustics of corridors multiplying sharp echoes; the ritual relationship between prisoners and jailors; the cold light of artificial illumination: my bodily sensations made me "comprehend" my father's sufferings in an instant. I lived through what I had not experienced myself, even though as a child I had spent almost five years in a Gulag prison camp (familiar in Western culture from the books of Shalamov and Solzhenitsyn) together with my mother and brothers and sisters, while my father was incarcerated elsewhere. So the experience of confinement was not unknown to me, but the tight space of the prison opened up to me, not in an abstract, but in an extremely sensory way, a very different aspect of the deprivation of freedom. "Culture is grounded in the human body," says Thomas Csordas:[2] the source of this recognition is not merely theoretical to me.

How might imagination transform the word into a bodily experience or into a concrete fact? The question is par excellence theatrical, and the history of theatre could probably be written as the answer of different theatrical periods and forms to this question. This essay would like to examine how barrack-dramaturgy[3] (a compound word coined at the end of the 1990s) and the praxis of theatre can help bring to our consciousness and create an open discussion around past events that were not directly experienced by us, but that have shaped our identity and determined our social life, our common discourse, and our public space. Is the prison experience of the "remorseless destroyer," as Alain Badiou called the twentieth century,[4] which has by no means run its course for the societies of Eastern Europe, transferable to human relationships, to different dependency games, to social relations that we have not experienced ourselves, but which we have inherited from our parents? Could a theatrical analysis of this heritage that weighs upon us all return to theatre its prevailing desire to be a culture-molding agent?

Although our inquiry refers to discourses in the field of contemporary aesthetics, it also goes beyond this and assumes a political significance, insofar as we take into account the notable fact that after the political changes in Romania, considered by Jean Baudrillard as an exaggeratedly "theatrical event" and a "simulacrum,"[5] the theatre in Romania did not attempt to process the experiences of the recent past for a surprisingly long time. The representative performances from the 1990s basically continued the previous metaphorical approach of the 1980s and mostly built on classic texts, examining on a philosophical level the relationship between authority and the individual. A totalitarian heritage shows itself in the amnesia of civic duty, in the autocracy of symbolic thinking, in a skepticism concerning political activity, as well as individual and collective human rights. In practical terms, here in Romania it took the artistic act out of the sphere of social efficacy.[6]

Barrack-dramaturgy was born out of the need to make imprisonment a common experience. Contrary to how it was culturally embedded at that time, theatre is a "hard" place. It is not the institutional form of weekend culture-consumption or celebrations traditionally supported here by the state. Questions related to the near past – What happened to us? Should we consider ourselves simply as victims, or were we also supporters of the system? How does our subordination develop and grow? – may have a special significance in societies where a right-winged totalitarianism was replaced by a leftist one without any real transition, and where public opinion considers both as primarily an imported power establishment forced on the populace from outside, a populace which avoids the relevance of questions concerning personal, responsible, politically efficient acts and the possibility of social cleansing, of reconciliation: in other words, the possibility of catharsis.[7]

According to barrack-dramaturgy, theatre is a place where we shut ourselves in. We become prisoners of our own free will. Then, as a result of the event that happens to us, that takes place with our cooperation, we are "set free," and so we consider ourselves as subjects and not as faceless objects of history who have no identity. The event of being shut in represents a radical breaking away from the theatrical practice that interprets and faithfully enforces texts, representing and honoring the author in a religious manner as the trustee and lord of primordial logos. This act focuses on the performance as an event in the present, as the bodily co-presence of actors and spectators,[8] moreover, as the proximity of "heavy bodies" and a "real gathering."[9]

To the extent that we present captivity as a universal experience, without necessarily connecting it to the actual reality of jails and prison camps, we define it in the following way: captivity is a state of being in which we are dislocated from our bodies. In this state, freedom, the essence of our identity, is highly fictionalized, and the body, compressed in a tight space, expresses itself by obsessive rituals. We can see that this definition permeates the boundaries of the merely historical-political-social interpretations and offers the possibility of a participatory understanding of different forms of dependencies which are characteristic of a consumer society also. We need to emphasize that even though the audience is encouraged to some kind of participation, sometimes even through explicitly "strong" means, barrack-dramaturgy remains a gentle event, carefully avoiding any kind of fashionable violence or provocation, any situations which might humiliate or degrade the audience. The spectator's moment of understanding might be delayed, but the performance does not call the spectator to account for their delay or partiality of recognition (*anagnorisis*).

Later we will attempt a short description of the characteristics of barrack-dramaturgy. For now, we will restrict ourselves to four elements: space, time, body, text.

Separation and participation

The usually confined space comes to life in the form of performative spaces. The special arrangement of the audience and the actors makes the event of being shut in unequivocal. Unavoidably, the spectators have to relinquish their freedom, their role as viewers, the safety and privacy generously assured them by traditional theatrical convention and the arrangement of the space. The space of barrack-dramaturgy does not segregate the auditorium as a safe place from which to gaze. Escape routes are blocked off both by the configuration of the space and by the first actions of the audience and actors that actually start the performance. Leaving the space during the performance inevitably makes the spectator a protagonist of the performance: the space does not impede one's leaving, but makes it significant without stigmatizing it. The arrangement of the space serves the intimate proximity of the audience and the actors, offering them the possibility of forming a single group, unlike the familiar practice of mainstream theatre where the relationship between the two groups is firmly hierarchical. The stage is in front of, behind, above, and underneath the audience, offering actors and audience the option of looking at each other and giving up the voyeur-like separation.[10] The contemporary look, the exchanging glances of the audience, the recognition of our presence become essential moments in experiencing the challenging immediacy of the performance. Singularity made common and shared – both the spectators' and the actors' – is the universal constant of the theatre phenomenon. In this space the ethical dimension replaces, or at least completes, the purely aesthetical attitude: the spectator is an active, self-reflective subject.

In search of present time

The time management of barrack-dramaturgy aims to restore the spectator's own present that has been lost and fictionalized. The event of the performance is unable to do this without the active participation of the spectator. The basic situation of the performance is determined by amnesia, the question that is usually hidden or aggressively monopolized by politics, the question that is placed outside of our self-reflective horizon by our suppressions and suicidal self-protective strategies against the past so characteristic of Eastern Europe. The theatrical situation is built around the "What happened to us?" question, and the process of answering the question marks the way back to ourselves, and starts with the recognition that we cannot tell our own stories, because we have no language, we have no words for it. Consequently, we are unable to return to our own present. "We yearn for a sense of the presence of our lives," writes Martin Seel, and he continues, "We want to experience the presences in which we exist as sensual presences."[11] Time processes are represented by fragmented language, broken syntax, and the dynamics of suddenly found sentences, the relationship between speech and silence, as well as compulsive-repetitive rituals, the rhythm of the falling apart and coming together again of a radically alienated body. We imagine this more as choreography, rather than a faithfully realistic representation.

Body, remembrance, experience

The body has the most important role in experimenting with the rebuilding of our own story. Language regains its meanings through the memories of the body: what can the body remember? The trauma of losing freedom or the lack of freedom alienates us from our own body. The prison–freedom relationship is taken out of its mythical frame by barrack-dramaturgy and is transferred into the immediate. The proof of our own existence is our body, and not just our own, but the bodies of others too. Language returns to us through our bodily experiences: it is put together there, so usually barrack-theatre is related to infinite loop–dramaturgy known mostly from video art: a compulsive return to the time, to the situation when we were conscious of ourselves, before that self broke apart in an unrecognizable way due to personal choices and traumas caused by history. Barrack-dramaturgy removes the border between the literary theatre dominated by speech and the theatre of the body (movement, dance). Language comes into being as a material of the body, so the actor needs to find in their own body that language that will occur on stage as one of the elements of the performance.

Text, reconstruction and doing justice

Barrack-dramaturgy gives up the illusion of a coherent story and resists the film and theatre industry pressure that demands new and never before heard stories. In a theatre space, the "document" organized into a text, *nolens volens*, becomes fiction. Barrack-dramaturgy accounts soberly for this theatre constant, so it sets the highest value on the community and the togetherness of people gathered in a theatre space. Linear structure becomes impossible because of the conflict between the project of the precisely told personal story and the language at hand having no significance. Speech becomes splintered, fragmented, and explicitly painful due to attempts and repetitions, even when the text has a poetic character, since speech reveals its own musical character: understanding becomes the experience of the body at the same time. Fragmented dramaturgy relies expressly on the spectator as a partner: the story that is difficult to put together is built by everybody in their own way to achieve an integral whole. The precisely told story that is different from a text with a linear structure is at the same time a true story too, because it contains the traces of the impossibility of telling it. The true story does justice as well, and this is a liberating event in itself. The well-told story gives the experience of identity found or at least tasted. However, the miracle is not performed by the actors, since they are also part of what will come to pass, an event that may fail to come about because the performance becomes extremely vulnerable and sometimes does not fulfill itself entirely. Our experience of identity given by the performance could be momentary; however, it remains a life fact and demonstrates a real possibility of gaining a personal identity.

Barrack-dramaturgy redefines the everyday meaning of success in a radical way. In the present situation of our theatres, suspending, or at least questioning, the performance as an occasion for culture to celebrate itself, or as a consumable product, creates difficulties on the recipient's side. However, the existential stake of the issues to be raised and the difficulty of the adapted stories come into an ethical conflict with the expectation of immediate success. Extreme reactions are very frequent: either passionate refusal or an eye-opening discovery and acceptance. The most valuable sign of the real effect of the performance – at least from our point of view – is the serial spectator. Returning to the scene of the performance and engaging in repeated participation puts the spectators and the actors into the position of perpetrator. Consequently, it becomes impossible to consider the past as part of a faceless, homogenized, distant history, but the subject of individual and active reflection.

Notes

1 Alain Badiou, *The Century* (London and New York: Continuum, 2006), 42.
2 Erika Fischer-Lichte, *The Transformative Power of Performance. A New Aesthetics*, trans. S. I. Jain (London and New York: Routledge, 2008), 89.
3 The term barrack-dramaturgy was born during the staging of my plays, written at the end of the 1990s, during the course of an extremely inspiring and fruitful collaboration with the company of the Hungarian Theatre of Cluj. The world premieres are connected primarily with stage director Gábor Tompa. Part of the experiment of barrack-dramaturgy was that I contributed to the performances as the dramaturg too, so that during rehearsals the plays could remain open and flexible. In addition to Gábor Tompa's revelatory performances (set and costumes: Carmencita Brojboiu), the productions of my plays by Mihai Mǎniuțiu, Christopher Markle, Stephanie Sandberg, Karin Coonrod, and Éva Patkó also helped me to achieve a clearer grasp of the concept. Special thanks to Erzsébet Daray and Ailisha O'Sullivan for the final English version of this essay. Previous essays on barrack-dramaturgy include András Visky, "Dramaturgia de baracă (articol de dicționar)," in *Teatrul Azi* 7-8-9 (2006): 110–20; "Le théâtre de baraques," in *Alternatives théâtrales* 106–7 (2010): 84–5; *Megváltozhat-e egy ember* (Cluj-Kolozsvár: KOMPRESS-Korunk, 2009), 11–19.
4 Badiou, 227.
5 J. Baudrillard, *The Illusion of the End*, trans. Charles Turner (Cambridge: Polity Press, 1994), 60.
6 As used by Richard Schechner in *Performance Theory* (London and New York: Routledge, 2003).

7 Péter György gives an excellent analysis of the "living in it and ignoring it" phenomena in the first chapter of his book, *Apám helyett* (In place of my father) (Budapest: Magvető, 2012), 9–69.

8 Fischer-Lichte, 69.

9 Hans-Thies Lehmann, *Postdramatic Theatre,* trans. Karen Jürs-Munby (London and New York: Routledge, 2006), 17.

10 Let us remember the decision of Grotowski, who in *Kordian* pushed the audience into a position of voyeurism. By separating them from the performance with a wooden fence, he forced the spectators' inevitable reflection on their own situation.

11 Fischer-Lichte, 96.

78

Framing the theatrical experience

Lobby displays

Miriam Weisfeld

Little documentation is available on when exactly lobby displays established a presence in American resident theatres, what percentage of theatres regularly use them, and how common the practice is in other countries. However, the tradition was likely inspired by museum exhibits. Currently studied in Museology and Museum Studies training programs, exhibit design is itself a storytelling art. Exhibits are typically created to educate the public about their subject matter through some combination of physical objects, images, and text. In the twenty-first century, two major innovations have greatly influenced exhibit design: digital media and a rise in the popularity of interactive experiences. Interactive experiences differ from passive experiences in that they include two-way communication instead of a one-way delivery of information. For example, whereas a twentieth-century exhibit on journalism might include a one-way delivery system of information in the form of a newspaper that visitors may read, a twenty-first-century exhibit might offer the visitor a chance to create his/her own newspaper, either on paper or on a computer screen. The increasing variety of delivery systems used by exhibit designers reflects the diversity of learning styles among children and adults. As museums seek to engage more – and more types of – visitors, they have placed increasing emphasis on providing exhibit experiences that appeal to a range of learners; these learners have varying desires to engage with technology and contribute (or "co-author") content for themselves. Many of these innovations are documented in Nina Simon's 2010 book *The Participatory Museum*, which can be accessed at www.participatorymuseum.org.

Theatrical lobby displays may serve many different missions. Most commonly, a lobby display is meant to educate audiences about aspects of a play they may be unfamiliar with: the history of the playwright, the environment in which the story takes place, or significant previous productions of the play. But lobby displays are increasingly motivated by other goals: to spur animated discussion among audience members; to empower them to interpret aesthetic strategies in the production they may find esoteric; or to fuel enthusiasm, loyalty, and viral marketing for the theatre. This chapter provides four contemporary examples of lobby displays with different goals and formats. The formats are categorized by the materials used (analogue vs. digital) and the nature of the engagement with the audience (passive vs. interactive). Again, diversity in lobby design abounds, and new experiments and vocabulary – "co-authorship," "entanglement," "connectivity," etc. – are further refined each day. In addition to describing the goals and format of each display, this essay attempts to place each display in context vis-à-vis the theatre's broad goals for engaging with its community at the time of the production. The mid-Atlantic region and the author's home theatre, Woolly Mammoth, are disproportionately represented here; it should be noted that innovative examples of lobby displays may be found in university, community, and professional theatres far beyond the American East Coast.

Although many resident theatres consider lobby displays a helpful tool, there is also a significant number of artists and administrators who believe the production should "speak for itself." According to this philosophy, attempts to deliver educational or interpretive tools outside the production itself – in the form of lobby displays, playbill notes, post-show discussions, etc. – are incompatible with the artists' goals. In this case, the artist may believe these tools may undercut the impact of the production or limit the range of possible interpretations the performance may spark. In a practical setting, a candid conversation with the artists about their goals and opinions is an absolutely essential first step toward determining if and how a lobby display may be useful.

Analogue/passive displays: Two River Theater's *Our Town*

In 2007, Aaron Posner began his first season as the new artistic director of Two River Theater in Red Bank, New Jersey. As newcomers in a small town, Posner and his new staff sought out ways to learn about the local community and integrate its values into the life of the theatre. They opened the 2007–8 season with a production of Thornton Wilder's *Our Town*, directed by Posner, and incorporating 13 bunraku-style full-body puppets designed by Aaron Cromie. The production was accompanied by a lobby display meant to evoke a spirit of nostalgia for the town of Red Bank that would parallel and deepen the audience's experience of Grover's Corners, the small New England town in which Wilder's play is set.

Additionally, this lobby display served public relations and aesthetic purposes. The year 2008 would mark Red Bank's centennial, and the display, titled "Relive 100 Years of Red Bank," was – according to a Two River press release – intended to "reflect and celebrate the *Our Town* in all of our lives." Posner's staff hoped it would communicate the theatre's respect for the history and citizens of Red Bank, building their affinity for the theatre's new leadership. Finally, the display served an aesthetic purpose. The production's use of life-sized puppets alongside live actors was a more theatrically innovative strategy than those traditionally seen on Two River's stage. By evoking nostalgia for the audience's own town as they entered the theatre, Posner hoped to diffuse any feelings of alienation or skepticism provoked by the anticipation of a new theatrical style.

The lobby display was conceived by Associate Artistic Director KJ Sanchez, an associate artist with The Civilians and founder/CEO of American Records Theater.

Sanchez's experience devising theatre from interviews and other source material provided the model for gathering material from the community and assembling it into an ambitious exhibit of photographs and oral history. Two River Theater partnered with Kathy Dorn Severini, the owner of Dorn's Classic Images, a photography company founded by the Dorn family in Red Bank in the late nineteenth century. The Dorn collection includes roughly five thousand images, taken from land and airplanes, dating back to glass plate negatives from 1885. Many of these images depict iconic moments from Red Bank's history: turn-of-the-century carnivals; ice boat races; regattas; visits by Theodore Roosevelt, King George VI, and Bob Hope; and many images of local businesses owned by longtime Red Bank families.

With the help of the Dorn family, a local paper called *The Red Bank Red Hot*, and the Red Bank Public Library, the Two River staff identified roughly ten citizens familiar with the history of businesses and occasions from the town's past. Theatre staff presented these citizens with images from the Dorn collection and tape-recorded the memories associated with the photographs. The interviews were then transcribed and edited into short chapters of oral history and placed alongside relevant photographs as captions. The photographs, lent by Dorn's Classic Images and enlarged to poster size, were hung with the captions along the walls of the theatre during the run of *Our Town*. The tools of this display were analogue: printed material hung on walls. Although this material was initially gathered through an interactive process in which community members co-authored the text, the display itself created a passive experience of viewing and reading. Audience response was generally enthusiastic, and theatre staff reported multiple comments from audience members who suggested the show's intermission be extended to allow for more time to see the lobby display.

Analogue/interactive: Woolly Mammoth Theatre Company's A *Bright New Boise*

Woolly Mammoth Theatre Company's 2011 production of Samuel D. Hunter's play *A Bright New Boise* began the second season of the theatre's new Connectivity initiative. Primarily inspired by a conference on theatre, democracy, and engagement which marked the theatre's thirtieth anniversary, Connectivity became a distinct staff department at Woolly Mammoth. The chief goal of the Connectivity Department was to activate the theatre's mission to create an "explosive engagement" between each performance and its audience. This was attempted via several means including:

- the creation of an "audience design" to identify and recruit the most highly invested mix of local stakeholders to see the play;
- the creation of engagement tools such as lobby environments, innovative playbills, blogs, podcasts, and other mechanisms for illuminating both the form and the content of the production;
- various forms of post-show discussions, surveys, and other means for experts and lay people in the community to compare their experiences of the production.

The first production of *Boise* after the New York premiere, Woolly Mammoth's show presented its audience with a story and a playwright brand new to the

Washington DC community. Woolly Mammoth's core audience was accustomed to unfamiliar and quirky new plays; but this worldly, highly educated, and generally liberal audience was not accustomed to plays tackling this subject matter. Playwright Samuel D. Hunter grew up in a conservative Christian community in rural Idaho. His play features an Evangelical protagonist struggling to reconcile his religious worldview with his agnostic and alienated teenage son. In consultation with Hunter and director John Vreeke, Woolly Mammoth's Connectivity director, Rachel Grossman, envisioned an audience design that would bring practicing believers together with secular and atheist audience members in a constructive dialogue about the role of faith in our public and private lives. But Grossman soon encountered challenges. Based on the theatre's marketing materials and reputation, faith-based groups feared the play would present a disrespectful or critical picture of religion. Secular audience members, on the other hand, were surprised when they were promised an un-ironic and sympathetic portrayal of Evangelism. Grossman, Woolly Mammoth production dramaturg, John M. Baker, and the rest of the theatre's staff set out to create tools to diffuse this skepticism and create an even playing field for both types of audiences to approach the show.

One of the most important tools was the lobby display, co-created by Grossman and Woolly Mammoth props master, Jenn Sheetz. Grossman and Sheetz created several stations in the lobby designed to capture the response of individual audience members to highly personal questions about faith and values. The questions included multiple-choice answers, and audience members could cast a vote for the answer they believed by making a physical mark on the display: rubber stamping a poster, dropping a bead in a jar, or tying a ribbon to a tree branch. Each station offered a different way to state how faith was manifest in one's public or private life. The nature of the stations was highly interactive – the marks left by audience members co-authored both the meaning and the physical shape of the stations – while the mechanisms for leaving those marks were simple analogue objects such as beads and ribbons.

Because the stations accumulated marks from the audience, they became more colorful and intriguing as the run of the play progressed. Ultimately the stations became visual surveys of how Woolly Mammoth's patrons thought about faith, and audience members showed great interest in learning how other audiences had responded. The playfulness of the lobby display diffused much of the reluctance that both religious and secular audiences felt about discussing matters of faith in public. But perhaps most provocative was the number of couples in the audience who apparently had never discussed these questions privately: many patrons were overheard expressing surprise at the bead or ribbon chosen by a spouse or parent in response to a question about their own beliefs. After several patrons inquired about the cumulative results of these responses, the numbers were posted on the theatre's website and members of the production's artistic team wrote responses to the patterns that emerged.

Digital/interactive: Woolly Mammoth Theatre Company's *Civilization: All You Can Eat*

Woolly Mammoth's world premiere of Jason Grote's *Civilization: All You Can Eat* appeared in the latter half of the 2011–12 season. At this point, the theatre had begun to add digital tools to their lobby experiments, and connectivity assistant Melanie Harker had taken over the creation of the displays. Grote's play was a sweeping satire of American consumerism, mixing a Robert Altman-esque cross-section of characters with abstract modern dance sequences and a talking hog on the run from an industrial farm. Harker and director Howard Shalwitz developed goals for the lobby display that would embolden the audience to grapple with the play's unconventional aesthetic strategies. Additionally, they hoped the lobby display could help the audience make meaning of a play with a somewhat submerged narrative and themes. Finally, they hoped to create a tool to fuel online discussion and viral marketing for the production.

Harker recruited the help of Woolly Mammoth's Claque: a group of highly engaged and youthful patrons who volunteered to gather several evenings each season to contribute their perspectives, networks, and expertise to the theatre's Connectivity work. She spoke with the Claque about how to entice Washingtonians who had strong opinions about economics, world history, anthropology, and sociology to participate in the critique of American civilization at the heart of Grote's play. A playful idea emerged: to create a "March Madness"-style bracket, modeled on NCAA tournaments, in which patrons could vote on which world civilization was the greatest. Claque member Jonathan Zucker, CEO of a web-based political fundraising platform called Democracy Engine, quickly helped flesh out the details: in order to recruit the maximum number of patrons in this "audience design," anyone should be able to nominate a civilization – but only patrons who attended the performance could vote on them. The voting would begin on the evening of the show's first preview; each winning civilization would advance to the next round of voting at the following performance; on closing night, the two civilizations with the most votes would go head to head.

With the help of Zucker and Woolly Mammoth operations manager Paul Kappel, Harker created a social media strategy to set the "Civilization Smackdown" in motion. The team identified experts from Washington's academic, museum, and policy worlds to nominate civilizations and spread the invitation to others in their networks. To make the game as fun as possible, any civilization – including extinct or fictional ones – could qualify, as long as nominators answered a series of questions about them that related to Grote's play. The questions included:

- What does this civilization produce?
- What does it consume?
- What will cause its downfall?

These "stats" were made available for patrons to view before casting their vote. Each evening – before the performance, during intermission, and for a brief period after the show – patrons could view a "bracket" of the nominated civilizations that was projected onto the lobby wall. Voters cast their ballots via Twitter, text message, or the bracket website, and the winner was announced each night via social media. Each component of this lobby display was digital, from the web platform projected onto the lobby wall to the voting mechanisms; and it was fully interactive, as the audience authored the content within the framework provided by the theatre. Forty-eight "civilizations" were nominated, ranging from Ancient Greece and the USA to Middle Earth and Ikea. Over the course of the play's run 863 patrons voted, many of whom participated in lively and humorous debates about the merits of our civilization and others in the context of the play.

Hybrid: the Pershing Square Signature Center

In 2012, New York City's Signature Theatre moved from their 160-seat house to a new building on 42nd Street, designed by Frank Gehry, which includes three performance spaces. Founded in 1991, Signature's mission is devoted to deeply exploring a living playwright's body of work; in the past, this had meant devoting each season to the work of one playwright at a time. The move to a three-theatre building allowed Signature to expand from one playwright residency per season to three different types of residencies: single year, five-year, and returning appearances by past resident playwrights. In order to expand on Signature's desire to deeply immerse patrons in the work of their playwrights, a team of architects, technologists, and theatre staff conceived a lobby that unifies all three performance spaces and encompasses a café, bookstore, concierge desk, and "media wall." The lobby now contains examples of three types of the displays described in this chapter: analogue/passive, digital/passive, and digital/interactive.

In their previous space, Signature's literary staff had created "show panels" for each production: two-dimensional analogue posters assembled from photos and text from the playwright's archive. With the help of Pop, a Seattle-based experience design and technology company, the staff converted their show panels into a dual digital and analogue dramaturgical showcase. The staff correctly surmised that patrons would at first regard the new high-tech lobby tools with trepidation. The analogue show panels were designed to help lower this barrier to engagement with an emphatically tactile design. Whereas the analogue show panels in the old space had been slick posters in frames, the new analogue panels were made of cork, with artifacts obviously attached with thumbtacks. These artifacts are typically two-dimensional photos or quotations, but sometimes included three-dimensional props or costume pieces that could be felt by hand. To compliment these analogue panels, the literary staff also began creating content for digital panels. Hung alongside the cork boards outside each theatre, the digital panels display a continuous slideshow of photographs and text related to the writing, rehearsal, and performance of the play currently running inside the house. Like the analogue panels, the digital screens invite passive consumption of the dramaturgical material, allowing patrons to view and read material chosen by the literary staff.

In addition to these show-specific panels, the staff and technologists designed two types of screens to immerse patrons in the broader context of the playwright residencies and encourage them to respond to their experience at the Signature Center. Two "storytelling screens" invite patrons to select more information about current and past shows, as well as current and past seasons and playwrights. Patrons select a topic from these three layers of Signature history via a touch-screen to access deeper information about one subject or return to a menu of several. The available information includes photos, videos, and text. For example, the information on Tony Kushner's 2011–12 residency included information about Signature's productions of *The Illusion*, *The Intelligent Homosexual's Guide to Capitalism and Socialism with a Key to the Scriptures*, and *Angels in America, Parts 1 and 2*. Additionally, the staff gathered interviews with artists who had been involved in previous productions of Kushner's plays, creating a rich multimedia illustration of the impact of Kushner's oeuvre. In addition to educating patrons about the work of Signature's past and current resident playwrights, the storytelling screens deliver institutional messaging about the theatre's work, reinforcing Signature's brand as a passionate champion of American playwrights and a chronicler of the legacies of living artists.

The third interactive panel, called the "reflection screen," invites patrons to co-author this institutional messaging and add a personal touch. Signature's staff designed multiple-choice questions asking patrons to describe their experience with various activities at the Signature Center, from the shows to the activities in the lobby. To respond to the questions or add a comment, patrons may tweet using the hashtag #sigwall; patrons who are not Twitter-savvy may select a multiple-choice answer on the touchscreen. If the patron chooses to make this response public, it is added to a digital scroll that runs continuously across the bottom of the reflection screen, as well as on additional screens elsewhere inside and outside the building. Finally, patrons may push a button on the reflection screen to take their own photograph and add their image to their verbal response. In addition to adding to the fun factor of a visit to the Signature Center, these visual and verbal reflections powerfully reinforce the theatre's brand as a home for diverse patrons to participate in the exploration of contemporary theatre.

Signature's marketing staff is currently working to refine analytical tools to capture data on who uses these lobby displays and how they are most often used. Their anecdotal observations indicate that many patrons who were initially hesitant to engage with the digital screens have become comfortable navigating them. Patrons of all ages are often seen turning from one lobby resource to another: reading about a playwright on a storytelling screen and then finding that playwright's anthology in the bookstore, or asking the concierge about a current production and then watching a slideshow about it on a show panel. The staff also continue to discuss how best to curate the content on each panel. The marketing staff members who manage the app that powers the screens have the ability to edit text contributed by patrons. They initially discussed erasing comments that might reflect negatively on the productions and the theatre. But so far no comments that patrons have elected to share have been censored by the staff, and there are no plans to do so in the future.

79

Dramaturg as public relations manager

Katie Rasor

The Hilton Head Island New Play Festival was initially informed as much by practical considerations as it was by artistic ideals. In 2009, one year into the recession, regional theatres specializing in new works were being forced to tighten their budgets, send out broad appeals for help, or even close their doors. Seeing the increasing dearth of script development opportunities for American playwrights, fellow ART alumnus Nick Newell proposed that we start our own new play festival. Where did he want to do this? There was a small regional theatre with an active audience base on Hilton Head Island, South Carolina. In preparing to pitch the festival to playwrights, we asked ourselves: What does this festival have to offer beyond a staged reading with professional actors and a weekend on a resort island? There would be no agents there and not much likelihood of being "discovered" hours away from any major theatrical hub. What, if anything, could feedback from a regional Southern audience offer playwrights that they could not get from American audiences living in major theatre cities? We did not realize it at the time, but what we feared would be the festival's weakness, its location in the American South, turned out to be its biggest strength.

Our inaugural festival took place in August 2010. The weekend-long event featured a staged reading of a new, full-length play by an American playwright and a dramaturg-moderated talkback with the director and playwright each evening. My work as a dramaturg started with the curation of the festival. After the plays were chosen, I would provide introductions between the playwright and director and facilitate conversations in the month leading up to the performance. The festival was slated to begin with a reading of Kansas-born, London-based playwright Stacia Saint Owens' *Catholic Girl Gun Club*, which explores issues of race, gender, religion, and war. Before opening night, however, concerns were raised that the piece was too experimental and political for Hilton Head Island audiences, who were accustomed to a theatrical diet of musicals and well-tested staples of the regional theatre circuit. Fears arose that audiences would be offended, confuse the hosting theatre, South Carolina Repertory Co., with the Hilton Head Island New Play Festival, and express their wrath at the SCRC box office that fall. These fears were not without foundation. *Catholic Girl Gun Club*, dedicated to the playwright's veteran sister, would be broaching the subject of war when the United States was fighting wars in both Iraq and Afghanistan and race during the first term of America's first African-American president, Barack Obama. In 2008, Blake White, the artistic associate who raised these concerns, had had to remove the Obama/Biden bumper sticker from his car after finding threatening notes tucked under his windshield wipers.

White feared that as a Boston-based dramaturg from the Midwest, I was not equipped to tailor a lineup of readings to an audience base that I had not worked with on a regular basis. I could fly in, shock everyone, and go back to Boston, leaving my hosts to deal with the public relations and financial fallout. To some degree, he was right. I did not choose the plays with SCRC's audience base in mind; I simply chose the pieces I found most interesting that I thought we could stage most effectively with the resources we had at our disposal. The only audience tailoring I did was based on Newell's advice that this community was quite capable of enjoying plays that engaged with all manner of controversial subjects, provided that there was an element of comedy involved.

Fortunately, Saint Owens is brilliant at creating moments of humor while dealing with challenging themes, and the reading went well. The rest of the weekend was sold out. The next play we featured was *Ephemera*, LA-based comedian Bryce Wissel's non-linear farce set in outer space (complete with a love-struck robot and a Creationist ape-man); it was received with enthusiasm. The final piece of the weekend, South Carolina playwright James Rasheed's *Baristas*, a cutting look at issues of class and politics in the South, so charmed the audience that plans were made to include a full production in SCRC's 2011–12 season.

Since August of 2010, the Hilton Head Island New Play Festival has showcased nine new plays in a broad range of styles. In that time, I have discovered that features of the South that I initially perceived as drawbacks to a new play development process were, on the contrary, potential assets. One concern was that Hilton Head Island audiences would not appreciate any piece that was unconventional or stylistically unfamiliar. Regional American audiences – particularly Southern ones – are often saddled with the reputation of being less sophisticated than audiences from New York or Chicago. While it is fair to say that they do not benefit from as broad a range of theatrical opportunities, this is not necessarily a detriment. I have found that this difference has allowed playwrights to receive particularly frank feedback about their work. For example, Marshall Botvinick's *Beckett in Jackson* is an unconventional blend of Southern comedy and cerebral references to the works of Samuel Beckett. This combination had proven confusing to a handful of Botvinick's friends from Harvard, who feared that an audience base would be able to enjoy the Southern jokes or the Beckett humor, but not both. As it turns out, not only could the Hilton Head Island audience provide feedback regarding the satire of Southern customs, they felt no pressure to prove their familiarity with Beckett's oeuvre. While an audience in New York or another urban theatre center might feel the need to live up to their "sophisticated" reputation, a cheerful show of hands in this case revealed that less than half of the audience had read a Beckett play. Were they bored during the Beckett parody dream sequence? No, they appreciated the absurdity even if they could not name the piece upon which it was based.

The fear that feedback from a less theatrically experienced audience base would prove useless to our playwrights, most of whom had already received extensive feedback from more established sources, was completely dispelled with our reading of Elena Zucker's *O Walter, My Walter* at the 2011 festival. The piece had already won the Rita and Burton Goldberg Prize in Playwriting and received a staged reading in New York. While, indeed, the Hilton Head Island audience was not interested in providing feedback on the dramatic structure of this dark comedy, based on the 2007 scandal at Walter Reed Army Medical Center, they were keen to provide insight from a different vantage point: the perspective of US Military veterans and their families. According to the US Census Bureau, 11.5 percent of South Carolina's population are veterans, compared to the national average of 9.6 percent and 1.0 percent of South Carolinians are currently employed by the Armed Forces – twice the national average.[1] As a community informed by a large veteran presence, our audience base was uniquely equipped to comment on the issues raised by this piece and did so with enthusiasm. Many audience members had spent time at Walter Reed and wanted to discuss the similarities of their experiences there to what they had seen in the play. An audience member's concern that the veterans were being mocked in this satire was quickly mollified, not by the playwright, director, or myself, but by other audience members eager to explain to her that the soldiers were not the objects of ridicule but the people and system that do not treat them well. They lauded the absurd style of the piece, likening it to the frustrations of military bureaucracy. Instead of being confused by the fact that all male characters were named "Walter" and all female characters "Winnie," an audience member pointed out that this choice captures the anonymity of being just one of many patients in a huge ward and overwrought system. The talkback ended with enthusiastic calls that the play be staged at a military hospital. While the audience did not provide the playwright with feedback in a literary sense, their contributions regarding the themes of the piece were invaluable.

New play development in the American South has posed a unique and sometimes unexpected set of challenges, including a lack of ethnic diversity. While we at the festival seek to connect playwrights to a region and cultural group that they would not normally encounter, we also seek to connect our audience to the voices and experiences of ethnic minorities in an area in which they often go unheard. In our pursuit to give the region access to developing American drama in all its diversity, we strive to extend this inclusion to the small community of professional actors in the South Carolina area. In largely ethnically homogeneous communities like Hilton Head Island, however, actors of color can be difficult to find. Often it is necessary to cast plays with minority characters from other parts of the region or even out of New York, which increases the production costs and impedes efforts to bring local voices into multiple aspects of the play development process.

In terms of ethnically diverse plays themselves, however, the Hilton Head Island audience has been welcoming to the artists of color who have been featured at the festival and their work. This is encouraging as the challenges to staging plays with ethnically diverse casts have not been political or social, but simply financial. While the audience's openness does not solve the economic conundrum, it does give us hope that when the opportunity arises to bring artists of color to the festival, our audiences will continue to receive them well. We hope as well that in an area that has a history of racial tension, the more opportunities that we are able to provide for minority artists locally, the more artists will feel comfortable coming forward and joining the artistic conversation.

Another challenge is that Southern audiences' tolerance for strong language has turned out to be more nuanced than initially expected. For example, at the Hilton Head Island New Play Festival, we maintain a policy of presenting plays as written, including the strong language, so that playwrights could get an uncensored reaction from this particular audience base. Generally, we've been able to maintain that principle and have found our audiences more tolerant to strong language than we had expected. There is one word, however, for which our audience seems to have a zero tolerance policy: "goddamn." We have actually had the same audience that laughed riotously at a comic delivery of the word "cunt" one night walk out the following evening over the use of the word "goddamn." The use of "cunt" was not even raised in the talkback, but I fielded multiple complaints both at the talkback and via phone and e-mail about the language in the show that used the word "goddamn." Such is our audience aversion to this word that should playwrights offer to change any language for the reading, they are surprised by the suggestion that "goddamn" be changed to "fuck" or "fucking" in situations that call for a generic strong explicative. Preston Lane, a North Carolina native and the artistic director of Triad Stage in Greensboro, North Carolina, recounts a similar intolerance of this particular word from his audience base, despite it being a younger and more financially and ethnically diverse group than typical audiences on Hilton Head Island, "Profanity is always going to get a little pushback. Just a little bit. But if the word 'goddamn' is used, I'll get letters and emails … It was a big surprise to me the first time."[2]

This extreme, specific intolerance often confuses theatre practitioners from other areas of the United States who have a hierarchy of offensiveness topped by racial, sexuality, or gender-related slurs (including the word "cunt"). When one considers the religious demographics of the American South, however, an explanation begins to emerge. According to a 2009 Gallup Poll,[3] the Southeast is home to America's highest concentration of people who self-identify as non-Catholic Christians: 75.2 percent of South Carolinians call themselves Christians, 23.8 percent above the national average. This information provides an insight into the cultural and religious values of this audience base and helps to explain their preferences. To this largely religious audience base, "goddamn" has connotations of eternal suffering and separation from God, a much weightier meaning than "fuck," which they understand simply as a crass verb for sexual intercourse.

In reading this, some playwrights will argue that they should be able to use whatever language they choose without catering to the preferences of a particular social group. Although I agree with that sentiment, it is worth noting that a playwright equipped with sensitivity and appreciation for this sort of variation will be better able to create verisimilitude in pieces that occur in or include characters from the South, much in the way that playwrights carefully consider the slang of a specific neighborhood when setting a piece there. This information also empowers playwrights interested in the marketability of a piece to a regional audience. Cultural knowledge of a particular audience base should be considered one of many tools available to a playwright, and the pursuit of new play development in the South serves to improve playwright access to such resources. In working in South Carolina, I came to understand that providing a cultural understanding of a target audience is yet another important way in which a dramaturg working in new play development can help serve the playwright.

Indeed, I do not share such information with the goal of making Southern audiences more comfortable, but more engaged. In fact, Lane describes learning to be comfortable with some measure of audience discomfort during Triad's first season: "We made a big decision. We looked at people leaving, and we thought: we can chase after them, or we can look at the people who are staying and we can ask 'where can we find more of them?' ... [W]e are in the process of growing an audience rather than chasing after one."[4] Lane's phrase "growing an audience" captures the greatest potential benefit of new play development in the American South: by inviting new groups to join the national conversation about American drama, we develop and cultivate, not just the pieces, but the audiences as well. In reading their plays in the South, playwrights enjoy the benefits of hearing from a group of people that they normally do not. This allows them a broader range of perspective and a better understanding of an often untapped, potentially profitable audience base. Audiences benefit, not only from exposure to new plays, but from the opportunity to join the actual process by which a play takes shape. In giving new parts of the country a greater sense of artistic ownership in contemporary American theatre, we encourage a larger group of Americans to become better, more engaged theatre patrons.

Notes

1 "State and Country QuickFacts," United States Census Bureau, available online at http://quickfacts.census.gov/qfd/states/45000.html, accessed March 28, 2013.
2 Preston Lane, telephone interview with the author, February 21, 2013.
3 Frank Newport, "Religious Identity: States Differ Widely," *State of the States Midyear 2009*, Gallup, available online at http://www.gallup.com/poll/122075/religious-identity-states-differ-widely.aspx#2, accessed March 28, 2013.
4 Lane, interview.

80
Talkbacks
Asking good discussion questions

Jodi Kanter

For many, a good discussion question is simply one that gets people talking. This is not a ridiculous criterion; community engagement of any kind is a rare commodity in the professional theatre, and one to be highly valued. But as we work toward more sophisticated engagement around our productions, it is worth asking what we hope our audiences will talk *about* and for what purpose. Bad post-show discussions fall into one of two categories: either they are insufficiently structured by the dramaturg – or whoever is leading them – and so susceptible to being taken over by audience members eager to share their own responses indiscriminately; or they are organized around a panel of experts who have a great deal to say about a given theme or content area but nothing whatsoever to say about the production. There are, in fact, appropriate situations for each of these types of discussions, but they arise much more infrequently than the discussions themselves would suggest. It is incumbent upon the dramaturg, first of all, to ask what or who the discussion is for. The answer to this question will inform what questions are asked and how the success of the discussion is assessed.

The play and its galaxy

In her well-known essay on reading plays, reprinted in this volume, Elinor Fuchs imagines the play as a planet to which the reader is paying a visit.[1] Through this wonderful conceit, Fuchs dramatizes the extent to which a play must be understood on its own terms in order to meaningfully evaluate it. She instructs the reader to ask about space, time, climate, and mood on this planet. She instructs us to ask, too, who has power on this planet and how it is exercised. Her essay has become the basis for many subsequent formulations for reading plays well.

To talk well about plays, I believe we need to situate the planet in its larger environment, its galaxy as it were. This is not as complicated as it may sound.

Fig 80.1 shows a diagram that indicates what I take to be the other major bodies in the play's orbit and, in parentheses, the inhabitants of those bodies who are most concerned with interplanetary relations. Below, following this simple scheme, I want

Figure 80.1 Play diagram

to elaborate what I think are the three most commonly productive types of post-show discussion, when each type is most useful, and how the dramaturg might shape the discussion so that it goes in the intended direction.

A discussion about the production

Typically, a post-show discussion about a production is framed as a service to the audience, a privileged visit behind the scenes and an opportunity to converse with (often self-selecting) professional artists. Such discussions are often warmly received. Naturally enough, audiences are eager to respond to and process the immediate experience at hand. They want to share their own emotional responses – when they cried, when they wanted to throw something, when they fell asleep. They also want to ask their own questions about the artistic process. They want to ask the director, "Why an aerial *Death of a Salesman*?" They want to ask the designer, "How did you ever think to create the Sahara with neon?" And they want to ask the actor, "Was it hard to memorize all those lines?"

Although these kinds of discussions can be fun and satisfying in so far as they give audience members access to privileged behind-the-curtain information, they rarely serve the audience in more meaningful ways. While sharing emotional responses to the production may be gratifying for both the audience member and the director/designer/actor, it is not an optimal use of communal time. Audience members can get as much and probably more gratification from sharing these kinds of responses with a friend. Those who really want to share their responses with the artists can do so more carefully, more completely, and more meaningfully in written form. Second, while the kinds of questions audience members ask of theatre professionals may satisfy individual curiosity about how theatre works, they do not serve in any substantive way to deepen audience appreciation for either the production or the process. Many professional theatres have open rehearsals, workshops, or mid-rehearsal lectures that provide much more substantive insight into the artistic process.

In general, we ought to stop having these kinds of discussions, with two important exceptions. First, a conversation about the production may be of real value to audiences in certain unusual circumstances, when the population has had little to no exposure to theatre as an art form or when the population has undergone some kind of trauma, individually or collectively. Productions of great dramatic texts in prison settings, for example, can serve this purpose, as can theatrical productions in war zones. In these situations, the post-show discussion can facilitate self-expression that has been socially or environmentally restricted. Indeed, it might persuasively be argued that in these situations, the production is merely a catalyst for a more meaningful exchange. Most often, however, discussions with these kinds of audiences go well beyond responding to the production itself, forging deep connections between the play and the community. In doing so, they become part of the final category of conversation discussed below.

A conversation about the production can also be of real value to the artistic team in those circumstances when the production itself is in process – that is, when it is in a "tryout" phase or is expected to move in the short term to another theatre or another city. The dramaturg should tailor the discussion to those elements of the production that remain adaptable and should, therefore, consult with the director extensively in formulating questions. Depending on the situation – not only the production schedule but the temperament and adaptability of the individual artists involved – it may be appropriate to pose questions around fairly major production choices such as the setting or the interpretation of a key scene. However, as the time when the next iteration of the production must be completed nears, this kind of feedback becomes less and less useful to the production team.

A discussion about the play

The "why" of the new play development discussion is relatively clear: to elicit responses that will serve the playwright, helping her to clarify the action of the play and deepen the audience's investment in it. But do new play development discussions actually work in this way? In "Talking Back," playwright David Rush suggests that the answer may be no. For his own part, he confesses that for many years he "sat through most discussions only because I felt I had to."[2] Rush argues that the problem with many such discussions is that they are shaped too little by the playwright and too much by the audience. He suggests that the dramaturg asks the writer to generate a list of discussion questions. "This is crucial because it forces the playwrights to stop and think seriously about the play. In order to determine what they want to learn, the writers have to articulate what they're trying to achieve."[3]

On the whole, general audiences do not understand clearly how best to serve the playwright. Therefore, one way that dramaturgs can be helpful is in laying down ground rules for the discussion. Rush offers three key suggestions: a prohibition of playwright response; a prohibition of judgments beginning with either "you should" or "I liked/I didn't like"; and a plea for brevity. After offering a particular question for discussion, the dramaturg can continue to guide responses by asking audience members to clarify their responses according to several key and commonly elided distinctions. First, the distinction between the play and the production. Dramaturgs can ask audience members to reflect on whether their response was primarily shaped by the play itself or by some element of the production. Second, the distinction between ambiguity and confusion. In unpacking audience members' responses to moments of ambiguity in the play, the dramaturg can ask audience members to reflect on whether these moments heightened audience engagement or diminished it. The playwright will want to know about moments of confusion in the play when a lack of clarity in the script takes audience members out of the action of the play. Third, the distinction between what the audience member wants and what the playwright wants. In my favorite song in the musical *You're A Good Man, Charlie Brown*, Linus responds to a school assignment to write a book report on *Peter Rabbit*. Not at all interested in *Peter Rabbit*, he solves the problem by writing that the book reminded him of *Robin Hood* and then goes on to write a dissertation about *Robin Hood*. This is the musical theatre illustration of the truism that all criticism is autobiography. In a new play discussion, this kind of response often takes the form of an audience member offering an idea for an alternate turn in the play's action than the one they have seen played out on stage. The dramaturg can help the audience member get back on track with a statement about the dramatic action or central thematic concern of the play such as, "I think what so-and-so is really interested in is ... " Of course, this requires laser clarity on the dramaturg's part about what the playwright wants to do with the play.

A discussion about the community

We visit the small planet of a play because we hope to return to our own, larger planet somehow illuminated. For me, this is the most important reason to hold a post-show discussion with a general audience. The dramaturg's most valuable role in post-show discussions is to guide audience members to make connections between the world of the play and the community or larger world around her. These connections foster both more creative participation in the real world and deeper engagement in finding meaning in the theatre.

Robert Scholes identifies this connection as that which makes reading (or viewing) a text an ethical act. Using George Eliot's *Middlemarch* as an example, he writes:

> To read in this way – which I would call ethical – the reader must bring the text of Vincy and the text of his life together in a metaphorical connection ... That is, I must freely accept the character Vincy as a metaphor for myself if this reading is to become ethical – and then I must seek to change my behavior so as to eliminate, or at least reduce, the validity of that metaphor in my life as it continues. For any of this to be possible, of course, it must be assumed that I have some power to change my life, that – to some extent – I am free and therefore responsible.[4]

Or, as Boal said, the theatre itself is not revolutionary; it is a rehearsal for revolution.

What kinds of questions, then, best serve to engage an audience in the kind of ethical reading of a play that leads to ethical participation in the world? The answer will depend on who the audience is; the world looks different to a high school student in a cultural enhancement program for economically disadvantaged young people than it does to a middle-aged professional with the disposable income to subscribe to a LORT theatre. But in any case, the search for relevance must begin with and continually return to the play itself.

A good dramaturg prepares for a post-show discussion by mining the play for themes and selecting from among those themes based on everything she knows about the audience. Through this process, she illuminates for audiences the most salient big ideas behind the drama. For example, a dramaturg might ask a young audience to think about *Romeo and Juliet* in terms of some of its big themes: love, trust, obedience, betrayal. This might be of interest to bright students with an affinity for abstract thinking. The dramaturg might even encourage the audience to think more concretely about how the action of the play relates to their own lives. She might ask, have your parents ever told you not to do something that you did anyway? Have you ever loved (or liked) the wrong person? Have you ever risked your life for something you believed in? Similarly, a good dramaturg mines the play for those themes most salient to the time and place in which the production is happening. This is the impulse behind post-show panels where *Romeo and Juliet* audience members might hear from a family psychologist, the director of a local violence prevention center, and an expert on drug abuse.

But the best discussion questions will challenge audience members of all ages and experience levels to evaluate the metaphorical connections that Scholes describes. What if, for example, both the drug counselor on the post-show panel and the disadvantaged young person on the school field trip were invited to respond to the question of whether the world of *Romeo and Juliet* is more violent than their own? What if the gay teenager handing out programs and the divorce lawyer on the theatre's board were asked whether it's easier to be in love today than it was in Shakespeare's time?

Creative staging of the discussion itself also has an impact on engagement. In recent years, there has been an explosion of experimentation in the area of "audience development," of which performance discussions are an important part. Many theatres have begun to push the boundaries of the post-show discussion format, holding, for example, round-robin impression-gathering sessions in which every voice is heard, or a series of targeted pre-show happy hours focused on particular topics. Other theatres have held book club-style discussions following the run of the show or sponsored discussion forums online in which audience members can engage with the performance as early as intermission. Theatres are also recognizing the importance of getting the audience talking before they walk into the building, and are extending many of their discussion formats backwards to make use of them before the production process even begins. Whatever form the discussion takes, it is by encouraging audiences to do the ethical work of making these connections between the play and the community that dramaturgs can best help audiences find meaning in the theatre. In that dark space between worlds lies wonder.

Notes

1 See Chapter 68 in this volume; Elinor Fuchs, "EF's Visit to a Small Planet: Some Questions to Ask a Play," *Theater* 34.2 (Summer, 2004): 4–9.
2 David Rush, "Talking Back: A Model for Postperformance Discussion of New Plays," *Theatre Topics* 10.1 (March, 2000): 53.
3 Rush, 56.
4 Robert Scholes, *Protocols of Reading* (New Haven, CT: Yale University Press, 1989), 152.

81

Talkbacks for "sensitive subject matter" productions

The theory and practice

Martine Kei Green-Rogers

Preparing for a post-show talkback may be a nerve-racking experience for most dramaturgs. However, that nervousness may turn into fear when one knows that the subject matter of the play, or the concept of the production, has the potential to arouse visceral, and potentially physical, reactions in an audience during a talkback experience. I am defining this type of subject matter as concepts that are controversial in today's society and politics. These concepts include, but are not limited to racism, sexism, ageism, homophobia, and extreme political agendas. When leading a discussion that incorporates potentially sensitive subjects, a dramaturg should view this as an opportunity to learn how the theatre's constituents view these issues, as opposed to succumbing to fear and anxiety. This article seeks to provide a practical guide to frame audience conversations on productions that address volatile subjects or representations. In addition, this article seeks to discuss the categories of audience members who may attend a talkback and how to use the strength and weaknesses of those categorizations to create a valuable educational experience for the participants.

To facilitate the transition from fear and anxiety to education, the most important question to ask is not "why" are these conversations so difficult but "how" do you deal with these difficult moments. Preparation for this moment must occur prior to the commencement of the talkback. Essentially, the dramaturg needs to create a sense of trust, safety, and openness *before* the talkback begins. I want to quickly define these key terms (trust, safe, and open) in order to create a baseline understanding of the environment that needs to be cultivated before the talkback begins. We are going to define "trust" as "one in which confidence is placed."[1] "Safe" is defined as "secure from the threat of danger, harm or loss."[2] With this particular definition, I want to point out that I am purposefully avoiding the definition of "safe" that includes "unlikely to produce controversy or contradiction."[3] The reasoning behind not including this particular definition is that it is difficult to avoid controversy and contradiction if one is facilitating a conversation about sensitive subject matters. However, a dramaturg should strive to create an environment that allows for any opinion to be voiced without the fear of retaliation. The idea here is to foster a challenging of ideas, not people. "Open" is defined as "characterized by ready accessibility and usually generous attitude; willing to hear and consider or to accept and deal with."[4] In this same instance, I am avoiding the definition that includes "exposed or vulnerable to attack or question," not that questioning is unwarranted, the concern in this particular instance is on "attacking."[5]

Ground rules are essential for a trusting, safe, and open talkback. Using the production's playbill is an ideal manner to disseminate the talkback's ground rules. The reasoning for this is three-fold; it allows talkback participants easy access to the rules before and during the talkback; it allows the dramaturg a physical item to direct talkback participants to when discussing the ground rules; and it provides an official way for all participants to recognize when a participant is in violation of those ground rules. To introduce the ground rules at the beginning of a talkback, I suggest stating, "In order to run this talkback as efficiently as possible and to make sure that we have time for as many questions and answers as possible, please take the next minute to review the ground rules for the discussion, as found in your playbill insert."

The following ground rules, some of which I have modified from the suggestions in *The Process of Dramaturgy* by Scott Irelan, Anne Fletcher, and Julie Felise Dubiner, *Theatre for Community, Conflict and Dialogue* by Michael Rohd, and my own personal experiences are:

1 Respond with "I" statements instead of "you" statements.
2 If you are responding to a question posed, attempt to avoid veering off topic with your answer.
3 If you are responding to the answer of someone else, please identify what idea you are responding to but not the person who originated the idea.
4 Always feel free to share what is on *your* mind. (Emphasis on your!)
5 Foster a spirit of non-judgment and respect.

Once the audience understands the ground rules, the process turns to facilitating the conversation by asking open and non-leading questions. For example, "Who wants to tell us in one word/sentence what the play was about for them?"[6] or "What was your experience when watching this play?" These questions have a similar purpose: to make the comments personal to their individual play-going experience. At this point, your job as dramaturg is to remain open to the audience's responses. This may require some acting skills, since you can never anticipate people's thoughts. However, you must also maintain your human connection to the production and talkback. If someone shares a thought that causes any emotional response from you, you must acknowledge it and move forward, remembering to address the idea or comment, not the person.

An audience's participation in conversations is not always automatic. When posing a question, one has to allow time for participants to process the question. Therefore, give them that time. Preface your questions with "I want to give you a minute to think about the following question." Then, after posing the question, your job as a moderator is to listen. As Rohd states, "a good facilitator … is a good listener. The group must know you care about their thoughts and their responses and that you are willing to learn as well. This is all signaled by the way you listen."[7] However, even if you give the audience time to ponder a question, there may be a reluctance to share. Yet you must resist the urge to talk to fill the silence. The reason is that you may, unintentionally, make a statement that is polarizing, compromising your position as the neutral moderator.

While in the beginning stages of the conversation, a dramaturg must be aware of potential distractions that may interfere with her ability to maintain the focus of the conversation. For example, you may have actors and other members of the artistic team appear onstage. Normally their entrance is not problematic except in a couple of instances. One is if the space in which the talkback occurs requires people to enter the space between you and the audience. Since you are in the position of needing to engender trust, having people continually crossing in between you and the audience begins to erode the foundation of trust you are cultivating. If it is at all possible, attempt to alleviate this by positioning yourself in a manner in which other members of the artistic team do not need to cross your path in order to join the conversation. This allows you to continue establishing a relationship with your audience even as people enter and exit the space. This also allows you to control the focus of the audience and acknowledge the people entering the conversation at a point that is useful to you and the audience. The other instance is if one of your fellow artists joins the stage in a moment of "crisis," a moment in which someone may have said something that triggered an emotional and/or vocal response by others in the audience. When this occurs, you must acknowledge the newcomer and the outburst. Have the newcomer sit down (without introduction) and then give the outburst, and the emotions that created it, the space it deserves. I find that statements such as, "I see that many people had an emotional connection to the idea of (insert idea here). I find that connection interesting and worth exploration." However, if it is not appropriate to continue that conversation, such as in the initial moments of gathering feedback from audience members, follow the previously mentioned statement with "I want to continue exploring other people's reactions and then return to this idea." However, do not forget that when this verbal contract (the promise to return to the idea) is created, it must be honored to maintain an atmosphere of trust. I advocate for returning to the idea because it gives people the opportunity to respond but also have the time to process their emotion. Also, when you return to the idea, make sure you remind people to use their "I" statements so that it is about their personal reaction as opposed to making generalized statements about the audience as a whole or attacking the original speaker. After the conversation has addressed the outburst, use that moment to introduce your newcomer to the audience.

Now that you are equipped with some techniques of approaching this type of talkback, understanding the audience types you may find at a talkback becomes important. David Rush, in reference to new play discussion, identifies several types of discussion participants, who you may also see at a play dealing with sensitive subject matter. These include the *destroyer*, "those long-winded, digressive, nit-picking nuisances who quickly derail a session," the *grandstander*, who "seizes the floor and babbles incomplete thoughts and unfinished sentences," the *wannabe* who claims "not to want to rewrite the play but then does," the *nitpicker*, "who specializes in molehills, launching into great diatribes," the *contender*, "who always disagrees with someone else," and the *sidetracker*, "who responds to a play, just not the one that was presented."[8] Since discussions about sensitive subject matter have a tendency towards people expressing a personal connection to the events represented, there is a context in which incomplete thoughts and molehills may be warranted, depending on a person's connection to the idea and the material presented in the play. However, when a dramaturg only has 20 minutes to an hour to facilitate a conversation that engages the entire audience, statements and diatribes that move the conversation away from the play become harmful since the space needs to be created for everyone who is interested in participating to do so.

The ability for dramaturgs to accomplish this egalitarian conversation lies in their ability to discern their body's semiotic and ideological place within the space in relation to the audience members and the type of talkback participant they represent. Cathy Royal has a sociologically based theory, the Quadrant Behavior Theory (QBT), that when applied within the context of a talkback may help a dramaturg simply, and quickly, identify these semiotic and ideological factors. Within the QBT, Royal identifies categories she deems the "big eight," which are defined as "race (skin color), gender, sexual orientation, class, age, ability, nationalism/ethnicity, and religious beliefs."[9] With these "big eight," Royal creates a matrix in which these categories are designated with a plus or a minus sign in order to create a visual understanding of how varying people within the audience may read the dramaturg's body. If a dramaturg understands, for example, the power and privilege of their body being read as "white male," which is classified with two plus signs (in the QBT), versus the potential devaluing that may come from having another person's body read as "woman of color," which is classified as two minuses, this dramaturg may begin to understand and anticipate how people may respond to the posed questions. For a possible scenario, would a person in a circumstance that designates them as two minus signs (a black woman audience member in an audience full of white men) feel as comfortable speaking out about their relationship to a play about lynching? Or for an opposite scenario, would (in this particular circumstance) a white male in an audience of black women feel comfortable speaking out about his relationship to a play about lynching? The answer to this is complicated, but understanding the mechanics behind the hesitance a minority voice may have in addressing the audience, or the power in statements made by a majority voice in any audience group, becomes important in creating a balanced audience talkback.

In order to effectively use this theory in another context, a dramaturg must determine which (and how many) of these "big eight" are found in the play and then determine whether the play uses a dominant (plus) or oppressed (minus) voice to represent that "big eight" category. Then the dramaturg must analyze whether their own signified body runs parallel or contrary to that "big eight" idea/voice in order to be able to anticipate how their body and ideology will be interpreted by the talkback participants. For example, in the case of *Clybourne Park* by Bruce Norris, if the dramaturg wanted to open a discussion about the changing face of racism in the play as seen through the characters of Francine/Lena (double minus), women of color (double minus) may be more open and honest with their response to the question if the moderator is a person of color (either single or double minus) because of the observed (and assumed) shared identity/oppressed connection. To bring up another possibility, as a result of the desire for political correctness in the same situation, a white male (double plus) audience member may be more inclined to remain silent in a scenario such as the previously mentioned one. However, the goal of a conversation, such as this one, is to not purposefully exclude a particular population during the conversation. Therefore, acknowledging the dramaturg's signified body and its perceived scale on the "big eight" will allow the implementation of strategies to create a more egalitarian conversation. These strategies include, for example, the crafting of questions that will help include a range of people when the conversation has become focused in on one particular group for an extended time. Such a question may be, for example, "Where may a person find the universality in a story such as this?" As long as the dramaturg is paying attention to the power and privilege dynamics in the room and responding proactively to any "crisis" moments, the talkback should feel similar to any other talkback.

In essence, the main points to remember when facilitating a conversation on plays that deal with sensitive subject matter are 1) establish ground rules; 2) physically position yourself and address the audience in a manner that helps establish trust; 3) open the conversation with icebreaker questions that establish the audience's personal response to the play (while remembering how your signified body may influence the conversation); and 4) thank everyone for their thoughts and acknowledge the vulnerability involved in participating in the conversation by congratulating them on their willingness to engage in the conversation.

Notes

1 *Merriam-Webster OnLine*, s.v. "trust," http://www.merriam-webster.com/dictionary/trust, accessed March 20, 2013.
2 *Merriam-Webster OnLine*, s.v. "safe," http://www.merriam-webster.com/dictionary/safe, accessed March 20, 2013.
3 *Merriam-Webster OnLine*, s.v. "safe," http://www.merriam-webster.com/dictionary/safe, accessed March 20, 2013.
4 *Merriam-Webster OnLine*, s.v. "open," http://www.merriam-webster.com/dictionary/open, accessed March 20, 2013.
5 *Merriam-Webster OnLine*, s.v. "open," http://www.merriam-webster.com/dictionary/open, accessed March 20, 2013.
6 Scott Irelan, Anne Fletcher, and Julie Felise Dubiner, *The Process of Dramaturgy: A Handbook* (Newburyport, MA: Focus Publishing/R. Pullins Company, 2010), 90.
7 Michael Rohd, *Theatre for Community, Conflict and Dialogue: The Hope Is Vital Training Manual* (Portsmouth: Heinemann, 1998), 113.
8 David Rush, "Talking Back: A Model for Postperformance Discussion of New Plays," *Theatre Topics* 10.1 (March 2000): 54–5.
9 Cathy Royal, "Quadrant Behavior Theory: Edging the Center (The Potential for Change and Inclusion)," *OD Practitioner* 42.2 (2010): 27.

82

Dramaturgies for the digital age

Ilinca Todoruţ

The array of media, venue types, and levels of audience engagement contained by performances today – be it the type to be seen/heard/interacted with/experienced on the proscenium stage, in a black box, inside a mall, in a gallery space, in the street, on the screen of a laptop, tablet, or mobile phone – calls for models of dramaturgies that take into account such structural diversity. Since theatre can take many shapes, the question arises if it's possible to construct a framework for thinking about dramaturgy in the larger context of digital culture.

The concern cannot be extricated from the ways in which the widespread use of digital technologies altered our engagements with inhabited realities and manners of communication and inter-relation. The familiar validation of theatre as eminently live and alive, present and co-present – and thus community inducing – rings untenable when many people rely on the internet to maintain connections across great distances or even search online for liveness, presence, and community that are slipping through the cracks in quotidian life. On the other hand, live theatre in its production and reception is inescapably mediated – think not only of technologies used on stage, but also the manners in which the audiences relate to a performance: through watching trailers, recordings, reading about it on blogs.

Digital technologies enable a plethora of practices in embodied staged performances or strictly online projects or performances relying on a mix of both virtual and physically materialized aspects. The fields of theatre and computer studies started a fruitful dialogue as early as 1991, when Brenda Laurel's innovative *Computers as Theatre* urged interface designers to think of the human-machine interaction in terms of Aristotelian dramatic concepts, where the primacy of action reigns. Laurel pursued the endowment of the human user with the feeling of taking action within the representational world of the computer. The study into the poetics of human-computer interaction continued through the late 1990s, when Janet Murray coined the term "cyberdrama" in her book *Hamlet on the Holodeck* to denote a computer-based narrative form shaped "as a dynamic fictional universe with characters and events."[1] The computer game Façade that she helped design unfolds as a domestic drama, where the player enters the game as a visitor to a couple's house. Through dialogue with the fictional characters and the range of actions afforded by the game, the player interacts with the couple, enters a love triangle, discovers their marital problems, and through the course of the game participates in the unfolding of a story. The gist of this neo-

Aristotelian interactive drama is that the participant is aware of the story and actively manipulates it.

From the perspective of other theatre practitioners, this conception of theatre as narrative-based Aristotelian drama seems limited. Taking advantage of the rapid developments in digital media, the range of tech-savvy performances has been enlarged outside conceptions of simulations and interactive dramas. Virtual theatres benefitted greatly from the affordances of Multi-User Domain platforms, which allow for a large number of people logging on from their own devices into the same virtual space. MUDs may be the main innovation that allowed for a model of theatre not as one player entering a computer-generated interactive world or simulation, but for a community of people experiencing an event together. The online world Second Life, for example, hosts a large number of performances where virtual personas, or avatars, perform for avatar-spectators. The Second Life theatre companies rehearse online, which entails not only learning lines, but programming the more spectacular actions done by the actors, such as metamorphoses into different creatures. The shows can take place on stages in familiar-looking theatre structures or in especially constructed environments. A production of *The Tempest* took their audience on the storming sea to witness the shipwreck. The performances range from original productions written for avatar theatre companies to adaptations of much loved literature such as *Alice in Wonderland* and stagings of classic plays.

Intermedial performances that happen simultaneously in physical spaces and virtual ones are facilitated through live streaming and videoconferencing platforms. A veteran of such telematic and networked performances, Helen Varley Jamieson (who prefers the term cyberformance for her practice) conceives events that are physically staged and spectated in one or multiple venues (often in different countries), which are then simultaneously live-streamed online and mixed with a staged virtual component. The resulting screen performance can be viewed by remote spectators, who in their turns can interact with performers and with each other through chat windows. The themes often engage with urgent political aspects of our interconnected global society, issues that seem particularly relevant when presented in the form of networked cyberformances. Together with collaborator Paula Crutchlow, Jamieson staged the project *make-shift* simultaneously in two different households linked through an online platform, accessible for viewing to anyone around the world with an internet connection. The UpStage online platform, accessed as any other website, united live streaming from the households with sounds, visuals, and computer-generated performers. Images and sounds from a beautiful island suffering ecological disaster mixed with avatar performer Dave, a regular Joe middle-class consumer. Remote spectators could chat among themselves, with Dave, and with the audience members in the households busy with small tasks such as following instructions to build a small kite from the plastics they've used that day. The networked event made palpable certain aspects and consequences of transnational consumerism.

Social media generate another type of digital culture performances. While these performances may not unfold entirely online, they are made possible only through online channels of information and communication. Flash mobs rely on social media to organize the surreptitious events when a large number of people in crowded public spaces suddenly coordinate at a specific hour and perform the same action, to the surprise of the inadvertent audience who happens also to be in the space. Flash mobs don't have to be complex to be effective: in 2006, *Frozen Grand Central* caused a real stir in the busy New York train station when more than two hundred people stood completely still together for a few minutes, caught in various actions of walking, checking time, and even embracing.

So-called viral theatres similarly rely on the prodigal dissemination of information in the digital age, an exponential spread mimicking contagion. Artists like Eva and Franco Mattes bet on the unchecked proliferation of bits of information to stage digital hoaxes. In 2001, for the Slovenian Pavilion at the Venice Biennale they "presented" a computer virus let loose into the network to spread into computers around the world, the project measuring its success against the paranoia induced into the public. Lastly, social media and portable networked devices create not only new performative modes, but leave imprints on traditional dramatic practices, such as playwriting. The dramaturgical format of online Twitter plays use the word-count restrictions imposed by the social media platform to construct often hilarious texts through status updates. The plays can be followed by subscribing to the performative Twitter channel.

Digital culture has long permeated live theatre practices, from technologically savvy Broadway productions, where the human actors are often just a cog in the image- and sound-producing machine, to lower budgeted productions by various theatre companies. The Builders Association famously mix live onstage computer-generated components with the material environment and embodied performers. Other shows like *Call Cutta in a Box* conceived by Rimini Protokoll rely on computer-mediated connections to stage one-on-one encounters between performers and spectators who are physically apart. In *Call Cutta in a Box*, the "first world" consumer enters a simple room equipped with table, chair, and a laptop and engages in teleconferencing with a "third world" service provider, a call center employee based in India.

Another type of digitally colonized live theatre practice employs artificial intelligence entities such as chatbots, which are capable of complex verbal interactions with each other or with humans, resulting in uncannily life-like conversations. Chatbots often star in online performances, but now they also do so in physical venues. In 2011, a show conceived by Annie Dorsen entitled *Hello Hi There* replaces human performers on stage with two very capable and entertaining chatbots. Represented as screens sitting on stage on two mounds of Astroturf, the chatbots engaged with each other and with a recording of the famous 1971 Chomsky–Foucault debate projected in the background.

As evidenced from the wide range of performative modes above, a dramaturg's role in virtual theatres cannot be fixed to a particular set of responsibilities. An obvious prerequisite is fluency in new media, while in the case of online performances even a basic grasp of programming is necessary in order to know what can be made possible and what not. For example, in Second Life performances there's still a lot of programming that goes into facilitating handing a piece of paper from one avatar to another, whereas an actor can turn into a dragon in two seconds flat. The dramaturg's familiarity with new media practicalities and concepts, which can be compared to the more traditional knowledge of scenography, is often induced simply by living in today's society, surrounded by and depending on digital devices. In the cultural discourse at large, discussions prevail on how digital technologies impact diverse spheres of human activity, from basic cognitive functions and inter-human relationships, to production modes and work practices. As always, a dramaturg's quality is an omnivorous curiosity.

A core idea of both Laurel and Murray was that programmers and game designers need dramaturgical training, useful in knowing how to plot a range of actions that users can easily engage with. In Second Life, avatar theatre companies often designate traditional production roles: performers, director, playwright, and even a dramaturg, while the place of designers is taken over by the programmer. In intermedial performances such as *make-shift*, Jamieson and Crutchlow hover over the project, aided by a mishmash of skills servicing the multimedia format. With a background in theatre, Jamieson is self-taught in basic programming and low-tech, DIY, free and accessible technologies like videoconferencing. Besides coming up with the concept for a performance and designing the online component, during the performance Jamieson and Crutchlow take the role of master of ceremonies, calling themselves "brokers" who negotiate and manage relationships with the physical audience. Traditional production roles in such intermedial performances are fluid, sharing directorial, dramaturgical, design, and acting functions. In contrast, Twitter plays can be the sole creation of a single playwright, although a dramaturgical flair is useful in deciding the frequency of posts or in adapting a well-known book, film, or TV series for the smart phone format. A flash mob dramaturgy is largely a work of facilitating communication. For the Mattes' viral theatre, devised in the niche of fine arts, the performance as a concept put in motion is a familiar mode of creation. In other conceptual types of performances like *Call Cutta in a Box*, Helgard Haug and Daniel Wetzel from Rimini Protokoll don't fulfill the traditional roles of a theatre director, just as the project doesn't involve traditional actors. It could be argued that what they do is closer to dramaturging than anything else: surveying a concept and orchestrating communication.

But the one dramaturgical concern relevant across different modes of digital per-formances is spectatorship. Relevant questions include: what are the particularities of the channels through which the performance reaches the spectator (smart phones, computers, screens on stage)? Who is the audience, particularly of online and inter-medial performances? How does the project relate to sometimes inadvertent audiences (like in flash mobs and viral performance)? How much agency should the spectator be given? If the former basic features of theatre can be easily dispensed with, such as physical venue (with performances taking place online), uninterrupted duration experienced in a physically doable length (which is not a constituent in, let's say, Twitter plays, which are generated through the laconic sentence format over days), and even the existence of a human actor (replaced by intelligent entities like chatbots), the one remaining unchallenged precondition for the theatrical situation is the necessary presence of the spectator.

The inherent interactivity of digital technologies encourages models for the increased participation of spectators, consumers, and receivers in other spheres of activity. For computer theorists like the aforementioned Murray, theatre using the computer as a representational medium offers the empowering gift of choice to the spectator turned protagonist, merging the player of computer games with the player as actor in dramatic history lingo (a figure known today under various names as "actant," "experiencer," "immersant"). The entertainment industry picked up on the trend and empowered the viewer in live TV dramas, where spectators from home vote which "actor" to eliminate. Businesses were quick to profit from the availability of free input through crowdsourcing practices, putting up open calls for always "fun" volunteer contributions. The spectator and his or her agency and participation are often at the center of performances fostered by digital technologies.

Fresh theoretical debates delve into audience studies, such as Jacques Rancière's collection of essays *The Emancipated Spectator*. He challenges the fad for participation in theatre by demonstrating that the assumptions between passive and active spectator correlated with merely watching and taking part in the show are too hastily drawn. Rancière doesn't want to devalue audience participation altogether, only the instant assumption that it makes for automatically better art if it's interactive and across-the-board political efficiency if spectators have agency to influence the course of the performance. The peculiar activity of the spectator is not to act, reminds Rancière, but the ability to move in and out of various forms of involvement, to associate and dissociate, to receive and to interpret: "That is what the word 'emancipation' means: blurring the boundary between those who act and those who look; between individuals and members of a collective body."[2]

Although Rancière's notions of spectatorial emancipation speak the lingo of in-betweenness and fluidity, he writes against "the idea of hybridization," which according to him results in elitist forms of "hyper-activism." But the spectator of hybrid performances does not have to be enslaved in representation any more than other audiences. The telematic viewer too can be a so-called emancipated spectator, watching a performance happening on screen, while having the option if he or she so desires to exchange impressions with other remote spectators and with the performers via chat. The conditions for fostering an emancipated spectator are not to be found in the affordances and limits of a specific medium, but in the thoughtfulness accorded to form and content in performance works across media. Comprehensive definitions of theatre might be less important than encouraging a versatile, challenging practice across representational media.

The concept and rising research field of intermediality, which refers first of all to the plethora of material means of representation and reproduction at our disposal and the correlative widening of the capacity for multi-channeled communication through several sensory fields, valorizes the positive values of the in-between, the hybrid, the fluid, and the open-ended. In pondering performance in a digital age, a careful consideration of reception in the rich array of practices taking newest technologies as material supports can be fruitful in enriching the entire spectrum of performance, in a time when boundaries are porous and the in-betweens are rich in possibilities.

Notes

1 Janet H. Murray, *Hamlet on the Holodeck* (New York: The Free Press, 1997), 6.
2 Jacques Rancière, *The Emancipated Spectator* (London and New York: Verso, 2008), 19.

83

Digital engagement
Strategies for online dramaturgy

Tanya Dean

The goal of this article is to offer resources to any dramaturg or literary manager seeking to take advantage of the internet as a medium to facilitate critical thinking and dialogue about theatre. For theatres that are committed to maintaining a dynamic online presence, successful digital dramaturgy is not necessarily reliant on cutting-edge technology. The three companies interviewed for this article – the Guthrie Theater in Minneapolis, Oregon Shakespeare Festival, and the National Theatre in London – each have very different digital presences, but they share one common factor: a strategic focus on what their available digital resources could offer audiences, and how they might extend dramaturgical conversation beyond the theatre space.

Guthrie Theater

The Guthrie Theater enjoys a long-standing reputation for producing carefully curated and researched Play Guides to accompany their productions. The first Play Guide was produced in 1975, intended as a resource primarily for teachers to supplement their classroom work, and by the mid 1980s Play Guides were being created for most productions in the season. These guides are primarily the remit of the dramaturg for any given production; he/she is in charge of curating and producing the Play Guide, aided by a literary intern to assist in the research and writing. For the 2000–2001 season, the Guthrie decided to make the Play Guides available online. This meant that the format of the guide had to adjust to consider the legal repercussions of publishing on the internet. "Previously we'd used several longer pieces, sometimes of several pages. Because we were doing very limited print runs (300 perhaps), we could ask permission for those pieces and if a fee was required it was often minimal," explains Carla Steen, publications manager/dramaturg for the Guthrie.[1] But since a digital publication has the potential to live in perpetuity online and be readily accessible to anyone, this changed the relationship with copyright holders. "So the content has taken the form of many smaller quotes that can be used within fair-use copyright guidelines."[2]

In keeping with their origins as hard-copy study guides, the Play Guides available on the Guthrie website are primarily print-driven in terms of format and style, but designed to be appealing and navigable as an online resource as well. Steen explains that the PDFs of the Play Guides also "have links within the documents and are iPad compatible."[3] The Play Guides are posted under the education section of the website and linked to the corresponding show page's resources. The Play Guides are also all archived online as PDFs, serving as both a digital memory of the Guthrie's production history and as a valuable resource for students and professionals alike who might be working on these plays in the future.

"Because each show will have different needs and information available, each guide will be different," explains Steen. "But we generally include information in these categories: the play, the playwright, cultural context and the Guthrie production."[4] A standard Guthrie Play Guide would generally include under the following headings:

- The Play: a synopsis, list of characters, literary analysis (quotes about the play from reviews, from academic journals, etc.), quotes by the playwright about the play.
- The Playwright: a biography, quotes by and about the playwright if available, perhaps a timeline of the author's life and major cultural events (usually just for classic plays but not always).
- Cultural Context: usually material that has been generated because of the needs of the production (glossary of terms from the script, culturally relevant information about the world of the play).
- The Guthrie Production: focuses on the specifics of the Guthrie production of the play (director's and designers' statements, perhaps something from the playwright if applicable).
- Then there are the potential extras that a Play Guide might offer: Building the Production might include production photos and backstage information about the set, costumes, props, sound, wigs, etc. This is usually added about two weeks later, as the information is gathered during tech week and can't be completed until production photos are taken, edited, and made available. Most guides will also include a For Further Reading section that will include books, articles, websites, films, and other additional resources that a reader or playgoer may find useful. Some guides may also include a Questions for Discussion page, usually for productions that would have a particular appeal to student groups.

While some dramaturgical materials are also made available in the program that is handed out when the audience physically arrives at the theatre, these can only "skim the surface," says Steen. "The play guide is intended to be a deeper dive into the material. We have an intelligent audience that enjoys knowing more about the work they see ... enriching the experience onstage is definitely embraced by our audience and, I think, Twin Cities audiences in general."[5]

Oregon Shakespeare Festival

When Julie Felise Dubiner, an associate director at Oregon Shakespeare Festival (OSF), is working on online dramaturgical content for OSF, she enjoys knowing that this content is being created for a "rabidly loyal audience." "OSF is blessed with a core audience of theatrelovers who are more interested in the intellectual stuff. There are people who have been coming to OSF for generations, people who have seen the entire Shakespeare canon … twice!"[6] For OSF, online dramaturgy is part of an ongoing conversation that is passionate and enthusiastic on both sides. OSF has had a website since the mid 1990s, which underwent a major redesign in 2012, with the intent of making the format less formal and more accessible. Key to this is the "Connect with Us" blog section of the website, which offers dramaturgical supplements such as articles, interviews, audio, and video clips. As OSF has a company photographer, they also always have high-quality, beautiful photos to share online. The Marketing and Communications Department maintain the website, but the dramaturgs and associate directors have been given direct access, allowing them to upload dramaturgical materials as they become available. Dubiner admits that there have been adjustments to this instant online publication, but feels that overall they are positive: "There's probably less good writing coming out, but the immediacy of the conversation makes it more powerful than any beautiful sentence I could construct over the course of three months."[7]

OSF has an active Twitter (@OSFashland) and Facebook page, where the idea of interacting with the audience really comes into play. These are maintained by the Marketing and Communications Department, with a number of people who participate or who are linked in (such as dramaturgs or guests from the cast or creative team). Dubiner says that these not only keep the dialogue between OSF and its audience vivified, they also bring them into a larger discourse: "Being in nowheresville, Ashland, it's great letting people across the country know what the function of our festival is, and it helps keep a conversation going nationally."[8] Dubiner's ambition is that this conversation will also help propel productions and playwrights towards life beyond OSF: "I get a lot of requests from people for scripts that I didn't hear from before I joined Twitter. We get a lot of interest from people who can't make it out here to see things, and want to learn more."[9]

OSF strives for regular postings on Facebook and Twitter, explains Eddie Wallace, the membership and sales manager at OSF: "We plug upcoming events, highlight good reviews, share new photos from dress rehearsals, share interesting articles from out in the arts industry or about Shakespeare, have the occasional contest, show fun photos from our Archives."[10] And Facebook followers offer immediate engaged feedback, posting comments on OSF Facebook posts. "When someone is fabulously effusive about the work they've seen, we thank them and encourage them to come back soon," says Wallace. "We don't have a written policy about responding to digital comments, but our overall company policy is that every letter or question or deep comment should get a response."[11]

As a "destination theatre," there is also a marked difference in how the website is valuable to both audience and festival. "People plan their trips to this festival differently from how they would plan trips to regional theatres. Our Marketing Department says that people tend to spend more time on our website than on the average 5–6 show season website," explains Dubiner. "If an audience member is coming for 5 days, and choosing from 11 shows, they will spend more time on website planning."[12] As such, digital content and dramaturgical resources become valuable tools to the theatrical pilgrims who journey to OSF every year. Dubiner says she feels that the website has replaced the idea of the old-school dramaturgy packet, meaning that the audience, cast, and creative team can now all become part of the dramaturgical conversation behind a particular production or a season theme. "The same pictures that I would previously have been photocopying 20 times for a rehearsal room dramaturgy packet, now I can post them online and suddenly the world can see what we're thinking about with this production. And we have a magnificently dedicated audience who will pay attention to these things."[13]

National Theatre

The average footfall through the National Theatre (NT) in London is approximately 600,000 people per year, according to Digital Content Producer Maya Gabrielle.[14] Online, however, the NT reaches a vast international audience; on average, the NT's views/downloads/streams average 1.6 million hits annually.[15] And that is going up exponentially each year, says Gabrielle, largely due to the extensive presence that the NT has worked to build on the web. The key, in Gabrielle's opinion, is to find the online hubs for audiences who are interested in and/or passionate about theatre (such as iTunes, iTunes U, YouTube, Sound Cloud) and make sure that the NT's dramaturgical materials are made available there as well as on the NT website. "This is one of the reasons why we are particularly good at developing digital content," she concludes. "We don't wait for people to come to us; we go to them."[16]

The NT employs a dedicated Digital Media Department; in addition to Gabrielle and David Sabel (head of Digital and executive producer of NT Live broadcasts), there is also an assistant producer, two in-house camera operators, film editors, and a pool of freelancers. The department produces dramaturgical materials on several different strands, including Digital Classroom, YouTube videos, podcasts (related to live events), and iTunes U. The Digital Media Department also invests considerable time in researching the impact and efficacy of their work and finding potential new avenues to explore. For example, the NT has a teacher focus group from a variety of schools and educational institutions from across the UK that meets quarterly and shares feedback on the NT's supplemental dramaturgical offerings. Gabrielle clarifies that the Digital Media Department is not a service department; rather, it is a creative department. "It's not about marketing, it's about sharing the excellence of the artists that we're lucky enough to have in this building."[17] This is in part related to the NT's status as a government-subsidized body, Gabrielle observes, "In response to the tax payer giving a little bit of money from their purse, we want to share as much as possible with them of what's happening."[18]

As the NT produces between 23 and 26 performances per year, spread across 3 different auditoria within the South Bank complex, the Digital Media Department has to be selective about which productions they produce supplemental video materials for.[19] As such, the focus is on productions that will reach the widest audience (such as the NT Live broadcasts, of which there are eight per year) and productions that are important educationally, particularly in the UK syllabus (with Shakespeare unsurprisingly a priority).[20] Rather than focus on the specifics of the production itself, Gabrielle tries to find larger themes within the play that will resonate with audiences long past the final performance. "Digital content is not cheap to make and we don't charge people to view it. So if production is only up for three months, I try and produce films that will have a shelf-life of between five to ten years, so I can justify the expense of making it."[21]

In a talk entitled "The Power of Online Video" (available on YouTube) she gave in 2011 for a digital seminar at Sadler's Wells, Gabrielle noted the serendipity of the popularity of the NT's videos beyond the obvious audience of passionate theatregoers.

> We were expecting Danny Boyle's *Frankenstein* and *War Horse* (seen by over a million people) to be the most popular. [But] the most popular collection of content that we put up on iTunes U was a simple voice collection with some warm-up exercises and how to breathe and articulate, because people ... do want to learn, they want basic instructional stuff ... It hadn't even occurred to us that that was valuable until we put it into that forum.[22]

At the same talk, Gabrielle also discussed the potential for collaboration offered by online platforms, citing the example of a project that the NT initiated with the Royal College of Art in tandem with *Frankenstein*, where students created short videos based on their experience of the production. This, emphasized Gabrielle, was an example of digital dramaturgy that was a cost-effective way of both engaging the audience and broadening the experience of a production. "None of this content cost any money ... this is user-generated content. We provided a platform to put it up; it's very good quality, it's on brand, it's absolutely connected to one of our productions."[23]

As an example of cost-effective online dramaturgy, Gabrielle showed a short video diary with rehearsal room footage from *One Man, Two Guvnors*, filmed by one of the actors with a Flip camera. Gabrielle explained that the Digital Media Department often give Flip cameras to members of the cast or staff directors or dancers (such as Fela) who are happy to film their experiences. She explained that the poor quality of the video becomes secondary to the insight into the rehearsal room that is being offered, because the people making the footage are a part of the creative experience. "[These videos] all cost nothing to shoot ... and what you sacrifice in quality video product, you can regain in the interest of the subject and the kind of access that you're giving the video viewer."[24] Gabrielle also offered key advice for smaller arts organizations that do not have the personnel or the resources to produce high-level digital content.

> You need to think, who are your audiences? What is the asset you are offering? If you can't spend a lot of money on having a great crew with great sound and making it look slick, what can you offer that somebody else can't? You can offer something; all of you who've got different creative processes that you're exploring, or different artists that you're working with, all of you have something unique and it doesn't necessarily need to be expensive to expose it.[25]

Notes

1 Carla Steen, publications manager/dramaturg, Guthrie Theater, interview by Tanya Dean, March 27, 2013.
2 Steen, interview.
3 Steen, interview.
4 Steen, interview.
5 Steen, interview.
6 Julie Felise Dubiner, associate director, Oregon Shakespeare Festival, interview by Tanya Dean, April 1, 2013.
7 Dubiner, interview.
8 Dubiner, interview.
9 Dubiner, interview.
10 Eddie Wallace, membership and sales manager, Oregon Shakespeare Festival, interview by Tanya Dean, April 1, 2013.
11 Wallace, interview.
12 Wallace, interview.
13 Wallace, interview.
14 Maya Gabrielle, digital content producer, National Theatre, interview by Tanya Dean, May 2, 2013.
15 Gabrielle, interview.
16 Gabrielle, interview.
17 Gabrielle, interview.
18 Gabrielle, interview.
19 Gabrielle, interview.
20 Gabrielle, interview.
21 Gabrielle, interview.
22 Maya Gabrielle, "The Power of Online Video" (2011), available online at https://www.youtube.com/watch?v=TvQ33v4GA_U, accessed May 10, 2013.
23 Gabrielle, video.
24 Gabrielle, video.
25 Gabrielle, video.

84

Digital dramaturgy and digital dramaturgs

LaRonika Thomas

In 1977 Yale established an M.F.A./D.F.A. program in dramaturgy, the first in America. During the same period, beginning around 1974, the first consumer computers came on the market. By the mid 1980s, professional dramaturgs formally founded Literary Managers and Dramaturgs of the Americas (LMDA), a sign that the field was growing in North America and that there was a desire among dramaturgs to share ideas and practices with each other and with the theatre field as a whole. In 1984, Apple released the Macintosh computer, and by 1985 the internet as we know it was becoming available to the general public.

While these events may be coincidental, it is clear that the development of the professional dramaturg in the US and the development of the digital social world and its accompanying technology have been concurrent. Today, dramaturgs use many digital tools in their work on individual productions, in the literary offices of theatre companies across the country, and as part of the national dialogue on theatre and new play development.

As the theatre artist who most conspicuously straddles the divide between the more private interactions of artist and artist and the more public interactions between artist and audience, dramaturgs have taken on these digital tools most enthusiastically and in a wide variety of creative ways, changing the field as they innovate. This interaction between digital technology and dramaturgy is influencing and transforming both. For dramaturgs, our dual role has been symbolized by two locales: the rehearsal hall and the library. Over the past several decades we have added a third location: the virtual space.

Digital tools and production dramaturgy

One of the great satisfactions of the digital age is the ability to find books and conduct dramaturgical research on the internet. While the chance discoveries that can be made when browsing a section of the library's shelves is still valuable, now many dramaturgs' searches begin – and sometimes end – online. In addition to conducting research digitally, a dramaturg can also distribute production research digitally. The large binders holding the dramaturg's protocol, notes, and endless research have not disappeared, but they are no longer absolutely necessary or proliferate. One physical copy of the protocol might live in the rehearsal room, but a copy may also live, along with supplemental materials such as (digital-friendly) videos and discussion forums, on a Googlegroup created for our work. This software is now so common that it almost seems unnecessary to describe it – a digital space, open only to those with permission, where one can post documents, links, images, and other items, and where the production team can communicate with each other as well as post items for each other. Actors can now download a PDF of the research packet and send it to their e-reader (possibly along with their script).

While basic digital workspaces such as Yahoogroups, Googlegroups, Google Docs, Microsoft SkyDrive, Dropbox, Box.com, and others are examples of online storage and communication sites, there are other, even more interactive programs that can be utilized for production dramaturgy. Jane Barnette, a professor at Kennesaw State University, has championed the use of wikis and software like PBworks to create online collaborative spaces that reach beyond file sharing and allow production teams to edit, comment on, and enhance each other's work. An early example of this can be seen in the University of Puget Sound's Oberon Project,[1] a wiki initially designed in 2006 for use with the university's production of *A Midsummer Night's Dream*. In these types of digital spaces, the text can be uploaded and worked on by a team of dramaturgs or by the production team as a whole. The script itself becomes a space for the director, actors, and designers to play with ideas. Set and costume designers can upload their sketches and designs. Dramaturgy packets become collaborative documents that continue to grow and change during the rehearsal process. Dramaturgs become editors of the digital space and process.

This kind of digital space can be especially useful for devised work, for situations where one or more members of the team are working from a remote location, and in educational settings. These digital workspaces allow for many editors and, as such, are good pedagogical tools for university dramaturgy courses. Students can share and comment on work, in both a classroom and production setting. This in turn creates dramaturgs who are comfortable sharing their work and creative ideas for a production; and it creates dramaturgs who are collaborative artists, with a place at both the physical table and the virtual one. And since dramaturgs are often responsible for introducing these kinds of digital tools into the rehearsal space, they are often the ones at the head of the virtual table. These digital tools provide dramaturgs with a stronger voice in the collaborative process, offering opportunities for the growth of the role of dramaturgy within professional theatre production.

Social media and audience outreach

Websites and social media are now used by many theatres to both market productions to potential audience members and give them access to contextual information related to the production. If audience members are interested in a particular production or theatre, one of their activities prior to attending the theatre will probably include visiting the theatre's website or its Facebook page or blog or Twitter feed or Tumblr.

Collaborations between the marketing and literary departments of a theatre come together in these digital spaces. A dramaturg may supply the play synopsis for the show's information page, for example, and the website can be an effective way to let patrons know about any post-show discussions or other activities that are planned around the production. A theatre's website might host an entire set of documents for each show that contextualizes and enhances the audience member's experience with the show.

Janine Sobeck, the former literary manager of Arena Stage, describes just this type of site in her discussion of Sub/Text: Your Virtual Dramaturg, the website she created for Arena Stage:[2]

> Based on the model of the Extra Features sections that are common on DVDs, I wanted to create an interactive experience that provided a wide range of information, ... while providing the tools for any audience member who wanted to delve more deeply into any of these subjects. Working with the publications director and web designer, we created a subsection of the Arena Stage website that, thanks to our existing web contract, allowed me unlimited space at no cost.[3]

Sobeck notes that Google Analytics showed more than 57,000 hits to the site and that audience members would quote from the site during post-show discussions.[4] Sobeck is now the dramaturgy specialist at Bringham Young University, where she has created a website similar to Sub/Text called 4th Wall Dramaturgy.[5] Meanwhile, Arena Stage's Sub/Text has been rechristened Extras and Insights.[6]

Baltimore's Center Stage also has a wide array of digital dramaturgy resources. A recipient of a Mellon grant for their dramaturgical work, Center Stage uses their digital dramaturgy site to post items such as the production's program, essays from the director or the production's dramaturgy team, links to further reading, images, and so forth. The theatre's Dramaturgy Department also uses Tumblr[7] to post shorter entries, quotations, images, and videos tracing the production process from a variety of angles. For instance, for the most recent production at the time of this writing, The Raisin Cycle – two shows, Clybourne Park and Beneatha's Place running in rep. – there is a link to an obituary for Chinua Achebe, a video montage from the costume designer, and a link to a series of conversations on race by the production company California Newsreel.

Both examples, Sub/Text and Center Stage's Digital Dramaturgy, illustrate how these digital spaces can change quickly, adapting to both the theatre's needs and also to the interests and manpower available to the theatre. What was on a website today may be gone tomorrow, or at least archived in the theatre's pages, further from public view. Or a theatre that relied on an assistant dramaturg for this type of digital work – time consuming and detailed – may suddenly lack the womanpower to keep a blog current if budget cuts eliminate that staff position. Or the theatre's priorities may shift with a new artistic director who does not value these kinds of digital tools.

These digital dramaturgy websites, hosted by individual theatre companies and centered around their production season, are resources for other dramaturgs and theatres as well as for audience members. As these resources become more detailed and more common, they will in turn affect dramaturgs' production work. What happens when one theatre's dramaturg can find much of what they need from another theatre's website? How might these inevitably shared resources free up dramaturgs' time for other, more individualized work on productions?

Online archives, databases, and new play development

Both the possibility for sharing information and the serendipitous availability of digital dramaturgy affects larger national conversations and collaborations regarding online archives, databases, and new play development. I had the opportunity to encounter the digital humanities and work with digital archives and encoding first-hand thanks to a University of Maryland course titled Technoromanticism. This course, taught by the director of the Maryland Institute for Technology in the Humanities (MITH), Professor Neil Fraistat, was an examination of the relationship between founding concepts of Romanticism and the anxieties, hopes, fears, and joys surrounding the way contemporary culture interacts with technology. Students encoded Mary Shelley's novel, *Frankenstein*, which required downloading and learning special software called GitHub. The software permitted each student to encode her assigned pages while also seeing the rest of the team's pages and making decisions regarding common notation.[8]

Encoding is not just a matter of taking an image of a page of text and uploading it to a website or typing handwritten pages into a computer program. Rather, it involves turning text into code – making a handwritten manuscript digital and searchable and also preserving the marginalia and various edits made by a variety of authors (Mary and Percy Shelley, in this case). Transforming text into code allows scholars and practitioners to ask different questions than they might have previously, or to ask questions in a different way.[9] Encoding text creates digital archives – databases that allow dramaturgs to approach research material and plays differently than they previously could. And whereas most theatre text throughout history would need to be encoded in order to be accessed in this manner, most recent (and future) theatre texts now begin as digital documents – they are "born digital."

Now, dramaturgs, imagine for a moment that you could go to a website, view or download a play script that has just been produced for the first time by X theatre company. Now imagine that you could read not only a clean copy of that script but also a marked up version containing the playwright's rewrites throughout the rehearsal process. And imagine you could also view the stage manager's prompt book, with all of her notes. And the dramaturgy packet and the program and see the designer's sketches, and so on – all in one place. And imagine that the collection of data for this play was just one among thousands. And that they were all searchable, graph-able, and map-able. While this sort of website is still only an idea, existing digital dramaturgy technology allows us to imagine the possibility. For instance, the American Theatre Archive Project (ATAP),[10] created by archivist Susan Brady and dramaturg Ken Cerniglia, is a national push to identify all of the analog and digital theatre archives in the country. 2amtheatre[11] and HowlRound[12] are online forums for national discussions of issues pertinent to the state of American Theatre.

HowlRound has also created the New Play Map,[13] a searchable map of the United States of current productions, presentations, workshops, and readings that is user-sourced. These types of digital dramaturgy efforts are not limited to the United States – Teatr w Polsce, a website dedicated to collecting Polish performance, is a good example of international forays into digital theatre archiving.[14] And, as covered in another article in this volume, the New Play Exchange, a crowdsourced literary management tool, is currently under development (see Chapter 45).

The work of Doug Reside, the New York Public Library's (NYPL) first digital curator for performing arts also deserves mention. Reside is encoding the librettos and additional materials from out-of-copyright musicals in NYPL's collection and posting them to the archive website.[15] Reside has also done work reconstructing and examining Jonathan Larson's digital documents related to the development of *Rent*. These documents were "born digital" but were on outdated floppy discs and needed to be accessed through older computers. As Reside notes in his own writing on the project, there is a "very real possibility that a large portion of our cultural history will be lost unless we solve it quickly."[16] Reside highlights one important question: with technology changing so quickly, how do we ensure that the materials of our work are accessible to those in the future? As Diana Taylor notes, both archive and repertoire are mediated.[17] We must be aware of that mediation now lest we lose the ability to access work in the future and it will become lost to us simply because our technology has advanced beyond the point where such access is possible. Also of concern, since most playwrights' work is now "born digital," is, in what way, if at all, will others have access to rewrites of future playscripts, with handwritten marginalia that indicates the playwright's thought process? How will this alter what we are able to learn about the process of play production in the future?

Digital dramaturgy

These new digital technologies are also influencing the very notion of what dramaturgy (and theatre) is, and the possibilities contained in the two. What changes about theatre when it moves to a digital space, either in part or entirely? Can we still call this type of performance "theatre"? Many theatre companies have a presence as an organization on Facebook or Twitter. But some take individual productions into these platforms, creating Facebook pages for characters from their current productions or staging entire plays on Twitter. While this is also certainly a marketing effort, with the ultimate goal to get audience members to the theatre to see the play, it is also its own performance. For instance, Romeo and Juliet's relationship status: "It's complicated."

Theatre artists are beginning to conceive of stories that cross boundaries between many mediums, and new movements are pushing form and structure. Last year a group of artists from Woolly Mammoth Theatre in DC, along with members of the Black Women's Playwrights Group and the Carnegie Mellon Entertainment Technology Center gathered to explore new ideas in transmedia theatre. They discussed their collaboration on a video game to accompany the production of *The Elaborate Entrance of Chad Deity* at Woolly Mammoth and a website created as part of Lynn Nottage's new play, *By the Way, Meet Vera Stark*. Or consider the work of German artist Kris Verdonck, who creates wordless performances involving interactions between human performers, machines, and digital video, often in collaboration with a dramaturg.[18] A dramaturg's work is redefined when encountering a play without a script, or one that relies upon the chance movements of a machine.

These ambitious projects are changing the notion of what dramaturgy and theatre are and can be in the twenty-first century. Dramaturgs are at the forefront of many of these conversations and projects, mapping where we have been and where we are on the digital terrain, and plotting the frontier of where we may be headed.

Notes

1 The Oberon Project, http://oberon.pugetsound.edu/oberonwiki/index.php/Main_Page, accessed May 10, 2013.
2 Janine Sobeck, "Creating Sub/Text," *Review: The Journal of Dramaturgy* 20 (2009/2010): 7–10.
3 Sobeck, 8.
4 Sobeck, 10.
5 4th Wall Dramaturgy, http://4thwalldramaturgy.byu.edu/, accessed May 10, 2013.
6 Extras and Insights, http://www.arenastage.org/artistic-development/extras-insights, accessed 10 May 10, 2013.
7 The Thaumaturgy Project, http://thaumaturgy.tumblr.com, accessed 10 May 10, 2013.
8 See "Team MARKUP: Encoding Frankenstein for the Shelley-Godwin Archive," Technoromanticism, http://mith.umd.edu/eng738T/team-markup-encoding-frankenstein-for-the-shelley-godwin-archive-2, accessed May 10, 2013.
9 See "Data Analysis Group Post," Technoromanticism, http://mith.umd.edu/eng738T/data-analysis-group-post, accessed May 10, 2013. See also Mining the Dispatch, http://dsl.richmond.edu/dispatch, accessed May 10, 2013.
10 American Theatre Archive Project, http://americantheatrearchiveproject.org, accessed May 10, 2013.
11 2amT, http://www.2amtheatre.com, accessed May 10, 2013.
12 HowlRound, http://www.howlround.com, accessed May 10, 2013.
13 New Play Map, http://newplaymap.org, accessed 10 May 10, 2013.
14 Also see, www.e-teatr.pl/pl/index.html, accessed May 10, 2013. For other European websites, see New International Theatre Experience, www.nitecorp.com; and the Information Centre for Drama in Europe (ICDE), http://www.playservice.net. For another US source, see also The Playwrights' Centre, www.pwcenter.org.
15 "Announcing: Musical of the Month," www.nypl.org/blog/2011/05/18/announcing-musical-month, accessed 10 May 10, 2013.
16 Doug Reside, "No Day But Today": A Look at Jonathan Larson's Word Files," www.nypl.org/blog/2011/04/22/no-day-today-look-jonathan-larsons-word-files, accessed May 10, 2013.
17 Diana Taylor, *The Archive and the Repertoire: Performing Cultural Memory in the Americas* (Durham, NC: Duke University Press, 2003).
18 A Two Dogs Company, www.atwodogscompany.org/en, accessed May 10, 2013.

85

Can technology save theatre?
Tweet seats, YouTube auditions, and Facebook backstage?[1]

Randi Zuckerberg

Those who know me well know that I have two great passions: technology and theatre. And when those two forces come together, I can't stop talking about it.

Something that's been on my mind a lot lately is the trend of "tweet seats" at operas, ballets, and shows. "Tweet seats" are seats where you're not just allowed, you're encouraged, to text during the show. While I applaud theatres for trying to engage younger audiences, this one has me worried. I feel like there's a fine line between embracing social media and just encouraging rude behavior. Broadway, at the best it can be, isn't just about asking people to tweet during shows. It's about using social media and technology to inspire, thrill, and engage millions of people every single evening.

In January 2013, I got to live a dream of mine when I appeared on Broadway. But I wasn't singing, acting, or dancing. I was giving a TED talk at TEDxBroadway, an event focused on what the future of theatre and Broadway might look like. I got to hear from some excellent speakers, including Thomas Schumacher (Disney Theatrical), Terry Teachout (well-known theatre critic), and George Takei (yes, Mr. Star Trek himself). And I got to stand on the stage of the "Avenue Q" Theatre and speak to a packed house about how Broadway can be better with social media and technology. Below are a few of the thoughts I covered in my talk.

In an age where I can watch virtually any movie on my laptop or read virtually any book on my tablet, why is it so darn hard to see a Broadway show?

We live in an incredible age of innovation. Seventy percent of the world's population has a mobile phone. And you can be connected anywhere, from the top of Mount Everest to outer space. So why is it that Broadway is still so limited by physical space in theatres, exorbitant ticket prices, and a lack of fresh, new content?

More people will see a mediocre movie on its opening night than a great Broadway show over the course of an entire year. For those who do make it to Broadway, the price of taking a family of four to a show is equivalent to multiple car payments. And even then, it's likely that your only options will be revivals of old Broadway shows or Disney movies turned into theatre. If Broadway is truly going to realize its potential and move into the twenty-first century, this has got to change.

Here are 10 ideas for how Broadway can use social media to reach those billions of internet and mobile-connected people around the world

1 YouTube auditions. Why not cast the net as far and wide as possible when casting for shows? This enables talented people worldwide to engage with Broadway, while allowing producers to see which people get a lot of video views and will likely bring a large audience with them to the box office!
2 Mobile programs. Instead of having the program be a piece of paper you flip through only when you've run out of conversation topics with the person sitting next to you, make it a living, breathing mobile app that can keep audiences engaged, long after they've left the theatre.
3 Crowdsource aspects of the show. Let your fans help "decide" a few small parts of the show, such as a costume, a small set piece, or a dance move. This gives your fans a sense of ownership and pride over the show, which means they'll tell all their friends about it.
4 Stream the show online with a cheap ticket price. Not everyone can travel to NYC. And those who do might not be able to afford a $200 ticket. Streaming a show online and charging $10 or so brings more people into the experience, while also generating a new revenue stream. Winning!
5 Partner with local businesses to create an "experience." By working together, local businesses can tap into each other's social media audiences and fan base to grow their own!
6 Photos, Photos, Photos. Photos are the things that go most viral online because they are easy to share and don't need to be translated. Consider setting up photo booths in the lobby at intermission or have a roaming photographer taking photos for your Facebook page.
7 Live-tweet the show! Consider having someone backstage whose entire job is to live tweet the show. Imagine if you could sing along to a musical from the comfort of your living room, *while* it was being performed on Broadway, just by following along on Twitter?
8 Social media walk-on roles. I recently had a small walk-on role in the *Anything Goes* touring production in SF. It was a win/win for everyone. I got a once-in-a-lifetime opportunity, and the production got some great marketing because I was Facebooking and Tweeting up a storm!
9 The @ reply is the new autograph. Gone are the days of standing outside the stage door in freezing temperatures to have a lead actor sign your playbill. Now your actors can engage with thousands of people online!

10 Make your fans feel like stars. With social media, you can now know if it's the birthday of someone sitting in the audience, or if someone is visiting from across the world. Give them a special shout-out or offer discounted tickets for that special occasion, and they'll brag to all their friends.

So, what do you think? Have you been to a show lately that was doing something particularly cool with technology? What are some of your ideas for how theatre and tech can come together?

The one thing I do know is that Broadway has to innovate. After all, why should it just be a sliver of the world coming to Broadway … when we can bring Broadway to the entire world?

Note

1 This article is reprinted from www.dotcomplicated.com, February 3, 2013, with permission.

INDEX OF NAMES

INDEX OF TERMS

action 1, 32–33, 45–46, 48, 53, 96, 152, 154, 159, 177, 182, 198, 205, 215–16, 238, 316, 318–20, 330–33, 351–52, 356, 360–61, 367, 370–72, 405–6, 408–9, 411, 415–16, 439, 462–63, 487–88

adaptation 2, 6, 11, 25–26, 58–59, 61, 62, 69–70, 73–74, 76–77, 79, 97, 154, 161, 165, 171, 180, 187, 203, 210, 226, 276, 280, 286, 294–303, 305, 310–12, 325–26, 332, 343, 347, 355–56, 367, 394, 427, 448, 451–52, 454, 470, 496, 498, 508

aesthetic 2, 4, 47, 48–49, 63–64, 69–70, 73, 80, 100, 109–10, 115–16, 164, 171, 219–20, 245, 253, 267, 278, 306–7, 312, 330, 336, 348, 351, 364, 367, 375, 377–78, 392, 416, 418, 433, 436, 467, 472–73, 476; architecture 382, 366; dramatic 365; experience 202–3, 205–7, 301–2, 304, 331; interruption 102; new 14, 33, 62, 243, 470; performance 33, 391; political 308; postdramatic 391, 393; postmodern 49; representation of life 105; strategies 472; techniques 352; theatre 5, 352

analysis 4–5, 8, 12–14, 26, 32, 42, 58, 72, 74, 79, 92, 158–60, 162, 174, 203, 215–17, 219–20, 283–84, 286, 297, 310–11, 318–20, 333–34, 342, 344, 346–47, 361, 365, 378, 381–82, 394, 402–3, 415, 418, 426–27, 430, 433–34, 436, 448–55, 467, 501; dramaturgical 4, 72, 92, 219, 310, 334, 381; internal, external 311; literary 501; literary character 318; parallel-text 448–49; play 12, 203, 403, 427; psychological 32; research 217; script 159, 426, 427, 430; text 215, 216; textual 158, 162, 220, 320, 433–34, 436, 450; theatre text 79

arrangement 1–2, 4–5, 12, 36, 41, 48, 64, 232, 246, 329, 332–33, 370–72, 379, 405, 438–39, 444, 446, 460, 468; dramatic actions 1; geometric 379; mathematical 439; of events 4; of performance roles 64;

of the audience and the actors 468, 460; of the incidents 1, 2; of the space 468; social 329, 332

audience 3, 5, 6, 8–14, 21, 26–31, 34–38, 40–49, 54, 57, 60, 69, 70, 72, 76–79, 84, 88–92, 95–97, 100–103, 113–15, 121, 124, 126–28, 131–34, 138–39, 141–45, 147–49, 158–63, 165, 169–72, 176, 180, 184, 189, 192, 194, 202, 204, 206, 214–15, 218–21, 225–28, 231, 234–39, 245–58, 262, 277–78, 285–86, 288–90, 292, 295, 297, 301, 306, 308, 310–11, 316, 319, 320, 322–26, 335–39, 343, 345–46, 348, 351–52, 355, 359, 361–63, 365–67, 375–76, 379, 381–82, 384, 386–87, 392, 394, 408, 409–11, 418–19, 426, 431–34, 446, 448, 452, 460, 464, 466–69, 472–76, 479–88, 490–504, 506–8, 510, 512–14; development 251–54; diverse 237, 251, 256, 326; education 219, 363, 472; engagement 158, 162, 194, 221, 257, 326, 487–88, 495, 504; experience 206, 246, 473, 508; global 124; international 69, 503; local 114, 255; national 10, 57, 72, 78, 131, 134, 144, 161, 277, 290, 479; new 8, 31, 169, 252, 258, 410; outreach 6, 8, 11, 13, 218, 297, 507; participation 34, 499; reception 202, 310, 325, 381, 433; response 44, 101, 325, 474, 491, 494; target 322–24, 483; white 9

authority 36, 45, 48, 66, 68–69, 102, 105–10, 163, 187–88, 209, 242, 282, 298, 305, 329, 332, 386, 397–98, 401–2, 420–21, 467; intellectual 45; in performance 305, 420; in the making process 108; of artistic invention 48; of a text 329, 421; of structuring 109; of the dramaturg 298, 420; of the playwright 106

body 32–34, 43, 47, 71, 96–97, 146, 148–49, 170–71, 180–82, 197–99, 205–6, 217, 308, 330, 335, 350, 352–53, 37–38, 392, 416–19,

527